Chicago Portraits

JUNE SKINNER SAWYERS

CHICAGO PORTRAITS

FOREWORD BY RICK KOGAN

Northwestern University Press
Evanston, Illinois

Northwestern University Press
www.nupress.northwestern.edu

Photography credits appear on page 361.

Book and cover design by Marianne Jankowski

Printed in the United States of America

10 9 8 7 6 5 4 3 2 1

Library of Congress Cataloging-in-Publication Data

Sawyers, June Skinner, 1957–
    Chicago portraits / June Skinner Sawyers ; foreword by Rick Kogan. — [Updated ed.].
        p. cm.
    Includes bibliographical references and index.
    ISBN 978-0-8101-2649-7 (pbk. : alk. paper)
    1. Chicago (Ill.)—Biography. 2. Chicago (Ill.)—Biography—Portraits. I. Title.
F548.25.S28 2012
920.0773'11—dc23

2011038716

♾ The paper used in this publication meets the minimum requirements of the American National Standard for Information Sciences—Permanence of Paper for Printed Library Materials, ANSI Z39.48-1992.

Key to Frontispiece Collage

Row 1: Harriet Monroe, John Belushi, Louis Sullivan, Mahalia Jackson, Louis Armstrong, Richard J. Daley

Row 2: Studs Terkel, Cap Anson, Richard Wright, Ann Landers, L. Frank Baum, Gene Siskel

Row 3: Earl Dickerson, Mary Garden, Mike Royko, Ben Hecht, Harold Washington, Carl Sandburg

Row 4: Joseph Cardinal Bernardin, Harry Caray, Al Capone, Potter Palmer, Ben Reitman, Jane Addams

In loving memory of my mother, Elizabeth Muir Lawson Porter Sawers

(born 1920 in Glasgow, Scotland; died 2000 in Chicago, Illinois)

and M. J. Jones (1966–2011), whose bravery, grace, and wisdom will be fondly remembered

Contents

Foreword
Rick Kogan

Imagine the difficulties of winnowing down the many millions of people who have shaped and shared this place we call Chicago to the relative handful you now hold in your hands. When my friend June Sawyers deemed more than 300 Chicagoans worthy of inclusion in this book, finding my father Herman—historian, journalist, and author (among many things)—among them was a special, personal bonus.

Before I was old enough to read any of his books about Chicago's history (to learn what those books were, please go to page 182), he wrote those books in my spirit. There we would be, standing on the Michigan Avenue Bridge, and I would be hearing from him the tales of the massacre at Fort Dearborn. There we would be, driving down 63rd Street, and I was listening to stories about the amusement park named White City, which led to stories about the first Ferris wheel and the World's Fair of 1893. That old garage on Clark Street . . . well, you know what happened there on Valentine's Day 1929.

Wherever we went and whatever we did, it was possible to feel the pulse of the past. In reading my father's section in this book, I came to realize how difficult it is to capture any life in a few hundred words and how artfully Sawyers accomplishes her more than 300 tasks.

William Faulkner, understandably not in this book, once said this: "The past is never dead. It's not even past." He was talking about the South but he could have been talking about Chicago.

For those of us who call this place home, Chicago's past is always with us. It does, as it should, echo through the years. There is the unmistakable voice of Carl Sandburg in the poetry of those on stage at the Uptown Poetry Slam that raucously holds forth on Sunday nights at the Green Mill. There's Muddy Waters alive in the fingers of a young West Side bluesman. There's William Le Baron Jenney whispering to a young architect dreaming of buildings in the sky.

History courses through the city. It is not something that can be destroyed by wrecking balls swung by greedy developers or politicians whose pockets are not fully stuffed. You can show me a Maxwell Street made dull and quiet, but tell me you cannot still get there a whiff of sausages grilling. You can tell me Gwendolyn Brooks is dead, but try to tell me her voice—"We real cool . . ."—is not alive along the streets of Bronzeville.

To understand the past is to have a better grip on where we are now and perhaps even get clues to where we might be going. Sawyers's biographies can be digested in bits and pieces, and you will be satisfied and enlightened. Taken whole and in order, as I decided to consume them over the course of two pleasant days (and nights), is to be stunned by the variety of people who have helped make Chicago Chicago and to be proud of the city's ability to nurture all manner of characters—of lofty, lusty, and low ambitions—and to keep moving onward.

Preface

Chicago has such a rich and varied history, so full of vivid and fascinating characters, that the most difficult task was deciding who not to include. An even thornier problem was more fundamental: How exactly do you define "Chicagoan"? How about someone who was born and raised elsewhere but spent many fruitful years here? Does that person qualify?

There were no easy, cut-and-dried solutions, so I had to rely on the counsel of valued colleagues and on the sound research of respected historians for guidance. Primarily, though, I used my own judgment. Not everyone will, of course, agree with my selections. Many undoubtedly will take issue ("Why wasn't so and so included?"). Those are the chances one has to take when assembling such a project. As the saying goes, it comes with the territory.

Essentially, I chose individuals who, either negatively or positively, made a substantial impact on the city. The entries fall primarily into two categories: those who were born and bred in Chicago and those who were born or raised elsewhere but, nevertheless, contributed to the vitality of the city.

The big names are here—Jane Addams, Nelson Algren, Charles A. Comiskey, Clarence Darrow, Richard J. Daley, George Pullman, Harold Washington, and, yes, Al Capone—as are the familiar ones that Chicagoans tend to take for granted, or know very little about, such as Marshall Field, James Kraft, Charles Walgreen, A. Montgomery Ward, and William Wieboldt.

I've also included people that the general reader may not immediately recognize but whose lives and deeds made a difference. Their contributions should be remembered. I'm referring to such people as Saul Alinsky, Albert and Lucy Parsons, and Ida B. Wells, among others. Then there are those who we sometimes forget had strong Chicago ties, including Louis Armstrong, L. Frank Baum, Nat King Cole, Sam Cooke, Bob Fosse, and Mahalia Jackson.

Obviously, a work that contains more than 300 names cannot possibly include every notable person who ever lived or worked in Chicago—that would require several hefty volumes and is beyond this book's scope and intention. Because of space and time restrictions, I could not include everyone that I had initially considered. In a perfect publishing world, I would have liked to include singer, playwright, and civil rights activist Oscar Brown Jr. (1926–2005), DuSable Museum cofounder Margaret Burroughs (1917–2010), artist and activist Carlos Cortez (1923–2005), former First Lady Maggie Daley (1943–2011), politician William L. Dawson (1886–1970), blues guitarists David "Honeyboy" Edwards (1915–2011) and Hubert Sumlin (1931–2011), improv pioneer Josephine Forsberg (1921–2011), sax player Franz Jackson (1912–2008), editor and publisher Curt Johnson (1928–2008), television anchorman Floyd Kalber (1924–2004), singer Abbey Lincoln (1930–2010), blues club owner Theresa Needham (1912–1992), naturalist Donald Culross Peattie (1898–1964), novelist and journalist Elia Peattie (1862–1935), singer Minnie Riperton (1947–1979), labor scholar and poet Franklin Rosemont (1943–2009), radio host Eddie Schwartz (1946–2009), artist Hollis Sigler (1948–2001), Ojibwa poet and playwright E. Donald Two-Rivers (1945–2008), improvisational acting pioneer Viola

Spolin (1906–1994), Old Town School of Folk Music cofounder Win Stracke (1908–1991), sportscaster Tim Weigel (1945–2001), and Chicago mayor "Long" John Wentworth (1815–1888), among others. *Chicago Portraits* does, however, strive to be representative of the people—to capture the essence of a life in a few paragraphs can be a challenge—who, at one time, made Chicago their home.

Also, does one include only people from the city proper or does one adopt a more expansive approach and include individuals whose lives straddled both city and suburbs? Granted, some of the older suburbs have a rich heritage of their own. Oak Park, for example, has claimed Ernest Hemingway while Frances Willard has strong associations with Evanston. In order to address the city/suburb dichotomy, I have, sparingly, included entries describing the famous sons and daughters of the vast region beyond the city limits.

The individuals portrayed in the following pages capture the many faces of Chicago's past. They were athletes and coaches, social workers and community activists, writers and editors, politicians and gangsters, pioneers and entrepreneurs, philosophers and musicians, judges and lawyers, priests, ministers, and rabbis.

These Chicagoans came from Glasgow and Rome, from St. Paul, Minnesota, and Galesburg, Illinois. They were descendants of people from lands all over the world. Generation after generation, they swept across the Illinois prairie, first by foot and wagon, then by train and automobile, and finally by airplane. They came from throughout the United States and from across the seas, all with their own heritage, all with their own dreams, all with their own individual story to tell. Whether native or foreign-born, they had one thing in common: They were all Chicagoans, as diverse and vibrant as the city itself.

JSS
Chicago, Illinois
January 2012

Acknowledgments

A book of this scope could not have been written without the assistance of many individuals and institutions and the work of historians and journalists who have spent their time and talent chronicling Chicago's past.

For this revised edition, I would particularly like to thank my sister, Margaret Batson, for typing the manuscript, an arduous task that she did with grace and speed. In addition, for research and photo assistance I would like to thank Debra Bade and Randall Weissman at the *Chicago Tribune;* Alison Hinderliter, manuscript and archives librarian at the Newberry Library; Nathaniel Parks, assistant archivist at Ryerson & Burnham Libraries at the Art Institute of Chicago; Caitlin Kolb, archives and collections assistant at the Frank Lloyd Wright Preservation Trust; and Karen Widi and Amy Hawkinson at Skidmore, Owings & Merrill.

Numerous people took time out of their busy days to read a version of the manuscript in draft form and/or offered their own insights and opinions or simply helped in ways both large and small. They include Arnie Bernstein, Amy Brent, Michele Casper at Lands' End, Ed Holstein, Gary Houston, Thomas Joyce, Ann Durkin Keating, Greg Kot, Richard Lindberg, Bill Savage, Kathryn Tutkus, John von Rhein, and Steve Young. I thank them. I also thank Theresa Albini and Jane Samuelson for their invaluable input.

Finally, thank you to my editor, Mike Levine, and managing editor Anne Gendler for their unflagging commitment to the project as well as their considerable patience; to Mary Klein and Dan Lindstrom for their thorough copyediting; and to interns Hana Bajramovic, Dana Leib, Elizabeth Male, Jessica Tackett, and Renee Zambo.

Chicago Portraits

Grace Abbott

Social Reformer

BORN: November 17, 1878
Grand Island, Nebraska

DIED: June 19, 1939
Chicago, Illinois

One of the illustrious women of Hull House, Grace Abbott exposed the exploitation of immigrants and children to city officials and went on to have a distinguished career in both public service work and as a professor of public welfare at the University of Chicago.

Abbott came from an enlightened Quaker family that stressed social justice and social equality. Her mother, Elizabeth Griffin Abbott, told her daughter that "the rights of women belong with the rights of the Indian and the Negro. Everyone must be free and equal, and everyone should be dealt with on the basis of equality and justice."

In 1898 Abbott graduated from Island College, Nebraska, and later completed graduate work at the University of Nebraska. In 1908 she moved to Chicago to work at Jane Addams's Hull House on the West Side. Her sister, Edith, was already affiliated with the University of Chicago's School of Social Work. Abbott continued graduate studies at the University of Chicago and received her Ph.D. in political science in 1909.

Abbott became the director of the Chicago Immigrants' Protective League while she was at Hull House. The league helped thousands of young immigrant families adjust to life in the New World. The league also established waiting rooms at railroad stations where new arrivals were greeted by men and women who helped them get acclimated to their new surroundings.

Soon after arriving at Hull House, Abbott investigated private employment agencies in Chicago, many of which were located along Canal Street in an area referred to as the "slave market." Unsuspecting immigrants used these agencies only to be charged high fees for jobs that often didn't even exist. Abbott published her findings in the report "The Chicago Employment Agency and the Immigrant Worker." Her hard work led to the passage of a law in 1909 that controlled such unscrupulous practices.

Abbott feverishly rallied for the passage of a fair and just immigration policy for the nation's "new" immigrants, a euphemism at the time that referred to immigrants from primarily eastern and southern Europe who were considered "foreign" as much for their religion as for their physical appearance: many, if not most, were Catholic. In January 1912, she testified before a congressional committee in Washington, D.C., on their behalf. She joined the faculty of the Chicago School of Civics and Philanthropy in 1911 but left in 1917 to work for various governmental agencies. From 1917 to 1919 she was the director of the Child Labor Division of the Children's Bureau in Washington, D.C. In 1918 she served as an adviser to the War Labor Policies Board. From 1920 to 1921 she was the executive secretary of the Illinois Immigrants' Commission and was chief of the United States Children's Bureau from 1921 to 1934. In this position she was able to ensure the passage of important child labor laws.

Following her departure from government work, Abbott returned to Chicago, where from 1934 until her death in 1939 she was professor of public welfare at the University of Chicago. She also edited, from 1934 to 1939, the university's *Social Service Review*. In 1917 Abbott wrote *The Immigrant and the Community*, a sympathetic account of the often-shameful treatment of immigrants in Chicago, and in 1938 she completed the massive, two-volume *The Child and the State,* which discussed child labor and the role of the state.

Abbott died of cancer in Chicago in June 1939.

See also: Jane Addams, Alice Hamilton, Florence Kelley, Mary McDowell, Agnes Nestor

Further reading: Jane Addams, *Twenty Years at Hull-House* (1910); Lela B. Costin, *Two Sisters for Social Justice: A Biography of Grace and Edith Abbott* (1983); June Sochen, *Movers and Shakers: American Women Thinkers and Activists, 1900–1970* (1973).

Robert S. Abbott

Newspaper Owner and Publisher

BORN: November 28, 1868
St. Simon's Island, Georgia

DIED: February 29, 1940
Chicago, Illinois

By crusading against racism and urging the black community to fight injustice, Robert Sengstacke Abbott revolutionized black journalism and, in the process, became the city's first African American millionaire.

The son of slaves, Abbott was reared on the outskirts of Savannah, Georgia. His father, Thomas, died when Robert was an infant, and his mother, Flora, later married Joseph Sengstacke, the son of a German-born white merchant and a black slave. Sengstacke, an ordained minister, instilled in his stepson a love of books and learning. Young Abbott attended the Beach Institute, a small Congregational institution in Savannah, before transferring to Claflin University in Orangeburg, South Carolina, in 1887 and then enrolling at the Hampton Institute in Hampton, Virginia—the famous African American center of learning founded by Booker T. Washington—to learn the printing trade.

After graduation, Abbott returned to Georgia to help his stepfather publish the *Woodville* (Georgia) *Times* before deciding to study law at Chicago's Kent College of Law, where he graduated, the only African American in his class, in 1899. Frustrated by the lack of opportunities for blacks—especially for a man as dark-skinned as he who had experienced rejection both by whites and by light-skinned African Americans—Abbott toyed with the bold idea of starting his own newspaper.

"I wanted to create an organ that would mirror the needs, opinions, and the aspirations of my race," said Abbott. At that time there were three African American newspapers in the city: Julius C. Taylor's *Broad Ax,* S. B. Turner's *Illinois Idea,* and Ferdinand I. Barnett's *Conservator,* but they functioned more as mouthpieces for their editors than as bona fide news-gathering organizations.

The *Chicago Defender,* the newspaper that Abbott eventually created, was different. It had a specific mission—the eradication of racial prejudice—and, in Robert Sengstacke Abbott, it had an indefatigable fighter. Abbott started from scratch. With 25 cents worth of capital (it cost $13.75 to print 300 copies, according to Abbott's biographer Roi Ottley, which he paid in installments), a folding card table, and a kitchen chair as the sole equipment, he launched the first issue on May 5, 1905. Middle-class whites in positions of power and members of the black elite with strong economic ties to the white establishment dismissed it as inflammatory journalism, but to the vast majority of the African American populace it was a source of pride. Although the *Defender* employed journalistic practices to attract attention that would be considered rather dubious by today's standards—such as the use of screaming yellow headlines—it was always taken seriously among its constituency. The *Defender* was there to goad, preach, and inspire.

Acutely aware of the widespread discrimination and severe unemployment in the South, Abbott encouraged rural blacks to migrate to the great industrial cities of the North. Indeed, his paper helped spur the Great Migration, when hundreds of thousands of African Americans moved from the South to Chicago and other northern cities. They came in droves, riding the Illinois Central passenger trains north from Louisiana, Mississippi, Alabama, and Tennessee. Between 1916 and 1970, seven million blacks left the rural South.

Abbott arranged for the Illinois Central to drop off copies of the paper along its route. Indeed Abbott would often hire railroad employees to distribute the paper in the South, notes historian James R. Grossman. In Chicago, the *Defender* was read in churches and in barber shops, anywhere African Americans congregated. Through aggressive reporting and a vigorous advertising campaign, the *Defender* became known as the bible of the African American community. By 1918 the *Defender* was able to boast a national circulation of 125,000, making it the best-selling black newspaper in the country. What's more, its passionate editorials and fearless reporting earned it the reputation as the most militant black newspaper in Chicago. In addition to its seminal role in encouraging the Great Migration, it also supported the desegregation of the armed forces, and sponsored virulent anti-lynching campaigns.

Abbott didn't forget his younger readers either. In 1929 he suggested the first Saturday in August be set aside as Bud Billiken Day. "Bud" was reportedly the nickname of Lucius Harper, executive editor of the newspaper, while "Billiken" was named after a mythical Chinese figurine—said to be the guardian of children—that sat on Harper's desk. Whatever its origins, today Bud Billiken Day remains a durable and popular Chicago tradition and, indeed, has since grown to be the largest African American parade in the country.

Abbott died in his sleep on February 29, 1940, in his house at 4742 South Parkway (now Martin Luther King Jr. Drive). Abbott Avenue is named in his honor.

The *Defender* has had several locations over the years. It was in a former synagogue in the Bronzeville neighborhood at 3435 South Indiana Avenue and, for more than forty years, at 2410 South Michigan Avenue. In 2005 the paper moved to a downtown office at 200 South Michigan Avenue. Four years later, in May 2009, the *Defender* returned to its South Side roots when it relocated to 4445 South King Drive, housed in a building—a former funeral home—that, according to African American historian Timuel Black, "was built by and for black businesses." Although competition from other black publications has led to reduced circulation—in 2008 it went from daily to weekly circulation—the *Chicago Defender* continues to cover news and events of importance to Chicago's African American community.

In late May 2009 the Abbott-Sengstacke Family Papers at the Woodson Regional Library, 9525 South Halsted Street, were opened to the public. Housed as part of the permanent collection of the library's Vivian G. Harsh Research Collection, it consists of more than 4,000 photographs and other memorabilia as well as 100 Sengstacke family home movies.

See also: Claude A. Barnett

Further reading: St. Clair Drake and Horace R. Cayton, *Black Metropolis: A Study of Negro Life in a Northern City* (1945); James R. Grossman, *Land of Hope: Chicago, Black Southerners, and the Great Migration* (1989); Roi Ottley, *The Lonely Warrior: The Life and Times of Robert S. Abbott* (1955); Allan H. Spear, *Black Chicago: The Making of a Negro Ghetto 1890–1920* (1967); Dempsey J. Travis, *An Autobiography of Black Chicago* (1981).

Wallace C. Abbott

Physician and Scientist

BORN: October 12, 1857
Bridgewater, Vermont

DIED: July 4, 1921
Chicago, Illinois

In 1888 Wallace Calvin Abbott founded what was to become Abbott Labs during a time when the pharmaceutical industry was in its infancy. From first-year sales of $2,000, the firm has grown into a $29.5 billion global health care company employing nearly 72,000 people in more than 130 countries.

Educated at Dartmouth College and the University of Michigan's Medical School, Abbott came to Chicago in 1886 and settled in the Ravenswood neighborhood. In 1888 he started the People's Drug Store in the kitchen of his small apartment and began manufacturing "granules" or pills. Early medications were imprecise and unreliable and their side effects so severe—such as their nauseating taste—that Abbott borrowed the idea of using the "alkaloid," or active part of a plant, from a Belgian-born surgeon named Adolphe Burggraeve and compressed this into pill form (previously medicinal fluids were extracted from herbs or plants and given to the patient in liquid form). Initially, he bought the granules but then, frustrated by their inferior quality, he began to make his own.

He formed the Abbott Alkaloidal Company and hired family members and friends to assist him. His sister filled the orders and answered inquiries, his parents placed shipping labels on the bottles, and a boyhood chum, Henry Shattuck, kept the books. Abbott edited a professional medical journal, *Medical World,* and in 1892 produced his first catalog, which consisted of 14 pages of text and 150 advertisements. Two years later, he assumed the editorship of the *Alkaloidal Clinic*—later changed to the *American Journal of Clinical Medicine*—which became one of the leading medical and surgical journals in the country. In 1897 he collaborated with Dr. William Waugh on the *Text Book of Alkaloidal Therapeutics,* a standard reference work on the subject at the time.

By 1914 the demand for alkaloids had peaked as the industry turned away from merely supplying remedies to actually manufacturing chemicals. Encouraged by members of his staff, Abbott entered the new field of synthetic medicines. Up until then, the manufacture of synthetic chemicals was confined to saccharin and aspirin, mostly manufactured by German companies. The outbreak of

World War I forced the United States to manufacture its own products. Abbott began producing a new wonder drug called Chlorazene, an antiseptic developed by an English doctor that helped save the lives of countless soldiers. In later years, the company produced the anesthetic Pentothal and the antibiotic erythromycin.

In 1921 all chemical manufacturing was transferred to a twenty-six-acre industrial site in the northern suburb of North Chicago. But the man behind the Abbott Labs was not to fully experience the fruit of his labor. In poor health and suffering from rheumatism and chronic kidney disease, Abbott walked home from his Ravenswood office one final time on July 1, 1921. Three days later, at the age of sixty-three, he died in his bed.

Some famous Abbott products include Murine eye drops, Selsun dandruff remedy, Similac infant formula, and Sucaryl sweetener.

Further reading: Herman Kogan, *The Long White Line: The Story of Abbott Laboratories* (1963); William D. Pratt, *The Abbott Almanac: 100 Years of Commitment to Quality Health Care* (1987).

Gertrude Abercrombie

Artist

BORN: February 17, 1909
Austin, Texas

DIED: July 3, 1977
Chicago, Illinois

I like to paint simple things that are a little strange.

—Gertrude Abercrombie

Artist Gertrude Abercrombie was known for her eccentric dress—her dark clothes and pointed velvet hats—as much as for her surrealist artwork. She remains one of the most important, and underappreciated, artists of the twentieth century. She had a distinctive personal style too, at turns humorous, eerie, and evocative as well as self-reverential and full of haunting portraits and landscapes.

Gertrude Abercrombie was born in Austin, Texas, the only child of Tom and Lula Jane Abercrombie, an opera singer. The family moved briefly to Berlin before returning to the United States on the eve of World War I, when they moved to the small town of Aledo, in western Illinois, and then to Chicago where her father found work as a salesman, settling in Hyde Park.

Abercrombie earned a bachelor's degree in Romance Languages from the University of Illinois at Urbana-Champaign. After graduating, she took classes in figure drawing and commercial techniques at the Art Institute of Chicago and the American Academy of Art. In 1931 she worked as an illustrator drawing glove advertisements for $15 a week at the Mesirow department store in Chicago and later served as an illustrator for the Sears, Roebuck catalog.

She did not turn to painting until the early 1930s when she began exhibiting at progressive Chicago art galleries. In 1935 she worked for the Works Progress Administration (WPA), which she attributed to validating her career as an artist. Around this time, she befriended a circle of bohemian friends, including the writer and playwright James Purdy (1914–2009). In 1940 she married a lawyer named Robert Livingston and they moved two years later to 5728 South Dorchester Avenue, in the Hyde Park neighborhood, where she would reside until her death.

Abercrombie, in fact, had a special affinity for Hyde Park. She helped establish the popular 57th Street Art Fair and ran a bohemian salon for artists, musicians, and writers in her Hyde Park home where she played the festive hostess of racially diverse parties. She became famous for Saturday night parties and Sunday afternoon jam sessions. Jazz musicians would often stop by the house, including Dizzy Gillespie, Sonny Rollins, Charlie Parker, Max Roach, and Sarah Vaughan. Abercrombie not only loved jazz—she was considered a fine piano player in her own right.

An idiosyncratic artist, Abercrombie is considered by critics to be a surrealist artist although she herself did not use that term to describe her work. Susan S. Weininger notes that surrealist painting was practiced as "a unique mode . . . in Chicago between 1910 and 1945 that was marked by local concerns and interests." These artists, she offers, were not part of any movement but rather moved from one style to another. Abercrombie, in particular, created mysterious, dreamlike landscapes. She thought of herself as a self-taught artist with Midwest sensibilities. On the other hand, critics have referred to her work as regional magical realism that plumbs the hidden world of the subconscious; indeed, Abercrombie often used supernatural elements in her work such as black cats, broomsticks, and full or crescent moons as well as personal motifs and symbols such as long black gloves and a bunch of grapes. A case in point is *Design for Death (Originally Charlie Parker's Favorite Painting)* (1946), in which she portrays an eerie landscape that consists of a bare tree, an empty ladder, a noose hanging from a branch, a box, and a full moon. Her paintings were famous for their lack of human beings—except, that is, for herself. "It's always myself that I paint," she reportedly said.

Abercrombie died at the age of sixty-eight at her home in Hyde Park. Before her death a retrospective exhibition of her work was held at the Hyde Park Art Center.

See also: Ivan Albright, Henry Darger

Further reading: Elizabeth Kennedy, ed., *Chicago Modern 1893–1945: Pursuit of the New* (2004); Susan Weininger and Kent Smith, *Gertrude Abercrombie* (1991).

Jane Addams

Social Reformer

BORN: September 6, 1860
Cedarville, Illinois

DIED: May 21, 1935
Chicago, Illinois

As founder and director of Hull House, Chicago's first settlement house, Jane Addams's fame has spread far beyond her native Illinois. Of all Chicago's historical figures, she is one of its most honored citizens.

By the time Addams enrolled at Rockford Female Seminary, where she met her lifelong friend and colleague, Ellen Gates Starr, she had developed a deep-seated desire to do something meaningful with her life, although exactly what her calling would be was still unclear.

After the sudden death of her father in 1881, Addams decided to attend the Women's Medical College in Philadelphia, but, near physical collapse herself—due to back problems and emotional distress caused by her father's death—she returned to her hometown of Cedarville in northwestern Illinois to regain her strength. In 1883 she departed on her first trip to Europe. It wasn't until her second visit, almost four years later, that she, accompanied by Starr, visited Toynbee Hall, a settlement house in the London slum of Whitechapel, an area made famous by the Jack the Ripper slayings in the late nineteenth century. Returning to the United States, the two women made plans to transfer the bold and novel idea of a settlement house to the streets of Chicago. All that was needed was a house in the right neighborhood.

They found it at the corner of Halsted and Polk Streets—a brick, two-story, dilapidated mansion built in 1856 by real estate developer Charles J. Hull and located in an overcrowded West Side neighborhood. On September 18, 1889, Addams, Starr, and a housekeeper, Mary Keyser, moved in.

Addams and Starr were not missionaries—they had no great desire to "uplift" the masses. Rather, Hull House was an experiment in social living. Addams and her colleagues maintained that poverty and lack of opportunity—not racial or ethnic inferiority—determined a person's success or failure. Their goal was to improve the area and better the lives of their neighbors. Although inspired by London's Toynbee Hall, Hull House was also part of a larger and indigenous American movement. By 1911 more than 400 social settlements existed in the United States—36 in Chicago alone.

Serving an average of 9,000 people a week, Hull House percolated with around-the-clock activity. There were lectures, art classes, and music lessons—Benny Goodman, Art Hodes, and James Petrillo were among the many students there, while Laura Dainty Pelham's Hull House Players, a professional theater group, pioneered the little theater movement in the United States. Also on the premises was the Jane Club (a boarding club for working girls), a boys' club, an assembly hall, a coffeehouse, a dining room, a day nursery, a kindergarten, an employment bureau, a basketball team, and an orchestra. Cognizant of the need for physical fitness and good personal hygiene habits, especially since many homes at the time lacked hot water and bathing facilities, Hull House offered public baths, a public gymnasium, a public playground—Chicago's first, established in 1893—and a public swimming pool.

The women of Hull House—Addams and Starr as well as Florence Kelley, Dr. Alice Hamilton, Grace Abbott, and Julia Lathrop, among others—were instrumental in the passage of much pioneering social legislation in the city and state, including the first factory inspection laws in Illinois, the first model tenement code in Chicago, and the first juvenile court in Chicago.

Blunt and outspoken, Addams's honesty often got her into trouble. During World War I, for example, she urged world leaders to end hostilities through arbitration rather than violence. For this, she was branded a traitor and Hull House was chastised as a "hotbed of anarchism." Despite such charges, Addams generally was venerated during her lifetime—some even called her a saint. Among her many accomplishments, she established, in 1915, the Women's International League for Peace and Freedom, wrote nearly a dozen books, received fourteen honorary degrees, and became the first American woman to win the Nobel Peace Prize (she shared it with Nicholas Murray Butler in 1931).

Addams died in May 1935 of cancer at the age of seventy-four. For two days, thousands of Chicagoans filed past her coffin on the Hull House grounds to pay their last respects.

Other people have followed in her footsteps, but Jane Addams remains a Chicago original and the institution she founded remains, in many ways, just as relevant today as when it first opened its doors in 1889. Hull House Museum at 800 South Halsted Street, owned by the University of Illinois, attracts more than 20,000 visitors each year. The original 1856 house and the residents dining hall, added in 1905, are all that remain of the thirteen-building complex. In 1989 Hull House celebrated its centennial with an exhibition, *Opening New Worlds*.

The Jane Addams Homes, which opened in 1938 as part of the federal Public Works Administration housing developments that housed mostly Italian immigrants, were occupied from 1938 to 2002. The last remaining of the Jane Addams Homes, located on the Near West Side at 1322 West Taylor Street, is scheduled to open as the National Public Housing Museum in 2012. The International Center for the Study of Housing and Society also will be based there.

On September 8, 2010, the city of Chicago celebrated the 150th anniversary of Addams's birth with a giant cake at Daley Plaza and a "People's Block Party" at the Chicago campus of the University of Illinois.

See also: Alice Hamilton, Florence Kelley, Mary McDowell, Ellen Gates Starr, Graham Taylor

Further reading: Jane Addams, *Twenty Years at Hull-House* (1910); Jane Addams, *The Second Twenty Years at Hull-House* (1930); Allen F. Davis, *American Heroine: The Life and Legend of Jane Addams* (1973); Allen F. Davis and Mary Lynn McCree, *Eighty Years at Hull-House* (1969); Louise W. Knight, *Citizen: Jane Addams and the Struggle for Democracy* (2006) and *Jane Addams: Spirit in Action* (2010); James Weber Linn, *Jane Addams: A Biography* (1935).

George Ade

Humorist and Playwright

BORN: February 9, 1866
Kentland, Indiana

DIED: May 16, 1944
Brook, Indiana

George Ade was an American humorist whose wry commentary and gently satiric portraits of Midwestern types won national recognition. "Early to bed, early to rise and you'll meet very few of our best people," was a typical Ade remark. His unadorned writing style and essentially optimistic outlook brought him both fame and fortune, and he was praised in his time by the likes of Mark Twain and William Dean Howells. His biggest success was *Fables in Slang*, a collection of short sketches that poked good-natured fun at turn-of-the-century manners in the vernacular of the common man and woman.

Ade arrived in Chicago in 1890 and joined the staff of the *Chicago Morning News* (later the *Chicago Record*). Within less than two years, the hard-working Hoosier rose from cub reporter to feature columnist. From 1893 to 1900 Ade wrote a popular newspaper column, "Stories of the Streets and of the Town," illustrated by his friend and college chum, John T. McCutcheon. McCutcheon accompanied Ade on his rounds—in the courts, in the parks, at the theaters, in the shops, and down the alleys—and sketched what he saw. The prolific Ade churned out 1,500- to 1,800-word essays six days a week, creating broad characterizations of easily recognizable human beings in a colorful, slangy idiom. Like his fellow Chicago columnists Finley Peter Dunne, Eugene Field, and Ring Lardner, Ade convincingly captured the texture of American urban life—its nuances, its jargon, its milieu—and presented it in such a way that it appealed to a broad readership. He wrote about newly arrived immigrants striving to find their niche, about wayward souls living in rundown hotels, about brash young men eager to make their mark in the world. Artie Blanchard, Pink Marsh, and Doc Horne were some of his most popular creations. Many of Ade's characters were odd sorts and eccentric types who lived on the frayed edge of society, yet were able to maintain a sunny disposition.

In 1897 the *Morning News* published "The Fable of Sister Mae, Who Did as Well as Could Be Expected," a humorous tale of two sisters from opposite sides of the track. The public liked what it read and wanted more. Ade responded with hundreds of these "Fables in Slang"—short and breezy morality pieces that ended with a flippant remark. This was the pattern he would follow the rest of his career, and it served him well. Ten books of fables were eventually published and several were made into silent films.

Ade enjoyed the status that fame brought. A lover of the theater, he and a group of local actors formed a supper club where visiting thespians could relax after work. He also wrote the comic opera *The Sultan of Sulu*, which opened at the Studebaker Theater in March 1902 and enjoyed a long run on the New York stage, and several plays including *The County Chairman* in 1903 and *The College Widow* in 1904.

Ade retired in 1920 to his 2,400-acre estate, Hazelden, near Kentland, Indiana, where he entertained his friends and enjoyed a life of leisure. He died in his home in 1944 at the age of seventy-eight.

See also: Finley Peter Dunne, Eugene Field, Ring Lardner, Victor Lawson, John T. McCutcheon

Further reading: George Ade, *Chicago Stories* (1963); Lee Coyle, *George Ade* (1964); James DeMuth, *Small Town Chicago: The Comic Perspective of Finley Peter Dunne, George Ade, Ring Lardner* (1980); Fred C. Kelly, *George Ade: Warmhearted Satirist* (1947).

Ivan Albright

Artist

BORN: February 20, 1897
North Harvey, Illinois

DIED: November 18, 1983
Woodstock, Vermont

Modeling his techniques after the classics of the Old Masters, Ivan Albright created images that captured the effects of time. Best known for his still lifes, character studies, and self-portraits, Albright's haunting compositions are most often noted for their idiosyncratic combination of intricate detail and dark, mottled surfaces, as is clearly evident in his masterpiece and most famous work, *The Picture of Dorian Gray*. Meticulously detailed and executed, Albright's paintings often took years to complete.

Albright and his identical twin brother, Malvin, were born in North Harvey, Illinois, in 1897. Their father was a landscape painter who studied under Thomas Eakins. After serving as a medical draftsman in France during World War I, Albright returned to Chicago to enroll at the Art Institute of Chicago, where he graduated in 1923. After attending Northwestern University, he studied architecture at the University of Illinois at Urbana-Champaign. By the early 1930s he had already developed his singular style of elaborate still lifes and melancholy figures who fought valiantly, if unsuccessfully, with the relentless passage of time.

Over his long career, Albright was called many things: a realist, a surrealist, an expressionist. And yet, despite his reputation as a painter of the macabre, he considered the Old Masters of classic European art his true mentors. He observed and was inspired by their techniques and often by their themes. Albright loved rambling titles; indeed, many of his paintings have exceedingly long ones. Among his best works are *Poor Room—There Is No Time, No End, No Today, No Yesterday, No Tomorrow, Only the Forever, and Forever and Forever without End (The Window)* (1942–63), which took more than twenty years to complete; *Into the World There Came a Soul Called Ida* (1929–30), a portrait of an elderly woman looking into a mirror; and *That Which I Should Have Done I Did Not Do (The Door)* (1931–41), an eight-foot-tall painting.

In 1943 he was commissioned to create the title painting of Albert Lewin's film adaptation of Oscar Wilde's 1891 novel *The Picture of Dorian Gray*, which starred the youthful-looking American actor Hurd Hatfield. The painting depicts Dorian Gray's physical transformation as the character leads an increasingly decadent life while his physical appearance remains that of a young, handsome man. At the climax of the film, Hatfield as Gray stabs a knife through its heart in an attempt to kill himself. Lewin shot the film in black and white but he depicted Albright's portrait in color in order to emphasize the rotting and decay of Dorian Gray's moral life. In 2008 Lifeline Theatre in Rogers Park presented the world premiere of an especially haunting adaptation of the Wilde classic by ensemble member Robert Kauzlaric.

Albright died in 1983 in Woodstock, Vermont, at the age of eighty-six. During the one-hundredth anniversary of his birth the Art Institute sponsored a major exhibition on his work. His most famous piece, *The Picture of Dorian Gray* (1943–44), is part of the museum's permanent collection. Other Albright works at the Art Institute include such Chicago-themed works as *Nude Portrait of Gertrude Abercrombie* (1935) and *Self-Portrait at 55 East Division Street* (1947). The Ivan Albright Collection at the Ryerson & Burnham Libraries at the Art Institute of Chicago houses Albright's archives.

Further reading: Michael Croydon, *Ivan Albright* (1978); Courtney Donnell, Susan Weininger, and Robert Cozzolino, *Ivan Albright* (1997); Elizabeth Kennedy, ed., *Chicago Modern 1893–1945: Pursuit of the New* (2004); Susan F. Rossen, ed., *Ivan Albright* (1997).

Nelson Algren

Novelist

BORN: March 28, 1909
Detroit, Michigan

DIED: May 9, 1981
Sag Harbor, New York

A realist in the tradition of Theodore Dreiser, Frank Norris, and James T. Farrell, Nelson Algren graphically portrayed the darker side of life. His gallery of characters included prostitutes, drug addicts, loan sharks, bookies, hobos, con men, and the other outcasts and rejects who haunted the pool halls, taverns, bowling alleys, and tenements of Chicago's underbelly. He wrote of betrayed dreams and lives lost, but the central theme of his work was, says his biographer, Bettina Drew, "the failure of love."

Algren's lifelong ambition was to be a great artist. Born in Detroit, Algren spent his early boyhood in a mostly Irish neighborhood on Chicago's South Side near 71st Street and Cottage Grove Avenue before moving with his family in 1913 to 4834 North Troy Street on the Northwest Side. In 1931 he graduated with a degree in journalism from the University of Illinois at Urbana-Champaign as the nation learned to cope with the full brunt of the Depression. Unable to find work, he rode the rails and hitchhiked across the country laboring at various odd jobs—door-to-door coffee salesman, migrant worker, gas station attendant, carnival shill. Two years later, his first piece—"So Help Me"—ran in *Story* magazine.

On the basis of "So Help Me," Algren received a $100 advance from Vanguard Press to write a novel about hobo life in the American Southwest. No stranger to the road, he hung out with thieves, petty criminals, and vagrants, asking questions, collecting stories, recording their observations, and listening to their patter. Bumming his way to Texas, he ended up serving a four-month prison term for stealing a typewriter from a rural college. From such picaresque experiences came his first novel, *Somebody in Boots*.

Along with novelist Richard Wright, Algren was an important member of the Chicago leftist literary establishment in the 1930s. He joined the Chicago John Reed Club, an intellectual social club that met at 1427 South Michigan Avenue, became secretary of the local chapter of the League of American Writers, and with Jack Conroy, edited a literary magazine, *The New Anvil*. In 1936 Algren was hired as a field worker for the Works Progress Administration's Illinois Writers' Project, compiling neighborhood studies and case histories. Later, in a similar capacity, he roamed the streets tracking down infected victims for the Venereal Disease Control Program. From 1942 to 1945 he served in the army with tours of duty in Wales, Germany, and France.

Algren's career picked up with the publication of his second novel, *Never Come Morning*, a devastating indictment of life in Chicago's Polish American slums, which the *New York Times* described as "brilliant." The deeply offended Polish community, however, condemned the book as Nazi propaganda. So unrelenting a portrait was *Never Come Morning* that the Polish Roman Catholic Union succeeded in banning it from the Chicago Public Library system for several years.

In 1950 Algren won the first National Book Award for Fiction for *The Man with the Golden Arm,* further securing his reputation as an important novelist. But by the time *A Walk on the Wild Side* was published in 1956, Algren's star had set. Critics, weary of his obsession with society's outcasts, dismissed it as a lurid, overly written potboiler, populated with stock characters and tired clichés and prompting one journalist to uncharitably ridicule him as "the bard of the stumblebum."

By the 1960s Algren had given up writing serious fiction and instead earned the bulk of his income from writers' conferences and lecturing. In 1968 he served an undistinguished stint as war correspondent in Vietnam for the *Atlantic Monthly.* Five years later, *The Last Carousel,* a collection of stories and sketches, appeared to enthusiastic reviews but disappointing sales. His last novel, *The Devil's Stocking,* a fictionalized account of the life of boxer Rubin "Hurricane" Carter, was published posthumously in 1983. Other prominent Algren works include the short story collection *The Neon Wilderness* (1947), which features the wonderful "How the Devil Came Down Division Street," and the lengthy prose poem, "Chicago: City on the Make" (1951).

In 1974 Algren moved to the East Coast. That same year he received the Award of Merit for the Novel from the American Academy of Arts and Letters. Several months before his death due to a heart attack in 1981, Algren was elected into the American Academy of Arts and Letters.

For a short period following his death, a segment of West Evergreen Street in the Wicker Park neighborhood was changed to West Algren Street (he had lived in a red brick walk-up at 1958 West Evergreen Street). But when residents complained vehemently—many fumed at the inconvenience of changing their address and just as many questioned the worthiness of Algren's work—the city felt compelled to revert to the original name.

Notwithstanding, in October 1989 a handful of Algren enthusiasts formed the Nelson Algren Committee with its purpose to "further the recognition of Nelson Algren as a major American writer of the twentieth century." Part of their mission is to have "appropriate" parks, streets, and libraries named in his honor and to urge the city to declare his birthday "Nelson Algren Day."

In April 2009, Steppenwolf Theatre sponsored "Nelson Algren Live: 100th Birthday Celebration at the Steppenwolf

Theatre" on the one-hundredth anniversary of his birth. Algren's "The Lightless Room" was read in public for the first time at Steppenwolf by prominent members of the Chicago and non-Chicago creative community, including actor Willem Dafoe, Steppenwolf artistic director Martha Lavey, and novelist Don DeLillo. The evening also included readings by Russell Banks, Barry Gifford, and editor and publisher Dan Simon. That same year, *Entrapment and Other Writings*, a new collection of Algren's work, which featured fiction, poetry, essays, and an interview, was published. In 1999 and again in 2008 the Lookingglass Theatre Company presented *For Keeps and a Single Day*,

John Musial's fascinating multimedia homage to Algren, which incorporated film and an onstage jazz combo. In 2001 the University of Chicago Press published a newly annotated fiftieth anniversary edition of *Chicago: City on the Make* by David Schmittgens and Bill Savage with an introduction by the late Studs Terkel.

See also: Jack Conroy, Theodore Dreiser, James T. Farrell, Richard Wright

Further reading: Martha Heasley Cox and Wayne Chatterton, *Nelson Algren* (1975); Bettina Drew, *Nelson Algren: A Life on the Wild Side* (1989); Art Shay, *Nelson Algren's Chicago* (1988).

Saul Alinsky

Community Organizer

BORN: January 30, 1909
Chicago, Illinois

DIED: June 12, 1972
Carmel, California

Opinionated, profane, and acid-tongued, Saul David Alinsky, the father of community organizing, was given many sobriquets in his day—communist, atheist, fascist—but, above all, he was called an agitator and was proud of it. More than anyone (with the possible exception of Barack Obama), Alinsky put the occupation of community organizer on the map and aroused what many considered a radical, and dangerous, philosophy: that ordinary people could take charge of their own lives by working together.

The child of Russian Jewish immigrants, Saul Alinsky studied sociology at the University of Chicago and graduated in the early 1930s. His fieldwork had included conducting interviews with juvenile delinquents and gangsters on the Near West Side. Along with Joseph Meegan, Alinsky organized the Back of the Yards Neighborhood Council (BYNC) in 1939 under the banner: "We the people will work out our own destiny." It wasn't the first neighborhood-based organization in the city, but it was one of the most influential. With so many obstacles to overcome—a stubborn nationalist pride among area ethnics; a fierce attachment to the local parish—it's remarkable that it got off the ground at all. Yet BYNC proved that by working toward a common goal neighbors could overcome even the most ingrained of Old World antagonisms. Holding its first meeting in July 1939, Alinsky challenged the community to find its own solutions to inadequate housing, unemployment, and crime.

Throughout his career, Alinsky's strategy remained essentially the same. By throwing the enemy off-guard ("mass jujitsu," he called it) using the confrontational tactics of sit-ins, protest demonstrations, and boycotts, he

hoped to force a showdown. "If the end doesn't justify the means," he would ask, "what the hell does?" His weapons were ridicule, sarcasm, and rudeness—all of which he used to devastating effect.

First in the Back of the Yards neighborhood during the Great Depression and then in Woodlawn, Alinsky campaigned for decent housing. In the Back of the Yards he recruited leaders of previously hostile ethnic groups—Lithuanians, Czechs, Slovaks, and Poles—by appealing to their mutual self-interests, something that Barack Obama (a student of Alinsky's methods) would use to his great advantage on his way to winning the presidency many years later in 2008. What's more, Alinsky's methods and tactics of marches and street theater, or threats of using both, were employed by future generations of organizers, in Chicago and elsewhere, from the maverick Catholic priest Father Michael Pfleger to the Reverend Al Sharpton.

In 1940 Alinsky established the Industrial Area Foundation (IAF), an activist organization whose initial aim was "to unite dispossessed peoples into power groups." His approach was simple but effective: to confront or embarrass institutions to achieve his desired aims. While he agreed that ordinary people might not have clout or money, they did have the advantage of numbers: they could get things done with their feet. They had, in other words, the capacity to disrupt. Today, IAF works with sixty affiliated organizations by hosting weeklong workshops. Other groups, such as the Chicago-based National People's Action, used Alinsky's tactics in the 1970s to make the public aware of the biased lending practices at local banks. It was IAF that trained Obama in the 1980s.

Following his success at IAF, Alinsky turned his attention to the racially troubled Woodlawn community, south of Hyde Park. When the University of Chicago announced plans to buy up property in Woodlawn, which would essentially uproot large numbers of poor black families, Alinsky raised funds from Catholic and Protestant churches and formed, in 1961, The Woodlawn Organization (TWO).

TWO's protests were marvelous examples of the power of negative publicity. When Woodlawn residents complained in vain to the school board of severe overcrowding in their elementary schools while classrooms in white neighborhoods stood half empty, Alinsky mounted a "Truth Squad" campaign, which consisted of battalions of mothers armed with cameras who descended upon the schools and took photographs of the unoccupied desks for all to see. On another occasion, caravans of black Woodlawn residents were bused to the homes of white slumlords on the North Side, where they picketed up and down the streets, distributing leaflets and generally raising a ruckus. Bluntly but effectively, Alinsky got his point across.

Alinsky traveled throughout the country organizing community groups—in Kansas City, Kansas; South Saint Paul, Minnesota; Lackawanna, New York; and Rochester, New York. He also wrote several books, including two primers of community organization—*Reveille for Radicals* (1945) and *Rules for Radicals* (1971)—and authored, in 1949, a sympathetic biography of union leader John L. Lewis. In his last years, Alinsky began organizing among the white middle class, calling that vast group of Americans the most alienated in the country. "They don't have a spokesman and the values they were brought up with are gone," he said.

Although Alinsky died in 1972 of a heart attack, his legacy is very much alive. Training centers and grassroots organizations, whose very existence would have been inconceivable without his work, are scattered across the country. The Industrial Area Foundation continues to train organizers by conducting intensive workshops, while the group Alinsky is most closely identified with, the Back of the Yards Neighborhood Council, celebrated its seventieth anniversary in 2009. In January 2009, friends and advocates gathered to celebrate what would have been Alinsky's one-hundredth birthday. Alinsky's centennial was marked by yearlong series of programs not only in Chicago but across the United States.

Today's generation of activists, organizers, and social workers, whether they realize it or not, owe a large debt to Saul Alinsky.

Further reading: P. David Finks, *The Radical Vision of Saul Alinsky* (1984); Sanford D. Horwitt, *Let Them Call Me Rebel: Saul Alinsky, His Life and Legacy* (1989); Robert A. Slayton, *Back of the Yards: The Making of a Local Democracy* (1986); Nicholas von Hoffman, *Radical: A Portrait of Saul Alinsky* (2010).

Fran Allison

Television Entertainer

BORN: November 20, 1907
LaPorte City, Iowa

DIED: June 13, 1989
Sherman Oaks, California

Along with Burr Tillstrom, Fran Allison formed the team that comprised *Kukla, Fran, and Ollie*, one of the most popular shows in television history. Allison's warm personality and reassuring presence earned her the nickname "First Lady of Chicago Broadcasting."

Allison made her singing debut at age four before a meeting of the Grand Army of the Republic in her native Iowa. She attended Coe College in Cedar Rapids, Iowa, where she earned degrees in music and education. While teaching the fourth grade, she began producing amateur contests and sang live on small Iowa radio stations. In 1937 Allison auditioned as a vocalist on Don McNeill's *Breakfast Club* program on the NBC radio network. Impressed with her singing voice and ebullient personality, NBC executives signed her to a long-term contract. On the *Breakfast Club* Allison began to develop further the character of Aunt Fannie, the town gossip, a role that she had originated on the Iowa stations.

When her husband, a music publisher representative, entered the service during World War II, Allison contributed to the war effort by selling war bonds at Chicago stage shows. At one of those shows she met a young puppeteer named Burr Tillstrom. After the war, Tillstrom began developing a children's television program in Chicago that featured an unusual cast of puppets with rather exotic names: Kukla, Oliver J. Dragon, Beulah Witch, Fletcher Rabbit, Cecil Bill, and Madame Oglepuss. But he felt something was missing. What the program needed, said Tillstrom, was a human touch. He immediately thought of the young woman he had met at the war bonds shows.

Kukla, Fran, and Ollie premiered in 1947 on the ABC affiliate, WBKB. That same year it moved to the NBC affiliate, WNBQ-TV (which later changed its call letters to WMAQ). In 1954 the Kuklapolitans left NBC to rejoin ABC. The program's nonhuman characters usually stole the show—Kukla, the earnest little Everyman; Ollie, the cocky know-it-all dragon; pompous Madame Oglepuss; gossipy Beulah Witch; and an assorted collection of pranksters and tricksters. No matter how mischievous or outrageous Tillstrom's motley characters were, though, the calm figure of Fran Allison was always there to maintain control. Whether rolling her eyes at the latest antics of Oliver J. Dragon or feigning shock at a remark by Madame Oglepuss, Allison displayed ample doses of patience and wisdom. Although poor ratings eventually led to the show's cancellation in 1957, for ten years the television audience was willingly swept away by the humorous adventures and good-natured fun of Kukla, Fran, and company. In 1961 Allison and the famous puppets returned to television—in a nationally syndicated show from New York—in five-minute installments on NBC five days a week.

Allison had a palpable connection to her nonhuman colleagues. She treated them with the utmost respect and dignity. She never considered them mere cloth. "Kukla, Ollie, and the others are as real to me as people," she once remarked.

Allison continued to appear on Chicago television after the demise of *Kukla, Fran, and Ollie.* In the late fifties she hosted the Emmy-winning *Fran Allison Show* and occasionally appeared in local plays, commercials, and television specials. She left Chicago in the late 1960s, first settling in New Jersey, and later moving to Los Angeles, where she hosted a television program for senior citizens. Occasionally Allison and Tillstrom appeared in revivals of *Kukla, Fran, and Ollie* at various Chicago theaters. In 1970 the show aired over public television stations for a five-week run and in 1978 the Chicago Historical Society (now the Chicago History Museum) staged a weeklong *Kukla, Fran, and Ollie* festival. The following year the Kuklapolitans put together a holiday special, *Tis the Season to Be Ollie,* on Channel 5. For several years, beginning in 1979, Kukla and Ollie—without Fran—were a Christmas tradition at the Goodman Theatre.

Allison died of leukemia in her Sherman Oaks, California, home at the age of eighty-one.

See also: Dave Garroway, Burr Tillstrom
Further reading: Daniel Berger and Steve Jajkowski, eds., *Chicago Television* (2010).

John Peter Altgeld
Politician

BORN: December 30, 1847
Nieder Selters, Germany

DIED: March 12, 1902
Joliet, Illinois

Honest, courageous, and scrupulously fair, John Peter Altgeld was that rare breed of politician who stood by his principles, refusing to bow to public opinion. His accomplishments while in office were many—during his tenure, the University of Illinois was built, the public park system of Chicago was enlarged, and the powers of state government were extended—but he is primarily remembered as the man who pardoned the Haymarket "martyrs."

Brought to the United States as an infant by his German immigrant parents, Altgeld was raised on a farm in Ohio. Following a stint in the Union army, he headed first to Cincinnati, then to St. Louis, and later to Kansas and Arkansas before settling in Savannah, Missouri, to study law. Admitted to the bar in 1872, he became a prosecuting attorney but left in 1875 to settle in the rapidly growing city of Chicago to practice law. With no connections, however, he had a difficult time landing on his feet. But he was determined to make his way.

As soon as he accumulated sufficient savings, Altgeld began to purchase lots of land in the Lakeview neighborhood where he had settled, subdividing and selling the property at a considerable profit. In 1877 he married and moved into a two-story frame house on Wellington Street between Halsted and Clark Streets. As his financial status improved, so did his living conditions. Altgeld and his wife moved into a brick house on West Grace Street. Altgeld then became a builder. His most ambitious project by far was the sixteen-story Unity Building in downtown Chicago: in 1890 he purchased a ninety-nine year lease on an expensive lot at 127 North Dearborn Street for the structure. A costly construction error, however, forced him to sell most of his other properties in order to pay for the construction of the Unity Building. This building, which had been praised as Chicago's new "skyscraper," was demolished in 1989.

In 1884 Altgeld, a Democrat, ran for Congress representing the Fourth District, a largely Republican area on

the North Side, but lost to Republican George Adams. The publication of the booklet *Our Penal Machinery and Its Victims,* however, soon brought him public attention. A brilliant indictment against the criminal justice system—and wildly ahead of its time—it boldly claimed that incarceration not only failed to rehabilitate criminals, but actually turned them into repeat offenders.

In 1886 Altgeld was elected judge of the superior court of Cook County and served five years before resigning to devote his time to real estate matters, with which he accumulated a tidy sum. In 1892, bored with the business world, he returned to politics and was nominated as the Democratic candidate for governor of Illinois. His opponents, however, branded him as a radical sympathizer and ardent socialist. Altgeld refused to respond to the accusations, choosing instead to run a low-key and cautious campaign. The strategy worked, for he won by a surprisingly large margin over the Republican incumbent Joseph Fifer. The victory earned him the honor of being the state's first foreign-born governor and the first governor to reside in Chicago.

Altgeld's term contained two of the most divisive moments in Chicago history. On May 4, 1886, a crowd of spectators gathered in Haymarket Square near Randolph and Desplaines Streets to protest the treatment by police of workers at the McCormick Harvesting plant the previous day. During the meeting, a bomb was thrown by an unknown figure, killing several people. Four men—Albert Parsons, August Spies, Adolph Fischer, and George Engel—were arrested, convicted, and, ultimately, on November 11, 1887, executed.

After reviewing the transcripts from the Haymarket Riot trial, Altgeld, on June 26, 1893, pardoned Samuel Fielden, Michael Schwab, and Oscar Neebe, the three surviving prisoners convicted of murder, including the murder of police officer Mathias Degan. In Altgeld's briefs, he denounced the selection of the jurors, presented irrefutable evidence that the police had introduced perjured testimony, and concluded that Judge Joseph Gary had conducted the trial with "malicious ferocity."

Now viewed as a courageous act of justice, Altgeld's decision was immediately condemned as the work of an anarchist, except, of course, in labor circles where he was hailed as a hero. Across the country, the reaction was much the same: "Governor Altgeld has encouraged anarchy, rapine, and the overthrow of civilization," said the *Toledo Blade* while the *Chicago Tribune* charged that "Governor Altgeld has apparently not a drop of pure American blood in his veins." Residents of Naperville, Illinois, burned his figure in effigy. There was even talk of impeachment.

Altgeld weathered the storm, but soon another crisis erupted. When wages were cut in the company town of Pullman without a commensurate reduction in rent, the employees voted to strike. Many joined locals of the American Railway Union, which, led by Eugene Debs, agreed to boycott Pullman cars. To make matters worse, President Grover Cleveland ordered federal troops, stationed in nearby Fort Sheridan, into Chicago—despite the vehement objection of Governor Altgeld—to maintain order and ensure the delivery of the U.S. mail. Affronted, Altgeld assured the president that Illinois was able to take care of itself. The strike finally ended, but not until Debs and other union leaders were imprisoned, former Pullman employees were blacklisted, and many lives were lost.

Altgeld ran for reelection in 1896 but lost by an overwhelming margin to Republican nominee John R. Tanner. Virtually bankrupt, he settled into semiretirement. Despite losing his gubernatorial reelection bid, Altgeld was still recognized as the leader of the Democratic Party in Illinois. One year after the loss, he handpicked Carter Harrison II as the Democratic nominee for mayor of Chicago, an office that the young Harrison won handily. But Altgeld, who believed in public ownership of streetcar franchises, was persuaded to run for mayor in 1899 when Harrison retracted campaign promises and aligned himself with the Democratic ward bosses in support of private ownership of the streetcar franchise. Again Altgeld lost.

On March 11, 1902, Altgeld suffered a cerebral hemorrhage while delivering a speech in Joliet, Illinois, and died early the next morning. Ironically, the very same press that once damned him so vehemently during the Haymarket episode mourned his passing as a great loss. Only in death did he earn the praise that eluded him in life.

Altgeld Street is named in his honor.

See also: Eugene Debs, Carter Harrison II, Albert and Lucy Parsons, George Pullman, Charles Tyson Yerkes

Further reading: William J. Adelman, *Haymarket Revisited* (1976); Paul Avrich, *The Haymarket Tragedy* (1984); Harry Barnard, *Eagle Forgotten: The Life of John Peter Altgeld* (1938); William H. Carwardine, *The Pullman Strike* (1973); Ray Ginger, *Altgeld's America: The Lincoln Ideal Versus Changing Realities* (1958).

Arthur Andersen

Accountant

BORN: May 30, 1885
Plano, Illinois

DIED: January 10, 1947
Chicago, Illinois

Arthur Edward Andersen founded a public accounting firm that was once a member of the so-called Big Five accounting firms. Andersen promoted the one-firm concept. From Chicago to London, San Francisco to Santiago, the firm applied uniform accounting principles. By the time of his death, Arthur Andersen and Company had branches in sixteen American cities as well as offices in London, Paris, and Mexico City. However, because of its tragic association with the Enron scandal, first revealed in November 2001, the firm no longer exists. The consultancy arm of Arthur Andersen is still operating, though, and is known as Accenture.

The fourth of eight children, Arthur Andersen was born in the town of Plano, Illinois, about fifty miles west of Chicago. His parents, John William and Mary Aabye Andersen, emigrated from Norway in 1882. After his birth, the family returned to Norway for several years and then came back to the United States and settled on Chicago's West Side. In 1901 Andersen found work as a mail boy at Fraser and Chalmers Company, which later became a part of the Allis-Chalmers Manufacturing Company. He attended night school and received his high school diploma in 1903. By 1906 he had risen to the position of assistant to the controller.

In 1907 Andersen joined the Chicago staff of Price Waterhouse and Company. The following year he passed the certified public accountant (CPA) examination, earning the distinction of being the youngest CPA in Illinois. At that time accounting was still a relatively new profession (it was not recognized by the state of Illinois until 1903). Andersen also enrolled in Northwestern University's night school program. He was such a conscientious student that the university asked him to teach a few accounting classes.

In 1911 Andersen commuted between his evening classes at Northwestern and his position as controller of Joseph Schlitz Brewing Company in Milwaukee. When several key faculty members left the university in 1912, the school appointed Andersen assistant professor and head of the accounting department. He reorganized the department. It was, he later recalled, a particularly stressful period as he was forced to prepare the courses on a weekly or monthly basis. "More frequently than not, the notes came off the mimeographing machine just before the class hour; there was not even sufficient time to allow them to dry," he recalled in his biography.

In 1913 Andersen and Clarence M. DeLany formed Andersen, DeLany, and Company with offices at 111 West Monroe Street. From the beginning, they stressed professionalism by hiring a staff of full-time accountants at a time when the accounting profession felt that such a move would lead to soaring fees and dwindling clients. While maintaining his practice in Chicago, Andersen continued to teach accounting classes at Northwestern. In 1915 he was promoted to professor of accounting. Four years later, his partner, Clarence M. DeLany, left and the name of the firm was changed to Arthur Andersen and Company. By 1922 the firm had grown so rapidly that Andersen felt it necessary to resign from the Northwestern teaching staff to devote more time to his own practice.

As the firm grew, so did its reputation. Andersen served an impressive list of clients, including Goldblatt Brothers, Hershey Chocolate Corporation, Marshall Field and Company, Walgreen Company, Stewart-Warner Corporation, and Texaco. In addition, Andersen's expertise in federal tax laws and practices contributed much to the firm's early success.

Andersen's one-firm concept streamlined the workload and made for smoother business practices among branch offices throughout the world. The one-firm concept integrated company policy, training, and operations so that all Andersen employees—no matter where they were located—learned the same principles. From office procedure to office design, Andersen stressed consistency in all matters.

After World War II, Andersen concentrated on establishing overseas branch offices to serve his international clients. In 1963, twenty-seven offices were operating outside the United States. By 1990, Arthur Andersen and Company had 243 offices in 54 countries, employing more than 51,000 people worldwide. Each member firm was privately owned and controlled by the partners in each particular country. Andersen knew that a company is only as good as its employees. With that in mind, the firm established an employee training school in 1970 in west suburban St. Charles, Illinois. Now called the Q Center, it is essentially a conference and training facility.

Andersen was active in civic and philanthropic affairs such as the Chicago Home for the Friendless, the First Methodist Church of Evanston, the Salvation Army, and the American Red Cross. From 1936 to 1942 he served as president of the Norwegian-American Historical Association. In addition, he was chairman of the Illinois Board of CPA Examiners and was president of the Illinois Society of Certified Public Accountants from 1918 to 1919.

In 1939 King Haakon of Norway awarded Andersen the Commander's Cross of the Royal Order of Saint Olav. In 1953 he was elected posthumously to the Accounting Hall of Fame at Ohio State University. A company history,

Arthur Andersen and Company: The First Fifty Years, 1913–1963, was published in 1963.

Andersen died in January 1947 at St. Luke's Hospital in Chicago. He was sixty-one.

See also: Arthur Young

Further reading: Walter H. Andersen and others, *Arthur Andersen and Company: The First Fifty Years, 1913–1963* (1963); Kenan Heise and Michael Edgerton, *Chicago: Center for Enterprise.* 2 vols. (1982).

Fred Anderson

Musician

BORN: March 22, 1929
Monroe, Louisiana

DIED: June 24, 2010

Jazz: what might fascinate about the music is how it rides over the edges, how it touches in between.

—Gerald Majer,
*The Velvet Lounge:
On Late Chicago Jazz*

Fred Anderson was many things: a tenor saxophonist, a club owner, a jazz advocate, a mentor to generations of jazz musicians. He started out as a disciple of Charlie Parker before finding his own voice and becoming one of the most influential jazz musicians in Chicago history. Anderson and the organization that he cofounded, the Association for the Advancement of Creative Musicians (AACM), are widely credited with establishing Chicago as an important center of experimental jazz.

Born in Monroe, Louisiana, Anderson came to Chicago with his mother—his father had abandoned them before the move up north—when he was still a boy. They settled into a one-room apartment in Evanston. A tenor saxophone that belonged to his cousin led to Anderson's lifelong interest in the instrument. A high school dropout, Anderson never played in a band or participated in school ensembles. "I was always an independent cat," he told AACM biographer George E. Lewis. "Me being an only child, maybe that was it. I sort of, like, taught myself music." Instead he received only a matter of months of training on the sax and some rudimentary instruction in music theory—he attended the Roy Knapp Conservatory on Wabash Avenue in Chicago's Loop and for a short time had a private tutor—otherwise Anderson was a self-taught genius. His jazz "textbook" consisted not of books per se but rather the classic recordings of Charlie Parker and tenor saxophonist Lester Young. Other influences included Dexter Gordon, Coleman Hawkins, Jay McShann, Duke Ellington, and Gene Ammons.

It wasn't until Anderson was in his thirties before he actually performed in a jazz club. In the early 1960s he formed his own group and, after a rather lengthy period of not releasing records or having his own band, he put together another outfit in 1972, the Fred Anderson Sextet. In the meantime, he supported his family by doing odd jobs as a waiter, a carpet installer, and a bartender. But jazz always remained his true love. Unfortunately, the kind of jazz he admired and excelled in—a demanding style of jazz

that combined the bebop of Parker with the so-called free jazz of the 1960s—was not commercially viable. Thus, in 1965, with fellow jazz aficionados and musicians—pianists Muhal Richard Abrams and Jodie Christian, drummer Steve McCall, and composer Phil Cohran—he created the nonprofit AACM. The organization evolved out of Abrams's Experimental Band. "We wanted to have a place where we could sponsor each other in concerts of our original compositions," another band member, the saxophonist Roscoe Mitchell, told the *New York Times.* AACM also offered a training program for young, aspiring Chicago musicians and provided exchange programs. In addition to Anderson, Abrams, and Mitchell, AACM membership includes or has included Lester Bowie, Joseph Jarmon, Malachi Favors, Jack DeJohnette, Leroy Jenkins, Henry Threadgill, Anthony Braxton, Mwata Bowden, Billy Brimfield, Kahil El'Zabar, Douglas Ewart, and Edward Wilkerson.

In May 1977, Anderson and Sharon Friedman opened a short-lived performance space called the Birdhouse (Gerald Majer described it as "a big empty room with folding chairs and couches along the walls"). It was named in honor of Anderson's hero, Charlie Parker, and located in the 4500 block of North Lincoln Avenue in the Lincoln Square neighborhood. But zoning issues, rising costs, low turnout, and objections from local residents—as well as not-so-vaguely veiled racial discrimination—led to its closing in late June 1978. In 1982 Anderson took over the Velvet Lounge, at 2128½ South Indiana Avenue, on the edge of Bronzeville, the historic African American neighborhood on the South Side. Its name was said to have derived from a comment that a customer once made about Anderson's sax playing as sounding as "smooth as velvet." By day it was a working-man's bar, by night a jazz club. Every Sunday Anderson held informal jam sessions, which soon became a mainstay for Chicago jazz musicians. He also served as the club's unofficial doorman and gatekeeper as well as its headliner.

Over the years Anderson was a mentor to many young musicians, including drummer Hamid Drake, flutist Nicole Mitchell, bassist Harrison Bankhead, trombonist

George Lewis, vocalist Dee Alexander, and saxophonist Ken Vandermark.

When the Velvet Lounge was set to be demolished to make room for a condominium development, Anderson's many admirers and fellow musicians raised enough money to allow the club to reopen around the corner. The old Velvet Lounge closed in April 2006, and a remarkably short three months later the new Velvet Lounge, at 67 East Cermak Road, opened. *Chicago Tribune* jazz critic Howard Reich has rightly called the Velvet Lounge "ground zero for avant-garde jazz in Chicago."

Anderson recorded more than two dozen albums, either with his own bands or with other musicians. His recordings include *Birdhouse* (1996), *Blue Winter* (2005), *Timeless: Live at the Velvet Lounge* (2006), *From the River to the Ocean* (2007), *The Missing Link* (2008), *Live at the Velvet Lounge Vol. III* (2008), *80th Birthday Bash: Live at the Velvet Lounge* (2009), and *Black Horn Long Gone* (2010).

On June 14, 2010, Anderson suffered a massive heart attack. He died ten days later. He was 81 years old.

Prior to falling ill, Anderson had been scheduled to appear at the Vision Festival, an annual celebration of free jazz, which was held on June 24, 2010, at the Abrons Arts Center on New York's Lower East Side (Muhal Richard Abrams had started a New York chapter of the AACM in 1983). As a eulogy, Abrams and festival director Patricia Nicholson asked for a ten-minute silence in Anderson's honor. A few days later, on Tuesday, June 29, 2010, hundreds came together in Chicago to offer their own celebration, giving testimonials and playing jazz for more than three hours at Leak and Sons Funeral Home at 7838 South Cottage Grove Avenue on the South Side.

Further reading: Nate Chinen, "Four Decades of Music that Redefined Free," *New York Times*, May 2, 2008; George Lewis, *A Power Stronger than Itself: The Association for the Advancement of Creative Musicians* (2008); Gerald Majer, *The Velvet Lounge: On Late Chicago Jazz* (2005); Ben Ratliff, "Honoring Heroes of Jazz, with Words, Silence, and Improvisation," *New York Times*, June 26, 2010; Howard Reich, "Saxophonist Nurtured Jazz in Chicago," *Chicago Tribune*, June 25, 2010; Neil Tesser, "A Jazz Great Who Left More than His Music," *New York Times*, June 27, 2010.

Margaret C. Anderson

Editor

BORN: November 24, 1886
Indianapolis, Indiana

DIED: October 19, 1973
Le Cannet, France

Margaret Caroline Anderson edited the seminal literary magazine, *The Little Review*, during the heady days of the Chicago literary renaissance of the early twentieth century. In those pages she introduced the works of Sherwood Anderson, Ernest Hemingway, and many others, and she championed cubism, Dada, surrealism, and anarchism. For a few brief but colorful years, Margaret Anderson was the toast of the town and the undisputed queen of the city's bohemian community.

The eldest of three daughters, Anderson received a conventional Midwestern upbringing in Indiana. She attended high school in Anderson, Indiana, and enrolled at a two-year junior preparatory class at Western College for Women in Oxford, Ohio. She left college with dreams of pursuing a career as a pianist. In 1908 she moved to Chicago with her sister Lois and worked as a book reviewer for the *Continent*, a religious weekly, before joining the staff of the *Dial*, a literary review. By 1913 she was the book critic for the *Chicago Evening Post*. Dissatisfied by the direction of her career, she became determined to establish her own magazine, even though she had no previous experience editing a magazine nor did she have the financial backing. But such details were obstacles to be overcome, which she most defiantly did.

In 1914 Anderson founded *The Little Review* and moved into room 917 (and later room 834) of the Fine Arts Building. The first issue, which contained articles on Nietzsche, feminism, and psychoanalysis, made a big splash. The magazine's motto too was bold and unconventional: it promised to make "no compromise with public taste." Living up to its motto, it published the best poetry, criticism, and artwork available without regard to fashion, politics, or convention. Devoted to art for art's sake, *The Little Review* introduced many of the best-known American, English, and Irish writers of the twentieth century to its readers, including the aforementioned Hemingway and Anderson as well as T. S. Eliot, Hart Crane, André Breton, Jean Cocteau, Emma Goldman, Amy Lowell, Carl Sandburg, Ford Madox Ford, Malcolm Cowley, W. B. Yeats, James Joyce, Wallace Stevens, William Carlos Williams, and Gertrude Stein.

In 1916 Anderson met jane heap (heap preferred the use of lowercase), who soon became her business as well as life partner. The following year poet Ezra Pound became

the magazine's foreign editor. Through Pound's many connections, *The Little Review* published works by Yeats, Eliot, Crane, and Joyce. In 1917 Anderson moved the magazine to New York, where she again caused a stir when, in 1918, she began serializing excerpts of James Joyce's controversial masterpiece, *Ulysses*. The U.S. Post Office seized and burned the offending issues and then, in 1921, convicted Anderson and heap on obscenity charges; each was fined $50.

Although the writers who contributed to *The Little Review* were paid nothing, they agreed to appear in her magazine: *The Little Review* had cachet, and Margaret Anderson was rapidly becoming the queen of the little magazine movement. She believed life could be lived as a work of art, and her unconventional magazine reflected that sentiment. Once, bored by the lack of good works available, she decided to publish an entire issue of 64 blank pages. She was nothing if not true to her word, and to her vision for the magazine.

In 1923 Anderson turned over the editorship of *The Little Review* to heap and moved to Paris. *The Little Review*

began to publish quarterly in 1923 and by 1926 only sporadically. It shut down that same year, although a final issue was published in Paris in 1929.

Anderson died in 1973 from heart failure in France. She is buried in the Notre Dame des Agnes Cemetery.

Anderson wrote a three-volume autobiography: *My Thirty Years' War* (1930), *The Fiery Fountains* (1951), and *The Strange Necessity* (1962). She also wrote a work of fiction, *Forbidden Fires*, which was published in 1996. *The Little Review Anthology* was published in 1953.

From October 1, 2006, to January 5, 2007, the Beinecke Library at Yale University, which houses her letters, exhibited *Making No Compromise: Margaret Anderson and the Little Review*.

See also: Harriet Monroe

Further reading: Don Darnell, "Martie: A Feminist Before Her Time, Margaret Anderson Was the Spark Who Turned Chicago into the Hottest Literary Town in the World," *Chicago Tribune Sunday Magazine*, January 20, 1991.

Sherwood Anderson

Novelist

BORN: September 13, 1876
Camden, Ohio

DIED: March 8, 1941
Colon, Panama

Dreamer, hustler, businessman—Sherwood Anderson played many roles during his lifetime, but it is as hero of the bohemian set during the Chicago literary renaissance of the early twentieth century that he is best remembered.

Anderson's early years in Chicago were disappointing. He had come to the city in 1896 at the age of twenty to "make his mark" in life. Instead of finding Easy Street, he encountered drudgery and destitution, rolling barrels of apples in a North Side factory. Two years later he returned to his native Ohio when his regiment of the National Guard was called into active duty during the Spanish-American War, and he was sent to Cuba. In 1900 he moved once again to Chicago and found work as a copywriter for an advertising firm.

Bored with his job, Anderson returned to Ohio to establish a mail-order paint firm. As business waned, he retreated more and more into his writing—he had made a habit of scribbling down his thoughts and observations during the workday and in his spare time. He was careful to separate his creative identity from his practical side; he did not wish one to interfere with the other.

The strain of toiling at his day job and writing fiction at night proved too much for him, though. In November 1912, he suffered a nervous breakdown. He wandered for four days—no one knows exactly where—until he turned up at a Cleveland hospital, apparently suffering from amnesia brought on by nervous exhaustion. Abandoning his wife and his business career in Ohio in order to pursue what he called "a life of truth," Anderson returned to Chicago, found an apartment at 735 Cass Avenue (now Wabash Avenue), and rejoined his old advertising firm. In this quest he was encouraged by Floyd Dell, editor of the *Friday Literary Review* and the city's resident bohemian. Dell took Anderson under his wing, referring to the businessman and writer as Chicago's "great unpublished author," and attempting to find a publisher for his first novel, *Windy McPherson's Son*.

With the publication of *Windy McPherson's Son*, the story of a small-town dreamer who goes to the big city, Anderson began to be taken seriously as a writer. Although *Marching Man*, his second novel, received mostly poor notices and stalled the momentum, the release of *Winesburg, Ohio*, a collection of short stories published in 1919 that captured the numbing conformity of small-town America, put him back on track; in fact, it changed everything for him. Not only was it hailed as Anderson's masterpiece—it is still regarded as an American classic—it also confirmed Chicago's growing reputation as a literary center. In 2006 a musical adaptation of *Winesburg, Ohio,* by Eric Rosen of the About Face Theatre, was mounted at Steppenwolf Theatre.

As his name grew, Anderson's link with Chicago loosened. Traveling to Paris in 1921, he discovered he was more famous abroad than at home. In 1922 he left Chicago altogether and began a peripatetic existence, lecturing and traveling across the country before finally settling in 1927 in Marion, Virginia, where he bought and edited two weekly newspapers. By 1933 he had become a national institution—though more celebrity than writer—whose time had come and gone.

In February 1941, Anderson visited South America as the government's unofficial goodwill ambassador. He became sick en route and died from peritonitis in Panama on March 8, 1941. *Sherwood Anderson's Memoirs* was published posthumously the following year.

See also: Floyd Dell, Edgar Lee Masters

Further reading: Dale Kramer, *Chicago Renaissance: The Literary Life of the Midwest 1900–1930* (1966); Alson J. Smith, *Chicago's Left Bank* (1953); Kim Townsend, *Sherwood Anderson* (1987); Kenny J. Williams, *A Storyteller and a City: Sherwood Anderson's Chicago* (1988).

Cap Anson

Baseball Player and Manager

BORN: April 17, 1852
Marshalltown, Iowa

DIED: April 14, 1922
Chicago, Illinois

Adrian Constantine "Cap" Anson earned a reputation as baseball's greatest slugger and player-manager of the nineteenth century. He won three National League batting championships and five pennants with the Chicago White Stockings (who later became the Cubs).

Anson attended the University of Iowa but in 1869 switched to the University of Notre Dame, where he organized the school's first baseball team. He began his professional career with the Rockford Forest Citys. His friend and colleague, Albert G. Spalding, played with the same team. In 1871 the Philadelphia Athletics of the National Association, predecessor of the National League, acquired Anson. He stayed with Philadelphia until 1875. The following year Spalding, then a pitcher for the Boston team, became manager of a new Chicago club, the White Stockings, and invited Anson to join as both player and captain. Dubbed the White Stockings (no relation to the present-day White Sox baseball club) because the players wore white hose, the team played at six different locations between 1870 and 1894, according to historian Steven A. Reiss, including the West Side Grounds bounded by Polk Street and Wolcott Avenue.

In 1879 Anson became manager and switched from third base to first. Under his leadership, the White Stockings became baseball's first "dynasty." The team captured five league pennants. Anson had an eye for talent. He signed Billy Sunday, who later became a popular evangelist, and groomed John G. Clarkson, considered by many to be one of baseball's greatest pitchers. In 1880, Anson and Spalding signed Larry Corcoran, Fred Goldsmith, Tommy Burns, and the great Mike "King" Kelly.

Anson retired in 1898 to become the nonplaying manager of the New York Giants. Shortly after, he finally decided to hang up his baseball mitt permanently. In 1890 he wrote his autobiography, *A Ball Player's Career.*

Anson introduced several key innovations into the game of baseball. He was the first manager to use two pitchers regularly, and he introduced the practice of spring training. Like Spalding, Anson was a stern disciplinarian, imposing strict curfews and meting out heavy fines to transgressors. Sometimes he used his considerable clout to maintain the status quo, such as when he wielded his power to bar African American athletes from playing major league ball.

Besides being a great coach, Anson was a gifted athlete. According to Chicago sports writers Eddie Gold and Art Ahrens, Anson boasted a lifetime batting average of .333. By the time he retired, he had 3,041 hits, including 532 doubles, 124 triples, and 97 home runs.

Anson had other interests besides baseball. From 1905 to 1907 he served as the city clerk of Chicago. Later, he performed on the vaudeville stage with his two daughters, and then he opened a billiard hall. But baseball remained his first love. At one point, he formed his own semipro team, Anson's Colts.

Anson died in April 1922. By then baseball had become such an indelible part of American life that it was difficult to imagine a time without it. Under Anson, Chicago had earned a solid reputation as a good baseball town. By 1903 the White Stockings name was changed to the Chicago Cubs (after being known by several other names, including the Orphans and the Colts). In April 1914, the Cubs opened the season in their new home, Weeghman Park, at the corner of Clark and Addison Streets. In 1926 the name was changed to Wrigley Field.

Anson was elected to the National Baseball Hall of Fame in 1939. Anson Place is named in his honor.

See also: Albert Spalding, Billy Sunday, William Wrigley Jr.

Further reading: Eddie Gold and Art Ahrens, *The Golden Era Cubs 1876–1945* (1985); Larry D. Names, *Bury My Heart at Wrigley Field: The History of the Chicago Cubs* (1996); Randy Roberts and Carson Cunningham, eds., *Before the Curse: The Chicago Cubs' Glory Years, 1870–1945* (2012); Steven A. Reiss, *City Games: The Evolution of American Urban Society and the Rise of Sports* (1989).

Philip Danforth Armour

Industrialist

BORN: May 16, 1832
Stockbridge, New York

DIED: January 8, 1901
Chicago, Illinois

Along with competitors Gustavus Swift, Nelson Morris, and the Cudahy brothers, Philip Danforth Armour helped make Chicago the meatpacking center of the country. Armour, a Yankee farm boy from upstate New York, firmly believed in the value of thrift, hard work, and perseverance. Keeping emotions in check also played a part in his attitude. "Most men talk too much," said the taciturn Armour. "Most of my success has been due to keeping my mouth shut."

In the early 1850s, Armour left upstate New York to pan for gold in California. Returning briefly to his hometown of Stockbridge, New York, he then moved to Milwaukee and entered the soap business. When his soap factory burned down, the restless Armour picked up again, this time settling in the 1860s in St. Paul, Minnesota, where he stayed for two years selling hides. Still not quite satisfied, Armour returned to Milwaukee to form a partnership with packer John Plankinton. With the Civil War raging and fresh meat in demand, business prospered.

Following the war, the meatpacking industry, which had been centered in Cleveland, shifted to Chicago. Sensing that Chicago was a city on the move, Armour transferred his base of operations in 1875 from Milwaukee to the booming metropolis and shrewdly began manipulating the pork market, buying when the price was low and selling at a handsome profit. Thus, Armour made a quick fortune—reportedly as much as $6 million during a twelve-month span. He expanded further into grain shipping, adding to his already impressive empire. An inventive businessman, Armour canned meat and exported it to Europe and shipped fresh beef to the East in the newly invented refrigerated cars.

In the early days of the packing business, animal wastes were promptly discarded. But Armour realized that by-products could actually bring in additional revenue. In this way, nothing—save the squeal of the pig, as he reportedly once said—would be wasted. Thus, the fat of the cattle was turned into lard, the intestines cleaned and salted and used for sausage casings, the blood and animal refuse converted into fertilizer.

By 1892 Armour could observe his empire from afar and boast of offices not only in Chicago but also in Omaha and Kansas City with 20,000 people in his employ. Still looking for ways to diversify, he began manufacturing toilet soaps, violin strings, medicines, and hospital accessories.

Armour harbored little sympathy toward unions and even less toward strikers. "As long as we are heads of our own houses," said Armour, "we shall employ what men we choose, and when we can't, why we'll nail up our doors—that's all." He was a creature of habit who rarely veered from his rigid schedule. He would rise each morning punctually at 5 A.M. to eat a hearty breakfast and would arrive at his office by 7 A.M. After a full day's work, he would leave at 6 P.M. and was ready to retire by 9 o'clock in the evening at his Prairie Avenue mansion. Said to be a humorless man, he had no time—and little patience—for pastimes or hobbies. "What interests can you suggest to me?" he once asked. "I do not read. I do not take part in politics. What can I do? Making money. It is my vocation and my avocation." It was not, however, the money itself that appealed to him. Rather it was "the getting of it," according to biographers Harper Leech and John Charles Carroll.

A devout churchgoer, Armour always found time to attend services at the Plymouth Congregational Church. One Sunday, the popular pastor, the Reverend Frank Gunsaulus, delivered a sermon with the provocative title "If I Had a Million Dollars," in which he looked to the future and pointed out that a city such as Chicago was in dire need of educated, well-trained employees. Gunsaulus's lecture apparently struck a nerve with Armour, because afterward the old man confronted the minister. "Young man, do you believe what you have just preached?" he reportedly asked. "I do, or I would not have preached it," replied Gunsaulus. Convinced of his sincerity, Armour offered the clergyman $1 million in return for "five years of your life." With a clasp of the hand, the deal was sealed. From such an informal encounter emerged the Armour Institute.

In 1940 the Armour Institute merged with the Lewis Institute to form the Illinois Institute of Technology (IIT).

Ludwig Mies van der Rohe, the renowned architect and an instructor at the school, carved a modern campus along South State Street between 31st and 35th Streets on what were once slum lands. Today IIT is a major institution that continues to specialize in architecture, science, and engineering.

Armour died in January 1901. He was sixty-eight.

See also: Ludwig Mies van der Rohe, Gustavus F. Swift
Further reading: Harper Leech and John Charles Carroll, *Armour and His Times* (1938); Louise Carroll Wade, *Chicago's Pride: The Stockyards, Packingtown, and Environs in the Nineteenth Century* (1987).

Louis Armstrong

Musician

BORN: August 4, 1901
New Orleans, Louisiana

DIED: July 6, 1971
New York, New York

Louis Daniel Armstrong was a great jazz trumpeter as well as a marvelous improviser who exerted a major influence on several generations of jazz musicians. By bringing New Orleans–style jazz to Chicago, the Louisiana native contributed greatly to the local jazz scene. Indeed, "Satchmo" helped make Chicago the jazz capital of the world. Armstrong took a new sound—jazz—and perfected it. By World War II, he was the most famous musician in the United States and one of the most recognizable figures in the world.

Born in the black Storyville section of New Orleans, Armstrong was the son of an unmarried fifteen-year old country girl. He grew up in a New Orleans surrounded by a motley mix of devout churchgoers, prostitutes, and gamblers. In the city's honky-tonk saloons the young Armstrong sneaked in to listen to such black cornet players as Buddy Bolden, Joe "King" Oliver, and Bunk Johnson.

Armstrong first played the cornet at thirteen when he was given one at the Colored Waifs' Home for Boys, where he had been sent for shooting a pistol into a New Year's Day parade. At the home, he joined a band. The band's director, Peter Davis, gave young Armstrong his first training in the rudiments of musical technique. After his release eighteen months later, he worked at an assortment of odd jobs—coalman, milkman, ragpicker—until he formed his own six-piece band. His first break came when he secured a six-month gig with Fate Marable's orchestra aboard the New Orleans excursion steamer, *Dixie Belle*. The Karnofsky family, his Russian immigrant neighbors, gave him the money he needed—$5—to purchase his first cornet, effectively changing his life.

In 1917 Armstrong's idol, the famous cornetist Joe "King" Oliver, left New Orleans and settled in Chicago. Armstrong replaced Oliver in the Kid Ory band back in New Orleans. In 1922 Oliver sent a telegram asking Armstrong to come to Chicago to join his Creole Jazz Band as the second cornetist at the Lincoln Gardens nightclub, formerly the Royal Gardens, at 459 East 31st Street.

Armstrong wasted no time and headed north. Arriving in Chicago late at night, he took a taxi to the café. From the street corner he could hear the music. Standing there in the dark, he paused and wondered if he was good enough to join a band that consisted of Johnny Dodds on clarinet, Honore Dutrey on trombone, and Lil Hardin on piano. No one else seemed to harbor such thoughts, however.

In 1924 Armstrong joined Fletcher Henderson's orchestra—Henderson pioneered a new sound that came to be known as swing—at the Roseland Ballroom in New York. But he returned to Chicago the following year. In late 1925 he joined the Erskine Tate orchestra at the Vendome Theater at 31st and South State Streets, switching from cornet to trumpet. A few months later he played with Carroll Dickerson's orchestra at the Sunset Café at 35th and Calumet Streets, where he was first billed as the "World's Greatest Trumpet Player." Enjoying much success, Armstrong gained enough confidence to form his own band, the Hot Five, which later became the Hot Seven, and made several revolutionary recordings. On them, Armstrong played solo improvisations, whereas earlier ensembles played in unison. These improvisations changed the sound of music. He also extended the range of jazz singing. He was a trailblazer. The records, now considered classics, were also made with some of the best jazz musicians of the day—Earl Hines on piano, Kid Ory on trombone, Johnny Dodds on clarinet, Lil Hardin on piano, and Johnny St. Cyr on banjo. Armstrong's star—and reputation—soared. His future looked bright, indeed.

By the mid-1920s jazz in Chicago had reached its historic peak. The best musicians who had paid their dues were ready to try their luck in the Big Apple. Armstrong himself left Chicago in the late 1920s, as did several other prominent figures on the local scene, including the Creole jazz pianist Ferdinand "Jelly Roll" Morton and the wunderkind from Iowa, Bix Beiderbecke.

By this time, though, no one city could claim Armstrong's prodigious talent. He already belonged to the world. During the 1930s he toured Europe, headlining the London Palladium in 1932. Several years later, in 1935, Armstrong moved back to Chicago but was forced to give up the trumpet temporarily because of lip problems. Two years later he underwent minor throat surgery at Chicago's Provident Hospital. After decades on the road, in 1956 he made one of the biggest tours of his career, a sweeping ambitious visit to Europe and Africa, which was filmed and released as *Satchmo the Great.*

Some of Louis Armstrong's most popular recordings include "Shine," "Chinatown," "Potato Head Blues," "When It's Sleepy Time Down South," "I Can't Give You Anything But Love," "West End Blues," and "Ain't Misbehavin'." His own compositions include "Sister Kate" and "If We Never Meet Again." In addition, Armstrong appeared in or contributed musically to more than thirty films, including *Pennies from Heaven* (1936), *Cabin in the Sky* (1943), *The Glenn Miller Story* (1953), and *Hello Dolly* (1969).

To much of the world, Louis Armstrong epitomized jazz. As a bandleader, he played, sang, and acted as the genial host. He developed a whole school of jazz singing called "scat," in which nonsensical sounds and phrases are used instead of words. During the Depression years when Armstrong played the "black and tan" clubs (nightclubs frequented by both African American and white patrons) of the northern cities, his popularity in Europe soared. Throughout the 1940s and 1950s Armstrong became known as the "goodwill ambassador" of the United States and was a top concert and nightclub draw well into the 1960s.

Armstrong's repertoire changed little over the years. Rather than compete with the bebop musicians of the 1940s, he continued to perform the straight-ahead melodic jazz that had made him so popular. Consequently, his critics belittled his sunny disposition and his crowd-pleasing demeanor—some considered it ingratiating, a form of pandering to the white man. Dizzy Gillespie, for example, complained of what he considered Armstrong's "Uncle Tom–like subservience." To younger black musicians Armstrong was a groveler, not much better than the African American comic film actor, Stepin Fetchit. But even his detractors could not ignore his influence.

In truth, Armstrong was a quiet revolutionary. In recent years, scholars such as Terry Teachout and John McWhorter have begun to acknowledge his immense contributions to popular music. McWhorter, in the *New Yorker,* has called Armstrong "the founder of jazz as we know it."

The first jazz musician to achieve mass popularity, he changed the face of popular music through his pioneering sense of rhythm, his virtuosity, and such masterworks as "St. Louis Blues," "Potato Head Blues," "West End Blues," and "Star Dust." The Hot Five's recordings, in particular, are considered to be the single most creative and innovative force in jazz history. Because of his popularity and his gregarious, larger-than-life persona, he was able to integrate the airwaves. During his career he performed with virtually every important name in popular music, from such early jazz pioneers as Sidney Bechet, Joe "King" Oliver, Bix Beiderbecke, Johnny Dodds, and Kid Ory to performers as diverse as Leonard Bernstein and Johnny Cash. What's more, his vocal style and his trumpet playing would influence countless generations of musicians, composers, and bandleaders, including Frank Sinatra, Bing Crosby, Ella Fitzgerald, and Billie Holiday. He was also the most influential soloist in jazz and the first black man to appeal to a white audience on a mass scale.

Armstrong died in his sleep in his New York home in July 1971. His house in the Corona section of Queens is now a museum.

See also: Earl Hines, Joe "King" Oliver

Further reading: George D. Bushnell Jr., "When Jazz Came to Chicago," *Chicago History,* Spring 1971; James Lincoln Collier, *Louis Armstrong: An American Genius* (1983); Gary Giddins, *Satchmo: The Genius of Louis Armstrong* (1988); John McWhorter, "The Entertainer," *New Yorker,* December 14, 2009; David Stricklin, *Louis Armstrong: The Soundtrack of the American Experience* (2010); Terry Teachout, *Pops: A Life of Louis Armstrong* (2009).

Gerald Arpino

Choreographer

BORN: January 14, 1923
Staten Island, New York

DIED: October 29, 2008
Chicago, Illinois

The cofounder of the Joffrey Ballet and its artistic director from 1988 to 2007, Gerald Arpino helped to popularize dance. Known for his eccentric, warm, and exuberant personality, Arpino also became the public face of one of the most well-known dance companies in the United States.

In 1956 Arpino founded the Joffrey Ballet in New York with its namesake Robert Joffrey as a small touring troupe. Joffrey was its original artistic director while Arpino was the resident choreographer. When Joffrey died in 1988, Arpino took over. He moved the company from New York to Chicago in 1995.

Under Arpino, the Joffrey became known for its youthful energy as well as its tendency to gravitate toward social statements. Arpino tried to reach a wider audience. The Joffrey's new works, for example, embraced counterculture rock in such ballets as Arpino's 1970 *Trinity*. But he also presented political protest pieces and plotless ballets.

Born and raised on Staten Island and the youngest of nine children of Italian immigrants, Arpino was proud of his heritage. His father, who died when Arpino was a boy of seven, owned beauty salons and greyhound racing dogs, and he dabbled in real estate. Arpino attended Wagner College on Staten Island for one year and, in 1942, enlisted in the U.S. Coast Guard Reserve. Meanwhile, Joffrey, who was the son of an Afghan father and an Italian mother, met Arpino in Seattle after World War II (their mothers were friends). It was Joffrey who introduced Arpino to ballet. But both men had a vision for what Arpino would call an Americanized ballet.

In 1953 Arpino joined the faculty of the Joffrey School, studying with Joffrey's ballet teacher, Mary Ann Wells. He also studied at the School of American Ballet with the modern dancer May O'Donnell. An injury in 1963 ended his dancing career, however. By that time he had already been studying choreography.

As directors, Arpino and Joffrey presented European revivals of ballet classics but with a strong American accent. Both men also tried to retain control of their company. It was a bit of a messy, ugly struggle. At one point, in 1964, Rebekah Harkness, chief patron of the Joffrey, even tried to change the company's name. Joffrey left and formed a newly reorganized Joffrey Ballet in 1965. Years later, when Joffrey died of AIDS in 1988, Arpino had to convince the ballet's board that he could continue Joffrey's legacy on his own. In 1990, amid a financial crisis, the anti-Arpino faction of the board tried to remove Arpino as its artistic director—but his popularity and the support of the other members of the board shored up his position. He then reorganized the company as Joffrey Ballet Chicago when supporters in Chicago offered financial support.

The move to Chicago revitalized the Joffrey, and Joffrey, in turn, revitalized Chicago's cultural scene. Chicago could now boast that it had its own internationally known ballet company with Arpino, its larger-than-life figure, as its head.

The company's works were sometimes controversial, even as Arpino insisted on making ballet more accessible to a mainstream audience. Throughout his tenure, the Joffrey continued to explore unconventional themes: nuclear war in *The Clowns* (1968) and love in the counterculture era in *Trinity* (1970). *Light Rain* (1981) was an erotically charged mixture of Eastern music and mysticism with a Western sensibility while *Round of Angels* (1983) was an artistic response to the AIDS epidemic. *Italian Suite* (1983) served as homage to Arpino's Italian heritage. *Billboards* (1994) was set to music by Prince, and a duet called *Ruth, Ricordi per Due* (2004) was an elegy. The pieces were uniformly exciting, lyrical, powerful, and emotional expressions as seen through the world of dance. In total, Arpino created about forty ballets.

Arpino stepped down from his post in 2007 and was succeeded by Ashley C. Wheater.

A forceful personality, Arpino was portrayed by Malcolm McDowell in Robert Altman's elegant 2003 film about the Joffrey called simply *The Company*. Most of the dancers played themselves. In the movie, Arpino's character was called Alberto Antonetti but there was no doubt that McDowell, an Englishman, was channeling the spirit of Arpino, even capturing his very idiosyncratic intonations and extravagant gestures.

In 2005 and 2006 the Joffrey celebrated its 50th anniversary as a company with festivities held at Chicago's Millennium Park. And in September 2008 the Joffrey moved into its new headquarters at a new high-rise called the Joffrey Tower at 10 East Randolph Street. A frail Arpino attended. In November 2008, the company presented three excerpts from Arpino's repertoire, *Round of Angels, Light Rain,* and *Trinity* as a tribute. Some 500 people gathered at the Auditorium Theatre. In his opening remarks, Mayor Richard M. Daley said that Arpino "enriched Chicago's reputation as a world-class city."

Arpino died at his home in Chicago in 2008 after a long battle with prostate cancer. He was eighty-five.

In late 2008 the Joffrey Ballet announced the opening of its own education and training center, the Academy of Dance, Official School of the Joffrey Ballet, part of its new facilities at the Joffrey Tower in downtown Chicago. The school offers instruction in ballet, jazz, tap, hip-hop, and Latin dance to students three years of age and older, as well as classes for adults in ballet, jazz, tap, and Pilates.

See also: Gus Giordano, Ruth Page

Jacob Arvey

Politician

BORN: November 3, 1895
Chicago, Illinois

DIED: August 25, 1977
Chicago, Illinois

For many years, this son of a Maxwell Street peddler was one of the most powerful and influential politicians in Illinois. Jacob Meyer Arvey attributed his success to simple hard work and the old political system of handing out favors. "Put people under obligation to you," he said. "Make them your friends."

Arvey was a self-made man. A graduate of John Marshall Law School in Chicago, he was appointed assistant state's attorney in 1918 and later served as prosecutor to the municipal court. In 1922 Arvey joined the regular Democratic organization as a precinct captain. That same year Ward Committeeman Mike Rosenberg ran for sanitary district trustee and asked Arvey to manage his campaign. Rosenberg won and Arvey rapidly rose to prominence. In 1932 he was elected Twenty-Fourth Ward alderman in the predominantly Jewish North Lawndale neighborhood. Arvey held this position for the next eighteen years. Historian Michael Funchion described Arvey as "the most powerful Jewish ward leader in the city." During the 1932 presidential election, Chicago chose a Democratic leader, Franklin Delano Roosevelt, for the first time since 1892. It was also the year that another Chicago Jew, Henry Horner, won the governor's seat. Arvey and his army of patronage workers in the Twenty-Fourth Ward helped carry the day for the Democratic Party in Illinois. Four years later, the Twenty-Fourth Ward came through again, which prompted Roosevelt to call it "the best Democratic ward in the country."

When World War II broke out, Arvey was serving as finance committee chairman in the city council. Despite his age, he requested a leave of absence from his law practice and resigned from his aldermanic post to enlist in the Thirty-Third Infantry Division of the Illinois National Guard as a judge advocate. He passed the physical only after faking an eye examination ("I memorized the chart," he later admitted). Arvey served admirably in the South Pacific, attaining the rank of lieutenant colonel, and was awarded the Bronze Star and the Legion of Merit. He then returned to Chicago, planning to retire from politics, but he couldn't resist the offer to succeed Mayor Edward Kelly as chairman of the Cook County Democratic Committee.

An innovative party chairman, Arvey slated such reform candidates as Martin H. Kennelly for mayor; Paul H. Douglas, an economics professor at the University of Chicago and later an alderman from the Fifth Ward, for U.S. senator; and Adlai E. Stevenson for Illinois governor. Such choices earned Arvey a national reputation as a savvy and shrewd leader. Arvey's success also lay in his ability to turn a handicap into an advantage.

In 1948, convinced that President Harry S. Truman—who had fallen behind in the polls—couldn't win reelection, he tried unsuccessfully to persuade war hero Dwight D. Eisenhower to head the Democratic ticket. Eisenhower ultimately rejected the offer and chose to join the Republican Party. Although some leaders expressed misgivings about Truman's candidacy, Arvey, reconsidering, became convinced that Truman could be turned into a winner. The real turning point came when Truman agreed to recognize the state of Israel in March 1948. Arvey then gave his full, unconditional support. That November the scrappy Missourian toppled Republican front-runner Governor Thomas E. Dewey of New York in one of the biggest upsets in American presidential politics.

Similarly, Arvey's quietly effective, behind-the-scenes influence convinced Governor Stevenson, the "reluctant candidate," to accept the Democratic nomination for president in 1952 in his ill-fated run against Eisenhower. Other Illinois candidates that Arvey slated for public office included Sidney Yates for congressman, Abraham Marovitz for federal court judge, Otto Kerner Jr. for governor, and Michael Howlett for secretary of state.

His power waned after Mayor Richard J. Daley assumed office in 1955. As Democratic National Committeeman, Arvey was little more than a figurehead. By 1960 Arvey disagreed with Daley over the national leadership of the Democratic Party, favoring Adlai Stevenson's third attempt for the presidency over Daley's choice, a young senator from Massachusetts named John F. Kennedy.

Arvey continued to serve on the Chicago Park District board until 1967 and was an Illinois member of the Democratic National Committee until 1972. He devoted his last years primarily to various Jewish philanthropic causes, serving on the boards of the Friends of Tel Aviv University, Israel Bonds Committee, and the World Jewish Council.

"I made mistakes," the dapper gentleman from Maxwell Street would later say. "I made a lot of them. But they're mistakes in judgment and not of the heart. I can live with them."

Arvey died in 1977 at the age of eighty-one. At the time of his death, the longtime West Side resident was living at 2300 North Lincoln Park West.

See also: Richard J. Daley, Paul Douglas, Henry Horner, Edward J. Kelly, Otto Kerner Jr.

Further reading: Ira Berkow, *Maxwell Street: Survival in a Bazaar* (1977); Roger Biles, "Jacob M. Arvey, Kingmaker: The Nomination of Adlai E. Stevenson in 1952," *Chicago History*, Fall 1979; David K. Fremon, *Chicago Politics Ward by Ward* (1988); Edward Mazur, "Jewish Chicago," in *Ethnic Chicago: A Multicultural Portrait* (1984), Melvin G. Holli and Peter d'A. Jones, eds.; Milton Rakove, *Don't Make No Waves—Don't Back No Losers: An Insider's Analysis of the Daley Machine* (1975) and *We Don't Want Nobody Nobody Sent: An Oral History of the Daley Years* (1979).

Barney Balaban

Theater Owner

BORN: June 8, 1887
Chicago, Illinois

DIED: March 7, 1971
Byram, Connecticut

Barney Balaban got his start in the movie business in 1908 when he and members of his family opened their own theater on the Near West Side. From such humble beginnings would grow the city's largest movie theater chain, Balaban and Katz.

Balaban grew up in the Maxwell Street neighborhood. His parents, Russian-born Jews, operated a tiny grocery store there. He left school at the age of twelve and went to work to earn money for the family. He held down many jobs—office boy in a hotel grocery shop, messenger, and clerk in a cold storage company. To escape the numbing squalor of daily life, Balaban and his brothers would visit the Yiddish theaters and the rundown nickelodeons strung out along Halsted Street and elsewhere. They weren't much to look at—usually old storefronts converted into theaters—but for young Balaban and his siblings they offered precious hours of entertainment and magical flights of fancy into another, seemingly perfect, world.

Barney's brother Abe, or A. J., as he was known, had a fine voice and secured a job singing at the Kedzie Theater at Kedzie Avenue and Roosevelt Road. It was an enjoyable way to make some money, and around the Balaban household the extra dollars were always welcome. Enticed by the aura of wealth that stood within easy reach outside their door, the brothers talked boldly about going into the movie business, perhaps even buying their own theater.

Together they scrimped and saved until they had accumulated the tidy sum of $750, approached the owner of the Kedzie, and, in a bold move, offered to buy it. To their surprise, he agreed to sell. They cleaned it up and hired a violinist for $1 a night. The rest they did themselves—running the theater, managing the box office, even performing.

It worked. Gradually the receipts rose, and the Balabans borrowed money to build another theater one block away. The Circle Theater opened in 1909, considered the finest in its day. The Balabans installed a pipe organ, hired a four-piece orchestra, and began booking the best vaudeville talent available—from Groucho Marx to Sophie Tucker.

The Balaban brothers acquired more theaters, and their income grew. Before long, business was so good that Barney quit his full-time job at the storage company to devote all his energy to a life in the theater. In 1915 Balaban teamed up with another entrepreneur named Sam Katz, and together they made plans to build a deluxe theater. The Central Park Theater could boast velour seats, chandeliers, and murals. In addition to offering movies, it presented stage shows, musical acts, and dancing. More theaters followed, each one more extravagant than the last—the Riviera (modeled after the chapel of Versailles), the Granada, the Century, the Paradise, the State-Lake, the Roosevelt, and finally, in 1921, the crown jewel of them all, the Chicago.

Moviegoing at a B&K theater was a special experience. The biggest theaters had exceptionally large staffs—sometimes as many as thirty ushers, uniformed and white-gloved, in addition to janitors, stagehands, projectionists, candy girls, cashiers, and ticket takers. The success of the B&K chain piqued the interest of the owners of Paramount Pictures, who admired Balaban's hands-on management style and efficient fiscal policies. Eventually the studio bought two-thirds of B&K stock for $13 million. Balaban became a member of the stockholders' protective committee, and, in 1936, he became chairman of the board. He was named president of Paramount one month later.

Balaban was an able administrator. When other studios faced financial ruin, Paramount stayed afloat, earning a reputation as one of the best-run companies in the movie industry. But whereas some called Balaban a financial wizard, others were less kind. Noted director Frank Capra once referred to him as "money-wise" but "art-foolish."

As early as 1948, Balaban warned that runaway production costs could imperil the future of the motion picture industry. Indeed, he had arrived at the unfounded conclusion that no movie could—no matter how big a hit—gross more than $3 million. Accordingly, no Paramount budget could exceed $1.5 million. Balaban dictated all policy decisions, business and creative, from the initial story treatment to the final hiring of cast and crew. Anything above the allotted budget required his approval in writing. Unfortunately, Balaban's taste in movies was rather pedestrian. Movies, he thought, perhaps remembering his old days growing up on Maxwell Street, should be entertaining. He had originally rejected, for example, *The Lost Weekend* as being too downbeat before Paramount executives convinced him otherwise. Ultimately Ray Milland, who played a down-on-his-luck alcoholic, won the Oscar for best actor in this 1945 classic. Balaban much preferred films like *Gulliver's Travels* and *The Ten Commandments*.

In 1967 Balaban was named honorary chairman of the board of Paramount, a title that he retained until his death in 1971. B&K changed its name to ABC–Great States in 1968 and, in 1974, to Plitt Theaters, which eventually sold its interest to the Toronto-based Cineplex Odeon.

An Orthodox Jew, Balaban was active in the Jewish community and made major charitable contributions to many organizations, especially the Westchester Jewish Center. Philip Bregstone, in *Chicago and Its Jews*, quotes Balaban as saying, "We Orthodox Jews have a duty to perform, an obligation to pay. In the early period of Jewish immigration most of our people came here poor and destitute. Now that many of us possess wealth it is time that we take up the responsibility ourselves, to build and maintain the charitable and philanthropic institutions and to create such others as modern American Jewry may require."

Balaban died of a heart attack in 1971 at age eighty-three in his idyllic Connecticut home, far removed from the crowded alleys and pungent aromas of his native Maxwell Street.

Further reading: Carrie Balaban, *Continuous Performance: The Story of A. J. Balaban* (1964); Ira Berkow, *Maxwell Street: Survival in a Bazaar* (1977); Arnie Bernstein, *Hollywood on Lake Michigan: 100 Years of Chicago and the Movies* (1998); Philip P. Bregstone, *Chicago and Its Jews* (1933); Hyman L. Meites, *History of the Jews of Chicago* (1924); J. I. Fishbein, ed., *The Sentinel's History of Chicago Jewry, 1911–1986* (1986).

Margery Barker
Rare Book Dealer

BORN: January 8, 1901
Michigan City, Indiana
DIED: May 6, 1980

Frances Hamill
Rare Book Dealer

BORN: March 30, 1904
DIED: October 21, 1987

Among the first female rare book dealers in the United States, Margery Barker and Frances Hamill were also the first rare book dealers to acquire the papers of Virginia Woolf and the Bloomsbury group—and thus were the first to introduce those works to an American audience.

Barker was born in Michigan City, Indiana, where she grew up. She attended Bryn Mawr College in Bryn Mawr, Pennsylvania. Hamill grew up in Clarendon Hills, Illinois, but went to Miss Porter's, an upscale boarding school in Farmington, Connecticut. In the early 1920s both took business courses at Northwestern University. For reasons still unclear, Barker was expelled from Bryn Mawr. Despite legal suits filed on her behalf by her mother, Barker never did discover the reasons behind her dismissal.

In 1922 Barker worked as a clerk in Fanny Butcher's famous Chicago bookstore. At the time Butcher was the *Chicago Tribune*'s book critic as well as an influential figure in the thriving Chicago literary scene. Within three years, Barker was promoted to store manager. In 1926 she hired Frances Hamill. Meanwhile, *Tribune* brass felt that Butcher's work at the paper and her position at the bookstore constituted a conflict of interest. So they issued an ultimatum: choose between the paper and the store. Butcher chose to remain at the *Tribune* and sell the bookstore. Although Barker and Hamill expressed interest in buying it, Butcher instead sold it to the Doubleday Company. Barker and Hamill were disappointed at Butcher's decision, but by that time they had already learned enough about the book business that they considered entering the rare book business on their own. Thus, they traveled to Europe in early 1928 to buy inventory. Eight months later they returned to Chicago and opened Hamill & Barker on the city's North Side.

Their catalogs during their early years in business contained two works by Virginia Woolf: a first edition of *Mrs. Dalloway* in 1933 that sold for $6 and *Jacob's Room* the following year for $8.50. They formed a legal partnership in 1941. When World War II broke out, they joined the war effort by setting aside their book business to work in factories as tool grinder trainees at the General Motors Electro-Motive Division in La Grange, Illinois, working the night shift. After the war ended, they reopened their bookstore in Chicago but at a different location.

In 1953 Hamill was elected president of the Antiquarian Booksellers Association of America, the first woman and the first Midwesterner to hold that position. Despite her highly respected reputation in the field, it took many years before she became a member of other bibliophilic clubs, such as the Grolier Club in New York and the Caxton Club in Chicago (neither club, it should be noted, admitted women as members until as recently as the mid-1970s).

Barker and Hamill made many book purchases over the years but none as famous, or influential, as their purchases of various Woolfian collections. It was an arduous process. From 1957 until 1970, they bought twenty-five volumes of Woolf's diaries. They also purchased manuscripts of Woolf's *The Voyage Out, Jacob's Room,* and *To the Lighthouse,* as well as hundreds of letters from Woolf to her sister, Vanessa Bell, and to her occasional lover, Vita Sackville-West. Many of these documents were eventually deposited in the Berg Collection at the New York Public Library. Barker and Hamill also purchased books and manuscripts from George A. Poole, owner of the Chicago printing firm Poole Brothers, Inc.; and rare books from Europe, the United States, and China that spanned the centuries from the fifteenth to the twentieth. These books included a rare Gutenberg Bible and a 1484 printing of Geoffrey Chaucer's *Canterbury Tales* by the English printer William Caxton, for whom the Chicago-based Caxton Club is named.

In 1975, Hamill and Barker met Terence Tanner, who was working at the time as a book scout. Eventually he became the sole owner of Hamill & Barker. Initially located in the Wrigley Building, it eventually moved to 1719 Howard Street in Evanston.

Barker died of cancer in 1980 and Hamill of a stroke in 1987.

See also: Stuart Brent, Fanny Butcher

Further reading: Rima Lunin Schultz and Adele Hast, eds., *Women Building Chicago, 1790–1990: A Biographical Dictionary* (2001).

Claude A. Barnett
News Service Owner

BORN: September 16, 1889
Sanford, Florida

DIED: August 2, 1967
Chicago, Illinois

A prominent leader in the black community for many years, Claude Barnett founded the Associated Negro Press (ANP) in 1919 when race riots and other violence against blacks filled the pages of the mainstream press. "After World War I, there was practically no news about Negroes except lynchings and tragedy. I wanted to change that," he said. During its heyday, the ANP—the black equivalent of UPI and AP—supplied news stories, features, essays, columns, poetry, book and record reviews, cartoons, and photographs to scores of black newspapers across the country.

Claude Barnett was born in Florida, the son of a hotel worker, but he was raised in Illinois, where he attended elementary schools both in downstate Mattoon and later in Chicago. In 1902 he attended Oak Park High School while working as a servant in the home of Richard W. Sears, cofounder of Sears, Roebuck and Company. Two years later he went back South and enrolled at the influential Tuskegee Institute in Alabama, where he became profoundly influenced by the black self-help principles of Booker T. Washington.

After graduating, Barnett got a job at the post office in Chicago before establishing his own advertising agency. He later formed a chemical company that manufactured cosmetics. For a short time, he sold advertising space for the *Chicago Defender,* Chicago's premiere black newspaper. In 1919, lacking capital but imbued with a personal vision, Barnett contacted black editors, civic leaders, and businessmen with the idea of establishing a news service of, for, and by blacks. Barnett called it the Associated Negro Press. Its watchwords were "progress, loyalty, truth."

The response was so good that by the end of its first year ANP had eighty-eight subscribers. At its peak, it provided news to 150 black newspapers across the nation, reaching an estimated two million readers per week. In addition, Barnett maintained a Washington, D.C., bureau, employed correspondents in New York and Los Angeles, and utilized scores of volunteer stringers.

Barnett was always looking for a black success story. He profiled black entertainers, politicians, clergy, and athletes—anyone who projected a positive image. He also ran national news stories but covered them from a black perspective. Later on, he carried some of the first news reports from the African continent.

Barnett wore many hats during his lifetime. In addition to his ANP duties, he acted as a special assistant to the secretary of agriculture, and from 1938 to 1942 he served as president of the board of Provident Hospital. In 1947 Barnett and his wife, singer and actress Etta Moten, made their first visit to Africa, a land they would come to love and admire. Over the years, they made many trips there, establishing strong ties with African leaders, clergy, editors, and businessmen. Barnett and Moten even became experts in African art and culture, collecting and exhibiting African crafts and delivering speeches before civic, religious, and fraternal groups.

Barnett's work on behalf of the worldwide family of blacks did not go unnoticed. In 1949 his alma mater, the Tuskegee Institute, awarded him an honorary doctorate in the humanities, and the governments of Haiti and Liberia honored him in a similar way.

For decades, ANP fulfilled a need that was sorely lacking in the African American community. It provided a national forum in which black leaders could express their views directly to their constituencies, and equally important, it gave black journalists an invaluable opportunity to develop their skills. All of that changed during the 1960s, when the white mainstream media increased its coverage of issues affecting the African American community. By this time, Barnett was in poor health, and he had neither the strength nor the time to devote to the news service. When he retired in 1964, the ANP ceased operations. He died three years later.

Barnett built a major news-gathering operation from scratch. Not only did the Associated Negro Press document the achievements of African Americans, it fostered pride and self-esteem in black communities throughout the United States. It also served as a precursor to such African American magazines as *Ebony* and *Jet*.

See also: Robert S. Abbott, John H. Johnson

Further reading: Linda J. Evans, "Claude A. Barnett and the Associated Negro Press," *Chicago History*, Spring 1983; Lawrence D. Hogan, *A Black National News Service: The Associated Negro Press and Claude Barnett* (1984); Roland E. Wolskey, *The Black Press, U.S.A.* (1971).

Mary Bartelme

Judge

BORN: July 24, 1866
Chicago, Illinois

DIED: July 26, 1954
Carmel, California

As the first woman judge in Illinois history and the second in the nation, Mary Margaret Bartelme was a pioneer in the field of helping underprivileged children. Nicknamed "Suitcase Mary" for the practice she had of providing young ladies en route to foster homes with suitcases packed with clothes and other necessities, Bartelme set new standards for treating wayward girls. Her philosophy was simple: "There are no bad children. There are confused, neglected children, love-starved and resentful children, and what they need most I try to give them— understanding and a fresh start in the right direction."

Mary Bartelme first planned to enter the medical profession. A woman doctor, however, advised her to consider law and set up an appointment for her with Myra Bradwell, founder of the *Chicago Legal News*. "One visit to her and I was determined to take up the study of law," Bartelme recalled.

Bartelme taught in Chicago's public schools for five years. Then, defying convention, she enrolled at Northwestern University Law School. She was admitted to the bar in 1894 and appointed public guardian of Cook County by Governor John Tanner in 1897—a post she held for sixteen years. In 1913 she was assigned to the juvenile court to hear girls' cases as an assistant to Judge Merritt W. Pinckney.

In 1923, three years after women won the right to vote, Bartelme was asked to run for the office of judge of the circuit court. In an unusual display of camaraderie, women from all walks of life rallied around her and provided the necessary margin of victory. Bartelme was supported by various women's organizations, several of which even staged rallies on her behalf. Male voters also supported

her, since many felt that a woman was the ideal choice for offering guidance to wayward girls.

Bartelme was a special friend to troubled girls everywhere who, through no fault of their own (generally due to divorce, death, or a separation in the family), found themselves homeless and with no place to turn. "I believe that the young girls of Chicago and of all of Cook County are entitled to at least one judge who can deal with them in terms of real sympathy and understanding rather than in terms of legal lore and technicalities," she explained.

Her unorthodox beliefs attracted worldwide attention. Social workers from around the globe wanted to visit the judge who spoke so eloquently on behalf of the nation's have-nots. Strong emotions were often played out in Bartelme's courtroom. It was not unusual for youngsters as well as jurors to lose their composure. Bartelme was prepared. She always had an ample supply of handkerchiefs on hand.

Rather than see unfortunate youngsters spend a night in jail, Bartelme formed what came to be known as "Mary clubs": institutions without bars, where girls were "helped, encouraged, corrected, but not reformed." In 1914 she converted her own house into the first "Mary club." Some girls stayed for as little as six months, some for as long as a year, and others for several years. Most went on to lead productive lives.

In 1927 Bartelme was unanimously elected president of the Women's Bar Association of Illinois. That same year she served as fund-raising chairwoman for the Mary Thompson Hospital for Women and Children.

In 1933 Bartelme retired from the bench and moved to Carmel, California, where she died in 1954. The Mary Bartelme Papers, part of the Jane Addams Memorial Collection, are housed at the University of Illinois at Chicago.

See also: Myra Bradwell

Further reading: Babette Inglehart, ed., *Walking with Women Through Chicago History* (1981); Herman Kogan, *The First Century: The Chicago Bar Association 1874–1974* (1974); Rima Lunin Schultz and Adele Haste, eds., *Women Building Chicago 1790–1990* (2001).

Ann Barzel

Dance Critic

BORN: December 13, 1905
Minneapolis, Minnesota

DIED: February 12, 2007
Chicago, Illinois

Dance critic, teacher, and historian, Ann Barzel was considered the doyenne of Chicago dance critics and a consistent presence at dance events around town. She attended dance concerts well into her nineties.

Barzel was born in Minneapolis but moved in 1914 with her family to Des Moines, Iowa, where she grew up. At the age of nine, her world changed when she discovered dance. She took her first dance lessons at the Jewish Settlement House and also took dance lessons from Elizabeth Werblosky, who had studied with the Denishawn Company. Barzel was so diligent that she clipped and saved discarded dance magazines from the local library.

In 1920, the family moved to Chicago, taking up residence at 3134 West 16th Street. She attended Crane Technical High School and Junior College (now Malcolm X College). She graduated from the University of Chicago in 1925 with a bachelor's degree in the humanities and did two additional years of graduate work. At the same time she taught at Hebrew school in the afternoons and took dance classes on weekends.

Her first dance teachers in Chicago were Mark Turbyfill and Adolph Bolm. She studied various styles of dance in Chicago as well as in New York, London, and Paris. She studied with Michel Fokine, Alexandre Volinine, Doris Humphrey, the School of American Ballet, Vecheslav Swoboda, Nicholas Legat, and others. For more than a decade, from 1931 to 1943, she performed as a dancer with the Chicago Civic Opera Ballet and with a group directed by Berenice Holmes, who took over Adolph Bolm's dance school when Bolm left Chicago. In addition to her various dance activities, Barzel also taught school at Penn Elementary School at 1616 South Avers Avenue, near 16th and Pulaski, where she remained until 1967.

In the 1940s Barzel became a lecturer on dance history at the University of Chicago, Columbia College Chicago, and other institutions as well as a teacher of dance technique. At the same time she reviewed dance, theater, and shows for many dance journals and encyclopedias. From 1946 to 1950 she was the dance critic of the *Chicago Times,* the predecessor to the *Chicago Sun-Times,* and from 1951 to 1974, of the *Chicago American* (later *Chicago Today*). She wrote for *Dance Magazine* for some forty years, covering dance events not only in Chicago but also in the greater Midwest. In addition, she wrote for the neighborhood Lerner newspaper chain from 1974 to 2003 as well as for

Ballet Review, Ballet Annual, Dance News, and other international dance publications.

From 1956 to 1975 Barzel served on the advisory panel for dance for the State Department's International Cultural Agency as well as serving from 1966 to 1974 as the dance consultant for the Illinois Arts Council. In 1979 she founded the Ballet Guild of Chicago. During the same year she received the Governor's Award for her service to the arts. Barzel was also a bit of a filmmaker. She shot films of touring ballet performances, from the wings, in the 1940s and 1950s, which today are considered an incalculable contribution to the field. Her films were used as an important source for the 2005 documentary *Ballet Russes* and were sometimes used by choreographers, including Jerome Robbins, as cues to help restage early works.

Barzel donated her dance collection, which consisted of archival dance materials in the United States and in Europe from as far back as the 1890s, to the Newberry Library. The collection includes 30,000 feet of film and 200 shelves of documents, books, periodicals, scrapbooks, programs, and photographs, as well as audiovisual material and artifacts. Her films are also in the dance collection of the New York Public Library for the Performing Arts at Lincoln Center. Barzel was a generous supporter of the Newberry Library, and the Ann Barzel Dance Reading Room in the Roger and Julie Baskes Department of Special Collections is named in her honor. Her ninety-seventh birthday was celebrated at the Athenaeum Theatre in Lakeview with performances by members of Hubbard Street, Joffrey, River North, and Trinity Irish dance companies. On April 23, 2007, the Newberry sponsored "A Tribute to Ann Barzel in Celebration of Her Life" at Chicago Sinai Congregation on West Delaware Place. Speakers included the theater critic Richard Christiansen, Gerald Arpino of Joffrey Ballet, Lou Conte of Hubbard Street Dance Chicago, Daniel Duell of Ballet Chicago, and Joel Hall of the Joel Hall Dancers.

Barzel died at St. Joseph Hospital in Chicago at the age of 101.

Mathias "Paddy" Bauler

Politician

BORN: January 27, 1890
Chicago, Illinois

DIED: August 20, 1977
Melrose Park, Illinois

The last of the saloon-keeping politicians, Mathias J. Bauler was a true Chicago character, a flamboyant and brash alderman of the old school who gained international notoriety when he uttered the immortal words, "Chicago ain't ready for reform." For over thirty years he ruled the Forty-Third Ward on the city's North Side from the back room of a saloon. As "clown prince" of the city council, he was more renowned for his wild parties than for any contribution he made to the public sphere. Instead, he drank, caroused, and reveled his way into Chicago history—and folklore.

Bauler's parents owned a saloon, and Paddy—nobody called him Mathias—early on learned the joys of poker, pinochle, and pool. When he was old enough, Paddy worked behind the bar. During Prohibition, he ran a speakeasy at the corner of Willow and Howe Streets where Chicagoans could rub shoulders with entertainers, politicians, and socialites, including Rudy Vallee, Anton J. Cermak, and Edith Rockefeller McCormick. But Bauler also pursued a political career, beginning as a part-time timekeeper in the Cook County treasurer's office.

After an unsuccessful run for alderman in 1925, Bauler was finally elected to the city council in 1933. When Prohibition was repealed, Bauler opened a saloon, the De Luxe Gardens, on the corner of North Avenue and Sedgwick Street. Bauler's saloon was the scene of wrestling matches, ribald storytelling sessions, and late night victory parties. When a political victory was assured, Bauler would don a silk top hat and frock coat, twirl a cane, and croon the opening lines of "Chicago (That Toddlin' Town)." An avid traveler, he and his long-time pal, Alderman Charles Weber of the Forty-Fifth Ward, would take off at a moment's notice to Munich, Vienna, Paris, Hong Kong—it didn't really matter where—and return with an armload of gifts for their cronies. "Who knows where he got the money?" the late Alderman Leon Despres asked. No one seemed to care. Controversy followed the rambunctious alderman in 1933 when he was indicted and charged with assault during a scuffle involving a Chicago policeman. Bauler, who fired two shots into the officer, claimed the shooting was in self-defense. All charges were eventually dropped.

Bauler, who always believed that one favor deserved another, had no patience with reformers, referring to them as "political science kids," and one can only imagine what he would have thought of the so-called honest services fraud charges that led to the corruption trial of former Illinois governor Rod Blagojevich in 2010. According to Bauler, the duties of an alderman were simple: collect the garbage, repair the streets, and clean the sidewalks, and the citizenry will show their appreciation with their votes. The people, he said, want service, not reform.

Chicago has seen many dirty campaigns in its time, but one of the dirtiest occurred in 1939 when Bauler campaigned against Republican James B. Waller. Bauler was declared the winner in the April runoff by a scant 243 votes. Waller cried foul and listed a litany of transgressions, including bribery, fraud, and intimidation of voters. He demanded a recount. Bauler's colleagues in the city council thought otherwise and dismissed the plea by a vote of 37 to 6. "It was a victory for the people," beamed Bauler.

By the time Bauler stepped down from his aldermanic post in 1967, he was an anachronism, the last in a long list of colorful saloon-keeper politicians such as Michael "Hinky Dink" Kenna and "Bathhouse John" Coughlin. During his later years, Bauler spent some time in New Mexico. In 1976 he returned to Chicago and moved into a high-rise retirement facility in Northlake. He suffered a stroke, apparently triggered by an earlier car accident in Santa Fe, New Mexico, and he died in August 1977 at the age of eighty-seven in Melrose Park.

See also: "Bathhouse John" Coughlin, Leon Despres, Michael "Hinky Dink" Kenna

L. Frank Baum
Author

BORN: May 15, 1856
Chittenango, New York

DIED: May 6, 1919
Los Angeles, California

Lyman Frank Baum created the American children's classic *The Wizard of Oz*. A prolific writer, Baum also wrote adventure novels and fantasies as well as some fourteen books about the magical land of Oz.

The son of a Scots Irish mother and a German American father, Baum spent his childhood in comparative luxury at his father's estate, near Syracuse, New York. Privately tutored, he briefly attended Peekskill Military Academy in New York. Baum became a cub reporter for the *New York World* at seventeen. Two years later he opened his own printing shop in Bradford, Pennsylvania, where he established a newspaper called the *New Era*. For a while he managed a small chain of opera houses in New York and Pennsylvania, and one time he even acted with a traveling stock company.

Baum, a friendly and outgoing man, enjoyed telling stories to his children. Soon he began writing down Mother Goose rhymes. In 1877 a collection of these stories called *Mother Goose in Prose* was published by the Chicago firm Way and Williams with illustrations by Maxfield Parrish. Several years later, in 1881, Baum wrote an Irish musical comedy. *The Maid of Arran* enjoyed a respectable run in New York but didn't provide enough money to live on. Baum then settled in Syracuse and established a small company that manufactured "Baum's Castorine," used for greasing axles. In the meantime, he wrote three more Irish melodramas: *Matches, Kilmourne,* and *The Queen of Killarney.* Only the first two were produced.

In 1887 Baum moved his family to Aberdeen, South Dakota, where he ran a general store, Baum's Bazaar, and published a weekly newspaper, the *Aberdeen Saturday Pioneer.* In 1891 the peripatetic writer moved to Chicago and found work as a reporter for the *Chicago Post.* He then worked as a salesman traveling throughout the Midwest selling china and glassware for a Chicago importing company. In 1897 he resumed his journalism career when he founded the *Show Window,* a monthly magazine for window trimmers. The following year he published, set the type, and printed in his own workshop another collection of children's stories, *By the Candelabra's Glare.* In 1899 he wrote *Father Goose, His Book,* which was illustrated by Chicago cartoonist William Wallace Denslow and hand-lettered by Ralph Fletcher Seymour, another local artist. It sold well.

The turn of the century was a busy year for Baum. He wrote four children's books: *The Army Alphabet; The Navy Alphabet;* a fantasy called *A New Wonderland,* set in the beautiful valley of Phunnyland where it snowed popcorn and rained lemonade "and the thunder is usually a chorus from the opera of *Tannhauser*"; and, most importantly, *The Wonderful Wizard of Oz,* which he wrote in the summer of 1900 while living at what is now 1667 Humboldt Boulevard, on the city's Northwest Side. It was issued by George M. Hill, the small Chicago house that published *Father Goose. The Emerald City of Oz,* the sixth in the series, reflected Baum's love of Ireland. It was a place where there was no illness or disease, where no one grew old, where animals could talk, where there were no rich or poor, and where there was no need for money. There was no sickness, poverty, or death in Oz.

Initially Baum had great difficulty finding a publisher for *The Wizard of Oz*. Indeed, the book was turned down by most of the local houses because, said Baum's wife, it was "too different, too radical." Hill agreed to distribute the book, but Baum and Denslow shouldered all the printing expenses. By the end of the year, the adventures of Dorothy Gale from Kansas, who was blown into Oz by a twister, had become the fastest-selling children's book in the country, and by 1902 it had sold five million copies.

Baum gave up his trade journal work to devote himself full time to creative writing. Collaborating with fellow Chicagoans Paul Tietjens, who wrote the music, and William Wallace Denslow, who designed the costumes (Denslow's office was located in Room 1021 of the Fine Arts Building on Michigan Avenue), Baum wrote the book and lyrics to the musical *The Life and Adventures of Santa Claus*.

Due to public demand, though, Baum returned to the Oz books. In 1903 he wrote *Enchanted Island of Yew* and in 1904 *The Marvelous Land of Oz*. Other books in the Oz series were *Ozma of Oz* (1907), *Dorothy and the Wizard in Oz* (1908), *The Road to Oz* (1909), *The Emerald City of Oz* (1910), and *The Patchwork Girl of Oz* (1913).

A prolific writer, Baum also wrote several adult novels (under the pseudonym Schuyler Staunton), two boy's adventure books, six novels about young fortune hunters, seventeen novels for teenage girls (under the pseudonym Edith Van Dyne), and six books of fantasy using the name Laura Bancroft.

In 1909 Baum moved to Los Angeles; his last Chicago residence before his departure for the West Coast was an apartment building located at 5243 South Michigan Avenue. Several years later his musical *The Tik-Tok Man of Oz* opened. It enjoyed profitable runs in San Francisco and Chicago. In 1914 Baum formed the Oz Film Manufacturing Company in order to produce movie versions of his fantasies. Five films were completed: *The Patchwork Girl of Oz*, *His Majesty the Scarecrow of Oz*, *The Magic Cloak*, *The Last Egyptian*, and *The Gray Nun of Belgium*.

In 1910 *The Wizard of Oz* was shot as a one-reeler by the Chicago-based Selig Pictures, and, in 1925, a silent version starring Oliver Hardy as the tin man was released. The film version that is indelibly etched in the national consciousness is, of course, the MGM musical of 1939 starring a young Judy Garland as the lost girl from Kansas, Dorothy Gale. Ironically, it was a commercial dud. Only later did it become the children's classic that we all know so well. It continues to cast its spell as evidenced by the phenomenal success of one of its offspring, Geoffrey Maguire's book and subsequent musical *Wicked*.

During his last years, Baum wrote *The Tin Woodman of Oz*, *The Magic of Oz*, and *Glenda of Oz*. *The Royal Book of Oz* was released posthumously. He died in his Hollywood home, which he had named, appropriately enough, "Ozcot," in May 1919, a week shy of his sixty-third birthday.

In 1976 a local bookseller, John Lenhardt, proposed naming a North Side park under construction at Webster Avenue and Larrabee Street after the mythical land of Oz. Today Oz Park serves as the city's tribute to the man and his enduring fantasy.

Further reading: Frank Joslyn Baum and Russell P. MacFall, *To Please a Child: A Biography of L. Frank Baum* (1961); L. Frank Baum, *The Annotated Wizard of Oz* (2000), edited with an introduction by Michael Patrick Hearn; Martin Gardner and Russel B. Nye, *The Wizard of Oz and Who He Was* (1957); Rebecca Loncraine, *The Real Wizard of Oz: The Life and Times of L. Frank Baum* (2009); Alberto Manguel and Gianni Guadalupi, *The Dictionary of Imaginary Places* (1987).

Bob Bell

Clown

BORN: January 18, 1922
Flint, Michigan

DIED: December 8, 1997
Lake San Marcos, San Diego County, California

Robert Lewis Bell may not have been the first Bozo the Clown but he was the most famous one. Bell played the role of the popular clown from 1960 to 1984 on WGN-TV.

The character of Bozo was created in 1946 by Alan W. Livingston, a businessman who later became an executive at Capitol Records (it was Livingston who signed the Beatles to Capitol in 1963). In 1949 Livingston sold rights to the character to various television stations. KTTV-TV in Los Angeles was the first station to broadcast the show *Bozo's Circus*. Here already were the characteristics that were to make the character famous: the flaming orange-red hair, the whiteface clown makeup, the ebullient personality, the distinctive laugh. In 1956 actor Larry Harmon bought the licensing rights to the character, which allowed local stations to hire actors to create their own versions of Bozo.

Bob Bell was born in Flint, Michigan, the son of a General Motors factory worker. After high school he enlisted in the marines and later, during World War II, in the navy. He became an announcer at WMRP (now WWCK) before moving to WHOT (now WDND) in South Bend, Indiana. In 1950, he worked at the WFBM-TV station (now WRTV) in Indianapolis before moving to WLW radio and WLWT-TV, both in Cincinnati, in 1953, where he joined the cast of the *Wally Phillips Show,* playing Phillips's sidekick. Phillips and Bell had an on-air chemistry that charmed audiences. In 1956 Bell followed Phillips to WGN radio and WGN-TV in Chicago. While Phillips would soon leave television altogether to concentrate on radio, Bell found another outlet for his talents: he joined the circus.

Bell first wore his Bozo costume for WGN-TV and also hosted a cartoon on the station in 1959. *Bozo's Circus* made its official premiere as a live one-hour show on September 11, 1961, just as the station was preparing to move from its Tribune Tower location to new studios at 2501 West Bradley Place on the Northwest Side. Simultaneously, Bell also hosted WGN's *Three Stooges* show, where he played the character of a neighborhood theater owner named Andy Starr who played old Three Stooges short films. He also was the voice heard in the early morning announcements on Channel 9.

WGN producer Don Sandburg developed the circus format for the new Bozo show. It was Sandburg who introduced the idea of the Grand Prize Game wherein two contestants, one boy and one girl, attempted to throw a Ping-Pong ball into six buckets all lined up in a row. To encourage competition, each successive bucket contained better and better toys. If the contestant successfully threw the ball into the last bucket, the magical Bucket #6, he or she would win a Schwinn bicycle as well as a bevy of silver dollars—that is, all the silver dollars that were placed in the bucket since the last winner. Or, as the avuncular ringmaster Ned Locke reminded his young contestants, "One silver dollar in bucket number six until someone wins them all!" This new *Bozo's Circus* was wildly popular; so popular in fact that at one point there was a ten-year waiting list for tickets. It even spawned, in 1966, a short-lived prime-time version called *Bozo's Big Top.* Chicago's version of *Bozo's Circus* was broadcast nationally in 1978.

In 1976, Ned Locke left the show and was replaced by Frazier Thomas, host of WGN-TV's own *Garfield Goose,* who brought with him the motley cast of characters from that show. In another major change, WGN moved the show from its long-held noon spot to weekday mornings and then, in an even more drastic change, chose to air a taped version rather than continue to broadcast it live. It was renamed *The Bozo Show* and aired after Ray Rayner's

Ray Rayner & His Friends. When Rayner retired in 1981, *The Bozo Show* ballooned to a bloated ninety minutes and included news and weather reports. The latter were spoken by Bob Bell, but without his Bozo costume.

In 1984 Bell retired to the San Diego area and was replaced by comedian Joey D'Auria. The final version of the show was known as *The Bozo Super Sunday Show.* In 1997 the Federal Communications Commission (FCC) required broadcast television stations to air a minimum of three hours of educational children's programming per week, which affected the content of the Bozo show as educational material led to less air time for Bozo and his antics. Competition from children's cable networks, such as Nickelodeon and the Disney Channel, also cut into the ratings. By the time WGN announced in 2000 that it was cancelling the show, *Bozo* was the last locally produced children's show in Chicago. The show's final broadcast was on August 26, 2001. In 2005 a two-hour retrospective, *Bozo, Gar & Ray: WGN TV Classics* was broadcast nationally.

In 1996 Bob Bell was inducted into the Clown Hall of Fame. He died of a heart attack in 1997 at the age of seventy-five. Ringmaster Ned Locke retired in 1976 and died from cancer in Kimberling City, Missouri, in 1992. Businessman Alan Livingston died in Beverly Hills, California, in 2009 at the age of ninety-one.

See also: Wally Phillips, Ray Rayner, Frazier Thomas

Further reading: Larry Bozo Harmon with Thomas Scott McKenzie, *The Man Behind the Nose: Assassins, Astronauts, Cannibals, and Other Stupendous Tales* (2010).

Saul Bellow

Author

BORN: June 10, 1915
Lachine, Quebec

DIED: April 5, 2005
Brookline, Massachusetts

*I am an American,
Chicago born—Chicago,
that somber city—and go
at things as I have taught
myself, free-style, and will
make the record in my own
way: first to knock, first
admitted; sometimes an
innocent knock, sometimes
a not so innocent.*

—The eponymous
character in
Saul Bellow's
*The Adventures
of Augie March*

Saul Bellow was a Nobel laureate and one of the major American novelists of the twentieth century. Although he was born in Quebec, the center of his fictional universe was Chicago. Bellow grew up in Chicago and spent most of his adult life in Chicago, and many of his works were set here. His characters were a diverse group but usually consisted of dreamers or seekers who lived in a corrupt world of fast-talking salesmen and con men. Bigger-than-life characters, they were filled with big ideas and Bellow's big-themed novels reflected that.

Born Solomon Bellow in Lachine, a poor, immigrant suburb of Montreal, he was the youngest of four children. His parents had emigrated from Russia to Canada. His father, Abram, tried but failed at whatever task he attempted, while his mother, Liza, was a very devout woman who hoped her son would become a rabbi or, failing that, a concert violinist. In 1924, when Bellow was nine, they immigrated to Chicago. His father found work in a bakery, but he also delivered coal and did some bootlegging on the side to make ends meet. Although young Saul was steeped in Jewish tradition, he eventually rebelled against what he considered his parents' "suffocating orthodoxy" and discovered—and relished—the rough street life of Chicago. In much the same way that James Joyce was irrevocably linked with Dublin, Bellow was linked with Chicago. Chicago, in fact, became his Dublin. Indeed, the city that he knew so well would later become a character in his own work.

Bellow began writing in elementary school despite the disapproval of his father, who did not think his son's literary aspirations would lead anywhere. His mother, though, was more supportive and understanding of her son's profound literary bent. Unfortunately, she died when Saul was seventeen. He took the loss hard, especially when his father remarried. Although devastated by his mother's death, Saul felt strangely liberated at the same time.

In 1933 Bellow enrolled at the University of Chicago. Two years later he transferred to the less expensive Northwestern University. Graduating in 1937 with honors in anthropology and sociology, he went on to attend graduate school at the University of Wisconsin–Madison for several months but quit to join the Works Progress Administration's Federal Writers' Project in Chicago, preparing biographies of Midwestern novelists. Then he joined the editorial department of Encyclopaedia Britannica and worked on Mortimer Adler's Great Books series.

In the late 1930s Bellow moved to New York and lived for a time in Greenwich Village, where he wrote fiction—with little success. During World War II he was rejected by the army because he had a hernia, but he later joined the merchant marine. It was during this time that he wrote his first novel, the largely autobiographical *Dangling Man,* about a young Chicagoan waiting to be drafted. It was published in 1944 before he had even turned thirty. He followed it up with *The Victim,* a novel about anti-Semitism that was heavily influenced by the work of Dostoevsky. From 1946 to 1948 he taught at the University of Minnesota.

In 1948 Bellow received a Guggenheim Fellowship and went to Paris, where he had something of an epiphany. An idea came to him: he would create a larger-than-life character who always had some sort of wild scheme in the works. The idea would eventually become *The Adventures of Augie March.* Published in 1953, Bellow's comical picaresque tale became his breakthrough novel and his first best seller. A meticulous craftsman, he was hailed as a new voice in American fiction: bold and lively but with inflections of both Yiddish and idiomatic American English. *Augie March,* like virtually all of his works, was written in a distinctive style, colloquial yet graceful, that somehow blended high art with low.

Throughout his long career, Bellow created a pantheon of vivid characters. In addition to Augie March, there is Wilhelm Adler, an unsuccessful actor who learns to accept his own limitations, in *Seize the Day* (1956); Eugene Henderson, an unlikely combination of violinist and pig farmer (as well as American millionaire) who travels to Africa in search of "a higher truth," in *Henderson the Rain King* (1959); Moses Herzog, a Jewish Everyman who despite being cuckolded by his wife and his best friend still remains an optimist (and who, it has been said, is the most like Bellow himself), in *Herzog* (1964); Artur Sammler, a Holocaust survivor living in New York City when it is in the midst of cultural and economic turmoil, in the dark *Mr. Sammler's Planet* (1969); Charlie Citrone in *Humboldt's Gift* (1975), about a successful Pulitzer Prize–winning author whose mentor, the alcoholic poet Von Humboldt Fleischer, dies a lonely death in a Times Square area hotel room; and Albert Corde, the main character in *The Dean's December* (1982), a meditative novel about power, death, and the fragility of the human condition.

Bellow's other works include the novels *More Die of Heartbreak* (1987), *A Theft* (1989), *The Bellarosa Connection* (1989), *The Actual* (1997), and *Ravelstein* (2000). His short story collections include *Mosby's Memoirs* (1968), *Him with His Foot in His Mouth* (1984), *Something to Remember Me By: Three Tales* (1991), and *Collected Stories* (2001). His nonfiction works include *To Jerusalem and Back* (1976), a memoir about his trip to Israel; *It All Adds Up* (1994), a collection of essays; and *The Last Analysis* (1964), a play.

Bellow once said, "Fiction is the higher autobiography." Consequently, he often adapted incidents and characters from his own life and the lives of people he knew. The character of Humboldt, for example, was modeled after the poet Delmore Schwartz; Henderson was based on the son of the writer John Jay Chapman; Gersbach in *Herzog,* a professor at Bard College who seduced Bellow's wife; and the eponymous character in *Ravelstein,* about a professor dying of AIDS, was inspired by the life of his good friend Allan Bloom, the author of *The Closing of the American Mind.*

In 1962 Bellow left New York to return to Chicago, moving into the Hyde Park neighborhood, to teach at the University of Chicago as a professor at the Committee on Social Thought. In 1993 he decided to move to Boston to teach at Boston University. He left Chicago for numerous reasons. Many of his closest friends had passed away, he said, including Allan Bloom, and he wanted a fresh start. He was also upset by the ugly racial climate in Chicago at the time. Several people in the black community had spread a repulsive story that Jewish doctors were deliberately infecting black children with HIV. Bellow found this "blood libel" charge to be offensive and wrote about it in the *Chicago Tribune.*

Bellow always denied he was a Jewish writer—he had little patience for categories of any sort. Nor was he much of a joiner. When he was younger he was briefly and very loosely linked with the *Partisan Review* crowd in New York but, in idiosyncratic fashion, chose to follow his own path; he did not pursue any particular school. But he was a man of paradox. Despite being closely associated with cities, he spent a great deal of his time on a Vermont farm. He was a cook, gardener, violinist, and also an avid sports fan.

Bellow felt strongly about things, and he made his opinions known. He dismissed the concept of multiculturalism or political correctness, an increasingly popular stance to take especially on American college campuses. Rather, Bellow firmly believed in the great books of Western civilization. His uncompromising attitude often led to controversy. A request from fellow author Richard Stern to have a monument named after Bellow in Hyde Park was turned down by Alderman (now Cook County Board president) Toni Preckwinkle. The request was denied because she considered comments he had made to the press to be racist. Bellow had feared the racial changes that had taken place in his Hyde Park neighborhood, and he had made his feelings clear. In addition, charges of insensitivity and elitism were leveled against him, especially when he asked an interviewer in *New York Magazine,* "Who is the Tolstoy of the Zulus? The Proust of the Papuans?" Bellow, in turn, responded to the criticism in an op-ed piece that appeared in the *New York Times,* calling the brouhaha a misunderstanding, and maintaining that he was referring to "the distinction between literate and pre-literate societies."

Bellow was the recipient of numerous awards during his lifetime. In 1976 he won the Pulitzer Prize in Fiction for *Humboldt's Gift* and the Nobel Prize in Literature. He is the only writer to have won the National Book Award three times and the only writer to have been nominated for the award six times. Married five times, he became a naturalized U.S. citizen in 1941.

Bellow died in 2005 at his home in Brookline, Massachusetts, at the age of eighty-nine. He is buried at the Jewish cemetery Shir HeHarim in Brattleboro, Vermont.

Further reading: James Atlas, *Bellow: A Biography* (2000); Malcolm Bradbury, *Saul Bellow* (1982); Michael K. Glenday, *Saul Bellow and the Decline of Humanism* (1990); Benjamin Taylor, ed., *Saul Bellow: Letters* (2010); James Wood, ed., *Saul Bellow Novels 1970–1982* (2010).

John Belushi

Comedian and Actor

BORN: January 24, 1949
Chicago, Illinois

DIED: March 5, 1982
Los Angeles, California

John Belushi clowned his way through Chicago's Second City, the legendary Old Town comedy improvisation club, and spent several sparkling seasons on NBC-TV's *Saturday Night Live* until attaining movie stardom at a relatively young age. Critics praised Belushi as a marvelous physical comedian who was also capable of great tenderness. He combined a robust blend of irreverent humor with a good-natured machismo filtered through a Midwestern sensibility. Belushi was a shooting star. He shone brightly for a few good years, and then he was gone.

Born in Chicago but reared in west suburban Wheaton, Belushi was the son of Albanian immigrants. At Wheaton Central High he won praise as an outstanding athlete in football, wrestling, track, and baseball. He sang in the school choir and played drums in a rock band called the

Ravins. Belushi, who attended several colleges in Illinois and Wisconsin, began his acting career performing in summer stock, including an improbable part in *Anne of the Thousand Days,* in which he played Cardinal Wolsey.

Belushi then formed, along with two friends, Steve Beshekas and Tino Insana, a comedy group called the West Compass Players. In 1970, after graduating with an associate of arts degree from the College of DuPage, Belushi enrolled at the University of Illinois at Chicago and found an apartment on Taylor Street. The West Compass Players, where Belushi wrote, directed, and starred in wickedly satirical skits, proved to be ample training ground for his next move. In 1971, he joined the cast of the Second City, at twenty-two, becoming its youngest member.

Belushi was a popular member of the critically acclaimed troupe. His devastatingly funny and deadly accurate impressions of Mayor Richard J. Daley won favor with audiences. "You did eight performances a week," Belushi once remarked, "so you didn't have to get desperate . . . you learned to write on your feet." In 1972 he appeared in National Lampoon's *Lemmings* in New York. He also wrote, directed, and performed in the *National Lampoon Radio Hour,* a nationally syndicated FM radio program. In 1975 Belushi joined the cast of *Saturday Night Live* (*SNL*), the groundbreaking NBC television show that revolutionized late-night programming.

SNL brought the Wheaton native fame and fortune. Among his most famous characters were a killer bee, a Samurai warrior, an imitation of rock musician Joe Cocker, and a waiter in a Greek diner—inspired by Chicago's Billy Goat Tavern—who constantly shouted "cheezborga, cheezborga!" Belushi and his colleague and best friend, Dan Aykroyd, left *SNL* in September 1979.

Belushi scored a hit with his first motion picture, the frat house comedy *National Lampoon's Animal House* (1978). The manic antics of "Bluto" Blutarsky grossed nearly $80 million. In *The Blues Brothers* (1980), another smash, Belushi and Aykroyd played their alter egos, Jake and Elwood Blues, two blues musicians on a "mission from God." In addition to the wildly successful movie, the Blues Brothers also spawned a hit album, *Briefcase Full of Blues* (1978), and a hit single, a rendition of Sam and Dave's "Hold On (I'm Comin')." In *Continental Divide (*1981), Belushi played a gruff Chicago newspaper columnist reportedly modeled after Mike Royko. His last film, *Neighbors,* was released in December of 1981. Other Belushi films include *Goin' South* (1978), *Old Boyfriends* (1979), and *1941* (1979).

A self-proclaimed "party animal," the beefy actor lived a life of excess. He overdosed on heroin and cocaine in March 1982 at the Chateau Marmont hotel on Sunset Boulevard, a popular hangout of movie and rock stars in West Hollywood. He was buried on Martha's Vineyard, Massachusetts. At the time of his death, the thirty-three-year-old actor was learning a role for a Paramount picture *Noble Rot.*

In 1989 the motion picture *Wired,* based on Bob Woodward's best-selling biography of Belushi, was released to largely disastrous reviews.

Further reading: Jeffrey Sweet, *Something Wonderful Right Away* (1986); Mike Thomas, *The Second City Unscripted: Revolution and Revelation at the World-Famous Comedy Theater* (2009); Bob Woodward, *Wired: The Short Life and Fast Times of John Belushi* (1984).

Joseph Bernardin
Cardinal

BORN: April 2, 1928
Columbia, South Carolina

DIED: November 14, 1996
Chicago, Illinois

Joseph Cardinal Bernardin was the first Italian American to head a major American diocese. A consensus builder, he made an impact on the national scene as he influenced Catholic teaching on pro-life issues, including such hot-button topics as the use of nuclear weapons and abortion.

Bernardin was born in the predominantly Protestant city of Columbia, South Carolina, the son of Giuseppi and Maria who hailed from the village of Tonadico di Primiero in the Dolomite Mountains of northern Italy. He attended both Catholic and public schools growing up. During his senior year of high school, he earned a scholarship to the University of South Carolina. Deciding initially to study medicine, he switched to philosophy and earned a bachelor's degree in 1948. He then changed his mind and decided to enter the seminary. He studied at Saint Mary's College in Kentucky and Saint Mary's Seminary in Baltimore, and in 1952 earned a master's degree in education at the Theological College at the Catholic University of America in Washington, D.C.

After being ordained to the priesthood in 1952 for the diocese of Charleston at Saint Joseph Church in Columbia, South Carolina, he spent fourteen years in the diocese of

Charleston. In 1966 he was appointed auxiliary bishop of Atlanta by Pope Paul VI—just thirty-eight years old, he became the youngest bishop in the country at the time. Two years later he was elected general secretary of the National Conference of Catholic Bishops of the United States Catholic Conference and moved to Washington, D.C. He served in that position until 1972, when Paul VI named him archbishop of Cincinnati. From 1974 to 1977 he was elected to a three-year term as president of the National Conference of Catholic Bishops and the United States Catholic Conference. In 1982 John Paul II named him archbishop of Chicago. Six months later he became a cardinal.

Not long after becoming cardinal, Bernardin introduced the concept of the Consistent Ethic of Life, or what became known as the "seamless garment" in which he declared that all life is sacred. He also avidly promoted peace. In 1983 he chaired a committee that released the pastoral letter, "The Challenge of Peace: God's Promise and Our Response." The letter questioned nuclear weapons policies even as it gave conditional approval of America's nuclear arsenal. Still, the pastoral called for a bilateral halt in the development and deployment of any new nuclear weapons. It was a controversial position to take.

Starting in the mid-1980s the Catholic Church was embroiled in a series of sexual abuse scandals involving priests throughout the United States. Bernardin himself was accused of sexual abuse in 1993 by Steven Cook, a former Catholic seminarian. The abuse was alleged to have taken place when Bernardin was still archbishop of Cincinnati. The scurrilous charge devastated Bernardin and soiled his up until then pristine reputation. He called it the most painful experience of his life. "The accusation startled and devastated me," he wrote.

In late December 1994 Bernardin met with his accuser at St. Charles Borromeo Seminary in Overbrook, a suburb of Philadelphia. Cook apologized to Bernardin and recanted his charges. Cook died on September 22, 1995, from AIDS. Bernardin felt liberated; a great weight had been lifted from his shoulders.

In response to the sex scandals plaguing the church, Bernardin released, in August 1996, "Called to Be Catholic: Church in a Time of Peril." Part of the Common Ground Initiative, the document encouraged open debate and transparency within the church on a variety of theological and social issues, including the changing roles of women, human sexuality, health care reform, and immigration. The project met with criticism. Cardinal Law of Boston, Cardinal Hickey of Washington, Cardinal Maida of Detroit, and Cardinal Bevilacqua of Philadelphia, for example, issued their own statements, strongly disagreeing with Bernardin and insisting that the church was not a place to discuss such matters.

In June 1995 Bernardin announced that he had been diagnosed with pancreatic cancer and planned to undergo surgery. Four months later, in October 1995, he released a pastoral letter on health care, "A Sign of Hope." After fifteen months in remission, Bernardin declared on August 30, 1996, that not only had the cancer returned, it had spread to his liver and was, in fact, inoperable.

In the final two months of his life, Bernardin shared his personal reflections on faith and mortality in *The Gift of Peace*, which was released posthumously the following year and became a national best seller. He clearly stated that he did not consider the book an autobiography but rather a reflection on his life and ministry during the three years before his passing. The book, he wrote, "is intended to help others understand how the good and the bad are always present in the human condition and that, if we 'let go,' if we place ourselves totally in the hands of the Lord, the good will prevail."

Two months before his death, he received the Presidential Medal of Freedom from President Bill Clinton. His final months were spent comforting other terminally ill cancer patients. On October 29, 1996, Loyola Medical Center dedicated the newly named Cardinal Bernardin Cancer Center. Despite his illness, Bernardin appeared at the press conference.

Bernardin completed *The Gift of Peace* on November 1, 1996. Thirteen days later, on November 14, he passed away. Before his death, he managed to find the strength to write the title of the book and sign his name on the front cover.

In 1997 the Catholic Theological Union in Hyde Park established the Joseph Cardinal Bernardin Center for Theology and Ministry to build upon his work and signature issues, including the Bernardin Scholarship, which provides graduate theological education; interreligous dialogue among Catholic, Jewish, and Muslim faith communities; and the Peacebuilders Initiative, which encourages and prepares high school students for a life of ministry and service.

See also: Arnold Damen, George Mundelein, James Quigley
Further reading: Joseph Cardinal Bernardin, *The Gift of Peace: Personal Reflections* (1997).

Frank Billings

Physician

BORN: April 2, 1854
Highland, Wisconsin

DIED: September 20, 1932
Chicago, Illinois

A noted physician, Dr. Frank Billings counted among his patients some of the leading citizens of Chicago. More importantly, Billings pioneered the study of medicine in the city with his greatest gift to medical education—the Medical School of the University of Chicago.

In 1832 Henry M. Billings migrated from New York State to southwestern Wisconsin, settling in Mineral Point and, with a partner, opening a general store. Frank Billings was born on farmland near the town. His father died in an accident when the boy was just eight. Frank Billings briefly taught in a country school before teaching at a public school for two years.

In 1878 Billings enrolled at the Chicago Medical College, which later merged with Northwestern University. In 1881 he graduated with a degree of doctor of medicine. Billings completed his internship at then Cook County Hospital and joined the Chicago Medical Club, whose purposes were "the promotion of good fellowship, harmony, and unity among the members, the advancement of medical science, and the maintenance of high professional standards." After three years of medical practice and teaching anatomy in Chicago, Billings went to Vienna in 1885 for a year of postgraduate study. He also attended lectures in London and Paris. It was in Paris where he met the great scientist Louis Pasteur. In 1886 Billings returned to Chicago to resume his career. Before long he decided to restrict his practice to general medicine and some consulting work.

In 1888 Billings joined the attending staff at Mercy Hospital and established a practice on the North Side where business flourished. As his reputation spread, he began to attract some of the city's wealthiest clientele, including many along posh Prairie Avenue. The meatpacker Philip Danforth Armour was one of his patients, as were George Pullman, Marshall Field, W. W. Kimball, the McCormicks, and the Palmers.

Billings served on the faculty of the Chicago Medical College as a professor of physical diagnosis from 1886 to 1891 and then as a professor of medicine from 1891 to 1898. He was also an attending physician at St. Luke's Hospital. In 1898 Billings was appointed professor of medicine at Rush Medical College on the West Side. He then met with William Rainey Harper, the president of the University of Chicago, to discuss a possible affiliation between Rush and the university. That year the two institutions agreed to merge. The new school, the Medical School of the University of Chicago, offered advanced training in medical research, including anatomy, physiology, and biochemistry.

Billings was appointed professor of medicine at the school and served as dean until 1920. Among its distinguished faculty were surgeons Nicholas Senn and Christian Fenger. Billings also acted as chief physician at the Presbyterian Hospital for many years. Under his tutelage, both institutions earned reputations as first-class centers for teaching, training, and research. In 1917, at the age of sixty-three, Billings joined the medical corps of the Armed Forces and was appointed chairman of the Red Cross Commission to Russia. In December 1921, he was promoted to Brigadier General in the Medical Officers' Reserve Corps of the United States Army.

Due to Billings's influence, the McCormick Institute for Infectious Diseases, which was located at 637 South Wood Street, was established by Harold F. and Edith Rockefeller McCormick. In addition, Billings fought for better-quality health care at what was then Cook County Hospital and helped improve the conditions of state mental institutions. He edited the second edition of the five-volume set *Therapeusis of Internal Diseases* (1914), and, with collaborators, edited the *General Medicine of the Practical Medicine* series (1901–21).

In 1924 Billings retired from active teaching but was appointed professor emeritus of medicine at the University of Chicago. "The main contributions of medical science in the past may be said to have been made to youth in the prevention of infant mortality and in the victory over diseases to which children are susceptible," he said in 1929. "The next step is to aid adults in battling their physical enemies."

In September 1932, Billings slipped on a rug in his North Side home at 1550 North State Parkway. He suffered severe internal bleeding and died as a result of his injuries at the age of seventy-eight.

See also: Morris Fishbein, William Rainey Harper, Mary Harris Thompson

Further reading: Thomas Neville Bonner, *Medicine in Chicago 1850–1950, A Chapter in the Social and Scientific Development of a City* (1957); Edwin Hirsch, *Frank Billings: The Architect of Medical Education, an Apostle of Excellence in Clinical Practice, a Leader in Chicago Medicine* (1966).

Jesse Binga
Banker and Realtor

BORN: April 10, 1865
Detroit, Michigan

DIED: June 13, 1950
Chicago, Illinois

Chicago's leading African American businessman during the 1920s, Jesse Binga was also a successful real estate agent and banker and one of the city's wealthiest African Americans. Binga symbolized a new type of black leader. His fortune came not from sports or entertainment—the typical route to African American success at the time—but from the business world.

Born in Detroit, Binga was the youngest of ten children. After high school he studied law for two years in the office of attorney Thomas Crisup. Restless, Binga left in 1885 and wandered west as an itinerant barber. After working as a porter on the Union Pacific Railroad, he invested in real estate in Pocatello, Idaho. It proved a lucrative deal. In 1896 Binga returned to Chicago, and with only $10 of capital he established a real estate business at 3331 South State Street in the heart of the city's Black Belt. In 1908 Binga established the Binga Bank, the first African American–owned bank in the city and the financial rock of the black community. In 1920 it became a state bank.

Proud, shrewd, and somewhat of a braggart, Binga was a controversial figure. Some called him a crook and an opportunist who used people whenever he had the chance. Others said he was simply an innovative businessman who wasn't afraid to take risks. A South Side booster and philanthropist, Binga helped scores of African American families acquire homes in the burgeoning Black Belt.

In 1912 Binga married Eudora Johnson, the sister of the notorious gambling overlord, John "Mushmouth" Johnson. She had inherited $200,000 from her brother before the marriage. The match boosted Binga's social standing and income significantly. In 1929 he built the Binga Arcade on the northwest corner of 35th and State Streets. The arcade was a five-story building that included office space and a dance hall on the roof. That same year Binga became chairman of a successful insurance company.

Racial tensions flared during the summer of 1919 as African Americans left the Black Belt and settled into the predominantly white neighborhoods of Kenwood and Hyde Park. Binga, who lived at 5922 South Parkway (now King Drive) and rented apartments to blacks in the area, received his share of attacks. His home and office, according to historian Allan H. Spear, were bombed seven times.

The Depression hit Binga and the African American community particularly hard. On July 31, 1930, Binga's bank was shut down by the state examiner. As as result, many members of Chicago's black community lost their savings and their hope. The bank, notes Spear, stood as a role model for a new confident generation of enterprising black businessmen. Consequently, the collapse of the bank shattered the dream of black empowerment—at least for a time.

Binga was convicted in 1933 of embezzling $22,000 from the bank and sentenced to ten years in the Illinois State Penitentiary in Joliet. Many felt he was too harshly treated and requested leniency. Petitions from prominent men and women, including the famed attorney Clarence Darrow, circulated calling for an early release in recognition of Binga's considerable contributions to the African American community. Released in 1938, the once prominent citizen found work as a lowly handyman in a Catholic church. He died penniless in June 1950 in St. Luke's Hospital. He was buried in Oakwood Cemetery.

Further reading: Commission on Chicago Historical and Architectural Landmarks, *Black Metropolis Historic District* (March 7, 1984); Rayford W. Logan and Michael R. Winston, eds., *Dictionary of American Negro Biography* (1982); Allan H. Spear, *Black Chicago: The Making of the Negro Ghetto 1890–1920* (1967); Dempsey J. Travis, *An Autobiography of Black Chicago* (1981).

Timothy Blackstone
Businessman

BORN: March 28, 1829
Branford, Connecticut

DIED: May 26, 1900
Chicago, Illinois

Timothy Beach Blackstone was a businessman, a mayor, and a founding president of the Union Stock Yards. The hotel that bears his name, the Blackstone Hotel on South Michigan Avenue, is located on the site of his former mansion.

Born in Branford, Connecticut, in 1829, Blackstone attended a local common school, as was the custom at the time, then enrolled at a nearby academy. Failing health, though, forced him to drop out in 1847. On the advice of his physician he sought outdoor employment and soon began working for Roswell B. Mason as a surveyor for the New York and New Haven Railroad. A year later he became an assistant engineer on the Stockbridge and Pittsfield Railroad. In 1851, Mason (who would later become mayor of Chicago) invited Blackstone to supervise construction of the Illinois Central Railroad between downstate Bloomington and Dixon. Accepting the position, Blackstone moved

to the town of La Salle, Illinois. In 1854–55 he served one term as La Salle's mayor. He returned to the railroad business, first as chief engineer and then as president of the Joliet and Chicago Railroad (it later changed its name to the Chicago and Alton Railroad). He served as president for twenty-five years. Blackstone was also the first president of the Union Stock Yards.

Blackstone died of pneumonia in Chicago in May 1900 at the age of seventy-one. His funeral was held at the Second Presbyterian Church and then transferred to Norwich, Connecticut, for burial services.

In 1904 his wife, Isabella, donated the T. B. Blackstone Memorial Branch Library on the South Side to the city of Chicago. Blackstone Avenue is named in his honor.

Blackstone built a mansion at what was then 252 Michigan Avenue. This property later became the site of the Blackstone Hotel and the Blackstone Theatre. The hotel, which was built from 1908 to 1910, was added to the National Register of Historic Places in 1986, and in May 1998 it was designated an official Chicago landmark. During the twentieth century it became famous for the number of American presidents—about a dozen—who stayed there. It also hosted more presidential nominating conventions—twenty-six—than any other American hotel. In popular culture, it contributed the phrase "smoke-filled room" to the political vernacular, referring to the secretive, behind-the-scenes deal making that led to Warren G. Harding being selected as the Republican nominee for president in 1920. After closing in 2000, the Blackstone reopened in March 2008 as part of the Marriott International Renaissance Hotels chain. During the renovation process, two of the historic guest rooms were preserved, including the infamous "smoke-filled room" on the ninth floor and the original presidential suite on the tenth floor.

Further reading: Miles Berger, *They Built Chicago: Entrepreneurs Who Shaped a Great City's Architecture* (1992).

Louise DeKoven Bowen

Social Reformer

BORN: February 26, 1859
Chicago, Illinois

DIED: November 9, 1953
Chicago, Illinois

As a child of privilege, Louise DeKoven Bowen could have had anything she wanted. Vast wealth and an easy, trouble-free existence were hers if she so desired. But Bowen was different. Imbued with a fierce social conscience and boundless energy, she chose instead to devote her life to helping the needy. As president of the Juvenile Protective Association, treasurer of Hull House, and vice president of the United Charities, she wielded great influence on social welfare programs in Chicago for almost sixty years.

Bowen was a member of many philanthropic, civic, and social organizations and was a leading figure in the woman suffrage movement. Furthermore, she was instrumental in the formation of the juvenile, boys', and domestic relations courts. She was also a founding member of the Visiting Nurses of Chicago and one of the organizers of the Woman's Board of Passavant Hospital.

Louise DeKoven was born at Wabash Avenue and Monroe Street, the only child of a wealthy Chicago pioneer family. She graduated from the Dearborn Seminary in 1875. As a young woman, DeKoven led a sheltered life. In her memoirs, *Growing Up with a City* (1926), she recalled that "the church . . . was the only outlet for social work." Following her marriage in 1886 to Joseph T. Bowen, a successful financier and banker, Louise Bowen played the role of a socialite. But unlike other women in her position, she used her power and wealth to help those in need. In this, she was greatly influenced by social reformer Jane Addams. During the 1890s Bowen and others brought about a statute establishing the first juvenile court in Chicago. When she became president of the Juvenile Court Committee, she convinced the city to erect a juvenile court building and a detention home.

In 1907 the Juvenile Court Committee became the Juvenile Protective Association whose function, said Bowen, was "to keep children out of the court by removing many of the demoralizing conditions which surrounded them." In many ways she was ahead of her time. She advocated stronger punishment for rape offenders, for example, and proposed that couples be required to have a medical certificate when applying for a marriage license. Bowen was also an early advocate of improving the quality of life for African Americans in Chicago. In 1912, in memory of her late husband, she established the Bowen Country Club, a seventy-two-acre summer camp near Waukegan, Illinois, for the underprivileged children of the Hull House neighborhood.

Bowen was a leading figure in the cause for woman suffrage. Not only was she president of the Chicago Equal

Suffrage Association, she also acted as vice president of the Illinois Equal Suffrage Association and served as auditor of the National American Woman Suffrage Association. In June 1916 she led a march of 5,000 women carrying placards that demanded votes for women. They marched on the Republican National Convention being held at the Coliseum in Chicago. Bowen also championed improvements in women's working conditions and in the welfare of children, and promoted efficiency and honesty in government.

At the time of her death, at the age of ninety-four, Bowen was still active in local affairs. She was the honorary president of Hull House, of the Juvenile Protective Association, and of the Woman's City Club. In 1941 the Rotary Club of Chicago awarded her its gold medal for distinguished service, the first woman ever honored with this award.

See also: Jane Addams, Mary Bartelme
Further reading: Sharon Z. Alter, "A Woman for Mayor?" *Chicago History*, Fall 1986; Muriel Beadle, *The Fortnightly of Chicago: The City and Its Women, 1873–1973* (1973); Louise DeKoven Bowen, *Open Windows: Stories of People and Places* (1946) and *Growing Up with a City* (2001); Rima Lunin Schultz and Adele Hast, eds., *Women Building Chicago, 1790–1990: A Biographical Dictionary* (2001).

James C. Bracken

Record Executive

BORN: May 23, 1909
Oklahoma

DIED: February 20, 1972

Vivian Carter

Record Executive

BORN: March 25, 1921
Tunica, Mississippi

DIED: June 12, 1989
Gary, Indiana

Before Motown, there was Vee-Jay. Founded by the husband-and-wife team of James Bracken and Vivian Carter, Vee-Jay Records was, for one brief shining moment, the biggest independent black-owned record label in the United States. Most famously, though, in 1962 Vee-Jay became the first American record label to sign the Beatles. In addition, Vee-Jay played a critical role in creating the uniquely Chicago sound of R&B, blues, doo-wop, and early rock and roll in the 1950s and 1960s.

James Bracken was born in Oklahoma and raised in Kansas City. Vivian Carter was born in Mississippi and moved to Gary, Indiana, as a child. In 1948 she won a deejay talent contest in Chicago. She worked at WGES radio in Chicago and then WJOB in her native Gary.

Bracken met Carter in Chicago in 1944. In 1950 they founded Vivian's Record Shop in nearby Gary, Indiana. Three years later they borrowed $500 from a pawnbroker and started their own record label, Vee-Jay. The name was taken from the initials of their first names. Both had a knack for spotting talent. Bracken himself also wrote some of the songs on the label. Eventually Carter hired her brother, Calvin Carter, as talent scout and producer. Success allowed the company to move from a converted garage space on South 47th Street to an office on Michigan Avenue and, in the late 1950s, to settle in at 1449 South Michigan Avenue in an area then known as Record Row. There was an easygoing camaraderie among artists and staff.

The first artist the Brackens signed was bluesman Jimmy Reed. At the time, Reed was a slaughterhouse worker in the Chicago Stockyards, cutting cattle. Reed's first session included "High and Lonesome" and an instrumental, "Roll and Rhumba." Vee-Jay followed up Reed's success with "Baby It's You" and "Bounce" by the Spaniels. The Brackens, though, were not set up to distribute their records beyond the metropolitan area. Thus these early records were leased to the Chicago-based Chance label.

Vee-Jay boasted a diverse catalog, including more than 400 jazz, gospel, and rock recordings. In addition to Reed and the Spaniels, its acts included Memphis Slim, John Lee Hooker, the Dells, the El Dorados, Jerry Butler, Gene Chandler, Dee Clark, and Betty Everett. Vee-Jay was also the first label to release a record by the Pips, who, in 1962, became known as Gladys Knight and the Pips. It had a jazz roster too, including Eddie Harris and Wayne Shorter, as well as a gospel lineup, including the Staple Singers, the Swan Silvertones, and Maceo Woods. Other artists included Lou Rawls, who recorded with the Pilgrim Travelers, and the poet Langston Hughes. At one point, the label even released comedy recordings by Dick Gregory and signed folk artists such as Hoyt Axton.

After the success of Gene Chandler's "Duke of Earl" in 1962, Vee-Jay expanded yet again, this time to include white pop artists. The first non-black artists to be signed to the label were the Four Seasons. But the unexpected success of their hit song "Sherry" caught the Brackens off-guard. Hampered by cash flow problems, they were without the financial means to press more copies of the record. The last thing the label needed was another hit.

And then, unbidden, the Beatles arrived on their doorstep.

In mid-1962, EMI, the British-owned parent company of the American label Capitol, approached Vee-Jay, offering the Brackens the option to acquire the rights in a licensing deal to accept a group that Capitol had turned down. Vee-Jay very much wanted the right to release Frank Ifield's "I Remember You," a worldwide hit at the time. But there was a catch: in order to get Ifield they had to agree to take an unknown band, a four-piece outfit from Liverpool known as the Beatles. Carter and manager Ewart Abner agreed. Thus, Vee-Jay unwittingly distributed "Please Please Me," "From Me to You," "Love Me Do," "Twist and Shout," and "Do You Want to Know a Secret" as well as, in late 1963, the group's first American album, *Meet the Beatles*. They set the Beatles masters aside and essentially forgot about them until one Sunday night in February 1964, when they turned on their television set and saw them on *The Ed Sullivan Show*. After that, everything changed. For Vee-Jay, the arrival of the Beatles was the beginning of the end.

In one month alone, Vee-Jay sold some 2.5 million Beatles records. But the label did not have enough money available to pay the artists their royalties or press enough records to meet the public demand. What's worse, Capitol quickly realized it had made a huge mistake and tried to make up for lost time by issuing a cease-and-desist order.

By spring 1963 rumors began circulating that Vee-Jay was in deep financial trouble. Despite their success, Vee-Jay was still being run as a small mom-and-pop operation. Basically, the Brackens had no available cash to distribute the records. Consequently, the Four Seasons filed suit against Vee-Jay for nonpayment of royalties.

With the hits no longer coming and creditors banging on their doors, a decision to move part of their operations to Southern California in 1963 caused even more headaches. Despite their success, or, more accurately, because of it, cash flow problems ultimately led to the company's downfall. Bracken and Carter were forced to temporarily cease operations in 1963. What's more, royalty disputes led the Four Seasons to move to Philips Records while Capitol Records, EMI's American branch, picked up the American rights to release both the Beatles and another EMI artist, Frank Ifield. Finally, in May 1966, Vee-Jay closed their Chicago office and filed Chapter 11 with some $3 million in debt. Its assets were purchased by executives Betty Chiapetta and Randy Wood.

Vee-Jay continues to license releases for its back catalog. The current distributors are P-Vine/Blues Interactions in Japan and Rhino Records in the United States. In 2007, Shout! Factory, a sublicensee of Rhino, released the *Best of Vee-Jay* box sets. In 1990, Daniel Pritzker, president of the Rockwood Music Group, acquired all the Vee-Jay masters.

Bracken died in 1972. After his death, Carter returned to Gary, where she was active in radio into the 1980s. She died in a Gary nursing home in 1989 after suffering a stroke.

In addition to the Beatles and Four Seasons records, Vee-Jay released many other hits, including "Goodnite Sweetheart, Goodnite" by the Spaniels, "Oh What a Nite" by the Dells, "The Shoop Shoop Song (It's in His Kiss)" by Betty Everett, "Let It Be Me" by Jerry Butler and Betty Everett, the original version of "Tainted Love" by Gloria Jones, and "Have I the Right?" by the Honeycombs. The Honeycombs were a London-based quintet distinguished by the power drumming of Honey Lantree, one of the few female drummers at the time.

See also: Leonard Chess, Curtis Mayfield
Further reading: Robert Pruter, *Chicago Soul* (1992).
Discography: *Vee-Jay: The Definitive Collection* (2007), a four-disc set.

Preston Bradley

Minister

BORN: August 18, 1888
Linden, Michigan

DIED: June 1, 1983
Morrisville, Vermont

Author, columnist, and broadcaster, Preston Bradley served as pastor of the Peoples Church of Chicago at 941 West Lawrence Avenue in the Uptown neighborhood for sixty-five years. With his velvet baritone and unorthodox viewpoints, Bradley stood out from the crowd—he frequently departed from traditional Christian teaching—and indeed proved to be one of the most controversial clergymen in Chicago history.

Bradley's father was from County Antrim, Northern Ireland, and his mother was of English descent. Both were Presbyterian, and both believed that Christianity brought joy and cheer into the world. In their eyes, religion celebrated the spiritual and the earthly, the sacred and the profane. In his autobiography, Bradley admits that he could not remember the time when he did not want to be a preacher—or an actor. "There's a little bit of the actor in every preacher, of course," he wrote.

Bradley attended Alma College in Alma, Michigan. After one year, he dropped out and studied law in Flint, Michigan. Inspired by a biography of evangelist Dwight Moody, he decided to move to Chicago to enroll at the Moody Bible

Institute. In 1912 Bradley was ordained as a Presbyterian minister and installed as pastor of the Church of Providence on the North Side. At the same time, he enrolled at Hamilton College of Law. Later he received his doctor of laws degree from Lake Forest College and, in 1939, received his doctor of divinity from Meadville Theological Seminary.

"I am not orthodox about anything," he once remarked during a sermon in 1912. "I am thoroughly, completely, adequately, gloriously, and triumphantly a heretic." Living up to his self-proclaimed title of heretic, he was charged with heresy for preaching that baptism is not a prerequisite for salvation. Bradley resigned from his position at the Church of Providence and instead founded his own congregation, the Peoples Church of Chicago.

The Peoples Church was a progressive institution. From the day it opened its doors, it welcomed Chicagoans of all races, creeds, and nationalities. Bradley, a religious maverick, defied orthodox religion of any kind. Each Sunday he presided over a growing congregation of followers who were attracted by his provocative opinions, stirring speeches, and unconventional attitude toward established religion. Unlike most clergy, Bradley was not afraid to take a stand on controversial issues. In 1923 Bradley became a Unitarian and the Peoples Church was accepted into the American Unitarian Association. The church, which remained nonsectarian, retained its unusual character. At its peak, the Peoples Church boasted a membership of 4,000 people.

Bradley did not separate politics from religion. He believed that it was the duty of the clergy to become involved in political affairs, to be knowledgeable, and to express an opinion. He advocated birth control, for example, when only the most radical thinkers would venture such an opinion. In 1919 he marched with Jane Addams in a woman suffrage parade, spoke out against the Ku Klux Klan during the 1920s, defended the leftist policies of Roosevelt's New Deal in the 1930s, and during World War II spoke out against Hitler and the growing anti-Semitism that was spreading throughout the world. Bradley's followers urged him to enter politics and run for mayor. He declined.

The Peoples Church was the first church in Chicago to broadcast regular services across the radio. Bradley acted as senior pastor at the church until 1968 and continued his weekly radio show until 1976 when failing health forced him to resign. A prolific writer, among his many books are *Courage for Today* (1934), *Mastering Fear* (1935), *Power from Right Thinking* (1936), *Life and You* (1940), *New Wealth for You* (1941), *Meditations* (1941), *My Daily Strength* (1943), *Happiness Through Creative Living* (1955), and *Between You and Me* (1967). He also edited *Liberalist* magazine.

Bradley was also founder and president of the Izaak Walton League, a conservationists' club, and a charter member of the Chicago Human Relations Commission. Further, he served on the board of the Chicago Public Library for more than half a century. In 1962 the Chicago City Council awarded him its award of merit for distinguished service to the community.

Bradley died in June 1983 at the age of ninety-four in a Vermont nursing home.

Today the Peoples Church continues to serve the diverse population of the Uptown community with social service programs, lectures, and consultation.

See also: Dwight L. Moody, David Swing, Billy Sunday
Further reading: Preston Bradley with Harry Barnard, *Along the Way: An Autobiography* (1962).

Myra Bradwell

Legal Reformer

BORN: Circa 1831
Manchester, Vermont

DIED: February 14, 1894
Chicago, Illinois

Although she practiced law, Myra Bradwell was an articulate and passionate crusader for legal and other types of reform. As founder of the weekly *Chicago Legal News*, Bradwell worked vigorously to improve the reputation of the legal profession and to encourage the highest standard of professionalism.

Born Myra Colby in Vermont, Bradwell moved with her family to western New York State as a child. When she was twelve, the family settled in Chicago. She was educated in Kenosha, Wisconsin, and at the Ladies Seminary in Elgin, Illinois, eventually becoming a teacher at the latter institution. She also taught in the Memphis, Tennessee, school system before returning to Chicago. During the Civil War years, Bradwell raised funds for wounded soldiers and their widows and children by arranging and managing fairs.

In 1852 she married James B. Bradwell, a prominent member of the Illinois bar, and studied law in order to help her husband further his career. She, too, wished to practice law but because she was a married woman, her admission

to the bar was refused by both the supreme court of Illinois and the United States Supreme Court. The nation's highest court held that "the peculiar qualities of womanhood, its gentle graces, its tender susceptibility, its purity, its delicacy, its emotional impulses, its subordination of hard reason to sympathetic feeling are surely not qualifications for forensic strife. Nature has tempered woman as little for judicial conflicts of the courtroom as for the physical conflicts of the battlefield. Woman is molded for gentler and better things." The judges declared that a woman, especially a married woman, did not belong in a court of law because the "married condition" amounted to a "disability" that would somehow prevent a woman from maintaining the proper client confidentiality, according to historian Charlotte Adelman.

Nevertheless, as a result of Bradwell's pioneering efforts, a woman—Alta Hulett—was finally admitted to the Illinois bar in 1873. Ironically, Bradwell had to wait more than fifteen years before the Illinois Supreme Court finally granted her a license in 1890. Due to poor health, however, she never actually practiced law. Bradwell, though, was the first woman in the United States to apply for admission to the bar, the first woman to become a member of the Illinois Press Association, and, according to contemporary newspaper accounts, the first woman to become a member of the Chicago Bar Association. In 1868 she established the *Chicago Legal News,* a newspaper intended for "every lawyer and businessman in the Northwest." The paper published a summary of cases heard in various U.S. courts as well as legal information and news items. Her constant attempts to further the legal profession inspired a group of men to found the Chicago Bar Association. Bradwell welcomed the new group and encouraged any organization that would elevate the standards of her calling and rid the profession of the "disreputable shysters."

An ardent feminist, Bradwell campaigned for woman suffrage and helped establish the Midwest's first woman suffrage convention in 1869. Bradwell was one of the founders of the Illinois Industrial School for Girls and one of the first women to suggest an official Women's Department at the World's Columbian Exposition in Chicago in 1893.

The temper of the times changed gradually as did the conservative mindset of the male-dominated courts. In 1890 the Illinois Supreme Court granted Bradwell a license, and in 1891, the United States Supreme Court admitted her to the Illinois bar. Other significant changes in the judicial system soon followed, notes historian Adelman. In 1894 the first African American woman, Ida Platt, was admitted to the Illinois bar. During the next few decades great strides were made in the women's movement. In 1914 the Women's Bar Association of Illinois (WBAI) was formed and, in 1919, Illinois became the first state to ratify the Nineteenth Amendment, which granted women the right to vote. Finally, in 1939, Governor Henry Horner signed a bill that gave women the right to sit on Illinois juries.

Bradwell died in February 1894 in Chicago at the age of sixty-three.

See also: Mary Bartelme, Henry Horner

Further reading: Charlotte Adelman, "A History of Women Lawyers in Illinois," *Illinois Bar Journal,* May 1986; Herman Kogan, *The First Century: The Chicago Bar Association 1874–1974* (1974); Rima Lunin Schultz and Adele Hast, eds., *Women Building Chicago, 1790–1990: A Biographical Dictionary* (2001).

James H. Breasted

Archaeologist

BORN: August 27, 1865
Rockford, Illinois

DIED: December 2, 1935
New York, New York

A brilliant scholar of Egyptology, James Henry Breasted was the first American to receive a Ph.D. in archaeology, held the first chair of Egyptology in the United States, and helped share modern archaeology as a science. He was professor of Egyptology and Oriental history at the University of Chicago from 1894 to 1925 and founded the Oriental Institute Museum in 1919.

The second child of Charles and Harriet Newell Garrison, Breasted spent his early childhood in Rockford, Illinois. In 1873 his parents bought a seven-acre tract in Downers Grove and built a small house. He entered North-Western (now North Central) College in Naperville at the age of fifteen and then served an apprenticeship in a pharmacy owned by his brother-in-law in Rochelle, Illinois. From 1882 to 1886 Breasted attended the Chicago College of Pharmacy. In 1886 his brother-in-law offered him a position as prescription clerk at his store in Omaha, Nebraska. Breasted accepted. Not satisfied by the pharmaceutical profession, he returned to Downers Grove the following year and decided to pursue another line of study.

In 1888 Breasted enrolled at the Congregational Institute (now the Chicago Theological Seminary) to study Hebrew and the Scriptures under Dr. Samuel Ives Curtiss. Determined to master Hebrew, he also taught himself Greek, Latin, Babylonian and Assyrian cuneiform, ancient Egyptian, French, German, and a smattering of Italian. At this point, he realized that a life in the ministry was not for him, and he changed course again in order to devote his life to the study of Oriental history and languages.

In 1890 Breasted transferred to Yale to study under William Rainey Harper. Harper suggested Breasted accept a chair in Egyptology at the newly proposed University of Chicago, of which Harper had just been named president. Breasted graduated from Yale in 1892 and, two years later, received his Ph.D. in Egyptology from the University of Berlin. Berlin was, at that time, the teaching and research center of the world in Oriental languages. He was at the top of his field but he felt scared, lonely, and confused, according to his son and biographer Charles Breasted. Recalling his Berlin days forty years later Breasted mused, "I shall never forget the dark shadow of uncertainty that always hung over me—uncertainty as to my own ability to make good and about following a science of which there was not a single professorship or post of any kind in any American university."

Breasted returned to the United States in 1894 and, accepting Harper's offer, became an assistant in Egyptology at the University of Chicago. In 1905 he became professor of Egyptology and Oriental history, the first chair in that subject in America. In the early days, according to Charles Breasted, Egyptology was, at best, a maddeningly inaccurate science, full of half-truths and populated by a "handful of competent" scholars who often disagreed among themselves over even the most fundamental of matters. During the early years of the century Breasted worked primarily in Europe, developing with other colleagues a dictionary of ancient languages. Collecting and collating about 1,000 historical documents, he produced *A History of Egypt* in 1905 and the five-volume *Ancient Records of Egypt* in 1907.

Breasted mounted his first major expedition to Egypt in 1905. In 1912 he published *Development of Religion and Thought in Ancient Egypt* and then wrote, with James Harvey Robinson, several high school textbooks, including *Outlines of European History* (1914) and *Ancient Times: A History of the Early World* (1916). In 1919 and 1920 he undertook an exhausting eleven-month journey through the Middle East. Following the excavation of King Tutankhamen's tomb in 1922 in Egypt, Breasted began working closely, mainly as a consultant, with the English archaeologist and noted Egyptologist Howard Carter and with the English aristocrat Lord Carnarvon, who financed the excavations. The discovery of the ancient Egyptian king's tomb fascinated the American public and, indeed, fired the imaginations of people throughout the world. All the artifacts taken from the tomb are in the Cairo Museum in Cairo, Egypt.

In 1919 the Oriental Institute at the University of Chicago was founded with a grant from John D. Rockefeller Jr. A great deal of the artifacts came from Breasted's Middle East sojourn during that year and the following year. In 1923 Breasted became the first archaeologist to be elected into the National Academy of Sciences. Two years later he began to devote all of his time to the institute and its various research projects.

Breasted's other writings include *Oriental Forerunners of Byzantine Painting* (1924), *The Conquest of Civilization* (1926), and *The Dawn of Conscience* (1933). He died from a throat infection at the Rockefeller Institute for Medical Research in New York City in December 1935.

Breasted, who lived at 5811 South Dorchester Avenue in Hyde Park, played a significant role in the growth and development of Egyptology and the museum he founded, the Oriental Institute, is an internationally recognized pioneer in the history and study of Egypt and the Near East. The museum, located at 1155 East 58th Street, houses objects from Egypt, Mesopotamia, ancient Persia, Syria, and Palestine, and is considered one of the foremost centers of Egyptology in the world today. Most of the objects in the museum's collection were discovered by institute scholars during archaeological excavations. In January 2010, the Oriental Institute celebrated its 90th anniversary with an exhibit, "Pioneers of the Past," which retraced Breasted's adventures in the Middle East.

See also: William Rainey Harper

Further reading: Abt, Jeffrey, *American Egyptologist: The Life of James Henry Breasted and the Creation of His Oriental Institute* (2011); Charles B. Breasted, *Pioneer to the Past: The Story of James Henry Breasted, Archaeologist* (1943).

Stuart Brent

Bookseller

BORN: April 8, 1912
Chicago, Illinois

DIED: June 24, 2010
Ashland, Wisconsin

An intellectual with a strong pugilistic side, Stuart Brent was a passionate and oftentimes difficult man. He became a bookseller not to make money but because he simply loved books; he considered bookselling a calling, not a business.

Born Stuart Brodsky in the Douglas Park neighborhood on the West Side in 1912, Brent was the youngest child in a family of six. He lived at 1639 South Central Park Avenue, a predominantly Jewish neighborhood at the time that consisted "of houses and trees and good back yards," he wrote in his memoir, *The Seven Stairs: An Adventure of the Heart* (1962). His father, Joseph, a blacksmith in his native Russia who found work in Chicago as a janitor and then as a tool and dye maker, believed in two things, love and work. "He mistrusted those who did not," Brent recalled.

Brent was a bookish boy who was seldom seen without a book in his hands. As a teenager and young man, he worked at various jobs. He was an usher at the Chicago Theatre. He was a newsboy, selling papers at the corner of Wabash and Van Buren from 7 P.M. to midnight. He worked in a grocery store, a hardware store, and a department store. He was a busboy and a dishwasher. One of his brothers was a prizefighter. Brent himself considered following in his sibling's footsteps and, while he did some boxing, he soon realized it was not meant to be (his lack of success in the ring led to his being given the dubious moniker of "the Horizontal Kid").

Brent attended Crane Junior College, the now defunct Lewis Institute, and graduate courses at the University of Chicago. He had ambitions of becoming an English professor. It was while he was still an undergraduate that an instructor, learning of his professorial ambitions, suggested he change his name from the Jewish-sounding Brodsky to something more Anglophilic. He chose "Brent," legally changing it when he was 19. He taught at the Chicago Teachers College and lectured on literary ideas at the downtown campus of the University of Chicago before entering the military.

Books were always on his mind. After serving in the army during World War II, where he reached the rank of master sergeant, Brent opened his first bookstore in August 1946, with a G.I. loan of $300. Called the Seven Stairs, it was located in a brownstone building on North Rush Street. No one in his family knew how to run a business, Brent the least of all. "How do you go about getting people to buy books?" he asked himself, as has every bookseller since. "Every morning I opened the store bright and early. Every night I closed very late. And no one came," he wrote in his memoir.

Eventually, though, Brent developed several techniques—laborious by today's standards—for selling books. He sent a postcard to everyone on his mailing list when he came across a book that he liked—inviting customers to visit his store to buy the book. He also made telephone calls to people but soon realized that it could not be done "indiscriminately." He made sure he didn't waste anyone's time. Brent observed that you "must know exactly what to say and say it quickly."

Brent had a reputation as being a difficult man. He himself admitted as much. Consequently, his customer relations were less than perfect. "I demanded that customers buy books for the same reasons that I sold them—out of a serious regard for greatness." To Brent, books were not disposable toys but rather almost sacred objects. Indeed, years later, at his memorial service, Brent's eldest son, Jonathan, referred to his father as "a stern moralist."

Brent cultivated a following among the city's literary elite. He supported the careers of Philip Roth and Richard Stern, among others. Regular visitors to his shop included Studs Terkel, Jack Conroy, Saul Bellow, and especially Nelson Algren. He held periodic parties honoring Algren's work. When Algren's *The Man with the Golden Arm* was released in late 1949, Brent hosted a cocktail party that he called "one of our greatest." Brent used other techniques to bring people into his shop, such as sponsoring a series of lectures on the great men of literature after official closing hours.

Brent closed the Seven Stairs and moved into bigger space at 670 North Michigan Avenue in the early 1950s. He would stay in the new store, Stuart Brent Books, until it closed nearly half a century later, in 1996. But first he held a going-away party attended by the city's literary editors, including Fanny Butcher of the *Chicago Tribune*, Emmet Dedmon of the *Chicago Sun-Times*, and Van Allen Bradley of the *Chicago Daily News*. Also in attendance were Algren, Conroy, Terkel, and Herman Kogan.

The Michigan Avenue shop soon became the literary headquarters of Chicago bookselling. It had a basement where Brent immediately began scheduling lectures, parties, and art exhibits. He even installed a grand piano for concerts. On Saturday afternoons he invited gatherings of men and women "from a wide range of professions and disciplines" to stop by and talk to one another and served them coffee and strudel.

In addition to his bookstore, Brent also hosted in the 1950s a television program on books called, appropriately,

Books and Brent, which aired locally on WBKB and syndicated nationally.

The Michigan Avenue bookstore closed in 1996 largely because of changes in book buying habits and high rent. "I, Stuart Brent," he said at the time, "am an anachronism."

Brent died at the age of ninety-eight in an Ashland, Wisconsin, hospital near Bark Point, his beloved farm.

See also: Nelson Algren, Saul Bellow, Fanny Butcher, Herman Kogan

Jack Brickhouse

Broadcaster

BORN: January 24, 1916
Peoria, Illinois

DIED: August 6, 1998
Chicago, Illinois

Hey-hey!

—Jack Brickhouse

The voice of the Cubs, the Bears, and the White Sox, the versatile Jack Brickhouse was at home whether interviewing popes and presidents or reciting the statistics of athletes. Indeed, during his long broadcasting career he covered five national political conventions and conducted interviews with four U.S. presidents and even Pope Paul VI. He was a man for all broadcasting seasons and was considered one of the greatest broadcasters in Chicago history. His enthusiasm was never feigned.

Born John Beasley Brickhouse in Peoria, Illinois, he was the son of John William "Will" Brickhouse, a theater sales manager, and Daisy, a hotel cashier and hostess. His parents were different on many levels. His father was tall (six feet five), his mother short (five feet one), and they were separated by a vast chasm of age: he was thirty-nine and she fifteen when they married. They separated before his father died of pneumonia, leaving Daisy a teenage widow with a two-year-old son to raise on her own. He never took the sacrifices she made to him for granted. Years later, he dedicated his autobiography to her.

To help make ends meet, Brickhouse delivered newspapers while still in grade school. He attended Peoria Manual High School and served as the sports editor of the school paper. After high school, he enrolled at Bradley University, although he did not graduate. Instead, in 1934, he entered Peoria radio station WMBD's "So you want to be an announcer" contest. Although he failed to win any of the prizes, someone at the station was impressed enough with his voice—and enthusiasm—to allow him to try out for one week. Two weeks later he was hired as a part-time announcer and part-time switchboard operator. He rose up the ranks quickly. Within four years he was calling the play-by-play for the Bradley University basketball team. This led to an audition at WGN radio. Eventually he took over the WGN baseball broadcasts—both Cubs and White Sox games—until he left after the 1943 season for a short stint with the marines. He was discharged because of complications resulting from a bout of childhood tuberculosis.

Between 1943 and 1948, when he rejoined WGN, Brickhouse covered non-sporting events, including numerous Democratic and Republican national conventions for other radio stations. Back on the sports beat, he covered everything from Golden Gloves boxing at the Chicago Stadium to wrestling and baseball from both Wrigley Field and Comiskey Park.

From 1948 to 1981 Brickhouse did play-by-play coverage for the Chicago Cubs on WGN-TV. He broadcast the Chicago White Sox games on WGN radio from 1940 to 1943, on WJJD radio in 1945, and on WGN-TV from 1948 to 1967, as well as various national sporting events, including three World Series broadcasts for NBC. He called Chicago Bears football on WGN-AM radio with fellow broadcaster Irv Kupcinet and was also a boxing commentator and did Chicago Bulls basketball games for WGN-TV from 1966 to 1973.

"My strength is that I can take a piece of copy on a subject I know little about and sound authoritative," he once said. Known for his passion, he was friendly but, unlike other broadcasters, he did not describe in much detail the action on the field, preferring instead to allow the visuals to tell the full story.

In 1981 Brickhouse retired from Cubs' baseball broadcasting. He was inducted into the Baseball Hall of Fame two years later, in 1983.

On March 3, 1998, he had brain surgery to remove a tumor. He died less than six months later, in August 1998, at St. Joseph Hospital after experiencing cardiac arrest. He was eighty-two.

A bust of Brickhouse stands on Michigan Avenue near the Chicago River.

See also: Harry Caray, Irv Kupcinet
Further reading: Jack Brickhouse, *Thanks for Listening!* (1986); Janice A. Petterchak, *Jack Brickhouse: A Voice for All Seasons* (1996).

Gwendolyn Brooks

Poet

BORN: June 7, 1917
Topeka, Kansas

DIED: December 3, 2000
Chicago, Illinois

Although she won the Pulitzer Prize and earned many other accolades during her life, poet Gwendolyn Brooks gained the greatest satisfaction by mentoring other writers. Defying conventional wisdom, she chose as her subject the world that lay outside her front door in Chicago's Bronzeville neighborhood. "I wrote about what I saw and heard in the street," Brooks once said. "I lived in a small second-floor apartment at the corner, and I could look first on one side and then the other. There was my material." Her mother reportedly told her, "You are going to be the lady Paul Laurence Dunbar." Her prophetic statement came to pass, for by the early 1960s, Brooks was considered the grande dame of African American writers.

Born Gwendolyn Elizabeth Brooks in Topeka, Kansas, in 1917, she was the daughter of a former schoolteacher and a father who was the son of a runaway slave. When she was six weeks old, the family moved to Chicago where she grew up on the South Side, which remained her home until she died. She attended Hyde Park High School, then a virtually all-white high school, and it was here where she had her first serious encounter with prejudice. Until then she hadn't given much thought to different races since she had seen only glimpses of whites, in the movies and "on the streetcar." She was aware of their existence but not their presence. "It was my first experience with many whites around. I wasn't much injured, just left alone," she recalled. "I realized that they were a society apart, and they really made you feel it."

When she transferred to the all-black Wendell Phillips High School she experienced a different kind of racial prejudice: intraracial. She was not considered one of the "hip" students, something she was made sorely aware of. What's more, her natural shyness along with her dark skin made it easier for her fellow students to ignore her. She transferred one last time, to the integrated Englewood High School, where she had a much more pleasant experience, graduating in 1934.

At the age of eleven she had begun to keep notebooks of original poetry. She published her first poem, "Eventide," in the October 1930 issue of *American Childhood* when she was just thirteen. Encouraged by her mother, she sent her poems along to poets Langston Hughes and James Weldon Johnson. Hughes, who would become a lifelong supporter of her work, encouraged her to keep writing. Many of her earliest poems were published in the "Lights and Shadows" column in the *Chicago Defender*. It seemed reasonable then, to her, that since the paper had already acknowledged her literary talent by publishing her

work, it might consider her for a position as a reporter. Consequently, Brooks wrote to *Defender* editor Robert Abbott. Abbott seemed to encourage her interest. Yet when Brooks appeared for a face-to-face interview, Abbott's demeanor changed. The interview, according to Brooks, was cold, "almost hostile." She attributed his change of mind to her dark complexion. And indeed, according to Abbott's biographer, Roi Ottley, Abbott apparently had an aversion to dark-skinned black women.

In 1936 Brooks graduated from Wilson Junior College in Chicago. Three years later she married Henry L. Blakely Jr., a fellow writer. In the early 1940s she began taking part in various poetry workshops. In the meantime, though, to make ends meet, she worked at a series of unsatisfactory jobs: as a clerk, a domestic, and an assistant to a spiritual adviser, E. N. French (she would later write about her experiences in her book, *In the Mecca*).

Over the years her poetry changed both in form and content, especially after she attended a conference of black writers at Fisk University in 1967. After listening to Amiri Baraka and others, she came away convinced that as a black poet she should write about the black experience. An important influence was the Gold Coast socialite Inez Cunningham Stark, who conducted poetry workshops for African Americans at the South Side Community Center. She encouraged her students to write about what they knew and to avoid the literary cliché.

Brooks chose to stay in Bronzeville, the historic black neighborhood on Chicago's South Side where she grew up. Her first poetry anthology, *A Street in Bronzeville,* published in 1945 by Harper & Row, consisted of portraits of the neighborhood. Employing the rhythms of the street and using ample colloquialisms, the Bronzeville poems captured the heart and soul of her community and created fully fledged characters that came alive on the page. She used a rich range of literary styles, too, including quatrains, free verse, ballads, and sonnets.

In 1946 and 1947 Brooks was awarded a grant from the American Academy of Arts and Letters and also received fellowships from the Guggenheim Foundation. In 1949 she published her second volume of poetry, *Annie Allen,* a portrait of a Bronzeville girl in which she used an experimental form called the sonnet-ballad. *Annie Allen* won *Poetry* magazine's Eunice Tietjens Memorial Prize and the following year, in 1950, it earned her the Pulitzer Prize. She became the first black writer to receive the prize.

In her essay "They Call It Bronzeville," which appeared in the October 1951 issue of *Holiday* magazine—novelist Nelson Algren helped get the essay published—she lamented the housing conditions that forced African Americans to live in cramped quarters: "Because of its cramped housing conditions, Bronzeville keeps stretching, stretching—leaning, cutting farther north, farther south, farther east, farther west. When this happens, violence follows."

In 1953 her novel *Maud Martha* was published but, despite the Pulitzer and her considerable reputation, it was mostly ignored. In it she traced the life of a Bronzeville woman from childhood to motherhood in a series of thirty-four vignettes. Today it is now regarded as a novel that was ahead of its time and as an important influence on generations of contemporary female writers.

In 1956 Brooks published *Bronzeville Boys and Girls,* a collection of children's poetry. Another poetry collection, *The Bean Eaters,* was released in 1960, and *Selected Poems* in 1963. By the time she published, in 1968, *In the Mecca,* a lengthy poem about a mother searching for her child in a Chicago housing project, her style had changed: it was more direct with clipped lines and abstract, random rhymes. *In the Mecca* was nominated for a National Book Award.

Brooks has been called the poet of the unheroic, an apt description since the people she wrote about seldom earned attention in the public eye. Her poem "The Bean Eaters," for example, is a portrait of an older couple struggling to get by who remember better times, while "Jessie Mitchell's Mother" illustrates the conflict between a light-skinned mother and a dark-skinned daughter, a topic that she knew much about.

Despite all of the accolades and fame, Brooks chose to live and work on the South Side and devoted a great deal of her time to helping young people by reading at schools, prisons, and hospitals and attending annual poetry contests for young people. She was a role model and a mentor to younger poets. In addition, she conducted poetry and writing workshops in her Chicago home that included members of the Blackstone Rangers street gang—a controversial choice—and she acknowledged the achievement and supported the work of the Artists Workshop of the Organization of Black American Culture (OBAC). Ultimately, her goal was to write poetry that reached all members of black society, including folks who frequented bars and taverns—in other words, people who didn't usually read poetry. "I want to write poetry . . . that will be exciting to such people," she said. "And I don't see why it can't be 'good' poetry. All black people: black people in taverns, black people in alleys, black people in gutters, schools, offices, factories, prisons . . . *not* always to 'teach'—I shall wish often to entertain, to illumine."

Indeed, Brooks gained the greatest satisfaction by mentoring other writers, including, most famously, Haki Madhubuti, author, poet, and publisher of Third World Press. Madhubuti paid her back by creating a literary center, the Gwendolyn Brooks Center, and an annual writer's conference in her name at Chicago State University. Other Brooks protégés included Sonia Sanchez, Nikki Giovanni, Sterling Plumpp, and Quraysh Ali Lansana, former artistic director of Chicago's Guild Complex.

Brooks often wrote with a fierce racial consciousness. She composed poems on integration in Little Rock and on the murder of Emmett Till in Mississippi, and wrote memorial poems in honor of her father as well as such important historic figures as Medgar Evers, Malcolm X, Harold Washington, Langston Hughes, and even Robert Frost. She also commented on events in Africa itself, such as the murder of Stephen Biko in "Music for Martyrs."

In 1968 Brooks became poet laureate of Illinois, succeeding Carl Sandburg. In 1976 she became the first black woman to be elected to the National Institute of Arts and Letters. In 1985 she was appointed Poet Laureate Consultant in Poetry to the Library of Congress. Four years later she received a lifetime achievement award from the National Endowment for the Arts. In 1994 she received an award from the National Book Foundation and was selected by the National Endowment for the Humanities as its Jefferson Lecturer. In 1995 she received the National Medal of Arts award.

In 1990 the Gwendolyn Brooks Chair in Black Literature and Creative Writing was established at Chicago State University. In addition, there is a Gwendolyn Brooks Center for African American Literature at Western Illinois University.

Her other works include *We Real Cool* (1966) and *Blacks* (1987). In addition to her many volumes of poetry and nonfiction titles, she also wrote two autobiographical works, *Report from Part One* in 1972 and *Report from Part Two* in 1995. In addition, Brooks reviewed books for various publications, including the *Chicago Sun-Times.* She taught poetry, fiction, and writing at various colleges and universities, including Columbia College Chicago, Northeastern Illinois University, Elmhurst College, Columbia University, and the University of Wisconsin–Madison. She was a frequent guest lecturer and writer in residence. She read at the Carter White House and at Harold Washington's first and second inaugurations, and later published three Chicago-themed poems in *Mayor Harold Washington* and *Chicago: The I Will City.* In 1980 she became determined to publish her own work, including *Primer for Blacks, Young*

Poet's Primer, and *Riot.* The latter is a three-part poem about the riots that took place in Chicago after Martin Luther King Jr. was assassinated in 1968.

Over the years Brooks lived at many locations on the South Side, including 4332 South Champlain; the Tyson Apartments on 43rd and South Park; 6424 South Champlain; 623 East 63rd Street; the 6800 block of South Evans; and 32 West 70th Street. But she lived at 7428 South Evans Avenue for more than four decades. In February 2010 the Gwendolyn Brooks House at that location was granted landmark status.

Brooks died from cancer on December 3, 2000, at her South Side home at the age of eighty-three. She is buried at Lincoln Cemetery in Blue Island, Illinois.

Further reading: Elizabeth Alexander, ed., *The Essential Gwendolyn Brooks* (American Poets Project, 2005); Gwendolyn Brooks, *Selected Poems* (1963); George E. Kent, *A Life of Gwendolyn Brooks* (1990); D. H. Melhem, *Gwendolyn Brooks: Poetry and the Heroic Voice* (1988); Steven C. Tracy, ed., *Writers of the Black Chicago Renaissance* (2011).

Big Bill Broonzy
Musician

BORN: June 26, 1893
Scott, Mississippi

DIED: August 15, 1958
Chicago, Illinois

One of the greatest musicians in the history of the blues, William Lee Conley Broonzy incorporated African American spirituals and folk songs with country and urban blues to create a style that was solely his—he was among the most versatile musicians in American popular music at the time. As the most popular African American blues singer of his day, Broonzy dominated Chicago blues during the 1930s. Indeed, he came to epitomize the sound of big-city blues: a guitar-driven, extremely rhythmic music with its roots in the Deep South. He was a mentor to fellow bluesmen, including Muddy Waters, but also to numerous rock musicians, such as Eric Clapton, Pete Townshend, and Ray Davies. His biographer, Bob Riesman, goes so far as to call him "the first ambassador of the blues."

One of seventeen children, the Mississippi-born, Arkansas-raised Broonzy developed an interest in music at an early age. He learned to play the fiddle from relatives and a traveling blues singer named C. C. Rider. An uncle taught him such blues and folk standards as "John Henry," "Midnight Special," and "Oh, Susanna." While still in his teens Broonzy began performing at local picnics and barbeques. From 1912 to 1917 he worked as an itinerant preacher in Arkansas. He served one year in the army and after his discharge settled in Chicago.

Broonzy arrived in Chicago in 1920 at the age of twenty-seven. He learned to play the guitar from "Papa" Charlie Jackson, performing nightly at house parties while working for the Pullman Company as a porter during the day. House parties were an African American tradition that was especially popular during the Prohibition era. Tenants in private residences would charge guests a small admission

(plus the cost of the food and illegal liquor) and collect enough money to pay the musicians as well as their rent.

Within a few years Broonzy had made several recordings, including "Big Bill Blues" and "House Rent Stomp," and played frequently in South Side clubs. Like most traditional musicians, however, Broonzy held many day jobs over the years—molder, cook, porter, and even janitor at Hull House. During the 1930s, Broonzy toured with country blues singer Memphis Minnie. A prolific composer, he reportedly wrote as many as 350 songs during his lifetime, including the blues standard "Key to the Highway."

During the folk revival of the 1950s, when traditional musicians were "discovered" by a young, generally college-educated, white audience, Broonzy performed frequently at folk festivals across the country. He also appeared and recorded with such national folk and blues figures as Pete Seeger, Sonny Terry, Brownie McGhee, and Leadbelly. Broonzy recorded extensively after World War II—from 1925 to 1952 he made some 260 blues recordings on Mercury, Chess, Folkways, and other labels.

Broonzy made his first trip to Europe in 1951 and visited the continent regularly thereafter. He was also a frequent guest at the People's Song concerts—a Midwestern branch of the New York-based organization had been established in 1946——and later at the "I Come for to Sing" folk revues, hosted by Studs Terkel, which established a residency at the Blue Note, a famous jazz and blues club of the 1940s and 1950s. Through his friendship with Terkel and Win Stracke, a singer and eventual cofounder of the Old Town School of Folk Music, Broonzy was also an influential figure in the development of the school. In fact, when the school opened on December 1, 1957, at its original location

50

at 333 West North Avenue in the Immigrant State Bank Building, Broonzy was there. Unfortunately, he had undergone surgery the previous year for lung cancer and, unable to sing, he played a blues piece instead.

Broonzy's presence in Chicago went well beyond performing. For a time in the 1950s, he also ran a tavern with his business partner, Josephine Moore. Called Big Bill and Moore's Lounge and located at 3634 South Cottage Grove Avenue, it quickly gained a reputation for its Sunday jam sessions. Another southern bluesman, Muddy Waters, was known to stop by.

Broonzy died in August 1958 from lung cancer at age sixty-five. He was buried in Lincoln Cemetery in Blue Island, Illinois. "Nobody gave us lessons," he wrote in his autobiography, *Big Bill Blues* (1955). "It was just born in us to sing and play the blues."

In recent years, several of Broonzy's original recordings have been remastered and/or released as box sets, including *Trouble in Mind* (2000), *All the Classic Sides 1928–1937* (2003), *Big Bill Broonzy Part 2: 1937–1940* (2005), *An Introduction to Big Bill Broonzy* (2007), and *Big Bill Broonzy War & Postwar Years 3: 1940–1951* (2007)

See also: Leonard Chess, Howlin' Wolf, Studs Terkel, Muddy Waters, Sonny Boy Williamson I

Further reading: William Broonzy and Yannick Bruynoghe, *Big Bill Blues: William Broonzy's Story* (1955); Donald Clarke, *The Penguin Encyclopedia of Popular Music* (1989); Peter Guralnick, *The Listener's Guide to the Blues* (1982); Sheldon Harris, *Blues Who's Who: A Biographical Dictionary of Blues Singers* (1979); Bob Riesman, *I Feel So Good: The Life and Times of Big Bill Broonzy* (2011); Mike Rowe, *Chicago Breakdown* (1975).

William Bross

Editor and Politician

BORN: November 4, 1813
Sussex County, New Jersey

DIED: January 27, 1890
Chicago, Illinois

Often called the original Chicago booster, William Bross personified the spirit of the Midwestern frontier—that of a brassy, brazen, and confident citizen fueled by an indomitable optimism and an unswerving faith in the future of his adopted city.

Born in a log cabin in New Jersey, Bross moved with his family to Milford, Pennsylvania, when he was nine. In 1832 he entered Milford Academy. Two years later, he enrolled at Williams College in Williamstown, Massachusetts, where he graduated with honors in 1838. He taught for several years before becoming principal of Ridgebury Academy, near his birthplace.

In October 1846, he embarked on a tour of western towns, including St. Louis and Chicago. Impressed with the settlement by the lake, he decided to stay and opened a bookselling company, Griggs, Bross and Company. In 1849 he founded the *Prairie Herald* newspaper. Two years later he and John L. Scripps established the *Democratic Press*. Then, he began publishing a series of pamphlets that boasted the advantages of the city to potential settlers. "Go to Chicago now!" he exclaimed. "You will never again have such a chance to make money!" In 1854 Bross published *The Railroads, History, and Commerce of Chicago,* a pamphlet that contained extensive facts and figures detailing the rapid growth of the city from its pioneer days as a small settlement on the prairie to its incorporation as a city in 1833 and to what he considered its excellent prospect for further expansion.

As a prominent newspaper editor, Bross played an important role in Civil War history in Illinois. In 1858 the *Democratic Press* and the *Chicago Tribune* merged and the name changed to the *Press and Tribune* and, two years later, to the *Chicago Daily Tribune*. The *Tribune* was an early advocate of President Abraham Lincoln and, with the outbreak of war in 1861, Bross and his paper fiercely supported the Union cause. Subsequently, Bross raised the Twenty-Ninth United States Regiment of Colored Volunteers, under the command of his brother, Colonel John Bross, by providing for virtually all of the expense. Bross is credited with exposing a Confederate plot to free prisoners at Camp Douglas on the South Side in November 1864.

In 1864 Bross was elected lieutenant governor of Illinois. The following year he toured California and, in 1867, he spent six months in Europe visiting Ireland, Britain, France, Belgium, Germany, Austria, and Italy. Sketches from his European trip appeared in the *Tribune* and were widely read.

Even the devastating effects of the Chicago Fire of 1871 could not dampen Bross's enthusiasm for the city. "I tell you," he predicted, "within five years Chicago's business houses will be rebuilt, and by the year 1900 the new Chicago will boast a population of a million souls." The city did not disappoint him.

In 1876 Bross wrote *History of Chicago,* considered the most comprehensive history of the city at that time. He contributed generously to various cultural organizations, including the Chicago Library Association and the Chicago Academy of Science.

Bross died in Chicago in January 1890 due to complications from diabetes. He was seventy-six. Bross Avenue is named in his honor.

See also: Henry Demarest Lloyd, Joseph Medill, Wilbur F. Storey, John S. Wright

Further reading: A. T. Andreas, *History of Chicago from the Earliest Period to the Present Time,* 3 vols. (1884–1886); Bessie Louise Pierce, *A History of Chicago,* 3 vols. (1937–1957); David Ward Wood, *Chicago and Its Distinguished Citizens, or The Progress of Forty Years* (1881).

Roger Brown

Artist

BORN: December 10, 1941
Hamilton, Alabama

DIED: November 22, 1997
Beulah, Alabama

Roger Brown was one of the Chicago Imagists, a loosely connected group of artists whose work was known for its surrealism and grotesque imagery.

James Roger Brown was born and raised in Alabama. He felt close to his grandparents and great-grandparents and, consequently, had an intense interest in family history and genealogy—he claimed ancestral connections to both Elvis Presley and Tallulah Bankhead—as well as the indigenous folk culture of the American South. His religious upbringing in the fundamentalist Church of Christ had a profound impact on him. He even considered becoming a preacher but in 1961 decided instead to attend art school. By the next year he had moved to Chicago to attend the American Academy of Art and then the Art Institute of Chicago where he was a full-time student from 1965 to 1968 and again from 1969 to 1970. In 1968 he received his BFA and in 1970 his MFA from the school. In 1970 Phyllis Kind in Chicago became the first gallery to exhibit his work. The gallery continued to support him throughout his career.

In the meantime, Chicago curator Don Baum organized a series of exhibitions in 1966, 1967, and 1968 at the Hyde Park Art Center under the name of the Hairy Who? (the moniker was intended as a pun on the name of WFMT art critic Harry Bouras, whom many of the artists considered pompous) and also at the Museum of Contemporary Art. The Chicago Imagists were an informal group of artists that, in addition to Brown, included Ed Paschke, Christina Ramberg, and Barbara Rossi.

Ray Yoshida, a professor of painting at the School of the Art Institute, and the artist and art historian Whitney Halstead encouraged Brown to find and collect objects, especially objects that had nothing to do with Western art. Halstead also brought to Brown's attention the work of such self-taught artists as Joseph Yoakum. Yoshida took Brown and other artists on hunting expeditions to Maxwell Street market as well as to secondhand shops and neighborhood flea markets. Yoshida, who died on January 10, 2009, and taught at the Art Institute from 1959 to 2005, was an important mentor not only to Brown but to other members of the Chicago Imagists group. Yoshida's own work was greatly influenced by comic book art.

Through his connections with Yoshida and Halstead, Brown began a lifelong interest in collecting art and found objects which functioned as source materials for his own work. In 1974 he purchased a storefront at 1926 North Halsted Street, which became his first home and studio. Three years later he constructed a second home and studio in New Buffalo, Michigan.

Brown's reputation continued to grow throughout the 1970s and 1980s. His work was shown in numerous solo and group exhibitions not only in Chicago but also in New York and elsewhere. In 1987 a major retrospective was held at the Hirshhorn Museum and Sculpture Garden of the Smithsonian Institution in Washington, D.C.

Brown was interested in many themes and topics, including natural and urban landscapes, architecture, popular culture, and mortality. Among his major works in Chicago are several murals, including *City of the Big Shoulders* in the NBC Tower, and *Arts and Sciences of the Ancient World: The Flight of Daedalus and Icarus* and *Arts and Sciences of the Modern World: LaSalle Corridor with Holding Pattern* (an Italian glass mosaic), both at the Ahmanson Commercial Development Company at 120 North LaSalle Street. In 1994 his glass mosaic mural *20th Century Plague: The Victims of AIDS* was installed at the Foley Square Federal Building in Manhattan. In 1997 his glass mosaic mural *Hull House, Cook County, Howard Brown: A Tradition of Helping* was installed at the Howard Brown Health Center in Chicago.

In 1991 Brown and other artists, dealers, and collectors with an interest in self-taught artists founded Intuit: The Center for Intuitive and Outsider Art. He leased the organization to his Halsted Street building in 1995. In October 2004 the Chicago Commission on Human Relations' Advisory Council on Lesbian, Gay, Bisexual, and Transgender Issues inducted Brown into its Gay and Lesbian Hall of Fame.

In 1996 Brown donated his 1926 North Halsted Street house to the School of the Art Institute. The Roger Brown Study Collection (RBSC), housed in an 1889 two-story brick building, contains his art collection, his original furniture and sketchbooks, his slides and photographs, and his personal and professional correspondence, writings, and architectural drawings. It also contains artworks from other Chicago Imagists as well as works by Henry Darger, Joseph Yoakum, Bill Traylor, Lee Godie, William Dawson, Mose Tolliver, and Edgar Tolson, in addition to naive and primitive art, outsider art, and found objects.

See also: Gertrude Abercrombie, Henry Darger, Ed Paschke
Other resources: Roger Brown Study Collection, www.saic.edu /art_design/special_collections/rogerbrown/index.html.

"Slim" Brundage

*House Painter
and Bohemian*

BORN: November 29, 1903
Blackfoot, Idaho

DIED: October 18, 1990
El Centro, California

I've always been allergic to formal instruction. If you want to find something out, the easiest way is to ask someone who knows. The second easiest way is to look it up in the Newberry Library.

—"Slim" Brundage

Myron Reed "Slim" Brundage was a major figure in Chicago's outsider heritage. A dyed-in-the-wool Marxist and working-class intellectual, he opened his free-speech oasis called the College of Complexes, a no-holds-barred tavern that was the precursor to the early days of the Second City, so-called guerrilla theater, and performance art. The house rules at the college were simple: heckling was encouraged but guests could speak only one at a time. In this way, Brundage maintained his version of orderly mayhem.

A house painter by trade, Brundage literally was born in an insane asylum—his mother worked there—in Blackfoot, Idaho. His socialist journalist father placed him in an orphanage after his mother died. He dropped out of grade school and ran away from home, taking to the open road at all of fourteen to become a hobo. He exchanged his given name, Myron, for what he thought was a more appropriate moniker, "Slim," given the life he was determined to lead. He received his education in the flophouses and boxcars of the country. At sixteen he became a member and then organizer of the Industrial Workers of the World (IWW), the industrial union, in Aberdeen, Washington. The world, he thought, would be a better place without bosses or, for that matter, politicians. Incarcerated for his labor activities, he served on a chain gang.

He settled in Chicago in 1922, where he became a frequent visitor to the city's numerous bohemian haunts and open forums of free speech. At the time there were about twenty to thirty of them, including the Bug Club on the South Side, Bughouse Square on the North Side, and the nearby (and most famous) Dil Pickle Club across from Washington Square Park, where he also worked as a janitor. These venues helped him to sharpen his mind and made him good at thinking on his feet, a skill that would come in handy.

In 1933 Brundage opened a short-lived version of the College of Complexes at 1317 North Clark Street, but it only lasted three months. Three years later, he became the director of the Hobo College that had opened at 1118 West Madison Street, which Brundage called the Knowledge Box. Decorated with murals of Karl Marx, Mark Twain, and Charles Darwin, it held seminars, clinics, and forums every night. At one point, members of the Hobo College even debated the University of Chicago.

In 1951 Brundage tried again, opening the College of Complexes at 1651 North Wells Street in Old Town, using a $6,000 workman's compensation settlement he received. The tavern operated, he insisted, in the tradition of "the soapbox, the cracker barrel, the corner saloon, the opium den," and its aim was to inform and educate, provoke and inspire. It featured female speakers, unusual for the day. It was interracial and multicultural and boasted an egalitarian atmosphere. It was the center of Chicago beat culture and one of the few places in the city comparable to New York's Greenwich Village or San Francisco's North Beach.

The college consisted of two rooms with black walls. Customers were encouraged to vent and to write their thoughts with white chalk on the wall. It offered a mixture of art, poetry, music, debate, art exhibits, plays, lectures, skits, and poetry readings, always laced with ample doses of wicked humor. Brundage played the genial, if unconventional, host. With his booming voice, he had a presence. Typically he would offer a question and then open the floor up to debate. Speakers had one hour to talk followed by a half hour of questions from the audience.

Billed as the Playground for People Who Think, the college was the place for poetry readings in Chicago during the late 1950s. No subject was off limits, no theme taboo. Anything and everything could and often did happen. Speakers at the college included aldermen, judges, preachers, professors, lawyers, authors, Wobblies, Democrats, Republicans, socialists, anarchists, and pacifists. During the beat era, it hosted beatnik poetry nights and beat plays. In addition to lectures and discussions, the college also had its own College Players, which staged plays by Shakespeare, Chekhov, Ibsen, and Tennessee Williams. Ken Nordine presented several of his "word jazz" sessions. Painters, photographers, and sculptors exhibited their work. There was music from folk and jazz to blues and classical as well as dance programs, from African and Latin American to modern and square. Big Bill Broonzy frequently played at the Wednesday folk nights. College film nights featured the classic cinema of Chaplin and Fields and Laurel and Hardy. Studs Terkel and Bob Gibson stopped by. Other well-known visitors included Nelson Algren, Willard Motley, Elmer Gertz, Leon Despres, Jack Conroy, and labor activist Burr McCloskey, as well as less-celebrated judges, professors, lawyers, poets, and Communists. The college also hosted strippers, nudists, and female wrestlers, as well as one of the most colorful characters, the dean of the confidence men, Joseph "Yellow Kid" Weil. Folk singer Ella Jenkins, a regular, launched her career here at the Wednesday night folk music sessions. Carl Sandburg and Gwendolyn Brooks stopped by and even, when they were in town, Duke Ellington and Tony Bennett. Topics ranged from "Does Beatnikism Have a Philosophy?" to "The Chicago Police Department and Its Terrible Record of Civil Liberty Violations." Speakers included everyone from the ACLU to Jesse Owens, the Olympic track star.

In the late nineteenth century and into the early decades of the twentieth century, Chicago was considered the hobo capital of the United States. In addition to the college and various free speech forums, it was home to the Free Society Group (one of the largest anarchist groups in the country from the 1920s through the 1950s), numerous radical newspapers and little magazines, and several hobohemian bookstores—most famously the Radical Bookshop on North Clark Street in the 1910s and 1920s.

The College of Complexes was a community of scholars that was, according to the late Franklin Rosemont, based on "cooperation, mutual aid, humor, and the pleasure principle." There was something going on seven nights a week. A direct heir of the earlier Dil Pickle, it welcomed nonconformists, eccentrics, and oddballs of all stripes and provided a link between hobo culture and the Wobblies and the beats and the counterculture. The heart of the college's program was devoted to group discussions of current events. But it also sponsored courses on history and poetry plus round robins and debates on the offbeat and the unorthodox—the more radical the better.

In June 1957 Brundage opened a branch of the College of Complexes in Greenwich Village at 139 West 10th Street. James T. Farrell, who had moved to New York by then, was one of the speakers. Brundage was also the person behind the idea of the Beatnik Party during the 1960 presidential election. The party nominating convention was held in July 1960 at the college's New York campus at 139 West 10th Street. Bill Smith was nominated as the candidate for anti-president, Joffre Stewart as the candidate for anti-vice president. Smith was among the most frequent speakers at the college and, for a time, was manager of Maury's Beatnik Bookstore on North State Street in the 1950s. The party slogan, "Don't Get Out the Vote!" reflected the anarchist tendencies of Brundage while the party platform called for the immediate abolition of government, money, and work.

In 1955 the college moved to 862 North State Street, and then in January 1960 to 515 North Clark Street. But all was not well. The Chicago Police Department's so-called Red Squad made frequent visits to the college, apparently unhappy with the college's stance to end the Cold War. Finally, during the spring of 1961 the IRS notified Brundage that he owed $100,000 in back taxes and demanded immediate payment.

Brundage shut the college down in May 1961. Since its demise, the college has been resurrected numerous times over the years and at various locations, including the 800 block of North State Street, at 105 West Grand Avenue, on North Wells Street, at Hogen's at 4560 N. Lincoln Avenue, and, most recently, at the Lincoln Restaurant near the corner of Lincoln Avenue and Irving Park Road.

In 1975 Brundage retired to Guadalajara, Mexico, and then, in the late 1980s, to Southern California. He died of a brain hemorrhage while attending a senior citizens' bingo party in El Centro, California, in 1990. He was eighty-six. His ashes are interred near the Haymarket Martyrs' Monument at Forest Home Cemetery in Forest Park.

See also: Ben Hecht

Further reading: Ron Grossman, "Matters of Opinion: Friends to Toast the Late Slim Brundage, Whose College of Complexes Gave Chicago's Thinkers a Forum," *Chicago Tribune*, September 19,

1997; Cara Jepsen, "Champion of the Gabfest: Remembering Slim Brundage and the College of Complexes," *Chicago Reader,* September 19, 1997; William Leonard, "The College of Cut-Ups," *Chicago Tribune Magazine,* May 13, 1956, and "Chicago's New 'Left Bank,'" *Chicago Tribune Magazine,* November 23, 1958; Franklin Rosemont, ed., *From Bughouse Square to the Beat Generation: Selected Ravings of*

Slim Brundage (1997); Alson J. Smith, *Chicago's Left Bank* (1953); Lee Sustar, "When Speech Was Free (And Usually Worth It). Con Men and Communists, Lowlife and Literati, Blowhards and Bohemians: Reminiscences of Chicago's Soapbox Society," *Chicago Reader,* October 21, 1983.

Leo Burnett

Advertising Executive

BORN: October 21, 1891
St. Johns, Michigan

DIED: June 7, 1971
Lake Zurich, Illinois

Ad man Leo Noble Burnett founded the Chicago advertising agency that bears his name in 1935. Today the agency is part of the French group Publicis with ninety-seven offices in eighty-four countries.

Burnett attended the University of Michigan, where he was an editor of the student newspaper. He began his professional career as a police reporter for the *Peoria Journal* but soon left journalism to pursue the more lucrative field of advertising. In 1916 he became advertising manager at Cadillac Motor Company. After a stint in the navy, he joined the Lafayette Motors Company as executive advertising manager, later accepting the position of vice president at the Homer McKee agency in Indianapolis. In 1931 Burnett moved to Chicago to hold a similar title at the advertising firm of Erwin, Wasey and Company.

With eight associates, the young ad man founded the Leo Burnett Company four years later and proved that great advertising campaigns did not have to originate in New York. His so-called Chicago school of advertising took the subtle approach, stressing the positive aspects of a product and allowing the "drama" to flow naturally. In essence, he wanted the product to sell itself.

During Burnett's long career, his agency created some of the best-known characters in advertising for some of the industry's biggest clients: Charlie the Tuna, the Pillsbury Doughboy, the Jolly Green Giant, the Harris Lion, the Marlboro Man, Tony the Tiger, the lonely Maytag repairman, Morris the Cat, the Man from Glad, and the Keebler Elves.

Burnett strived to create an honest look, even going so far as to use Burnett employees rather than models in some of his ads. He abhorred phoniness in all its forms and encouraged employees to be themselves. "Any company . . . is too big when its ranks are riddled with cynicism," he said several months before his death. "When its heart pumps ink instead of blood and its arteries harden into bureaucracy. When it takes advantage of its bigness to become an economic bully. Especially, when its people feel that they shed their identity as individuals each working day from 9:00 A.M. to 5:00 P.M."

Burnett was a director of the Better Business Bureau of metropolitan Chicago and a trustee of the American Heritage Foundation. In 1963 he received the Distinguished Service Award in Journalism from the University of Missouri and that same year was given the Business Statesmanship Award of the Harvard Business School Association of Chicago. Burnett was also a director and former chairman of the national Advertising Council.

In 1967, at age seventy-six, Burnett stepped down from active management to take up the newly established post of founder/chairman. But he made it clear to his staff that he still intended to maintain a full schedule. "I expect to shave regularly and to remain fully active within the outer limits of my new status until senility clearly makes me either an old nuisance or a bench warmer," he said. He died four years later in June 1971 of a heart attack at his Lake Zurich country estate.

Burnett was listed as one of *Time* magazine's 100 most influential people of the twentieth century.

In May 1989, the Leo Burnett Company moved into its new international headquarters—designed by architect Kevin Roche—at 35 West Wacker Drive in Chicago's Loop. In 2010, Leo Burnett Worldwide, as it is now known, celebrated its seventy-fifth anniversary.

See also: Fairfax M. Cone
Further reading: Kenan Heise and Michael Edgerton, *Chicago: Center for Enterprise,* 2 vols. (1982).

Daniel H. Burnham

Architect and City Planner

BORN: September 4, 1846
Henderson, New York

DIED: June 1, 1912
Heidelberg, Germany

Although he was more administrator than architect, Daniel Hudson Burnham was also a bold visionary who dared to dream big. "Make no little plans; they have no magic to stir men's blood," he once said. Burnham saw the city and region as a single, organic framework and the entire lakefront as public space: it should, he believed, belong to everyone. It was a radical idea and vastly ahead of its time.

Of Yankee stock, Burnham moved to Chicago with his family in 1855 at the age of nine. During the Civil War he enlisted in the Nineteenth Illinois Regiment of the Union army, but his father protested that he was too young and prevented him from serving. An excellent athlete and artist, Burnham, however, was no scholar—he failed the entrance examinations to both Harvard and Yale.

In 1867 Burnham became a salesman at a mercantile house in Chicago, a position he detested. Changing directions, he accepted a job in the architectural office of Loring and Jenney as a draftsman apprentice. Still uncertain, he took up a friend's suggestion to head west to Nevada, where at age twenty-two he ran unsuccessfully for state senator on the Democratic ticket. Disheartened by this latest failure, Burnham returned to Chicago to resume his architectural career, determined more than ever to become a great architect.

He found a mentor in Peter Wright, an innovative and successful architect who helped young Burnham develop his drawing skills and bolstered his fragile ego. In 1873 a rejuvenated Burnham formed a partnership with John Wellborn Root, a brilliant young architect originally from a prominent family in Georgia. It was a marvelous pairing of personalities—Burnham's outgoing nature complemented Root's serene intensity. For the most part, Burnham found the clients and Root designed the buildings.

Burnham and Root soon became one of the most famous architectural firms in the nation. During their eighteen-year partnership, they built residences, office buildings, railroad stations, hotels, churches, stores, hospitals, and some of the finest structures to be erected in the city of Chicago, including the Montauk Building (1882); the Rookery (1886); the original Art Institute (1887); the Monadnock Building (1891), their most durable masterpiece and the tallest structure in Chicago made without steel reinforcement; and the Women's Christian Temperance Union (1892). He also worked with Charles Atwood to create the Reliance Building at State and Randolph (it has been converted into a boutique hotel and is now called Hotel Burnham with the upscale Café Atwood located at

street level). His other buildings include the Railway Exchange on South Michigan Avenue, Union Station, and the Peoples Gas Building, also on South Michigan Avenue.

Burnham's greatest fame was as director of works for the World's Columbian Exposition of 1893, that mammoth celebration that commemorated the 400th anniversary of Columbus's discovery of America. Given complete artistic and creative control of the grounds and buildings, Burnham hired some of the finest names working at the time, including architects Dankmar Adler, Louis Sullivan, and Henry Ives Cobb; landscaper Frederick Law Olmsted; and sculptors Augustus St. Gaudens, Daniel Chester French, and Frederick MacMonnies.

But Root died suddenly in 1891 before the designs for the exposition were finalized. Burnham was devastated by his friend and colleague's untimely death. He was despondent. To Burnham, Root was irreplaceable. "We had the perfect partnership," he said.

But the work had to go on. Burnham chose as Root's replacement Charles B. Atwood, a draftsman in the New York architectural firm of Herter Brothers. Burnham's concept of a dream-like city painted uniformly white and designed in a mostly classical, or Beaux Arts, style supplanted Root's modern vision. Through rainstorms, blizzards, and strikes, Burnham and his crew of 7,000 created a magnificent vision on a site that only two and a half years earlier had been a marshy bog. As the director of works, he lived mostly at the fairgrounds for the two years it took to build it. Nearly 20,000 men worked for Burnham. "It will be built," he told his doubters, and it was. But this achievement came at a high price. During the course of the construction, more than 700 accidents occurred, and close to twenty men died during the first year from malaria, typhoid, and pneumonia. Finally, though, opening day arrived: May 1, 1893. At first few came because of the dire economy, but eventually the fair witnessed some 600,000 visitors on a single day at its peak. In total, twenty-seven million visitors came, making it the largest tourist attraction in U.S. history.

The White City was universally admired for the timeless beauty and grandeur of its buildings. A great popular success, it attracted millions of customers and inspired countless speeches and essays, several full-length histories, and a spate of novels, including Henry Blake Fuller's *With the Procession* and Robert Herrick's *Memoirs of an American Citizen.* Years later, in 2003, Erik Larson would set his historical novel, *The Devil in the White City,* at the fair and choose as his two protagonists Burnham and H. H. Holmes, a serial killer who pretended to be a doctor.

Despite the economic depression that gripped the city at the time, thousands of Chicagoans and visitors from around the country flocked to the grounds when the fair opened on May 1, 1893. Once inside, they simply couldn't believe their eyes. With its brilliant white color and neoclassical design, the exhibition earned the sobriquet of "White City." The White City was nothing less than an urban Eden, a real-life utopia with no litter and no crime. But visitors who expected to see the achievements of contemporary Chicago architecture on display were bound to be disappointed, for the neoclassical structures faithfully imitated European models. Although certain people—ranging from Louis Sullivan to Harriet Monroe, Root's sister-in-law—criticized Burnham for the fair's slavish imitation of classical ideals (in contrast to Root's vision of a bold, democratic style of architecture that would serve as a break with the past), the public was clearly impressed. Over twenty-one million people attended, according to Burnham's biographer, Thomas S. Hines, ringing up total gate receipts of $10,336,065.

The popularity of the White City also influenced the City Beautiful Movement of the late nineteenth century, which was modeled after the French Beaux Arts. The movement, architectural critics insisted, was the expression of a newly confident country, a nation on the brink of greatness. The homogeneity of the architecture and its partiality toward classical facades reflected the desire to create a symbolic language of national unity in post–Civil War America. Its legacy lives on and can be seen even today in such contemporary examples as Lincoln Center in New York, the Kennedy Center in Washington, D.C., the Music Center in Los Angeles, and Millennium Park in Chicago. The significance of the fair was clear: cities could be orderly and beautiful. Classical architecture and natural landscape could exist side by side.

Some time after the success of the Columbian Exposition, Burnham developed and co-wrote, with Edward Bennett, the monumental *Plan of Chicago,* published in 1909, an ambitious attempt to chart the city's future. Among other things, Burnham proposed the straightening of the Chicago River, the erection of a bridge across the river on Michigan Avenue, the widening and extension of Michigan Avenue, the construction of a double-decked drive that would skirt the congested downtown, the development of additional parks, the promise to protect the natural beauty of the city's lakefront, the creation of a civic center at the intersection of Halsted and Congress Streets, and, curiously, given the city's later reputation, the halting of new skyscraper construction—twenty stories was the suggested maximum height.

The plan caused a sensation. Widely praised and accepted, it was officially adopted by Mayor Fred Busse in 1910. Charles H. Wacker, a wealthy brewer, was appointed chairman of the Chicago Plan Commission. Not all of Burnham's plans were realized—the civic center was never built and, of course, the Chicago skyline has continued to sprout skyscraper after skyscraper. But Burnham's vision was city planning at its best, an agile balance between the desire for growth and the need for continuity. He went on to create master plans for other cities too: Washington, D.C., Cleveland, San Francisco, and Manila. The Burnham Plan, however, was his greatest achievement.

Burnham was not a great architect in the way that, say, Wright or Sullivan were great architects, but he did have a special talent for bringing people together and for forging his complex ideas into reality. He was the ultimate pragmatist. Lynn Becker, in the *Chicago Reader,* has called him an "intellectual magpie" for the way he turned to various sources, picking and choosing the best elements, and bringing together the city's business elite as well as the top national architects to create a visionary whole.

In the spring of 1912, he and his wife, Margaret, sailed for Europe. It was his last trip abroad. He died in Heidelberg, Germany, from complications from colitis, food poisoning, and diabetes.

In 2009 the city celebrated the one-hundredth anniversary of the Burnham Plan in ways both big and small. The Burnham Pavilions, two designs commissioned by the city and on display from June to October in Millennium Park, consisted of designs by architects Ben van Berkel and Zaha Hadid. The Amsterdam-based van Berkel's design, partly inspired by Frank Lloyd Wright's cantilevered buildings, complimented the city's skyline. On the other hand, the Iraqi-born and London-based Hadid based her ultra-modern aluminum design on the city's diagonal streets, which contrast sharply with its otherwise regimented street grid.

In February 2009 the Chicago chapter of the American Institute of Architects announced a competition for the design of a public memorial to Burnham to be erected by the Field Museum. The winning entry was by the Chicago-based David Woodhouse Architects. The key features of the memorial are two twelve-foot-high granite walls that are set at right angles. A statue of Burnham will stand by the walls.

Other events during the centennial celebration year included the centennial edition of Burnham's *Plan of Chicago,* a joint collaboration between the Great Books Foundation and the Chicago History Museum; and the world premiere of composer Michael Torke's *Plans* for soprano solo, tenor solo, chorus, and orchestra, commissioned by the Grant Park Music Festival. Each of the five movements of the latter, a forty-minute choral work, was based on a sentence from Burnham's famous speech that begins, "Make no little plans; they have no magic to stir men's blood."

In October 2010, the Chicago Metropolitan Agency for Planning released its "Go to 2040" plan, which, inspired by as well as echoing Burnham and Bennett's 1909 *Plan of Chicago*, recommended the renovation of existing roads rather than the construction of new roadways, and raising the state gas tax to fund road maintenance and public transport, among other suggestions.

Burnham Avenue is named in his honor.

See also: Bruce Graham, John Wellborn Root, Louis Sullivan, Charles H. Wacker, Harry Weese

Further reading: Lynn Becker, "An Odd Way to Honor Burnham," *Chicago Reader*, July 16, 2009; Daniel Burnham and Edward Bennett, *Plan of Chicago: Centennial Edition* (2009); Carl Condit, *The Chicago School of Architecture: A History of Commercial and Public Buildings in the Chicago Area, 1875–1925* (1964); Thomas Hines, *Burnham of Chicago: Architect and Planner* (1974); Erik Larson, *The Devil in the White City: Murder, Magic, and Madness at the Fair That Changed America* (2003); *The Plan of Chicago @ 100: 15 Views of Burnham's Legacy for a New Century* (2009); R. Samuel Roche and Aric Lasher, *Plans of Chicago* (2010).; Carl Smith, *The Plan of Chicago: Daniel Burnham and the Remaking of the American City* (2006).

Other resources: *Make No Little Plans* (2009), an hour-long documentary by writer, producer, and director Judith Paine McBrien (see also www.danielburnhamfilm.com).

Edgar Rice Burroughs

Author

BORN: September 1, 1875
Chicago, Illinois

DIED: March 19, 1950
Encino, California

Master storyteller Edgar Rice Burroughs didn't start writing until he was thirty-five years old, yet there was no denying his magical touch. Book after book, with one adventure story after another, he transported his readers from familiar surroundings to the exotic worlds of the African jungle, the landscape of Mars, and the center of the Earth. A prolific writer, Burroughs completed seventy-one books in his lifetime that were eventually translated into thirty-six languages and sold more than one hundred million copies. The popularity of "sword and sorcery" literature in recent years has led to a revival of interest in, and to a reevaluation of, his work. Burroughs influenced many writers of this genre, from Robert E. Howard (creator of Conan) to Michael Moorcock (creator of Elric). One could even trace Burroughs's spirit down to the present day in the persona of the dashing, globe-trotting archaeologist Indiana Jones and his numerous successors.

Although not usually regarded as a Chicago writer, Burroughs was a native Chicagoan, born on West Washington Street, and he spent his boyhood years on the West Side. Occasionally he used the city as a setting. His best-known Chicago novel, *The Mucker* (1912), describes the adventures of a wayward West Side street urchin named Billy Byrne. According to some accounts, Byrne, not Tarzan, was Burroughs's favorite fictional character.

After graduating from a Michigan military academy, Burroughs wandered about the West, searching for gold and laboring at various occupations: cow puncher, policeman, salesman, railroad guard. Upon returning to Chicago, he ended up in a series of dead-end jobs. To relieve the boredom of his work, he would write wild adventure yarns. In 1912 he sold his first story, "Under the Moons of Mars," for $400 to *All-Story* magazine. Still secretive and apprehensive about his writing, he used the byline Normal Bean, which some conscientious copy editor changed to Norman Bean.

In December 1911, confined to his tiny North Side apartment, Burroughs began writing the story that would earn him literary immortality. It was set in Africa and told the fantastic tale of an infant, John Clayton, raised by a family of apes. "Tarzan of the Apes" was published in the October 1912 issue of *All-Story* magazine. The phenomenal success of Tarzan spawned sequels, movie and television interpretations, games, candy bars, and even an X-rated cartoon. The first Tarzan movie, *Tarzan of the Apes*, released in 1918, starred Elmo Lincoln as Tarzan and Enid Markey as Jane. Other screen Tarzans included Buster Crabbe, Johnny Weissmuller, and, on the small screen, Ron Ely. Although the character of Tarzan was reportedly influenced in part by Rudyard Kipling's *Jungle Books*, Burroughs always had an interest in mythology, and he admitted that the ancient story of Romulus and Remus, the founders of Rome, was the more likely inspiration.

Burroughs received much criticism for his casual approach to writing. He usually spent from one to three months writing a book. On the other hand, *The Chessmen of Mars* took twenty-one months to complete. In the early days, Burroughs wrote his stories out in longhand, did little outlining or advance planning, and rarely did any rewriting or polishing. With a wife and family to support, he was more concerned with paying the bills than courting critical acclaim. "I loathed poverty," he said later. "There is nothing honorable or fine about it."

In 1919 Burroughs moved to California and developed real estate in the San Fernando Valley. The community grew and eventually the residents had to choose a name. They voted to call it Tarzana in honor of the town's leading citizen.

Burroughs created thoroughly realized worlds and characters, such as John Carter, the Confederate officer who died on Earth only to be reborn on Mars, and David Innes, the young man from Connecticut who traveled to an underground continent 500 miles beneath the earth's surface. He encouraged his readers to become involved. In *The Chessmen of Mars*, he included a step-by-step description of how to play Jetan, or Martian chess ("The game is played with twenty black pieces by one player and twenty orange pieces by his opponent, and is presumed to have originally represented a battle between the Black race of the South and the Yellow race of the North."). In later years his attempts at serious fiction failed miserably. "I've often considered writing deeper stuff," he once said, "but why should I?" During World War II, at age seventy, Burroughs covered the war

in the Pacific from the Marshall Islands for the *Los Angeles Times*. He returned to California after the war ended.

On March 19, 1950, Burroughs died at his home in Encino, California, while reading the Sunday comics.

Other books in the Tarzan series include *The Return of Tarzan* (1914); *Tarzan and the Jewels of Opar* (1918); *Tarzan, Lord of the Jungle* (1928); and *Tarzan at the Earth's Core* (1930). The Pellucidar series includes *At the Earth's Core* (1922), *Pellucidar* (1923), and *Return to Pellucidar* (1941). The Martian series includes *A Princess of Mars* (1917), *The Gods of Mars* (1918), *The Warlord of Mars* (1919), and *John Carter of Mars* (1964), while the Venus series consists of *Carson of Venus* (1939) and *Escape on Venus* (1946). A feature-length motion-picture adaptation of *John Carter of Mars*, directed by Andrew Stanton and starring Taylor Kitsch in the title role, is scheduled for release in 2012 by Pixar/Walt Disney Studios.

See also: Johnny Weissmuller

Further reading: L. Sprague de Camp, *Literary Swordsmen and Sorcerers: The Makers of Heroic Fantasy* (1976); Geoffrey Johnson, "Edgar, the Ape-Man," *Chicago*, December 1989; Richard A. Lupoff, *Edgar Rice Burroughs: Master of Adventure* (1965); Alberto Manguel and Gianni Guadalupi, *The Dictionary of Imaginary Places* (1987).

Fanny Butcher

Literary Critic

BORN: September 13, 1888
Fredonia, Kansas

DIED: May 14, 1987
Chicago, Illinois

Fanny Butcher was considered the dean of Chicago literary critics. Historian Adele Hast has gone so far as to call Butcher the Oprah Winfrey of her day.

Born Frances Amanda Butcher in Fredonia, Kansas, she was the daughter of Oliver Butcher, a commercial artist, and Hattie Butcher. When Frances was a child, the family moved to Chicago, where her father attended classes at the Art Institute. After he fell ill, the family lived in poverty. Before she turned six, she had received a copy of *Black Beauty*, which led to her lifelong love affair with literature.

Butcher attended college at the Lewis Institute from 1906 to 1908, and graduated from the University of Chicago in 1910. For five months she served as a high school principal in Rolling Prairie, Indiana, but returned to Chicago and did publicity and secretarial work for the Little Theatre. She also wrote feature articles for *Morrison's Weekly* and other publications. Before long her book reviews were appearing in the *Chicago Evening Post*'s literary supplement

edited by Floyd Dell, a major coup since Dell and his section were considered among the best in the Midwest.

Butcher made all the right literary connections. She became a member of the Illinois Woman's Press Association and made sure her name was known around town. In 1913 she met Mary Eleanor O'Donnell, the women's editor of the *Chicago Tribune*. O'Donnell offered Butcher a job writing a column, "How to Earn Money at Home." Butcher jumped at the chance, and thus began a fifty-year career at the paper. During her tenure there, she wrote on music, fashion, theater, and society, but also did some crime reporting and even covered several murder trials.

In 1922 Butcher became literary editor, a position that she had long coveted. She wrote influential book reviews and wrote a weekly column called "The Literary Spotlight." For fifteen years she also wrote the society column, using the pseudonym "Thalia," the Greek muse of comedy. Her reviews were well written and insightful but, most importantly, they were noticed. People read her column and they listened to her. She made it her business to know people in the industry. Over the years she maintained friendships or acquaintances with many important literary figures, including Willa Cather, Bennett Cerf, Edna Ferber, Ernest Hemingway, Sinclair Lewis, H. L. Mencken, Gertrude Stein, George Bernard Shaw, T. S. Eliot, William Faulkner, Somerset Maugham, and Thornton Wilder. Many visited her at her unpretentious house on Ellis Avenue and 29th Street. Butcher was even mentioned in a cartoon by Helen E. Hokinson that ran in an issue of the *New Yorker* in 1940: the cartoon depicts a bookstore clerk showing a book to an elderly society woman with the caption, "Hugh Walpole liked it, Fanny Butcher liked it, Wm. Rose Benét liked it, and Mrs. Roosevelt liked it, but it *isn't* very good."

From 1919 to 1927 Butcher ran a bookshop, Fanny Butcher Book Store, in the Loop at the corner of Michigan Avenue and Adams Street, directly across the street from the Art Institute. It was a popular meeting place. "People met their friends there, left messages, sat (or mostly stood), and talked," she writes in her autobiography. Butcher tried to spend as many afternoons at the shop as she could. She went to her office at the *Tribune* as early as possible, worked "at top speed on my copy," and then read the books at night that she was going to write about in her column.

She loved being a bookseller, although she did more than simply sell books. She was a philosopher, friend, doctor, lawyer, and "purveyor of advice to the lovelorn," she recalled in her autobiography. She often did the shopping for "helpless male customers" who provided her with their entire Christmas gift lists. To her, books "were as important to mental health as food or vitamins were to the body, and should," she felt, "be prescribed with care." Some passersby, though, were apparently confused by her sign. Every week at least one person would ask, "Is this a butcher shop?" But when her connections to the *Tribune* became problematical she sold the shop to Doubleday in New York.

Butcher remained at the *Tribune* until her retirement in 1963. In 1972 she published her autobiography, *Many Lives, One Love*. In 1953 she became the first woman to be honored by the Friends of the Chicago Public Library; she served as its president for a decade. In 1981 she was inducted into the Chicago Press Club's Hall of Fame.

She died in 1987 at the age of ninety-nine.

The Fanny Butcher Papers are housed at the Newberry Library in Chicago.

See also: Margery Barker, Stuart Brent, Frances Hamill
Further reading: Fanny Butcher, *Many Lives, One Love* (1972).

Paul Butterfield

Musician

BORN: December 17, 1942
Chicago, Illinois

DIED: May 4, 1987
North Hollywood, California

Paul Butterfield, a white Chicago musician, played an amplified, rock-based version of the blues that influenced countless local bands and inspired rabid support on college campuses. Butterfield combined the virtuosity of jazz with the power of rock and the sensuality of the blues.

Butterfield grew up on the South Side, studied classical flute, and sang in the church choir. He taught himself how to play the harmonica and began gigging with such venerable Chicago bluesmen as Howlin' Wolf, Otis Rush, Magic Sam, Buddy Guy, Junior Wells, and Little Walter at various South Side clubs when he was still underage.

Butterfield attended the University of Chicago, where he met another musician, Elvin Bishop, and formed his own band. In 1964 he put together the Paul Butterfield Blues Band, which fused blues with folk, rock, and jazz and included Butterfield on harmonica, Bishop on guitar, and Mike Bloomfield on guitar. Butterfield became a

well-respected figure on the local club circuit, attracting a loyal following. Indeed, Butterfield and his band were the American equivalent of John Mayall's Bluesbreakers, that seminal English blues group of the sixties.

Their first album, *The Paul Butterfield Blues Band* (1965), elicited largely favorable reviews. In 1965 the group appeared at the Newport Folk Festival in Newport, Rhode Island. The first electric band to play the festival, they also were the band who backed Bob Dylan's controversial foray into electric folk. In 1967 Butterfield added a brass section. Band members fluctuated considerably during the late sixties. In 1969 the Paul Butterfield Blues Band played to thousands of fans at the famed Woodstock music festival in New York. Three years later Butterfield assembled yet another group, Better Days. In 1973 he recorded the soundtrack for the motion picture *Steelyard Blues*, starring Jane Fonda and Donald Sutherland.

During the early 1980s, Butterfield experienced some serious health problems that were aggravated by his transient lifestyle and extensive drug use. In 1986 Amherst Records released *The Legendary Paul Butterfield Rides Again.*

Other Butterfield albums include *The Resurrection of Pigboy Crabshaw* (1968), *In My Own Dream* (1968), *Keep On Moving* (1969), *Butterfield Live* (1970), *East-West* (1971), *Golden Butter/The Best of the Paul Butterfield Blues Band* (1972), *It All Comes Back* (1973), *Paul Butterfield/Better Days* (1973), *Put It In Your Ear* (1976), and *North/South* (1981).

Butterfield, the white man who popularized the blues for a rock audience, died in his North Hollywood apartment in May 1987 of an accidental drug overdose.

"Butterfield was certainly one of the pivotal figures in raising the consciousness of blues in what was a white-dominated '60s rock world," wrote *Los Angeles Times* pop music critic Robert Hilburn, "and also helped make the idea of a white musician playing the blues credible."

See also: Howlin' Wolf, Muddy Waters

Further reading: Sheldon Harris, *Blues Who's Who: A Biographical Dictionary of Blues Singers* (1979); Irwin Stambler, *The Encyclopedia of Pop, Rock and Soul* (1989).

John Callaway

Broadcast Journalist

BORN: 1936
New Martinsville, West Virginia

DIED: June 23, 2009
Racine, Wisconsin

John Callaway liked to tell the story that he arrived in Chicago with only seventy-one cents in his pocket and from that humble beginning fashioned a near-legendary broadcasting career. Considered by his peers to be the best interviewer on television, he was insatiably curious about people and life in general. That curiosity formed the foundation of his remarkable career.

John Callaway was the son of a newsman. His father was the editor of the local newspaper in his hometown of New Martinsville, West Virginia. He grew up in a house filled with music—he loved the songs of Gershwin and Porter—and surrounded by books. Despite the trappings of middle-class respectability, however, all was not well. In 2001 he staged a one-man show that recalled his often-difficult upbringing—his father drank too much and money was oftentimes scarce. When his father became seriously ill, the money troubles worsened. Because he couldn't afford it, he dropped out of Ohio Wesleyan University after only one and a half years—he didn't earn enough at his job as a dishwasher to pay his bills. In fact, he was some $800 in debt, a princely sum at the time. "I told the dean I was going to Chicago to work in the steel mills," he told Charles Leroux of the *Chicago Tribune*. "I don't know where that came from. Maybe it was from reading [Carl] Sandburg, or from having read the *Studs Lonigan* trilogy as a kid," he said, referring to James T. Farrell's classic work of working-class Irish American life in Chicago. "I knew no one in Chicago—not a soul. The dean came up with $50 from the Bertha Enright fund for students who neither smoke nor drank, and that was my stake."

He hitchhiked across Ohio and most of Indiana before, through good fortune, a minister that he met along the way handed him a train ticket to Chicago on the South Shore Line. He had in his possession only a handful of items—some clothes, the New Testament, and a copy of David Riesman's *Individualism Reconsidered*. He arrived at Randolph Street station on February 6, 1956. "When I stepped out of the station, I suddenly sensed that this was my city, that I was in the right place at the right time."

He worked at odd jobs, took acting and playwriting classes—apparently he was not a very good actor—and even considered taking a job in the nearby steel mills. Before long he found work as a clerk at R. Cooper Jr., a General Electric distributor. He got his first job in journalism at the City News Bureau, the famous and now-defunct wire service that trained generations of Chicago journalists, where he worked as a police reporter.

In 1957 he joined CBS as a reporter and documentary producer for WBBM radio and television. He rose quickly through the ranks and learned the tricks of the trade that would serve him so well in the years to come. At CBS he won seven national awards for his thirteen-part documentary series on the civil rights movement, *The House Divided.* As news director at WBBM, he helped develop that station's all-news format and in 1968 was appointed vice president of CBS radio in New York. In 1973 he returned to Chicago to serve as the lead reporter for the new WBBM-TV newsroom. In the late 1970s he was the host of the nationally syndicated radio series *Conversations from Wingspread,* in which he discussed public policy issues.

Callaway then moved over to Chicago's public television affiliate, WTTW. He spent thirty-five years at Channel 11.

He created the *Public Newscenter,* the forerunner of *Chicago Tonight.* For fifteen years he was host of *Chicago Tonight,* a live newsmagazine show, which made its debut in 1984. His first guest was Mayor Harold Washington. A master interviewer, Callaway was famous for preparing exhaustively for his interviews, which meant reading entire books rather than just portions of them. A gentle but persistently dogged interviewer, he was an expert in posing follow-up questions. Callaway could interview anyone and often did. Guests included Norman Mailer, Henry Kissinger, Jonas Salk, Mike Ditka, John Updike, Oprah Winfrey, and Richard M. Daley.

Callaway left *Chicago Tonight* in 1999. His last *Chicago Tonight* broadcast was aired live from the Harold Washington Library on June 23, 1999. For a short time he offered commentary when Carol Marin was the anchor of the WBBM-TV newscast. Beginning in 2006, he hosted *Friday Night,* a half-hour one-on-one interview program on Channel 11. He also served as host and senior editor of his Emmy-winning "Chicago Stories" segment of *Chicago Tonight.* In addition, he hosted the monthly public affairs series *Front and Center with John Callaway* at the Pritzker Military Library in downtown Chicago.

Other Callaway series that appeared on PBS nationally were *Campaigning on Cue, Inside Television, Dilemmas of Disarmament,* and *The Paper Chase Addendum Interviews.* He was also the coproducer and host/reporter of the nationally broadcast documentary about America's voting habits, *None of the Above.*

Whether in front of the camera or on stage, Callaway was a natural showman. He created and performed in two autobiographical one-man shows, *Life Is . . . Maintenance* and *John Callaway Tonight.* Both productions were given their world premieres at the Pegasus Players Theatre in Chicago's Uptown neighborhood. In addition, he sang at benefits for the Chicago Symphony Orchestra and the Lyric Opera of Chicago.

Callaway won numerous awards, including a Peabody Award, sixteen Emmys, and ten honorary doctorate degrees, including degrees from Northwestern University, Loyola University, and the John Marshall College of Law. He was also the recipient of the Benton Medal from the University of Chicago and the National Academy of Television Arts and Sciences Chicago Silver Circle award, a member of the Chicago Journalism Hall of Fame, and the author of the best-selling *The Thing of It Is,* a collection of essays. Although a college dropout, he was the founding director of the William Benton Fellowships in Broadcast Journalism at the University of Chicago, a program for mid-career radio and television broadcasters.

Callaway died suddenly of a heart attack at the age of seventy-two after becoming dizzy at a Racine, Wisconsin, store.

Al Capone

Gangster

BORN: January 17, 1899
Brooklyn, New York

DIED: January 25, 1947
Palm Island, Florida

Few other names are as closely associated with Chicago as Al Capone. Even decades after his death, his exploits remain an endless source of fascination for millions of people worldwide.

Capone's father, Gabriel, had emigrated from the slums of Naples in 1893 to settle in a rough, working-class neighborhood of Brooklyn. Alphonse grew up on these mean streets, a big kid, cocky and hot-tempered. He quit school at fourteen, picking up odd jobs—a clerk in a candy store, a pin setter in a bowling alley—before joining a street gang, the Five Pointers, on Manhattan's Lower East Side. He then got a job as a bouncer and bartender before joining Johnny Torrio's powerful gang. In 1918 he married Mae Coughlin, a salesgirl in a department store. The following year their first and only child, Albert Francis, was born, with Torrio acting as the infant's godfather. Within a short time, Capone had earned a reputation as an impulsive and fearless punk who used whatever means necessary to get a job done. In 1919 Torrio, who had moved to Chicago in 1909, sent for Capone to act as bodyguard, chauffeur, and bartender at the Four Deuces at 2222 South Wabash Avenue. When mob boss "Big" Jim Colosimo was murdered in his own café on May 11, 1920, Torrio took over the underworld.

The election of reform candidate William E. Dever as mayor of Chicago in 1923 forced Capone and his cohorts to lie low for a while. At Torrio's behest, Capone set up shop in west suburban Cicero, where he ruled with an iron fist, eventually controlling the communities of Burnham, Chicago Heights, Melrose Park, Stickney, Berwyn, Posen, Blue Island, and Forest View.

In 1925 Capone inherited the gangland throne from his mentor, Johnny Torrio, when Torrio, after surviving

a near-fatal assassination attempt, retired from the "business." Torrio transferred everything to Capone: brothels, breweries, speakeasies, and gambling houses. By that time Torrio had built quite an empire, reaping an annual income in the millions of dollars from bootlegging and prostitution and from the manufacture, distribution, and sale of liquor and beer. Capone then established headquarters in the Metropolitan Hotel at 2300 South Michigan Avenue. It was convenient to both city hall and the central police department. He marshaled his forces and began to methodically eliminate his enemies—a long list that included Dion O'Banion, Hymie Weiss, and the O'Donnell brothers.

In 1928 Capone moved across the street to the imposing Lexington Hotel and occupied the entire fourth and most of the third floor. By this time the reelection of Mayor William Hale Thompson reasserted Chicago's status as a "wide-open" town. Capone took full advantage of the situation. Indeed, Capone enjoyed a rather cozy relationship with both the mayor and the men in blue. Daniel Serritella served as the gangster's "representative" in the city council, while his henchmen were furnished with officially stamped cards that read: "To the Police Department—You will extend the courtesies of the department to the bearer."

Meanwhile, gang killings continued unabated on the street. It took the deaths of several high-profile figures—the shooting of assistant state's attorney William H. McSwiggin in 1926, the killing of *Chicago Tribune* reporter Jake Lingle in 1930, and the ferocity of the St. Valentine's Day massacre in 1929—for the citizens of Chicago to demand that something be done. For many years the public had simply looked the other way, refusing to acknowledge the daily horror that was taking place on the city streets. In fact, many people saw Capone as a folk hero, an underdog harassed by law enforcement officers. Almost despite themselves, ordinary citizens rather admired Capone's chutzpah, envied his wealth, and coveted his apparently glamorous lifestyle. Indeed, millions of Americans actually sympathized with him. He reportedly received letters from all over the world. But to a large number of Italian Americans, Capone's exploits were a constant embarrassment and a reminder of how far removed they were from the mainstream of American society. Even to this day, Italian Americans often cringe at the very sound of his name.

By 1930, at the age of thirty-one, Capone had reached the pinnacle of his blood-stained career. His personal income was conservatively estimated at $50 million a year—by his accounts. He owned an extravagant home in Florida, and he was king of an immense criminal empire. Ironically, bad bookkeeping, not murder, led to Capone's fall.

Capone was able to elude the law for so long because he never filed a tax return, nor did he keep paper records. Eventually, though, the paperwork—or rather, the lack of it—caught up with him. When George Johnson of the Bureau of Internal Revenue, along with the able-bodied assistance and persistence of Eliot Ness, assembled enough information, which included interview transcripts, letters, Western Union money orders, and telephone bills, they were able to put a strong enough case together to send him to prison.

In 1931, due to the perseverance of Ness and his fabled "Untouchables" team of popular legend, the government was able to gather enough evidence to indict Capone for conspiracy to violate the Volstead Act, which prohibited the manufacture, sale, or transportation of liquor within the United States. More damaging were the charges of income tax evasion leveled against the gangster. Ultimately, Capone was fined $50,000 and sentenced to eleven years, first in a prison in Atlanta and finally in the federal penitentiary on Alcatraz Island in San Francisco Bay. During his jail term, the syphilis he had contracted as a young man worsened, and due to poor health, he was released from prison after serving only eight years.

On January 10, 1947, Capone collapsed from a brain hemorrhage. Less than a week later, he developed bronchial pneumonia and died in the presence of his family at his Florida estate at the age of forty-eight. He was originally buried in Mount Olivet Cemetery at 2755 West 111th Street, but because of uproar from the community, his remains were later moved to Mount Carmel Cemetery in Hillside, Illinois.

In 2009 Capone's Park Manor two-flat at 7244 South Prairie Avenue was put on sale at an asking price of $450,000.

Much to the chagrin of the Chicago tourism office, Capone's legacy—and popularity—still endures, even though Mayor Richard J. Daley, the father of Richard M. Daley, sought to raze most of the buildings that had any connection to Capone. Still, the gangster-themed Untouchables Tour, which tour owner Craig Alton founded in 1989, attracts a local, national, and increasingly international clientele.

See also: William E. Dever, William Hale Thompson

Further reading: Herbert Asbury, *Gem of the Prairie: An Informal History of the Chicago Underworld* (1942); Jonathan Eig, *Get Capone: The Secret Plot That Captured America's Most Wanted Gangster* (2010); John Kobler, *Capone: The Life and World of Al Capone* (1971); Humbert S. Nelli, *Italians in Chicago 1880–1930: A Study in Ethnic Mobility* (1970); Eliot Ness with Oscar Fraley, *The Untouchables* (1969); Fred D. Pasly, *Al Capone: The Biography of a Self-Made Man* (1930); Virgil W. Peterson, *Barbarians in Our Midst: A History of Chicago Crime and Politics* (1952); Jessica Reaves, "Capone's Legacy Endures, to Chicago's Dismay." *New York Times*, April 23, 2010; Robert J. Schoenberg, *Mr. Capone* (1992).

Harry Caray

Broadcaster

BORN: March 1, 1914
St. Louis, Missouri

DIED: February 18, 1998
Rancho Mirage, California

Born Harry Christopher Carabina, Harry Caray was a radio and television sports broadcaster but also a master entertainer. He covered four major league baseball teams during his career: the St. Louis Cardinals, the Oakland Athletics, the Chicago White Sox, and the Chicago Cubs. A fan's broadcaster, he was known for his larger-than-life persona, his wide-rimmed glasses, and his trademark use of the phrase "Holy Cow!"

Caray began his broadcasting career with the St. Louis Cardinals in 1945, where he stayed for twenty-five years until he was fired in 1969. He then spent one year broadcasting for the Oakland Athletics before accepting a broadcasting position with the Chicago White Sox. With the White Sox, he was popular as much for his on-camera enthusiasm as for his off-camera hijinks. On the other hand, unlike his colleague, friend, and fellow broadcaster Jack Brickhouse, Caray could be critical of the performances of the home team—some thought excessively so. During his tenure he partnered with various color analysts, including Bob Waller, Bill Mercer, and J. C. Martin, but the chemistry didn't always work. It wasn't until he had former outfielder Jimmy Piersall in the booth with him that sparks flew. Management couldn't help but notice and, consequently, Piersall was hired, in 1977, as Caray's partner on both radio and television.

During his years covering the White Sox, Caray contributed many dramatic performances. But no night was quite as memorable as what happened on July 12, 1979: Disco Demolition Night. At a time when disco was at the peak of its popularity, Disco Demolition Night, the brainchild of Chicago radio personality Steve Dahl, prompted die-hard rock fans to condemn the disco craze. Between the games of a doubleheader between the White Sox and Detroit Tigers, Dahl blew up a crate of disco records that fans had been encouraged to bring. In the aftermath of this stunt, thousands of irate fans stormed the Comiskey Park outfield. Startled by the response, Caray tried to calm the crowd by encouraging them to sing "Take Me Out to the Ball Game"—but to no avail. The result was that the White Sox forfeited the second game of the double header.

In 1981 Caray switched to covering the Cubs on WGN-TV. His broadcasting partners with the Cubs included Milo Hamilton, with whom he had a strained relationship, and Steve Stone, whom he partnered with successfully for fourteen years. Because WGN had outlets throughout the United States, Caray became known nationwide. During Caray's tenure in the booth, the Cubs, in 1984, won the National League East division title. While with the Cubs,

he continued the practice that began when he was with the White Sox of singing "Take Me Out to the Ball Game" during the seventh-inning stretch. Using a hand-held microphone, he held it outside the booth's window so the crowd could hear his idiosyncratic rendition of the song. After his death, the Cubs continued the tradition and even invited celebrity guests to join in.

During his long career, Caray also broadcast University of Missouri football, Boston Celtics and St. Louis Hawks basketball, and Cotton Bowl games on national radio.

In 1987 Caray suffered a stroke. Although he made a remarkable recovery, age and carousing—he was known as "The Mayor of Rush Street" in some quarters—had clearly taken their toll on his health. On February 14, 1998, Caray was celebrating St. Valentine's Day with his wife Dutchie at a restaurant in Rancho Mirage, his winter home in California, when he collapsed and hit his head on the side of a table. He never regained consciousness. He died of cardiac arrest on February 18 at the age of eighty-three. His funeral at Holy Name Cathedral on February 27, 1998, was attended by sports royalty, including Sammy Sosa and Mike Ditka. He was buried in All Saints Cemetery in Des Plaines, Illinois.

On October 23, 1987, Harry Caray's Italian Steakhouse opened in Chicago. Today the franchise consists of six restaurants, including locations in Lombard and Rosemont. Harry Caray's Tavern in Lakeview is a casual alternative.

In 1989 the Baseball Hall of Fame awarded Caray for his "major contributions to baseball."

See also: Jack Brickhouse
Further reading: Harry Caray with Bob Verdi, *"Holy Cow!"* (1989); Steve Stone and Barry Rozner, *Where's Harry?* (1999).

Anton J. Cermak

Politician

BORN: May 9, 1873
Kladno, Bohemia (now Kladno, Czechoslovakia)

DIED: March 6, 1933
Miami, Florida

As Chicago's first and only foreign-born mayor, Anton Joseph Cermak took advantage of the city's changing demographics to organize various groups into a cohesive political organization that led straight to city hall. It was a lesson that others—from Richard J. Daley to Harold Washington and beyond—did well to remember.

Cermak's family first settled at 15th and Canal Streets in Chicago, but they later moved to the small mining town of Braidwood, Illinois, some sixty-five miles south of the city, where Cermak attended elementary school. After a short period of working in the coal mines in Will and Grundy counties, Cermak hopped a boxcar to Chicago. He found a job tending horses for the railway in the old Bohemian neighborhood of Pilsen. Soon he was able to buy a horse and wagon and began selling kindling wood. He moved to Lawndale on the West Side and dabbled in other occupations—trucking, banking, and real estate mostly.

Like other politicians before him, Cermak started his political career as a precinct captain. In 1902 he was elected to the Illinois state legislature. He then became secretary of the United Societies for Local Self-Government. A firm believer in personal liberties, Cermak was known around town as a staunch advocate in the fight against Sunday closing laws and state prohibition—the *Chicago Tribune* once referred to him as "the wettest man in Chicago."

In 1909 Cermak won the aldermanic seat for the Twelfth Ward (which later became the Twenty-Second). Three years later he was elected to the office of municipal court bailiff. In 1918, however, he was defeated in his bid for election as sheriff of Cook County. A bit shaken, Cermak returned to the city council in 1919. In 1922 he was elected president of the Cook County Board. During his tenure—he was reelected in 1926 and 1930—a new Criminal Courts Building and county jail were erected in his ward, new highways were constructed, and additional forest preserves were acquired.

In 1928 Cermak suffered two devastating blows. He was defeated in his bid for a seat in the Illinois Senate and his beloved wife, Mary, died. Then, in a miraculous political recovery, Cermak clinched the leadership role of the Democratic Party following the death of his friend and mentor, George Brennan. In 1931 he became Chicago's thirty-sixth mayor, sweeping past his Republican rival, "Big Bill" Thompson.

Cermak ran an efficient, cost-conscious, and well-oiled machine. He promised good government to all Chicagoans, and good government was what he delivered. Cermak was essentially a shrewd businessman and, like any good businessman, he learned the ways of acquiring power and played the role of the great compromiser very well. By pleasing his constituency and appeasing his enemies, he broadened his political base until anyone foolish enough to challenge his authority met with certain political death.

On the evening of February 15, 1933, Cermak was fatally wounded while appearing with President-elect Franklin D. Roosevelt in Miami, Florida. A disgruntled Italian immigrant, Giuseppe Zangara, had fired shots at Roosevelt, his intended victim, but struck Cermak instead. As he was being taken to the hospital, Cermak reportedly uttered the famous line to Roosevelt, "I am glad it was me instead of you."

The city of Chicago and the nation stood vigil and waited as the mayor struggled valiantly for life. He lost the battle in the early morning of March 6. However, according to his biographer, Alex Gottfried, the direct cause of death was not the gunshot wound but ulcerative colitis.

Zangara, the self-proclaimed enemy of kings and presidents, was executed by the state of Florida in speedy fashion—just two weeks after Cermak died. "Lousy capitalists," he reportedly uttered, as the switch was pulled.

See also: Richard J. Daley

Further reading: Alex Gottfried, *Boss Cermak of Chicago: A Study of Political Leadership* (1962); Paul M. Green, "Anton J. Cermak, The Man and His Machine," in *The Mayors: The Chicago Political Tradition* (1987), Paul M. Green and Melvin G. Holli, eds.; Frederick F. Rex, *The Mayors of the City of Chicago* (1934).

Leonard Chess

Record Producer

BORN: March 12, 1917
Motele, Poland

DIED: October 16, 1969
Chicago, Illinois

Leonard and his brother Phil Chess, Polish Jews who immigrated to the United States with their family, formed a record label that signed some of the greatest names in the history of blues and rock and roll. Chess Records was a hands-on operation in which the brothers worked closely with the artists. Indeed, on at least one occasion, Phil reportedly played drums during a recording session. The label's roster of talent included Muddy Waters, Howlin' Wolf, Robert Nighthawk, Jimmy Rogers, Little Walter, Sonny Boy Williamson II, Johnny Shines, J. B. Lenoir, and Willie Dixon. In 1964, Chess even welcomed the bad boys of rock—the Rolling Stones—into its South Michigan Avenue studios. To Rich Cohen, Leonard Chess had assembled "the greatest catalog in the history of the Blues," and had "reinvented popular music twice, first by ushering in the electric Blues, then by ushering in Rock and Roll."

In Poland, the Chess, or Czyz family, to use its original spelling, had been merchants, rag pickers, and junk collectors. In 1928 the family immigrated to the United States. The father, Yasef Czyz, Americanized the name to Joseph Chess while his Polish-born sons, Leizor and Fiszel, became Leonard and Phil, respectively. The family lived at 1425 South Karlov in the Lawndale neighborhood on the South Side. Leonard attended Crane Technical High School; Phil went to Marshall High School, then known as "the Jewish school." Leonard developed an early taste for black music since he was a young boy walking along South Cottage Grove, hearing, on the one hand, music wafting from the church choirs and, on the other, blues riffs radiating from the neighborhood dives. Leonard combined both worlds. Or as Rich Cohen notes, "When Leonard learned English, he learned syntax and grammar in school, but he learned the rhythm of the Negro streets near his apartment. The result was a once-in-a-history hybrid, a Polish Jew with the voice of the cotton fields."

After graduation, Leonard labored as a shoe salesman before working with his father at the family-owned business, the Wabash Junk Shop, at 2971 South State Street. But Leonard, ambitious and on the lookout for other opportunities, was not happy being a junk dealer. He wanted more out of life. He ran a liquor store at 5060 South State Street in the heart of the black community and then later moved to 47th and South Parkway (now Martin Luther King Jr. Drive), in the heart of the so-called black downtown. Meanwhile, Phil was attending college at Bowling Green State University on a football scholarship. He dropped out of school after three years to join the family business before being drafted, in 1943, into the army. He served the last few months of World War II in the Aleutian Islands.

Leonard, in the meantime, had branched out again. Borrowing money from his father, he purchased the Congress Street Buffet at 47th Street and South Karlov and converted it into a nightclub. He tore out the tables, added velvet booths, and installed a horseshoe-shaped bar, a barbecue pit, and a stage for performers. He changed its name, too, to the Macomba Lounge. By the time Phil was discharged from the military, Leonard had moved the Macomba to 3905 South Cottage Grove, "a small neighborhood bar with a big local reputation," as Nadine Cohodas describes it.

The nightclub scene had exposed the brothers to the raw sound of the Delta blues. When major record companies stopped releasing so-called race records, Chess filled the void, attracting a strong local market but also an international audience. Such Chess recording artists as Muddy Waters and Howlin' Wolf helped to influence the burgeoning rock and roll scene. Musicians who were part of the British invasion, from Eric Clapton to the Rolling Stones, later recalled growing up on their music.

The Chess brothers frequented the city's taverns and juke joints in search of new talent. "We heard some of the music and we started recording it," recalls Phil. The label began as a strictly two-man operation. "I didn't know what I was doing," Leonard admitted in a newspaper interview in 1969, "but I was doing it all myself, working days at the record company, nights at the club. Pretty soon I had to get out of the club, and I turned it over to Phil."

In 1950 Leonard and Phil became the owners of the Aristocrat record label. Aristocrat had been founded three years earlier by the husband-and-wife team of Charles and Evelyn Aron. Early releases on the Aristocrat label included polka music in addition to its stable of blues and jazz releases. The first record on Aristocrat was "Union Man Blues" by Andrew Tibbs. The brothers had invested both money and time in the company until buying the Arons out. They changed the label's name from Aristocrat to Chess. The first release on the Chess label was Gene Ammons's "My Foolish Heart"; the second, Muddy Waters's "Walkin' Blues/Rollin' Stone" was a considerable hit. Indeed, Waters put Chess on the musical map. Waters's "Hoochie Coochie Man" was a hit, and others followed. The brothers, to show their approval for his hard work, gave Waters a spanking new red and white Oldsmobile '98. "Giving a musician a car was not an uncommon form of payment at the time," notes Cohodas, "particularly if the tender was a Cadillac. Taking care of musicians' other needs—clothing, rent, medical and legal bills—was all part of the mix."

When it came to signing artists, the brothers relied on their broad instincts. Phil stayed at the office while Leonard went on the road, promoting and looking for new talent and making contacts with influential people. In 1950 he linked up with Sam Phillips, the legendary record producer in Memphis, Tennessee. Chess had the opportunity to sign a young, unknown singer from Tupelo, Mississippi, named Elvis Presley, but they weren't too impressed and turned him down flat.

Even after attaining nationwide commercial success, Chess remained a family business at heart. In the early years the label operated from a series of small storefronts at various locations on the South Side. The original location of Chess was at 5249 South Cottage Grove Avenue. But as the label grew, the brothers decided they needed bigger quarters. In 1951 the headquarters moved to the corner of 49th Street and Cottage Grove Avenue and then to an even bigger space, in 1954, at 4750 South Cottage Grove. In late 1956 Chess purchased a two-story building at 2120 South Michigan Avenue, the label's most famous address, and converted it into offices with their own shipping facilities and a second-floor recording studio (previously they used the recording facilities at Universal Studio).

Erected in 1911, Chess's new headquarters had previously housed a furniture slipcover manufacturer and a tire company. Chuck Berry recorded four of his seven Top Ten hits there, including "Johnny B. Goode" and "Rock and Roll Music," according to a Commission on Chicago Landmarks staff report. Chuck Berry's "Maybellene," which originally had been called "Ida Red," was also recorded there: it took thirty-seven takes before Leonard was satisfied with the sound. And still another early rock and roller, Bo Diddley, also recorded at the studio.

Other artists on the Chess roster included Elmore James, Sonny Boy Williamson II, Clarence Gatemouth Brown, Otis Rush, John Lee Hooker, Robert Nighthawk, Ahmad Jamal, Rufus Thomas, Bobby Bland, Memphis Slim, Big Bill Broonzy, and Washboard Sam. Chess even recorded sermons by C. L. Franklin (father of Aretha Franklin) of the New Bethel Baptist Church in Detroit.

The first sessions at the Michigan Avenue address, though, were with Muddy Waters, Little Walter, Howlin' Wolf, and Chuck Berry. Years later, in 1964, the Rolling Stones cut several records there, including the instrumental "2120 South Michigan Avenue," a variation of a Little Walter riff. The Chess label had its own unique sound. By rigging a loudspeaker and a microphone at both ends of a sewer pipe, the now familiar echo effect was created. In addition, the brothers hired a self-taught twenty-two-year-old

engineering wunderkind named Jack Wiener. Wiener covered the original wood floor with two inches of cork and then laid concrete over it. The walls were designed, according to Cohodas, to "float on resilient springs for complete isolation from the adjoining rooms" in order to maximize the soundproofing. Wiener also built two echo chambers for special effects.

Chess also had two subsidiaries: Checker for pop, rock, and blues; and Argo for jazz and comedy. Indeed, the label maintained a roster of jazz performers that included Ramsey Lewis, Ahmad Jamal, and Sonny Stitt in addition to its selections of Delta blues, country blues, doo-wop, gospel, and early rock and roll releases. Blues artist Willie Dixon also developed talent and acted as an arranger during the recording sessions. But with the growing popularity of rock and the widespread practice of white musicians covering the blues, Chess and other small independent labels went into decline. In an effort to appeal to a wider audience, the firm experimented with avant-garde and progressive rock in the late 1960s on the Cadet Concept label. One of the label's biggest successes was the Rotary Connection, a racially mixed group of four men and two women that featured the expressive vocals of the late Minnie Riperton—she died in 1979 at the age of thirty-one. Riperton turned solo and had a hit single in 1973 with "Loving You."

In addition to the record company, the brothers formed a partnership, L. and P. Broadcasting Company, that owned radio stations WVON-AM and WSDM-FM in Chicago and WNOV-AM in Milwaukee. Leonard ran WVON, whose call initials meant "Voice of the Negro." The station went on the air in 1963.

In 1966 Chess moved into larger headquarters at 320 East 21st Street, which housed a business office, art department, recording studio, and pressing plant. But business was not what it used to be. Three years later Leonard sold Chess to General Recorded Tape, a California firm that had pioneered the cassette and eight-track tape technology, important innovations in the music industry at the time. By 1970 the executive offices relocated to New York, although the 21st Street studio remained in operation. In 1975 Chess was sold once again, this time to All Platinum, which became Sugar Hill. Finally, MCA Records, which had been distributing All Platinum, acquired the Chess catalog in 1985. MCA has reissued most of the Chess recordings, making the music available for future generations.

Leonard had his first heart attack in 1956 when he was only forty. He suffered a fatal heart attack in October 1969, two blocks away from the 21st Street building. He was fifty-two. Phil Chess is now retired and lives in Arizona.

After Leonard's death, Phil sold WVON to Globetrotter Communications.

In 1987 Leonard Chess was inducted posthumously as a "pioneer" into the Rock and Roll Hall of Fame, and in 1995 both brothers were inducted into the Blues Hall of Fame as nonperformers.

On June 7, 1990, the former Chess headquarters at 2120 South Michigan Avenue was dedicated as an official Chicago landmark. In 1993 Marie Dixon, Willie Dixon's widow, bought the South Michigan Avenue building to house the Blues Heaven Foundation; Dixon had created the foundation a few years earlier. In October 1999, the Clinton administration, as part of its "Save America's Treasures" program, granted special landmark status to the most famous home of Chess Records.

"Blues," said Phil Chess, "is nothing but the truth."

In 2008 the feature-length motion picture *Cadillac Records,* costarring Adrien Brody as Phil Chess, Beyoncé Knowles as Etta James, and Jeffrey Wright as Muddy Waters, explored the roots of the label. Another movie, the independent *Who Do You Love?*, offered a similar perspective. Made in 2008, it was released in the spring of 2010.

See also: Bo Diddley, Willie Dixon, Howlin' Wolf, Muddy Waters.

Further reading: Rich Cohen, *Machers and Rockers: Chess Records and the Business of Rock & Roll* (2004); Nadine Cohodas, *Spinning Blues into Gold: The Chess Brothers and the Legendary Chess Records* (2000); John Collis, *Chess Records* (1998); Commission on Chicago Landmarks, "Chess Records Office and Studio," July 1989; Peter Guralnick, *Feel Like Going Home: Portraits in Blues and Rock 'n' Roll* (1981); Robert Palmer, *Deep Blues* (1982); Mike Rowe, *Chicago Breakdown* (1975).

Discography: *And This Is Free: The Life and Times of Chicago's Legendary Maxwell Street* (CD/DVD); *Aristocrat of the Blues: Chess 50th Anniversary Collection* (1997); *Best of Chess: Original Versions of Songs in* Cadillac Records (2008); *Chess Blues* (1993); *Chess Blues Classics: 1947–1956* (1997); *Chess Blues Classics: 1957–1967* (1997).

Del Close

Actor and Director

BORN: March 9, 1934
Manhattan, Kansas

DIED: March 4, 1999
Chicago, Illinois

Actor, teacher, and mentor to such iconic comics and Second City alumni as John Belushi and Bill Murray, Del Close possessed a macabre sense of humor that reflected his darkly pessimistic view of the world. Despite his self-destructive tendencies, he lived long enough to become one of the pioneers of improvisational theater.

Del Close was born in Manhattan, Kansas, in 1934, the son of a jeweler (as well as the second cousin of Dwight D. Eisenhower). While still a teenager he joined a traveling carnival troupe as a fire swallower, but he also found the time to attend college at Kansas State. In the mid-1950s he joined the St. Louis branch of the Compass Players, an improv company created by Mike Nichols and Elaine May. After a brief stint on Broadway in a comedy about beatniks called *The Nervous Set*, he moved to Chicago in the early 1960s to perform and direct at the Second City.

After being fired from the Second City for substance abuse—Close was a heavy drug user—he spent a few years in San Francisco and became one of the founders of the San Francisco–based 1960s comedy troupe the Committee. He then returned to Chicago in the early 1970s. Close was hired again to direct at the Second City and taught many of the comic actors who would soon become famous. In the early 1980s he even worked closely with cast members of *Saturday Night Live* as a teacher and mentor. After being fired once again from the Second City, in 1983 he cofounded, with Charna Halpern, the ImprovOlympic, a theater school and performance space that developed a form of improvisation that employed long-form comedy, which they facetiously called the Harold (the Del Close Theater at I.O. is named in his honor). In his book *Truth in Comedy*, cowritten with Halpern, Close describes the structure of the Harold in detail. In the late 1980s, Close also occasionally acted in movies that were set in Chicago, such as John Hughes's *Ferris Bueller's Day Off* (1986) and Brian de Palma's *The Untouchables* (1987). He also acted in the nuclear war drama *Fat Man and Little Boy* (1989).

Close made two comedy albums, *How to Speak Hip* and *The Do-It-Yourself Psychoanalysis Kit*. In addition to his movie roles, he appeared in numerous plays. He played the role of Polonius in Robert Falls's seminal 1985 production of *Hamlet* at the Wisdom Bridge Theater. He also appeared in Peter Sellars's 1994 adaptation of *The Merchant of Venice* (set in Venice, California, not Venice, Italy) at the Goodman Theatre, and in Steppenwolf Theatre's revival of Sam Shepard's *Buried Child* in 1995.

Over the years Close had a love-hate affair with the Second City. He was a firm advocate of improv and thus his relationship with the comedy enterprise grew more intense as the troupe relied more on scripted sketches than on the improv method that Close preferred, which led to some wicked flare-ups. Indeed, Second City cofounder Bernard Sahlins fired Close on at least two occasions. Essentially, Close insisted that improv was an art form in its own right. To Sahlins improv was meant to be used as a tool, not as a final performance form. Sahlins believed it was a process, a way to create sketches, a means to an end; but to Close, on the other hand, it was the end.

Close continued his sparring with Sahlins until the very end. During his last days, some fifty of his friends gathered at Illinois Masonic Hospital. A dining room off the hospital's downstairs cafeteria was reserved for a private party "though little about it was private," notes Kim Johnson. "There were jazz musicians, nurses, caterers, pagan priests, reporters, celebrities, novice students, old friends, and even a Comedy Central camera sent by the Upright Citizens Brigade in New York." Harold Ramis was there, as were Bill Murray and his brother Brian Doyle-Murray. The Second City's Joyce Sloan and Bernard Sahlins were there, too. As Close was wheeled into his room wearing his oxygen mask and robe, with a tangle of tubes to monitor his breathing, Sahlins gave him a hug. Close was having none of it. Instead he wagged his finger in the air and insisted, with a wicked smile, "It *is* an art form." At last, Sahlins conceded, at least for a moment.

"Del, for tonight, it is an art form," Sahlins echoed.

Close died at the age of sixty-four of emphysema at Illinois Masonic Hospital in Chicago.

Close almost always got the last word—even after death. In his will he bequeathed his skull to the Goodman Theatre. "I give my skull to the Goodman Theatre, for a production of *Hamlet* in which to play Yorick, or for any other purposes the Goodman Theatre deems appropriate," it declared. Four months later, on July 1, 1999, Halpern handed over to the Goodman's artistic director Robert Falls a skull; it lay on a red velvet cushion inside a Lucite box. But, in fact, the skull did not belong to Close. It was all for show since both Illinois Masonic and the Illinois Society of Pathologists refused to remove Close's head. Instead, Halpern had Close's body cremated and bought a skull at the Anatomical Chart Company in Skokie, Illinois.

See also: John Belushi, Paul Sills, Viola Spolin

Further reading: Jeff Griggs, *Guru: My Days with Del Close* (2005); Kim Johnson, *The Funniest One in the Room: The Lives and Legends of Del Close* (1999); Sheldon Patinkin, *The Second City: Backstage at the World's Greatest Comedy Theater* (2000); Bernard Sahlins, *Days and Nights at the Second City: A Memoir, with Notes on Staging Review Theatre* (2002); Jeffrey Sweet, *Something Wonderful Right Away: An Oral History of the Second City and the Compass Players* (2004); Mike Thomas, *The Second City Unscripted: Revolution and Revelation at the World-Famous Comedy Theater* (2009).

Nat King Cole

Musician

BORN: March 17, 1919
Montgomery, Alabama

DIED: February 15, 1965
Santa Monica, California

The smoky-voiced singer whose hits included "Mona Lisa," "Too Young," "Rambling Rose," and the timeless Christmas classic "The Christmas Song," Nat King Cole was the first African American to host his own weekly television program. *The Nat King Cole* show premiered on NBC in 1956 and ran for sixty-four weeks. Cole was the first African American to cross over to the pop charts. The soft-spoken Cole was tops in his field in recording, nightclub performance, television, and motion pictures.

Born Nathaniel Adams Coles (he later dropped the "s" in his last name), he moved with his family to Chicago from Alabama when he was four years old. His father became pastor of the True Light Baptist Church located at 7302 South Maryland Avenue, and young Nathaniel sang in the choir. Cole's mother was also a church singer. As a youngster, Cole played the piano, and in high school he organized a fourteen-piece band. He attended both Wendell Phillips and DuSable high schools. Cole and his brother, Eddie, led a combo, the Rogues of Rhythm, at a tavern on 58th Street. Many evenings he would sit outside the Grand Terrace nightclub and listen to the likes of Earl Hines and Art Tatum. After graduating from high school, Cole went on tour with a musical revue called "Shuffle Along," and in 1937 he settled in Los Angeles.

Cole then began playing at California beer joints before forming the Nat King Cole trio, a strictly instrumental group that consisted of guitar, bass fiddle, and piano. The popular story is that during a show one night, a drunk shouted from the crowd, demanding that someone sing. Cole protested that there were no singers in the group. The heckler insisted, so Cole began warbling "Sweet Lorraine." Years later, Cole's widow, Maria, said the truth was a bit more mundane. Cole had been singing several songs per set and when the crowd responded positively to his voice, he simply began to sing more. Cole received his famous sobriquet when the manager of a club where he and his trio were playing was so impressed with the musician's nimble fingers on the keyboard that he christened him "King" Cole.

Although he first emerged as a jazz pianist of the first order, it is as a singer that Cole excelled. In 1942 Capitol signed the King Cole Trio and two years later they had their first hit, "Straighten Up and Fly Right." During the early 1950s, Cole enjoyed a string of solo hits that would make him one of the most popular stylists of his generation, including "Nature Boy," "Unforgettable," "Mona Lisa," "Too Young," and "Those Lazy-Hazy-Crazy Days of Summer."

Although Cole never injected politics into his music—he preferred to keep his personal opinions to himself—sometimes trouble followed him. At a show in Birmingham, Alabama, on April 10, 1956, members of the North Alabama White Citizens Council who were waging a campaign against bebop, rock and roll, and "Negro music,"

rushed the stage and knocked the singer to the floor, repeatedly kicking him. Understandably shaken, Cole said he couldn't continue and offered a refund. No one requested their money back.

Cole appeared in several motion pictures, including *China Gate* in 1957 and the Academy Award–winning *Cat Ballou* in 1965. In 1958 he portrayed W. C. Handy in *The St. Louis Blues*.

Cole, a heavy smoker, died in February 1965 in Santa Monica, California, after a two-month battle against lung cancer.

In 1968 Superintendent of Chicago Public Schools James F. Redmond asked the board of education to name a school after Cole. The Nathaniel Cole Child-Parent Center stands at 412 South Keeler Avenue. In the same year, a park at 85th Street and South Park Avenue honored the late singer.

See also: Sam Cooke, Earl Hines

Cyrus Colter

Author

BORN: January 8, 1910
Noblesville, Indiana

DIED: April 17, 2002
Evanston, Illinois

At a time when most people are looking forward to retirement, Cyrus Colter began a new career. In his novels and short stories he wrote about the often-invisible lives of ordinary African American working-class and middle-class folk. He also became the head of the Department of African American Studies at Northwestern University, the first black person at the university to hold an endowed chair.

Colter earned a bachelor's degree from Ohio State University and, in 1940, a law degree from Chicago-Kent College of Law. After graduating, he briefly became a deputy internal revenue collector for the city of Chicago before serving in the army in Europe during World War II, where he rose to the rank of field artillery captain. He returned to civilian life in 1946 and began a successful career as a lawyer. In 1950 Governor Adlai Stevenson appointed him to the Illinois Commerce Commission (ICC). He served in the position of commissioner for a good deal of his adult life, from 1950 to 1973.

Not quite satisfied with his career, at the age of fifty he began to seriously study Russian literature, particularly the work of Tolstoy, Dostoevsky, and Chekhov. In 1973 he resigned from the ICC to teach creative writing in the Department of African American Studies at Northwestern

University. He felt he could turn his own life experiences, as well as the greater African American story, into works of fiction. Encouraged by his wife, Imogene Mackay, he began to write. His first short story, "A Chance Meeting," was published in *Threshold,* a little magazine based in Belfast. But it wasn't until he was sixty when his first collection of stories, *The Beach Umbrella,* was published, in 1970. *The Beach Umbrella* won the University of Iowa's School of Letters fiction prize. The publication of two subsequent works of fiction, the novels *The River of Eros* in 1972 and *The Hippodrome* in 1973, led to his appointment as the Chester D. Tripp Professor of Humanities at Northwestern University, a position that he maintained from 1973 to 1978.

After leaving Northwestern, he continued to write. In 1979 *Night Studies* won the 1980 Carl Sandburg fiction prize, and in 1988 he published *A Chocolate Soldier.* His collected stories *The Amoralist and Other Tales* were published the same year. His last published work was the novel *City of Light* (1993), about an African American in Paris who attempts to establish an African homeland for diaspora blacks.

Colter died in April 2002 at the age of ninety-two.

The Cyrus Colter Papers are housed at Northwestern University in Evanston, Illinois.

Gary Comer

Entrepreneur and Philanthropist

BORN: December 10, 1927
Chicago, Illinois

DIED: October 4, 2006
Chicago, Illinois

A visionary entrepreneur, Gary Campbell Comer was the founder of the mail-order and casual-clothing retail giant Lands' End. Self-effacing and generous to a fault, he is also remembered for his philanthropic legacy of supporting children's health care and education, and for combating global climate change. He used his wealth to give back to his old neighborhood and to the city itself.

Comer was born and raised in the Grand Crossing neighborhood on the South Side, the son of a railroad worker and a homemaker. He attended Paul Revere Elementary School and Hyde Park High School. An avid sailor beginning in childhood, he learned to sail while taking lessons at a Chicago Park District beach house. Subsequently, he became a world-class sailor and won a number of competitions, including the North American Championships. He won a bronze medal in the Pan American Games.

Comer came from modest means. Since he couldn't afford to attend college, he worked at various odd jobs before joining the advertising firm of Young & Rubicam in 1950. He stayed there for a decade and, in 1960, quit and spent a year traveling in Europe. He returned to Chicago where he met his future wife, Frances Ceraulo; they married in 1962. By that autumn he had already started a business, selling sailboat equipment, hardware, duffel bags, rain suits, and several items of clothing from his apartment on North Kedzie Avenue. He called it Lands' End because, as he said, "It had a romantic ring to it." The misplaced apostrophe was a typo but it stuck. In spring 1963 Comer and five partners incorporated Lands' End Yacht Stores and moved to a rent-free basement office on Elston Avenue. By 1965 his upstart company was making a small profit and made enough money to print its first catalog. The catalog quickly became admired for its clever writing and graphics. Eventually he bought out two partners. In 1978 he moved the warehouse and telephone operations to Dodgeville, Wisconsin. In 1986 his company went public. Today Lands' End is the second largest apparel-only mail-order business and the world's largest clothing website.

Comer stepped down as president of Lands' End in 1990, although he remained chairman of the board and the majority shareholder until the company was sold to Sears, Roebuck and Company in May 2002.

Despite his phenomenal success as a businessman, Comer is perhaps best known, and most widely admired, for his philanthropy. He gave away millions of dollars. He funded CITY 2000, a yearlong photo project that led to 500,000 photos and a book. He donated more than $80 million to the creation and expansion of the Comer Children's Hospital at the University of Chicago, and at the University of Chicago Medical Center funded the Comer Pediatric Mobile Care program. Run by university physicians, it brings comprehensive primary and preventive health care to students at South Side public schools. In 2001 he and his wife Frances donated $21 million to help erect the six-story, 242,000-square-foot University of Chicago Comer Children's Hospital—it opened on February 19, 2005. He also gave a $20 million gift in 2003 to add a pediatric emergency room. In 2006 he made a $42 million donation to the University of Chicago to create the Comer Center for Children and Specialty Care, adjoining the Comer Children's Hospital. It was the largest single donation ever made to the University of Chicago.

In 2001 Comer supported several Chicago-based projects that advanced health and education, especially for children on his native South Side. He gave $50 million to the Paul Revere Elementary School community, including $30 million to create the Gary Comer Youth Center, an activity, performance, and education center for area youths located at 7200 South Ingleside Avenue. It is adjacent to the school and not far from his childhood home, and also serves as the home of the South Shore Drill Team. On September 14, 2010, Gary Comer College Prep, at 7131 S. South Chicago Avenue, officially opened its doors.

Comer died in his Gold Coast apartment from prostate cancer at the age of seventy-eight.

Charles A. Comiskey

Baseball Club Owner

BORN: August 15, 1859
Chicago, Illinois

DIED: October 26, 1931
Eagle River, Wisconsin

Baseball maverick Charles Albert Comiskey achieved many firsts in his life. He was the only player to become an owner, he changed first-base play by emphasizing the importance of fielding ground balls, and he introduced the idea of night games to a quizzical nation. Along with Byron Bancroft Johnson, he founded the American League and, in 1900, established a new baseball club, the Chicago White Stockings (not to be confused with the original White Stockings, which became the Cubs). Two years later, he shortened the name to "White Sox." Comiskey revolutionized the game of baseball.

Comiskey's father, John, arrived in Chicago from County Cavan, Ireland, in 1852, making his living first as a contractor and then as alderman for the old Seventh Ward. A baseball fanatic from his youth, young Charles Comiskey played amateur ball on West Side sandlots before going off from Holy Family parish to St. Mary's College in Kansas to acquire a proper education. After signing up with the Dubuque Rabbits, a minor league team, as a pitcher and reserve infielder, he became player-manager of the St. Louis Browns of the American Association, leading the team to four straight pennants. In 1890 Comiskey joined the Pirates of the Chicago Brotherhood, who played their games on an athletic field at 35th and Wentworth Streets.

From 1892 to 1894 Comiskey was captain, manager, and first baseman of the National League's Cincinnati Red Stockings (later called the Reds). There he developed a friendship with "Ban" Johnson, sports editor of the *Cincinnati Commercial-Gazette*. With Johnson, he helped found the renegade American League, raiding other teams to recruit the best available talent.

The Chicago White Sox made their local debut on a cold and blustery April 21, 1900, in a wooden grandstand at the 39th Street grounds. Comiskey Park, however, didn't open its gates to the public until July 1, 1910, when the White Sox played the St. Louis Browns, losing the opener 2–0. The first night game was played there on August 27 of the same year.

Those were good days for Comiskey and his White Sox. In 1906 they battled the Cubs in the city's only crosstown World Series, winning four games to two. In 1913, always looking for ways to promote the sport and his team, Comiskey arranged for a series of exhibition games to be played in Japan, Australia, Ceylon, Egypt, Italy, France, and England.

Nicknamed "The Old Roman" because of his pronounced nose, Comiskey was a complex, curiously enigmatic figure. Although known as a tightwad around his players—indeed, he often treated them like chattel—he could be quite generous when it came to members of the press. He lavished gifts and words of praise on sportswriters and provided them with free meals after every home and road game. In many ways an innovative and forward-thinking baseball strategist, he could just as easily be stubbornly conservative, as he was when he prevented blacks from playing in the major league.

In 1917 the White Sox brought home the pennant and the world championship aided by the powerful pitching of Eddie Cicotte, who won a dazzling twenty-eight games that year. As a result of their hard work, Comiskey had promised bonuses to the players, but he later changed his mind, rewarding them instead with bottles of champagne. Since their contract expressly forbade them from playing with any other team, they had little choice but to stay and endure. But their collective anger simmered.

In 1919 Comiskey assembled one of the greatest teams ever to play on a baseball diamond. There was pitcher Cicotte, outfielder "Shoeless" Joe Jackson, third baseman George "Buck" Weaver, center fielder Oscar "Happy" Felsch, southpaw pitcher Claude "Lefty" Williams, infielder Frederick McMullin, first baseman Charles "Chick" Gandil, and shortstop Charles "Swede" Risberg.

Frustrated and angry with the Old Roman's intransigence, Gandil approached Boston gambler Joseph "Sport" Sullivan and proposed, for a promise of $80,000 cash, to throw the upcoming 1919 World Series against the Cincinnati Reds. Already suspicious, Comiskey had received anonymous tips and had even hired private detectives to uncover the truth. A grand jury was convened but, in a private meeting with the Old Roman, Cicotte tearfully confessed. The White Sox owner expressed little sympathy for the fallen ballplayer. "Tell it to the grand jury," he snapped.

The "Black Sox" trial began July 18, 1921. Although they were acquitted of any wrongdoing in court, the new baseball commissioner Kenesaw Mountain Landis banned the eight players from the game for life. "Regardless of the verdict of juries, no player who throws a ball game . . . will ever play professional baseball!" he insisted. "The reason for the popularity of the sport," Comiskey said before the Black Sox Scandal erupted, "is that it fits in with the temperament of the American people and because it is on the square. Everything is done in the open."

The scandal broke the spirit of the usually indomitable Comiskey. He died a recluse at his Wisconsin home on October 26, 1931, an emotionally drained veteran of the baseball wars.

On September 30, 1990, Comiskey Park hosted its last baseball game with a White Sox victory over the Seattle

Mariners, 2–1. The new Comiskey Park opened across the street on April 18, 1991. In January 2003 it was renamed U.S. Cellular Field.

See also: Cap Anson, Kenesaw Mountain Landis, Ring Lardner

Further reading: Eliot Asinof, *Eight Men Out: The Black Sox and the 1919 World Series* (1963); Gustaf W. Axelson, *"Commy": The Life Story of Charles Comiskey* (1919); Richard Lindberg, *Who's on 3rd? The Chicago White Sox Story* (1983).

Other resources: *Eight Men Out* (1988), a dramatization of the Black Sox Scandal, directed by John Sayles.

Fairfax M. Cone

Advertising Executive

BORN: February 21, 1903
San Francisco, California

DIED: June 20, 1977
Carmel, California

Fairfax Mastick Cone, who cofounded the firm of Foote, Cone & Belding in 1942, was a major figure in Chicago advertising circles. Quick to condemn irresponsible advertising, he preferred to convey coherent and clear messages without the gimmicks. Above all, he wished to upgrade the much-maligned reputation of advertising. "We believed that advertising should be thoughtful and honest, with no exceptions, and that no other kind of [advertising] should ever play a part in the affairs of Foote, Cone & Belding," he once remarked.

Cone was born in San Francisco, the son of William H. Cone, a mining engineer and prospector, and Isabelle Williams, a teacher. Due to his father's peripatetic profession, Cone was tutored at home by his mother until the sixth grade. He attended high school in Oakland and at the age of sixteen went to sea for eight months on the SS *Haxtum,* a transatlantic freighter.

In January 1921, at his father's insistence, Cone enrolled at the University of California at Berkeley to continue his education. He edited school magazines and enjoyed cartooning. One summer he was hired as a copy boy at the *San Francisco Bulletin.* He then worked at the *San Francisco Examiner* for three years as an advertising salesman, writer, and illustrator before jumping to the L. H. Waldron agency as an artist. He left after one year when he realized his color blindness—he had sketched primarily in monochromatic black-and-white previously—would limit his opportunity to advance.

In 1929 Cone joined the San Francisco office of Lord and Thomas as a copywriter. In 1939 he became manager and in 1941 transferred to New York as vice-president and creative director, working directly with the owner Albert D. Lasker. In 1942 Cone moved to Chicago, where he became Lord and Thomas's executive vice-president. The firm dissolved when Lasker retired the same year.

The Chicago-based Cone, along with two other colleagues, Emerson Foote in New York and Don Belding in Los Angeles, formed their own ad agency, Foote, Cone & Belding, in 1942. Cone acted as chairman of the executive committee from 1942 to 1948, chairman of the board from 1948 to 1951, and president from 1951 to 1957. Under his leadership, the firm became one of the ten largest advertising agencies in the world.

Foote, Cone & Belding was formed at a crucial time in the history of advertising. The war economy didn't offer much opportunity for luxury goods. Advertising was, in effect, a dispensable industry. Cone, who learned very quickly to adapt with the times, did the most logical thing—he devoted advertising space in magazines and newspapers to the war effort "as a truly unselfish public service." When television came into its own in the years following World War II, Foote, Cone & Belding took advantage of the new medium by hiring cowboy Roy Rogers to sell Post Toasties and comedian Sid Caesar to promote Libby's canned pineapple.

Cone avoided anything that suggested even the slightest vulgarity or smacked of poor taste. Foote, Cone & Belding clients included Sunkist Growers, Dole Pineapple, Kraft Foods, the Paper Mate Company, the Ralston Purina Company, Sara Lee, Hills Brothers Coffee, and Trans World Airlines. The agency's clever and catchy advertising slogans saturated the airwaves and entered into American popular culture. Some familiar Foote, Cone & Belding campaigns were for Raid ("Raid kills bugs dead!"), Dial Soap ("Aren't you glad you use Dial? Don't you wish everybody did?"), Clairol ("Does she or doesn't she? Hair color so natural only her hairdresser knows for sure."), Hallmark ("When you care enough to send the very best"), Pepsodent ("You'll wonder where the yellow went"), the Toni Company ("Which twin has the Toni?"), and Zenith ("The quality goes in before the name goes on").

Cone typically worked sixty-hour weeks, yet still managed to read five to seven books per week. He was also active in civil affairs. He was a member of the Board of Trustees of the University of Chicago and acted as its chairman from 1963 to 1970, was a director of the Chicago Better Business Bureau, and was general chairman of Chicago's Crusade of Mercy. Cone also served as chairman of both the American Association of Advertising Agencies and the Advertising Council.

Cone was somewhat of a purist. He believed that advertising was not only a respectable profession but also a noble one. An outspoken critic of offensive advertising methods, Cone denounced billboards ("The peace and beauty of the landscape is interrupted and, in effect, violated by jungles of unsightly advertisements") and abhorred the use of advertising to "sell" political candidates.

In 1975 Cone was elected into the Advertising Hall of Fame and in 1976 into the Illinois Business Hall of Fame. He wrote two autobiographical books: *With All Its Faults:*

A Candid Account of Forty Years in Advertising (1969) and *The Blue Streak: Some Observations, Mostly About Advertising* (1973). "Advertising always follows, it never leads," wrote Cone in *With All Its Faults*. "Nevertheless, it should be used in the best traditions of our society and not the very questionable postures that evolve from time to time. . . . Advertising should never stoop to conquer."

Cone retired to Carmel, California, in 1970. He died in June 1977 at his home there after a prolonged illness. He was seventy-four.

In 2006, Foote, Cone & Belding merged with Draft to become Draftfcb. Its Chicago offices are located at 101 East Erie Street and 633 North St. Clair Street.

See also: Leo Burnett

Jack Conroy

Novelist

BORN: Circa 1899
Moberly, Missouri

DIED: April 30, 1990
Moberly, Missouri

During the 1930s and 1940s Missouri-born Jack Conroy was the foremost practitioner of what came to be called the "proletarian novel." He wrote his most important work in Chicago, where he befriended and found inspiration from such kindred spirits as Nelson Algren and Richard Wright, both of whom, like the jovial and hard-drinking Conroy, harbored ambitions of becoming the "American Gorki" (referring to the Russian writer renowned for his Bolshevik sympathies).

Conroy was born in the mining town of Moberly, Missouri. His father, a former Jesuit, died in a mining accident. At thirteen, Conroy worked at a railroad car shop, and at fifteen he served as recording secretary for the local branch of the Brotherhood of Railway Car Men. In 1922 Conroy led a column of laborers during the Great Railroad Strike of that year. When the strike was broken, Conroy lost his job and spent the next decade doing odd jobs throughout the country and living the life of a hobo. He worked in steel mills in Toledo and auto factories in Detroit, and in 1930 he returned to Missouri as a construction worker and there started *Rebel Poet* magazine. The "manifesto" of *Rebel Poet* eloquently expressed Conroy's leftist leanings. The magazine, he proclaimed, "championed the weak and defenseless" and condemned "the greed of industrial barons who are converting American laborers into abject serfs." His writing career received an additional boost when the Baltimore scribe H. L. Mencken published his work in *American Mercury*.

In May 1933, Conroy became editor of another small literary magazine, *The Anvil*, the first publication to print the work of African American author Richard Wright. Its motto was "We prefer crude vigor to polished banality." In 1935 it merged with the *Partisan Review*. Conroy then came to Chicago in 1938, at the invitation of his friend Nelson Algren, to edit the *New Anvil*, with Algren serving as managing editor. Conroy edited the *New Anvil* from 1938 to 1940. In addition to Wright and Algren, the *New Anvil*'s list of contributors included James T. Farrell, Langston Hughes, and William Carlos Williams. Along with Algren, Studs Terkel, Saul Bellow, and others, Conroy was a member of the Illinois Works Progress Administration Federal Writers' Project.

Conroy won critical acclaim in 1933 with his novel *The Disinherited*, a thinly disguised autobiographical work about life as a migrant worker in the 1920s. Another novel about American laborers, *A World to Win* (1935), was not as successful as *The Disinherited*. That same year Conroy was awarded a Guggenheim Fellowship to conduct research on African American migration to the North. Ten years later, in 1945, his hard work paid off with the release of *They Seek a City*, coauthored with Arna Bontemps. An impassioned account of the mass exodus of rural blacks into the great northern cities, it was the first literary collaboration between a white author and an African American author. A revised edition was published in 1966 under the title *Anyplace But Here*. Conroy also collaborated with Bontemps on several children's books, including *The Fast Sooner Hound* (1942) and *Sam Patch* (1951). In 1969 Conroy received the Illinois Literary Prize and in 1977 he won a National Endowment for the Arts grant.

Conroy also held important editing positions in Chicago: from 1946 to 1947 he was the literary editor of the *Chicago Defender* and from 1947 to 1969 the senior editor of the Chicago-based *New Standard Encyclopedia*. Literary historian Doug Wixson observed, "He was different from almost all the other proletarian writers. He wrote from within the experience. He was not an educated writer with political sympathies for the downtrodden and the worker. He was one."

In 1979 *The Jack Conroy Reader,* edited by Jack Salzman and David Ray, was published.

Conroy died in April 1990 in Missouri. He was ninety-one.

See also: Nelson Algren, Saul Bellow, James T. Farrell, Albert Halper, Richard Wright

Further reading: Arna Bontemps and Jack Conroy, *Anyplace But Here* (1966); Jack Salzman and David Ray, eds., *The Jack Conroy Reader* (1979).

Sam Cooke
Singer

BORN: January 22, 1935
Chicago, Illinois

DIED: December 11, 1964
Los Angeles, California

A pioneer soul singer, Sam Cooke was the first major gospel star to cross over to pop. Many critics now credit him with paving the way for a later generation of soul singers. His vocal style found favor with many performers, from Otis Redding and Al Green to Smokey Robinson and Teddy Pendergrass. Rock star Rod Stewart has often cited Cooke as a major influence, and, indeed, Stewart recorded several of Cooke's songs, including "Twistin' the Night Away" and "Bring It On Home to Me."

Sam Cook (he added the "e" later) grew up on the South Side of Chicago, one of eight sons of a Baptist minister. He began singing "as soon as he could talk," his father said in a newspaper interview. At nine, Cooke joined a gospel group, the Singing Children, and a few years later became a member of the Highway QC's. In the early 1950s, after graduating from Wendell Phillips High School, he sang with the gospel group the Soul Stirrers, replacing lead singer Rebert Harris. Later, he became the lead vocalist of the Pilgrim Travelers. A handsome and charismatic performer, Cooke considered switching to pop but hesitated for fear of offending his loyal gospel audience and disappointing his Baptist father. Hence, early pop recordings were released under the pseudonym Dale Cook, including his first pop song, in 1956, "Lovable."

In 1957 Cooke recorded an original composition, "You Send Me," for Keen Records, which became his first million seller, soaring to the top of both the R&B and pop charts. In 1960 Cooke moved to RCA. Some of his more memorable hits include "Everybody Loves to Cha Cha Cha" (1959), "Only Sixteen" (1959), "Wonderful World" (1960), "Chain Gang" (1960), "Cupid" (1961), "Twistin' the Night Away" (1962), "Bring It On Home to Me" (1962), "Having a Party" (1962), "Another Saturday Night" (1963), and the posthumously released "Shake" (1965).

An extremely likable performer, Cooke possessed a warm, sweet, and supple voice that soared, whispered, and lovingly caressed each syllable, giving even the most innocuous lyrics a depth that they otherwise lacked. Unlike many African American artists who came into prominence during the 1950s and 1960s, Cooke maintained creative control over his material. He not only ran his own publishing company and his own management firm, he also owned a record company, Sar/Derby Records, where he gave a break to many up-and-coming singers, including Bobby Womack, Billy Preston, Mel Carter, and fellow Chicagoan Lou Rawls.

Cooke died, in the prime of his career, under rather mysterious circumstances. He was shot to death in a Los Angeles motel room in December 1964 by the night manager, Bertha Franklin, during a scuffle. The singer, dressed only in a topcoat, reportedly attacked Franklin in an effort to find the whereabouts of a young woman he had taken to the motel. Franklin shot Cooke three times during the altercation. His body was brought back to Chicago, where thousands of screaming and crying fans at A. R. Leak's Funeral Home on South Cottage Grove Avenue tried to get one last glimpse of their fallen hero. He was buried at Forest Lawn cemetery in Glendale, California.

Despite the sordid circumstances surrounding his death, Cooke remained an idol to African Americans. In early 1965 RCA released the prophetic "A Change Is Gonna Come." Inspired by Bob Dylan's protest song "Blowin' in the Wind," it was an appropriate swan song, full of fire and righteous anger, and remains an enduring statement to Cooke's great talent.

See also: Nat King Cole
Further reading: Peter Guralnick, *Sweet Soul Music: Rhythm and Blues and the Southern Dream of Freedom* (1986); Gerri Hirshey, *Nowhere to Run: The Story of Soul Music* (1984); Joe McEwen, *Sam Cooke: A Biography in Words and Pictures* (1977); Jim Miller, ed., *The Rolling Stone Illustrated History of Rock & Roll* (1976); Daniel Wolff with S. R. Crain, Clifton White, and G. David Tenenbaum, *You Send Me: The Life & Times of Sam Cooke* (1995).

Discography: *Sam Cooke at the Copa* (1964); *Sam Cooke at the Harlem Square Club, 1963* (1985); *Sam Cooke—The Man and His Music* (1986); *Portrait of a Legend, 1951–1964* (2005).

Jack L. Cooper
Deejay

BORN: September 18, 1888
Memphis, Tennessee

DIED: January 12, 1970
Chicago, Illinois

Jack L. Cooper, a pioneer in his field, dominated black radio from the 1930s to the 1950s. The nation's first African American radio personality, he was also the city's first black sportscaster on radio, the first black newscaster on radio, and the first black executive of a radio station. Although not the first black deejay on the air, he was the first to offer radio from an exclusively African American perspective.

Cooper left school in the fifth grade and found work as a gofer, traveling the racetrack circuit through the Midwest and the South. Later he moved to Cincinnati, where he boxed in 160 amateur fights and won several championships, including the Negro Welterweight Crown of Ohio. Cooper also played second base for a semipro baseball team, managed theaters in Florida and Arkansas, and wrote for several African American newspapers, including the *Chicago Defender.* In 1924 he was hired as assistant theater editor of the *Defender,* and he wrote a regular column called "Coop's Chatter," which addressed issues of concern to the African American community.

"Were we to spend half the time between the pages of good books that we spend between the curbstone and the building, there would be less crime, more business, and better understanding," he wrote. More than anything, Cooper wished to see his fellow African Americans advance. Black self-help, he believed, was the only road to success.

Cooper got his start in the entertainment business performing in minstrel shows. He then branched out into acting and comedy routines before forming his own theater troupe in the early 1920s, the Cooper and Lamar Music Company. While working as East Coast correspondent for the *Defender* in Washington, D.C, Cooper made his radio debut on a local musical variety program on a white-owned radio station hosted by a German bandleader. Since black broadcasters were not allowed to work on white radio stations, Cooper cloaked his African American identity by performing comedy routines in various accents and dialects, including black dialect. The anonymity of radio thus offered opportunities for African Americans that did not otherwise exist in the entertainment field, yet it provided little outlet for self-expression. Frustrated with the program's restrictions and itching to reveal his true identity, Cooper returned to Chicago in 1926, determined to create a niche for African Americans on the local airwaves.

On November 3, 1929, his first show, *The All-Negro Hour,* premiered on WSBC. It was a live one-hour variety show that featured a diverse cast of characters as well as appearances from top local and national talent. In structure it resembled a vaudeville stage show. The program reflected the sentiment of its time. In response to the unprecedented success of *Amos 'n' Andy,* Cooper offered "Luke and Timber," a segment about two black migrants. He also aired live gospel and spiritual concerts and produced a mystery-drama serial called *The Nitemare.*

But Cooper's radio shows were not all just fun and games. In 1938 he launched a public service program, *Search for Missing Persons,* produced in cooperation with the Chicago Police Department. Listeners who tuned in to Cooper's various shows could hear advice about finding employment, learn about legal rights, and receive news from and about the African American community. Each August, Cooper aired special coverage of the annual Bud Billiken parade—the biggest event in the black community. In the days before African Americans were allowed to participate in the majors, Cooper aired play-by-play coverage of black baseball games. He also ran his own advertising agency and gave fellow African Americans their start in radio. The crowning achievement of Cooper's radio career was a news discussion show called *Listen Chicago,* says Mark Newman, author of *Entrepreneurs of Profit and Pride: From Black Appeal to Radio Soul.* Cooper bought airtime from many stations, including, at various times, WSBC, WHFC, WEDC, WJJD, WAAF, and WBEF. By the later 1940s—at the height of his career—he boasted more than forty hours of airtime on four different radio stations, notes Newman.

Cooper was extremely active in the black community, contributing time and money to various African American groups and organizations, including the South Side Boys' Club and the Morgan Park Youth Association.

Cooper retired in 1961. He died in his apartment at 1335 West 111th Place at the age of eighty-one in January 1970.

See also: Robert S. Abbott, Charles Correll, Freeman Gosden
Further reading: Chris Heim, "Riding the Waves: The Rise of Black Radio in Chicago," *Chicago Tribune Sunday Magazine*, February 12, 1989; Mark Newman, *Entrepreneurs of Profit and Pride: From Black Appeal to Radio Soul* (1988).

Paul Cornell

Real Estate Developer

BORN: August 5, 1822
White Creek, New York

DIED: March 3, 1904
Chicago, Illinois

In the 1840s a young lawyer named Paul Cornell came to Chicago from the East. He arrived with a bundle of clothes, a pack of business cards, $1.50 in his pocket, and a heart full of hope. Despite his youth—he was only twenty-five years old—he had a shrewd and far-reaching mind. As soon as he was able, he began to acquire property south of the city limits. He established the South Park system, which eventually evolved into Jackson and Washington parks. In 1854 he helped establish Oak Woods Cemetery. Eventually he became one of the largest suburban real estate developers in Chicagoland, but today he is best known as the person who laid out the streets and parks of the community he called Hyde Park.

In the early days, Hyde Park consisted of a series of oak ridges running across an open prairie, a low-lying area frequently under water. Cottage Grove was a dirt road. At the southeast corner of 63rd Street and Cottage Grove Avenue stood a barn where horses were kept. The main roads were Lake and Stony Island Avenues, but during or after a rainstorm, travelers were forced to use Vincennes Avenue.

Born in upstate New York, Cornell moved with his family to Adams County, Illinois, shortly after his father died. When he was old enough, he decided to study law. In 1847 he was admitted to the Illinois bar and moved to Chicago. On his first night in town, however, his entire savings were stolen from his hotel room. Fortunately, a sympathetic attorney came to his rescue, providing the young man with both a loan and a position in a Chicago law firm.

While working in the law office of Skinner and Hoyne, Cornell met Senator Stephen Douglas, who reportedly encouraged him to save all his money and invest it in land situated between the city limits and the Calumet area. Intrigued by this counsel, Cornell rode on horseback to the site and became convinced that a viable community could be built there. By 1853 Cornell had accumulated enough capital to buy 300 acres of land from 51st to 55th Streets, which he subdivided and sold to private investors. Although it was sparsely populated, Cornell assured the community's existence by selling sixty acres of land at its southern edge to the Illinois Central Railroad, with the provision that the railroad make six stops a day at the 53rd Street station. He also created an anchor in the community by building the Hyde Park Hotel. The community thus became a haven for weary Chicagoans who sought peace and tranquility and wished to get away from the city for a few days. To attract new residents, Cornell advertised the area as "beautifully situated on high ground interspersed with groves, on the lake shore six miles from Chicago."

In 1861 the residents petitioned the Illinois General Assembly to create the separate township of Hyde Park. About that time the townspeople erected their first public institutions: the First Presbyterian Church of Hyde Park in 1860, a public grammar school a few years later, and a high school in 1870.

After the Civil War, Cornell lobbied in Springfield for the creation of the South Park Commission, an agency that would purchase land and develop a public park system for the area. He hired renowned landscape architect Frederick Law Olmsted to create Jackson and Washington parks and the Midway Plaisance, and thus transform the marshy land into an attractive green belt. Although a lack of capital and the Chicago Fire of 1871 slowed the area's development, the broad boulevards and extensive parks became major selling points in the growth of Hyde Park.

In 1889 Hyde Park was annexed to the city of Chicago. The following year Chicago was chosen as the site of a world's fair, to be held in 1893, to celebrate the 400th anniversary of Columbus's journey to America. The influential architect and city planner, Daniel H. Burnham, suggested that nearby Jackson Park would be the perfect location to host such an event. In 1892 the University of

Chicago opened, and by the time Cornell died, Hyde Park was clearly no longer a sparsely settled village.

Cornell was a charter member of the South Park Commission and served on it for more than thirteen years. He also acted as the township's first supervisor. Later, he purchased land further south and developed the community of Grand Crossing, which was originally called Cornell.

Cornell, often called the father of Hyde Park, died in Chicago in March 1904. Cornell Drive is named in his honor. The elite suburb that he founded developed into one of the city's most prestigious and important neighborhoods, with quality housing, schools, shopping, and the much-respected University of Chicago. Many years later, the community and its neighbor, Kenwood, would become famous for another reason: for being the home of President Barack Obama.

See also: Daniel H. Burnham, Stephen A. Douglas, John Wellborn Root

Further reading: Jean F. Block, *Hyde Park Houses: An Informal History, 1856–1910* (1978); Glen E. Holt and Dominic A. Pacyga, *Chicago: A Historical Guide to the Neighborhoods: The Loop and South Side* (1979); Rebecca Janowitz, *Culture of Opportunity: Obama's Chicago: The People, Politics, and Ideas of Hyde Park* (2010); Dominic A. Pacyga and Ellen Skerrett, *Chicago: City of Neighborhoods* (1986).

Charles Correll

Radio Entertainer

BORN: February 2, 1890
Peoria, Illinois

DIED: September 26, 1972
Chicago, Illinois

Freeman Gosden

Radio Entertainer

BORN: May 5, 1899
Richmond, Virginia

DIED: December 10, 1982
Los Angeles, California

Two of the most popular and durable names in radio history were the characters Amos and Andy. Freeman F. Gosden as Amos and Charles J. Correll as Andy entertained America for more than thirty years until changing values and the advent of the civil rights movement forced them off the airwaves.

Charles James Correll was born in Peoria, Illinois. After graduating from Peoria High School, Correll worked as a stenographer for the state superintendent of public instruction. Later, he learned the bricklaying trade. But Correll had a creative side, too. He tinkered on the piano and participated in local amateur theater productions.

Freeman Fisher Gosden attended school in Richmond, Virginia, and Atlanta, Georgia, and then sold tobacco products and later automobiles. During World War I he served as a navy radio operator.

Gosden met Correll while he was working for a firm that staged amateur theater productions. They became fast friends and began traveling together for several years, putting on amateur shows. In 1924 the duo began singing on radio station WEBH, which broadcast from the Edgewater Beach Hotel in Chicago. The following year they joined the staff of WGN radio. Within two years they starred in their own radio show as two stereotypical African American characters named Sam and Henry.

Despite the success of the show, the pair decided to switch stations, jumping to WMAQ in 1928, and they changed the names of their characters to the more euphonious Amos and Andy. Gosden portrayed Amos Jones, the lazy but good-natured partner who was always making promises he couldn't keep, while Correll was the shrewd and mischievous Andy Brown. As co-owners of Fresh Air Taxicab, they ruled over a motley assortment of characters—most of them played by Gosden and Correll—including the Kingfish, Lightnin', and Madame Queen.

On August 19, 1929, *Amos 'n' Andy* aired nationally on NBC. By 1930 the show was running six nights a week with Gosden writing most of the scripts. It was said that during the 1930s the program was so popular that the country came to a halt for fifteen minutes every night. *Amos 'n' Andy* was on the air continuously, five nights a week, from 1929 until the spring of 1943, when it became a weekly half-hour show. It continued on radio until 1960. In 1948 CBS bought the rights to the characters from Correll and Gosden for a reported $2.5 million.

The pair appeared in blackface in two movies, *Check and Double Check* (1930) and *The Big Broadcast* (1936). In the late 1940s Correll and Gosden searched the country for African American actors to play the title roles in the television version, rather than portraying the characters themselves. "The truth is," said Correll, "we don't look believable in blackface. We look like something out of burlesque or a minstrel show." More than 800 African American actors were auditioned, according to a report in the *Chicago Tribune*. The TV show, which premiered in 1951, was the first network series with an all-black cast: Spencer Williams played Andy, Alvin Childress played Amos, and Tim Moore played Kingfish.

During its radio heyday, few African Americans actually protested the show. *Amos 'n' Andy* was, according to at least one veteran radio executive, possibly more popular among blacks than among whites. Scattered complaints did occur, of course, especially among black professionals who attacked the program as a stereotypical depiction of African American life. As early as 1931 the *Pittsburgh Courier* petitioned the FCC to cancel *Amos 'n' Andy*. The show continued, however.

In 1951, the National Association for the Advancement of Colored People (NAACP) charged that the television series portrayed African Americans "in a stereotypical and derogatory way." Correll and Gosden, who produced the program, denied the accusations. Rather, they insisted, they were merely satirizing human nature. Nevertheless, mounting protests during the mid-1960s forced the withdrawal of the television show from syndication.

In 1972 Correll died in Chicago of cardiorespiratory problems at the age of eighty-two. Gosden died in Los Angeles in 1982. He was eighty-three.

See also: Jack L. Cooper

Further reading: Melvin Patrick Ely, *The Adventures of Amos 'n' Andy: A Social History of an American Phenomenon* (1991); J. Fred MacDonald, *Don't Touch That Dial: Radio Programming in American Life from 1920 to 1960* (1979); Mark Newman, *Entrepreneurs of Profit and Pride: From Black Appeal to Radio Soul* (1988).

"Bathhouse John" Coughlin

Politician

BORN: August 15, 1860
Chicago, Illinois

DIED: November 8, 1938
Chicago, Illinois

Along with his partner, Michael "Hinky Dink" Kenna, "Bathhouse John" Coughlin held the aldermanic seat of the corrupt First Ward for more than forty-five years. Through bribery, chicanery, and a shrewd understanding of Chicago politics, Coughlin maintained control.

John Coughlin was Irish on both sides. His father hailed from County Roscommon, his mother from County Limerick. He grew up in an area east of the Chicago River between Adams and Monroe Streets known as Conley's Patch. His father made a respectable living as the proprietor of a small grocery store, but like many Chicagoans he lost everything in the Chicago Fire of 1871. Coughlin attended classes at the Jones School at Harrison and Federal Streets. After hours, he labored as an assistant to the school janitor. He left Jones at the age of thirteen and spent two years at the Christian Brothers' Industrial School. At fifteen he had had enough of schooling and was ready to go to work.

An amiable and easygoing lad, Coughlin took any job that came his way, such as when he secured a position as a delivery boy and then clerk in his father's store. He was ecstatic when his brother Joe got him a job as a "scrubber" in a Turkish bathhouse on Clark Street. Here young Coughlin got his first glimpse of the trappings of power and the men who ran the city. He was duly impressed. He scrubbed down politicians, prizefighters, merchants, and underworld figures, and he hoped that one day he would join their prominent ranks. "I formed my philosophy while watching and studying the types of people who patronized the bathhouses," he would later say. "I watched and learned never to quarrel, never to feud. I had the best schooling a young feller could have." One year later Coughlin got a job in the finest bathhouse in the city, located in the Palmer House, and met more of the city's movers and shakers. Through such connections, he was able to open his own establishment in 1882. A few months later, he opened another and earned the nickname "Bathhouse John."

The rough and tumble world of Chicago politics appealed to the young businessman. He became a member of the First Ward Democratic Club and then advanced to the role of precinct captain. Coughlin was a natural-born politician. He felt at home in the company of these brash men and enjoyed the privileges and status that political office brought. More importantly, he knew when to shut his mouth and play along, and in Chicago politics that virtually guaranteed success.

He wore the clothing of a young man on the rise—loud colors, silk bowler hat, frock coat, and mauve gloves. But Coughlin wanted more. Dissatisfied with being on the periphery of politics, he longed to see it from the inside. He got his wish on April 5, 1892, when he was elected alderman of the First Ward. The First Ward was the richest and most notorious of the city's wards since it contained the central business district and the extremely lucrative redlight district. Never one to rock the boat, Coughlin voted as he was told by fellow city council members on important city ordinances.

But the winds of Chicago politics frequently change course. Shortly after his election, Coughlin found himself at odds with the mayor. Carter Harrison I had just been reelected for the fifth time. A practical man, Harrison had chosen to distance himself from the underworld element ("I am for the people. I will not have anything to do with the bummers," he insisted). Coughlin, who made the fatal mistake of supporting the incumbent Mayor Hempstead Washburne during the campaign, was conveniently cast aside. Powerless and friendless, the hapless alderman turned to Michael "Hinky Dink" Kenna for help. Kenna was a taciturn saloonkeeper who kept to himself and spoke only when necessary, but he knew Chicago politics inside and out. All Coughlin had to do, advised Kenna, was stay out of trouble and warm up to Harrison. Harrison would eventually come around.

It worked. Coughlin soon found himself in Harrison's good graces again. Kenna was also elected alderman, in 1897, and with Kenna by his side—for twenty-six years, they co-ruled as aldermen of the First Ward—Coughlin made inroads into the lucrative underworld trade then thriving in the Levee, as the city's sprawling red-light district was called. Protection money from gamblers, saloonkeepers, brothels, and gaming houses helped to line the pockets of Coughlin and Kenna and the ward organization.

Despite the money that was flooding into the area, the First Ward was always hard-pressed for cash. Coughlin and Kenna devised an ingenious solution one day in Hinky Dink's saloon. Why not stage a lavish ball to bring revenue into the coffers of the Democratic ward organization? Why not indeed? And so began a colorful Chicago tradition, with the first ball taking place on Christmas in 1896.

For ten years the notorious First Ward balls were examples of Chicago at its most sinful. Truth be told, the city had never seen anything quite like it. The highlight of a typical First Ward ball, the moment that everyone waited for, was the arrival of Bathhouse John himself—dressed in lavender trousers, pink gloves, yellow pumps, and silk top hat—and leading the grand march at the stroke of midnight. While reformers recoiled in horror at the sight of pimps, burglars, and prostitutes mingling with police officers, politicians, and businessmen, historians tell us that Bathhouse John and Hinky Dink counted the proceeds all the way to the bank.

The days of the First Ward balls were soon to end, however. Public outrage and reformers like George E. Cole, president of the Municipal Voters' League, a watchdog organization, and Arthur Burrage Farwell, president of the Chicago Law and Order League, made sure of it. The last First Ward ball was held in 1910. The Everleigh Club, the Levee's most famous brothel, was shut down on October 24, 1911, by orders of Mayor Harrison. After constant raiding by the police, the Levee was finally shut down altogether in 1912.

With Coughlin and Kenna's influence waning in the 1920s, a new, more dangerous element gained control of the First Ward—gangsters with names like Colosimo and Torrio were taking over. Even Coughlin's self-proclaimed status as "Chicago's poet alderman" (he had earned a reputation in some circles as at least something of a poet) came under attack when newsman Jack Lait revealed that *Tribune* reporter Jack Kelley, not Coughlin, wrote all his poetry.

Coughlin spent his last years in city hall as a pawn for the bosses of the underworld. Kenna and Coughlin became mere puppets of Al Capone. Most of Coughlin's colleagues from the old days were gone, and the new breed expressed little interest in his incoherent ramblings. For months he lay sick and feeble in the Lexington Hotel. He died on November 8, 1938, with debts from his lavish spending habits totaling $56,000.

See also: Al Capone, Carter Harrison I, Carter Harrison II, Michael "Hinky Dink" Kenna

Further reading: Herman Kogan and Lloyd Wendt, *Lords of the Levee: The Story of Bathhouse John and Hinky Dink* (1943).

John Crerar

Industrialist and Philanthropist

BORN: March 8, 1827
New York, New York

DIED: October 19, 1889
Chicago, Illinois

John Crerar, the Andrew Carnegie of Chicago, made his fortune during the early days of the burgeoning railroad business, but his legacy lives on through his philanthropy.

Born in New York, Crerar was the son of Scottish immigrants and enjoyed a successful business career back East before partnering up in 1856 with another businessman, Morris K. Jesup, who ran a railroad supply company. After the Michigan Southern and Michigan Central Railroads partnered to open a branch of their operations to Chicago, Crerar became manager of the Chicago offices. In 1863 Crerar and J. McGregor Adams established their own firm of Crerar, Adams and Co. as manufacturers and dealers of railroad supplies.

In addition to his business dealings, Crerar also invested in George Pullman's revolutionary sleeping car cabins on trains. When the Pullman Palace Car Company was established in 1867, Crerar was a member of its board of directors. He also served as director of the Chicago and Alton Railway, and held directorships of the London and Globe Insurance Company, the Illinois Trust and Savings Bank, and the Chicago and Joliet Railroad.

A devout Presbyterian, Crerar was an elder and trustee of the Second Presbyterian Church on South Michigan Avenue. He also donated money to the Young Men's Christian Association (YMCA). The Crerar Memorial Presbyterian Church at 8100 South Calumet Avenue and King Drive is named in his honor.

But Crerar is best known today as a philanthropist. Over the years he contributed funds to numerous organizations and institutions, including the Chicago Relief and Aid Society, the Chicago Literary Club, the Chicago Historical Society (now the Chicago History Museum), and the Chicago Bible Society.

A lifelong bachelor, he lived at the Grand Pacific Hotel, which was built after the Chicago Fire of 1871 and located at Clark, LaSalle, Quincy, and Jackson. In September 1889 Crerar suffered a partial stroke. He died the next month. A few days before Christmas a memorial service was held at the downtown Central Music Hall. Many of the city's most prominent citizens attended. He was buried in Greenwood Cemetery, Brooklyn, in the family plot next to his beloved mother, Agnes.

In his will, Crerar bequeathed $2 million to fund the establishment of a library in the city of Chicago. He did not specify what kind of library—only that it be free and bear his name. He also preferred that it be located on the South Side since the city already had the Newberry Library on the North Side. What's more, he requested that it be "tasteful, substantial, and fireproof" and that the books and periodicals "be selected with a view to create and sustain a healthy moral and Christian sentiment." Crerar left no doubt as to what he intended the library to contain—and not contain. And as a Presbyterian Scot, he specifically asked "that all nastiness and immorality be excluded." By this, though, he did not necessarily mean "nothing but hymn books and sermons" but rather that no "dirty French novels and all skeptical trash and works of questionable moral tone" be housed in a library that had his name on it.

Thus, given these limitations, his executors decided that the John Crerar Library would be a library of science and medical books. Established in 1895, the John Crerar Library became one of the greatest research libraries in the United States. It opened its doors two years later on the sixth floor of the Marshall Field Annex at Wabash Avenue and Washington Street, which it occupied until 1920, when it moved to its own building at Randolph Street and Michigan Avenue. Consisting of seven floors, two reading rooms, and commercial space, it remained there until 1961. In 1962 the library moved to the campus of the Illinois Institute of Technology (IIT), where it was housed in a modern structure designed by Skidmore, Owings, and Merrill. A merger agreement signed in April 1981 with the trustees of the University of Chicago led to the construction of a new building for the library on the University of Chicago campus.

Today the John Crerar Library at 5730 South Ellis Avenue on the west side of the science quadrangle is home to more than 1.4 million volumes in the biological, medical, and physical sciences as well as collections in general science and the philosophy and history of science, medicine, and technology. In addition, the John Crerar Collection of Rare Books in the History of Science and Medicine contains nearly 30,000 volumes, including the classic texts of Galileo and Newton, and is permanently housed in the Special Collections Center at the University's Regenstein Library at 110 East 57th Street. In addition to honoring Crerar's memory, the John Crerar Foundation sponsors the annual John Crerar Foundation Science Writing Prize for College Students, rewarding excellence and clarity in science writing.

See also: George Pullman

Further reading: Wayne Rethford and June Skinner Sawyers, *The Scots of Chicago: Quiet Immigrants and Their New Society* (1997).

Richard J. Daley

Politician

BORN: May 15, 1902
Chicago, Illinois

DIED: December 20, 1976
Chicago, Illinois

Richard Joseph Daley ran Chicago for twenty-one years, from 1955 to 1976—longer than any other mayor in Chicago history except his son, Richard M. Daley, who served as mayor for twenty-two years. Indeed, many Chicagoans knew no mayor other than Richard J. Daley. By forging a multiethnic coalition that consisted of the working class, middle class, white ethnics, and African Americans, Daley was able to control city hall for more than two decades. Daley never coveted any higher office, never made any great fortune. He was simply the mayor.

Daley grew up in the ethnically diverse neighborhood of Bridgeport, the son of an Irish American metal worker and union activist father and a suffragist mother. Born at 3602 South Lowe Avenue, he was baptized at Nativity of Our Lord Catholic Church at 37th Street and Union Avenue. He attended a Catholic high school, De La Salle Institute, at 35th Street and Wabash Avenue, and later found work in the nearby stockyards while attending law school at night. In 1933 he graduated from DePaul University, becoming the first member of his family to earn a college degree. A lifelong resident of Bridgeport, Daley continued to reside in a brick bungalow at 3536 South Lowe—one block away from his place of birth—even after winning the mayor's seat.

At twenty-one, Daley became a precinct captain and, a bit later, a clerk in the city council. In 1927 he served as clerk-secretary to Eleventh Ward alderman Joseph P. McDonough, after which he held a variety of positions in local government: secretary to the county treasurer, deputy county comptroller, and ward committeeman. In 1936 Daley, a Democrat, was elected to the Illinois legislature as a write-in Republican when the state representative, David Shanahan, died. After assuming office, however, Daley returned to the Democratic fold. Two years later, he won a seat in the state senate.

In 1946 Daley lost in his bid to become county sheriff—his only defeat—but recuperated sufficiently to be appointed deputy comptroller of Cook County. Three years later, he was named director of the Illinois Department of Finance by Governor Adlai E. Stevenson. In 1950 he was chosen Cook County clerk, and in 1953 he became chairman of the Cook County Democratic Central Committee—a position with considerable clout. Two years later, in 1955, Daley was nominated for mayor of Chicago. He challenged and defeated the incumbent, Martin H. Kennelly, in the Democratic primary and then faced the Republican nominee, Robert E. Merriam, son of the educator and politician Charles E. Merriam. Daley defeated his opponent 708,222 to 581,255.

At the age of fifty-three, the native of Bridgeport had won his first mayoral election.

Daley inherited a political machine. He consolidated his power and extended his party influence to the state and national levels. Indeed, his enthusiastic support of John F. Kennedy for president in 1960 helped elect the New Englander to the White House. Subsequently, Daley became known as a kingmaker. He was reelected in 1959, 1963, 1967, 1971, and 1975.

Daley's longevity was due in no small measure to his ability to compromise. During his years in office, he initiated a massive program of public works, including the construction of O'Hare International Airport, the development of the expressway system, and the launching of extensive urban renewal projects in the Hyde Park–Kenwood, Near North, and Near West Side neighborhoods. He did the basics, too—making sure the streets were cleaned and repaired and the garbage was collected.

In 1968 Chicago and other American cities experienced ugly race riots following the assassination of Martin Luther King Jr. in Memphis. The intensity of the violence prompted Daley to issue his now infamous "shoot to kill" order. During the Democratic convention in August of the same year, the city again was the scene of violent demonstrations, this time between police and anti–Vietnam War demonstrators. Despite criticism from the press, newspaper polls revealed that public opinion supported Daley's hardnosed crackdown.

In 1974 Daley suffered two strokes, yet recovered. During the 1975 reelection campaign, he beat liberal alderman William Singer and black state senator Richard Newhouse in the primaries before easily defeating Republican challenger Forty-Seventh Ward Alderman John J. Hoellen in the general election, winning an unprecedented sixth term in office. Although it proved to be his highest margin of victory—75 percent—it was based on one of the lowest voter turnouts in the city's history.

The various Daley administrations saw their share of scandals over the years, including the notorious Summerdale police scandal of 1960—police officers from the Summerdale district were charged with being part of an extensive burglary ring—but none ever touched Daley personally.

Not known as a great orator, Daley frequently misspoke, often to devastatingly funny (if unintentionally so) effect. Consider these choice Daley malapropisms: "We must rise to ever higher and higher platitudes of achievement"; or "They have vilified me," he said, referring to yet another run-in with the press, "they have crucified me, yes, they have even criticized me"; and perhaps his most famous remark, "Gentlemen, get the thing straight, once and for all: the policeman isn't there to create disorder, the policeman is there to preserve disorder." The quote, however, that best sums up Daley's philosophy was a deceptively simple yet exceedingly wise statement he made in 1955: "As a leader of the Democratic Party of Cook County I pledge to continue a policy based on the principle that good government is good politics—and good politics is good government." His son Richard M. Daley apparently inherited his father's tendency toward malapropisms.

Daley suffered a fatal heart attack while in his doctor's office on December 20, 1976. He was seventy-four. His son Richard M. Daley became mayor in 1989. Like his father, Richard M. Daley was reelected numerous times, eventually serving in office even longer than his father and hence becoming the city's longest-serving mayor. Richard J. Daley's wife, Eleanor "Sis" Daley, died from a stroke at the age of ninety-six on February 16, 2003, in her Bridgeport home. Both are buried in Holy Sepulchre Cemetery in Alsip, as is Richard M. Daley's wife, Maggie Daley.

See also: Anton J. Cermak, Julius J. Hoffman, Edward J. Kelly, Ralph Metcalfe, Harold Washington

Further reading: John M. Allswang, "Richard J. Daley: America's Last Boss" in *The Mayors: The Chicago Political Tradition* (1987), Paul M. Green and Melvin G. Holli, eds.; Roger Biles, *Richard J. Daley: Politics, Race, and the Governing of Chicago* (1995); Adam Cohen and Elizabeth Taylor, *American Pharaoh: Mayor Richard J. Daley—His Battle for Chicago and the Nation* (2001); Bill Gleason, *Daley of Chicago: The Man, the Mayor, and the Limits of Conventional Politics* (1970); Eugene Kennedy, *Himself! The Life and Times of Mayor Richard J. Daley* (1978); Len O'Connor, *Mayor Daley and His City* (1975) and *Requiem: The Decline and Demise of Mayor Daley and His Era* (1977); Milton Rakove, *Don't Make No Waves . . . Don't Back No Losers: An Insider's Analysis of the Daley Machine* (1976); Mike Royko, *Boss: Richard J. Daley of Chicago* (1971).

Arnold Damen

Priest

BORN: March 13, 1815
Leur, Holland

DIED: January 1, 1889
Omaha, Nebraska

Arnold Damen pioneered Catholic education in the frontier town of Chicago. He was the founding father of Holy Family parish, often referred to as the "parish on the prairie." Holy Family was the first Jesuit parish in Chicago.

The seventh of nine children, the Dutch-born Damen was the son of John Damen, a prosperous builder. As a young boy, Damen leaned toward a life in the priesthood. He became determined to follow the path of God after hearing the words of Father Peter DeSmet, a missionary to the Native American community, and Damen offered himself as a candidate for Jesuit missions to America. The forthright and hardworking Damen was accepted. He trained at the village of Florissant, some fifteen miles from St. Louis, and was ordained in 1844 at the age of twenty-nine. After three years assisting in parish work, Damen was appointed the first pastor of St. Francis Xavier's Church in St. Louis, where he stayed for ten years.

Damen, a fellow clergyman noted, was "gifted with uncommon eloquence." He drew crowds to his sermons and became known throughout St. Louis and the state of Missouri. As his reputation spread, Damen was invited to conduct a series of sermons in Chicago. At the request of Bishop Anthony O'Regan, he conducted a mission in Chicago in August 1856 with three other Jesuits, Isidore Boudreaux, Benedict Masselis, and Michael Corbett.

O'Regan invited them to stay and to establish a parish and an educational system. They preferred, however, to form a new parish altogether rather than merely take over Holy Name Church at State and Superior Streets.

Damen acquired property near the intersection of Blue Island Avenue and 12th Street (later called Roosevelt Road) in May 1857 and began building a frame church, Holy Family, at 11th and May Streets—the only Catholic church on the West Side and, indeed, one of the few structures in the neighborhood. Many Jesuits criticized Damen's decision to settle in such a remote location. Nevertheless, the church was dedicated to Bishop James Duggan on July 12, 1857. The early parishioners were hardworking folk—mostly Irish but also of Bohemian and German heritage—who labored in the nearby railroad yards or along the Chicago River, loading and unloading boats or working as mechanics, blacksmiths, bricklayers, and carpenters.

The cornerstone of the present church was laid on August 23, 1857, and was dedicated on August 26, 1860. It was—and still is—a handsome church, said to be the third largest church in the country at that time. The interior was designed by the respected Chicago architect John Van Osdel. The *Chicago Tribune* called it "certainly one of the finest edifices of its class in the United States."

Damen, who was said to know everyone in the parish by name, then went about establishing a comprehensive school system in the parish—the Holy Family Free School for Girls in 1857 and, in the same year, the Holy Family Free School for Boys. In 1860 the Religious of the Sacred Heart order opened a parochial school at Taylor and Lyle Streets. In 1867 Father Damen invited the Sisters of Charity of the Blessed Virgin Mary from Dubuque, Iowa, to teach at the Holy Family parish. That summer they opened two schools, St. Aloysius and St. Stanislaus.

On September 5, 1870, St. Ignatius College, forerunner of Loyola University, opened on West Roosevelt Road with Father Damen acting as the school's first president. The school miraculously survived the Chicago Fire of 1871. While the fire raged outside, Father Damen, so it is said, made a promise at the shrine of Our Lady of Perpetual Help to keep seven lighted candles burning on the altar if the school and church were spared.

Damen served as president of the college until 1872 while retaining his title as pastor of the Holy Family parish. He established parochial schools in the frontier town and tried to instill in his congregation a love of the written word. More importantly, he resolved to preach and bring the word of the Gospel to the poor. Damen was such a dominant force in the community that Holy Family began to be known as simply "Damen's church" and the parish as "Damen's parish."

In 1877 Damen was appointed superior of the missions, headquartered at St. Ignatius College. Two years later, he was appointed pastor of Sacred Heart Church. By the following year, a new four-story brick school had been completed, and by 1890 Holy Family parish had become the largest English-speaking parish in the country.

In 1888 Damen was sent to Creighton College in Omaha, Nebraska. On June 4, 1888, while preaching in Evanston, Wyoming, he suffered a stroke. His condition deteriorated during the following months, and he died in Omaha on New Year's Day 1889. He was seventy-four.

In 1927 Robey Street was renamed Damen Avenue in honor of the clergyman.

In subsequent years, dwindling enrollment and financial hardship took such a heavy toll upon Holy Family that the Jesuit owners reluctantly decided to demolish the structure unless $1 million in cash was raised by a December 31, 1990, deadline. Racing against the clock, the Holy Family Preservation Society mounted a whirlwind eleventh-hour appeal. People from throughout the city, and indeed the country, responded generously, and Holy Family Church was saved from the wrecking ball.

See also: Jacques Marquette, George Mundelein, James Quigley

Further reading: Joseph P. Conroy, *Arnold Damen, S.J.: A Chapter in the Making of Chicago* (1930); Gilbert J. Garraghan, S.J., *The Jesuits of the Middle United States*, 3 vols. (1984); Rev. Msgr. Harry C. Koenig, S.T.D., *A History of the Parishes of the Archdiocese of Chicago*, 2 vols. (1980); George A. Lane and Algimantas Kezys, *Chicago Churches and Synagogues: An Architectural Pilgrimage* (1981); Ellen Skerrett, *Born in Chicago: A History of Chicago's Jesuit University* (2008).

Henry Darger

Artist

BORN: April 12?, 1892
Chicago, Illinois

DIED: April 13, 1973
Chicago, Illinois

An eccentric, obscure, and enigmatic figure during his own lifetime, Henry Darger became known after his death as the quintessential outsider artist. He is now widely recognized as a self-taught genius, a pop culture icon, and as one of the most-celebrated of outsider artists.

Henry Darger was born in 1892 at 350 West 24th Street. When he was four his mother died shortly after giving birth to a daughter. Since his father was impoverished, Darger was placed in a Catholic boys' home, and when his father died in 1905 he was institutionalized in an asylum for "feeble-minded children," to use the terminology of the day, in downstate Lincoln, Illinois. He escaped from the asylum when he was sixteen and made his way back to Chicago, where he found work in a Catholic hospital as a custodian, a job he maintained until he retired—aside from a brief stint in the army during World War I.

Descriptions of Darger's mental condition vary. He may have suffered from Tourette's syndrome or Attention Deficit Disorder (ADD). Some even suggest he had paranoid schizophrenia while others say he was autistic. Either way, Darger had obsessive habits and behaved oddly. He attended mass daily, often several times a day. He collected garbage, rummaging through trash cans. He wore a dirty overcoat and Scotch-taped glasses. In 1930 he moved into a second floor room at 851 West Webster Avenue in the Lincoln Park neighborhood; he lived there for more than forty years. When, at the age of eighty, he started having difficulty climbing the stairs to his room, his kindly landlords, Nathan and Kiyoko Lerner, helped him move to a charity nursing home. When the Lerners went back to clean Darger's room, they discovered that their quiet neighbor was no ordinary tenant.

Nathan Lerner was a photographer by profession and thus immediately recognized the quality of Darger's work. Darger left behind nearly 300 large-scale watercolor paintings, several hundred drawings and other watercolor paintings, and a 15,145-page manuscript with the unwieldy title *The Story of the Vivian Girls, in What Is Known as the Realms of the Unreal, of the Glandeco-Angelinnian War Storm, Caused by the Child Slave Rebellion*. Set in an imaginary Christian land, the epic tale and religious parable tells the story of three prepubescent Catholic girls on another planet who lead an uprising against the godless empire of the Glandelinians, males who want to enslave and kill children.

He also left behind *The History of My Life*, an eight-volume, 5,084-page autobiography; a ten-year daily weather journal; diaries; and another work of fiction called *Crazy Horse: Further Adventures in Chicago*, which consisted of more than 10,000 handwritten pages.

Darger's scroll-like paintings were originally bound in volumes often as wide as nine feet. He traced his images from books, popular magazines, newspapers, comic books, and various other sources, transferring the images using carbon paper and thus producing a collage-like look. Ken Johnson has described his style as an "eccentric, old-fashioned children's picture-book style." Darger was a mystifying amalgamation: William Blake meets Wizard of Oz meets Joseph Gould (Gould was the homeless twentieth-century Greenwich Villager who was said to be writing an oral history of the world).

Initially, Darger's first paintings sold for a few hundred dollars. Then word got out, and interest grew. Subsequently, the Lerners began to publicize his work, taking on the role of agents, and donating his works to various museums devoted to outsider art. They even contributed to the 2004 documentary on Darger, *In the Realms of the Unreal*.

Darger died a day short of his 81st birthday in April 1973. He was buried in All Saints Cemetery in Des Plaines, Illinois.

Since his death, references to Darger have frequently appeared in pop culture. Songs have been written about him by artists as diverse as Natalie Merchant and Sufjan Stevens. The poet John Ashbery published a book-length poem about him, *Girls on the Run*, in 1999 (inspired by Darger's *Vivian Girls* tale). He has been referred to in opera and ballet, and even *The Simpsons* television program referenced him in an episode when Lisa Simpson visited the Darger exhibit at the American Folk Art Museum (in 2001 the museum opened a Henry Darger Study Center).

When Darger's apartment was demolished in 2000, the Lerners gave many of Darger's belongings to the Chicago-based Intuit: The Center for Intuitive and Outsider Art. In January 2008, Intuit created the permanent Henry Darger Room Collection, which consists of a replica of his actual living and working space and includes Darger's tracings, clippings from newspapers and magazines, comic books, cartoons, children's books, coloring books, personal documents, and architectural fixtures and furnishings.

Darger's work is also included in the permanent collections of the Museum of Modern Art, the Art Institute of Chicago, the Museum of Contemporary Art, the New Orleans Museum of Art, and the Milwaukee Art Museum. In 2008 New York's American Folk Art Museum presented "Dargerism: Contemporary Artists and Henry Darger," an exhibition that explored the influence of Darger's work on contemporary artists.

See also: Gertrude Abercrombie, Roger Brown, Ed Paschke

Further reading: Brooke Davis Anderson, *Darger: The Henry Darger Collection at the American Folk Art Museum* (2001); Michael Bonesteel, ed., *Henry Darger: Art and Selected Writings* (2000); Ken Johnson, "An Insider Perspective on an Outsider Artist," *New York Times*, April 18, 2008; John M. MacGregor, *Henry Darger: In the Realms of the Unreal* (2002).

Other resources: *In the Realms of the Unreal* (2004), a documentary about Henry Darger, directed by Jessica Yu.

Clarence Darrow

Lawyer

BORN: April 18, 1857
Kinsman, Ohio

DIED: March 13, 1938
Chicago, Illinois

Clarence Seward Darrow, a magnificent orator and life-long dissenter, defended unpopular causes and handled the most sensational trials of his day. A celebrity lawyer during a time when the profession was populated by faceless figures in sterile courtrooms, Darrow befriended the poor, the weak, the powerless, the disenfranchised, and the forgotten.

Born in northeastern Ohio, Darrow came from a family of freethinkers. His father was an agnostic and an ardent abolitionist as well as the village cabinetmaker, furniture dealer, and undertaker. Darrow studied at Allegheny College and at the University of Michigan Law School. Admitted to the bar in 1878, he practiced law in northeastern Ohio. Several years of practicing small-town law, though, convinced him to move to a bigger city.

In 1888, Darrow arrived in Chicago, where he met a fellow liberal thinker and judge, John Peter Altgeld. Darrow had greatly admired Altgeld's impassioned critique, *Our Penal Machinery and Its Victims,* which urged prison reform. The two men became fast friends and eventual business associates. Later Darrow formed a partnership with the lawyer and poet Edgar Lee Masters.

In 1890 Darrow was appointed assistant corporation counsel for the city. He resigned to become general counsel for the Chicago and Northwestern Railway and then left in 1895 to defend Eugene Debs in the Pullman Strike trial. The trial was a turning point in Darrow's career. "The decision to defend Debs led me away from the world of wealth to that of wretchedness and misery," he wrote later. "For making it I have no regrets."

In 1902 Darrow was elected to the Illinois House of Representatives on the Public Ownership ticket, an independent party that advocated public ownership of the city's streetcar lines. He served one term. By this time Darrow had gained a national reputation as a labor lawyer. He represented miners in the anthracite (coal) strike of 1902 in Pennsylvania and, in 1907, successfully defended William D. Haywood, who was accused of the murder of former Idaho governor Frank Steunenberg. In 1911 he defended the McNamara brothers, siblings accused of bombing the *Los Angeles Times* building in a labor dispute that ultimately killed twenty innocent workers. Darrow once again emerged victorious but, in the process, he himself was accused of jury tampering. Although acquitted, the experience devastated him to such an extent that it took some time for the famed attorney to get back on his feet again. He returned to Chicago in 1913, in his words, "pretty near done."

Darrow's biggest case came in 1924. Nathan Leopold and Richard Loeb were teenage sons of prominent Chicagoans; they kidnapped and murdered fourteen-year-old Bobby Franks for "kicks." Loeb, seventeen, had long wanted to commit the "perfect crime." He persuaded his friend Leopold, a year older, to assist. While the public clamored for the death penalty, Darrow pleaded for mercy. He avoided a trial by jury by pleading that the defendants were guilty. Then he argued before the judge that they were too young to be executed and that their behavior was swayed—indeed, distorted—by the teachings of the nineteenth-century German philosopher Friedrich Nietzsche, who challenged the foundations of Christianity and traditional morality. "It is hardly fair," Darrow maintained, "to hang a 19-year-old boy for the philosophy that was taught him at the university." In the end, he won. On September 10, 1924, the court sentenced the defendants to life imprisonment.

The Leopold and Loeb case has been an inspiration for numerous movies and plays. Among the most notable are Meyer Levin's novel *Compulsion* (1956) and its movie adaptation three years later, John Logan's play *Never the Sinner* (1988), Tom Kalin's film *Swoon* (1992), and Stephen Dolginoff's quirky off-Broadway musical, *Thrill Me: The Leopold and Loeb Story* (2005).

Another sensational case associated with Darrow was the infamous Scopes "monkey trial." In 1925 a twenty-four-year-old Tennessee schoolteacher, John T. Scopes, was indicted and charged with a misdemeanor for teaching Charles Darwin's theory of evolution in a public school. The Scopes trial tested the constitutionality of a new "anti-evolution" law that had just passed the Tennessee General Assembly. Broadcast over WGN radio, the landmark case mesmerized Chicago and, indeed, the rest of the country. In one corner stood the "infidel" Darrow on the side of science and free speech; in the other the true believer, William Jennings Bryan, a former statesman and a great orator in his own right. Although the case was later dismissed by a Tennessee court on a technicality, it remains one of the most famous trials in American history.

Early in his career, Darrow opposed the principle of capital punishment. He tried unsuccessfully, for example, to stop the execution of Eugene Prendergast, who was convicted of the assassination of Chicago mayor Carter Harrison I in 1893. Darrow sincerely believed that poverty caused crime and other forms of antisocial behavior. "If everybody had a minimum wage of $50 a day," he said back in 1932, "there would be no crime." Punishment, as such, he deemed an ineffectual way of handling transgressions.

Darrow wrote many novels and essays. Among his books are *An Eye for an Eye* (1905); *Crime, Its Cause and Treatment* (1925); and his autobiography, *The Story of My Life* (1932).

Darrow died of heart disease in March 1938 at his home at 1537 East 60th Street, overlooking the bridge over the Jackson Park lagoon. He was eighty years old. Funeral services were held in the Bond Chapel on the University of Chicago campus, and his ashes were scattered in the lagoon. On May 1, 1957, the bridge was dedicated as the Clarence Darrow Bridge in his honor. Every year a wreath-laying ceremony is held commemorating the life of the celebrated lawyer.

Such a larger-than-life figure couldn't help but attract the attention of Hollywood producers and screenwriters. Several actors, including Spencer Tracy in *Inherit the Wind*, portrayed Darrow on the big screen, while Henry Fonda played the lawyer on the stage in a popular one-man show during the 1970s.

The Clarence Darrow Digital Collection is housed at the University of Minnesota Law School.

See also: John Peter Altgeld, Eugene Debs, Meyer Levin, Henry Demarest Lloyd, Edgar Lee Masters

Further reading: Simon Baatz, *For the Thrill of It: Leopold, Loeb, and the Murder That Shocked Jazz Age Chicago* (2009); Clarence Darrow, *The Story of My Life* (1932); John A. Farrell, *Clarence Darrow: Attorney for the Damned* (2011); Andrew E. Kersten, *Clarence Darrow: American Iconoclast* (2011); John Logan, *Never the Sinner: The Leopold and Loeb Story* (1999); Irving Stone, *Clarence Darrow for the Defense* (1941); Kevin Tierney, *Darrow: A Biography* (1979); Arthur Weinberg, ed., *Attorney for the Damned: Clarence Darrow in the Courtroom* (1957); Arthur Weinberg and Lila Weinberg, *Clarence Darrow: A Sentimental Rebel* (1980).

Charles Gates Dawes

Politician

BORN: August 27, 1865
Marietta, Ohio

DIED: April 23, 1951
Evanston, Illinois

Charles Gates Dawes served as comptroller of the currency during the McKinley administration and as vice president of the United States under Calvin Coolidge from 1925 to 1929. But more than this, Dawes was a lawyer, banker, diplomat, soldier, statesman, and philanthropist, something of a Renaissance man who scorned convention and despised pomposity in all its forms.

Among his other achievements, Dawes served as brigadier general during World War I; was the first director of the federal budget in 1921; developed the Dawes Plan, for which he was awarded the Nobel Peace Prize in 1925; served as ambassador to Great Britain from 1929 to 1932; and acted as the finance chairman of the 1933 Chicago World's Fair.

Dawes came from a long line of military men. The son of a Civil War general, he was a descendant of William Dawes, who made the famous midnight ride with Paul Revere to warn the Americans of the British advance. Dawes spent his boyhood in the river town of Marietta, Ohio, and at age nineteen he received a bachelor of arts degree from Marietta College. He then attended the Cincinnati Law School, was admitted to the Ohio bar, and moved to Lincoln, Nebraska, to set up a law practice.

In 1894 he left the legal profession and entered the natural gas supply business, first in La Crosse, Wisconsin, and then in Evanston, Illinois. Two years later he entered politics and campaigned for presidential hopeful William McKinley. His business acumen did not go unnoticed, for when McKinley won the election he appointed Dawes, at age thirty-one, comptroller of the currency.

In 1902 Dawes made his first try for elected office, running for the Republican nomination for the Illinois senate, but he was decisively beaten. His political curiosity satisfied, he returned to banking and established the Central Trust Company. During World War I, Dawes joined the army, earned the rank of major in the Corps of Engineers, and was given the responsibility of purchasing supplies for the American Expeditionary Force in Europe. In this capacity he was especially good at cutting through government bureaucracy. Later he was appointed brigadier general under General John J. Pershing. In 1923 he authored the Dawes Plan, an ambitious attempt to rebuild Europe and to collect German reparations. For this he was awarded the Nobel Peace Prize in 1925, sharing it with Sir Austen Chamberlain, British foreign secretary.

After returning to the United States, Dawes was appointed the first director of the budget under President Warren G. Harding. His career improved considerably in 1924 when Calvin Coolidge chose him as his vice-presidential running mate. Dawes spent most of his time on the campaign trail attacking the Ku Klux Klan. In 1929 President Herbert Hoover made Dawes ambassador to Great Britain.

As ambassador, he caused a minor diplomatic row when he refused to wear knee breeches at the Court of St. James.

Dawes retired from public life in 1932 and returned to Chicago to help his brother Rufus organize the Century of Progress Exposition for the 1933 world's fair. He was then appointed the first chairman of the Reconstruction Finance Corporation, which attempted to restore financial stability in Europe. He resigned when he discovered that the Central Trust Company he had founded was encountering financial difficulties. Always an outspoken statesman, the old soldier opposed American involvement in World War II.

Dawes wrote eight books on banking and government, including *The Banking System in the United States, Journal of the Great War*, and *First Year of the Budget*. His personal fortune, derived from banking and public utilities, was reportedly one of Chicago's largest.

Dawes married Carol Blymyer in 1888. In 1912 their only son, Rufus, drowned. In 1913 Dawes built a $100,000 hotel for the homeless at 12 South Peoria Street in Chicago as a memorial to his son.

Dawes lived in a twenty-eight-room mansion at 225 Greenwood Street in Evanston from 1909 until his death in 1951. The mansion is now maintained by the Evanston Historical Society and was declared a National Historic Landmark in December 1976. It is open to the public.

Further reading: Bascom N. Timmons, *Portrait of an American: Charles G. Dawes* (1953).

Eugene Debs

Labor Activist

BORN: November 5, 1855
Terre Haute, Indiana

DIED: October 20, 1926
Elmhurst, Illinois

Eugene Victor Debs, the foremost leader of the American socialist movement, began his public life as a Democrat. He earned the Socialist Party's nomination for president on four occasions (and the Social Democratic Party's once) and traveled the country speaking on many controversial subjects: women's rights, equality for blacks, birth control, and child labor. An outspoken foe of capitalism, Debs spent his entire life fighting against what he considered the tyranny of corporations, who judged employees solely in terms of their profit value.

Debs came from a close-knit French family who had settled in the largely French community of Terre Haute, Indiana. He quit school at fourteen to work for the railroad, scraping paint and grease from locomotives. Laid off during the recession of 1873, he tried to find work in Evansville, Indiana, but when he did not succeed there, he went to St. Louis, where he was hired as a locomotive fireman. The death of a friend in a locomotive accident and the prodding of his mother, who feared for his safety, convinced Debs to abandon railroading altogether in 1874. He returned to Terre Haute and took a job as a loader at a wholesale grocery company.

In 1875 Debs joined his first labor union, the Brotherhood of Locomotive Firemen. He was elected city clerk of Terre Haute, and in 1884 he won a seat in the Indiana House of Representatives. During his term there he supported various civil rights measures, including a bill to abolish race discrimination and one that extended suffrage to women. Both bills were defeated. Not willing to compromise his ideals, he decided not to seek reelection. In 1893 Debs was one of the founders of the American Railway Union (ARU), and he later became its president. "Labor," he said, "can organize, it can unify, it can consolidate its forces. This done, it can demand and command."

A devastating war broke out between capital and labor in 1893 and 1894. There were many skirmishes across the land, but the eyes of the nation were focused on Illinois. The battle was fought in the company town of Pullman, with Eugene Debs acting as the ARU's field commander. For this reason, the Pullman boycott of 1894 was nicknamed "The Debs Rebellion."

Pullman was portrayed by the popular press as a model community run by a benevolent and just manager. In reality, George Pullman was hardly the kind figure he was made out to be. In 1893 a severe economic depression gripped the nation. In order to maintain the company goal of a six percent profit, Pullman dismissed workers and cut their wages but refused to lower their rents. The workers grew angrier and more resentful. Meanwhile, Pullman remained in his plush Prairie Avenue mansion, unyielding and implacable in his resolve to weather the storm.

In May 1894 the workers voted to strike despite an injunction forbidding it. Pullman was adamant. He refused to talk with the ARU. In retaliation, Debs ordered the ARU's 150,000 members not to handle any Pullman cars or equipment although he did caution them to avoid violence. Debs's defiance landed him in the McHenry County

Jail in Woodstock, Illinois, under the charge that he had conspired to obstruct the mails. It would not be the last time he served a jail sentence. The strike ended in July, and, for the moment, Pullman emerged victorious.

For a brief period in his life, Debs supported the Populist Party (a profarmer, proworker party popular in the 1890s), but finding it an inadequate answer to the inequities of American society, he abandoned capitalism altogether and converted to socialism. On June 10, 1898, the Social Democracy of America party met in Chicago. Its manifesto called for the public ownership of all industries controlled by monopolies and trusts, the public ownership of all railroads, national insurance for workers against accidents and unemployment, and the replacement of war with international arbitration. Several years later—on June 27, 1905—a new industrial union was formed, also in Chicago. The members, who included Debs, William Haywood, Lucy Parsons, and "Mother" Jones, called themselves the Industrial Workers of the World (IWW).

Despite Debs's leadership, the Socialist Party in America was in trouble from the start. Its direction was unclear, its goals wavered, and the radical ideology that occasionally surfaced clashed with that of the more conservative members. On June 16, 1918, at the Ohio Socialists' state convention in Canton, Ohio, Debs delivered a speech urging workers to oppose the war effort. A government reporter in the audience zealously wrote down the labor leader's every word and gesture. Debs was arrested on June 30, 1918, and indicted for violation of the Espionage Act.

The trial began in Cleveland that September. The jury deliberated for six hours and found him guilty.

Despite Debs's confinement in an Atlanta penitentiary, the members of the National Socialist Convention in New York renominated him for a fifth term as president of the union. As time went on, more and more petitions for Debs's release arrived on the desk of President Woodrow Wilson. Many feared that the feeble sixty-five year old man might die in prison. Wilson, however, denied parole. It wasn't until Warren G. Harding took office that the labor leader was freed, on Christmas Day in 1921. He had spent almost three years in jail.

After his release, despite rheumatism, kidney trouble, and heart problems, Debs continued to speak and write on behalf of socialism. In September 1926 he checked into the Lindlahr Sanitarium in west suburban Elmhurst, Illinois, hoping to regain his health. But his condition deteriorated and by mid-October he lapsed into a coma. The man who abhorred poverty, had an abiding faith in the sanctity of human fellowship, and served as an inspiring role model for a generation of labor leaders died on October 20, 1926. He was eulogized from Chicago to Moscow.

See also: John Peter Altgeld, Clarence Darrow, William "Big Bill" Haywood, Henry Demarest Lloyd, Lucy and Albert Parsons

Further reading: Bernard J. Brommel, *Eugene V. Debs: Spokesman for Labor and Socialism* (1978); William H. Carwardine, *The Pullman Strike* (1973); Ray Ginger, *Altgeld's America: The Lincoln Ideal Versus Changing Realities* (1958) and *The Bending Cross: A Biography of Eugene Victor Debs* (1949).

Floyd Dell

Writer and Editor

BORN: June 28, 1887
Barry, Illinois

DIED: July 23, 1969
Bethesda, Maryland

Dell cut a dashing figure in early twentieth-century Chicago. As editor of the influential *Friday Literary Review,* he furthered the careers of Sherwood Anderson, Robert Herrick, Vachel Lindsay, and other local writers. He hired a number of book reviewers who would become famous authors in their own right, including Fanny Butcher, later the *Chicago Tribune's* literary critic, and Margaret C. Anderson, founder of the *Little Review* magazine.

Before he was twenty-five, Dell was already editor of and chief contributor to the *Friday Literary Review,* a supplement of the *Chicago Evening Post.* Cosmopolitan in approach, the *Review* was distributed nationally, which helped put Chicago on the national literary map and was instrumental in the Chicago literary renaissance. In his articles and essays—he was a prodigious contributor to the publication—Dell took great pleasure in defying literary convention as much as he could.

Dell was ahead of his time. His first book, *Women as World Builders: Studies in Modern Feminism* (1913), consisted of essays on leading figures of early twentieth-century feminism. But he was also a paradox: he was a womanizer who supported women's rights. With his wife, Margery Currey, a schoolteacher, he hosted a salon that was one of the most popular bohemian gatherings in the city. First on Morse Avenue in Rogers Park and then at the corner of Stony Island Avenue and 57th Street in Jackson Park, the salon attracted writers, poets, journalists, and artists, including

Margaret Anderson, Harriet Monroe, Carl Sandburg, Vachel Lindsay, Edgar Lee Masters, and Sherwood Anderson. According to his biographer Douglas Clayton, Dell and Currey practiced an unconventional marriage: they divided their tasks more or less equally and handled financial matters jointly. "I was assistant cook and bottle-washer," Dell remarked, "expert in making a salad, lobster Newburg, and other dishes—I was assistant home-maker."

The Dell salon had its heyday in Rogers Park in 1909 and 1910, but flourished briefly in Jackson Park when the Dells moved there in early 1913. The salon played a significant role in what was known as the Jackson Park arts colony, which consisted of an entire block on both sides of 57th Street near the Illinois Central Railroad and then toward Stony Island Avenue. Artists and writers moved into the one-story buildings that were left over from the 1893 World's Fair and converted the spaces into cheap studios ($12 a month) and living quarters. In addition to Dell, other residents included the University of Chicago economist and social critic Thorstein Veblen, and painter Bror Nordfeldt (his portrait of Dell is in the Newberry Library), as well as an assortment of painters, sculptors, writers, musicians, and dancers. The fragile buildings were demolished in the 1960s.

Dell moved to New York in October 1913, settling in Greenwich Village, and joined the staffs of two leftist publications, *The Masses* and *The Liberator*. His defense of conscientious objectors during World War I led to the suppression of *The Masses* and his indictment, in 1917, under the Sedition Act. The charges were later dropped.

A brief experience with psychoanalysis around 1918 allowed him to finish *Moon-Calf* (1920), his best-known work, which he was writing in fits and starts, and it even seemed to keep his personal life in check as he settled down, marrying B. Marie Gage in 1919 (he had divorced Currey in late 1915). He had outgrown his "vagabonding" phase, as he called it. He moved out of Greenwich Village and settled in Croton-on-Hudson.

Dell published eleven novels, although his first, *Moon-Calf*, was the best received. In addition, he wrote *Were You Ever a Child?* (1919), which was his response to John Dewey's theories on education. In 1935, his twelfth novel was rejected by his publisher as being out of touch with the times. To keep himself afloat, he accepted a job in the Works Progress Administration. He remained there until he retired in 1947. He also wrote several plays and an autobiography, *Homecoming* (1933). He died in 1969 at the age of eighty-two.

The Floyd Dell Papers are housed at the Newberry Library in Chicago.

See also: Margaret C. Anderson, Fannie Butcher

Further reading: Douglas Clayton, *Floyd Dell: The Life and Times of an American Rebel* (1994); Floyd Dell, *Intellectual Vagabondage* (1990).

Oscar De Priest

Politician

BORN: March 9, 1871
Florence, Alabama

DIED: May 12, 1951
Chicago, Illinois

Oscar Stanton De Priest was a popular figure in Chicago's African American community and one of its most powerful politicians. A Republican, De Priest became the first black alderman in Chicago, the first black Cook County commissioner, and the first African American elected to Congress from a northern state. This latter victory proved a landmark in the history of the black community, inspiring other African Americans across the country to follow his example.

Born in rural Alabama, De Priest received his education in the Salinas, Kansas, public school system. At the age of seventeen he ran away with two friends to Dayton, Ohio. He eventually settled in Chicago in the 1890s where he found work as a house painter. He entered politics as a candidate for county commissioner in the early 1900s and served two terms on the county board before being defeated for reelection in 1908.

For many years the city's white power structure thwarted the ambitions of black politicians. White bosses such as Martin Madden and George Harding ruled over predominantly black wards. As black people became more vociferous, however, and began demanding representation in their neighborhoods, the Republican organization could no longer ignore them. Succumbing to this pressure, party leaders nominated De Priest for alderman of the Second Ward in 1915. He won the election.

In 1916 De Priest garnered tremendous support from the black community when he introduced a civil rights ordinance in the Chicago City Council. It was a valiant try but clearly ahead of its time, for it was loudly ridiculed and soundly defeated. Black politicians still bowed to the wishes

of the white bosses instead of serving the needs of their own people. In this regard, De Priest was a typical politician. Indeed, his critics found his voting record particularly deficient. The Municipal Voters' League, a watchdog group whose aim was to rid the city council of corrupt aldermen, censured De Priest and charged that he voted against virtually every reform bill that came his way. "No alderman in Chicago's history (has) piled up a more notorious record in so short a time," they said, and they described him as "a colored politician who for years has been used by white politicians to line up colored votes; has considerable force and ability, but is thoroughly self-seeking."

Further controversy followed De Priest in 1917 when he was indicted for accepting payoffs from gamblers and for bribing police officers. The embattled alderman insisted that the alleged payoffs were, in fact, campaign contributions and charged that he was the victim of racism. Thanks to the brilliant defense of his lawyer, Clarence Darrow, De Priest was acquitted, but his reputation was severely damaged. He decided to sit out the 1917 aldermanic race. The next year, though, he was ready to make a comeback.

Party leaders, however, wanted no part of his plan, and they chose to support another African American, Robert R. Jackson. Despite De Priest's popularity with black voters, who still considered him a hero and their friend, Jackson won by a narrow margin. In a bold move that presaged the tactics of a later generation of black politicians, De Priest formed an independent party—the People's Movement, which preached racial pride and solidarity—and ran against Jackson in the general election. He still failed to win.

De Priest maintained a low profile until 1928 when he successfully gained the congressional seat from the First District. As congressman, he tentatively championed civil rights. He fought against Jim Crow and sought to enact a national anti-lynching law. De Priest was reelected to Congress in 1930 and 1932. In 1934, however, he was defeated by the Democratic candidate, Arthur W. Mitchell. De Priest continued to serve as Republican committeeman and regained his aldermanic seat in 1943, this time in the Third Ward, but lost it again in 1947.

In January 1951 De Priest was knocked down by a Chicago Motor Coach bus while crossing an intersection near his home. He died several months later in Provident Hospital. He was buried in Graceland Cemetery.

See also: Ralph Metcalfe, William Hale Thompson, Harold Washington

Further reading: St. Clair Drake and Horace R. Cayton, *Black Metropolis: A Study of Negro Life in a Northern City* (1962); Harold F. Gosnell, *Negro Politicians: The Rise of Negro Politics in Chicago* (1935); Allan H. Spear, *Black Chicago: The Making of a Negro Ghetto, 1890–1920* (1967); Dempsey J. Travis, *An Autobiography of Black Politics* (1987).

Leon Despres

Politician

BORN: February 2, 1908
Chicago, Illinois

DIED: May 6, 2009
Chicago, Illinois

The lone wolf of Chicago politics, Leon Despres was known as the conscience of the Chicago City Council. He represented Hyde Park as the alderman of the Fifth Ward from 1955 to 1975.

A South Sider of French-Jewish heritage, Despres's father was in the clothing business but died when he, Despres, was still a boy. After his father's death, his mother took him to Italy and France. Returning to Chicago, he graduated from the University of Chicago and the school's law school. In 1929 he began practicing law, representing labor unions during the Depression.

Despres had a love-hate relationship with the University of Chicago. Although it gave him a strong educational foundation, he fought the administration on civil rights and housing grounds. As urban decay encroached on the Hyde Park neighborhood, the university began gobbling up more and more property and sponsored an urban renewal program that Despres felt priced poor African Americans out of their own neighborhood.

Despres was elected alderman from the Fifth Ward in 1955. As alderman, he had big shoes to fill—his predecessor was Senator Paul H. Douglas. But Despres was a worthy successor. His causes were many—fighting segregation; supporting women's rights, architectural preservation, and fair elections; and ending patronage. He fought so-called restrictive residential covenants, a legal technique that fostered racial segregation in the 1940s and was, essentially, a blatant attempt to keep blacks out of white areas of Hyde Park. Sometimes his reform efforts led to unintentionally humorous encounters. One December, he offered resolutions against gender discrimination, which prompted the mayor to cry, "Let's not discuss sex at Christmastime."

Despres's voice often was the most radical in the room and just as often the lone voice against racism in the city council. He was known as "the only Negro in the city council" at a time when the council, in the 1950s, had six African American members. Black aldermen were often loyal to Mayor Richard J. Daley and helped to maintain the status quo. But this didn't stop Despres from making his objections quite vocal. Consequently, Daley frequently turned his microphone off, which only encouraged him to speak louder for those who he felt had no voice.

Although Despres lost more battles than he won, he never stopped trying. Much of what he once fought for has now come to pass or, at least, has come closer to fruition. He learned to be patient. He knew that, eventually, he would get his way, if indirectly. Everyone knew who originated the bills; his opposition just conveniently chose to ignore them. Thus, legislation sponsored by Despres was defeated only to be passed later by Daley loyalists.

Despres also served on the Chicago Planning Commission and, under Mayor Harold Washington, as city council parliamentarian.

Despres continued to practice law until a few years before he died at the age of 101. He even wrote an online diary for the web magazine *Slate*. In early 2008 at a downtown law office, several friends, including former senator Adlai Stevenson, former U.S. attorney general Tom Sullivan, and former Illinois comptroller Dawn Clark Netsch, honored Leon Despres with a 100th birthday party by placing him on mock trial for heresy and sedition. Among the charges: that he felt the city was ready for reform and conspiring to take down the Chicago machine.

Despres gleefully pled guilty on both counts.

Despres died of heart failure in his Hyde Park apartment in 2009 at the grand old age of 101.

See also: Richard J. Daley, Harold Washington

Further reading: Leon Despres and Kenan Heise, *Challenging the Daley Machine: A Chicago Alderman's Memoir* (2005); Rebecca Janowitz, *Culture of Opportunity: Obama's Chicago; The People, Politics, and Ideas of Hyde Park* (2010).

William E. Dever

Politician

BORN: March 13, 1862
Woburn, Massachusetts

DIED: September 3, 1929
Chicago, Illinois

By all accounts William Emmett Dever was considered a good man, a highly respected man. And when he became mayor of Chicago in 1923, he had nothing but the people's best wishes. Encouraged by this sincere display of goodwill and support, he set about putting Chicago on course. He sponsored massive public works, revitalized public services, and fought an unrelenting battle to rid the city of bootleggers. What's more, his administration had no hint of scandal—a remarkable achievement for a city that took peculiar pride in its flaws. These accomplishments made Dever a subject of admiration throughout the world, and in his own country it earned him the accolade of America's best mayor. From coast to coast he became known as the man who "cleaned up" Chicago. Yet despite these considerable accomplishments—or, perhaps, because of them—he only served one term, from 1923 to 1927, losing his bid for reelection to his nemesis, William Hale Thompson. To this day Dever is probably the least-remembered of Chicago's twentieth-century mayors.

Dever was educated in the Woburn, Massachusetts, public school system. At fourteen, after one year of high school,

he entered the family tannery. After five years of working for his father, he moved to Boston, and then spent two years on the road. On a business trip to Olean, New York, he met Kate Conway, whom he later married, and the two settled in Boston. One day Kate noticed a newspaper clipping that claimed Chicago tanners could make good money—as much as $24 per week. The ad piqued her husband's interest.

The couple arrived in Chicago in 1887, and Dever began work at a tannery on Goose Island while going to law school at night. Following his graduation from the Chicago College of Law in 1890, he began his own law practice. He later attended discussion groups at the Chicago Commons settlement house. Its president, Graham Taylor, liked the young man and tried to persuade him to run for alderman. Dever gently refused the offer, but after much prodding he finally agreed. He lost the election in 1900 but ran again two years later and was elected alderman from the Seventeenth Ward.

Dever soon earned a reputation as one of the city council's most hardworking and well-respected members. He built parks, installed public baths, and improved the streets of his ward. In 1910 he was elected judge of the Superior Court of Cook County and was reelected in 1916 and 1922.

Dever enjoyed his status as a judge. In 1911 he and his family moved into a new apartment at 708 West Buena Avenue in what was then fashionable Uptown. Four years later he purchased a brick three-flat at 5901 North Kenmore Avenue in Edgewater.

With the exception of the fraud trial of former Illinois Senator William Lorimer, most of the cases Dever handled were routine and hardly newsworthy. In 1916, while still a sitting trial judge, Dever was appointed to the Illinois Appellate Court for the First District, an influential position, where he heard appeals from lower court decisions. In early 1903 George Brennan, chairman of the Democratic Party, chose Dever as the mayoral candidate with the best chance to defeat the incumbent, William Hale Thompson, in the upcoming campaign.

With his impeccable credentials and liberal tendencies, Dever became the darling of reformers and independents. "Chicago needs a mayor who has the courage to say 'no' and say it to all his best friends," Clarence Darrow declared. Unable to withstand the pressure, Thompson eventually withdrew from the race, and Dever, backed by the full force of the Democratic party, easily defeated the Republican candidate, Arthur C. Leuder.

Dever's first days in office were jovial and imbued with a great spirit. He wanted to be remembered, he said, as the mayor who did "something big, something worthwhile" for the city. He wasted no time in assembling a strong cabinet—Francis X. Busch, dean of the DePaul University Law School, was named corporation counsel, and social reformer Mary McDowell was appointed welfare commissioner. He filled the school board with his own appointees, a largely progressive group; and he chose a new police chief, Morgan A. Collins, who had a reputation as an honest cop and who promised to bring discipline and integrity back to the department.

Dever's term was full of public works accomplishments. Under his leadership Wacker Drive was completed; the northern section of Ogden Avenue was extended; Ashland and Western Avenues were widened; Union Station was opened; the Chicago River was straightened; the South Water Street market was improved; and the city's first airport, Municipal Airport (later renamed Midway) was built. A major disappointment was his failure to solve the city's protracted public transportation problem. Dever fought for municipal ownership of the city's bus and rapid transit lines, at that time privately owned, but his measures were overwhelmingly defeated in a public referendum.

Dever devoted a large part of his time to combating the bootleggers and gangsters who threatened to take over the city. Although he described himself as "wet," he made it his business to enforce the Prohibition laws and thereby unwittingly caused his own downfall. "It's the law. What else can I do but enforce it?" he explained in an address delivered to the Chicago Bar Association.

Dever's initial attempts to crush the bootleggers met with success. The media labeled it "The Great Beer War." It made the mayor something of a national celebrity. The police raided saloons and nightclubs, shut down breweries, suppressed the bootlegging trade, and revoked thousands of licenses. The people supported his efforts, and, for a time, crime subsided. But the truce was short-lived. By 1925 Chicago was in the middle of a full-fledged gang war. Not only were crime statistics on the rise, but the crimes were more vicious and daring than ever. Chicagoans who opened their newspapers in the morning were greeted with reports of shootouts on downtown streets in broad daylight, of robberies at elegant hotels, and of murders of public officials. Dever's political career was one of the casualties.

The last two years of his term were spent trying to stem the tide of gangster violence. Still, the violence escalated. Although Dever admitted in 1926 before Senate hearings on Prohibition that "the great experiment" was a "tremendous mistake," he still believed he had no choice but to try to enforce the law.

Democratic Party leaders and prominent citizens persuaded Dever to run against William Thompson for a second term. Out of a sense of duty, he agreed. "Big Bill" Thompson, forever the street fighter in tune with the pulse of the voters, promised to return Chicago to its "wide open" status.

Dever lost by 83,000 votes, and the nation, unfamiliar with Chicago's brand of politics, was understandably stunned. Dever, for one, was glad to leave. "I have always felt that being mayor was a four-year job," he said. "Any man faithfully performing the duties of the office must be prepared to serve only a single term."

Dever accepted the position of vice president of the Bank of America but was forced to leave due to illness. He died of cancer in 1929 only two years after leaving office.

See also: Al Capone, Mary McDowell, William Hale Thompson

Further reading: Paul M. Green and Melvin G. Holli, eds., *The Mayors: The Chicago Political Tradition* (1987); Melvin G. Holli and Peter d'A. Jones, eds., *The Biographical Dictionary of American Mayors, 1820–1980: Big City Mayors* (1981); Frederick F. Rex, *The Mayors of the City of Chicago* (1934); John R. Schmidt, *"The Mayor Who Cleaned Up Chicago": A Political Biography of William E. Dever* (1989).

Earl Dickerson

Businessman and Political Activist

BORN: June 22, 1891
Canton, Mississippi

DIED: September 1, 1986
Chicago, Illinois

Throughout his long life, Earl Dickerson wore many hats. But one theme remained constant: whether serving as alderman—he was Chicago's first elected African American Democratic alderman, representing the Second Ward from 1939 to 1943—lawyer, or businessman, he sought social justice and fought segregationist policies. Known for his civility and sense of decorum, he was also a role model for later generations of ambitious young black professionals, including John H. Johnson.

Born in the small Mississippi town of Canton in 1891, Earl Burrus Dickerson was the grandson of a former slave. An avid reader, Dickerson attended the Canton public school system before fleeing to Chicago in 1907 as a stowaway on an Illinois Central train, "clothed with little else than a burning sense of outrage and a driving resolve," observed biographer Robert J. Blakely. Through hard work and good fortune, he was able to attend various preparatory schools, first in New Orleans and then in Chicago. He attended the Laboratory Schools of the University of Chicago and then the Evanston Academy, the prep school for Northwestern University. The only black student at the Evanston Academy, he graduated in the spring of 1909. That fall he enrolled at Northwestern University, where he took courses in Latin, English, and oratory. Continuing his education, in 1914 he earned a bachelor's degree and teaching certificate at the University of Illinois at Urbana-Champaign. He taught English, debate, and mathematics for a year at the famous Tuskegee Institute in Mississippi under Booker T. Washington.

During World War I, Dickerson received training at a segregated officers' training school. Commissioned as a second lieutenant in the Ninety-Second Division and sent to France, he acted as an interpreter and later commanded an infantry platoon where he saw battle. Returning to Chicago in 1919, he organized the first American Legion post of African American veterans. He then resumed his law school studies and became, in early 1920, the first African American to receive a degree from the University of Chicago Law School.

In 1920 Dickerson was admitted to the Illinois bar. When he tried to find work at various Chicago law firms but was turned down because of racial discrimination, he opened his own private practice with an office located at 184 West Washington Street. Five years later, the National Bar Association (NBA) was organized as a response to the discriminatory practices of the Chicago Bar Association (CBA), which refused to accept blacks. In 1939, Dickerson became the first African American member of the Illinois

State Bar Association. In 1945 he led a movement to integrate the CBA, becoming in that year one of its first African American members. (Dickerson served as president of the NBA in 1945 and 1946.) In addition, he was president of the National Lawyers Guild from 1951 to 1954, the first African American to be so elected. He was also elected to the National Association for the Advancement of Colored People (NAACP) board in 1941 and remained a member until 1971.

Dickerson also played a crucial role in the development of the Chicago Urban League. In 1925 he was elected to its board of directors. By 1936, he became vice president of the league and, three years later, president; he was re-elected in 1940. During his presidency, he was a staunch advocate of fair employment practices, pressuring President Franklin D. Roosevelt to issue an executive order to eliminate discrimination in employment. Dickerson's efforts succeeded: FDR issued the order in June 1941. He was a member of FDR's first Fair Employment Practices Committee.

In the late 1920s Dickerson entered politics. He was a candidate in 1927 for alderman of the Second Ward, which, along with the Third and Fourth Wards, made up the heart of the historic Black Belt. Running as an independent, he lost. In 1939, Dickerson made a successful bid for alderman of the Second Ward when he ran in the primary against two veteran black politicians—William L. Dawson and William E. King—and won the April runoff election.

As alderman, Dickerson made concerted efforts to address the serious housing shortages in the overcrowded Black Belt and attempted to rescind racially restrictive residential covenants. Also while still an alderman, he argued the first case, *Hansberry v. Lee,* against racially restrictive housing covenants before the Supreme Court in 1940. The covenants essentially referred to contracts by property owners who agreed not to sell, rent, or lease to African Americans. In 1937, Carl Hansberry, a real estate broker and board member of the Chicago branch of the NAACP, expressed an interest to Dickerson that he wanted to buy property at 6140 South Rhodes Avenue in the Woodlawn neighborhood. At the time Dickerson was also general counsel of the Supreme Liberty Life Insurance Company, one of the largest African American–owned life insurance companies in the United States. When Hansberry asked to borrow money from Supreme Liberty in order to buy the property, Dickerson informed him that the Woodlawn Property Owners Association, which held a restrictive covenant in the neighborhood, would likely bring the case to court. Unfazed by that daunting prospect, Hansberry agreed he would pursue a lawsuit if it should come to pass. It did. In late 1940, Dickerson argued the *Hansberry v. Lee* case before the Supreme Court. Although Dickerson won on a technicality—for violation of due process—the Hansberry decision set the stage for the subsequent landmark 1948 Supreme Court *Shelley v. Kraemer* case that prohibited judicial enforcement of racially restrictive covenants. The case inspired Carl Hansberry's daughter, Lorraine Hansberry, to write her historic play *A Raisin in the Sun*.

After the Supreme Court decision, and faced with the very real threat of white flight, Dickerson encouraged South Side institutions to remain in their respective South Side neighborhoods. Although George Williams College chose to move to the suburbs, Michael Reese Hospital and the University of Chicago stayed and became strong stabilizing influences promoting integrated communities. Years later, in August 1963, Dickerson continued his social justice battles by taking part in the historic March on Washington for Jobs and Freedom. The following year the Civil Rights Act was passed in Congress.

In 1942 Dickerson ran for Congress but lost to William L. Dawson after a vicious campaign. In 1948 he tried again, running this time on the Progressive Party ticket. He again failed to win but, in 1952, was nevertheless made chairman of the Platform and Resolutions Committee of the Progressive Party.

Dickerson was also a successful businessman. He served as general counsel of the Supreme Liberty Life Insurance Company, at 3517 South Indiana Avenue, the first insurance company owned and operated by African Americans. In 1955 he was elected president of the company.

Dickerson died in September 1986 at the age of 95 in his apartment at 4800 Chicago Beach Drive. He is buried in Burr Oak Cemetery in south suburban Alsip, a village that he helped establish.

See also: Lorraine Hansberry, John H. Johnson

Further reading: Robert J. Blakely with Marcus Shepard, *Earl B. Dickerson: A Voice for Freedom and Equality* (2006).

Bo Diddley

Musician

BORN December 30, 1928
McComb, Mississippi

DIED: June 2, 2008
Archer, Florida

He invented his own name, his own guitar, and his own persona. Along with Chuck Berry and Little Richard, Bo Diddley helped to reshape the sound that would become known as rock and roll, using blues, gospel, and R&B as his foundation. He had a big, booming voice and a guitar known for its distortion and tremolo, which he designed himself. His wisecracking and playful songs came with a forthright cockiness. He was also a great showman with a preference for loud, plaid jackets. What's more, Diddley popularized one of the most enduring rhythms in rock and roll. It even bears his name: the Bo Diddley beat. The name of a song, "Bo Diddley," was also the name of a performer—him.

The man who came to be known as Bo Diddley was born Ellas Otha Bates in Mississippi to a poor farming family. His father died soon after his birth, and his teenage mother handed him over to the care of her cousin, Gussie McDaniel, who adopted and raised him. In 1934 the McDaniels moved to the South Side of Chicago when Ellas was still a young boy. He was active in the local Ebenezer Baptist Church, studying the trombone and violin under O. W. Frederick, a music teacher at the church where

Gussie McDaniel taught Sunday school. When he was twelve he started playing guitar and joined the church's orchestra. But hearing John Lee Hooker's 1949 R&B hit "Boogie Chillen" changed his world as he, like many other musicians before him, combined the sounds he heard on the street with the sounds he had learned in church. He would later say that playing the violin influenced his style of rhythm guitar.

He attended the Foster Vocational School but dropped out at the age of fifteen. Initially he played on street corners with his friends. Then he formed a band called the Hipsters that later changed its name to the Langley Avenue Jive Cats. During the summer of 1943–44 he played for tips in Maxwell Street, that famous training ground of up-and-coming blues musicians. In 1951 Diddley secured a regular gig at the 708 Club at 708 East 47th Street. By 1954 he was playing with harmonica player Billy Arnold, drummer Clifton James, and washtub player Roosevelt Jackson; they recorded demos of "I'm a Man" and "Bo Diddley." To augment his income, Diddley held a series of menial jobs—at a grocery store, a picture-frame factory, as an elevator operator, a meatpacker, a laborer, and a truck driver. He even earned some money as a light heavyweight boxer.

Diddley's distinctive sound came from a pounding beat punctuated by a tremolo guitar. By transferring the neck and the circuitry of a Gretsch guitar and connecting it to a square body, Diddley essentially built his own guitar. In 1958 he asked the Gretsch Company to make him an improved version built to the same specifications. "My technique," Diddley told his biographer George R. White, "comes from bowing the violin, that fast wrist action."

Diddley combined the musical styles of two regions—the Deep South and the South Side of Chicago—to create a unique, singular sound. The Bo Diddley beat was an African-based 4/4 rhythm pattern similar to a style called hambone that street performers used by slapping their arms, legs, chest, and cheeks while chanting rhymes. The beat was picked up by countless other rock and roll musicians. He reportedly came across it while learning to play a Gene Autry song, "(I've Got Spurs that) Jingle, Jangle, Jingle."

Diddley's recordings were groundbreaking in the way they straddled the line between R&B and rock and roll. One record in particular, "Say Man" (which was also his only top twenty pop hit), was ahead of its time. In the song, an exuberant musical dialogue takes place between Diddley and his maraca player Jerome Green—numerous music critics consider it a precursor to rap. Diddley and Green's sparring was inspired by the African American tradition of "doing the dozens," the good-natured insults that form the foundation of rap and hip-hop. He was ahead of his time in other ways, too. His band featured a female guitarist at a time when very few women were in rock bands.

Diddley had been turned down by Vee-Jay and other record labels before being accepted at Chess Records. He sent demo tapes to Chess. Leonard Chess liked what he heard and asked Diddley to stop by the studio. On March 5, 1955, Diddley and his band went to Chess to record four songs, including the record that bore his name. "Bo Diddley" reached number one on the R&B charts. In another session he recorded "Diddley Daddy," which featured Little Walter on harmonica, Willie Dixon on bass, and the doo-wop sound of the Moonglows on backing vocals.

In 1963 Diddley went on a successful tour of Britain, performing with the Everly Brothers, Little Richard, and the Rolling Stones. In the early 1970s he moved to New Mexico and became a deputy sheriff. Even so, he continued to make albums for Chess on the Checker label until the mid-1970s. Although Diddley's recording career fizzled, he was not forgotten. He appeared in a cameo, for example, in the Eddie Murphy film *Trading Places,* and toured with the Clash in 1979. He also performed at two inaugural balls,

one for President George H. W. Bush and one for President Bill Clinton.

He was also an influential guitarist and developed innovations in both tone and style. His trademark instrument was the rectangular-shaped Gretsch guitar. He wrote clever and witty lyrics adapted from folk songs: "Bo Diddley" was based on the lullaby "Hush Little Baby" while "Who Do You Love" was a riff culled from the New Orleans hoodoo tradition. Diddley's influence on other musicians was profound. He influenced Jimi Hendrix, the Rolling Stones, and Eric Clapton, while his Bo Diddley beat can be heard in everyone from Buddy Holly ("Not Fade Away") and the Strangeloves ("I Want Candy") to U2 ("Desire") and Bruce Springsteen ("She's the One").

Bo Diddley's other hits included "Pretty Thing" in 1956 and "You Can't Judge a Book by the Cover" in 1962. He also cowrote the pop hit "Love Is Strange" in 1957.

In 1987 Bo Diddley was inducted into the Rock and Roll Hall of Fame. Several years later his song "Bo Diddley" was inducted into the Grammy Hall of Fame as a recording of lasting significance.

Bo Diddley died in June 2008 of heart failure at the age of seventy-nine at his home in Archer, Florida.

See also: Leonard Chess, Willie Dixon, Little Walter

Further reading: George R. White, *Bo Diddley: Living Legend* (1998).

Discography: *The Chess Box: Bo Diddley* (1990); *His Best: The Chess 50th Anniversary Collection* (1997); *Ride On: The Chess Masters, Vol. 3 1960–1961* (2009).

Walt Disney

Cartoonist and Motion-Picture Producer

BORN: December 5, 1901
Chicago, Illinois

DIED: December 15, 1966
Burbank, California

Walter Elias Disney revolutionized the art of animated film and in the process became one of the most iconic figures in motion-picture history—a Midwestern boy with a love of drawing, a vivid imagination, and an irrepressible will to succeed.

Born in Chicago, Walt Disney lived with his family at 1249 North Tripp Avenue (now 2156 North Tripp) in the Hermosa neighborhood. They later moved to Marceline, Missouri, and then Kansas City, Missouri, but returned to Chicago in 1917, living at 1523 Ogden Avenue on the Near West Side. Disney attended McKinley High School in Chicago while taking night classes at the Art Institute. For a short time, Disney worked at Filmack, a production company that creates cinema trailers, as an animation artist in the 1920s.

After moving out west, Disney achieved his first commercial success with *Steamboat Willie* (1928), which featured a character named Mickey Mouse. Over the years he introduced to the world such endearing figures as Donald Duck, Goofy, and Pluto. Some Disney classics include *Snow White and the Seven Dwarfs* (1938), the first feature-length cartoon motion picture; *Fantasia* (1940), a perennial favorite, but surprisingly, a commercial failure when first released; *Pinocchio* (1940); *Dumbo* (1941); *Bambi* (1953); and *Sleeping Beauty* (1959). He produced several television shows, including *The Mickey Mouse Club* and *The Wonderful World of Disney*, and built the Disneyland amusement park in Anaheim, California, as well as Disney World in Orlando, Florida.

Disney's first company went bankrupt while his second company, created with his brother Roy, nearly collapsed because of professional rivalry with staff. But with his first feature-length film, *Snow White and the Seven Dwarfs,* Disney transformed animation.

Disney lived a remarkable life and accomplished much during his life. But one of his last wishes never came to fruition: an urban utopia near Disney World was never built.

In October 2009 the Walt Disney Family Museum, a $10 million complex based in a former army barracks and devoted to telling the story of Disney's life and career, opened in San Francisco. The museum was created by the Walt Disney Family Foundation.

Disney died from lung cancer in Burbank, California, at the age of sixty-five.

The Walt Disney Magnet School at 4140 North Marine Drive, the city's first magnet school, is named in his honor. In 2004 Disney's daughter, Diane Disney Miller, dedicated a $250,000 animation lab at the school.

Further reading: Neal Gabler, *Walt Disney: The Triumph of American Imagination* (2002); Richard Schickel, *The Disney Version: The Life, Times, Art, and Commerce of Walt Disney* (1997).

Willie Dixon

Musician

BORN: July 1, 1915
Vicksburg, Mississippi

DIED: January 29, 1992
Burbank, California

William James Dixon, bluesman extraordinaire, wrote songs that made other people famous. They include "Little Red Rooster," "Hoochie Coochie Man," "Back Door Man," "I Just Want to Make Love to You," "I Ain't Superstitious," and "Wang Dang Doodle." But he was more than just a songwriter. He was the complete bluesman. Indeed, in addition to Muddy Waters, Dixon is considered the most influential bluesman of the post–World War II era as well as an important link between blues and rock and roll.

One of fourteen children, Dixon served time in state prison farms for the minor offense of stealing plumbing supplies when he was still a teenager. But music was his saving grace. As a boy in Vicksburg, Mississippi, Dixon listened to sacred and profane music—both spirituals and the blues. He set his poetry to music and sold the songs to traveling hillbilly and country and western performers. He learned how to sing harmony and sang bass in the Jubilee Singers, a local gospel quartet.

Dixon went north to Chicago in 1936, ostensibly to become a boxer. In 1938 he won the Illinois State Golden Gloves Heavyweight Championship as an amateur and then turned professional, working briefly as Joe Louis's sparring partner before once again turning, this time seriously, to music. He played bass in a group called the Five Breezes, performing on Maxwell Street and around town. He was a conscientious objector during World War II. "Why should I fight to save somebody that's killing me and my people?" he asked at the time, and was subsequently imprisoned for ten months. After the war, he formed the Four Jumps of Jive and then joined the Big Three Trio before going solo in 1951. Around that time he accepted an offer from the Chess brothers to work for their eponymous

record label. He wore many hats at Chess: he was a talent scout, he helped with arrangements, he produced sessions, and he wrote songs. He played bass on sessions for Chuck Berry, Muddy Waters, Howlin' Wolf, Little Walter, and Sonny Boy Williamson. He was also a producer for the Chess subsidiary, Checker Records. He was at Chess off and on for many years, roughly from 1948 to the early 1960s. Years later, when Chess's Michigan Avenue building was condemned, Dixon bought the building and transformed it into a blues museum.

Dixon was a prolific songwriter. He wrote "My Babe" for Little Walter, "Back Door Man" for Howlin' Wolf, and "Hoochie Coochie Man" for Muddy Waters. Many rock artists have covered his songs, including Bob Dylan, Cream, Led Zeppelin ("Bring It On Home"), the Yardbirds, the Rolling Stones ("Little Red Rooster"), and the Doors ("Back Door Man"). In addition, Led Zeppelin's heavy rock classic "Whole Lotta Love" is based on the lyrics of Dixon's "You Need Love."

Dixon also wrote and worked with such non-Chess artists as Otis Rush, Buddy Guy, and Magic Sam. His first solo album, *Willie's Blues,* on the Bluesville label, was released in 1960. His next album did not appear until a decade later, *I Am the Blues* (1970), on Columbia Records.

Essentially Dixon was a goodwill ambassador for the blues. He founded the Willie Dixon Blues Heaven Foundation, which is now run by Dixon's widow, Marie. In 1997 the former Chess Records headquarters at 2120 South Michigan Avenue became the Blues Heaven Foundation's official home. The foundation attempts to preserve the legacy of the blues and secure copyrights and royalties for blues musicians. It also provides emergency medical financial assistance to musicians. Tours of the Blues Heaven Foundation are available.

"The blues are the roots of all American music," Dixon once said. "As long as American music survives, so will the blues."

In 1988 Chess released *Willie Dixon: The Chess Box,* a two-disc set that featured his greatest songs as performed by other artists, from Muddy Waters to Bo Diddley. The following year he published his autobiography, *I Am the Blues.*

Dixon's health deteriorated in the 1970s and 1980s. A diabetic, he had to have his leg amputated, which severely compromised his already-precarious condition. He died of heart failure in 1992 at the age of seventy-six.

Dixon was inducted into the Blues Hall of Fame in 1980. In 1989 he received a Grammy Award for his album *Hidden Charms.*

See also: Leonard Chess, Bo Diddley, Howlin' Wolf, Little Walter, Muddy Waters

Further reading: Willie Dixon, *I Am the Blues: The Willie Dixon Story* (1990).

Discography: Willie Dixon, *The Chess Box* (1988).

R. R. Donnelley
Publisher

BORN: November 15, 1836
Hamilton, Ontario

DIED: April 8, 1899
Chicago, Illinois

Richard Robert Donnelley, one of the city's first commercial printers, aspired to be the best in his profession. The "Donnelley way" required that one devote the proper time, energy, and talent necessary in order to do a good job. Donnelley dedicated both his personal and business life to these principles.

Donnelley was apprenticed to a printer in his native town of Hamilton, Ontario. He was offered a partnership in a shop while still a teenager. In 1857 he decided to relocate to New Orleans, and he eventually became a partner in a shop owned by the *True Delta* newspaper. When the Civil War erupted, however, he returned to Canada, where he and his partner, Joseph Lawson, established a successful printing business.

In October 1864, Donnelley accepted an offer from Chicago publishers Edward Goodman and Leroy Church to join them. The firm of Church, Goodman, and Donnelley, located at 108–110 Dearborn Street, soon became one of the major publishing houses in the Midwest, producing some twenty-three weekly, monthly, and quarterly publications. In 1870 the company was renamed the Lakeside Publishing and Printing Company.

Plans were made to erect a Gothic structure to house the thriving company. The double impact of the Chicago Fire of 1871 and the panic of 1873, however, forced the business to close. Donnelley, like countless other Chicagoans, lost everything. A determined Donnelley traveled to New York in search of financing. Due to his strong character and impeccable reputation, he was able to secure enough credit to rebuild and reorganize.

In 1886 the company decided to diversify by publishing its first directory for the Chicago Telephone Company, the predecessor of Illinois Bell. (Ten years earlier, the Scots-born inventor Alexander Graham Bell had applied for a patent on a new invention he called the telephone.) Their first telephone directory was 244 pages long and included 6 pages of advertisements, 88 pages of Chicago listings, 25 pages of suburban listings, and 108 pages of classified listings.

Branching out into fiction, the firm operated a successful business producing inexpensive paperbacks. This was a significant accomplishment since Donnelley made good literature, including the works of major American and European writers, accessible to the general public. In 1903, after Donnelley's death, the first volume of the Lakeside Classics, Benjamin Franklin's autobiography, was published.

Donnelley believed printing and publishing to be two separate functions. In 1880 he formed a subsidiary, the Chicago Directory Company, to handle the publishing side of the business. In 1882 the printing firm was named R. R. Donnelley and Sons Company and continued to grow. The company printed circulars and catalogs for many of the city's big department stores, including Montgomery Ward and Company. In 1897 the firm moved into larger headquarters at the Lakeside Press Building, designed by noted architect Howard Van Doren Shaw, at Polk Street and Plymouth Court.

Donnelley died in 1899. The presidency of R. R. Donnelley and Sons, the printing branch, fell to his son, Thomas Elliott Donnelley. Another son, Reuben Hamilton, joined the publishing end of the business as a clerk in 1882 and eventually took it over.

In 1908 Thomas established the Apprentice School of the Lakeside Press, a comprehensive seven-year training program for aspiring printers. The first class of twenty-four apprentices graduated in 1915. In 1916 the publishing firm changed its name to the Reuben H. Donnelley Corporation, and it eventually became the largest publisher of telephone directories in the country.

Eventually two separate companies were created, R. H. Donnelley, a subsidiary of Dun and Bradstreet, which publishes the Donnelley directories; and R. R. Donnelley and Sons, which prints, among other things, the Donnelley directories and the Sears catalog.

In May 2009, R. H. Donnelley filed for bankruptcy. By February 2010, though, the company returned as Dex One Corporation, a print and interactive marketing firm.

See also: Howard Van Doren Shaw

Thomas A. Dorsey
Gospel Music Pioneer

BORN: July 1, 1899
Villa Rica, Georgia

DIED: January 23, 1993
Chicago, Illinois

The father of gospel music, Thomas Dorsey wrote more than 2,000 blues songs and about 1,000 gospel songs and was the founder and president of the National Convention of Gospel Choirs and Choruses. Dorsey was the music director of Pilgrim Baptist Church on the South Side from 1932 until the late 1970s.

Born in the small Georgia town of Villa Rica in 1899, Thomas Dorsey was the son of a Baptist preacher. He began playing the piano professionally at the age of twelve while occasionally, despite his young age, working in bordellos.

After a brief stopover in Atlanta, his family moved north to Chicago in 1916 and joined the Pilgrim Baptist Church. He studied at the Chicago College of Composition and Arranging. During the 1920s, Dorsey adopted the stage name of "Georgia Tom" and played barrelhouse piano in one of Al Capone's speakeasies. He also toured with the great blues singer Ma Rainey and performed with slide guitarist Hudson "Tampa Red" Whittaker. In 1926 Dorsey composed his first gospel hit, "If You See My Savior, Tell Him That You Saw Me," which combined the sacred with the secular. Mahalia Jackson made the song famous; it has been translated into fifty languages. Gospel combined Christian themes with the rhythms and cadences of blues and jazz; in essence, it brought together the sacred and the profane. Dorsey recorded another hit song, the racy blues hit "Tight Like That," with Rainey and Whittaker in 1928.

Dorsey tried to peddle his songs via song sheets but, frustrated by the racism of the industry, he decided to try selling his songs on his own. Dorsey became the first independent publisher of black gospel music when he established the Dorsey House of Music in Chicago in 1932. Thus, Dorsey began recording gospel while still playing the blues—but his dual existence would eventually take its toll on both his life and his music. When his first wife, Nettie, died during childbirth along with his son in 1932, Dorsey began to rethink his lifestyle. It was a turning point in his life. He circumvented his grief by writing his most famous song, and one of the best-known gospel songs, "Take My Hand, Precious Lord."

Initially the mainline Protestant churches frowned upon Dorsey's songs—which were, after all, blues-based—as controversy erupted between role of the church in African American society and the expression of a distinctive African American culture and religion. But by the late 1930s, the majority of African American congregations embraced this new type of music.

Dorsey's influence, however, was not limited to just African American musicians. His songs were also recorded by white musicians, from Tennessee Ernie Ford to Elvis Presley. His greatest hit, "Take My Hand, Precious Lord," was sung at the funeral of slain civil rights leader Martin Luther King Jr. in 1968.

In October 1979, Dorsey was the first black elected to the Nashville Songwriters International Hall of Fame. Several years later, in September 1981, he was elected to the Georgia Music Hall of Fame. The following year the Thomas A. Dorsey Archives opened at Fisk University in Nashville.

Dorsey's other songs include "Peace in the Valley," "Jesus Is the Light of World," "How About You," "Angels Watching Over Me," and "My Savior Carries Me Home."

Dorsey died in 1993 at the age of ninety-three from Alzheimer's in Chicago. He is buried in Oak Woods Cemetery.

In 2002 the Library of Congress added Dorsey's 1973 album, *Precious Lord: New Recordings of the Great Songs of Thomas A. Dorsey,* to the National Recording Registry.

See also: Mahalia Jackson

Further reading: Horace Clarence Boyer, *How Sweet the Sound: The Golden Age of Gospel* (1995); Michael W. Harris, *The Rise of Gospel Blues: The Music of Thomas Andrew Dorsey in the Urban Church* (1992); Tony Heilbut, *The Gospel Sound: Good News and Bad Times* (1997); Bernice Johnson Reagon, *We'll Understand It Better By and By: Pioneering African-American Gospel Composers* (1992).

Paul Douglas

Politician

BORN: March 26, 1892
Salem, Massachusetts

DIED: September 24, 1976
Washington, D.C.

During a long and varied career, Paul Howard Douglas was an economist at the University of Chicago and a United States senator from Illinois from 1949 to 1967.

Paul Douglas graduated from Bowdoin College in 1913 and earned a master's degree two years later from Columbia University and a Ph.D. in economics in 1921. In 1919 he accepted a position teaching economics at the University of Chicago. Over the years, though, he became increasingly involved in politics on both the regional and national levels. He was an economic adviser to Republican Governor Gifford Pinchot of Pennsylvania and Democratic Governor Franklin D. Roosevelt of New York. He also campaigned against Samuel Insull's stock market manipulations, helped draft laws that regulated utilities and created unemployment insurance, and established pensions for older workers.

An independent at heart, he nevertheless ran for mayor of Chicago in 1935 as a Republican, but he failed to gain the support of the party. Four years later, he ran as an independent for alderman of the Fifth Ward and won a narrow victory. A reformer on the city council, his attempts to transform public education and lower public transportation fares were unsuccessful. In 1942 he ran for the U.S. Senate, this time as a Democrat, but lost in the primary.

After this unsuccessful Senate bid, Douglas resigned from the city council and enlisted in the marines as a private. He was fifty years old. He was quickly promoted to corporal and then to sergeant. He wrote training manuals, and so his desk job effectively kept him out of the war zone. Eventually, though, he became an officer and was sent to the Pacific with the First Marine Division. There he saw action at the Battle of Peleliu and won a Bronze Star for his bravery—he carried ammunition to the front lines under enemy fire. He earned his first Purple Heart when he was grazed by shrapnel and his second Purple Heart when he was wounded while carrying the injured. The injury to his left arm left it permanently damaged. Douglas was given an honorable discharge as a lieutenant colonel.

Returning to civilian life, Douglas reentered politics and ran for the open Illinois seat in the U.S. Senate during the 1948 election. Employing a populist campaign, he traversed the state for six months in a battered Jeep. A staunch liberal, his issues included civil rights, the construction of more public housing, and reform of social security programs. He supported environmental protection, public housing, and truth-in-lending laws and opposed real estate redlining. His campaign was effective. He beat the incumbent, Senator C. Wayland Brooks, in an upset victory.

Despite his strong liberal credentials, Douglas was an unconventional liberal. He was also fiscally conservative. Appointed as chair of the Joint Economic Committee, he led a series of investigations into fiscal mismanagement. In 1952 he was encouraged to make a presidential run to seek the Democratic nomination, but Douglas refused the offer, supporting instead Senator Estes Kefauver of Tennessee.

Douglas was, at heart, a maverick who often flouted party lines and party convention. His heroes tended to be other like-minded nonconformists. They included the controversial Illinois governor John Peter Altgeld, but also Republicans such as Abraham Lincoln and Robert LaFollette Sr., of Wisconsin. He also admired social reformer Jane Addams and attorney Clarence Darrow. Douglas believed in fighting the good fight, and if that offended party loyalists, so be it. He was also an ardent conservationist long before the popularity of the environmental movement. He helped, for example, to save the Indiana Dunes from ruin.

Douglas served the state of Illinois in the United States Senate for nearly twenty years. He was reelected in 1954 and 1960. In 1966, at the age of seventy-four, Douglas ran for a fourth term but lost to the forty-seven-year-old liberal Republican Charles H. Percy.

In the early 1970s Douglas suffered a stroke. He died in 1976 at his home in Washington, D.C., at the age of eighty-four. His body was cremated and his ashes scattered in the Japanese gardens in Jackson Park near the University of Chicago campus.

Further reading: Roger Biles, *Crusading Liberal: Paul H. Douglas of Illinois* (2002); Paul Douglas, *Ethics in Government* (1952), *In the Fullness of Time: The Memoirs of Paul H. Douglas* (1972), and *In Our Time* (1967).

Stephen A. Douglas

Politician

BORN: April 23, 1813
Brandon, Vermont

DIED: June 3, 1861
Chicago, Illinois

Stephen Arnold Douglas was the first Chicago politician to make a name for himself on the national scene. Although small in size, Douglas possessed a great spirit. Like many diminutive men, he made up in personality what he lacked in stature. For several years, he was considered the country's foremost statesman. With his magnificent speaking voice and forceful personality, Douglas earned the nickname "the Little Giant."

Douglas spent his boyhood years on a Vermont farm. His father had died when Douglas was still an infant. At fifteen, he was apprenticed to a cabinetmaker. After his mother remarried, the family moved to Canandaigua, New York, where he enrolled at the local academy. He then studied law in the office of one of the town's leading attorneys. Working his way westward, Douglas settled in Jacksonville, Illinois, in 1833 and was admitted to the Illinois bar the same year.

Douglas held a succession of prestigious positions throughout his career—lawyer, member of the Illinois legislature, state prosecutor, land office commissioner, secretary of state of Illinois, and judge of the Illinois Supreme Court. He rapidly ascended the ladder of success and prominence. He became a congressman at age thirty and a senator at thirty-four.

A firm believer in "manifest destiny," Douglas strongly supported western expansion. He encouraged the federal government to acquire California and to annex Texas during the Mexican-American War (1846–1848). He also urged the construction of a transcontinental railroad that would link Chicago to the West.

Douglas pushed through Congress the Kansas-Nebraska Act of 1854, a controversial piece of legislation that repealed the Missouri Compromise of 1820, which had set boundaries between slave states and free territories. Douglas, a devout states' rights advocate, dubbed the new law "popular sovereignty." Douglas felt that by allowing freedom of choice he could avert tragedy. It was a costly error from which his career would never fully recover.

During his campaign for reelection to the U.S. Senate, Douglas faced a formidable challenger by the name of Abraham Lincoln. Lincoln, a member of the new Republican Party, favored keeping slavery out of the territories. Seven Lincoln-Douglas debates were scheduled during the summer of 1858, including one in Ottawa, Illinois, where more than 10,000 people came to witness the confrontation of the two politicians. At stake was not only the future of both men's careers but also the future of an entire country. The major issue during the debates was the concept of popular sovereignty. Although Lincoln won the popular vote during the general election, Douglas emerged triumphant when the Democratic state legislature voted to return him to Washington.

By today's standards, Douglas harbored blatantly racist views. "This is a white man's government made by white men, for white men and their descendants," he once said. The slavery issued tore the country apart and split the Democratic Party. In 1860 Douglas won the Democratic nomination for president but lost to Lincoln in the general election. Douglas had always considered himself a patriot. Although he disagreed with Lincoln over the issue of slavery during the campaign, he could not turn his back against the government when Lincoln was finally elected. When war was declared in 1861, Douglas rallied behind the new president and encouraged his followers to do the same.

Douglas, who lived in Chicago during the last fourteen years of his life, invested heavily in Chicago real estate, especially along the lakefront and in the Lake Calumet area. He also established the Illinois Central Railroad. In 1852 he bought seventy acres between 31st and 35th Streets west of the Illinois Central tracks. Two years later he built his home, which he called Oakenwald, near Cottage Grove Avenue and 35th Street. Douglas also made donations and was one of the incorporators of the original University of Chicago, which opened in 1860 at 34th Street and Cottage Grove Avenue but closed due to financial difficulties in 1886. In 1892 another University of Chicago opened—it had no ties to the old school—in Hyde Park.

Douglas died in Chicago of typhoid fever in 1861 at the age of forty-eight.

In 1861 a federal prison camp was established between 31st Street, Cottage Grove Avenue, 33rd Street, and Forest Avenue (now Giles Avenue) on land owned by Douglas. It was named Camp Douglas in honor of the late senator. The camp, which had earned a notorious reputation due to overcrowding and unsanitary conditions, closed in late 1865.

Around the turn of the century the Douglas neighborhood had evolved into a thriving African American commercial and entertainment center. Black-owned businesses and scores of nightclubs proliferated along 35th and South State Streets. After the Depression, the area drastically deteriorated. Nevertheless, a number of late-nineteenth-century homes still stand in the Douglas neighborhood, primarily between 31st and 35th Streets and along Calumet, Giles, and Prairie Avenues, which comprise the Douglas Historic District.

At the eastern end of 35th Street, between Lake Park Avenue and the Illinois Central railroad tracks, stands a memorial to Douglas. Perched atop a 104-foot column is a statue of the man they called the Little Giant. The sculpture, completed by Leonard Wells Volk in 1881, is visible from the Illinois Central line and from nearby Lake Shore Drive. It is a popular destination for Civil War and Chicago history buffs.

Douglas Boulevard, Douglas Drive in Douglas Park, and Stephen A. Douglas Drive are all named in honor of the late senator.

Further reading: Robert W. Johannsen, *Stephen A. Douglas* (1973).

Theodore Dreiser

Novelist

BORN: August 27, 1871
Terre Haute, Indiana

DIED: December 28, 1945
Los Angeles, California

Herman Theodore Dreiser's best work contained a biting and bitter condemnation of the hollowness at the core of the American Dream. Obsessed with the "brittle cruelty" of life, Dreiser didn't shy away from harsh realities. His novels were denounced as obscene and immoral, and several were banned. Despite this reception, Dreiser remained a singular literary voice, widely imitated and grudgingly admired even by his fiercest critics. By the time of his death, he was considered one of the most influential American novelists of the twentieth century.

Dreiser spent most of his boyhood in Warsaw, Indiana, the twelfth child in a family of thirteen. His first taste of big-city life came in the 1880s when his mother and the other children moved to Chicago, living in a six-room apartment at Madison Street and Throop Avenue. The family decided to return to Indiana after only a short time. Determined to stay on in Chicago, though he was only a teenager, Dreiser held a succession of odd jobs: dishwasher, cook, boxcar tracer, and stock boy.

The generosity of a former teacher allowed Dreiser to enroll at Indiana University. One year later he dropped out and returned to Chicago, convinced that journalism was the only profession in which he could shine. He tried his hand at reporting at the *Chicago Daily Globe* and then moved to the *St. Louis Globe-Democrat* where, in addition

to his regular duties, he reviewed as many as three plays per evening. On one occasion, he was scheduled to attend three different performances, but he was then unexpectedly told to cover a holdup. Even so, he wrote glowing reviews, mostly culled from press agency releases. The next morning he awoke to the ghastly news that none of the troupes had performed that night due to a delayed train. Too embarrassed to face his editor, he left an apologetic note, gathered his belongings, and kept a low profile until he joined the second-rate morning newspaper, the *Republic.* When he eventually left St. Louis, he landed a job on the *Pittsburgh Dispatch.*

Although still a young man in his early twenties, Dreiser feared that time was running out. In 1894 he moved to New York where he joined the staff of the *World* newspaper. His reporting skills hadn't improved—he was still careless with facts—and he quit before he was fired. After an unsuccessful attempt to publish a music magazine with his brother Paul, who gained fame as the composer of "On the Banks of the Wabash"—Dreiser left New York to stay with a friend, Arthur Henry, in Maumee, Ohio. Henry, city editor of the *Toledo Blade,* was working on a novel at the time. According to Dreiser's biographer, W. A. Swanberg, Henry encouraged Dreiser to do the same. "Finally I took out a piece of yellow paper and to please him wrote down a title at random—*Sister Carrie,*" Dreiser later recalled. He had no plot, no characters—just a name.

Sister Carrie provoked violent reactions. Condemned for its frank portrayal of sex, it is credited with bringing the American novel into the twentieth century. It told the tale of Carrie Meeber, a young country girl who moves to Chicago, sets up house with a married man, and becomes a prominent actress. Dreiser never apologized for Carrie's behavior, nor did he punish her, as required of the "respectable" fiction of the day. His publisher, Doubleday, Page, and Company, was so dismayed with him that it initially tried to be released from its contractual obligations. After Dreiser threatened to file a lawsuit, however, the company agreed to print a nominal number of books—only 1,000 copies.

Early reviews were disappointing; most critics called the book immoral and unrelentingly downbeat. A few, however, praised Dreiser for his courage and some even suggested greatness. In September 1901, *Sister Carrie* was published in Britain to generally favorable reviews. In 1907 a tiny New York publisher, B. W. Dodge and Company, reissued the book. This time the reception was considerably better. The *World,* Dreiser's old paper, called it a book of "uncommon quality," and the *San Francisco Call* referred to it as "a work of genius."

After *Sister Carrie* was first published Dreiser continued jumping from job to job—assistant feature editor of the *New York Daily News,* editor of *Smith's* magazine, editor of *Broadway* magazine. Following the successful reissue of *Sister Carrie,* Dreiser was offered a high-salary position as editor-in-chief at the prestigious Butterick Publishing Company, which published women's magazines.

Dreiser's second novel, *Jennie Gerhardt* (1911), received mostly positive reviews. Literary critic Floyd Dell called it a great book, and H. L. Mencken compared it favorably with the works of Tolstoy, Zola, and Conrad. Dreiser then turned his pen to the turbulent career of Chicago traction tycoon Charles Tyson Yerkes. In 1912 he returned to Chicago to research Yerkes's career. The result was the Frank Cowperwood trilogy, which consisted of *The Titan* (1912), *The Financier* (1914), and *The Stoic* (1947). Dreiser depicted Cowperwood as a ruthless robber baron who turned self-gratification and the relentless pursuit of power into a career.

Dreiser's most successful novel was *An American Tragedy* (1925), which explored American society's insatiable thirst for wealth and pleasure. Like his earlier novels, it reflected Dreiser's continued fascination with class and status. Based on a true story, it recounted the tale of a vacuous young man, Clyde Griffiths, who leaves his working-class girlfriend, Roberta Alden, for a wealthy woman after Alden becomes pregnant with his child. He plots to murder her by taking her to a deserted lake and staging an accident, but he is unable to follow through. The boat somehow overturns, however, and the young woman drowns. Though he maintains he is innocent, Griffiths is sentenced to die in the electric chair. *An American Tragedy* was an unqualified success and was hailed as one of the greatest novels of the twentieth century. The film *A Place in the Sun* (1951), starring Montgomery Clift, Elizabeth Taylor, and Shelley Winters, was based on Dreiser's classic.

Dreiser's literary output during the last twenty years of his life was minimal. Just prior to his death, he resumed writing and completed two novels, *The Bulwark* and *The Stoic.* His other works include several one-act plays.

Dreiser died in Los Angeles in 1945 of a heart attack at the age of seventy-four.

See also: Floyd Dell, James T. Farrell, Charles Tyson Yerkes

Further reading: Robert H. Elias, *Theodore Dreiser: Apostle of Nature* (1949); Dale Kramer, *Chicago Renaissance: The Literary Life of the Midwest, 1900–1930* (1966); Richard Lingeman, *Theodore Dreiser: At the Gates of the City 1871–1907* (1986) and *Theodore Dreiser: An American Journey 1908–1945* (1990); Jerome Loving, *The Last Titan: A Life of Theodore Dreiser* (2005); Donald Pizer, *The Novels of Theodore Dreiser: A Critical Study* (1976); W. A. Swanberg, *Dreiser* (1965).

John Drury

Broadcaster

BORN: January 4, 1927
Aurora, Illinois

DIED: November 25, 2007
Wheaton, Illinois

John Drury was one of the most popular and enduring broadcasters in Chicago television history. Known for his devilish sense of humor, he instilled both a sense of gravitas and gentle wit to his daily broadcasts.

Born in Aurora, Illinois, Drury grew up during the height of the Great Depression. He graduated from Aurora High School in 1945 and served in the navy during World War II. After graduating from the University of Iowa, he secured his first job in broadcasting in 1950 with radio station KSTT in Davenport, Iowa. He also held radio and television jobs in Fort Wayne and Indianapolis, Indiana, and spent half a dozen years at WTMJ-TV in Milwaukee.

But Drury considered these stations as mere stepping stones to finding a job he really coveted: one in Chicago. He finally received an offer to go to the Chicago area when WBBM-TV offered him a position in 1962. He spent five years there, working with Bill Kurtis and Walter Jacobson and also serving as Fahey Flynn's first coanchor. In 1967 he moved to WGN-TV to anchor the 10 P.M. news broadcast but three years later moved again, to WLS. He was also the evening news anchor for the ABC affiliate in Chicago and a frequent weekend anchor for their national news broadcasts from New York. The rest of his broadcast career was spent between WGN and WLS. He retired from WLS in 2002.

Despite his good looks and traditional broadcaster's voice, Drury considered himself first and foremost an investigative reporter. He wanted to be remembered as a serious broadcast journalist rather than a mere anchorman.

Over the years Drury received numerous Emmy Awards. In 2002 he was inducted into the Chicago Journalism Hall of Fame and given the prestigious Silver Circle Award for his many years in television broadcasting. Two years earlier the Museum of Broadcast Communications also granted him an award for his services.

Drury was a realist about his profession. At one point, in the late 1970s, he was so discouraged by the business side of the industry, where profit meant more than journalism, that he seriously considered leaving it altogether. In fact, he enrolled in a training class as a potential McDonald's franchise owner. During a two-year period, he spent his weekends at McDonald's, even taking customers' orders at the drive-ups. Several unsuspecting customers, not recognizing him but impressed with his voice, encouraged him to try another profession. "You ought to be in radio," they told him.

In 2003, shortly after he retired from WLS, Drury was diagnosed with amyotrophic lateral sclerosis (ALS), commonly known as Lou Gehrig's disease. As the disease took its toll, eventually he was able to speak only with the assistance of a voice box. Despite his illness, he became a staunch advocate for research, raising awareness of the disease. He died at the age of eighty at his home in Wheaton, Illinois, after a four-year struggle.

Ruth Duckworth

Sculptor

BORN: April 10, 1919
Hamburg, Germany

DIED: October 18, 2009
Chicago, Illinois

Ruth Duckworth was an iconoclast who worked primarily in clay and bronze. She created large sculptures and smaller works, as well as murals.

Born Ruth Windmüller in Hamburg, Germany, she was the daughter of a Jewish father. As a result, she was not allowed an education under the Nazi regime. In 1936 she left Germany for England to study at the Liverpool School of Art. During World War II she traveled with her own puppet show in the north of England and found work in a munitions factory. She later studied stone carving at the City and Guilds of London Art School and carved tombstone decorations. In 1949 she married Aidron Duckworth.

Ruth Duckworth was an iconoclast, although her sculpture was profoundly influenced by the work of such quite different modernists as Henry Moore, Constantin Brancusi, and Isamu Noguchi. She started as a stonemason in England who didn't turn to ceramics until she was in her forties. But once she became enamored with ceramics nothing could deter her. Determined to become a ceramist, she enrolled in 1956 at the Central School of Arts and Crafts in London and began studying glazing. Initially she produced tableware in stoneware and porcelain, but gradually her work became more abstract and grander. She hand-shaped her work, which puzzled contemporary ceramists in England, who were not accustomed to the process that she preferred. What's more, sculptors typically worked in wood, stone, or metal, and thus denigrated clay as a medium. And yet Duckworth's work was greeted positively by some of the younger artists. Even so, since her large-scale ceramic work was not popular in England at the time, she accepted a teaching position at the University of Chicago in 1964. In Chicago, she began executing massive ceramic murals and, later, bronze sculptures.

Duckworth taught ceramics at the University of Chicago from 1964 until 1977, working out of a studio in the Pilsen neighborhood. In Chicago she was commissioned to create a series of stoneware murals at the entryway of the university's Geophysical Sciences Building. She used topographical illustrations of Mount Fuji and various satellite photographs of the earth to create one of her best-known pieces, *Earth, Water, and Sky,* which involved a series of murals that covered four walls. Indeed, many of her works consist of large-scale murals. They are located in lobbies, airport terminals, and other large public spaces.

In the 1970s Duckworth was commissioned to do her most important large-scale work to date, *Clouds Over Lake Michigan,* in the Chicago Board Options Exchange Building. The work featured abstract and figurative elements. In 1982 and 1983, Congregation Beth Israel in Hammond, Indiana, commissioned *The Creation,* another major ceramic work. Duckworth also created several monumental bronze sculptures on the campuses of Eastern Illinois University in Charleston, Illinois; Northeastern Illinois University in Chicago; and Lewis & Clark Community College in Godfrey, Illinois.

After she retired from teaching, Duckworth remained in Chicago and worked from the 1980s until her death in a former pickle factory in the Lakeview neighborhood on the North Side.

Her work was rarely represented in galleries (although her work was shown at the Exhibit A Gallery in Evanston, Illinois, in the early 1980s)—and she preferred it that way. "I don't like to be owned by anybody," she once said. In 2005 she was the subject of a retrospective exhibit, *Ruth Duckworth: Modernist Sculptor,* at the Museum of Arts and Design in New York and the Cultural Center in Chicago.

Duckworth died at the age of ninety at the Seasons Hospice and Palliative Care in Chicago after a brief illness. Her work is in the collections of several major museums, including the Art Institute of Chicago.

Finley Peter Dunne

Humorist and Journalist

BORN: July 10, 1867
Chicago, Illinois

DIED: April 24, 1936
New York, New York

In Martin Dooley, the fictitious barkeep of a working-class Bridgeport saloon, Finley Peter Dunne created a Chicago character who won instant acceptance in his hometown and renown nationwide. At the peak of his popularity in pre–World War I America, Dunne was hailed as an Irish American Mark Twain and one of the great humorists of his day.

Dunne was born and raised in St. Patrick's parish on the Near West Side of Chicago. His father owned a small lumberyard, and his relatives were active in Democratic ward politics and included a number of prominent Chicago priests. After graduating from West Division High School, young Pete—he added Finley, his mother's maiden name, after her death—entered the newspaper business at age sixteen as a copy boy at the *Chicago Telegram.* Later he was promoted to police reporter. His knowledge of the city and his skill as a journalist allowed him to advance quickly. He left the *Telegram* to join the *Chicago Daily News* where, among his general assignment and editorial duties, he covered the sports beat. In 1888 he became political reporter on the *Times* and was quickly promoted to city editor—at twenty-two the youngest in Chicago. From there he jumped to the *Daily Tribune* and, in 1892, he joined the staff of the *Chicago Evening Post* as an editorial page editor.

In October 1893, Dunne began writing in Irish dialect for the *Evening Post.* Literary historian Charles Fanning calls Dunne's great creation, Martin Dooley, bartender and philosopher from the South Side neighborhood of Bridgeport, the first dialect voice of genius in American literature. From 1893 to 1898 these weekly columns created a full picture of Irish American working-class urban life. The portraits of laborers, streetcar drivers, and mill workers contain memorable dignity and depth. Sage, satirist, social critic, philosopher, and thinker, Mr. Dooley was immensely popular. Readers identified with his resourcefulness, his quick wit, and his ordinary common sense. Modeled after a real life Chicago bartender, Mr. Dooley tended bar in a mythical Irish tavern along Archer Road, or as he referred to it, the "Archey Road."

Through Mr. Dooley, Dunne examined the customs, habits, and attitudes of a working-class Chicago neighborhood and explored other themes too—the great Irish potato famine of the 1840s, the plight of the immigrant, the fight for Irish independence, the struggle of the Irish to attain respectability in America, and the pains of assimilation.

But Dunne was not only concerned with Irish topics—he also addressed other themes such as social reform, the Pullman strike, and Chicago politics. Dunne's satirical columns on the Spanish-American War in 1898 were widely reprinted and ushered in the second phase of his career. In 1900 he moved to New York and his columns became nationally syndicated. The wise old sage of Bridgeport was quoted across breakfast tables throughout America, so that by World War I Dunne was the most famous columnist in the country.

Dunne wrote approximately 700 Mr. Dooley columns. He died in his New York apartment in the Delmonico Hotel in 1936 after a long illness. By that time, Dunne had fallen into relative obscurity. The fictitious Mr. Dooley, however, was still fondly remembered.

Dunne's first anthology, *Mr. Dooley in Peace and War* (1898), was followed by *What Dooley Says* (1899), *Mr. Dooley in the Hearts of His Countrymen* (1899), *Mr. Dooley's*

Philosophy (1900), *Mr. Dooley's Opinions* (1901), *Observations by Mr. Dooley* (1902), *Dissertations by Mr. Dooley* (1906), *Mr. Dooley Says* (1910), *Mr. Dooley on Making a Will and Other Necessary Evils* (1919), and *Mr. Dooley at His Best* (1936).

In 1996 Finley Dunne's Tavern, at 3458 North Lincoln Avenue in the Lakeview neighborhood, opened. A no-frills neighborhood bar, it honors the memory of the late columnist.

See also: George Ade, Eugene Field, Ring Lardner

Further reading: Jerry DeMuth, *Small Town Chicago: The Comic Perspective of Finley Peter Dunne, George Ade, Ring Lardner* (1980); Elmer Ellis, *Mr. Dooley's America: A Life of Finley Peter Dunne* (1941); Charles Fanning, *Finley Peter Dunne and Mr. Dooley: The Chicago Years* (1978) and "The Literary Dimension," in *The Irish in Chicago* (1987), Lawrence McCaffrey et al., eds.; Charles Fanning, ed., *Mr. Dooley and the Chicago Irish: An Anthology* (1976); Barbara C. Schaff, *Mr. Dooley's Chicago* (1977).

Elmer E. Ellsworth

Army Officer

BORN: April 11, 1837
Malta, New York

DIED: May 24, 1861
Alexandria, Virginia

Colonel Elmer Ephraim Ellsworth was Chicago's first war hero: the first Union officer killed in the Civil War. As the leader of Chicago's Zouave Cadets, Ellsworth offered an ideal, romantic portrait of war that today may appear naive and sentimental. For a time though, Ellsworth and his Zouaves epitomized the nation's best qualities—patriotism, self-sacrifice, and unswerving loyalty. Songs were composed about them, and Zouave dolls, dressed in tiny scarlet trousers, flooded the market.

Ellsworth moved to Chicago in 1854 when a young New Englander, Arthur F. Devereux, offered him a position as a clerk in his patent-soliciting business. "My life has been a constant struggle between duty and inclination," he wrote to a friend. Chronic health problems prevented him from attending West Point. Although disappointed, he pursued the study of law, living very frugally in order to save money for his education.

Ellsworth had always dreamed of military glory. In 1859 he was hired as a drillmaster for volunteer regiments in Chicago. Ironically, he was too poor to join these companies, which consisted mostly of young men of high social standing and some wealth. Their uniforms were expensive, and they staged lavish balls and participated in parades and elaborate drills for the entertainment of the public.

The dashing, handsome Colonel Ellsworth wanted to be a nineteenth-century King Arthur. When perusing European magazines, he came across the colorful uniforms of the French Zouaves, named after a mountain tribe in Algeria. The French adopted this tribe's system of warfare and thus distinguished themselves during the Crimean War. Ellsworth obtained a copy of a Zouave drill manual from his fencing master, Dr. Charles A. DeVillers, who had served as a surgeon in a French Zouave regiment.

The Zouave drill required top physical fitness, precision, and skill. The soldiers were taught to load and fire on the run, when lying down, and when kneeling. They also learned how to bayonet effectively. And although some people dismissed their training as nothing more than "idle and foolish recreation," Ellsworth disciplined his troops unsparingly, four hours every evening, except Sunday, in order to make them combat-ready. Later, many Zouaves distinguished themselves in the Civil War as a result of their elaborate training.

Word of this exciting new unit and their handsome leader circulated within Chicago's military circles. Their uniforms, too, became the subject of conversation: beaded blue jackets, red vests, collarless blue shirts, gold-trimmed jackets, yellow sashes, baggy scarlet trousers, and blue caps. Colorful though they were, these uniforms were hardly made for combat duty. Eventually the uniforms were discarded altogether and the soldiers ordered to don regular Union army clothing.

Ellsworth's cadets won the drill championship of the United States and Canada in 1860. That same year Ellsworth published *Manual of Arms for Light Infantry,* arranged for U.S. Zouave Cadets. Following the Zouaves's successful national tour, Ellsworth came to the attention of Abraham Lincoln, then a prominent lawyer. Lincoln, impressed with Ellsworth's integrity, invited the young man to join his law firm in Springfield, Illinois, but the outbreak of war the following year ended Ellsworth's brief legal career.

In 1861 Ellsworth was appointed adjutant and inspector general of militia for the United States Army. He later quit as drillmaster to train Illinois troops, but later still he returned to his native New York where he trained the New York Zouaves.

In May 1861, Ellsworth and his men traveled to Alexandria, Virginia. When he saw a Confederate flag waving atop the Marshall House hotel, he turned to his men and cried, "Boys, we must have that down before we return." This simple act of patriotism cost him his life. He was fatally wounded by the hotel's manager, James W. Jackson. Jackson was in turn slain by Ellsworth's troops.

Chicago was "profoundly agitated" upon learning of Ellsworth's death, according to an editorial in the *Chicago Tribune.* "No man has been watched by our citizens with warmer interest than Colonel Ellsworth."

See also: James Mulligan, Philip Sheridan
Further reading: Ruth Painter Randall, *Colonel Elmer Ellsworth: A Biography of Lincoln's Friend and First Hero of the Civil War* (1960).

Ada Everleigh

Madam

BORN: February 15, 1866
Near Louisville, Kentucky

DIED: January 5, 1960
Roanoke, Virginia

Minna Everleigh

Madam

BORN: July 13, 1878
Near Louisville, Kentucky

DIED: September 16, 1948
New York, New York

For over a decade Minna and Ada Everleigh were the proprietors of the most celebrated brothel in America, a fifty-room mansion at 2131–33 South Dearborn Street.

The Everleigh Sisters (their original family name was reported to be Lester) enjoyed an aristocratic upbringing. Their father was a wealthy Kentucky lawyer who spared no expense in providing his daughters with a proper education, which included finishing school. But the prospect of married life—social custom of the day dictated their future—held little interest for either sister. Instead, they had other ideas of how they wanted to occupy their time. After acting in several repertory companies in Washington, D.C., they opened their first brothel—in Omaha, during the Trans-Mississippi Exposition. When the exposition closed in 1899, they headed for Chicago.

The Everleigh Club opened its doors on February 1, 1900, without any advance publicity or advertisements. It was as elegant as any first-class hotel. True to their proper upbringing, culture was very important to the sisters, as was maintaining a refined atmosphere. There was a library lined with rare books, an art gallery, a dining room, oil paintings, silk curtains, mahogany staircases, gilded bathtubs, and gold-plated spittoons. There was also a waiting list to work at the Everleigh Club. According to historian Charles Washburn, in order to be hired a girl needed to be in perfect health, possess a pretty face and figure, and look good in evening clothes. The girls were also given daily drills in proper behavior. "Be polite, patient, and forget what you are here for," Minna directed. "Remember the Everleigh Club has no time for the rough element, the clerk on a holiday, or a man without a checkbook. Your youth and beauty are all you have. Preserve it. Stay respectable by all means."

There were fourteen soundproof rooms (or parlors), each with its own name: Moorish, Gold, Silver, Copper, Red, Rose, Green, Blue, Oriental, Japanese, Egyptian, Chinese, Music, and Ballroom, according to Washburn. To gain admittance, a prospective guest had to produce a letter of recommendation, an engraved card, or a formal introduction. The prices were not cheap: $12 bought a bottle of champagne, $50 an evening with dinner.

In October 1909, the English evangelist Gipsy Smith led a parade into the heart of the Levee, as the city's red-light district was called. The Levee, prepared for the invasion, was on its best behavior. The blinds were drawn, the lights dimmed. Not even the sound of a tinkling piano could be heard. Smith and his cadre of reformers knelt outside the infamous Everleigh Club and prayed and prayed. After the marchers departed, though, the Levee resumed its old character. The doors of the Everleigh Club opened, the lights went on, and the music spilled out into the streets. It was reportedly the busiest night the district had ever had.

In 1910 a vice commission, consisting of some of the most respected names in town, including Julius Rosenwald, the Rev. Frank W. Gunsaulus, and Graham Taylor, was appointed by Mayor Fred A. Busse to probe Chicago's escalating vice problem. The commission concluded that "the problem will remain just as long as the public conscience is dead to the issue or is indifferent to its solution. The law is only as powerful as the public opinion which supports it."

Disregarding the vice commission's study, *The Social Evil in Chicago*, the sisters published a brochure advertising the finer points of their club. It fell into the hands of Mayor Carter Harrison II. Incensed, Harrison issued an order to shut it down on October 24, 1911. Segregated vice was no longer regarded as an appropriate solution to the problem of prostitution, and politicians, bowing to public pressure, could no longer afford to look the other way. The sisters knew the end was in sight. "Well, boys, we've had good times, haven't we," said a bejeweled Minna to the men of the press. "You have all been darlings. You've played square. And we thank you sincerely." At one o'clock

on the morning of October 25, 1911, the order came down. "Nothing we can do about it," uttered a police officer. Within a week the Everleigh sisters had boarded the Twentieth Century Limited at LaSalle Street Station and headed with their $1 million in savings for sunny Italy. They returned to Chicago six months later with hopes of reopening their old club. But it was not to be.

Minna died in 1948 in New York's Park West Hospital. Ada lived a quiet life until the age of ninety-three. She was buried next to her beloved sister near Roanoke, Virginia. The building that housed the notorious Everleigh Club was demolished in 1933.

See also: "Bathhouse John" Coughlin, Carter Harrison II, Michael "Hinky Dink" Kenna

Further reading: Karen Abbott, *Sin in the Second City: Madams, Ministers, Playboys, and the Battle for America's Soul* (2008); Herbert Asbury, *Gem of the Prairie: An Informal History of the Chicago Underworld* (1942); Herman Kogan and Lloyd Wendt, *Lords of the Levee: The Story of Bathhouse John and Hinky Dink* (1943, 2005); Charles Washburn, *Come Into My Parlor: A Biography of the Aristocratic Everleigh Sisters of Chicago* (1936).

James T. Farrell

Novelist

BORN: February 27, 1904
Chicago, Illinois

DIED: August 22, 1979
New York, New York

James Thomas Farrell was a novelist, critic, essayist, short story writer, poet, and journalist as well as a first-rate social historian whose powerful novels captured the frustration, humiliation, and anger of a generation of working-class Irish Americans.

One of fifteen children born to James Francis Farrell and Mary Daly, James Thomas Farrell was raised by his maternal grandmother when his father could not afford to feed yet another hungry mouth. He lived with the Dalys at 4816 South Indiana Avenue. He later lived at 5704 South Indiana Avenue and 5816 South Parkway Avenue (now King Drive). Farrell graduated from St. Cyril (now Mount Carmel) High School. He worked as a clerk for the American Realty Express Company, as a cigar store clerk, and as a service station attendant before enrolling at the University of Chicago in 1927. He dropped out two years later to devote all of his energy to writing.

His first novel, *Young Lonigan* (1932), was a brutally frank depiction of an Irish American youth in Chicago's Washington Park neighborhood. It sold millions of copies and brought Farrell early fame. The Lonigan trilogy—which

also included *The Young Manhood of Studs Lonigan* (1934) and *Judgment Day* (1935)—made a tremendous impact on the literary world. Farrell's sympathetic but scrupulous portrayal of the life of ordinary people set his novels apart from proletarian literature of the thirties, and he exerted a profound influence on generations of American writers from Norman Mailer and Kurt Vonnegut to Tom Wolfe and Bette Howland.

Farrell's output was significant. He wrote twenty-five novels, seventeen collections of short stories, and many books of nonfiction. The Studs Lonigan series, however, overshadowed everything else he created. "Writing is my life and 'Studs' is part of my life as a writer," he once said, "but I do resent having other works compared with *Studs Lonigan*. I don't think of myself as a pole vaulter who must break my own record with each book. . . . To examine life, and to explore the nature of experience, is my aim."

The critical tide is now turning and Farrell's other novels are beginning to receive the attention they deserve, including Farrell's largely autobiographical novels, beginning with *A World I Never Made* (1936). The O'Neill-O'Flaherty novels, which follow Danny O'Neill from the South Side of

Chicago to New York literary circles, include *No Star Is Lost* (1938), *Father and Son* (1940), *My Days of Anger* (1943), and *The Face of Time* (1953).

An outspoken man with strong leftist views, Farrell served as chairman of the American Committee for Cultural Freedom from 1954 to 1956, but his early repudiation of Stalinism earned him the enmity of prominent literary critics and intellectuals.

The Death of Nora Ryan, the last novel published in Farrell's lifetime, appeared in 1978. The following year, NBC-TV aired a critically acclaimed three-part series based on the Lonigan trilogy. Several other books remained in manuscript form, one of which, *Sam Holman,* was published in 1983.

Farrell was the first American novelist to put Irish ethnic life into a coherent urban context. Not only did he examine the thoughts, aspirations, and values of working- and middle-class Irish Americans in the half century between 1900 and 1950, but he depicted in stunning detail the neighborhoods in which they lived. Throughout his long literary career, Farrell's constant aim was "to write so that life may speak for itself." His novels did precisely that.

Other novels include *Tommy Gallagher's Crusade* (1939), *Ellen Rogers* (1941), *Bernard Clare* (1946), *The Road Between* (1949), *Yet Other Waters* (1952), *This Man and This Woman* (1951), *A Brand New Life* (1972), *The Dunne Family* (1976), and the Eddie Ryan series of novels, including *The Silence of History* (1963), *What Time Collects* (1964), *Lonely Future* (1966), and *When Time Was Born* (1967).

Farrell died of a heart attack in his Manhattan apartment on August 22, 1979. He is buried in the Farrell family plot in Calvary Cemetery in Evanston.

A portion of Indiana Avenue west of Washington Park is named in his honor.

See also: Jack Conroy, Theodore Dreiser, Finley Peter Dunne
Further reading: Edgar Marquess Branch, *James T. Farrell* (1963); Charles Fanning, "The Literary Dimension" in *The Irish in Chicago* (1987), Lawrence McCaffrey et al., eds.; Charles Fanning and Ellen Skerrett, "James T. Farrell and Washington Park: The Novel as Social History" in *Chicago History,* Summer 1979.

Edna Ferber

Novelist

BORN: August 15, 1887
Kalamazoo, Michigan

DIED: April 16, 1968
New York, New York

A popular novelist and short story writer, Edna Ferber launched her literary career in Chicago. Her most popular novel, *So Big,* had a Chicago setting, as did many of her early short stories, including "The Gray Old Dog," "Home Girl," and "Mother Knows Best."

Ferber was the daughter of a Hungarian immigrant, Jacob Charles Ferber, and a second-generation German, Julia Neumann, and was raised in the Jewish faith. After high school, Ferber made $3 a week as a reporter for the *Appleton* (Wisconsin) *Daily Crescent* but was fired from the job by an editor who did not like having a woman on his staff. She later secured a post with the *Milwaukee Journal,* but had taken up fiction writing for therapeutic reasons after suffering a nervous breakdown. She met with some success, and a number of her short stories were published in various magazines.

Ferber arrived in Chicago in 1910 and found work as a reporter for the *Chicago Tribune.* Pounding away on a $17 used typewriter, she sat down and wrote, in 1911, her first novel, *Dawn O'Hara,* based on her newspaper experience in Milwaukee. It was rejected so many times that she gave up and threw it into the furnace. Fortunately, her mother rescued it from the flames.

In 1917 she wrote *Fanny Herself* about a young woman who comes to Chicago to work in a mail-order firm. By the mid-1920s, Ferber had settled in New York and had become a successful playwright. She collaborated with George S. Kaufman on *The Royal Family* (1927), *Dinner at Eight* (1932), *Stage Door* (1936), *The Land Is Bright* (1951), and *Bravo!* (1949).

In 1924, her next novel, *So Big,* returned to Chicago themes. Set on a truck farm in South Holland, just south of the city, *So Big* earned her the Pulitzer Prize for fiction (she was the first Jew to win the highly coveted award) and catapulted her to national attention. The novel, a classic of American literature, soon became required reading on high school and college campuses. Ferber was as surprised as anyone at the book's monumental success. "Not only did I not plan to write a best seller," she confessed, "but I thought I had written the world's worst seller. I didn't think anyone would ever read it." *So Big* is still considered an American classic.

Among her other novels were *Showboat* (1926), which captured theatrical life on the Mississippi and was adapted into a successful musical by Jerome Kern and Oscar Hammerstein; *Cimarron* (1930), about the early days of

Oklahoma; *Come and Get It* (1935), which was set in the lumber camps of Wisconsin and Michigan; and *Great Son* (1944), which was set in the Pacific Northwest. In addition, she wrote the novels *Saratoga Trunk* (1941), *Giant* (1952), and *Ice Palace* (1958). Many of her books were turned into movies, including *Giant,* which starred Elizabeth Taylor, Rock Hudson, and, in his last role, James Dean.

Other Ferber works included *Cheerful—By Request* (1918), *The Girls* (1921), *Gigolo* (1922), *American Beauty* (1931), and *They Brought Their Women* (1931).

Ferber died in her Park Avenue home in New York City in 1968 at the age of eighty.

Enrico Fermi

Physicist

BORN: September 29, 1901
Rome, Italy

DIED: November 28, 1954
Chicago, Illinois

The nuclear age began in 1942 in a converted squash court beneath the stands of Stagg Field on the campus of the University of Chicago. Its unlikely hero was a quiet, soft-spoken Italian immigrant named Enrico Fermi.

The son of an Italian railroad official, Fermi studied at the University of Pisa from 1918 to 1922. Later on he attended the universities of Leyden and Gottingden in the Netherlands. He was appointed professor of theoretical physics at the University of Rome in 1927. In 1934, in his laboratory at the University of Rome, he studied the effects of bombarding atoms with negatively charged neutrons. Using simple equipment, Fermi and his team decided to experiment further by bombarding all the elements of the periodic table. His persistence paid off when, four years later, Fermi received the Nobel Prize for successfully splitting the uranium atom.

Fermi traveled with his family to Sweden to receive the award but later decided not to return to Italy because of the growing threat of fascism there. First he went to London. Then, in 1939, he accepted an offer to join the faculty of Columbia University as a professor of physics, where he continued his pioneering atomic research. In 1942 he transferred from Columbia to the University of Chicago and was placed in charge of constructing the world's first atomic bomb—code name: the Manhattan Project. Fermi and his team of scientists worked diligently in secrecy until December 2, 1942, when they achieved the first controlled nuclear reaction.

Because of the urgency of the situation—the United States was in a desperate race to build an atomic bomb before Germany could develop one—there was no time to build a proper lab. Instead, a makeshift reactor, molded in the shape of a giant beehive and consisting of graphite blocks interspersed with chunks of uranium, was constructed. To control the reaction, rods of cadmium were inserted into the pile. When the rods were removed, a chain reaction took place and fission resulted.

On that cold December day, Fermi and other members of his team stood on a balcony at one end of the squash court, opposite the reactor. A three-person "suicide squad" suspended a bucket of boron solution over the pile should the heat become intolerable. On the squash court floor, another scientist handled the master control rod. At 3:20 P.M. Fermi ordered the rod removed. After a tense moment and several adjustments, he matter-of-factly announced, "The reaction is self-sustaining." The precise time was 3:25 P.M.

The world would never be the same again.

In 1944 the federal government moved Fermi and other scientists associated with the Manhattan Project to Los Alamos, New Mexico, in total secrecy and under false names (Fermi's new name was Eugene Farmer). On July 16, 1945, the years of hard work reached fruition when the first atomic bomb was exploded in a test at Alamogordo Air Base. Three weeks later, the United States dropped atomic bombs on Hiroshima and Nagasaki, forcing a Japanese surrender and ending World War II.

It is uncertain how Fermi felt about the mass destruction caused by the atomic bomb. He tended to keep his opinions to himself. Laura Fermi once remarked that her husband believed that nothing was served "by trying to halt the progress of science." Further, he asserted, "Whatever the future holds for mankind, however unpleasant it may be, we must accept it, for knowledge is always better than ignorance."

In December 1945 Fermi returned to the University of Chicago as a professor in the Institute of Nuclear Physics, where he remained until he died of cancer in 1954. He was only fifty-three years old. There is no concrete evidence that the cancer was caused by exposure to radiation. *Nuclear Energy,* a sculpture by Henry Moore, now marks the spot where Fermi and his team of scientists conducted their famous experiment.

"His needs were few," recalled a friend and fellow scientist, Dr. Herbert Anderson, at a memorial service shortly after Fermi's death. All he needed were "chalk, a blackboard, and an eager student."

Further reading: Pierre de Latil, *Enrico Fermi: The Man and His Theories* (1964); Laura Fermi. *Atoms in the Family: My Life with Enrico Fermi* (1954); Emilio Segre, *Enrico Fermi, Physicist* (1970).

Eugene Field

Journalist and Poet

BORN: September 2, 1850
St. Louis, Missouri

DIED: November 4, 1895
Chicago, Illinois

"I am a Yankee by pedigree and education but I was born in that ineffably uninteresting city of St. Louis," wrote Eugene Field. Poet and merry prankster, Field wrote the "Sharps and Flats" column in the *Chicago Daily News* for over a dozen years. He was the first of the so-called literary journalists of Chicago—including George Ade, Finley Peter Dunne, and Ring Lardner—to achieve national recognition. Field presented two faces to the world: the gentle man who wrote children's poetry and the worldly journalist who professed a penchant for drink.

Both of Field's parents hailed from Vermont. When his mother died in 1857, a cousin took care of him and acted as his foster mother. His love of practical jokes got him expelled from three schools: Williams College, Knox College, and the State University of Missouri. Field began his journalism career at the *St. Louis Evening Journal* in 1872. Three years later he joined the *St. Joseph* (Missouri) *Gazette*. He returned to St. Louis to assume an editorship on the *Times-Journal*. He then joined the staff of the *Kansas City Times* but left in 1881 to become managing editor of the *Denver Tribune* at the age of thirty-one. At the *Tribune* he initiated a popular column, "Odds and Ends," for which he was the principal contributor.

In 1883 Field accepted an offer from Melville E. Stone to join the staff of the *Chicago Daily News*. His column debuted on August 15, 1883, under the banner of "Current Gossip." Two weeks later the title was changed to "Sharps and Flats." It was a wide-ranging column and, according to historian Alson J. Smith in *Chicago's Left Bank*, it was the first daily newspaper column in the country. Field commented upon politics, the arts, and sports. He didn't care much about facts and figures; he preferred instead anecdotes and the rather imprecise art of describing the idiosyncrasies of human nature. The whimsical side of life appealed to him.

Field developed a curious ritual when he was ready to begin his day's work. "Getting ready to write" is how his editor, Charles H. Dennis, described it. He seldom arrived at the office before 11 A.M. and never wrote down a single word until 3 P.M., but he always managed to finish his column by 6 P.M. He spent the hours between 11:00 and 3:00 socializing, gossiping, and chatting among his colleagues. After finally entering his office, he would discard his coat, take off his shoes, don a pair of comfortable slippers, and roll up his trousers above his ankles. Then he would sit down, place his feet on the desk, and cross his legs. Only then would he *begin* to write.

Although Field did not complain, historian Kenny J. Williams maintains that the columnist was heavily censored by his editor, John Ballantyne, who deleted any copy that was too critical of the moneyed establishment. The unspoken rule was that Field could gently ridicule but could not overtly criticize.

At the same time he was earning a living as a columnist, Field began to write children's verse and compose poetry, mostly of a sentimental nature. Although his poetry is largely forgotten today, there was something about it—its innocence and cheerfulness perhaps—that appealed to nineteenth-century American tastes. Field may have been a newspaperman, but it was his poetry that made him famous. A devout bibliophile, Field and a circle of literary friends often met at the Saints' and Sinners' rare book corner of McClurg's Bookstore at Wabash Avenue and Monroe Street to discuss books and literature.

During his last years, Field, in ill health, wrote his column from home. His son delivered it to the office each day.

Field wished to be recognized as a serious writer of fiction, but instead he became one of the best-loved columnists and poets of his day. Kenny J. Williams calls him the first Chicago journalist to receive national fame. Field died in his sleep due to heart failure in November 1895. He was only forty-five.

Among his books of verse and poetry were *Denver Tribune Primer* (1882), *Culture's Garland* (1887), *Little Book of Western Verse* (1889), *A Little Book of Profitable Tales* (1890), *Second Book of Verse* (1893), and *Echoes from the Sabine Farm* (translations of Horace, 1893).

In 1922 a statue dedicated to Field was unveiled in Lincoln Park Zoo. The sculpture by Edward McCartan, which is east of the Small Mammal House, depicts the figure of an angel dropping flowers over two sleeping children. Verses from two of Field's most popular children's poems, "Wynken, Blynken, and Nod" and "Sugar Plum Tree," were carved in the granite.

For many years Field lived at 4240 North Clarendon Avenue on the North Side. He was buried in Graceland Cemetery. In 1926 his remains—with the consent of the Field family—were moved to the Church of the Holy Comforter in Kenilworth, Illinois.

See also: George Ade, Finley Peter Dunne, Ring Lardner, Victor Lawson, Melville E. Stone

Further reading: Alson J. Smith, *Chicago's Left Bank* (1953); Slason Thompson, *Eugene Field: A Study in Heredity and Contradictions*, 2 vols. (1901); Kenny J. Williams, *Prairie Voices: A Literary History of Chicago from the Frontier to 1893* (1980).

Marshall Field

Merchant

BORN: September 18, 1834
Conway, Massachusetts

DIED: January 16, 1906
Chicago, Illinois

Mandel Brothers; the Fair; Carson, Pirie, Scott—all were (and the last still is) big Chicago department stores. But none quite matched the grandeur and dignity of Marshall Field and Company. Like Potter Palmer and John G. Shedd, Marshall Field was a Yankee who made good in Chicago. The quiet-mannered Field reminded his employees, "Always remember, we are the servants of the public." The company motto? "Give the lady what she wants."

Marshall Field was working for a dry goods store in Pittsfield, Massachusetts, when talk of a rough and ready town, a thriving center of commerce on the Midwestern prairie, captured his imagination. Field had saved some money, and by 1855 he was ready to leave Massachusetts to seek his fortune out west.

Field arrived in Chicago in 1856 and soon found work at the wholesale firm of Cooley, Wadsworth and Company as a clerk. His employer, John Farrell, observed, "He had a merchant's instinct . . . and he never lost it." Field worked hard and lived frugally, devoting all of his time to learning the business. He soon rose to be a junior partner and was placed in charge of sales and credit. Within a year he was offered a full partnership, and the new firm of Farwell, Field and Company was formed. Potter Palmer, founder of the company and in ill health at the time, sold his retail and wholesale business to the new firm. Thus the firm of Field, Palmer, and Leiter was created. Settling on State Street, Field encouraged other retail businesses to open there also.

On October 12, 1868, Field's grand new store at State and Washington opened to a huge throng who gathered eagerly outside the doors. Field wanted to please his new clientele, and so he guaranteed their money back if customers were not entirely satisfied. Furthermore, Field introduced free delivery service and opened a bargain basement store. Most of all, he carefully nurtured an irresistible atmosphere. Women, especially, enjoyed the attentiveness and respect of the well-mannered and efficient store clerks.

Field and his partner, Levi Leiter, soon clashed over policy matters, and in 1879 Field bought Leiter out. In 1881 Field, Palmer and Leiter became Marshall Field and Company. In 1887 the wholesale division moved into a new building designed by the noted Boston architect H. H. Richardson. A massive Romanesque structure, it filled the entire city block bounded by Adams, Quincy, Wells, and Franklin Streets. It was demolished in 1930.

Field reportedly attracted the most aggressive men in the retail business. John G. Shedd, a New Hampshire farm boy, rose through the organization to become president of the company. Another important figure was the quick-tongued, ambitious Harry Gordon Selfridge, who started with the company in 1879 as a stock boy in the wholesale house. It was Selfridge's idea to open a restaurant in the store. At first Field objected. "This is a dry-goods store," he said, "we don't feed people here." Then he reconsidered, and in April 1890 a tearoom was opened. As manager of the retail division, Selfridge is credited with transforming Marshall Field and Company from a dry goods store into the full-fledged department store that made it famous. Selfridge later founded the equally famous department store in London that bears his name.

A generous benefactor, Field donated money to the University of Chicago to be used toward an athletic field. For years the students referred to it simply as "Marshall Field" until it was renamed Stagg Field, in honor of the great University of Chicago football coach Amos Alonzo Stagg. The Field Museum of Natural History was founded in 1893 during the World's Columbian Exposition with a $1 million gift from Field. Initially located in the old Palace of Fine

Arts building in Jackson Park, it was moved to its present site at Roosevelt Road and Lake Shore Drive in 1921.

On January 16, 1906, the merchant prince fell fatally ill, a victim of pneumonia. A bell rang through the State Street store at the news of his death, and the shades were drawn. On the day of his funeral, all the stores along State Street closed, out of respect to his memory. Field was buried in Graceland Cemetery.

When Marshall Field IV died in 1965 at the age of forty-nine, the Field family relinquished control of the company with the sale of its last remaining stock. In 1982 BAT Industries, a London tobacco conglomerate, acquired the firm, and in April 1990, the Minneapolis-based Dayton Hudson Corporation took over.

On August 30, 2005, Macy's, Inc. acquired Marshall Field's. On September 9 of the following year, Marshall Field's was officially renamed Macy's; it is one of Macy's flagship stores nationwide. However, many loyal Marshall Field's customers refused to accept the name change and boycotted the store. In 2005 the grassroots organization FieldsFansChicago.org staged protest rallies and letter-writing campaigns: its goal is to restore Marshall Field's in name as well as in quality and service. The organization continues its campaign through blogging and the maintaining of a website, www.fieldsfanschicago.org.

See also: Potter Palmer, John G. Shedd
Further reading: Lloyd Wendt and Herman Kogan, *Give the Lady What She Wants! The Story of Marshall Field and Co.* (1952).

John Fischetti

Cartoonist

BORN: September 27, 1916
Brooklyn, New York

DIED: November 18, 1980
Chicago, Illinois

Pulitzer Prize–winning cartoonist John Fischetti was considered by many in his profession to be one of the best editorial cartoonists in the country.

Giovanni Fischetti knew by the time he was twelve that he wanted to be a newspaper cartoonist. Born in Brooklyn to an Italian immigrant family, Fischetti ran away from home at sixteen. He hopped freight trains, toiled as a cabin boy on a ship bound for South America, and mopped hallways. In 1919 he returned home to study commercial art at the Pratt Institute in Brooklyn.

Fischetti's first cartooning job was with Walt Disney's studio on the West Coast animating Mickey Mouse. While there, he picked up several assignments on the *Los Angeles Times*. Later, Fischetti moved to San Francisco and then Chicago where he freelanced for *Coronet* and *Esquire* magazines.

In 1941 the *Chicago Sun* hired Fischetti as an editorial cartoonist, but the outbreak of World War II cut short his career plans. From 1942 to 1946, he served in the army and worked for *Stars and Stripes* in Paris. When he returned to the United States, he joined the *New York Herald Tribune* as an editorial cartoonist. From 1951 to 1961 he was a syndicated editorial cartoonist but returned to Chicago in 1966 to join the *Chicago Daily News*. He won the Pulitzer Prize two years later for general excellence in cartooning. When the *Daily News* ceased publication in 1978 Fischetti moved to the *Chicago Sun-Times*.

Fischetti was a pioneer of what he referred to as the "new look" cartoons. He drew wide horizontal cartoons, a departure from the more vertical styles of traditional cartooning, and satirized everything from fads and fashions to contemporary mores and values. He reserved his most acerbic bite, however, for politics and politicians, whom he described as the "linchpin of most of the social ills."

Fischetti often created his best work under deadline pressure. One of his most critically acclaimed—and poignant—cartoons depicted the figure of a weeping Abraham Lincoln on the floor of the Lincoln Memorial on the day of John F. Kennedy's assassination. Another was his drawing of an African American man, bound with chains labeled "white racism," and accompanied by the caption: "Why don't they lift themselves up by their own bootstraps like we do?"

In 1973 Fischetti published his autobiography, *Zinga Zanga Za!*, which was profusely illustrated with 150 of his cartoons.

During the early 1970s Fischetti's health faltered. He suffered heart attacks in 1972 and 1973 and underwent triple bypass surgery in 1979. He died in November 1980 at the age of sixty-four after collapsing in his Near North Side home.

In 1980 a John Fischetti Scholarship Dinner was established in his name. Proceeds from the annual event, held each November, go toward a scholarship fund for outstanding Columbia College journalism students.

See also: John T. McCutcheon

Morris Fishbein
Physician

BORN: July 22, 1889
St. Louis, Missouri

DIED: September 27, 1976
Chicago, Illinois

For many years Dr. Morris Fishbein was the most influential person in American medicine. As editor of the *Journal of the American Medical Association* for almost forty years, Fishbein helped the American Medical Association (AMA) grow into a powerful organization that still greatly affects both medical practices and health legislation.

Fishbein's father, Benjamin, a glassware merchant, wanted his son to become a rabbi, but young Morris had other ideas. He received a bachelor's degree from the University of Chicago in 1910 and an M.D. in 1912 from Rush Medical College.

Fishbein began his clinical career in Durand Hospital at the McCormick Institute for Infectious Diseases, located at 637 South Wood Street, as a house physician in 1912. In 1913 he became assistant to Dr. George H. Simmons, editor of the *Journal of the American Medical Association*. He held that post until 1924, when he was promoted to editor.

Fishbein turned the journal into one of the most influential and well-read medical publications in the country. In its pages he attacked quacks, promoted good medical practices, and disparaged socialized medicine—including subsidized medicine for the poor and the elderly—as a threat to professional standards, a position that he would later retract. By 1965 he supported Medicare and other federal health programs as necessary aspects of health care. "As conditions change we must adapt to the changes," he explained. "When conditions become so severe they can no longer be handled by private initiative, government must step in."

In addition Fishbein founded a lay magazine, *Hygeia*, and established the American Medical Association's public relations department. In 1921 he became *Time* magazine's first medical editor. From 1924 to 1950 he edited the *Journal of the American Medical Association*, founded the weekly *Medical World News*, and wrote a popular syndicated medical column. From 1958 to 1967 he acted as editor of *World-Wide Abstracts of General Medicine*. He was also president of the Chicago Medical Society and president of the Chicago Heart Association.

In 1950 Fishbein retired but continued his work as a medical editor with Encyclopaedia Britannica. During a speech to the graduating class of the Chicago Medical College in 1965, Fishbein said the old-time physician who made house calls was dead. "The modern doctor must combine the tactfulness of a diplomat, the eloquence of a lawyer, the impartiality of a judge, the decision of a general, the frankness of a witness, and the astuteness of a man on trial for his life with the precision of a mathematician, the imagination of an artist, the altruism of a philanthropist, and the tenacity of a pawnbroker."

In 1969 Fishbein published his autobiography, *Morris Fishbein, M.D.: An Autobiography*. Among his forty books are *Do You Want to Become a Doctor?* (1939), *History of the American Medical Association* (1947), and *The Handy Home Medical Advisor and Concise Medical Encyclopedia* (1953).

In 1970 a new professorship for the teaching of history of science and medicine was established at the University of Chicago in his name. Five years later Fishbein was honored by Jackson Park Hospital and the medical division of the State of Israel Bonds for his contributions to medicine and the economic development of the Jewish state.

Fishbein, who lived at 5454 South Shore Drive, died in Jackson Park Hospital in 1976. He was eighty-seven.

See also: Frank Billings

Dannie Flesher
Record Label Owner

BORN: May 20, 1951
Hope, Arkansas

DIED: January 10, 2010
Hope, Arkansas

Dannie Flesher and his partner Jim Nash were the founders and owners of one of the most important independent record labels in Chicago popular music history, Wax Trax, which was both a record store and a record label. Wax Trax served as the unofficial headquarters of Chicago's new wave, punk rock, and industrial music scene and pioneered the industrial music movement in the United States.

Flesher and Jim Nash, his business partner and longtime companion, opened a record store in Denver called Wax Trax in the 1970s. By 1978 they moved their base of operations to Chicago at 2449 North Lincoln Avenue. They concentrated on imported punk records and electronic music. *Chicago Tribune* rock music critic Greg Kot once referred to Wax Trax as "the city's island of misfit toys, where punks, freaks and outsiders gathered to buy music, advertise shows and plot their futures."

The Wax Trax record label started slowly, almost imperceptibly. The first releases were limited edition records, including Brian Eno's seven-inch recording *Wimoweh/*

Deadly Seven Finns in 1974. The first official release in 1981 was the experimental punk band Strike Under's *Immediate Action,* which was followed later that year by the seven-inch record *Born to Be Cheap*, by the disco/dance artist Divine. But it was the release of Ministry's *Cold Life* (1981) that put Wax Trax on the musical map.

As the store become more popular, Flesher and Nash began sponsoring shows and selling (handmade) concert tickets at such now-defunct venues as Gaspar's, O'Banion's, and Tut's. The store stocked the records of well-known English acts, including Roxy Music, David Bowie, Eno, the Human League, and Heaven 17, but they also carried artists on independent labels such as Stiff, 2 Tone, and Sugar Hill. Admirers of Ian Curtis and his band Joy Division, Flesher and Nash made Wax Trax the unofficial headquarters of the band's label, Factory Records. In fact, Wax Trax sponsored the band's first-ever American tour with a concert at Tut's, which was scheduled to occur on May 27, 1980. Unfortunately, by then Curtis had committed suicide on May 18, the eve of the tour.

During the 1980s, Flesher and Nash were enjoying their glory years. Nash was the flamboyant frontman; Flesher handled the behind-the-scenes work. Their modest offices on Lincoln Avenue—their apartment was above the store—in fact became the label's international headquarters. Wax Trax was known for its cutting-edge and boundary-pushing music and artists; the music combined elements of disco, electronic music, rock, and the avant-garde, and eventually came to be known as industrial disco. Among the artists they represented were Front 242, KMFDM, My Life with

the Thrill Kill Kult, Throbbing Gristle, and, most famously, Ministry. In 1993 Wax Trax moved from Lincoln Avenue to 1657 North Damen Avenue in Wicker Park.

The underground artists on Wax Trax went on to sell millions. Despite the outward success of the label, Flesher and Nash were not very good businessmen. They never did sign contracts with the musicians they discovered, for example. Consequently, most of their more successful acts went elsewhere to do work for the major labels. In 1992, Wax Trax declared bankruptcy and was bought by the New York–based TVT Records. Still, Flesher and Nash retained creative control.

After Wax Trax folded and his business partner and life partner Jim Nash died on October 10, 1995, from AIDS-related complications at the age of forty-seven, Flesher left the music business altogether and, in 2005, returned to his native Arkansas.

In 1994, TVT released *Black Box—Wax Trax! Records: The First 13 Years,* a three-CD box set of Wax Trax's biggest sellers.

Flesher died from pneumonia in January 2010 at the age of fifty-eight, in Arkansas.

In April 2011, a series of tribute concerts entitled "Wax Trax! Records Retrospectable" were held at Metro, a live-music club at 3730 North Clark Street.

See also: James Bracken and Vivian Carter, Leonard Chess
Further reading: Greg Kot, "A Wax Trax for the 90s: Underground Institution Is Still Making Noise," *Chicago Tribune,* October 23, 1994.

Fahey Flynn

Television News Broadcaster

BORN: August 6, 1916
Escanaba, Michigan

DIED: August 8, 1983
Chicago, Illinois

His trademarks—the bow tie, the jaunty "Howwww do you do, ladies and gentlemen"—branded Fahey Flynn as a newsman of the old school. For more than thirty years, Chicagoans invited Flynn into their living rooms. Said one admiring colleague at a 1981 testimonial dinner in his honor, "Can you imagine any station manager today hiring a man who is five-foot-five-inches high, overweight, with a leprechaun face, wearing a bow tie and bearing his unlikely name?" Perhaps not, but by the end of the 1970s, Fahey Flynn had become a local broadcasting institution.

The broadcaster's unusual name was a combination of the surname of his father, Flynn, and that of his mother,

Fahey. Flynn was a graduate student in economics at the University of Wisconsin during the late 1930s when he found part-time work at radio stations in Fond du Lac and Madison. He then joined WEMP radio in Milwaukee as a $60-a-week announcer and broadcasted the minor league Milwaukee Brewers baseball games. Flynn eventually earned a bachelor's degree in history and English from the University of Wisconsin–Oshkosh.

In 1941 Flynn auditioned for a broadcasting job at WBBM radio in Chicago—and got it. After a tour of duty in the navy during World War II, Flynn resumed his radio career. In 1948 he won several radio journalism awards for his series "Report Uncensored," an exposé on conditions at a delinquent boy's school in St. Charles, Illinois. Two years later, he won more acclaim for his program on race relations, "The Quiet Answer."

On March 3, 1953, Flynn made his television debut on WBBM-TV, sporting one of his favorite polka-dot bow ties. A new Chicago tradition was born. For a decade, Flynn teamed up with meteorologist P. J. Hoff, an affable sort who drew cartoons to illustrate the weather, on the 10 P.M. WBBM newscast.

Flynn won six Chicago Emmy awards, including, in 1958, the first Chicago Emmy award for newscasting. He also received an Emmy for Outstanding Spot Coverage during the May 1979 crash of American Airlines flight 191 at O'Hare International Airport. In 1980 he was honored as the Chicago Variety Club's Man of the Year.

Flynn left WBBM-TV in 1968 when the general manager, in an effort to upgrade the newscast's image, forced him to wear regular ties. Instead, Flynn bolted to rival station WLS-TV, and was replaced at WBBM by a young, personable newsman named Bill Kurtis. In time, he, too, became a local broadcasting tradition.

At WLS, Flynn, along with coanchor Joel Daly and meteorologist John Coleman, launched a new format called "Eyewitness News." Although some critics disparagingly referred to it as "Happy Talk," Chicagoans found the friendly repartee and the apparently genuine camaraderie among the newscasters refreshing. The ratings soared. Flynn and company were credited, along with others, for leading WLS's Eyewitness News to the top of the ratings for virtually all of the 1970s.

Flynn died of complications from internal hemorrhaging at Northwestern Memorial Hospital in Chicago. He was sixty-seven.

Flynn was praised for his professionalism, his integrity, and his grace under pressure. Said his friend and colleague, Joel Daly, at the funeral mass, "In our peculiar world of prima donnas, Fahey Flynn was one of a kind. A man of tact, a man of sensitivity for whom rank had no particular privileges."

See also: John Drury

Leon Forrest

Author

BORN: January 8, 1937
Chicago, Illinois

DIED: November 6, 1997
Evanston, Illinois

Author and professor Leon Forrest wrote complex novels about the African American experience that combined myth, history, legend, and black music traditions. His works had many influences—from Ralph Ellison and William Faulkner to Dylan Thomas and Eugene O'Neill—but he was especially moved by the blues, jazz, and gospel music of Charlie Parker, Billie Holiday, Mahalia Jackson, and Thomas Dorsey. Forrest considered the act of reinvention an essentially African American cultural attribute, and he used black music, specifically jazz, as a structural framework. He employed two of its most basic concepts—improvisation and syncopation—to reflect the journeys of his characters, and as a metaphor for the broader African American experience.

Born in Cook County Hospital to Leon Forrest and Adeline Green, Forrest was the biracial son of a musician and songwriter who also worked as a bartender for the Santa Fe Railroad. His mother, a Catholic Creole from New Orleans, wrote short stories, although they were never published. He never knew his white father but was nevertheless influenced by the Protestant faith of his father, who was a

member of the Pilgrim Baptist Church and director of its youth choir. Indeed, faith and intraracial tension were prominent themes in Forrest's work.

Forrest attended the all-black Wendell Phillips elementary school. There his teachers exposed him to black history and such black writers as Langston Hughes, Countee Cullen, Richard Wright, and W. E. B. DuBois. He also attended Hyde Park High School, newly integrated at the time, and from 1955 to 1956 Wilson Junior College. From 1956 to 1957 he briefly studied accounting at Roosevelt University before enrolling in 1960 at the University of Chicago. Drafted into the army the next year, he completed his basic training and became a public-information specialist while serving in Germany for two years. Forrest returned to Chicago in 1962 and resumed his studies at the University of Chicago, where he took creative writing courses and even occasionally sat in on Ralph Ellison's lectures. While at the university he met and befriended Professor Allison Davis, a social anthropologist, and English professor John G. Cawelti. While attending college he worked at 408 Liquors, his mother's bar and liquor store, which provided good material for his later fiction, especially *Divine Days* (1995), where he captured the voices and stories of ordinary people from the neighborhood.

With his racial consciousness raised by his studies at the University of Chicago, Forrest participated in the historic 1963 March on Washington and then moved into the Avon, a rooming house that was occupied by other artistic types, including musicians, painters, writers, and retired professors. He purchased a typewriter and began work on his first novel, while at the same time working as an office boy for the Catholic Interracial Council's Speakers Bureau. He did not complete the novel, though, until 1971.

In the meantime, he continued to ply his trade as a working journalist. From 1964 to 1968 Forrest wrote for several community weekly newspapers, including the *Woodlawn Booster,* the *Englewood Bulletin,* and the *Woodlawn Observer.* From 1969 to 1972 he was also a contributor and editor of *Muhammad Speaks,* the news organ of the Nation of Islam in which he frequently wrote about racial injustices. Through his contacts there he personally met Ellison and was introduced to an editor at Holt, Rinehart, the publisher of Toni Morrison's 1970 novel *The Bluest Eye.* That editor in turn referred Forrest to Morrison herself, who was an in-house editor at the time at Random House.

In 1966 his first short story, "That's Your Little Red Wagon," was published in the literary magazine *Blackbird.* It would later become a part of his novel *There Is a Tree More Ancient than Eden,* published in 1973. In 1967 his three-act play, *Theatre of the Soul,* was performed at the Parkway Community House. He also wrote *Re-Creation,* a one-act verse play set to music by T. J. Anderson, which was presented at the African American architect Richard Hunt's Chicago studio in 1978. In 1982 he collaborated again with Anderson by writing the libretto for *Soldier Boy, Soldier,* an opera composed by Anderson that was produced at the University of Indiana at Bloomington.

Forrest's novels borrow from jazz and blues sensibilities while using modernist techniques. In particular, black music provided Forrest "with inspiration, form, and style," notes Dana Williams, especially the work of Mahalia Jackson and Billie Holiday. In fact, Forrest wrote "Solo Long-Song: For Lady Day," an homage to Holiday, and he even once said that he was "weaned" on her music. Other musical influences included Thomas Dorsey, the father of gospel music. Forrest was a great admirer of gospel. It was the only music, he believed, that truly expressed the complexities of African American life after the Great Migration.

In 1972 Forrest resigned his position at *Muhammad Speaks* to devote his life to full-time creative writing. That same year he accepted an associate professorship at Northwestern University. In 1985 he became chair of the university's Department of African American Studies, which he held until 1994 while also a professor in the English department. He lectured too at numerous American universities, including Yale, Brown, Tufts, Wesleyan, Notre Dame, and Harvard.

There Is a Tree More Ancient than Eden (1973) is about the troubled relationships between the illegitimate offspring of a former slave-owning family and uses the nonlinear and improvisational style of jazz to create its mesmerizing effect. It contains many modernist influences. With its feelings of displacement and isolation and interracial tension between darker- and lighter-skinned blacks, it employs too a stream-of-consciousness, experimental style within a modern jazz narrative. As Forrest's first novel—it was endorsed by Saul Bellow and introduced by Ralph Ellison—it was an attempt to come to terms with the devastating antilynching song "Strange Fruit" that Billie Holiday made famous in narrative form and that affected him so much. "The eloquence she achieved on stage, the thrilling effect she had on her audience, he desired to achieve on paper," observes Williams. Forrest used jazz, and its various muted forms, as a jumping-off point, as a way to reinvent or reinterpret lives. To Forrest, the spiritual, or the sorrow song, is the African American's attempt at reinvention since the spiritual is a retelling of biblical stories but sung in the African American vernacular—so much so that it gains social, religious, and cultural significance.

With his second novel, *The Bloodworth Orphans* (1977), Forrest used blues songs and blues artists to inform both the plot and the characters, especially the life of the legendary bluesman Lightnin' Hopkins. The character of Carl-Rae here and Hopkins Golightly in the later *Meteor in the Madhouse* (2001) both pay homage to Hopkins. In *Orphans,* six major characters represent various aspects of African American life and their diverse responses to racial discrimination. To tell the story of being orphaned in America, Forrest adopts black musical impulses—jazz as both theme and structure here—borrowing music as a metaphor to reintegrate experience. But the novel also has echoes of Greek and Latin mythology with its search by three orphaned siblings striving to understand the source of their roots.

In *Two Wings to Veil My Face* (1984), Forrest once again turns to the blues as a metaphor for African American life. He not only uses a blueslike storytelling structure, he also incorporates blues and slave history, combining storytelling and the blues to examine his character's struggles, "which, like the blues song, laments but shows no signs of surrender," says Williams, as an ex-slave tells her life story to her great-grandson. *Two Wings to Veil My Face* won numerous awards, including the DuSable Museum Certificate of Merit and Achievement in Fiction and the Carl Sandburg Award. Following its critical success, Mayor Harold Washington even proclaimed April 14, 1985, as Leon Forrest Day in Chicago.

His next novel, *Divine Days* (1992), uses a technique that Forrest called reinvention, as he used black cultural traditions to explore various shades of blackness and the diversity of blackness. Considered by many to be his masterwork and set in 1966 Chicago, it was once again influenced by blues, jazz, gospel, and spirituals. It tells the story of an African American playwright investigating the disappearance of another black man.

Forrest's other works include *Furious Voice for Freedom*, a collection of essays originally published in 1992 that was reprinted as *Relocations of the Spirit* in 1994. His novel *Meteor in the Madhouse* was published posthumously.

Forrest died in November 1997 after a long battle with prostate cancer. He was honored in a memorial ceremony at Northwestern University on January 30, 1998.

The Leon Forrest Papers are housed at Northwestern University in Evanston, Illinois.

See also: Gwendolyn Brooks, Richard Wright

Further reading: John C. Cawelti, ed., *Leon Forrest: Introductions and Interpretations* (1997); John Edgar Wideman, "In Memoriam: Leon Forrest, 1937–1997," *Callaloo* 21, Winter 1998; Dana A. Williams, *"In the Light of Likeness—Transformed": The Literary Art of Leon Forrest* (2005).

Bob Fosse

Choreographer and Film Director

BORN: June 23, 1927
Chicago, Illinois

DIED: September 23, 1987
Washington, D.C.

A hard-driving, fiercely competitive song-and-dance man, Robert Louis Fosse was one of the most widely acclaimed choreographers of the Broadway stage as well as a respected motion picture director. Although his theatrical work usually consisted of upbeat and energetic musicals, his movies—especially *Lenny, All That Jazz, Cabaret*, and *Star 80*—traveled down darker paths.

The son of a salesman who moonlighted as a vaudeville singer, Fosse received his first dance lesson at age nine above a drugstore at Ashland and Montrose Avenues in Chicago. Though especially fond of baseball, Fosse idolized not an athlete but a dancer, Fred Astaire. By the time he was thirteen, Fosse had formed his first nightclub act and began performing in clubs around the Midwest. He did stints as a teenage hoofer in Chicago burlesque houses and nightclubs. "I got $10 a night, six nights a week, and that makes you a very interesting figure in high school," said Fosse, who attended Amundsen High School on the city's North Side and performed in the school's variety shows.

While serving in the navy during World War II, Fosse appeared in several productions that toured the Pacific. Upon his discharge, he teamed up with Mary Ann Niles, his first wife, in several road-show productions. In 1953 Fosse left for Hollywood and appeared in several films, including *Kiss Me Kate*, with Howard Keel and Kathryn Grayson. *Kiss Me Kate* was the first film in which Fosse's own choreography appeared. Although he was allowed to stage his own

dance numbers, Gower Champion, the film's choreographer, was given the actual credit. Fosse later admitted that he began doing his own choreography out of self-defense, because there weren't enough good choreographers to go around. His aim was to blend dancing and dialogue so that "you can't tell where one stops."

In 1954 Fosse headed for Broadway, where he choreographed *Pajama Game* (for which he won his first Tony) and *Damn Yankees*. Other shows followed—*New Girl in Town* with Gwen Verdon, and *Redhead* and *Sweet Charity*, which he both choreographed and directed. *Sweet Charity*, in particular, was a Broadway smash. Its songs included such showstoppers as "Big Spender" and "If My Friends Could See Me Now." Fosse also choreographed *Little Me* and *How to Succeed in Business Without Really Trying*. Among these successes, he only suffered one flop, *Pleasures and Palaces*, about the unlikely pairing of Catherine the Great and John Paul Jones.

Fosse's debut as a movie director in 1968 was far from promising. Critics panned *Sweet Charity*, starring Shirley MacLaine as the prostitute with a heart of gold, as being downbeat and confusing. While they praised his innovative choreography, they criticized his "choppy" direction. The 1987 Broadway revival of *Sweet Charity*, however, was a hit and was considered the definitive production.

Everything came together with Fosse's next film, the Oscar-winning *Cabaret* (1972), starring Liza Minnelli as an American singer in a cabaret in Berlin during the waning days of the Weimar Republic and Joel Grey as the sneering master of ceremonies. By allowing the songs to comment on the action and foreshadow the lives of the characters, *Cabaret* breathed new life into a moribund art form and, in the process, broke every rule in the movie musical tradition. Pioneering, brash, and unsentimental, *Cabaret* was called the first "adult" musical. The scenes inside the Kit Kat Klub captured Fosse's choreography at its most provocative with its finger-snapping rhythm, deliberately jerky movements, and a sensual, almost vulgar, earthiness.

In 1973 Fosse won every major award in the entertainment industry. In addition to his Oscar for *Cabaret*, he brought home a Tony for *Pippin* and an Emmy for the television concert film *Liza with a Z*. Fosse's next film, *Lenny* (1974), starred Dustin Hoffman as the acid-tongued comedian Lenny Bruce. Though flawed and uneven, it was further evidence of the director's fascination with the underside of American society. The largely autobiographical *All That Jazz* (1979) was a thinly veiled account of Fosse's near-fatal heart attack, which occurred in 1974 while he was rehearsing the Broadway musical *Chicago* and editing *Lenny*. The late Roy Scheider played the overworked song-and-dance man with great aplomb. *All That Jazz* received nine Oscar nominations and won four awards. Fosse's last movie, *Star 80* (1983), was a harrowing account of the murder of *Playboy* model Dorothy Stratten by her jealous husband. A box office failure, it nevertheless received generally positive reviews for its unflinching examination of the dark side of human nature.

Despite his cinematic success, Fosse always felt more at home on the stage. His most popular efforts include *Chicago* (1975), *Pippin* (1972), and *Dancin'* (1978). *Chicago* is a musical ode to the city of Fosse's birth. *Pippin*, a sort of medieval coming-of-age tale, was Fosse's longest-running show (it ran for five years), and one for which he won Tonys for best director and best choreographer. *Dancin'* is a joyous celebration of the Broadway musical and its hard-working chorus line, and it won Fosse another Tony for best choreographer. In 1986 Fosse directed his last Broadway show, *Big Deal*. Set in the Chicago of his youth, the show used popular songs of the thirties and forties. Although Fosse won another Tony for best choreography, it was ultimately both a critical and commercial flop and closed after only seventy performances.

Fosse suffered a fatal heart attack at George Washington University Hospital in Washington, D.C., minutes after the opening of the revival of *Sweet Charity* in 1987.

In November 2009, the Chicago-based Thodos Dance company presented *Fosse Trilogy*, a revival by Fosse protégé and choreographer Ann Reinking. It was presented at Centre East at the North Shore Center for the Performing Arts in Skokie, Illinois, and at the Harris Theater in downtown Chicago. *Fosse Trilogy* consists of three short Fosse dances—"Cool Hand Luke," "Mexican Breakfast," and "Tijuana Shuffle"—that were staged by Fosse himself for various 1960s television variety programs. Two of the dances made their premieres on the live stage.

Fosse believed the fewer the words, the better. He felt the images on the screen should say it all. What's more, he always maintained that work would be his way of attaining a piece of immortality. Ironically, it was both his saving grace and his downfall.

Further reading: Martin Gottfried, *All His Jazz: The Life and Death of Bob Fosse* (2003); Kevin Boyd Grubb, *Razzle Dazzle: The Life and Work of Bob Fosse* (1989).

Steve Fossett

Aviator and Adventurer

BORN: April 22, 1944
Jackson, Tennessee

DIED: September 3, 2007
Near Mammoth Lakes,
California

A retired Chicago commodity options trader who made his fortune in soybean futures, James Stephen Fossett wanted to be remembered for doing things that most people would like to do but never got around to doing—adventuring was his way of becoming immortal. Fossett was a man out of time but also a timeless adventurer who followed in the spirit of adventurers of earlier eras. He set more than one hundred world records (although many have since been broken). In his autobiography he wrote, "My appearance is strictly average, my athletic ability is mediocre, and there is nothing dramatic about my speech or demeanor. I am bemused when people are surprised that I am such a low-key person because it adds to their curiosity."

Fossett grew up in Garden Grove, California, in Orange County. His father was a soap production supervisor at the Procter & Gamble soap factory. When young Fossett climbed Mt. Jacinto as a boy of twelve, one could say his future was set for him. He got the adventure bug.

Graduating from Garden Grove High School in 1962, he spent that summer hiking the John Muir Trail. He earned a bachelor's degree in economics from Stanford University in 1966—during his senior year he took a break from his studies by swimming to Alcatraz Island—and an M.B.A. from Washington University in St. Louis two years later. Then he programmed computers at IBM in New York, held a management job at Deloitte & Touche in Detroit, and consulted for Drexel Burnham & Co., also in Detroit, where he was fired. Dusting himself off, he took a job in Chicago as a systems analyst at Marshall Field's. Bored, he soon quit and decided instead to drive a Yellow cab to make ends meet—all the while still looking for something more exciting to occupy his time.

In 1973 Fossett joined Merrill Lynch before jumping to the Chicago Board Options Exchange. While there he made his first million. The year was 1977, and he was only thirty-three. He lost all of it, though, in 1979, due to the vagaries of the marketplace. Still he was not deterred. Instead he started his own brokerage firm, Lakota Trading, later founded Marathon Securities and, later still, Larkspur Securities.

But the adventure bug still lay dormant. In college Fossett had read *The Royal Road to Romance,* published in 1925 about the globetrotting Richard Halliburton—he went missing in 1939 and was never found. As it turns out, Halliburton proved to be his role model in more ways than one.

Despite his reputation as a reckless celebrity adventurer, Fossett spent a considerable amount of time and preparation trying to avoid unnecessary risks. He cheated death so many times that it was hard to keep track. He climbed 350 mountains in his lifetime, including Mount Everest, where he tried unsuccessfully to reach the summit on two occasions.

Fossett's adventures were legendary. In August 1998, on his fourth attempt to fly around the world in a balloon, he got caught in the middle of a violent thunderstorm off northeast Australia. The balloon fell nearly 30,000 feet into the Coral Sea. There he was—surrounded by sharks while the balloon's capsule itself was on fire, with Fossett still in it. He managed to cling onto his life raft and swam through the capsule's hatch, now submerged under water. He was picked up after a waterlogged ten hours at sea. That same year, in December, Fossett, along with Richard Branson and Per Lindstrand, tried again. And when they floated perilously close to Chinese airspace—it was too late to change their plans—they grew fearful that fighter jets might shoot them down. Fortunately, they flew over China without any bodily harm. He also set a record by gliding more than 50,000 feet above the Andes Mountains. In addition, he swam the length of the Golden Gate Bridge—at night.

According to his own website, Fossett held 115 world records. In 2002 he became the first person to circumnavigate the world solo in a hot-air balloon, this after five failed attempts, including one that ended in a crash landing in a remote village in India. In July 2002, he completed his first solo balloon flight around the world: 20,626 miles in thirteen days, eight hours. In April 2004, he sailed around the world in fifty-eight days and nine hours. It was the fastest sailing trip around the world. In March 2005, he completed the first solo flight around the world, some 25,294 miles, without stopping or refueling. It took sixty-seven hours after a leak drained a goodly amount of his spare oxygen and fuel. Flying solo from Florida to England and back (the flight included two Atlantic crossings), in 2006 he set the nonstop distance record for an aircraft. In the same year, with copilot Einar Enevoldson, he became the first to fly a glider into the stratosphere, reaching an altitude record of more than 50,000 feet. He also set twenty-one world records at sea, including the round-the-world speed record for vessels under sail. And he holds the record for speed in a zeppelin (71.5 miles per hour).

But Fossett didn't always finish first. In 1985 he swam the English Channel, and it was the slowest crossing of the year. Once, he drove a dogsled in the Iditarod race in Alaska, placing forty-seventh.

But whether first, last, or somewhere in between, Fossett never gave up. His resiliency and good fortune remained with him until September 3, 2007, when his luck finally ran out.

It was supposed to be a routine flight, a short pleasure jaunt—the equivalent, his wife Peggy later said, of a Sunday morning drive, "no more challenging for Fossett than a dip in the hot tub for [Olympic gold-medal swimmer] Michael Phelps." He wore sweats, a T-shirt, and tennis shoes and carried a bottle of water, but for some inexplicable reason he did not wear his GPS-equipped Breitling watch, nor did he bring a cell phone.

Fossett was reportedly scouting locations for a dry lake bed for his upcoming attempt to break the world land-speed record. He took off alone at 8:45 A.M. from the Flying-M Ranch in a borrowed Bellanca Citabria Super Decathalon, a single-engine two-seater made of fabric and steel tubing, "a sort of glorified barnstorming stunt plane," writes Bryan Smith. Located near Yerington, Nevada, about ninety miles southeast of Reno, the ranch was owned by hotel magnate Barron Hilton. Fossett was scheduled to return by noon but he never showed up.

That evening an extensive search began. Crews from nine surrounding counties searched for him as well as Civil Air Patrol pilots from six states and dozens of volunteers, including NASA test pilot Einar Enevoldson and astronaut Neil Armstrong. Even Blackhawk helicopters equipped with infrared technology were used. But nothing was found. At least $3 million was spent on the search ($1 million by his wife Peggy) that involved hundreds of planes and people on foot who scoured some 17,000 square miles. It was reportedly the most extensive search for a missing aircraft in American history.

Finally, the search was called off in October 2007. On September 29, 2008, a hiker in a remote area of the Inyo National Forest in east central California, near the town of Mammoth Lakes, found Fossett's pilot's license and more than $1,000 in $100 bills. Two days later a helicopter pilot spotted wreckage on a mountainside 200 feet below; it was scattered over an area 400-feet long. Somehow the debris had been missed in nineteen previous searches. Fossett's plane had apparently crashed at a high speed into the mountainside.

According to the National Transportation Safety Board, the official cause of the accident was blamed on likely downdrafts of at least 400 feet per minute. On February, 15, 2008, Judge Jeffrey A. Malak of the Circuit Court of Cook County declared Fossett legally dead. He was sixty-three.

In July 2007, Fossett was inducted into the National Aviation Hall of Fame. At the time of his death he owned a condominium with his wife at Water Tower Place. In addition, he had homes in Beaver Creek, Colorado, and Carmel, California.

When asked why he did what he did, Fossett replied, "I have a very low threshold for boredom."

Further reading: Steve Fossett with Will Hasley, *Chasing the Wind* (2006); James Janega, "Driven by Soaring Dreams," *Chicago Tribune*, October 3, 2008; Bryan Smith, "Without a Trace," *Chicago*, March 2008; James Vlahos, "Steve Fossett: The Aviator," *New York Times Magazine*, December 28, 2008.

Bud Freeman

Musician

BORN: April 13, 1906
Chicago, Illinois

DIED: March 15, 1991
Chicago, Illinois

As a member of the legendary Austin High Gang, tenor saxophonist Lawrence "Bud" Freeman played a crucial role in the development of what came to be known as the Chicago style of jazz, a style modeled after the great African American jazz musicians but marked by a fluent and strong rhythmic beat. Freeman, one of the most influential figures in Chicago jazz history, continued to perform until he was well into his eighties.

Freeman, the son of a Jewish garment cutter and a French Canadian woman, grew up in the Austin community on the Far West Side. While attending Austin High School, he befriended several young men who would form the nucleus of the seminal Austin High Gang. The Austin High Gang consisted of Freeman on saxophone, Jimmy McPartland on cornet, Dick McPartland on guitar, Jim Lannigan on bass, Frank Teschemacher on alto sax and clarinet, Dave North on piano, and Dave Tough on drums. Occasionally a reserved young man from the Maxwell Street neighborhood by the name of Benny Goodman would sit in with the gang. Most of the boys were already taking violin and piano lessons. Freeman, who didn't play an instrument but had grown up surrounded by music in his home, took saxophone lessons from McPartland's father.

In his autobiography Freeman recalls the times he and his friends would spend at the Spoon and Straw soda parlor in Oak Park, listening to records on the jukebox by the New Orleans Rhythm Kings. "We were so excited by that first record that we decided that afternoon to become jazz musicians and form our own band," noted Freeman. Freeman would travel to the Lincoln Gardens on the South Side to hear cornetist Joe "King" Oliver's Creole Jazz Band and an unknown trumpeter named Louis Armstrong. Another favorite was Bix Beiderbecke, the trumpet genius from Iowa who lived in Chicago for a brief period and performed in North Side clubs.

In 1924 Freeman made his professional debut playing with Dave Tough in a Sheboygan, Wisconsin, roadhouse. Back in Chicago, the gang rehearsed together and honed their skills by playing at parties and dances. In December 1927, Freeman, Teschemacher, Jimmy McPartland, Lannigan, pianist Joe Sullivan, guitarist Eddie Condon, and drummer Gene Krupa went into the studio and recorded several classic examples of Chicago jazz: "Liza," "Nobody's Sweetheart Now," "China Boy," and "Sugar." Although influenced by Armstrong and Beiderbecke, as well as contemporary French composers, Freeman by this time had developed a distinctive style that incorporated the rhythmic swing of the great jazz masters and the complex harmonies of classical music, yet was marked by a mellow and lyrical tone.

Freeman continued to perform with local dance and jazz bands until 1928, when he joined Ben Pollack in New York. In 1935 he formed the Windy City Five with Bunny Berigan, Claude Thornhill, Eddie Condon, Grachan Moncur, and Cozy Cole. The following year he teamed up with Jimmy and Tommy Dorsey, but left in 1937 to join Benny Goodman's band. It was not a pleasant experience, recalls Freeman, who refers to it in his autobiography as "the biggest mistake of my life. Benny liked to do all the playing, as well he should have. There wasn't much for me to do there, and he was very difficult to work for." He stayed only one year.

In 1943 Freeman was drafted and sent to the Aleutian Islands, where army brass took advantage of his talent and made him the leader of the military band. After the war he returned to New York to resume his career. During the next few decades, Freeman lived a nomadic existence, spending a large portion of his time playing clubs and concerts across the United States, in Canada, and in Europe.

In the late 1960s Freeman formed the World's Greatest Jazz Band, a ten-piece outfit based in New York. The World's Greatest Jazz Band performed at the best nightclubs in the country. A noted Anglophile, Freeman moved to London in 1974, staying for six years. After a prolonged absence from Chicago, Freeman returned in 1980 to perform at the Chicago Jazz Festival. At this point he fell in love with his hometown all over again and decided to stay.

Freeman recorded with many bands during his long career. Some titles include *Bud Freeman and His Orchestra* (1928), *Bud Freeman and His Windy City Five* (1935), *Bud Freeman Trio* and *Bud Freeman and His Gang* (1938), *Bud Freeman and His Summa Cum Laude Orchestra* (1939), and *Bud Freeman and His Famous Chicagoans* (1940). *The Compleat Bud Freeman*, an anthology of career highlights, was released in the early 1970s.

Freeman denied inventing the Chicago school of jazz—he always gave Armstrong and Oliver their proper due. "Our own contribution," he recalled several years ago in the *Chicago Tribune*, "was really to popularize the tenor saxophone in a band setting."

Freeman died of cancer a month before his eighty-fifth birthday at the Warren Barr Pavilion nursing home at 66 West Oak Street in Chicago.

See also: Louis Armstrong, Benny Goodman, Earl Hines, Gene Krupa, Mezz Mezzrow, Joe "King" Oliver

Further reading: Donald Clarke, *The Penguin Encyclopedia of Popular Music* (1989); Bud Freeman, as told to Robert Wolf, *Crazeology: The Autobiography of a Chicago Jazzman* (1989); Dempsey J. Travis, *An Autobiography of Black Jazz* (1983).

Henry Blake Fuller

Novelist

BORN: January 9, 1857
Chicago, Illinois

DIED: July 28, 1929
Chicago, Illinois

A distinguished Chicago blue blood, Henry Blake Fuller had an elegant, graceful writing style that epitomized the short-lived genteel tradition of Chicago literature that was prominent during the late nineteenth century.

Fuller was born near Van Buren and LaSalle Streets on the future site of the La Salle Street railroad station. With the exception of one year spent at the Allison Classical Academy on the shores of Lake Oconomowoc, Wisconsin, Fuller received his entire education in Chicago's public schools. After graduating from South Division High School, Fuller held a quick succession of clerical jobs—clerk in a kitchenware shop on State Street, messenger for the Bank of Illinois, and bookkeeper for the Home National Bank—before he left Chicago to spend one year in Europe.

Upon his return, Fuller began writing a fantasy romance, *The Chevalier of Pensieri-Vani* (1891). Written in an office on Lake Street, Fuller's first novel was an episodic work set in the Italy of his imagination. It didn't attract much reader interest—few Fuller novels did, esoteric as they were—but it was appreciated by a small segment of the literary set.

The Cliff-Dwellers (1893), Fuller's second novel—and his first set in Chicago—received virtually unanimous acclaim. *The Cliff-Dwellers* (the name refers to the skyscraper office where its main characters worked) has often been identified as the first important American urban novel. Not only was it one of the first credible portraits of the business world in American literature, it was also one of the first to use Chicago as a fictional setting. The Cliff-Dwellers is also the name of the prestigious social club, founded in 1907 by Fuller and fellow writer Hamlin Garland, that had its headquarters on the ninth floor of Orchestra Hall. In 1996 it moved to the Borg-Warner Building at 200 South Michigan Avenue.

Fuller's second Chicago novel, *With the Procession* (1895), received even more glowing reviews than *The Cliff-Dwellers.* Generally considered his most mature work, *With the Procession* chronicles Chicago's progress from isolated fort to bustling metropolis. *Under the Skylight,* a collection of short stories that contains descriptions of Chicago's artistic life, including a thinly veiled portrait of Hamlin Garland, was published in 1901. Fuller devoted the next two decades to writing primarily short stories, essays, and one-act fantasy plays.

During the last year of his life, Fuller experienced an energetic burst of creativity. Within a seven-month period he managed to complete two novels—*Gardens of This World* and *Not on the Screen*—and began work on a third. *Gardens of This World* returned to the romantic fantasy genre of his first novel while *Not on the Screen* satirized Chicago's fledgling motion picture industry. In addition, Fuller wrote a column of literary criticism for the *New York Evening Post* and was on the management staff of *Poetry* magazine. He was also a frequent contributor to the *New Republic.* His other novels include *On the Stairs* (1918) and *Bertram Cope's Year* (1919). The University of Chicago featured prominently in the latter.

Although not generally well known even among students of American literature, Fuller was an important figure on the Chicago literary scene. Theodore Dreiser placed Fuller in the "vanguard of the New Realism," and later such Midwestern writers as Thornton Wilder and Glenway Wescott acknowledged their debt to him. By the time of his death in 1929, his novels of manners were considered typical examples of nineteenth-century writing.

A painfully shy man who devoted most of his life to his work, Fuller felt comfortable around only a few close friends, though even they were expected to maintain a respectable distance. Fuller did, however, develop a good working relationship with Harriet Monroe, the publisher of *Poetry* magazine. He was a member of its publication advisory committee for three years.

After the death of his mother in 1907, Fuller lived in a succession of rooming houses in Hyde Park. When he died of heart disease in 1929 at the age of seventy-two, he was living at a friend's home at 5411 South Harper Avenue.

See also: Theodore Dreiser, Hamlin Garland, Harriet Monroe, Lorado Taft

Further reading: Bernard R. Bowron Jr., *Henry B. Fuller of Chicago: The Ordeal of a Genteel Realist in Ungenteel America* (1974); Constance Griffin, *Henry Blake Fuller: A Critical Biography* (1939); Henry Regnery, *The Cliff-Dwellers: The History of a Chicago Cultural Institution* (1990).

Mary Garden

Opera Singer

BORN: February 20, 1877
Aberdeen, Scotland

DIED: January 4, 1967
Aberdeen, Scotland

Mary Garden dominated Chicago opera for more than twenty years. Candid, temperamental, and always entertaining, she retired at the peak of her career in the early 1930s. "I began at the top. I stayed at the top and I quit at the top," said the unpredictable diva.

Born in Aberdeen, Scotland, Garden immigrated with her family to the United States, settling first in Chicopee, Massachusetts, and later in Hartford, Connecticut. The family moved to Chicago in 1888. At the age of sixteen Garden appeared in an amateur production of Gilbert and Sullivan's *Trial by Jury.* The wife of a local merchant heard her singing in a suburban church choir and, smitten with her voice, offered to pay for her to be trained in Paris.

Garden arrived in Paris in 1897 and made her professional debut three years later at the Opera Comique. As luck would have it, she was sitting in the audience when the star of the show fell ill. She went onstage in the third act of Charpentier's *Louise* and enraptured the audience—and continued to do so for one hundred successive nights. She filled houses in Brussels, London, New York, Boston, and eventually Chicago.

Although Garden put Chicago opera on the map, the first opera performed in the city was Bellini's *La Sonnambula* on July 29, 1850, at John Rice's theater on West Randolph Street. In the 1860s a young distiller from Massachusetts, Uranus H. Crosby, built a combined opera house, art gallery, and office building at Washington and State Streets.

In 1909 the city matured sufficiently to support its own resident company, the Chicago Grand Opera. Financed partly by Harold F. McCormick, head of the International Harvester Company, and Charles Gates Dawes, vice president of the United States, the new company launched its inaugural season on November 3, 1910, at the Auditorium Theatre with a production of *Aida.* Two days later Mary Garden made her Chicago debut in *Pelleas et Melisande.*

During her first year, Garden performed her most controversial role, Salome, in the opera of the same name. *Salome* was condemned from pulpit to editorial desk. Garden's sensual performance offended a significant portion of the opera-going public, notes Ronald L. Davis in *Opera in Chicago,* and prompted the president of the Chicago Law and Order League to protest to the chief of police. Although *Salome* played to two sold-out houses, the third show was canceled, apparently in a concerted effort to save the reputation of the fledgling company.

Despite the support of the opera-going public, the Chicago Grand Opera ended the 1913–14 season with a $250,000 deficit, notes Davis. The outbreak of World War I further aggravated its fragile economic situation, and the company was forced to declare bankruptcy. In the spring of 1915, a new company emerged, the Chicago Opera Association, with McCormick retaining his title of president.

In 1921 Garden became general director of the association, the first woman to head an opera company. Her tenure, a tempestuous one, lasted only one year. She brought in high-priced contemporary stars (moves that almost bankrupted the company), waged feuds, and carried on artistic squabbles with members. By the end of the year, her confrontational management style led to the resignations of her business executive, her artistic director, and many singers. Tired of the daily battle, she agreed to step down. "I am an artist and my place is with the artists," she explained. Despite a $1 million deficit, critics agreed that Garden delivered on her promise of going "out in a blaze of glory." The *Tribune* confessed, "There is no question but that the operatic season this year has been more brilliant than ever before."

In 1922 the Chicago Opera Association was reorganized into the Chicago Civic Opera. Unlike the older company, which was financed through the generosity of a handful of wealthy patrons, the new organization was bankrolled by contributors who pledged to pay a specific amount over a five-year period. Garden continued to perform with the new company and was a crowd-pleaser.

Garden gave her Chicago farewell performance on January 24, 1931, in *Le Jongleur de Notre Dame* at the Civic Opera House, which had opened two years earlier. When the curtain fell, she gathered her belongings and left, without saying goodbye to anyone. From Paris she cabled a succinct message: "My career in America is done."

After she retired, Garden visited Chicago frequently. She performed in an occasional vaudeville show in the city, something that she had always wanted to do, and, in 1935, she taught a course in opera at the Chicago Musical College.

Garden was a free spirit who did what she wanted—and damn the consequences—and lived where she wanted. When it came to choosing between marriage and a career, there was never any doubt which side would win. "I always put it in the scales and weighed it against art. It was always the same," she confessed. "Down went the gentlemen and up went art." After all, she reasoned, "If you have a great career, why do you want a man trailing you?"

Garden made her last public appearance in Chicago in January 1954 as a guest on WGN-AM radio while on a lecture tour of the United States. Although she professed to love America, she said she wished to live and die a Scot. Garden spent the last twenty-five years of her life in her native Aberdeen and died in January 1967, seven weeks short of her ninetieth birthday.

See also: Charles Gates Dawes, Samuel Insull, Ruth Page

Further reading: Robert L. Brubaker, "130 Years of Opera in Chicago," *Chicago History,* Fall 1979; Ronald L. Davis, *Opera in Chicago* (1966); Mary Garden and Louis Biancolli, *Mary Garden's Story* (1951); Edward C. Moore, *Forty Years of Opera in Chicago* (1930).

Hamlin Garland

Novelist

BORN: September 14, 1860
West Salem, Wisconsin

DIED: March 4, 1940
Hollywood, California

A pioneering novelist of American fiction, Hamlin Garland settled in Chicago at the time of the 1893 World's Columbian Exposition and became a major figure in the Chicago literary renaissance.

Garland was born on a farm near West Salem, Wisconsin, in 1860. When he was eight, he and his family traveled across the Mississippi River into Winneshick County, Iowa. As a youngster, he worked on his father's farm in the summer and attended Cedar Valley Seminary in the winter. In 1882 Garland moved to the East Coast but returned to the Midwest a year later and settled in McPherson County, North Dakota. After spending a year on the windswept Dakota prairie, he again headed back east. In 1899 he married Zulime Taft, sister of the Chicago sculptor Lorado Taft.

Garland's initial touch of fame came with the publication of *The Moccasin Ranch* (1909), the first of his Mississippi Valley stories. At that time he was teaching private classes in English and American literature in Boston. As a member of the Boston literary circle, he came into contact with some of the leading figures in American arts, letters, and public life, including Oliver Wendell Holmes, William Dean Howells, Edward Everett Hale, and Edwin Booth.

In 1887 he made a return visit to the Midwest from which emerged a series of sketches, *Main-Travelled Roads.* The following year he published his first novel, *A Spoil of Office.* In 1893 he decided to settle in Chicago; while there, he would eventually write a dozen novels in addition to a biography of General Ulysses S. Grant. *Rose of Dutcher's Coolly* (1895), considered by many critics to be his best novel, focuses on a rural Wisconsin girl who decides to pursue a poetry career in Chicago. He also wrote a largely autobiographical Midwestern trilogy: *A Son of the Middle Border* (1917), *A Daughter of the Middle Border* (1921), and *Trailmakers of the Middle Border* (1926).

In 1907 Garland approached several prominent friends, including novelist Henry Blake Fuller, sculptor Lorado Taft, and painter Ralph Clarkson, about establishing a prestigious social club for the city's literary elite, comparable to the Players Club in New York. At Garland's suggestion, they named it the Cliff-Dwellers Club, which was also the title of Fuller's 1893 novel. (Historian Emmett Dedmon argues that the name derives from the cliff-dwelling Indians of the American Southwest, not from Fuller's novel.)

On November 6, 1907, Garland, Fuller, Taft, bookseller Francis Browne, and Ralph Clarkson organized the prestigious social club and made their headquarters on the ninth floor of Orchestra Hall at 220 South Michigan Avenue. In 1930 Garland moved to Hollywood, where he lived across the street from film director Cecil B. DeMille. While in the movie capital, Garland worked on half a dozen books including one that probed psychic phenomena.

In his later years, critics sometimes referred to Garland as the dean of American letters. Writes literary historian Kenny J. Williams, "Mr. Garland's stories, though very powerful, are inexpressibly sad. They deal with the horror of hard work. His characters toil and droop and languish on the treadmill of fate."

Garland died in his Hollywood house at the age of seventy-nine due to a cerebral hemorrhage while completing the final chapters of his book *The Fortunate Exile,* which describes his ten years in California.

See also: Henry Blake Fuller, Lorado Taft

Further reading: Jean Holloway, *Hamlin Garland* (1960); Kenny J. Williams, *Prairie Voices: A Literary History of Chicago from the Frontier to 1893* (1980).

Dave Garroway

Broadcaster

BORN: July 13, 1913
Schenectady, New York

DIED: July 21, 1982
Swarthmore, Pennsylvania

Although he lived in Chicago for less than a decade, David Cunningham Garroway was the most distinguished representative of the so-called Chicago school of television, which was known for its easygoing informal approach to entertaining and was practiced by Fran Allison, Burr Tillstrom, Studs Terkel, and others. Garroway made his first splash in broadcasting on Chicago radio, where his wry sense of humor attracted a loyal following. In 1952 he launched NBC's durable talk-and-news program, *The Today Show.* With his bow tie, horn-rim glasses, and mild manner, Garroway won over the national audience too.

Garroway was born in upstate New York, the son of a mechanical engineer. The family later settled in St. Louis. In 1935 he graduated from Washington University with a bachelor's degree in English. He had a brief career as a piston-ring salesman before realizing that selling was not his strong suit. He then studied at Harvard University's business school for a short time.

In 1937 Garroway found work as a page at NBC for $16 a week. Although he fared poorly in the network's radio announcing class, he was hired as an announcer at station KDKA in Pittsburgh the following year. He served in the navy during World War II and taught at a school for radio technicians in Hawaii. Discharged in 1945, he came to Chicago as a staff announcer at station WMAQ, which broadcast from the Merchandise Mart. In January 1946, he made his radio debut with "The 11:60 Club," a late-night program that featured jazz and Garroway's distinctive nocturnal musings. In between records, Garroway dispensed advice and comments and uttered wise and witty observations. "The rapport he established with his audiences was nearly mystical," wrote Chicago columnist Bob Wiedrich in 1982. "You felt you had a friend behind the microphone who understood and identified with the loneliness of night people. He was an iconoclast of sorts. But most of all he lifted your spirits."

In April 1949 Garroway hosted an original variety show based in Chicago called *Garroway at Large*. The show departed from the usual television format. Instead of painted backdrops, Garroway's set featured a threadbare studio with a stagehand's ladder as the only prop. Soon his charm and intelligence earned him a national reputation. The success of the show led the top brass in New York to hire him as the host of the *Today Show*. During the 1953–54 season he also hosted his own variety program on NBC, *The Dave Garroway Show*. Later he was featured on NBC's *Wide, Wide World*.

The accidental death of his wife from an overdose of sleeping pills led to Garroway's premature retirement in 1961. A decade or so later, Garroway attempted a comeback, *The CBS Newcomers,* a one-hour summer replacement variety show. But no one seemed interested in the former talk show host.

"It was the most exciting rut in the world," said Garroway about his stint on the *Today Show*, "but you lived one kind of a life, and it made you think that you knew what was going on, but you really didn't."

Garroway committed suicide in his Philadelphia suburban home in 1982 after suffering complications from open-heart surgery. He was sixty-nine.

See also: Fran Allison, Studs Terkel, Burr Tillstrom

Henry Gerber

Activist

BORN: June 29, 1892
Bavaria, Germany

DIED: December 31, 1972
Washington, D.C.

A native of Germany, Henry Gerber started the first American homophile organization, the Society for Human Rights, in Chicago in 1924. It is considered the oldest gay organization in the United States. Although he was often publicly humiliated for his work, he set the stage for the emergence of later gay rights groups.

Gerber was born Henry Joseph Dittmar in Bavaria. He changed his name to Gerber after immigrating to the United States in 1913. He settled in Chicago because of its large German population. In 1917, though, he was committed to a mental institution because of his homosexuality. When the United States declared war on Germany during World War I, he had to make a difficult choice: either be interned as an enemy alien or enlist in the army during the American occupation of Germany. He chose the latter. While assigned as a printer and proofreader with the Allied Army of Occupation in Coblenz, Germany, he became active in the fledgling German gay civil rights movement and, in particular, was inspired by the work of Magnus Hirschfeld, a German national, and his Scientific-Humanitarian Committee. Hirschfeld was trying to change German law regarding its antihomosexual legislation.

After his service was completed, Gerber returned to Chicago and found work at the post office. But, inspired by Hirschfeld, he became more determined than ever to establish a similar organization in America. Between 1924 and 1925 he lived at 1710 North Crilly Court in Old

Town. It was there where he founded, in 1924, the Society for Human Rights (SHR), serving as its secretary. The SHR was the first gay civil rights organization in America, and its newsletter, *Friendship and Freedom,* the first documented gay civil rights publication in the United States. Its purpose was to "promote and protect the interests of people who by reasons of mental and physical abnormalities are abused and hindered in the legal pursuit of happiness . . . and to combat the public prejudices against them by discrimination."

But his organizational skills notwithstanding, Gerber still could not convince the authorities that the new institution that he founded was a legitimate one. Consequently, he was arrested for being a "degenerate." He was tried three times, and the charges against him were eventually dropped, although the trials required him to use up virtually all of his life savings. Worse, he was fired at the post office for "conduct unbecoming a postal worker."

Gerber moved to New York and, in 1927, reenlisted in the army, where he served until receiving an honorable discharge in 1945. He also continued writing articles supporting gay rights. He died on New Year's Eve 1972 at the age of eighty in Washington, D.C.

In 1992 Gerber was inducted into the Chicago Gay and Lesbian Hall of Fame. The Gerber/Hart Library at 1127 West Granville Avenue on the Far North Side is named in honor of Gerber as well as fellow civil rights activist Pearl M. Hart (1890–1975). President of the Women's Bar

Association of Illinois, Hart supported the legal and civil rights of both her gay and non-gay clients. She was also among the first inductees into Chicago's Gay and Lesbian Hall of Fame.

The library evolved from the work of historian Greg Sprague, who began his Chicago Gay History Project in 1978, and has been located at various sites over the years: first at 3225 North Sheffield Avenue (now the Center on Halsted), then to 3352 North Paulina Avenue, and currently at its Rogers Park location. Mostly volunteer-run and often billed as the Midwest's largest gay, lesbian, bisexual, and transgender archives, it houses more than 14,000 volumes, 800 periodicals, and 100 archival collections.

Further reading: Tracy Baim, ed., *Out and Proud in Chicago: An Overview of the City's Gay Community* (2008).

Gus Giordano

Dancer

BORN: 1923
St. Louis, Missouri

DIED: March 9, 2008
Chicago, Illinois

A dancer, teacher, and choreographer, Gus Giordano was one of the founding fathers of Chicago dance. He created his own dance technique now known around the world as jazz dance. A popularizer of American jazz dance, he organized the first Jazz Dance World Congress.

Gus Giordano was born in St. Louis, Missouri. Interested in dance as a child, he studied ballet and modern dance before joining the marines during World War II. During the war he performed at military bases across the United States. After being discharged from the service, he also performed on Broadway in such musicals as *Paint Your Wagon* and *On the Town*. In 1953 he moved to Chicago and started his own dance studio.

In 1962 Giordano began Dance Incorporated Chicago, which he renamed Giordano Dance Company in 1966, said to be the first dance troupe to dedicate itself solely to jazz dance. Jazz dance combined formal technique with a sense of looseness and fluidity coupled with a bit of soul. It is now known as Giordano Jazz Dance Chicago. Over the years he created hundreds of choreographic works. Company programs featured pieces by Giordano and such guest choreographers as Mia Michaels and Davis Robertson.

In 1990 Giordano organized the first Jazz Dance World Congress, which brought jazz dance companies together for a week of master classes and performances. Since then, annual conventions have been held in the United States but also in Japan, Germany, and Mexico. Giordano wrote several books, including *Anthology of American Jazz Dance* in 1975 and *Jazz Dance Class: Beginning thru Advanced* in 1992. He also won an Emmy in 1980 for the television special *The Rehearsal*.

Giordano died of pneumonia at the age of eighty-four at Northwestern Memorial Hospital in Chicago.

The company is now directed by his daughter, Nan Giordano, and located at 5230 North Clark Street.

See also: Bob Fosse

Arthur J. Goldberg

Judge

BORN: August 8, 1908
Chicago, Illinois

DIED: January 19, 1990
Washington, D.C.

The son of Russian immigrant parents, Arthur J. Goldberg was raised in the Maxwell Street neighborhood on the Near West Side at Halsted and O'Brien Streets and later at 13th Street and Lawndale Avenue. After graduating first in his class from Northwestern University Law School in 1929, he joined the Chicago law firm of Pritzker and Pritzker and for two years edited the *Illinois Law Review*.

In 1938 Goldberg started his own practice and from 1939 to 1948 served as a professor of law at the John Marshall Law School. Sympathetic to union causes, Goldberg represented several major unions in the 1930s and 1940s and was instrumental in the formation of the merger of the Congress of Industrial Organizations (CIO) and the American Federation of Labor (AFL).

Throughout his career, Goldberg held many important positions on a national level, including U.S. Supreme Court justice, ambassador to the United Nations, and secretary of labor in the Kennedy administration. As a Supreme Court justice, Goldberg coauthored a landmark case in 1965 that struck down a Connecticut ban on birth control devices and laid the foundation for the controversial *Roe v. Wade* decision in the early 1970s that legalized abortion. In 1965 he resigned from the bench to serve as U.S. ambassador to the United Nations. He advocated the admission of China into the United Nations, and urged the United States to adopt a harder line against apartheid in South Africa. Soon after moving his law firm to Washington, D.C., in 1971, he joined the faculty of American University as a professor of law and diplomacy.

Goldberg died in 1990 at the age of eighty-one.

Bertrand Goldberg
Architect

BORN: July 17, 1913
Chicago, Illinois

DIED: October 8, 1997
Chicago, Illinois

Architect and engineer, entrepreneur and public intellectual, Bertrand Goldberg had a lifelong interest in the role of architecture in society. His iconic Marina City remains the defining work of his illustrious career. It not only launched Goldberg's career, its exuberant and still-modern design continues to retain a hold on the popular imagination.

Born in Chicago, Goldberg trained at the Cambridge School of Landscape Architecture, now a part of Harvard University. He also studied at the Bauhaus, working alongside Ludwig Mies van der Rohe, as well as at the Armour Institute of Technology (now the Illinois Institute of Technology). He worked for various architects, including Keck & Keck in 1935 and Paul Schweikher from 1935 to 1936, before opening his architectural firm in Chicago the following year. During World War II Goldberg was active under the Lanham Act, designing housing and mobile penicillin laboratories for the government. From 1937 to 1950 he worked primarily by himself until he established a partnership with Leland Atwood in the firm Atwood and Goldberg. Finally, in 1954, he opened Bertrand Goldberg Associates (BGA), which remained open until his death in 1997. The firm grew from a modest group of ten people to thirty by the early 1960s. By the end of the decade the firm had some fifty employees with offices in Chicago, Boston, and, briefly, Palo Alto, California. At its height in the 1970s, Goldberg's firm employed more than one hundred people.

In addition to his architectural practice, from 1939 to 1942 Goldberg, along with fellow architect Gilmer Black, designed, built, and developed prefabricated houses. From 1949 to 1952 he served as design consultant for the Pressed Steel Car Company, developing the Unicel plywood boxcar and a housing project called Unishelter. Unishelter referred to a factory-built modular housing system that could be packed as a shipping container before its shipment to Alaska. In the 1950s he worked with real estate magnate Arthur Rubloff on privately built public housing such as the Drexel Home and Gardens project (1957), an affordable housing complex. In the 1970s and 1980s BGA concentrated on designing and building health care and educational facilities. Its distinctive designs required innovative technology. Thus, the firm had to devise solutions to complex materials and construction issues.

Goldberg firmly believed that cities contributed to the fabric of civilization. He attempted to create a synthesis of the physical, political, cultural, and intellectual in his buildings. Progressive and pragmatic with a strong utopian streak in him, he sought to democratize architecture. What's more, he designed buildings that appealed to the individualist: he created iconic buildings that transcended their time.

The simplicity of the circular form, in particular, appealed to him, and he used it again and again not only with Marina City but also at Prentice Women's Hospital for Northwestern Memorial Hospital (1974), River City (1982–86), and the Raymond Hillard Homes (1966). But Marina City remains his most famous and significant work.

The Chicago politician and labor leader William McFetridge asked Goldberg to find a site for a building that would house new union headquarters. Goldberg thought the Chicago River area would be conducive but too expensive. Instead he suggested a then-radical idea: that the needs of union members would be better served by developing a multiuse residential and workspace in downtown Chicago; in other words, a city within a city. Consequently, in 1959, Goldberg partnered with the International Plumbers' Union to develop a downtown mixed-use residential project on the north bank of the Chicago River. What eventually emerged was Marina City.

The circular, corn-cob-shaped Marina City (1959–1964, 1967) included the two tallest residential concrete buildings at the time of its completion. Consisting of a mixed-use complex of five buildings, it featured two sixty-story apartment towers, twenty lower floors of parking, and forty floors of apartments that featured a pie-shaped layout, an office building (now the Hotel Sax), and a theater (now the House of Blues) as well as parking space and a marina with boat storage. When it first opened it also boasted an ice-skating rink and a bowling alley. Before the towers were completed, there were 3,500 applications to rent one of the apartments. The first tower was finished in 1962, the second tower the following year. Radio station WCFL was located on the sixteenth floor of the State Street tower from 1965 to 1985.

Marina City is significant for many reasons, but it is especially noteworthy because of its many design and construction innovations. A building with all electric utilities, it was the first major use of slip-form construction. At the time of their completion, the two towers were the tallest apartment buildings in the world and the tallest reinforced concrete buildings. The complex's office building was supported with load-bearing concrete mullions and flush glazing. The theater was originally designed for live theater productions but ultimately was constructed as a television studio with three smaller movie theaters below. Eventually the rental units were changed to condominiums and the office building redeveloped into a hotel (first the House of Blues Hotel and now the Hotel Sax). The former ice-skating rink is now the Smith and Wollensky steakhouse.

Goldberg designed other famous buildings. The Raymond Hillard Homes (1966) are two sixteen-story circular towers originally intended for the elderly and two eighteen-story curved towers for low-income families. These structures were built to provide both a solution to the problem of inadequate public housing and buildings that residents would be proud to live in. In 1997 the development was listed on the National Register of Historic Places and is now mixed-income housing.

In 1974 Goldberg designed another circular building, Prentice Women's Hospital for Northwestern Memorial Hospital. Completed in 1975, this rectilinear building of column-and-beam construction housed the obstetrics and gynecology departments and the Northwestern Institute of Psychiatry. In 1975 his firm was given an award from the *Engineering News Record* for distinguished architectural and engineering development for innovations. In June 2011, the Washington, D.C.–based National Trust for Historic Preservation placed Prentice, vacant since 2007, on its list of America's Most Endangered Historic Places. Around the same time, Northwestern University had requested a demolition permit to raze the building to make way for a modern medical research tower.

Another innovative Goldberg building is River City, a mixed-use apartment complex. Its long, winding interior atrium is modeled after a Parisian street. The architect's original vision was much more ambitious. Using once again the city-within-a-city approach, he envisioned mixed-use of three seventy-two-story skyscrapers that were to be linked by sky bridges, housing everything from schools to shopping centers. Unable to acquire the proper zoning permits, however, he modified his designs over the ten years or so that it took to complete the building.

His Maxim's de Paris (1963) at 24 East Goethe Street was an exact replica of the famous Parisian restaurant of the same name. Located in Astor Towers, it featured red velvet banquettes, stained glass, brass, and mahogany. Goldberg's wife Nancy owned and ran this prestigious restaurant from 1963 until 1982. In 2000 the Goldberg family donated Maxim's to the City of Chicago. Now known as Maxim's: The Nancy Goldberg International Center, it is operated by the Chicago Department of Cultural Affairs and hosts special events.

Working with fellow architect Harry Weese, in 1984 Goldberg offered a proposal for the 1992 Chicago World's Fair. The Floating World's Fair was to extend from Chinatown to Goose Island and the lakefront on the east. The fair was intended to be a joint exposition between the United States and Spain in order to celebrate the 500th anniversary of Columbus's voyage to the New World. But Chicago pulled out of the bid due to public protests about the planned site and bureaucratic wrangling between the city and the state of Illinois.

BGA's last major work was an annex to Wright College. The pyramid-shaped building features an enclosed central atrium, glass-fronted computer rooms, faculty offices, and a library. It was completed in 1992.

In 1966 Goldberg was elected to the College of Fellows of the American Institute of Architects and in 1985 he was given the Officier de l'Ordre des Arts et des Lettres by the French government.

"I firmly believe," Goldberg said, "that the concept of total environment creates a pleasurable experience for the occupant. St. Augustine said that beauty is that which gives pleasure. I do not know if that which gives pleasure is also beauty. But we are closer to our objective by creating the pleasurable total life—both physical and spiritual."

Goldberg died in October 1997. His most famous building, Marina City, continues to be a pop culture icon. Over the years it has appeared in movies, on television, and on magazine covers as a symbol of Chicago and Chicago architecture. In 2002 the alternative rock band Wilco (which has roots in Chicago) featured it on the cover of their album *Yankee Hotel Foxtrot*. The Bertrand Goldberg Archive is housed at the Ryerson & Burnham Libraries, while the Bertrand Goldberg Collection, Department of Architecture and Design, is housed at the Art Institute of Chicago.

See also: Ludwig Mies van der Rohe, Harry Weese

Further reading: Igor Marjanovi and Katerina Rüedi Ray, *Marina City: Bertrand Goldberg's Urban Vision* (2010); Jay Pridmore and George A. Larson, *Chicago Architecture and Design* (2005); Zoë Ryan, ed., *Bertrand Goldberg: Architecture of Invention* (2011).

Maurice Goldblatt

Merchant and Philanthropist

BORN: Circa 1892
Stachev, Poland

DIED: July 17, 1984
Chicago, Illinois

Maurice Goldblatt was one of Chicago's most successful Jewish businessmen. He maintained two careers in his life: cofounder of one of the biggest department stores in Chicago history and chairman of the University of Chicago Cancer Research Foundation. Maurice Goldblatt and his brother Nathan were Polish-born Jews who served Eastern European immigrants in Chicago, much as they had in their homeland.

Goldblatt came to Chicago from Poland in 1905 and found work in a Milwaukee Avenue dry goods store. In 1914 the Goldblatt brothers—twenty-one-year-old Maurice and his nineteen-year-old brother Nathan—opened their first retail store in a wooden bungalow at 1617 West Chicago Avenue with $1,000 capital. Later their younger brother Louis ran errands while the youngest, seven-year old Joey, rang the cash register. By 1934 they operated a chain of seven stores and adopted the slogan "America's Fastest Growing Department Stores." The company incorporated in 1928. Goldblatt's flourished during the Depression by offering essential goods at low prices. Business was so good that in 1937 the firm opened its flagship store at 333 South State Street.

In 1944 Nathan died of cancer. Maurice had been extremely close to his younger sibling. Grief-stricken, Maurice decided to devote the rest of his life to raising funds for cancer and heart disease research. In 1948 Nathan's widow, Frances, founded the Nathan Goldblatt Society for Cancer Research, which became affiliated with the University of Chicago. Maurice initially donated $1 million to the university's Nathan Goldblatt Memorial Hospital for Cancer Research. In the late 1940s, Goldblatt served on the board of the National Heart Advisory Council—one of the few laypeople to do so—and in 1950, he was appointed to the National Advisory Cancer Council.

Goldblatt retired in 1946 as chief executive officer of the company but continued as chairman into the 1960s. At one time, the chain operated forty-seven stores that accounted for fifteen percent of the Chicago retail market. Falling on hard times, Goldblatt Brothers closed the firm's flagship store on State Street in 1981 and filed for bankruptcy. Family squabbles were allegedly commonplace and, according to newspaper accounts, may have actually contributed to the company's decline. In addition, the introduction of discount chain stores such as Kmart and Venture also cut considerably into the firm's profits.

In 1982 the administration of Mayor Jane Byrne purchased the vacant Goldblatt's building on South State Street for conversion into a new central library. Byrne's successor, Harold Washington, decided not to renovate the Goldblatt's building but to instead erect a new library building at the corner of State and Van Buren Streets. Finally, in 1989, the city and DePaul University announced plans to buy the Goldblatt's building and transform it into a part of the university's downtown campus, which is what it remains today.

In 1978 Goldblatt's had hired several outsiders with merchandising ability to rescue the firm from certain financial ruin. When a change in management proved insufficient, Goldblatt's returned to its original no-frills policy and, in a remarkable comeback, reopened six stores in March 1982. Rather than carrying furniture and major appliances, the new Goldblatt's concentrated on brand-name apparel, small appliances, and housewares. By the 1990s, however, dwindling sales and a changing retail marketplace—including the arrival of the big box stores—led to the sale of the remaining Goldblatt's stores to the discount department store retailer Ames. Goldblatt's finally shut down altogether in 2000, and liquidation took place in 2003.

Maurice Goldblatt died at the University of Chicago's Bernard Mitchell Hospital from a heart attack in July 1984. He was ninety-two.

See also: Marshall Field, Richard Sears, Aaron Montgomery Ward, William A. Wieboldt

Benny Goodman

Musician

BORN: May 30, 1909
Chicago, Illinois

DIED: June 12, 1986
New York, New York

Swing was the music of a generation between the Depression and World War II, and Benjamin David Goodman, the "King of Swing," was its monarch. Goodman, a high school dropout from the Maxwell Street ghetto, changed the course of popular music. He did not invent swing—a danceable type of big-band jazz that reached the height of its popularity during the pre–World War II era—but he was the one who developed it into a great and popular art form.

Goodman's parents, David Goodman and Dora Rezinsky, were Russian immigrants who had met and married in Baltimore but moved to the Maxwell Street area of Chicago in 1902. His father was a tailor. "Pop would get up before any of us, about six o'clock, make the fire and fix breakfast for us. We started to drink coffee as soon as we were weaned, because milk for so many kids cost more than he could afford," recalled Goodman in his autobiography, *The Kingdom of Swing.* The family moved frequently from cramped apartment to cramped apartment.

Young Benny received music lessons at Kehelah Jacob Synagogue, near his home at 1125 Francisco Avenue. Later, he joined the Hull House band and played John Philip Sousa marches. Goodman also took private lessons from Franz Schoepp, a brilliant clarinet teacher who coached members of the Chicago Symphony. Eventually Goodman was asked to join what would later be called the Austin High Gang, a group of musicians including sax man Bud Freeman. The members of the group attended Austin High School on the West Side—except for Goodman, who was a student at Harrison High School. Recalls Freeman, "He was no more than thirteen years of age. He played the clarinet so beautifully—it was not to be believed. He was a very pleasant little guy, who hadn't the faintest idea of the extraordinary talent he possessed."

Goodman's talents were in demand. He began performing polkas, waltzes, and popular tunes with small dance bands at high schools and colleges, and at local dances. Later he would play at cabarets, in dance halls, and at nightclubs such as the Green Mill Gardens (now called the Green Mill Jazz Club) at Broadway and Lawrence. By the time Goodman was fourteen he was so busy that he decided to drop out of school.

The music Goodman loved, the music he truly wanted to play, was the new phenomenon that was sweeping the country. Thursday was "Jazz Night" at Balaban and Katz's Central Park Theater, and Benny's brother, Charlie, persuaded the manager to let his talented sibling play clarinet there. The manager liked Benny so much that he hired Goodman as a fill-in.

The young clarinetist quickly built a reputation as one of the best musicians in Chicago. In 1925 he joined the Midway Gardens Orchestra. A large indoor-outdoor dance hall at Cottage Grove Avenue and 60th Street designed by Frank Lloyd Wright in 1913, the Midway Gardens was inspired by European beer gardens and offered extravagant food, drink, and entertainment.

Later that year bandleader Ben Pollack wired Goodman and invited him to come to California. After a successful tour, the band returned to Chicago in early 1926 and played in some of the city's top clubs. When not performing with Pollack, Goodman found work as a freelance musician. In 1934 he felt confident enough to form his own band. The Goodman Band made its debut at the Roosevelt Hotel in New York one year later. The manager—despite an enthusiastic response from the audience—was not impressed with this "new" sound, which, with its up-tempo beat and soaring rhythms, was a sharp departure from the romantic balladry and slick pop tunes then in vogue. Gradually the press began referring to this sophisticated and exciting style of dance music as "swing," and young people quickly embraced it as their own.

One of the historic moments in jazz was the Benny Goodman Orchestra concert at Carnegie Hall in January 1938. Although the hall was filled to capacity, the reaction of the New York press—mostly classical music critics—was lukewarm, at best. And yet Goodman's groundbreaking performance represented a turning point in the history of popular music. Jazz, once dismissed as primitive music, was now becoming accepted in "polite society."

Goodman was not the easiest man to get along with. Bud Freeman, who left Tommy Dorsey in 1937 to join Goodman's band, admitted as much. "Working for Benny was the most miserable experience of my life," said Freeman. Historian James Lincoln Collier describes Goodman as "self-absorbed, moody, irritable." A perfectionist, he hired and fired musicians so rapidly that it was virtually impossible to keep track of their comings and goings. Although a great improviser and technically proficient on his instrument, Goodman relied on outside arrangers—people like Fletcher Henderson, Dean Kincaide, Benny Carter, and Lyle "Spud" Murphy. Indeed, Henderson wrote some of Goodman's most important tunes, including "King Porter Stomp" and "Sometimes I'm Happy."

No matter how far he traveled, no matter how famous he became, Goodman never forgot his roots. In 1945, he donated $5,000 to the Hull House music school and, as late as 1976, performed a charity concert there.

Goodman, who made his first record in Chicago in 1926 on the Victor label, was credited with being the first white musician to utilize black talent. Pianist Teddy Wilson played with Goodman, as did drummer Lionel Hampton, among others. Indeed, over the years, Goodman's constantly changing personnel featured some of the greatest names in jazz—black or white—including Gene Krupa, Harry James, and Georgie Auld, as well as singers Helen Forrest and Peggy Lee.

Swing fell on hard times after World War II, the victim of both changing economics and changing tastes in music. A new generation of teenagers rejected the big band sound in favor of solo singers such as Frank Sinatra and Eddie Fisher, and hard-core jazz fans turned their ears to a brash new music—bebop—that was emerging from the nightclubs of Harlem. Swing, notes Collier, was perceived as old-fashioned, commercial dance music.

Yet Goodman continued to perform. Throughout the 1940s, 1950s, and into the 1960s he put together various bands to play at special events, including a tour of the Soviet Union in 1962. In the late 1960s Goodman performed classical music concerts, featuring the works of Brahms, Mozart, and Copland, and he recorded a number of classical pieces.

In 1955 a biographical film of Goodman's life and music, *The Benny Goodman Story*, starring Steve Allen, was released.

Goodman continued to play big band music until 1986 and had even scheduled a West Coast concert tour for that year, but he never made it. The old man of jazz, by this time a veritable American institution, died of a heart attack in the study of his New York apartment on June 12, 1986.

See also: Louis Armstrong, Bud Freeman, Earl Hines, Gene Krupa, Mezz Mezzrow, Joe "King" Oliver

Further reading: Ira Berkow, *Maxwell Street: Survival in a Bazaar* (1977); James Lincoln Collier, *Benny Goodman and the Swing Era* (1989); D. Russell Connor, *Benny Goodman: Listen to His Legacy* (1988); Stanley Dance, *The World of Swing* (1979); Bud Freeman, as told to Robert Wolf, *Crazeology: The Autobiography of a Chicago Jazzman* (1989); Benny Goodman and Irving Kolodin, *The Kingdom of Swing* (1939).

Kenneth Sawyer Goodman

Playwright

BORN: September 19, 1883
Chicago, Illinois

DIED: 1918
Chicago, Illinois

Kenneth Sawyer Goodman, a promising playwright, worked in the family lumber business, yet theater and the arts were his passions. In 1911 Goodman and another up-and-coming playwright, Thomas Wood Stevens, were among the founders of the Chicago Theatre Society, an arts support group. Stevens, who established the influential Blue Sky Press and taught art at the Art Institute, met Goodman in 1908. The two friends established a publishing house, the Stage Guild, to distribute their own one-act plays and masques. Goodman's plays were performed by theater groups in Detroit, New York, and as far away as Manchester, England.

Goodman often collaborated with Thomas Wood Stevens; their works include *Holbein in Blackfriars: An Improbable Comedy* (1913); *Rainald and the Red Wolf*, which was presented for the annual Mardi Gras festival of the Art Student's League; and numerous one-acts, including *Barbara* (1914), *The Hero of Santa Maria* (1920), *The Green Scarf* (1920), *The Game of Chess* (1914), *Ephraim and the Winged Bear* (1914), *Dust of the Road* (1912), *A Pageant for Independence Day* (1912), and *Back of the Yards* (1914). He also collaborated with journalist Ben Hecht in such works as *The Wonder Hat* (1920).

In 1917 Goodman enlisted in the United States Naval Reserve. He died while on leave at the family home on North Astor Street during the influenza epidemic of 1918 that swept through Chicago. He was only thirty-five. He is buried at Graceland Cemetery in a tomb designed by architect Howard Van Doren Shaw.

In 1922 Goodman's parents proposed to the Board of Trustees of the Art Institute to create a memorial theater in their son's memory. They donated $250,000 to the Art Institute to establish a repertory company and a school of drama. The Goodman Memorial Theatre, designed by Chicago architect Howard Van Doren Shaw, opened on October 20, 1925. The theater's professional company, the Repertory Company, presented three Goodman plays at the dedication performance: *Back of the Yards*, *The Green Scarf*, and *The Game of Chess*. Two nights later, it presented its first public performance, John Galsworthy's *The Forest*.

The Goodman's first artistic director was Goodman's former colleague and friend, Thomas Wood Stevens. Under his helm, the Goodman presented a mixture of classics, contemporary plays, experimental plays, and new works. Stevens resigned in 1930 and was replaced by Hubert Osbourne, who ran the theater for a year. Because of cost, the Art Institute decided to shut down the acting company while keeping the doors of the drama school open.

The head of the Goodman School of Drama, Maurice Gnesin, polished the school's reputation over a nearly thirty-year reign. Goodman students included Karl Malden, Sam Wanamaker, Geraldine Page, Shelley Berman, Harvey Korman, Jose Quintero, Linda Hunt, and Joe Mantegna.

When Gnesin died in 1957, John Reich took over, but with a caveat: that the acting company be re-established. After more than a decade of rebuilding the theater's subscriber base, the Goodman reopened in 1969. After a few bumps—Reich resigned in 1972 and his successor, Ken Myers, also resigned—William Woodman became artistic director in 1973. In 1978 the Goodman School was acquired by DePaul University. That same year Woodman resigned and his assistant, Gregory Mosher, assumed control. Mosher stayed until 1985, when he moved to the Lincoln Center Theater in New York and the current artistic director, Robert Falls, took over.

In December 2000 the Goodman Theatre moved into its new home on Dearborn Street on the former site of the Selwyn and Harris theaters. The first production was August Wilson's *King Hedley II*.

The Kenneth Sawyer Goodman Papers are housed at the Newberry Library.

See also: Ben Hecht

Steve Goodman

Musician

BORN: July 25, 1948
Chicago, Illinois

DIED: September 20, 1984
Seattle, Washington

One of Chicago's best-loved singer-songwriters, Steve Goodman's vibrant stage personality and gently satiric lyrics earned him a loyal following on the Chicago folk circuit during the late 1960s and early 1970s. Along with John Prine and Bonnie Koloc, Goodman helped put Chicago on the folk music map.

Goodman grew up listening to rock and roll, Chicago blues, Hank Williams, and Woody Guthrie. He spent his formative years on the North Side and in Evanston and attended high school at Roosevelt High and Maine East High School in Park Ridge, Illinois. By the time he graduated, he was composing his own songs. In 1971 he played a gig with Kris Kristofferson at the Quiet Knight at 959 West Belmont Avenue. In the audience sat Paul Anka, who was so impressed that he brought Goodman to New York for some recording sessions. Goodman then signed a deal with Buddah Records.

His self-titled debut album, produced by Kristofferson, featured contemporary folk material. Although it received generally positive reviews, it didn't do well commercially, prompting Buddah to drop Goodman from the label. He jumped to Asylum Records but again failed to attract a substantial following. Frustrated by the lack of response, he formed his own label, Red Pajamas.

In 1967, Goodman began playing at the popular Old Town hangout the Earl of Old Town, at North and Wells. At this time, he was also working as a clerk in the Park Ridge post office and attending Lake Forest College. Within two years, he was able to support himself with club dates and jingle work.

Goodman's most popular song, "City of New Orleans," became a top twenty hit for Arlo Guthrie in 1972. Many of Goodman's best efforts had Chicago themes, such as "Daley's Gone," "Go Cubs Go," "A Dying Cub Fan's Last Request," and "Lincoln Park Pirates," a tongue-in-cheek indictment of a local towing car company. A Lincoln Avenue bar, Somebody Else's Troubles, was named after a Goodman song.

Goodman was stricken with leukemia in 1969, but he kept his illness a secret until forced to go public many years later when he missed a Harry Chapin memorial concert in 1982. "The reason that I had kept a low profile about it for so long was that I didn't want any favors, didn't want to have to explain my special set of circumstances. I couldn't see dragging it around as part of my press kit," he explained the following year.

Goodman and his wife moved to Seal Beach, California, in 1980. The singer died at the University of Washington hospital in Seattle four years later at the age of thirty-six.

Goodman's albums include *Steve Goodman* (1971), *Somebody Else's Troubles* (1972), *Jessie's Jig & Other Favorites* (1975), *Words We Can Dance To* (1976), *Say It In Private* (1977), *High and Outside* (1979), *Hot Spot* (1980), *Artistic Hair* (1983), and *Affordable Art* (1984), as well as two posthumous releases, *Santa Ana Winds* (1984) and *Unfinished Business* (1987). He also produced fellow Chicagoan John Prine's critically acclaimed album *Bruised Orange* and had a minor hit with "The Dutchman," the opening cut on *Troubles,* composed by Chicago singer-songwriter Michael Smith. Goodman made some slight changes to the melody and lyrics, which initially annoyed Smith. However, more than half a dozen years after its release, Smith embraced "The Dutchman" as his "signature song."

Following Goodman's death, fellow Chicago musician Corky Siegel said, "The Steve on stage is the same as the Steve off stage. Steve had a philosophy that life is too important to take too seriously." Goodman was a musician's musician. Although widespread commercial success eluded him—he had only a handful of minor hits—he was held in high esteem by his fellow musicians both in Chicago and across the country. "He was truly a great musician," added singer Bonnie Raitt, "and he loved to play for anyone, anywhere, any time."

On January 26, 1985, friends of the singer—including Raitt, John Prine, Bonnie Koloc, David Bromberg, Arlo Guthrie, Jethro Burns, and Richie Havens—gathered at the Arie Crown Theater to perform a five-hour tribute. The proceeds of the show were donated to leukemia research. A live double album was released in December 1985 on Goodman's Red Pajamas label.

In July 2010, the Lakeview post office at 1343 West Irving Park Road was officially renamed in his honor. A formal ceremony took place several months later. Goodman's former colleagues and friends, including Ed Holstein, Bonnie Koloc, and Corky Siegel, performed in front of an audience of some 250 people.

See also: Fred Holstein
Further reading: Clay Eals, *Steve Goodman: Facing the Music* (2007).

Bruce Graham

Architect

BORN: December 1, 1925
La Cumbre, Colombia

DIED: March 6, 2010
Hobe Sound, Florida

When I was a child, my dream was to build cities.

—Bruce Graham

Bruce Graham integrated modernist design and intricate engineering and designed two of Chicago's most famous buildings, the Sears Tower (now the Willis Tower) and the John Hancock Center. He believed good buildings make good cities.

The son of a Canadian banker, Bruce John Graham was born in a small town outside Cali in Colombia. His father's position led him to settle in different parts of the world. After Colombia, the family moved to San Juan, Puerto Rico, where Graham spent his boyhood years. At fifteen, he won a scholarship to the University of Dayton to study engineering. In 1943 he enlisted in the navy, training as a civil engineer and a radar technician, before being shipped to the Philippines. After finishing his military service, he enrolled at the University of Pennsylvania, where he earned a degree in architecture in 1948.

An admirer of Mies van der Rohe, Graham moved to Chicago and was hired at Holabird, Root, and Burgee, where he worked on drawings for two years. In 1949, he joined the architectural firm of Skidmore, Owings and Merrill (SOM). He stayed there until his retirement in 1989. Graham moved up the ladder quickly at SOM, becoming a design partner by 1960.

In 1973 he was an active participant in the drafting of the Chicago 21 plan, an ambitious plan that recommended the transformation of Navy Pier into a recreation area, the straightening of the S-curve on Lake Shore Drive, and the creation of the Chicago Museum Campus, which consists of fifty-seven acres of gardens and walkways and three museums: the Adler Planetarium, the Shedd Aquarium, and the Field Museum.

Graham's other buildings include the Inland Steel Building (1957), which was based on an earlier plan by his SOM colleague Walter Netsch, as well as the Equitable Building and the Chicago Civic Center (now the Richard J. Daley Center), both completed in 1965. In the 1980s he designed Three First National Plaza (1981), Madison Plaza (1982), One Magnificent Mile (1983), the Chicago Tribune Freedom Center Printing Plant (1982), the Quaker Tower (1987), and McCormick Place North (1986). In addition to his work in Chicago, Graham also designed buildings across the United States as well as in Hong Kong, Cairo, Barcelona, Seoul, and London, including the master plan for the famous Canary Wharf in the city's Docklands area.

Graham offered a distinctive interpretation of the Miesian glass box. Working closely with SOM's chief structural engineer, Fazlur Khan, he devised a way to maximize office space at a minimum cost in the most innovative fashion. He conceived of a tapered tower with an exterior system of structural supports, and realized that by using X braces and exterior columns—used most famously in the Hancock building—he could free up interior space while lowering costs. The Willis Tower used a similar technique. Using the setback forms of older skyscrapers such as the Empire State Building, it consists of mutually supportive square tubes where two towers rise some 20 stories of the 110-story building.

In many ways, Graham was a visionary even when his plans did not come to fruition. In 1980 he was among a team of architects who drafted a plan for the 1992 World's Fair that would be held in Chicago. This new fair was intended to match, if not surpass, the fairs of 1893 and 1933. The ambitious plan called for a series of buildings that were to be constructed on the Near South Side with some 500 acres of lagoons and islands to be reclaimed from Lake Michigan. But many communities opposed it. What's more, poor economic conditions and lack of support from the mayor's office dashed the plans.

In 1989 Graham retired from SOM and opened his own firm, Graham & Graham, with his second wife, Jane Abend. In 1999 the John Hancock Center was awarded the American Institute of Architects' 25-Year Award.

Graham's buildings reflected his personal philosophy. Buildings, he believed, should be "clear, free of fashion, and simple statements of the truth."

On June 16, 2010, the Chicago Architecture Foundation sponsored a panel discussion called "Remembering Bruce Graham" with Richard Tomlinson, managing partner of SOM, architect Lucien Lagrange, and Franz Schulze, emeritus art professor at Lake Forest College. Tomlinson called Graham both a "poet" and a "great collaborator" while Schulze commented on his independent streak. "He built upon Mies but he was his own man," he said.

See also: Ludwig Mies van der Rohe, Walter Netsch, Harry Weese
Further reading: *Bruce Graham of SOM* (1989).

Red Grange
Football Player

BORN: June 13, 1903
Forkville, Pennsylvania

DIED: January 28, 1991
Lakes Wales, Florida

Football legend Harold Edward Grange, nicknamed "the Galloping Ghost" by sportswriter Grantland Rice, put the University of Illinois on the map. What's more, Grange—football's first superstar—helped turn professional football into a big business. Combining the grace of a gymnast with the speed of a runner, Grange was often called the best player to ever play the sport.

The son of a lumber dealer, Red Grange was born in a small Pennsylvania town. His mother died when he was five, and his father decided, several months later, to move the family to west suburban Wheaton. The red-haired Grange was a natural athlete. Known around town as the "Wheaton Ice Man," he worked his way through college by delivering blocks of ice every summer. He enrolled at the University of Illinois at Urbana-Champaign but had no desire to play football—at slightly under six feet tall and not quite 170 pounds he felt he was too small. Nevertheless he was accepted on the freshman squad, and he did well. He also found time to join the basketball and track teams.

On October 18, 1924, the Illinois-Michigan game catapulted Grange's name across the nation's sports pages as Illinois routed the undefeated and highly favored Michigan team 39–14. Grange scored four touchdowns in twelve minutes—all in the first quarter. In total he gained 402 yards, carried twenty-one times, and completed six passes for 64 yards.

College football was enjoying its glory days during the 1920s, and Grange was its star player. The halfback's fleetness of foot captured on grainy newsreels inspired imaginations in motion picture theaters across the country. Thousands of football fans flocked to university stadiums—crowds of 60,000 or more were not uncommon on some of the larger campuses—to watch their heroes in action. College athletes epitomized the purity and goodness of amateur sports. "Football," declared Grange's coach Bob Zuppke, "isn't meant to be played for money." Professional football, on the other hand, was floundering. What the game needed in order to survive was a big name to attract more customers to the stadiums. It has often been said that Red Grange made professional football respectable.

Grange played his final game as a college athlete on November 21, 1925, when Illinois defeated Ohio State 14–9. One day later, after much secret negotiation, Chicago Bears coach George Halas signed Grange to an unprecedented $25,000 contract. Grange's decision upset not only his father but also his college coach and his legions of fans that were aghast that the darling of the collegiate gridiron would deign to play "commercialized football." Grange was accused of selling out when, in fact, as he later admitted, he had a simpler and more compelling motive: he needed the money.

Some 36,000 Chicago fans—attendance at Bears games usually averaged 5,000 and was rarely more than 12,000—got their first glimpse of the Galloping Ghost several days later on Thanksgiving Day when the Bears played the Chicago Cardinals at Wrigley Field. It wasn't a very impressive debut. Grange gained only thirty yards in a 0–0 tie. Three days later, however, he redeemed himself when he gained 140 yards and led the Bears to a 14–13 victory over the Columbus Tigers.

Grange agreed to participate in a sixteen-game postseason barnstorming cross-country tour to promote professional football. By that time Grange was attracting crowds wherever he played. Advertisements encouraged fans to come out to "See Red Grange with the Chicago Bears." Promoters, taking advantage of the moment, made a small fortune by selling Red Grange dolls, sweaters, caps, and ginger ale to eager fans.

Due to Grange's unprecedented popularity, Grange's agent, C. C. Pyle, asked Halas for a five-figure salary and one-third ownership of the team. Halas balked at what he considered an outrageous request. Pyle countered by establishing in 1926 the nine-team American Football League (AFL), rival to the National Football League (NFL).

Grange initially played with the AFL's short-lived local franchise, the Chicago Bulls (no relationship to the current basketball team of the same name). But even Grange's formidable presence couldn't keep the team afloat. He then signed with the New York Yankees football club, also of the AFL. By the end of the 1926 season, the AFL had collapsed due to a lack of interest and the Yankees were allowed to join the NFL. The next time Chicagoans—more than 30,000 of them—saw the Galloping Ghost in person was at Wrigley Field in a Yankee uniform. During the game, which the Bears won 12–0, he suffered a debilitating knee injury and spent the 1928 season on the injured list.

When the Yankee franchise folded in 1929, Halas invited Grange to return to the Bears lineup at his old position of running back. When that proved too strenuous, he switched to defensive back. Grange retired in 1934, although he made his last appearance with the Bears during an exhibition game in January 1935. In the fall of that year Grange turned down an offer from Halas to become head coach, instead choosing the less stressful position of assistant coach. He retired from football altogether in 1937.

Grange's gridiron exploits thrilled the crowds and turned the then fledgling sport of professional football into big business. Grange was inducted into the Pro Football Hall of Fame in 1963. In addition to his football career, Grange tried his hand at other ventures, including managing a nightclub on Sheridan Road, managing sales of a bottling company, selling insurance, and broadcasting for radio and television for ten years. Grange also appeared in several movies, including *The Galloping Ghost, One Minute to Play,* and *The Racing Romeo.*

A modest man, Grange tended to downplay his fame. "If you have the football and eleven guys are after you, if you're smart, you'll run," he once said with characteristic good humor.

Grange died of complications from pneumonia in a Florida hospital. He was eighty-seven.

See also: George Halas, Sid Luckman, Bronko Nagurski, Walter Payton, Amos Alonzo Stagg

Further reading: George Vass, *George Halas and the Chicago Bears* (1971).

Marion Mahony Griffin

Architect

BORN: February 14, 1871
Chicago, Illinois

DIED: August 10, 1961
Chicago, Illinois

Marion Mahony Griffin was the first licensed female architect in the United States and the only woman in Frank Lloyd Wright's inner circle.

Born in Chicago in 1871, Marion Mahony Griffin grew up in Winnetka. She received her architecture training at the Massachusetts Institute of Technology but returned to Chicago to work with her cousin Dwight Perkins in a studio that was designed by Perkins and was shared by several architects, including Wright. In 1895 she became Wright's first employee.

A fellow architect in the Wright studio, Barry Byrne, once said that Griffin won most of the informal design competitions but that Wright "filed them away . . . for future use." In fact, she oversaw the completion of Wright's work after he left Oak Park for Europe in 1909. Numerous architectural historians, including Paul Kruty at the University of Illinois at Urbana-Champaign, now believe that she influenced Wright more than has been previously acknowledged.

The underappreciated Griffin was the first woman to obtain an architecture license in Illinois. Her style was similar to Japanese woodblock prints. Her drawings came to be known as the Wasmuth Portfolio, a collection of Wright's designs that was published in Germany in 1910. The portfolio established Wright's reputation in America but it also influenced such European modernists as Mies van der Rohe and Le Corbusier.

In 1911 Griffin persuaded her famous architect husband, Walter Burley Griffin, to enter the competition to design Australia's capital city of Canberra; she created fourteen drawings in ink on satin for the competition. These drawings in turn helped her husband win the commission. They moved to Australia in 1914. Only small portions of the plan were used, however. Her husband also worked in India beginning in 1935. She joined him six months later. He died in an accident there in 1937. After his death, she returned to Chicago. Complications caused by the outbreak of World War II prevented Marion Griffin from ever returning to Australia. Unfortunately, she failed to get much work after her return to America.

In her later years, Griffin suffered from dementia. She died a pauper at Cook County Hospital in 1961 at the age of ninety. She was buried at Graceland Cemetery in an anonymous grave. In 1997 Graceland moved her remains to a granite columbarium designed by the Chicago architect John Eiffler. In the same year the Kinnert Art Museum at the University of Illinois held an exhibit of Griffin's architectural renderings, many of which resembled Japanese prints.

In recent years the Art Institute of Chicago has made available a facsimile of her memoir, *The Magic of America*, which can be viewed at www.artic.edu/magicofamerica.

A few works attributed to her survive: a mural in the George B. Armstrong elementary school in Chicago and several Prairie-style private homes in downstate Decatur, Illinois. She was also known for her paintings of local flora.

See also: Walter Burley Griffin, George W. Maher, Frank Lloyd Wright

Further reading: Judith A. Barter, ed., *Apostles of Beauty* (2009); Debora Wood, ed., *Marion Mahony Griffin* (2005); David Van Zanten, ed., *Marion Mahony Reconsidered* (2011).

Walter Burley Griffin

Architect

BORN: November 24, 1876
Maywood, Illinois

DIED: February 11, 1937
Lucknow, India

As the planner of Canberra, Australia's capital city, Walter Burley Griffin's greatest achievement was carried out on another continent on the other side of the world. Yet Griffin was a local boy. He was educated in the Oak Park public schools and graduated from the University of Illinois. A disciple of Frank Lloyd Wright, Griffin designed Prairie-style homes that are scattered throughout Evanston and in Elmhurst, Illinois, where he lived from 1893 to 1914. The Beverly neighborhood on the Southwest Side has the largest concentration—twelve—of Griffin-designed houses.

Griffin was born in Maywood, Illinois, the eldest of four children of George Walter Griffin, an insurance adjuster, and Estelle Griffin. While still in high school he displayed an interest in landscape gardening, a trait that would follow him into his chosen profession. He studied architecture at the University of Illinois at Urbana-Champaign. His first job was working with the Chicago architect Dwight Perkins, where he was surrounded by some of the most progressive architects of the time. From there he worked at Frank Lloyd Wright's Oak Park studio as an assistant from 1901 to 1905 before setting up his own practice.

In 1912 Griffin submitted the winning entry in an international contest to plan the new capital city of Canberra, then little more than an oasis on the vast Australian continent. After seven years as a director of design, he left the city when government officials introduced a plan of their own. For various reasons, Griffin's original vision was compromised. Griffin chose to stay in Australia and established a private practice, first in Melbourne and then in Sidney. He was killed during an accident at a construction site at the University of Lucknow in India, when he fell and ruptured his gall bladder. He was sixty years old. In 1963 Griffin made Australian history when he became the first American to appear on an Australian postage stamp—after his death, his reputation had improved considerably.

In 1981 the 1600 block of West 104th Place between Wood Street and Prospect Avenue—the site of seven of his commissions—was designated a Chicago landmark and renamed Walter Burley Griffin Place.

See also: Marion Mahony Griffin, George W. Maher, Louis Sullivan, Frank Lloyd Wright

Further reading: Judith A. Barter, ed., *Apostles of Beauty: Arts and Crafts from Britain to Chicago* (2009); Mati Maldre and Paul Kruty, *Walter Burley Griffin in America* (1996).

Samuel E. Gross
Real Estate Developer

BORN: November 11, 1843
Dauphin, Pennsylvania

DIED: October 24, 1913
Battle Creek, Michigan

Master builder Samuel Eberly Gross billed himself as "The World's Greatest Real Estate Promoter." Gross is credited with building twenty-one suburbs, constructing more than 10,000 houses, and selling more than 40,000 lots. His most distinguished project, the Alta Vista Terrace block in Wrigleyville, is a landmark Chicago district.

Gross moved with his parents from Pennsylvania to Illinois in the mid-1840s. When the Civil War started in 1861, he joined the Forty-First Illinois Volunteer Infantry, but he was forced to leave because of his youth. After the war, Gross moved to Chicago. He graduated from Union College of Law in 1866 and was admitted to the Illinois bar the same year. While still practicing law, Gross opened a real estate office and purchased empty lots of land, intending to transform them into livable communities.

Gross managed to accumulate a fortune selling lots of land and homes to middle-class buyers and working-class immigrants. By the end of the 1890s the realtor was said to be worth an estimated $3 million to $5 million. Among the neighborhoods and communities he developed are Grossdale, an area west of the city limits in what is now Brookfield, Illinois; Gross Park on the North Side, bounded by Addison Street and Belmont, Western, and Ashland Avenues; Brookdale, west of the Illinois Central railroad tracks between 69th and 71st Streets; the southern suburb of Calumet Heights, Illinois; the Lakeview neighborhood around Wellington and Southport Avenues; McKinley Park, an area on the South Side near Hoyne Avenue and 34th Street; and the Back of the Yards, between 45th and 47th Streets and from Laflin to Ashland Avenue. This development included Gross Avenue, now known as McDowell Avenue.

Around the turn of the century, construction began on what has become his most enduring legacy—Alta Vista Terrace—from property that he purchased east of the Chicago, Milwaukee, Saint Paul, and Pacific Railroad tracks. Modeled after a street in the Mayfair section of London, Alta Vista Terrace is a charming and elegant example of late Victorian architecture within hailing distance of Wrigley Field. Forty brick row houses line the one-block stretch between Grace and Byron Streets.

Often called the "street of forty doors," Alta Vista Terrace is a marvel of architectural symmetry. A replica of every house is duplicated on the other side of the street. The mostly two-story townhouses feature such exquisite details as Gothic doorways, Ionic and Doric columns, coach-lights, and bay windows. Alta Vista Terrace was designated a landmark district by the Commission on Chicago Historical and Architectural Landmarks in 1971.

In addition to his thriving real estate ventures, Gross was also a playwright. In the 1870s he wrote a play, *The Merchant Prince of Cornville*, a comedy of manners that featured a character with a very large nose. Gross's play created quite a stir in late-nineteenth-century Chicago when he charged that Edmond Rostand's French comedy *Cyrano de Bergerac* (1897), based on the life of the seventeenth-century French poet, dramatist, and soldier, plagiarized *The Merchant Prince*. In 1902 a Chicago judge ruled that Gross was indeed the true author and that the popular French play was "clear and unmistakable piracy." Maintaining his innocence from his country estate in France, Rostand argued that "there are big noses everywhere in the world." Despite the ruling, Rostand's play is the one that is remembered while Gross's play has been completely forgotten.

Gross died in 1913 in Battle Creek, Michigan, at the age of sixty-nine.

See also: Arthur Rubloff
Further reading: Richard Cahan, *Landmark Neighborhoods in Chicago* (1981); Dominic A. Pacyga and Ellen Skerrett, *Chicago: City of Neighborhoods* (1986).

George Halas
Football Coach

BORN: February 2, 1895
Chicago, Illinois

DIED: October 31, 1983
Chicago, Illinois

One of the grand old men of sports, George Stanley Halas, or "Papa Bear," as he was called, revolutionized football. He founded and coached the Chicago Bears to National Football League (NFL) championships in 1933, 1941, 1946, and 1963 against the New York Giants; and in 1940 and 1943 against the Washington Redskins. He helped create the National Football League, and he was, until surpassed by Don Shula, the NFL's winningest coach, earning a league record of 318 wins, 148 losses, and 31 ties.

George Halas was the youngest son of a Bohemian tailor who owned his own shop around 18th Street and Ashland Avenue in the heart of Chicago's Pilsen neighborhood. Halas's life was one of good fortune and good timing. An avid athlete, Halas excelled at both baseball and basketball at Crane Technical High School. At the University of Illinois he joined the football team and graduated in 1918 with a civil engineering degree. During World War I he served one year in the navy, was stationed at the Great Lakes Naval Training Station, and played on the Great Lakes football team. The team was good enough to earn an appearance at the 1919 Rose Bowl against the Mare Island (California) Marines. Halas was named the most valuable player.

In 1919 Halas joined the New York Yankees as a promising outfielder. His baseball career was cut short, however, when he suffered a hip injury, causing him to miss many games. He played the remainder of the season for a Saint Paul, Minnesota, minor league team, then returned to Chicago and secured a job in the engineering department of the Chicago, Burlington, and Quincy Railroad.

Halas played professional football during the 1919–20 season for the Hammond Pros, at a time when football attracted few fans. In 1920 A. E. Staley, president of a Decatur-based corn products company, hired him to organize the Decatur Staleys, a semipro football team. In the same year, Halas became one of the founders of the American Professional Football Association (APFA). The group's first meeting took place in the automobile showroom of Ralph Hay, owner of the Canton Bulldogs, in Canton, Ohio. Hard times hit A. E. Staley in 1921. Looking for ways to save money, the company was forced to abandon its football team. Staley suggested that Halas move to Chicago, and he offered to provide the young coach with $5,000 in start-up costs. He had only one request, that Halas call the team the Chicago Staleys for one season. Halas promised he would and moved north. In 1922 he renamed the team the Chicago Bears, in a playful nod to the Chicago Cubs. The team's orange and blue colors he took from his alma mater, the University of Illinois. In the same year, the APFA changed its name, at Halas's suggestion, to the National Football League (NFL).

Professional football, however, failed to win many converts until the 1925 arrival of Red Grange, the halfback whose gridiron feats earned him the nickname of the "Galloping Ghost." Grange turned the game around entirely, drawing unprecedented crowds into the stadiums and creating a palpable excitement on the playing field and in the stands. One of Halas's greatest coaching moments, of which there were many, occurred during the 1940 championship game when the Bears routed the Washington Redskins in a 73–0 victory.

From 1942 to 1946, Halas served in the naval reserves and was awarded the Bronze Star. After the war he resumed his coaching position with the Bears, stepped down in 1955, and returned three years later. He retired as head coach on May 27, 1968. In 1963 Halas was chosen to be a charter member of the Pro Football Hall of Fame. In 1974 general manager Jim Finks took over day-to-day operations of the Bears while Halas retained the title of chairman of the board. But in 1979 he once again assumed the Bears' presidency. After witnessing too many miserable seasons, with Jim Dooley as coach from 1968 to 1972, Abe Gibron from 1972 to 1974, Jack Pardee from 1974 to 1978, and Neill Armstrong from 1978 to 1982, Halas hired Mike Ditka as head coach in 1982.

Some of the finest athletes ever to play for the Bears played during the Halas years. In addition to Grange, there were quarterbacks Sid Luckman, Johnny Lujack, and Jim McMahon; kicker George Blanda; fullback Bronko Nagurski; center Clyde "Bulldog" Turner; linebackers Bill George and Dick Butkus; tight end Mike Ditka; halfbacks John "Paddy" Driscoll and George McAfee; wide receiver Johnny Morris; and running backs Willie Galimore, Gale Sayers, and Walter Payton.

More than anything else, Halas was considered an innovator. He insisted, for example, that no player could be signed until he completed college. In the 1930s he pushed through rule changes that allowed for more forward passing. In 1940 he introduced the T-formation, the basis of all contemporary football offensive tactics, which helped open up the game. He recommended that throwing the football behind the line of scrimmage be legalized. Furthermore, the Chicago Bears were the first team to film and study their games, the first to hire their own band, the first to publish a team newspaper, and the first to practice every day.

Halas died in his North Side apartment in October 1983 at the age of eighty-eight.

See also: Red Grange, Sid Luckman, Bronko Nagurski, Walter Payton

Further reading: George S. Halas, with Gwen Morgan and Arthur Veysey, *Halas: An Autobiography* (1986); George Vass, *George Halas and the Chicago Bears* (1971).

Margaret Haley

Labor Activist

BORN: November 15, 1861
Joliet, Illinois

DIED: January 5, 1939
Chicago, Illinois

Margaret Haley grew up to be the leader of one of the country's most militant unions—the Chicago Teachers Federation—fighting the good fight to improve public education.

Raised on an Illinois farm, Haley was the eldest of a family of eight. Her mother was a native of Ireland and her father an Irish American who came to Chicago to work on the Illinois and Michigan Canal. When she was ten, her father moved the family to Channahon to operate a stone quarry. Haley attended a convent school in nearby Morris. At sixteen she began teaching at a country school near Minooka and then taught in Joliet before moving to Chicago to teach in 1882. Eventually Haley secured a job at the Hendricks School near the Union Stockyards. Later, she studied under Francis W. Parker, principal of the Cook County Normal School and one of the country's most progressive educators.

In 1900 Haley was elected district vice president of the Chicago Teachers Federation (CTF), an organization founded in 1897. She acted as the business representative until her death. The CTF's objective was "to raise the standard of the teaching profession." The CTF contributed greatly to the progressive reform movement then enveloping the city, and, through it, Haley campaigned vigorously for tax reform, municipal ownership, teacher benefits, an elected school board, and woman suffrage.

In 1902 members of the CTF voted to affiliate with the Chicago Federation of Labor. Many viewed this decision with alarm, calling it a "radical departure." Three years later, Haley welcomed the election to city hall of Edward Dunne, whom she considered a friend of labor. With Haley acting as Dunne's "silent" adviser, the mayor appointed one of the most progressive school boards in Chicago history, consisting of an unprecedented number of women, reformers, and civic leaders. Controversy followed Dunne's choices, however, especially among business interests. Tensions eased somewhat in 1909 with the appointment of Ella Flagg Young as superintendent of Chicago Public Schools. But by 1915 things had turned ugly again as the new mayor, the indomitable William Hale Thompson, assailed the policies of both Haley and the CTF. More trouble mounted with the appointment of William McAndrew in 1924 as superintendent. McAndrew's decisions, which included abolishing the advisory teachers' councils, proved immediately unpopular among teachers and drew fire from the CTF.

In May 1916, the American Federation of Teachers (AFT) was formed and the CTF chartered as Local #1 with Haley designated as the CTF's national organizer. The following year, however, the CTF withdrew from the AFT after the Illinois Supreme Court granted the Chicago School Board the power to hire or dismiss a teacher at will and for no cause. One day later, the Illinois governor, Frank Lowden, signed the Otis Law, which affected only the City of Chicago and which gave Chicago teachers the security of tenure. In 1937 a new organization was formed, the Chicago Teachers Union (CTU), but the CTF refused to join.

The CTF, which consisted entirely of female grade school teachers, clashed with various high school unions, including the Chicago Federation of Men Teachers and the Federation of Women High School Teachers. Haley favored granting the same standard wage for all teachers, regardless of grade level or sex, notes historian Robert L. Reid. Since high school salaries were substantially higher than grade school wages, Haley found little support outside the CTF. The CTF continued until 1968, when factionalism and bitter labor disputes led to its dissolution. The CTU, a combination of two high school federations and the Elementary Teachers' Union, remains a potent presence on the current labor scene.

Haley began her autobiography with the words, "I never wanted to fight." But a fighter she was—her enemies called her a "lady labor slugger"—until the day she died of heart disease in January 1939 at the age of seventy-seven. Through her vigorous leadership, Haley improved teacher salaries and benefits, provided job security, and helped raise the standard of the teaching profession.

See also: Francis W. Parker, William Hale Thompson, Ella Flagg Young

Further reading: Robert L. Reid, ed., *Battleground: The Autobiography of Margaret A. Haley* (1982).

Albert Halper

Novelist

BORN: 1904
Chicago, Illinois

DIED: January 19, 1984
Pawling, New York

Best known for his proletarian novels of the 1930s, Albert Halper grew up on the West Side and, after graduating from high school, held a succession of blue-collar jobs. The mechanized nature of the work only reinforced his attitude that the majority of laborers toiled in dead-end jobs that offered little economic relief or mental sustenance. Several of his early novels were set in Chicago. They include *The Foundry* (1934), about workers in a Chicago electrotype plant on the eve of the stock market crash of 1929; *The Chute* (1937), set in the Sears, Roebuck and Company mail-order plant on the West Side; and *The Little People* (1942), about employees of a Chicago department store.

In *On The Shore* (1934), his autobiographical collection of short sketches, Halper portrays the Jewish immigrant life of his family in Chicago, with such evocative titles as "A Herring for My Uncle" and "Hot Night on the West Side." He also recalls his own Chicago childhood when he used to go swimming in Union Park. "I was born on the West Side near the Northwestern tracks; there were factories and big livery stables and once a week I sprinkled sawdust on the floor, throwing out the grains like golden seeds."

Another Chicago novel is *Sons of the Fathers* (1940), an antiwar tract about the relationship between a Jewish immigrant and his son. *The Golden Watch* (1953) is a coming-of-age tale set in pre–World War I Chicago. His best-known novel, *Union Square* (1933), takes place in Depression-era New York. Halper also edited two Chicago anthologies: *This Is Chicago* (1952), a collection of fiction and essays that featured the work of Nelson Algren, James T. Farrell, Ring Lardner, Meyer Levin, and Richard Wright; and *The Chicago Crime Book* (1967), which contains nonfictional accounts of the city's criminals and gangsters.

Halper died in 1984 at the age of seventy-nine.

See also: Saul Bellow, Meyer Levin

Dina Halpern

Actress

BORN: July 15, 1909
Warsaw, Poland

DIED: February 17, 1989
Chicago, Illinois

A distinguished star of the Yiddish-speaking theater for more than half a century, Dina Halpern resided in Chicago from 1948 until her death. She began her career as a dancer and performed with the Warsaw Yiddish Art Theatre, and she was featured in the 1937 films *The Dybbuk* and *The Vow*. By the time she came to the United States in 1938, she was a household name in Poland and the Baltic countries. After the end of World War II (her entire family had perished in the Treblinka concentration camp), Halpern directed and guest starred in Yiddish theater productions in England, France, Israel, Argentina, and Australia.

Halpern set all-time long-run records for Yiddish theater in Chicago with starring roles in *Anna Lucasta* in 1949 and *The Little Foxes* in 1950, both presented at the Douglas Park Theatre at Kedzie and Ogden Avenues. As founder and artistic director of the Chicago Yiddish Theater Association—now defunct—from 1960 to 1970, she presented productions of classic Yiddish works. In 1985 Israel's Bar-Ilan University established the Dina Halpern Institute for the Yiddish Performing Arts, and in July 1988 Halpern received the Manger Prize, the most prestigious honor in Yiddish literature.

Halpern, who was married to the Chicago Lyric Opera publicist Danny Newman, died in 1989 at St. Joseph Hospital of cancer at the age of seventy-nine.

See also: Danny Newman

Further reading; Irving Cutler, *The Jews of Chicago: From Shtetl to Suburb* (1996).

141

Alice Hamilton

Scientist and Social Reformer

BORN: February 27, 1869
New York, New York

DIED: September 22, 1970
Hadlyne, Connecticut

Alice Hamilton played a major role in the development of industrial health legislation in Illinois and contributed to pioneering studies in the fields of public and industrial health. The New York–born, Indiana-raised Hamilton pursued a medical career because she felt the profession offered the best opportunity for women.

Hamilton received her medical degree from the University of Michigan in 1893 and studied pathology and bacteriology in Germany and, later, at Johns Hopkins University. Hamilton first encountered slum living conditions while working at the New England Hospital for Women and Children in the outskirts of Boston, where she made frequent house calls to patients living in tenements. In 1897 she moved to Chicago and became a resident at Hull House, the famous settlement house cofounded by Jane Addams and Ellen Gates Starr. By day she was a professor of pathology at the Women's Medical College of Northwestern University; in the evening she would return to Hull House, where she studied the sources of disease transmission and taught good hygiene to residents of the ethnically diverse neighborhood. Her published findings about the causes and transmission of tuberculosis provoked a public investigation and reevaluation of the city's health department.

From 1911 to 1921, Hamilton investigated industrial poisoning for the federal government while continuing to make occasional visits to Hull House. In 1919 she became an assistant professor of industrial medicine at Harvard University, the first woman to hold a position on the Harvard medical faculty. Her autobiography, *Exploring the Dangerous Trades,* was published in 1943.

Hamilton died in 1970 at the age of 101.

See also: Grace Abbott, Jane Addams, Florence Kelley, Ellen Gates Starr

Fred Hampton

Political Activist

BORN: August 30, 1948
Chicago, Illinois

DIED: December 4, 1969
Chicago, Illinois

Described by his admirers as a cross between Malcolm X and Dr. Martin Luther King Jr., and by his detractors as a dangerous revolutionary, Fred Hampton lived a brief life that ended tragically in violence. Chairman of the Illinois Black Panther Party, Hampton was killed in a police raid on party headquarters at a West Side apartment in 1969.

Born in Chicago but raised in west suburban Maywood, Illinois, Hampton attended Proviso East High School. During his years there he became a spokesman for African American youth—black enrollment at the school in the mid-1960s was approximately 30 percent—and led protests against the school administration, demanding that African American children be assured equal treatment. Hampton served as president of the youth council of the Maywood branch of the National Association for the Advancement of Colored People (NAACP). Under his leadership, says writer Dempsey Travis, membership rose from 40 to more than 500 members.

In June 1967, Hampton and several other young African Americans protested to Maywood officials about the lack of a swimming pool in their neighborhood (blacks were not allowed to use the whites-only pool). Hampton led a peaceful march to city hall, averting what may have turned into a violent confrontation. Even so, police arrested him and charged him with mob action. He was acquitted.

Hampton's transformation from suburban teenager to civil rights activist was a relatively rapid one. In June 1968, Hampton, Bobby Rush, Jewell Cook, and Billy Brook founded the Illinois branch of the Black Panther Party. Under Hampton's leadership, the organization grew to more than 1,000 members during a twelve-month period.

The Black Panther Party was founded by Huey Newton and Bobby Seale in Oakland, California, on October 15, 1966. Their ten-point program demanded "social change by direct action, including force, if necessary, to restructure the 'system' to permit blacks to control their own status." In March 1968, J. Edgar Hoover, director of the FBI, called the Panthers "the single most dangerous threat to the internal security of the United States."

But the Panthers did not only talk about revolution at the point of a gun. They also sponsored programs to help African American communities across the country. In the spring of 1969, the Chicago Panthers, led by Hampton, took a cue from their brethren on the West Coast, and sponsored a free breakfast program at the Better Boys Foundation on South Pulaski Avenue. By the end of May, reports writer Dempsey Travis, the program had been expanded to the Marcy-Newberry Association at 16th Street and Homan Avenue, the Peoples' Church at 201 South Ashland Avenue, the Precious Blood Church at Congress

Street and Western Avenue, and St. Dominic's Church at 357 West Locust Street in the Cabrini-Green housing project. In addition, the Chicago branch organized the Peoples' Medical Center at 3850 West 16th Street, which was affiliated with Mount Sinai Hospital.

On December 4, 1969, Hampton, 21, and Mark Clark, 22, died of gunshot wounds suffered during a police raid, orchestrated by Cook County State's Attorney Edward V. Hanrahan, on Panther headquarters at 2337 West Monroe Street. Four other occupants of the apartment were wounded. Black Panther members maintained that police murdered Hampton and Clark. An FBI investigation revealed that the police, who had a warrant to search for illegal weapons, fired more than ninety shots. The occupants, on the other hand, fired only one.

In 1982 the Cook County Board, after a year of negotiation between government attorneys and the plaintiffs, approved a $1.85 million settlement, which called for the federal government, Cook County, and the City of Chicago to each pay $616,333 in damages. The settlement, believed to be the largest in a civil rights suit, concluded that there was a conspiracy to destroy the Black Panther Party. The suit, originally filed in 1970 and dismissed in 1977 by U.S. District Court Judge Joseph Sam Perry, accused law enforcement officials of violating the civil rights of Black Panther members.

The Black Panther Party disbanded in the mid-1970s. In an example of how times change, former Black Panther Bobby Rush was elected alderman of the Second Ward in 1983. Since 1993 he has represented Illinois's First Congressional District in the House of Representatives. On June 9, 2009, Edward Hanrahan died of complications from leukemia at his home in River Forest, Illinois, at the age of eighty-eight.

See also: Julius J. Hoffman

Further reading: Jeffrey Hass, *The Assassination of Fred Hampton: How the FBI and the Chicago Police Murdered a Black Panther* (2009); Abe Peck, *Uncovering the Sixties: The Life & Times of the Underground Press* (1985); Jon F. Rice, *Up on Madison, Down on 75th: A History of the Illinois Black Panther Party* (1983); Dempsey J. Travis, *An Autobiography of Black Chicago* (1981).

Lorraine Hansberry

Playwright

BORN: May 19, 1930
Chicago, Illinois

DIED: January 12, 1965
New York, New York

"I was born on the South Side of Chicago. I was born black and female. I was born in a depression after one world war and came into adolescence in another." So begins Lorraine Hansberry's autobiographical play, *To Be Young, Gifted, and Black* (1969).

Lorraine Vivian Hansberry enjoyed a middle-class upbringing. Her father was a United States marshal and later a successful real estate broker and banker. Even so, he frequently was required to fight battles against city codes that enforced racial segregation. Hansberry was born at 5330 South Calumet Avenue and moved with her family when she was eight into the predominantly white Washington Park neighborhood. In 1938, when Illinois courts evicted the family from their home at 6140 South Rhodes Avenue on the grounds of racial housing codes, Hansberry's father appealed to the federal courts. Two years later the U.S. Supreme Court ruled in Hansberry's favor, prohibiting the practice of racially restrictive housing ordinances. The experience inspired Hansberry years later to write *A Raisin in the Sun* (1956).

Hansberry attended the Betsy Ross Elementary School at 61st Street and Wabash Avenue. From there she went to Englewood High School. At that time she wanted, she said, to be a journalist. After graduation she studied painting at the Art Institute of Chicago and attended classes at the University of Wisconsin and at the University of Guadalajara, in Ajijic, Mexico. She moved to New York at the end of her sophomore year, in 1950, where she met her future husband, Robert Nemiroff, on a New York University picket line, and the following year she joined the staff of *Freedom* magazine, a political journal published by the noted actor and singer Paul Robeson.

Although she had no training in theater aside from a few courses in set designing and theater history at the University of Wisconsin, Hansberry began writing plays soon after her marriage. In 1956 she wrote a three-act play, *A Raisin in the Sun*. Inspired by the Langston Hughes poem of the same name, *A Raisin in the Sun* incorporates elements from the author's own life. It tells the story of a poor black family on Chicago's South Side and their attempt to escape from the ghetto by purchasing a home in an all-white neighborhood.

A Raisin in the Sun made its Chicago debut in February 1959 during a tryout run at the Blackstone Theater. The cast included Sidney Poitier, Ruby Dee, Diana Sands,

Glynn Turner, Ivan Dixon, and Louis Gossett, artists who would later make names for themselves in television and film. *Chicago Tribune* theater critic Claudia Cassidy called the work "a remarkable play" performed by a "gifted" cast. "More important to Chicago," she wrote, "is that it has the fresh impact of something urgently on its way." The play won universal acclaim when it opened on Broadway the following month. *A Raisin in the Sun* became the first play by a black woman to be produced on Broadway, and Hansberry became the youngest American playwright—and the first African American—to win the New York Drama Critics Circle Award for best play. It was an outstanding achievement. In 1961 Poitier starred in the successful film adaptation and, in 1973, a musical version, *Raisin,* won a Tony Award for best musical.

Hansberry's second play, *The Sign in Sidney Brustein's Window* (1964), about the social awakening of a young Jewish intellectual in Greenwich Village, was not as successful and met with mixed reviews. Hansberry, too, was criticized among her peers for daring to write from the perspective of a white male.

Hansberry died from cancer in January 1965 at the height of her young career. She was only thirty-four. One of her last efforts, *To Be Young, Gifted, and Black: The World of Lorraine Hansberry,* was a distillation of her work—from a novel, letters, and plays—newly scripted and presented by her husband as a fitting memorial to her life and work. *To Be Young, Gifted, and Black* premiered in New York on January 2, 1969, at the Cherry Lane Theater in Greenwich Village. Her other works include *The Drinking Gourd* (1960), about slavery; an unproduced teleplay commissioned by NBC; and *What Use Are Flowers?* (1961),

a modern-day fable. Among her posthumous works is *Les Blancs,* about the making of an African American revolutionary.

Since the early 1980s, there has been a renewed interest in Hansberry's work. A revival of *A Raisin in the Sun* ran at Chicago's Goodman Theatre in 1983 and again in 2000, and a new biography of the playwright's life and work was published in 1991. In February 2010, Bruce Norris's Pulitzer Prize–winning satirical play *Clybourne Park* received its world premiere in a critically acclaimed production at the Playwrights Horizons theater in New York; in 2011, it played at Steppenwolf Theatre in Chicago. Norris offers a theatrical adaptation of the Hansberry family drama but set in the fictitious Chicago neighborhood of Clybourne Park. And in October 2010, Steppenwolf premiered Robert O'Hara's *The Etiquette of Violence,* another modern reworking of Hansberry's classic play.

Actor Douglas Turner Ward, who appeared in the original Broadway production of *A Raisin in the Sun,* called Hansberry a "pioneer" and further stated, "She broke new ground. She created new possibilities. Her impact and influence upon her own generation and succeeding ones are historic."

The house on South Rhodes is now known as the Lorraine Hansberry House. In February 2010, the Chicago City Council granted it official landmark status.

Further reading: Steven R. Carter, *Hansberry's Drama: Commitment amid Complexity* (1991); Anne Cheney, *Lorraine Hansberry* (1984); Steven C. Tracy, ed., *Writers of the Black Chicago Renaissance* (2011).

William Rainey Harper

Educator

BORN: July 26, 1856
New Concord, Ohio

DIED: January 10, 1906
Chicago, Illinois

William Rainey Harper was one of the cofounders and the first president of the University of Chicago. A gregarious man with a magnetic personality, he dominated the university like few others, expanding its influence beyond its Hyde Park campus and, in the spirit of unity, building a foundation based upon service to the community, to the city, and, by extension, to the world.

Born in Ohio of Scots-Irish stock, Harper was a precocious youngster. He entered Muskingum College at the age of ten and graduated at fourteen. He worked in his father's

dry goods store for a short time before enrolling at Yale as a graduate student in philology at seventeen, and he received his Ph.D. in 1875 just short of his nineteenth birthday. In the same year he married the daughter of the president of the college.

Harper then became the principal of Masonic College in Macon, Tennessee. The following year he moved to Granville, Ohio, to be a tutor in the preparatory department at Denison University, which ultimately became Granville Academy. Recognizing Harper's prodigious talents as an administrator, the new institution then made the young

scholar principal. In 1879 he accepted a position teaching Hebrew at the Baptist Union Theological Seminary in Chicago, which had relocated from Douglas Park to Morgan Park, on the Southwest Side, two years earlier. Harper founded two scholarly journals, the *Hebrew Student* and *Hebraica,* and established the American Institute of Hebrew. In 1886 Harper decided to teach at Yale as professor of Semitic languages in the graduate department and as instructor in the Divinity School.

Harper had grandiose visions of founding a great institution of higher learning, preferably in the Midwest. He persuaded several wealthy figures of the feasibility of his plan. In 1890 Chicago merchant Marshall Field donated a plot of land east of Ellis Avenue and north of 57th Street to the new venture while entrepreneur and philanthropist John D. Rockefeller provided the initial $600,000 to get the project off the ground. Field, businessman Martin Ryerson, and other prominent Chicagoans contributed additional money.

In September 1890, Harper was elected president of the new University of Chicago. An older university of the same name had stood at Cottage Grove and 34th Street since 1861, until it declared itself bankrupt in 1886. The new university was incorporated on September 10, 1890, and opened its doors on October 1, 1892. The success of Harper's university was built on the principle of service. Harper established a university press in order to spread the university's beliefs and philosophy throughout the world. Men and women, Harper agreed, should be admitted to the university on an equal footing. Further, Harper required all first-year students to pass an entrance examination. The university itself consisted of four undergraduate colleges, a nonprofessional graduate school, and schools of divinity, law, medicine, engineering, pedagogy, fine arts, and music. The University Extension was modeled after Cambridge University and consisted of lectures given outside the university proper, evening courses, correspondence courses, special courses, and a library extension. Harper divided the university year into four quarters of twelve weeks, each followed by a one-week break. Each quarter, in turn, was divided into two terms of six weeks each. Instruction was thus offered throughout most of the year, allowing for greater freedom and flexibility for both the student body and the staff.

Harper recruited the brightest and the best by offering good wages and the promise of freedom of expression to any and all prospective teachers. He would not take no for an answer. His perseverance paid off. Harper persuaded some of the best minds available to participate in his bold experiment in the heartland, including Albert A. Michelson, physics professor; Albion W. Small, head of sociology; Thorstein B. Veblen, assistant professor of political economy; Amos Alonzo Stagg, physical education teacher and coach of the Maroons football team; John Dewey, philosopher and educator; novelist Robert Herrick from the Massachusetts Institute of Technology; poet William Vaughn Moody; James Henry Breasted, the first teacher of Egyptology in the nation and the founder of the Oriental Institute; Emil G. Hirsch, Old Testament scholar; and Robert Francis Harper, the president's brother and famed Assyriologist. In addition, the University of Chicago founded the country's first university press, and it was one of the first institutions of higher learning to introduce graduate programs in such areas as business management, sociology, and social work.

Harper wrote many books, including *The Trend in Higher Education* (1905), *The Structure of the Text of the Book of Hosea* (1905), *A Critical and Exegetical Commentary on Amos and Hosea* (1905), *The Prophetic Element in the Old Testament* (1905), and *The Priestly Element in the Old Testament* (1909).

Harper died of cancer in 1906 at the age of forty-nine. He died before he achieved his greatest goal—to establish a medical school at the university—yet his legacy and his memory live on. He, no doubt, would be pleased to learn that the school he founded and the medical center, established in 1898, continue to be among the very best in the nation and, indeed, the world.

Harper Avenue is named in his honor, as is Harper College, which opened in 1967 in Palatine, Illinois.

See also: Frank Billings, Marshall Field, Robert Herrick, Emil G. Hirsch, Robert Maynard Hutchins, Albert A. Michelson, Amos Alonzo Stagg

Further reading: Thomas Wakefield Goodspeed, *The Story of the University of Chicago, 1890–1925* (1925); Rebecca Janowitz, *Culture of Opportunity: Obama's Chicago: The People, Politics, and Ideas of Hyde Park* (2010); Richard J. Storr, *Harper's University: The Beginnings* (1966).

Carter Henry Harrison I

Politician

BORN: February 15, 1825
Fayette County, Kentucky

DIED: October 28, 1893
Chicago, Illinois

A brilliant orator, "Our Carter" (a nickname referring to the close relationship between the mayor and the citizenry), served four consecutive terms as mayor of Chicago from 1879 to 1887 and won an unprecedented fifth term in 1893. A pragmatist, Carter Henry Harrison defended the right of anarchists to stage meetings as long as they were peaceful, and he tolerated vice as long as it was confined to a restricted area. Outgoing, genial, and charming, Harrison was a friend of the people. Despite his upper-class background, he was able to win the support of the common laborer, the burgeoning immigrant population, and the business class. Harrison was a Chicago booster from the moment he set foot in the city in 1855.

Harrison's father died when he was eight months old. Young Carter received most of his early education from his mother and from Kentucky country schools. He graduated from Yale in 1845 and then transferred to the law school of Transylvania University in Lexington, Kentucky. He spent two years traveling abroad in Europe, Asia, and Egypt. In 1855 Harrison came to Chicago, where he made his fortune in real estate during the land boom. In 1871 he entered politics and was elected a member of the first Board of Commissioners of Cook County. He held this post until December 1874, when he won the seat for Illinois's Second Congressional District in the United States House of Representatives. Reelected two years later, he declined the nomination in 1878.

In 1879 Harrison won his first term as mayor of Chicago and was reelected in 1881, 1883, and 1885. He sat out the 1887 election. That summer he quenched his passion for travel by setting off on a world tour. In 1889 he rejected the mayoral nomination, but two years later he agreed to run against Democrat Dewitt C. Cregier. He lost that bid. Determined, he ran as an independent, but lost again—this time to the Republican, Hempstead Washburne.

Carter Harrison was a larger-than-life figure as he galloped up and down the city streets on his horse. As mayor, his "live and let live" philosophy allowed saloons, brothels, and gambling houses to carry on business unimpeded by city hall and the police department. Harrison thought these "institutions" were just as important in their own way as churches, and he regarded gambling and prostitution as unfortunate but necessary evils. As long as the voters agreed with his laissez-faire thinking, it served him well.

In the latter half of 1891, Harrison bought the *Chicago Times* newspaper, primarily as an organ from which he could launch his still-considerable political ambitions. More than anything, Harrison wanted to be the mayor during the World's Columbian Exposition of 1893. He ran in a bitterly contested battle against Republican Samuel W. Allerton and emerged triumphant, enjoying the biggest margin of his colorful career. Although most of the daily papers dismissed him as the ally of gangsters and thugs, he still exuded great personal appeal and was well liked by the ordinary citizens.

The Mayor Harrison of 1893 proved vastly different from the Mayor Harrison of years past. Displaying a new face to the public, he disavowed any connection with the city's underworld. Yet he was always a practical man. When the reformers were in the spotlight, Harrison turned reformer, and when the public no longer demanded reform, Harrison turned the other cheek.

The opening of the World's Columbian Exposition in May of 1893 found the mayor in a jubilant mood. Visitors from throughout the country—indeed, the world—descended upon the city. At the closing of the fair in October 1893, Harrison made a confident speech before a convention of mayors. That night he returned to his Ashland Avenue mansion. When the doorbell rang, he opened the door and started to speak; an intruder drew a revolver and fired. Harrison fell, mortally wounded. Patrick Eugene Prendergast, a disappointed office seeker, was charged with the murder and was eventually convicted and hanged. Instead of celebrating Chicago's future, the World's Fair ended on a somber note as a mournful city buried its beloved mayor.

See also: "Bathhouse John" Coughlin, Carter Henry Harrison II, Michael "Hinky Dink" Kenna

Further reading: Claudius O. Johnson, *Carter Henry Harrison I: Political Leader* (1928); Herman Kogan and Lloyd Wendt, *Lords of the Levee: The Story of Bathhouse John and Hinky Dink* (1943); Erik Larson, *The Devil in the White City: Murder, Magic, and Madness at the Fair That Changed America* (2004); Frederick F. Rex, *The Mayors of the City of Chicago* (1934).

Carter Henry Harrison II

Politician

BORN: April 23, 1860
Chicago, Illinois

DIED: December 25, 1953
Chicago, Illinois

Like his father before him, Carter Henry Harrison II was a pragmatist and a natural politician. He also served five terms as mayor of Chicago. Yet his contributions have been sorely neglected, even ignored. His considerable achievements—he established playgrounds in slum neighborhoods, developed the outer harbor, and extended city services—have been eclipsed by the towering figure of his famous parent.

Carter Harrison II received his early schooling in Germany in the duchy of Saxe-Altenburg (a European education was highly valued among Chicago's elite). After his mother's death in 1876, he returned to Chicago and enrolled at St. Ignatius College, now Loyola University. He then earned a law degree from Yale. In 1886 he entered the real estate business with his brother, William Preston Harrison. For several years the brothers operated the *Chicago Times*, which their father had bought in 1891. It did not fare well, and they sold it at a loss.

Harrison served four consecutive two-year mayoral terms (from 1897 to 1905) and one four-year term (from 1911 to 1915). The 1897 campaign revolved around such emotional reform issues as the suppression of vice, the municipal ownership of public utilities, and the operation of an honest, efficient government. Harrison, tearing a page from his father's book of political etiquette, did not believe in legislating public morality; instead, he advocated the populist concept of "personal liberty."

Harrison attracted a broad constituency, from laborers to immigrants, and he was equally at home, as historian Edward R. Kantowicz so colorfully puts it, "in a poker game with party hacks or at a reception on the Gold Coast." Unlike his father, however, Harrison earned a reputation as somewhat of a reformer and thus attracted a modicum of middle-class support.

One of the biggest issues confronting the Harrison administration was the traction drama—the complex dispute over municipal ownership of public transportation—with the indomitable Charles Tyson Yerkes playing the role of villain. In 1881 Yerkes began purchasing streetcar lines. His goal was to buy all the lines in the city and reap the substantial rewards from such a monopoly. A series of bills were introduced in the state senate extending Yerkes's franchise for fifty years. The effort failed. Yerkes tried again and goaded a pliable representative to introduce a bill—the Allen bill—that authorized city councils to grant the franchises. It passed the Illinois Senate. However, through the valiant efforts of Mayor Harrison it was defeated in the Chicago City Council in 1898.

But the traction problem was far from over. There was widespread discontent with streetcars. Invariably they were overcrowded and usually late. The public demanded action, but the city, insisted the mayor, did not have the necessary funds to finance a takeover of the streetcars.

In 1905 Harrison, for health reasons, retired from politics and moved to California. Edward F. Dunne campaigned on the promise of immediate ownership by the city and won, but he, too, failed to settle the traction dispute. Two years later, the city council and the streetcar companies finally came to terms. Streetcar operators agreed to upgrade their cars and, in return, gave the city the option to buy at any time.

In 1911 Harrison resumed his political career with a narrow primary victory over ex-mayor Dunne. In the general election he faced the Republican challenger, the professor-turned-alderman Charles E. Merriam. Harrison won—but barely. The narrow margin indicated that all was not well. Harrison's last term was marred by partisan infighting and an ugly maneuvering for power, much of it due to the behind-the-scene machinations of the corrupt Democratic boss, Roger A. Sullivan. Harrison's most dramatic act occurred during his waning days in office in 1911, when he shut down the infamous Everleigh Club. In 1915 Harrison lost the Democratic primary to a Sullivan loyalist, Robert A. Sweitzer. Sweitzer, in turn, was defeated in the general election by the Republican, William Hale Thompson.

During World War I, Harrison served as a captain with the American Red Cross in France. There were rumors that he would run for a seat in the United States Senate in 1927, but he passed on the opportunity. In 1933 he was appointed Collector of Internal Revenue for the Northern District of Illinois. He resigned in 1944. Three years later, in 1947, he served as the chair of the Citizens of Greater Chicago Committee, which supported the mayoral candidacy of Martin Kennelly.

Harrison died at the age of ninety-three, on Christmas Day, 1953.

See also: John Peter Altgeld, "Bathhouse John" Coughlin, Ada and Minna Everleigh, Michael "Hinky Dink" Kenna, Charles E. Merriam, Charles Tyson Yerkes

Further reading: Carter H. Harrison II, *Stormy Years: The Autobiography of Carter H. Harrison, Five Times Mayor of Chicago* (1935) and *Growing Up with Chicago* (1944); Edward R. Kantowicz, "Carter H. Harrison II: The Politics of Balance," in *The Mayors: The Chicago Political Tradition* (1987), Paul M. Green and Melvin G. Holli, eds.; Herman Kogan and Lloyd Wendt, *Lords of the Levee: The Story of Bathhouse John and Hinky Dink* (1943); Frederick F. Rex, *The Mayors of the City of Chicago* (1934).

Paul Harvey

Broadcaster

BORN: September 4, 1918
Tulsa, Oklahoma

DIED: February 28, 2009
Phoenix, Arizona

News commentator and pioneer talk-radio host, Paul Harvey would begin his program with a hearty "Hello, America!" A heartland icon and national fixture since 1951, he delivered both news and commentary. He was often called the Walter Winchell of his day. He was plain-spoken and known for his folksy observations and brief human-interest stories that often ended with humorous one-liners. The world may have changed around him but neither he nor his format did. He ended each broadcast with his signature sign-off, "Paul Harvey" followed by a long pause and then "Good *day*!"

Born Paul Harvey Aurandt in Tulsa, Oklahoma, Harvey was the son of a police officer who was killed in the line of duty when Harvey was a youngster of three. As a teenager, Harvey so impressed a teacher at Tulsa Central High School with his voice that the teacher took him to a local radio station and told the manager, "This boy needs to be on the radio." Harvey was taken on as an unpaid gofer but it didn't take long before he was allowed to deliver commercials and read the news on the air. He also studied speech and literature at the University of Tulsa. In the 1940s he dropped his last name for professional reasons.

Harvey worked at KXOK radio in St. Louis and then as a reporter in Hawaii. After the attack on Pearl Harbor, he joined the army. Discharged in 1944, he moved to Chicago and obtained an announcing job at WENR-AM. In 1946 he became the host of a call-in program. Several years later, in 1951, ABC became the owner of WENR and consequently Harvey began broadcasting coast to coast. As he became more popular, New York executives took notice and asked him to relocate to New York. He refused.

Although Harvey appeared on television in the late 1960s and early 1970s his forte, and preference, was always radio. He also lectured extensively and wrote a syndicated column that appeared in hundreds of newspapers. His characteristics were legendary: he became famous for his pauses while on the air. He had said that those trademark pauses originally developed as "a lazy broadcaster's way of waiting for the second hand to reach the top of the clock." But dead air and silence became his best friends in ways that were unheard of on radio at the time.

Harvey was called the voice of Middle America and the voice of the "silent majority" and was known for his heartfelt conservatism or "political fundamentalism," as he called it. He was also considered the "most listened-to man in the history of radio," according to Bruce DuMont of Chicago's Museum of Broadcast Communications and host of the radio program "Beyond the Beltway." He personalized the news and also wrote and delivered his own commercials.

Harvey may have been a devout conservative but he was also a practical and fair-minded man. Initially he supported the anti-Communist activities of Sen. Joseph McCarthy during the 1950s, but he withdrew his support when he felt McCarthy had gone too far. He was full of surprises in other ways, too. He supported, for example, both the passage of the ill-fated Equal Rights Amendment and a woman's right to have an abortion. His most famous broadcast was in 1970, when he announced on the radio that he could no longer support President Richard M. Nixon and his expansion of the Vietnam War into Cambodia. In fact, he urged Nixon to withdraw forces, not escalate them. "Mr. President," he said, "I love you, but you're wrong." Harvey shocked his listeners—he had been an ardent supporter of the Vietnam War. His unexpected announcement led to an avalanche of criticism and a flood of letters and telephone calls.

In 1976 Harvey began broadcasting on his show a segment called "The Rest of the Story," which consisted of five-minute anecdotal descriptions of the lives of famous people, oftentimes with twist endings, such as the incident of the thirteen-year-old boy who received a gift of cash from Franklin Delano Roosevelt and turned out to be none other than Fidel Castro. Or the famous trial lawyer who never finished law school (that would have been Clarence Darrow). "The Rest of the Story" segments were his attempt to capture "the heartbeats behind the headlines."

In 2005 Harvey received the Presidential Medal of Freedom and in the same year was inducted into the Radio Hall of Fame.

Harvey's heyday occurred from the 1950s through the 1990s; his show was broadcast twice daily. At the height of his career he reached more than twenty-four million listeners on more than 1,200 radio stations nationally and 400 Armed Forces Radio stations around the world; his syndicated column was carried by more than 300 newspapers. In Chicago he was heard locally on WGN-AM. Disciplined and consistent, he rarely veered from his morning routine—he had oatmeal every morning. He lived in west suburban River Forest and rejected numerous offers to move his show from Chicago to the East Coast.

For several months in 2001 Harvey was not able to work because of a virus that weakened his vocal cords. He returned to work and was still working almost up until his death in February 2009. Harvey died at the Mayo Clinic Hospital near his winter home in Phoenix, Arizona. He was ninety.

Ben Hecht

Journalist and Playwright

BORN: February 28, 1894
New York, New York

DIED: April 18, 1964
New York, New York

Ben Hecht led the kind of life that legends are made of. During his multifaceted career, Hecht produced about seventy screenplays, twenty-six books, twenty plays, and hundreds of short stories and magazine articles. He is best remembered today for his vivid portrayal of wisecracking, cynical Chicago journalists in the play *The Front Page* (1928), which he coauthored with Charles MacArthur.

Born in New York of Russian-Jewish immigrants, Hecht moved with his family to Chicago when he was six and, in 1903, settled in Racine, Wisconsin. After high school Hecht moved in with his aunt and uncle in Chicago. He soon got a job on the *Chicago Daily Journal* as a "picture chaser"—a dubious start, perhaps, but one that gave him plenty of opportunity to display his ingenuity. His chief function was to secure photographs, by whatever means necessary, of noteworthy people who had fallen on bad times. According to biographer William MacAdams, Hecht did everything within—and outside of—the law to please his editors. He used fire escapes, crawled through open windows, posed as a gas meter inspector, and broke into locked houses. Hecht quickly earned a reputation as the best picture thief in the business.

In fact, Hecht's editors were so impressed that they sent him off to cover news stories. Unsure of how to gather the facts, Hecht did what many inventive news reporters of that era reportedly did—he made them up. As he gained more experience on the street, however, he turned into an ace reporter and covered several major stories, including the Dayton flood of 1913 and the founding of President Theodore Roosevelt's Bull Moose Party.

But Hecht had other ambitions. In 1913 he met Kenneth Sawyer Goodman, an aspiring dramatist and the son of a lumber millionaire. Goodman and Hecht collaborated on several one-act plays, including *The Wonder Hat* (1920). Hecht's full-length solo play, *The Egotist,* was produced in New York in 1922.

Meanwhile, in 1914, Hecht had secured a job at the *Chicago Daily News.* Editor Henry Justin Smith reigned over an impressive group of novelists and poets who disguised themselves as reporters. Smith, recalled Hecht, "loved our paper with an interest that ignored circulation and saw it as a daily novel written by a wild but willing bunch of Balzacs."

Hecht was the unofficial king of Chicago's literary world. His biting wit and devastatingly scathing tongue held forth at Schlogl's, the august downtown tavern that was home to a host of *Daily News* staffers and other literary types. The leading figure on Chicago's bohemian circuit, Hecht made fast friends with others in the close-knit circle—Carl Sandburg, Sherwood Anderson, Ring Lardner, and Margaret Anderson, among many others—and was a frequent visitor to the notorious Dil Pickle Club on the Near North Side in the shadow of the Newberry Library. With fellow bohemian Maxwell Bodenheim, he founded the Players' Workshop, an alternative theater on the South Side. In 1923 Hecht and Bodenheim teamed up again, this time to publish the *Chicago Literary Times,* an insolent biweekly newspaper that poked irreverent fun at posers, politicians, writers, artists, society types, hangers-on, and just about anyone and everyone that the pair deemed worthy enough to hold up to ridicule.

Writing newspaper stories and one-act plays or publishing saucy journals did not wholly satisfy the ambitious journalist. Hecht soon joined the other top literary talent who wrote for the silver screen, which included William Faulkner, George S. Kaufman, and Ring Lardner. Although he criticized the banality of the Hollywood machine, he was very much in demand. Among his many screenplays are *Underworld* (1927), *The Front Page* (1931), *Scarface* (1932), *Barbary Coast* (1935), *Wuthering Heights* (1939), *Gunga Din* (1939), *It's a Wonderful World* (1939), *Spellbound* (1945), *Notorious* (1946), and *A Farewell to Arms* (1957), as well as scores of uncredited films, including *The Prisoner of Zenda* (1937), *A Star Is Born* (1937), *Angels with Dirty Faces* (1938), *Gone with the Wind* (1939), *His Girl Friday* (1940), *Foreign Correspondent* (1940), *Mutiny on the Bounty* (1962), *A Walk on the Wild Side* (1962), and *Casino Royale* (1966). Hecht won Academy Awards for two scripts, *Underworld* (1927) and *The Scoundrel* (1935), which he also directed.

A prolific wordsmith, Hecht reportedly once wrote a screenplay in one night and dictated a novel in thirty-six hours. "I think it's better to keep writing than to labor over every word, trying to make it a gem," he once said.

Hecht's best-known work remains *The Front Page,* the hit play he coauthored with Charles MacArthur in 1928, which is set in the rough-and-tumble world of Chicago journalism. There have been several motion-picture versions of the play, including *His Girl Friday,* starring Cary Grant, Rosalind Russell, and Ralph Bellamy; *The Front Page* (1974), starring Jack Lemmon and Walter Matthau; and *Switching Channels* (1988), starring Burt Reynolds, Kathleen Turner, and Christopher Reeve. Another Hecht-MacArthur play, *Twentieth Century* (1932), was made into a movie in 1934.

Though politically neutral for most of his life, Hecht helped raise money for the establishment of a Jewish state in what was then British-owned Palestine and what is now

Israel, when the horrors of the Nazi concentration camps became known. The author's outspoken support of Zionism—the movement supporting the establishment and maintenance of a Jewish homeland—and his criticism of British policy in Palestine resulted in his movies being banned in Britain for four years.

In 1954 Hecht's massive 950-page autobiography, *A Child of the Century*, was published by Simon & Schuster. From 1958 to 1959 Hecht hosted his own talk show on a local New York City television station. In 1969 *Gaily, Gaily*, the colorful memoir of Hecht's days as a cub reporter originally published in 1963, was turned into a motion picture directed by Norman Jewison and starring Beau Bridges as the young Hecht.

Hecht's novels include *Erik Dorn* (1921), *Gargoyles* (1922), and *Count Bruga* (1926), among many others. In 1922 an anthology of his Chicago newspaper articles, *1001 Afternoons in Chicago*, was published. In 1998 Chicago playwright Paul Peditto adapted that anthology into a two-act play, which was presented at the Live Bait Theater and the Prop Theater in Chicago. One of his last plays, a gangland musical called *Chicago*, was never produced. His last book, *Letters from Bohemia*, a collection of letters, was published posthumously in 1964.

Hecht suffered a heart attack in April 1964 in his New York apartment.

Hecht's ex-wife, Marie Armstrong Hecht, was the editor of the short-lived magazine, *The Chicagoan*, Chicago's version of the *New Yorker*. She was also a translator and poet. *The Chicagoan* made its debut on June 14, 1926. Its pages consisted of articles, profiles, reviews, photographs, cartoons, and other news of the "metropolitan life."

See also: Margaret C. Anderson, Sherwood Anderson, Kenneth Sawyer Goodman, Ring Lardner, Carl Sandburg

Further reading: Doug Fetherling, *The Five Lives of Ben Hecht* (1977); Neil Harris, *The Chicagoan: A Lost Magazine of the Jazz Age* (2008); William MacAdams, *Ben Hecht: The Man Behind the Legend* (1990).

Ernest Hemingway

Novelist

BORN: July 21, 1899
Oak Park, Illinois

DIED: July 2, 1961
Ketchum, Idaho

Chicago suburb Oak Park has claimed Hemingway as its own, but for fifteen months in 1920 and 1921, the famous author lived on Chicago's North Side at several locations—1030 North State Street, 100 East Chicago Avenue, and in the 1300 block of North Clark Street—and edited an obscure magazine called *Cooperative Commonwealth*. Hemingway attended Oak Park and River Forest High School and delivered the *Oak Leaves* newspaper. Hemingway received his first taste of literary success in 1926 with the publication of *The Sun Also Rises*. Subsequent novels included *A Farewell to Arms* (1929); *To Have and Have Not* (1937); *For Whom the Bell Tolls* (1940); and *The Old Man and the Sea* (1952), which earned him a Pulitzer Prize in 1953 and the Nobel Prize in Literature the following year.

Hemingway's image remains enigmatic, that of an essentially rootless man whose incurable wanderlust led him to adventures and places far from his native Midwest. Oak Park may never have appeared in his novels, but, as writer Michael Reynolds argues, it existed as a moral presence "beneath the surface, invisible, and inviolate." Hemingway remains a larger-than-life figure to this day. His name still sells books and magazines, and journalists and scholars still discuss his merits.

After Hemingway's marriage to Hadley Richardson in September 1921 at the First Presbyterian Church in Horton Bay in northern Michigan, the couple returned briefly to Chicago before they moved to Paris. There, in the company of his fellow Lost Generation expatriates, Hemingway began the famous journey that the world would come to know. In the year of his death he was working on his Paris memoir, *A Moveable Feast*, in which he recalled the writing of his first Midwestern stories set in the north of Michigan.

Hemingway died of a self-inflicted shotgun wound at his home in Idaho. He was sixty-one.

Hemingway was born and lived in a two-story Victorian home at 439 North Oak Park Avenue in Oak Park until 1906. Now known as the Hemingway Birthplace Home, it is open to the public and has been restored by the Oak Park Hemingway Foundation. He then lived at 600 North Kenilworth Avenue in the suburb until 1919. His mother, Grace, designed the house herself. It included a two-story music room where she gave music lessons and held recitals. The boyhood home is not open to the public but remains a favorite stop among literary tourists. The

Hemingway Museum and Bookstore is housed in the Oak Park Arts Center while the Oak Park Library houses the Hemingway Archives and Research Room.

Further reading: Carlos Baker, *Ernest Hemingway: A Life Story* (1969); Michael R. Federspiel, *Picturing Hemingway's Michigan* (2010); Peter Griffin, *Along with Youth: Hemingway, the Early Years* (1985).

Robert Herrick

Novelist

BORN: April 26, 1868
Cambridge, Massachusetts

DIED: December 23, 1938
St. Thomas, Virgin Islands

Novelist and university professor Robert Herrick, a transplanted New Englander from Massachusetts, had a love-hate relationship with Chicago, his adopted city. Repelled by what he considered Chicago's physical ugliness, he was also attracted by its crude emotional vitality. He lived and taught in Chicago for thirty years and set many of his novels here. Herrick was a realist in the tradition of William Dean Howells and Henry James; he wrote what he saw.

A graduate of Harvard University, Herrick accepted an offer in 1893 from William Rainey Harper to teach in the English department of the new University of Chicago. In the early years, Herrick moved from one Hyde Park apartment to another. Among his Hyde Park addresses is 5735 South University Avenue.

Herrick was a member of the so-called Chicago school of writing, which referred not so much to a particular style as to an obsession with the city, its history, its mores, and its environment. Others in this category include Theodore Dreiser, Henry Blake Fuller, Sherwood Anderson, and Floyd Dell, as well as such individual works as Frank Norris's *The Pit* and Upton Sinclair's *The Jungle*. "Its members cannot be identified with a literary or philosophical creed, a program of reform, or even a particular physical community," writes Blake Nevius in *Robert Herrick: The Development of a Novelist* (1962). "If they are united at all it is in their common acknowledgment that the Chicago of their day provided the best example for the realist of the emerging urban and industrial civilization."

Most of Herrick's novels critique American culture and condemn greed and the mad rush to make more money. The typical Herrick hero, often wrestling with inner demons, struggles to maintain moral responsibility in a corrupt, materialistic society. Herrick felt that, of all American cities, Chicago best symbolized the dangers of unchecked capitalism. *The Gospel of Freedom* (1898), about the love between a woman and a Chicago businessman, makes liberal use of its Chicago locations. It was generally well received except among members of the local press,

who objected to the author's harsh treatment of the city. *The Web of Life* (1900) tells the story of a young doctor who rejects a lucrative practice to serve the poor on the far South Side and becomes disillusioned by the poverty and class hatred he finds there. In *The Common Lot* (1904), a Chicago architect enters into a partnership with a shady contractor to erect jerry-built structures. He suffers pangs of guilt when fire destroys one of his buildings, a hastily constructed hotel, and results in a tragic loss of life. *The Memoirs of an American Citizen* (1905), considered by many critics to be Herrick's best novel, chronicles the ascent and decline of a successful meatpacker who rises to the top of his profession through bribery and corruption. Set against the backdrop of the Union Stockyards and the Packingtown neighborhood, the book incorporates historical events and actual places into its narrative, including the Haymarket Affair, the World's Columbian Exposition, and the Pullman strike. Finally, the largely autobiographical *Chimes* (1926) follows the founding of an innovative university—clearly modeled after the University of Chicago—through its first three decades.

In December 1923, Herrick resigned from the University of Chicago in order to devote his time exclusively to writing. During the last years of his life, however, Herrick made a drastic change. He abandoned writing altogether to enter public service. In January 1935, he accepted the position of Government Secretary of the Virgin Islands. He died there at the age of seventy.

Herrick's works have not aged particularly well. Although Herrick was praised by his fellow writers, his reputation has fallen considerably in comparison to Dreiser, Anderson, Hemingway, Farrell, and other contemporaries.

Among Herrick's other novels are *A Life for a Life* (1910), *The Healer* (1911), *His Great Adventure* (1913), *Clark's Field* (1914), *Homely Lilla* (1923), and *The End of Desire* (1932).

See also: Sherwood Anderson, Floyd Dell, Theodore Dreiser, James T. Farrell, Henry Blake Fuller, William Rainey Harper, Ernest Hemingway

John Hertz

Entrepreneur

BORN: April 10, 1879
Ruttka, Austria

DIED: October 8, 1961
Los Angeles, California

Transportation king John D. Hertz gave Chicago its first organized taxicab service and founded the Hertz rental car agency.

The Austrian-born Hertz was brought to the United States by his parents when he was five years old. The family settled on Chicago's West Side where young Hertz attended public school. He quit in the sixth grade to find work to help support his family. Hertz began his career selling newspapers on Chicago streets and then became a $6-per-week wagon driver. Later he found work as a copy boy at the old *Chicago Morning News,* which later changed its name to the *Chicago Record.* Eventually Hertz was promoted to sports reporter and later to assistant sports editor, but he lost the job when the paper merged with another.

An athlete himself, Hertz took boxing lessons at a gym on North Clark Street. Because of the anti-Semitism prevalent at that time, he decided to use the name Dan Donnelly. As Donnelly, he won championships in amateur tournaments at the Chicago Athletic Association. Later he fought under his own name and managed Benny Yanger, a contender for both lightweight and middleweight titles. Hertz also operated weekly boxing shows at the Star Theater on Clark Street.

A friend convinced Hertz that the future lay in automobiles, and, indeed, few other inventions in history have so profoundly affected patterns of human life. Hertz couldn't even drive, but in 1904 he began selling cars. He was so successful that several years later he became a partner in an automobile agency. Much of the company's business involved trade-ins, or used cars. In a moment of inspiration, Hertz decided in 1907 to turn the secondhand vehicles into taxicabs. At that time, taxicabs were the province of the rich—ordinary citizens couldn't afford to pay the extravagantly high fares. Hertz responded by slashing prices and, to further lure customers, he boasted that he could have a cab at a particular destination within ten minutes. Hertz provided a service and, thus, demanded high standards from his employees. He insisted that his drivers be well dressed, polite, and personable, and maintain a clean car.

The taxicab, note historians Gorman Gilbert and Robert E. Samuels, "represented a new, faster, more convenient form of personal urban transportation." Mass transportation suffered as the automobile and taxicab industries expanded. The development of the taxi industry paralleled the popularity of the automobile and, in turn, affected public transportation. At the turn of the twentieth century more than 4,000 automobiles were manufactured in the United States. A decade later the number had risen to 181,000,

and four years later it jumped to more than 548,000. By 1930 the American automobile industry produced five million cars annually.

With seven limousine cars, Hertz established the Yellow Cab service in 1915. When the public complained that the fares were too high, he introduced smaller models at cheaper rates and he painted his cars yellow for easy identification. By 1940, he had a fleet of forty and was able to build his own manufacturing plant. The company prospered and eventually expanded into bus and truck manufacturing.

Hertz entered the car rental business in 1923 when he purchased a rental firm from a local salesman named Walter Jacobs. The following year he established the Yellow Drive-It-Yourself Company and began promoting a spacious automobile, called the "Ambassador," as a rental car. The idea floundered—customers apparently didn't want to be seen driving an obviously rented vehicle (the "Ambassador" was larger than most cars). In 1925 he sold both the manufacturing branch and the rental arm of the company to General Motors. Four years later Hertz sold the Yellow Cab Company to the Parmalee System, which, in turn, was bought by Checker Motors. In 1953 General Motors sold Yellow Drive-It-Yourself to Hertz's Omnibus Corporation, which then changed its name to Hertz Rent-A-Car.

Hertz held many positions in the business world: director of the First National Bank of Chicago, director of Keeshin Transcontinental Freight Lines, and director of Paramount Pictures Corporation. In addition, he was an active partner in the now-defunct investment firm Lehman Brothers for more than twenty-seven years. Hertz also served in various capacities during both world wars, as a civilian expert with the Motor Transport Division of the U.S. Army in World War I and as assistant in charge of motor vehicles to Undersecretary of War Robert Patterson in World War II, for which he received the Presidential Medal of Merit. In addition to his business interests Hertz was a successful breeder of horses. In 1928 his horse, the Reigh Count, won the Kentucky Derby. Another of his horses, Count Fleet, won the Derby in 1943.

In 1955 Hertz retired as chairman of the board of the Hertz Corporation. Two years later he and his wife, Fannie, founded the Fannie and John Hertz Engineering Scholarship Foundation, which provided cash scholarships to needy and deserving engineering students.

Hertz died in October 1961 in California at the age of eighty-two.

For many years, the Chicago-based Yellow Cab and Checker Cab—two of the largest taxicab fleets in the world—monopolized the taxi industry in Chicago. In 1963 a city ordinance granted 80 percent of the city's 4,600 cab licenses to Yellow Cab Company and Checker Cab Company. Twenty-five years later the city council finally broke the stranglehold by proposing an ordinance that added 500 new licenses, called medallions, per year for three years.

See also: Charles Tyson Yerkes

Further reading: Gorman Gilbert and Robert E. Samuels, *The Taxicab: An Urban Transportation Survivor* (1982); Harold M. Mayer and Richard C. Wade, *Chicago: Growth of a Metropolis* (1969).

Margaret Hillis

Conductor

BORN: October 1, 1921
Kokomo, Indiana

DIED: February 4, 1998
Evanston, Illinois

Margaret Hillis founded the Chicago Symphony Chorus in 1957 and was its highly acclaimed director for nearly forty years. Hillis was a disciplined and superb musician whose quest for musical excellence was uncompromising during her long career. The chorus performed the great choral works of Bach, Handel, Mozart, Haydn, Beethoven, Mendelssohn, Brahms, and Mahler along with such contemporary composers as Stravinsky, Schoenberg, Bartók, and Rorem. Hillis made history in other ways, too: she was the first woman to conduct the Chicago Symphony Orchestra (CSO) and ultimately exerted a huge influence on the performance of choral music in the United States. Under her direction, the chorus became the model for other choral organizations across the country. "The Chicago Symphony Chorus never sings a reading of a work: we sing a performance. There is a vast difference," Hillis once said.

Born in Kokomo, Indiana, Hillis knew as a child that she wanted to be a conductor, and studied the piano, saxophone, and French horn. As a teenager she taught herself to play the trumpet and string bass. (She had other interests too: she was a junior golf champion at the age of twenty.) In 1940 she entered Indiana University in Bloomington as a piano major. While at the university during those early years of World War II she became a pilot, and in 1943 she interrupted her studies to become a navy civilian flight instructor at the Muncie, Indiana, airfield. After the war she resumed her studies, graduating in 1947 with a bachelor of arts degree in composition. From 1947 to 1949 she attended the Juilliard School in New York. There, one of her students advised her to go into choral conducting because women were not offered positions with orchestras at the time. Consequently, she studied choral conducting with Robert Shaw, working as his assistant at the Collegiate Chorale from 1952 to 1954.

Hillis held many positions in many places simultaneously. In 1948 she became director of the Metropolitan Youth Chorale in Brooklyn. From 1950 to 1960 she served as a conductor and instructor at Union Theological Seminary in New York. In 1950 she founded the Tanglewood Alumni Chorus, which later performed as the New York Concert Choir and Orchestra. In 1954 she founded and became the first music director of the American Choral Foundation, which sought to raise the standards of choral performance. While in New York she also taught choral conducting at the Juilliard School.

In 1957 CSO music director Fritz Reiner invited Hillis to establish a symphony chorus, and by November auditions had been completed and the Chicago Symphony Chorus had begun rehearsals. Its informal debut occurred during a private concert on November 30 of that year. During the second half of the concert, Hillis took the podium to present, among other works, the "Servants' Chorus" from Donizetti's *Don Pasquale*, thus becoming the first woman to conduct the CSO. The Chicago Symphony Chorus made its subscription debut on March 13, 1958, with Mozart's *Requiem*, conducted by Bruno Walter, and in 1963 the chorus made its first appearance with the CSO at the Ravinia Festival in Highland Park, Illinois.

In 1972 the chorus made its first recording with Georg Solti, Beethoven's Symphony no. 9, and in 1979 its first recording with Daniel Barenboim, Bruckner's Psalm 150. In 1976 Hillis led the first Do-It-Yourself Messiah concert at Orchestra Hall, which became a popular annual event. In 1977 Hillis famously made headlines in newspapers across the country when—with only three days' notice—she stepped in for Solti and conducted the CSO and Chorus in Mahler's Eighth Symphony at Carnegie Hall. There had been no time for rehearsal, but critics and audiences alike enthusiastically lauded her great achievement. In 1988 Hillis cofounded the Association of Professional Vocal Ensembles, which later changed its name to Chorus America.

Hillis appeared as a guest conductor with many American orchestras, including the National Symphony, the St.

Paul Chamber Orchestra, the St. Louis Symphony, the Baltimore Symphony, and the Minnesota Orchestra. She was also, at various times, conductor and choral director of the Santa Fe Opera Company, choral director of Chicago Musical College at Roosevelt University, music director and conductor of the Kenosha Symphony Orchestra, resident conductor of the Civic Orchestra of Chicago, music director of the Choral Institute, director of choral activities at Northwestern University, conductor and choral director of the Cleveland Orchestra Choruses, music director and conductor of the Elgin Symphony Orchestra, artistic director of the Dame Myra Hess concert series, and director of choral activities for the San Francisco Symphony.

During Hillis's tenure, the Chicago Symphony Chorus appeared with the orchestra nearly 600 times, recorded forty-five works, won nine Grammy awards between 1977 and 1993, and accompanied the CSO on domestic and international tours, including the chorus's successful European debut in 1989 in London and Salzburg. Hillis's Grammy awards included awards for recordings of Verdi's *Requiem,* Beethoven's *Missa solemnis,* Haydn's *Creation,* Brahms's *German Requiem,* and Bach's Mass in B Minor.

In 1987 Governor James R. Thompson declared April 29 Margaret Hillis Day in Illinois in honor of the thirtieth anniversary of the chorus. Seven years later, Mayor Richard M. Daley proclaimed September 20, 1994, as Margaret Hillis Day in Chicago.

For many years Hillis was a member of the advisory council to the National Endowment for the Arts and was appointed by President Ronald Reagan to serve a six-year term on the National Council on the Arts. She was an indefatigable supporter of the importance of choral singers to Chicago, and with her extensive guest conducting throughout the United States, demonstrated her technical brilliance and musical vision to countless choral singers, both professional and amateur.

Hillis announced her retirement as director of the Chicago Symphony Chorus in 1991 but continued to work until Duain Wolfe succeeded her in June 1994; she then assumed the mantle of director laureate. She died in February 1998 at the age of seventy-six in Evanston, Illinois, of complications from lung cancer. On March 14, 1998, a memorial service was presented at Orchestra Hall.

In 2008 the Chicago Symphony Chorus celebrated its fiftieth anniversary with a special concert at the Symphony Center, formerly known as Orchestra Hall.

The Margaret Hillis Collection is housed in the Rosenthal Archives of the Chicago Symphony Orchestra.

See also: Georg Solti

Further reading: Jane Samuelson, "For the Love of Music," *Chicago,* April 1980.

Sidney Hillman

Labor Activist

BORN: March 23, 1887
Zagare, Lithuania

DIED: July 10, 1946
Long Island, New York

Called "the Rasputin of organized labor," Sidney Hillman rose from Chicago's West Side to the corridors of the White House and held several prominent positions in various labor organizations in both Chicago and New York. In the latter city he transformed the garment workers union into one of the country's most powerful.

The son of a merchant, Hillman initially studied to be a rabbi but for economic reasons accepted a position working in a chemical laboratory in Kovno, Lithuania. Hillman was imprisoned for eight months after his involvement in controversial labor activities. He fled to England upon his release and immigrated to the United States in 1907. He settled in Chicago and found menial work as a stock clerk at Sears, Roebuck and Company. Hillman then worked as a garment cutter at the clothing firm of Hart, Schaffner

and Marx. He joined the United Garment Workers Union of America and was an effective leader during the groundbreaking garment workers' strike of 1910, which essentially shut down the clothing industry—then Chicago's second-largest industry—for sixteen weeks.

In 1914 Hillman moved to New York to head the Amalgamated Clothing Workers of America, one of the largest trade unions in the country. One of the original members of the Congress of Industrial Organizations (CIO), Hillman served as labor adviser to President Franklin D. Roosevelt.

Hillman died in 1946 at his summer home in Long Island at the age of fifty-nine.

The New York-based Sidney Hillman Foundation continues Hillman's work to create a "better America," awarding prizes in journalism and offering grants for scholarships, research, and lecture series on college campuses, as well as supporting medical research at the Sidney Hillman Health Centers in New York and Philadelphia.

Further reading: Steven Fraser, *Labor Will Rule: Sidney Hillman and the Rise of American Labor* (1993); Matthew Josephson, *Sidney Hillman: Statesman of American Labor* (1952).

Earl Hines

Musician

BORN: December 28, 1903
Duquesne, Pennsylvania

DIED: April 22, 1983
Oakland, California

Earl "Fatha" Hines was one of the most influential pianists in jazz. As a bandleader, he launched the careers of such famous musicians as Dizzy Gillespie, Charlie Parker, Billy Eckstine, and Sarah Vaughan. As a musician, he revolutionized the role of the jazz piano during the 1920s by making it an important and integral component of jazz ensemble performance. "No musician has exerted more influence over the course of piano jazz history," noted critic Dick Hadlock.

Although it was an African American music, jazz did not receive widespread acceptance until white musicians (the first jazz recordings were made by a white group, the Original Dixieland Jazz Band, in 1917) brought it to the forefront. During the 1920s and 1930s, white musicians such as Benny Goodman, Artie Shaw, and Tommy and Jimmy Dorsey transformed jazz into America's popular music. Meanwhile, African American artists had obscure careers or, like Hines, played to predominantly white audiences in elegant clubs for a mere pittance.

Hines's love of music was nurtured from an early age. His father played the trumpet, his mother the pipe organ. Born in a suburb of Pittsburgh, the classically trained Hines started piano lessons at the age of nine. He quit high school and began accompanying singer Lois Deppe, who soon moved to Chicago and encouraged the young pianist to accompany her.

Hines's first Chicago gig was in 1923 at the Elite Club at 3030 South State Street. He landed a job with the Carroll Dickerson Orchestra, and it was there that he met a young man from Louisiana named Louis Armstrong. In 1926 the band played the Sunset Café at 315 East 35th Street. When Dickerson left, Armstrong took over and launched a new jumpy sound that became known as the Chicago style of jazz. Many young white pupils, including Benny Goodman, Gene Krupa, Tommy and Jimmy Dorsey, Dave Tough, Muggsy Spanier, Bud Freeman, and Bix Beiderbecke, came to learn a lesson or two from the jazz masters.

In December 1927, Armstrong, Hines, and drummer Zutty Singleton rented their own space at Warwick Hall at 543 East 47th Street and began performing, with other musicians, as Louis Armstrong's Hot Six. It was a short-lived venture, and Hines was soon back in the clubs. He became a featured soloist with clarinetist Jimmy Noone's quintet at the Apex Club on 35th Street between South Prairie and South Calumet Avenues. In 1928 he went into the studio and recorded with Armstrong under the name of the Hot Five. In the same year, he made a number of classic recordings with Noone as well as several solo piano records.

By the end of 1928, Hines formed his own unit, and it became the house band at the Grand Terrace, originally at 3955 South Parkway (now King Drive) and later at the southwest corner of 35th Street and South Calumet Avenue, where he remained for more than a decade. Nightly broadcasts from the Terrace gave the pianist a national reputation. Like many Chicago nightclubs in the 1920s, the Grand Terrace was owned by the Capone syndicate.

In 1940 Hines turned down an offer to join Benny Goodman's orchestra, opting, instead, to form another outfit. This was to be no ordinary band. In 1941 the Hines lineup boasted some of the most formidable talent in the history of jazz, including singer Billy Eckstine, who doubled on trumpet, trombonist Benny Green, trumpeter Dizzy Gillespie, and pianist and second vocalist Sarah Vaughan. Although the group stayed together for almost a year, they never cut a record because of the recording ban of 1942, when James C. Petrillo, president of the American Federation of Musicians, ordered union members not to record.

Hines joined Louis Armstrong's All-Stars in 1948, but he left in 1951 to play with his own group at the Hangover Club in San Francisco. In 1957 he toured Europe with trombonist Jack Teagarden. Hines continued to tour and recorded extensively with groups and as a solo act throughout the 1960s and 1970s. Among his recordings are *Quintessential Recording Session* (1970), *Quintessential Continued* (1973), and *An Evening with Earl Hines* (1973). Hines also recorded tributes to Louis Armstrong, Hoagy Carmichael, Duke Ellington, Cole Porter, and George Gershwin. Hines's most famous compositions are "Rosetta,"

"My Monday Date," "Piano Man," "57 Varieties," and his biggest hit, "Boogie Woogie on the St. Louis Blues."

Hines died of a heart attack in Oakland, California, in 1983.

"If 'genius' is a word that still has meaning," offered *Chicago Tribune* music critic Larry Kart a few days after the musician's death, "Earl Hines was just that—a man whose music not only tested the rules but left us in doubt as to whether there are any rules, other than the ones his inspiration managed to create."

See also: Louis Armstrong, Bud Freeman, Benny Goodman, Gene Krupa, James C. Petrillo

Further reading: Stanley Dance, *The World of Earl Hines* (1977); Nat Shapiro and Nat Hentoff, eds., *The Jazz Makers: Essays on the Greats of Jazz* (1957); Dempsey J. Travis, *An Autobiography of Black Jazz* (1983).

Emil G. Hirsch
Rabbi

BORN: May 22, 1851
Luxembourg

DIED: January 7, 1923
Chicago, Illinois

One of the foremost Jewish scholars of his day, Emil Gustav Hirsch articulated his unorthodox views as rabbi of the Chicago Sinai Congregation at 46th Street and Grand Boulevard for more than forty years. Reform Jews, said Dr. Hirsch, must work to rebuild their faith and continually question the fundamental ethic of their foundation.

Born in Luxembourg and educated in Germany, Hirsch came to the United States as a teenager and attended the Episcopal Academy of Philadelphia. Later he enrolled at the University of Pennsylvania, where he received his degree in 1872, and then spent four years of study in Berlin and Leipzig. He became a rabbi in 1877 and was assigned to a synagogue in Baltimore. One year later he was transferred to the Adath Israel Congregation in Louisville, Kentucky, and in 1880 he came to the Sinai Congregation in Chicago.

As a Reform Jew, Hirsch held unconventional views. He believed that the Sabbath need not be celebrated only on Saturday, and to the consternation of many, he established Sunday morning services for those who could not attend on Saturday. He held that scripture need not be treated as a museum piece but was, in fact, a living document, open to interpretation. Always outspoken, Hirsch suggested that a settlement house be built on the South Side for the sons of millionaires since, he felt, they were often more ignorant than the poor. He criticized wealthy Jews for being more concerned about showing off their jewelry than helping those less fortunate than themselves.

Hirsch was radical in other ways, too. At a time when women were segregated in Jewish synagogues, he invited two women—Jane Addams and Hannah G. Solomon, founder of the National Council of Jewish Women—to speak before the temple congregation. He also lectured on the need for workers' compensation and factory safety legislation. He founded the *Reform Advocate*, a weekly newspaper that gave him a national platform for his opinions. "He was not a Zionist," insisted his son, David Hirsch. "He felt Judaism was a universal religion and that its mission was everywhere."

"He was a master in the knowledge of comparative religions and in higher criticism, and he likewise knew the highest teachings of the morals of Judaism. He was especially a prophet in this industrial age. He stressed the ethical obligations of religion to do justice, love mercy, and walk humbly with God," observed Dr. Stephen S. Wise, rabbi of the Jewish Free Synagogue in New York, following Hirsch's death in 1923.

In addition to his religious duties, Hirsch served as president of the board of the Chicago Public Library and as a member of the board of commissioners of the Public Charities of Illinois. He became professor of Semitic languages and literature at the University of Chicago in 1892, the first American rabbi to teach at a secular institution of higher learning. He was also a lecturer at Johns Hopkins University in 1902.

The Chicago Sinai Congregation, now located at 5350 South Shore Drive, is one of the best-known Jewish congregations in the city. Hirsch High School, built in 1925 at 77th Street and Ingleside Avenue, was named in the rabbi's honor.

"He was the greatest Jewish preacher of his generation, a mighty and unafraid prophet of truth," said Wise.

Further reading: Irving Cutler, *The Jews of Chicago: From Shtetl to Suburb* (1996); David E. Hirsch, *Rabbi Emil G. Hirsch: The Reform Advocate* (1968).

Julius J. Hoffman

Judge

BORN: July 7, 1895
Chicago, Illinois

DIED: July 1, 1983
Chicago, Illinois

Julius J. Hoffman, nicknamed "Julius the Just," gained national attention as the cantankerous judge who presided over the raucous Chicago Conspiracy Trial in 1969.

Educated in Chicago's public schools, Hoffman attended the Lewis Institute and Northwestern University. He was admitted to the Illinois bar in 1915. Hoffman worked as an associate and partner in the law firm of White and Hawxhurst until 1936, when he became general counsel for the Brunswick-Balke-Collender Company. In 1944 he joined Markheim, Hoffman, Hungerford and Sollo and remained there until 1947, when he was elected a judge of the Superior Court of Cook County for a six-year term. During this period, Hoffman also served on the faculty of the Northwestern University Law School. In 1953 President Dwight D. Eisenhower named Hoffman to the United States District Court in Chicago.

Hoffman presided over a number of important trials, including the prosecution of the promoters of Krebiozen, a controversial anticancer drug; the desegregation suit against the South Holland school district; the tax evasion trial of mobster Tony Accardo, and the deportation suit against alleged Nazi war criminal Frank Walus. The U.S. Court of Appeals overturned Hoffman's guilty ruling on the Walus case and ordered a new trial.

The most notorious case of Hoffman's career was the Chicago Conspiracy Trial. In 1969 five of the Chicago Seven—Rennie Davis, David Dellinger, Tom Hayden, Abbie Hoffman, and Jerry Rubin—were convicted of conspiracy to cross state lines with the intent to incite riots during the 1968 Democratic Convention in Chicago. A reporter described the courtroom atmosphere as "unruliness disturbed by only occasional bouts of decorum."

The trial of the Chicago Seven reflected the sometimes frenzied, always tense atmosphere of the time as the United States was embroiled in a war in Vietnam and thousands of antiwar demonstrators took to the streets in protest. The original eight defendants were David Dellinger, Rennie Davis, Tom Hayden, Abbie Hoffman, Jerry Rubin, Lee Weiner, John Froines, and Bobby Seale. The government claimed that the defendants conspired to encourage people from throughout the United States to come to Chicago to protest during the Democratic Convention in August 1968 with the intent to confront the Chicago Police Department and other authorities in order to create riot conditions. Hoffman and Rubin disrupted proceedings during the one-hundred-day trial with frequent interruptions of name calling and mocked the legal system by donning judicial robes. Witnesses included everyone from poet Allen Ginsberg to novelist Norman Mailer. Judge Hoffman cited a total of 175 contempt of court charges against the defendants and their lawyers, which included such violations as commenting aloud without permission, laughing, applauding, and blowing a kiss to the jury. Hoffman's attempts to control the court often turned to extremes, as when he ordered Black Panther leader Bobby Seale gagged and bound and tied to his chair when Seale refused to obey an order to keep silent. The Seale incident prompted singer-songwriter Graham Nash two years later to release "Chicago," in which Nash observes, "So your brother's bound and gagged / and they've chained him to a chair."

The court sentenced Dellinger, Davis, Hayden, Hoffman, and Rubin to five years in prison and fined each $5,000. The appeals court later overturned the convictions. "The demeanor of the judge and the prosecutors," noted one judicial opinion, "would require reversal even if errors did not." Tom Hayden later insisted that the entire youthful generation of the 1960s was on trial. "Our crime was our identity," he wrote in *Trial*. "The charges against us made no sense. Our crime was that we were beginning to live a new and contagious life style without official authorization. We were tried for being out of control."

In 1982 the Executive Committee of the United States District Court ordered that the then eighty-six-year-old jurist be assigned no new cases, citing as evidence his age and frequent complaints that he had been acting increasingly erratic and abusive on the bench. Despite the censure, Hoffman continued to hear cases as senior U.S. District Court judge until his death in July 1983.

Hoffman was active in philanthropic and charitable affairs and served as vice-chairman of the Hospital Building Fund of the Jewish Federation of Chicago. He was also a member of the Chicago Sinai Congregation.

Hoffman died of natural causes at the age of eighty-seven at his home at 179 East Lake Shore Drive.

Further reading: Andy Austin, *Rule 53: Capturing Hippies, Spies, Politicians, and Murderers in an American Courtroom* (2008); *The Conspiracy Trial: The Extended Edited Transcript of the Trial of the Chicago Eight* (1970), introduction by William Kunstler and foreword by Leonard Weinglass; Tom Hayden, *Trial* (1970); Tom Hayden, Frank Condon, and Ron Sossi, *Voices of the Chicago 8: A Generation on Trial* (2008); Mark L. Levine, George C. McNamee, and Daniel Greenberg, eds., *The Tales of Hoffman* (1970); Abe Peck, *Uncovering the Sixties: The Life & Times of the Underground Press* (1985); John Schultz, *The Chicago Conspiracy Trial* (2009), rev. ed., introduction by Carl Oglesby and afterword by the author.

Other resources: *Chicago 10* (2007), a partly animated documentary, directed by Brett Morgen; *Medium Cool* (1969), directed by Haskell Wexler and partly set during the trial.

William Holabird

Architect

BORN: September 11, 1854
Amenia, New York

DIED: July 19, 1923
Evanston, Illinois

With its consistent, uniformly excellent designs, the firm of Holabird and Roche exemplified the mainstream approach of the Chicago school of architecture. "Individual buildings of Sullivan and Root are superior to anything they did; yet they discovered the simplest utilitarian and structural solutions to the problems of the big urban office block," wrote architectural historian Carl W. Condit.

Born in New York State, William Holabird graduated from high school in St. Paul, Minnesota. He attended West Point for two years but resigned in 1875 and moved to Chicago, where he became a draftsman at William Le Baron Jenney's architectural firm. In 1880 Holabird formed a partnership with Ossian C. Simonds; Martin Roche joined them the following year, and the firm changed its name to Holabird, Simonds and Roche. When Simonds left in 1883, the name became Holabird and Roche. The firm's first major commission, the Tacoma Building at the corner of LaSalle and Monroe Streets in 1889, was inspired by Jenney's Home Insurance Building, which was completed the previous year and is often acknowledged as the world's first skyscraper. The Tacoma improved and further developed Jenney's iron-and-steel skeleton method of construction. Indeed, the Tacoma was called one of the most advanced building designs of its time.

Other important Holabird and Roche works in Chicago were the Caxton Building (1890), an addition to the Monadnock Building (1893), the Marquette Building (1894), the Congress Hotel (1907), the LaSalle Hotel (1909), the Sherman Hotel (1912), and the John Crerar Library (1919).

Holabird died in 1923 in Evanston, Illinois, at the age of sixty-eight. He was buried in Graceland Cemetery. Today the firm that he founded is known as Holabird and Root and is located at 140 South Dearborn Street.

See also: William Le Baron Jenney

Fred Holstein

Folksinger

BORN: December 9, 1943
Chicago, Illinois

DIED: January 12, 2004
Chicago, Illinois

Fred Holstein was the "catalyst" of the Chicago folk scene. "He took a song apart and reconstructed it in the way he thought it would most move the listener," folk music critic and radio host Rich Warren said. "A song absolutely had to resonate in him before he would sing it." He was, in short, Chicago's troubadour.

Born and raised in the South Shore neighborhood, Holstein was the eldest of three sons of a pharmacist. His family ran a drugstore at 79th Street and Michigan Avenue. As a child he often frequented the House of Music, a record store in the neighborhood. The owner, George Silas, stoked young Holstein's interest in all kinds of music, but especially folk music. Holstein bought his first guitar at Lyon & Healy downtown for $14.95, and in 1961 he began hanging out at the Fret Shop in Hyde Park. Although it wasn't a club, the owner allowed customers to sit inside and play guitar all day. Self-taught, Holstein learned to play by singing along to records and studying various songbooks. His appetite whetted, he took guitar lessons at the Old Town School of Folk Music—he would later teach there off and on—and joined a group called the Frets. Attending a Pete Seeger concert at Orchestra Hall (now called the Symphony Center) changed his life and convinced him that he too could make a living as a folk singer. As a teenager he snuck into the numerous North Side folk clubs, soaking up the atmosphere and listening intently to the lyrics of the songs.

Holstein had a deep baritone and a charming stage manner. He also had the gift of instant recall. He reportedly had 1,000 songs memorized. In 1966 the Earl of Old Town, a club near the corner of North Avenue and Wells Street, began to feature folk music. The Earl, as it was known, soon became a fixture of the local folk scene and one of the most famous folk clubs in the country. Holstein was there as part of the opening night lineup. *Chicago Sun-Times* movie critic Roger Ebert has called the Earl "the holy ground of the Chicago folk music renaissance." In addition to Holstein, the Earl featured Steve Goodman, Bonnie Koloc, Michael Smith, Jim Post, Bob Gibson, Ginny Clemons, and John Prine, among others.

Holstein soon became a regular at the numerous folk clubs that sprouted up in the city and suburbs during the so-called folk scare. He first began performing in the early 1960s in Chicago bars. He was the house singer at the Earl of Old Town as well as at its branch outlet, the Earl on Harlem. In the early 1970s, with his brother singer-songwriter Ed Holstein, Steve Goodman, Bill Redhed, and Earl Pionke, he opened Somebody Else's Troubles on North Lincoln Avenue. After Troubles closed, he and Ed opened another folk club, Holstein's, in 1981, also on Lincoln Avenue. It enjoyed a successful seven-year run and booked virtually every reputable folk act in the English- (and sometimes non-English) speaking world, from Doc Watson to Queen Ida to Silly Wizard. Alan Holstein was the manager, Ed booked the talent, and Fred was the house act. It closed on New Year's Day 1988—appropriately with a singalong, led by Fred, of his rendition of "For All the Good People." It had become his signature song. After Holstein's closed in 1988, Holstein sang in and around Chicago.

Because Holstein was an interpreter of traditional and contemporary folk songs rather than a songwriter, his talents were often overlooked. "What I do is entertain people," he told journalist Rick Kogan, "and I use folk music as my way to do that. I see myself as a conduit."

Holstein did not tour much, preferring to stay close to home, nor did he make many recordings. What he did do was sing songs. He also introduced Chicago folk audiences to the work of Eric Bogle, Gordon Bok, Hazel Dickens, Ewan MacColl, Ralph McTell, Malvina Reynolds, Stan Rogers, Peggy Seeger, Cyril Tawney, and many others. After the folk boom ended, he continued to play occasionally and also booked acts at various clubs and tended bar at Sterch's, on Lincoln Avenue. In his later years he also performed on a regular basis, with his brother Ed, at the Abbey Pub.

The 2001 release of a double CD, *Fred Holstein: A Collection,* combined remastered songs from his previous two LPs, songs from the archives of WFMT-FM, and portions of interviews.

Holstein died in January 2004 of heart failure during stomach surgery at Swedish Covenant Hospital. At the time of his death he was still performing, occasionally, and tending bar at Sterch's, which has since closed.

See also: Steve Goodman

Discography: *Fred Holstein: A Collection,* 1977–1983; *Fred Holstein: Live at the Earl of Old Town* (2008), a live performance from June 30, 1969; *Remembering Fred: A Tribute to Fred Holstein* (2004), a double CD featuring live performances at the Fred Holstein Memorial Concert held on April 3, 2004, at the Old Town School of Folk Music.

Milton Horn

Sculptor

BORN: September 1, 1906
Kiev, Ukraine

DIED: March 29, 1995
Chicago, Illinois

Sculptor Milton Horn made an intentional effort to integrate his work as seamlessly as possible into the framework of public buildings and public settings.

Born in Kiev, Ukraine, Horn came to the United States with his family as a young boy in 1915, first settling in Massachusetts. He studied with the Copley Society in Boston and attended the Beaux Arts Institute in New York. He taught at Olivet College in Michigan before moving to Chicago with his wife, the former Estelle Oxenhorn, in 1949.

In 1927 Horn received his first commission: for a sculpted ceiling in the Savoy-Plaza Hotel in New York. In 1935 he began a series of commissions through the federal Works Progress Administration (WPA). His wood reliefs were integrated into the architecture of public buildings, including schools and post offices. In 1939 Horn began serving as Carnegie Professor of Art at Olivet College in Michigan, where he met Frank Lloyd Wright. He worked with Wright on numerous projects. In 1957 he organized a committee to save Wright's Robie House, located in Hyde Park, from almost certain demolition.

Horn's best-known sculpture is *Chicago Rising from the Lake* (1954), which was originally installed on the wall of a former city parking garage at Wacker and Dearborn. Later restored, it is now located along Chicago's Riverwalk on the west side of the Columbus Drive Bridge. The first piece of art purchased by the city since 1892, it symbolizes Chicago's roles in the commodities markets and transportation, as well as the former Union Stockyards.

Horn's other works include reliefs for the Jewish Federation of Metropolitan Chicago at 1 South Franklin Street and the *Hymn to Water* at the Central Water Filtration Plant. He also sculpted busts of Aaron Montgomery Ward and F. W. Woolworth for the Merchandise Mart; *Moses and the Burning Bush* at the Chicago Sinai Congregation, 15 West Delaware Place; *The Creation of Adam* at Fourth Presbyterian Church, 126 East Chestnut Street; and two bronze sculptures, *Jacob Wrestling with the Angels* and *Saint Francis,* inside St. Thomas the Apostle church, 5472 South Kimbark Avenue.

Horn, who lived in Lincoln Park, died in the Johnston R. Bowman Rehabilitation Center at Rush-Presbyterian-St. Luke's Medical Center in March 1995.

In late 1999 the Spertus Museum presented an exhibit of his work entitled "Rediscovering Milton Horn."

Further reading: Ira Bach and Mary Lackritz Gray, *Chicago's Public Sculpture* (1983); James L. Riedy, *Chicago Sculpture* (1981).

Henry Horner

Politician

BORN: November 30, 1878
Chicago, Illinois

DIED: October 6, 1940
Winnetka, Illinois

Judge of the Probate Court of Cook County since 1914, Henry Horner made history in 1932 when he was elected Illinois's first Jewish governor. In addition to attracting a broad constituency, Horner managed to unite the usually fractured Jewish vote, which had historically been torn between the desires of the more established German Jews and the recently arrived Eastern European Jews.

Horner's father, Solomon Levy, was brought to Kentucky from Bavaria in 1850 by his uncle. Settling in Chicago in 1870, he married Dilah Horner one year later. In 1878 Dilah gave birth to their third son, Henry, in their South Michigan Avenue apartment. By this time, though, the marriage was strained. Dilah filed for divorce, accusing her husband of physical cruelty. Hannah Horner, Dilah's mother, offered housing for her daughter and two of the children—the father received the custody of the eldest son—under one condition: that Dilah and the children's names be changed to Horner.

Young Horner attended the Chicago Manual Training School on the South Side. Then he enrolled at Kent College of Law at night and worked as a law clerk by day. Horner received his first taste of Chicago politics on the streets of the First Ward, where his uncle Isaac worked for aldermen Michael "Hinky Dink" Kenna and "Bathhouse John" Coughlin. When still a law student, he campaigned in 1897 for Carter Harrison II, further advancing his political education. Two years later he was admitted to the Illinois bar and began a lucrative law practice, specializing in real estate and probate law. Early in his career Horner realized the value of establishing relationships with important civic and political leaders. He joined, for example, the prestigious Standard Club—his maternal grandfather, Henry Horner I, had been one of its charter members. By the turn of the century Horner was a well-respected young man appreciated by both the diverse Jewish community and the regular Democratic machine.

In 1907 Horner was appointed attorney for the Cook County Board of Assessors and, in 1914, was elected judge of the Probate Court of Cook County, winning each contest by progressively wider margins. In 1930, notes his biographer, Thomas Littlewood, Horner received more votes than anyone else on the county ticket. Horner earned an excellent reputation as an honest and meticulous judge and a man of irreproachable integrity.

Such a loyal and reliable vote-getter did not go unnoticed. In 1932 the Democratic Party endorsed Horner for governor. A great compromiser, Horner enjoyed broad support, appealing to Democrats, Republicans, independents, reformers, Jews, and gentiles. He won by, at that time, the largest majority in Illinois history, aided considerably by the monolithic support of the Jewish electorate.

In 1933 the new governor clashed over control of the licensing of city saloons with the new mayor of Chicago, Edward J. Kelly, who was appointed chief executive by the city council following the murder of Mayor Anton Cermak in Miami. Kelly fought for local jurisdiction while Horner insisted that the state should manage the operations. The relationship between the two leaders deteriorated as Kelly increasingly felt threatened by Horner's stubborn independence. Despite the refusal of Kelly to endorse Horner for reelection, the governor managed to pull off a stunning upset during the 1936 Democratic primaries, defeating Kelly's choice, Chicago Health Commissioner Herman C. Bundesen, by a substantial margin. In the November general election, Horner easily beat the Republican candidate C. Wayland Brooks, carrying the city alone by more than 300,000 votes. Once again the Jewish community came to the aid of their favorite son.

In 1938 Horner, stricken with cerebral thrombosis (a blood clot of the brain), decided not to seek reelection for governor in 1940. A financial scandal among his staff exacerbated his weakened condition. Horner died of cardiovascular disease and inflammation of the kidneys at the age of sixty-one in October 1940.

Horner contributed his time and money to various charities and causes. He acted as president of the Young Men's Jewish Charities and served as chairman of the social service committee of Michael Reese Hospital.

The worth of Horner's administration cannot be measured in legislation alone. At Horner's funeral, Rabbi Louis L. Mann hailed the fallen politician as "a martyr to the cause of good government." His greatest strength, writes biographer Littlewood, was his character. He will be remembered not for what he did but for who he was. Said poet Carl Sandburg upon his death, "He was the real goods. In the realm of politics there have been too few like him. He collaborated with men who were purchasable without becoming purchasable himself. He had thoroughgoing integrity. He got to high places without selling his soul."

See also: "Bathhouse John" Coughlin, Carter Harrison II, Edward J. Kelly, Michael "Hinky Dink" Kenna

Further reading: Philip P. Bregstone, *Chicago and Its Jews: A Cultural History* (1933); Irving Cutler, *The Jews of Chicago: From Shtetl to Suburb* (1996); Thomas B. Littlewood, *Horner of Illinois* (1969); Charles J. Masters, *Governor Henry Horner, Chicago Politics, and the Great Depression* (2007); Edward Mazur, "Jewish Chicago: From Diversity to Community," in *Ethnic Chicago* (1984), Melvin G. Holli and Peter d'A. Jones, eds.

Howlin' Wolf

Musician

BORN: June 10, 1910
White Station, Mississippi

DIED: January 10, 1976
Hines, Illinois

A character unique in the annals of blues music—indeed, any music—is Howlin' Wolf, a.k.a. Chester Arthur Burnett. Although his music was very much in the tradition of Charley Patton and Robert Johnson, nobody else sang quite like him. An energetic performer and a ferocious singer, this huge hulking man (6 feet, 6 inches, and nearly 300 pounds) influenced a diverse group of white and black musicians, including the Paul Butterfield Blues Band, Cream, John Fogerty, the Rolling Stones, Johnny Shines, the Yardbirds, and Junior Wells, and popularized "Smokestack Lightning," "Back Door Man," and "Spoonful." Like fellow Mississippian Muddy Waters, Howlin' Wolf moved to Chicago and helped forge a new sound in the blues— a sound that was loud, raucous, and brash. Although he never achieved Waters's level of fame, Howlin' Wolf helped shape the sound of post–World War II Chicago blues.

Chester Arthur Burnett was named after Chester A. Arthur, the twenty-first president of the United States, but he received his famous nickname from his grandfather, John Jones, who used to tell him stories about the wolves that populated the area where he grew up. He warned young Chester that if he misbehaved, the wolves would get him. His religious mother threw him out of the house when still a child because he refused to do chores around the farm. He moved in with his uncle, Will Young, who mistreated him. He ran away when he was thirteen.

Burnett didn't pick up a guitar until he was almost eighteen. "At that time," he recalled, "I was working on the farm with my father, baling hay and driving tractors, fixing fences, picking cotton, and pulling corn. There was a lot of music around there, work songs." In the late 1920s, Howlin' Wolf met the enigmatic Charley Patton, who lived on a nearby plantation and gave him some rudimentary guitar lessons as well as some tips on showmanship. Other influences included Blind Lemon Jefferson, Ma Rainey, Lonnie Johnson, Tampa Red, Tommy Johnson, and country singer Jimmie Rodgers. He tried to emulate Rodgers's famous "blue yodel," but all that came out was a howl. Later he received informal coaching on the harmonica from Rice Miller (Sonny Boy Williamson II). In the early 1930s, Howlin' Wolf traveled with legendary bluesman Robert Johnson and with bluesmen Johnny Shines, Honeyboy Edwards, Robert Junior Lockwood, and Son House. In 1941, he was drafted into the army. Based mostly in Seattle, he was often asked to entertain the troops, but later admitted he never liked the experience.

After the war, Howlin' Wolf returned to a life of farming until he formed his own band in the late 1940s. Popular around Arkansas and Mississippi, he hosted a radio show on KWEM in West Memphis, Arkansas, beginning in 1948. In the early 1950s, he recorded some sessions for Sam Phillips's Sun label and, then, with the Chicago-based Chess label. His early Chess recordings, "I Love My Baby" and "All Night Boogie," garnered little attention in the North but were popular in the South. Subsequent Chess records, which included "Evil Is Going On," "I'll Be Around," and "Forty Four"—all released in 1954—met much the same fate.

By the time Howlin' Wolf had moved to Chicago, in late 1952, his style had matured. Critics have described it as a modern, almost jazzy style, accompanied by the singer's rough, intense vocals. Gradually his music began to soften. He experimented with a horn section and opted for slower rhythms. He was a popular performer on the Chicago club circuit during the 1950s and 1960s. In 1968 he appeared at the University of Chicago Folk Festival and, by the mid-1970s, he was playing a double bill with another great bluesman, B. B. King, at the International Amphitheater, at 42nd and Halsted Streets.

Howlin' Wolf made his first record, "Moanin' at Midnight," in 1951. He enjoyed his first hit, the darkly brooding "No Place to Go," in 1954 and released "Smokestack Lightning," which remains a critical favorite, two years later. In the early 1960s, Howlin' Wolf recorded a series of blues classics—many of them written by Willie Dixon—including "Wang Dang Doodle," "Back Door Man," "The Red Rooster," "I Ain't Superstitious," and "Goin' Down Slow."

In 1972 Howlin' Wolf was awarded an honorary doctor of arts degree from Columbia College in Chicago even though he was functionally illiterate for most of his life (he eventually did earn his GED). In poor health, he was admitted to the Veterans Administration Hospital in Hines, Illinois, in 1975 and died there from complications from kidney disease early the next year. He was buried in Oak Ridge Cemetery in Hillside, Illinois.

Howlin' Wolf was inducted into the Blues Hall of Fame in 1980 and the Rock and Roll Hall of Fame in 1991.

See also: Big Bill Broonzy, Leonard Chess, Little Walter, Muddy Waters

Further reading: Peter Guralnick, *Feel Like Going Home: Portraits in Blues and Rock 'n' Roll* (1981); Sheldon Harris, *Blues Who's Who: A Biographical Dictionary of Blues Singers* (1979); Robert Palmer, *Deep Blues* (1981); Mike Rowe, *Chicago Breakdown* (1975); James Segrest, *Moanin' at Midnight* (2005).

Discography: *The Chess Box* (1991), a three-disc box set; *Moanin' in the Moonlight* (1959); *Howlin' Wolf Sings the Blues* (1962); *The Howlin' Wolf Album* (1969); *The London Howlin' Wolf Sessions* (1971); *The Back Door Wolf* (1972).

Gurdon S. Hubbard

Pioneer

BORN: August 22, 1802
Windsor, Vermont

DIED: September 14, 1886
Chicago, Illinois

Fur trader, merchant, and statesman, Gurdon Saltonstall Hubbard was one of the greatest of the pioneers of early Chicago. He arrived when Chicago was but a remote village in the middle of the vast Midwest. When he died more than sixty years later, it had grown into an exciting and prosperous city. The city's first meatpacker and banker, he was also instrumental in the building of the Illinois and Michigan Canal. In addition, he reportedly wrote the city's first insurance policy, bought the first Chicago fire engine, built the first brick hotel in Chicago, and was a founder of the Board of Trade.

Of Yankee stock, Hubbard attended the Windsor school in Vermont at age six. Financial difficulties compelled his parents to send him to live with a relative in Bridgewater, Massachusetts. Finally, deep in debt, his father fled with the family to Montreal to avoid his creditors. In 1816 Hubbard apprenticed at a Montreal hardware store that supplied goods and equipment to fur traders. He ran errands, unpacked crates, delivered goods along the waterfront, and helped with the bookkeeping. And, when the day's work was done, he read. His favorite subject was French exploration in North America.

In early 1818 he left Montreal for the Indian territory with French-Canadian traders. At age sixteen Hubbard was a trading post clerk for the American Fur Company, owned by the famous trapper John Jacob Astor. After a summer in Mackinac, Michigan, he came to Chicago in late 1818. Eventually he established a successful fur trade from Danville to Chicago. It was called "Hubbard's Trail."

In 1824 Hubbard was appointed superintendent of the Illinois River trading posts of the American Fur Company, at the present-day location of Mackinac Island, where he came into regular contact with various Indian tribes—the Potawatomis, Winnebagos, and Chippewas, among others—and learned to respect and appreciate Indian ways and traditions. The Indians, in return, admired the young man's honesty and his great physical strength. They called him Papamatabe, the Swift Walker. Contemporary newspaper accounts reported that he could walk as much as seventy miles in one day. Three years later Hubbard became the owner of an American Fur Company franchise.

Representing Vermilion County, Hubbard introduced in the state legislature a bill creating what would later become the Illinois and Michigan Canal. The canal formed a link between the Great Lakes and the Mississippi River and thus opened up northern Illinois for future commercial development. After much debate and delay, the bill finally passed through both houses in January of 1836. Hubbard was appointed one of the commissioners of the Illinois and Michigan Canal Commission.

In 1834 Hubbard settled in Chicago permanently, becoming one of the village's first trustees. He purchased a log cabin on Lake Michigan from Billy Caldwell, the half-Potawatomi, half-Irish Indian chief. Often called Chicago's most "useful" citizen, Hubbard engaged in many productive activities. He built a warehouse and packing plant, which was dubbed "Hubbard's Folly" due to its tremendous size. He established a shipping line, organized an insurance agency, and speculated heavily in real estate. He was also a partner in Chicago's first hotel, the Lake House, at Rush and Kinzie Streets.

In 1860 Hubbard was elected alderman of the Seventh Ward. In the same year tragedy struck when his passenger ship, the *Lady Elgin,* was rammed by a schooner, the *Augusta,* off the Winnetka shore, resulting in 297 deaths. Two years later another of his ships, the *Superior,* went down in a storm.

Like many Chicagoans, Hubbard lost most of his possessions in the Chicago Fire of 1871. Near bankruptcy, he—again, like the city itself—began the painful and arduous process of recovery. In May 1883, Hubbard became critically ill. The following year excruciating pain resulted in the removal of his left eye. "True to his Indian training he resolutely refused an anesthetic," wrote his nephew, Henry R. Hamilton. "He simply lay down without a murmur or tremor and let doctors cut out his eye." In 1885 his other eye was removed.

When he died at the age of eighty-four in September 1886, the local press referred to him in glowing terms as the city's "oldest settler." He was buried in Graceland Cemetery.

Hubbard's career became synonymous with the growth of Chicago. When he settled in Chicago in 1834, the little village had a population of fewer than 200 inhabitants. By the time of his death in 1886 the town had blossomed into a booming metropolis of three quarters of a million people. In his massive three-volume history of Chicago, A. T. Andreas sums up Hubbard's accomplishments best: "He held nearly every office of trust that his fellow citizens could thrust upon him. It may be said here that he never violated any trust bestowed."

Hubbard Street is named in his honor.

See also: John Kinzie, Jean Baptiste Point du Sable

Further reading: A. T. Andreas, *History of Chicago from the Earliest Period to the Present Time,* 3 vols. (1884–1886); Ernest Poole, *Giants Gone: Men Who Made Chicago* (1943); Lloyd Wendt, *"Swift Walker": An Informal Biography of Gurdon Saltonstall Hubbard* (1986).

John Hughes

Filmmaker

BORN: February 18, 1950
Lansing, Michigan

DIED: August 6, 2009
New York, New York

John Hughes set many of his films on Chicago's North Shore, and one film in particular, *Ferris Bueller's Day Off* (1986), has achieved iconic status. Hughes helped put Chicago on the filmmaking map: before John Hughes, very few filmmakers shot in Chicago. Hughes changed that by choosing to work out of metropolitan Chicago rather than Hollywood. During the 1980s he directed, wrote, or produced a series of films that captured the essence of American teen culture before he faded into relative obscurity by the early 1990s. He had a major influence on youth culture. He was sometimes called the J. D. Salinger of filmmaking because of his perceived reclusiveness.

John Wilden Hughes Jr. was born in Lansing, Michigan. When he was thirteen, his family moved from the upper-middle-class Detroit suburb of Grosse Pointe, Michigan, to the Chicago area, living a middle-class existence in Northbrook, Illinois. He began his career as an advertising copywriter in Chicago at the ad agency of Needham Harper & Steers before moving on to become an ad copywriter and creative director at Leo Burnett, where he learned how to tell a story within minutes. During his tenure at Leo Burnett, he frequently traveled to New York and, unbeknown to his ad agency colleagues, hung out at the offices of the *National Lampoon* magazine, trying to attract some attention. His persistence paid off when the magazine began accepting his work and, eventually, hired him as a staff editor. Since they were so impressed with him, he was allowed to work from his home in the Chicago suburbs.

In early 1979, while snowbound in his home, Hughes wrote a short story for *National Lampoon* about a miserable family road trip that he had originally called "Vacation '58." After it was published in the magazine, it was bought by Warner Bros., and he was given the opportunity to write the screen adaptation even though he had never written a screenplay in his life. *National Lampoon's Vacation,* released in 1983, became a huge hit and put Hughes on the map. It was the beginning of a very intense and productive period in his life.

Hughes made different kinds of teen flicks. He used Chicago and Chicago-area locations in ways that people had never seen before. *Sixteen Candles* (1984) was shot in and around Skokie and Highland Park. *The Breakfast Club* (1985) is set in the fictional suburb of Shermer, Illinois, but was inspired by New Trier High School in Winnetka. The high school in the film was actually Maine North, which had been shuttered, in Des Plaines. The eponymous character in *Ferris Bueller's Day Off* drives around Chicago in a

Ferrari, attends a Chicago Cubs baseball game, visits the Art Institute, goes to the observation deck at the top of the Sears Tower (now the Willis Tower), and, in the film's rousing climax, participates in the German-American Appreciation Parade, singing a rendition of "Twist and Shout" and "Danke Schoen." Chicago became a character of its own in the movie.

Hughes was a prolific screenwriter. As soon as he finished one screenplay, he would start another. In addition to his own movies, he wrote the screenplays of *Career Opportunities* (1991), *Dutch* (1991), *Curly Sue* (1991), *Beethoven* (1991), *Home Alone 2: Lost in New York* (1992) , and *Maid in Manhattan* (2002; under the name Edmond Dantès).

His biggest success was the *Home Alone* series, which he wrote and produced. The first film in the series was released in 1990. A young boy, played by Macaulay Culkin, is left behind at home after his parents forget to take him with them on a family holiday. The film took in nearly $300 million in domestic box office receipts and led to two sequels.

But it is the teenage-themed films of the 1980s that set Hughes apart. His name is associated with an entire film genre: comedies about misunderstood youth. Hughes boosted the careers of Matthew Broderick, Molly Ringwald, Anthony Michael Hall, John and Joan Cusack, and Ally Sheedy. During the 1980s, the heyday of his career, one successful film followed after another. *Sixteen Candles* stars Molly Ringwald as a girl whose sixteenth birthday is forgotten amidst the chaos of her sister's wedding. It also features Anthony Michael Hall, John Cusack, Joan Cusack, and Jami Gertz. Both *The Breakfast Club* and *Weird Science* (1985) were released during this time. And Hughes's most iconic film, *Ferris Bueller's Day Off,* also from this period, stars Matthew Broderick as a mischievous high school student who plays hooky from school, spending the entire day sightseeing in Chicago. It made $70 million at the box office but, more importantly, lived on in the memory of many who saw it. The film is considered one of the great high school movies of all time.

Although Hughes's films did not always achieve critical acclaim, they did influence pop culture and made an indelible mark in particular on the attitudes of members of so-called Generation X, those post–baby boomers born in the late 1960s and early 1970s. *New York Times* film critic A. O. Scott has called Hughes "our Godard," referring to the iconic French filmmaker Jean-Luc Godard, "the filmmaker who crystallized our attitudes and anxieties with just the right blend of teasing and sympathy." *Chicago Sun-Times* film critic Roger Ebert has called him "the philosopher of adolescence."

Hughes's characters wrestled with issues of identity and conformity and the often-precarious relationship between parents and their misunderstood children. He portrayed American teenagers not as mindless stereotypes but as individuals with souls. And, in a departure from most teen films, he explored the subtle class distinctions within high school cliques.

Hughes also directed *Weird Science* and *Planes, Trains, and Automobiles* (1987) and wrote and/or produced *National Lampoon's European Vacation* (1985), *Pretty in Pink* (1986), *Uncle Buck* (1989), and *Some Kind of Wonderful* (1987). The last movie he actually directed, *Curly Sue* in 1991, was both a commercial and critical flop. Still he continued to write for the screen; sometimes using pseudonyms. As Edmond Dantès he shared story credit with Seth Rogen and Kristofor Brown on Owen Wilson's *Drillbit Taylor* in 2008. After the failure of *Curly Sue*, though, he began to withdraw from the industry. He never directed another film. During the last years of his life he was living quietly with his wife, Nancy Ludwig, on a large farm outside Harvard, Illinois.

Hughes collapsed on August 6, 2009, of a heart attack during a morning walk as he crossed 55th Street in Manhattan while visiting family. He was taken to Roosevelt Hospital, where he died later that morning at the age of fifty-nine.

In 2009 four young filmmakers made a documentary, *Don't You Forget About Me,* about their elusive search for him.

Further reading: Susannah Gora, *You Couldn't Ignore Me If You Tried: The Brat Pack, John Hughes, and Their Impact on a Generation* (2010); A. O. Scott, "An Appraisal: The John Hughes Touch," *New York Times,* August 8, 2009.

Robert Maynard Hutchins

Educator

BORN: January 17, 1899
Brooklyn, New York

DIED: May 14, 1977
Santa Barbara, California

Charming, erudite, debonair; a scholar, philosopher, and reformer—Robert Maynard Hutchins was all this and more. At thirty he became president of the University of Chicago—the youngest head of a major American university. Called the most celebrated intellectual of his time, Hutchins was also chairman of *Encyclopaedia Britannica* and editor of the 54-volume *Great Books of the Western World* (1952). Admirers praised him as the "boy wonder" of academe, while critics fumed that he was nothing more than an arrogant, trouble-making, Yankee iconoclast. Clearly, Robert Maynard Hutchins, the renegade scholar, ran resolutely against established academic practices.

Hutchins's father, a minister, imbued his son with a firm appreciation of the Protestant ethic. The elder Hutchins enrolled his son at Oberlin Theological Seminary in Ohio in 1915. During World War I, Hutchins enlisted in the army ambulance service, and in June 1918 he was assigned to Genoa as part of the American Expeditionary Force with the Italian army. After the war Hutchins resumed his education, receiving a bachelor's degree in 1921 and a law degree in 1925, both from Yale, and graduating magna cum laude in 1925. Hutchins then joined the Yale faculty, and within two years he attained the rank of associate professor. In 1927 he was appointed dean of the Yale Law School. And finally, on April 25, 1929, the University of Chicago chose the thirty-year-old Hutchins as its president.

Hutchins acted with bold strokes. He preached cultural literacy before it was fashionable to do so. He insisted, however, that his programs were merely continuations of the late William Rainey Harper's original vision. It was Harper, the champion of liberal arts and the university's first president, said Hutchins, who urged that "an essential element in the education of every man . . . is a study of the great heritage we have received from the past."

Hutchins revamped the entire curriculum and divided the university into an undergraduate college with separate graduate schools. What's more, he stressed the importance of a liberal education and unilaterally opposed vocational training at the university level, instituting instead an undergraduate curriculum based upon the Great Books program, which studied the great classics of Western civilization. Mandatory class attendance was abolished—rather, students had to pass comprehensive examinations. Hutchins was more concerned with what a student knew than with how many A's or B's he or she accumulated. In particular, he humanized the study of law. He introduced psychology, history, economics, political theory, and philosophy into the law curriculum in order to "produce educated lawyers and not merely lawyers who know the rules and how to manipulate them," he said.

In 1939 Hutchins abolished intercollegiate football at the University of Chicago, insisting that the school could no longer effectively compete with the big, public universities—during the final season, Chicago lost miserably to such opponents as Harvard (61–0) and Michigan (85–0). It was not exactly a surprising decision, considering Hutchins's Puritan past and his belief, according to his biographer, that enjoyment was a form of indolence. "There is no doubt on the whole that football has been a major handicap to education in the United States," he said. Understandably, Hutchins's controversial decision caused great dissension on campus. Years later, in 1969, varsity football returned to the Midway. In 1976 Chicago joined the Midwest Conference but left in 1986 to join the University Athletic Association.

In 1943 the University of Chicago obtained control of *Encyclopaedia Britannica,* and Hutchins was appointed chairman of *Britannica*'s board of editors. He took a leave of absence from the university to work in *Britannica*'s adult education program and served as director of the encyclopedia from 1947 to 1974. In 1947 Hutchins and Mortimer Adler introduced the "Great Books of the Western World" courses. Hutchins believed that studying the classics prepared one for "the good life," and that in order to consider oneself educated, a person must be aware of these works. He insisted, however, should anyone dare to brand him an elitist, that the courses be made available to everyone. In 1952 he became editor-in-chief of the *Great Books of the Western World.*

In 1945 Hutchins was appointed chancellor of the University of Chicago. He left the university in 1951, however, to become an associate director of the Ford Foundation. From 1954 to 1974 he served as chief executive officer of the Fund for the Republic, a civil rights organization that supported efforts to safeguard the freedom of the press, brought religious and racial discrimination to the attention of the American public, and attacked the abuses of McCarthyism, among other things.

In 1959 Hutchins organized the Center for the Study of Democratic Institutions, a California-based think tank. He retired in 1974 but returned when an effective successor could not be found. In 1975 the headquarters of the institute moved from Santa Barbara, California, to Chicago.

Robert Maynard Hutchins, the most celebrated educator of his generation, died in 1977 at the age of seventy-eight in Santa Barbara, California.

Among Hutchins's many books are *The Higher Learning in America* (1936), *The Conflict in Education* (1953), *Some Observations on American Education* (1956), *Education for Freedom* (1963), and *Education: The Learning Society* (1968).

"Education," Hutchins once said, "is not a substitute for experience. It is preparation for it."

Today, the Chicago-based Great Books Foundation continues Hutchins's legacy. Established by Hutchins and Adler in 1947, the foundation is an independent, nonprofit educational organization. It offers literary programs for kindergarten through high school and college, and sponsors hundreds of adult book groups.

See also: William Rainey Harper

Further reading: Harry S. Ashmore, *Unseasonable Truths: The Life of Robert Maynard Hutchins* (1989); Jonathan R. Cole, *The Great American University: Its Rise to Preeminence, Its Indispensable National Role, Why It Must Be Protected* (2010).

J. Allen Hynek

Astronomer

BORN: May 1, 1910
Chicago, Illinois

DIED: April 27, 1986
Scottsdale, Arizona

Joseph Allen Hynek was the leading authority on UFOs in the United States and the director, from 1948 to 1969, of the air force's Project Blue Book, a government-sponsored program that gathered, analyzed, and studied information about UFOs. Hynek was credited with coining the term "close encounter" to refer to an actual meeting with an extraterrestrial. Film director Steven Spielberg borrowed this term for the title of his 1977 blockbuster movie, *Close Encounters of the Third Kind*. Hynek adopted strict scientific principles for the study of UFOs, bringing a semblance of respectability to what many of his colleagues considered the dubious science of ufology.

Born in Chicago to Czech parents, Hynek attended public schools in Chicago. After graduating from Crane High School, Hynek enrolled at the University of Chicago, where he received his Ph.D. in 1935. The following year he accepted a position of assistant professor in the Department of Physics and Astronomy at Ohio State University in Columbus, Ohio. From 1946 to 1955 he was the director of the McMillin Observatory at Ohio State, and from 1956 to 1960 he was the associate director of the Smithsonian Astrophysics Observatory in Cambridge, Massachusetts.

In 1960 Hynek returned to the Chicago area to assume the chairmanship of the Department of Astronomy at Northwestern University. Five years later he became the director of Northwestern's Lindheimer Astronomical Research Center. In September 1947, the air force—under the code name Project Blue Book, with headquarters at the Wright-Patterson Air Force Base in Dayton, Ohio—asked Hynek to evaluate UFO sightings. Hynek took the assignment seriously. Rather than dismissing UFOs as figments of overworked imaginations, he discovered, to his complete surprise, that there were many more questions than answers. Although most reports could be explained as aircraft sightings or the result of atmospheric conditions, there were others that could not be so easily identified. But in December 1969, after two decades of investigation with no solid evidence, Secretary of the Air Force Robert C. Seamans officially terminated Project Blue Book based on the recommendation of Dr. E. U. Condon, a scientist who served as director of an air force–sponsored study group at the University of Colorado.

In 1975 Hynek founded the Center for UFO Studies in Evanston, Illinois. The center, a nonprofit organization that functioned as a clearinghouse for UFO reports, received the cooperation of municipal police departments as well as the support of scientists from a dozen American universities. In 1981, due to a lack of funds, Hynek was forced to shut down his office, and he moved the center into his Evanston home at 2623 Ridge Avenue. Hynek continually sought research funds from the National Science Foundation, NASA, and private foundations. Most requests, however, were met with a snicker and not-so-polite suggestions to try elsewhere.

Despite Hynek's impeccable reputation as a highly respected scholar, not everyone in the scientific community approved of his work. In 1975 scientist Carl Sagan, interviewed in the *Chicago Tribune*, referred to the study of UFOs as "a nonscience. It's entirely anecdotal. You have to have data other than hearsay for anything to be scientific." Even some members of Hynek's staff questioned his activities. In 1982 Rudolph H. Weingartner, dean of Northwestern's College of Arts and Sciences, stressed in a letter to a member of the university relations staff that "the Lindheimer Observatory has nothing to do with UFOs and never did. Hynek's UFO Center has always been a *non*-Northwestern affair. There are many who think that what he's up to has nothing to do with research."

Hynek's work received perhaps the greatest boost in 1977 when film director Steven Spielberg addressed the subject of UFOs in *Close Encounters of the Third Kind*. Hynek not only acted as consultant but also made a brief appearance during the film's climactic "encounter" scene.

Hynek retired from his teaching position at Northwestern in 1978, although he continued as professor emeritus until he moved his UFO headquarters from Evanston to Scottsdale, Arizona, in 1984. He died in Scottsdale of a brain tumor in 1986. He was seventy-five.

Hynek authored several books, including *Astrophysics* (1951), *Challenge of the Universe* (1962), and *The UFO Experience: A Scientific Inquiry* (1972).

Samuel Insull

Entrepreneur

BORN: November 11, 1859
London, England

DIED: July 16, 1938
Paris, France

Samuel Insull was one of the most powerful businessmen in the United States during the 1920s. For many years people idolized him as the embodiment of the great American success story. Here was a poor young Englishman who started with nothing and made a fortune through hard work, intelligence, and perseverance. At its height, the Insull empire included Commonwealth Edison, Peoples Gas, the elevated railways of Chicago, and the interurban lines connecting Chicago with its suburbs.

Insull possessed a boundless energy and a burning ambition to achieve respectability. A quick study, he had an inquisitive and agile mind. If he didn't know something, he would learn it, and he would memorize whatever he read. Insull began his career as an office boy in an English auction firm. Although he did well—and indeed was even promoted to clerical supervisor—he was unceremoniously fired one day when an important client insisted that his son have Insull's position. Crushed by this rejection, Insull answered an ad for a secretary to an American banker. He was hired. Several years earlier, Insull had read about a young American inventor named Thomas Edison. Edison became Insull's hero. And as it turned out, his new employer was not, in fact, a banker, but Edison's European representative.

In 1881 Insull arrived in the United States as Thomas Edison's private secretary. He traveled across the country promoting Edison's inventions and quadrupling his sales. In 1892 the Chicago Edison Company began looking for a new president. The directors asked Insull if he could recommend anyone. Insull thought it improper to mention himself. His mother, who was visiting at the time, had no such qualms and persuaded her son to offer his services. He did, and the directors accepted his offer.

At that time electricity was thought of as a luxury item. Insull reasoned that everyone should have electricity, and he promoted the somewhat radical idea that lower prices would create bigger sales and thus yield greater profits. As Chicago Edison grew, so did Insull's reputation. In 1889 he became vice president of the Edison General Electric Company, and three years later he was named president. In 1907 the Commonwealth Edison Company was formed. Six years later, in 1913, Insull assumed the chairmanship of the Peoples Gas, Light, and Coke Company. Between 1911 and 1914, according to his biographer, Insull became Chicago's leading traction magnate and began to acquire and modernize the interurban railroads that connected Chicago and the suburbs.

Insull was a practical man. A happy environment makes for happy employees, he reasoned. He treated his workers fairly, but he demanded respect and loyalty. In return he gave them many fringe benefits. In addition to a pension, disability compensation, medical care, and life insurance, he added such niceties as athletic teams and savings and loan plans. Furthermore, employees were urged to become stockholders. Insull had a highly sophisticated social conscience, and he subtly encouraged all of his employees to participate in some form of community service activity.

Insull attended the opera regularly. Offended by opera's elitist image, he sought ways to bring it to the people. When Harold and Edith Rockefeller McCormick chose to step down as the major patrons of the Chicago Opera Company in 1922, he saw his opportunity. Insull decided to build a new home for opera, this time along the Chicago River at Wacker and Madison. He hired the august architectural firm of Graham, Anderson, Probst, and White to design a combination opera house and office building. Construction began in January 1928 and was completed during the dark weeks following the stock market crash of 1929.

Insull's business interests fell apart as a result of the crash. He tried to buy up his own stock, but debt engulfed his holding companies, and scores of small investors—including many of his employees—lost everything. Exhausted and embarrassed, Insull fled temporarily to the safe refuge of Europe in order to avoid prosecution. In his absence, he was charged with fraudulent use of the mails and accused of violating the Bankruptcy Act. Insull insisted he would return but only when a fair trial was possible. He admitted no wrongdoing and felt his decisions were more a matter of taking care of business than any malevolent act. Insull was forced to return to Chicago in 1934 to face the court. He was tried three times for fraud, violation of federal bankruptcy laws, and embezzlement, but he was acquitted on all three counts.

Insull died of a heart attack in the summer of 1938, while waiting to board a Paris subway train.

See also: Carter Harrison II, Charles Tyson Yerkes

Further reading: Forrest McDonald, *Insull* (1962); Harold L. Platt, *The Electric City: Energy and Growth of the Chicago Area, 1880–1930* (1991).

Mahalia Jackson

Singer

BORN: October 26, 1911
New Orleans, Louisiana

DIED: January 27, 1972
Evergreen Park, Illinois

Mahalia Jackson popularized gospel music in the 1950s and 1960s, spreading its warmth and joy around the world. She sang at humble storefront churches as well as on the stages of the world's premier concert halls. Although her recordings sold millions of copies, and she performed for kings, queens, prime ministers, and presidents, including singing the national anthem at John F. Kennedy's inauguration, she remained a sincere person, genuinely surprised, and even touched, by the depth of her success. "I love singing. Period," she once said.

Born in a three-room shack in New Orleans in 1911, Mahalia Jackson was the granddaughter of a slave. Her father was a combination stevedore, barber, and minister. Several of his sisters performed in vaudeville routines, but his children were only allowed to listen to religious music. As a youth, Jackson joined her father's church choir. She dropped out of school after eighth grade to work as a servant. When she was sixteen, she left New Orleans for Chicago, where she worked as a hotel maid, a private servant, and a packer in a food plant. One day her aunt took her to a service at the Greater Salem Baptist Church at 215 West 71st Street. When she sang "Hand Me Down My Silver Trumpet, Gabriel," the pastor was so impressed that he asked the young girl to join the church's choir as a soloist. Jackson saved enough money to study at beauty school,

and she opened a small beauty shop, Mahalia's Beauty Salon, at 3252 South Indiana Avenue. Later she invested in real estate and opened a flower shop. But, of course, it was her magnificent voice that changed the course of her life.

Jackson made her professional singing debut at the Olivet Baptist Church, at 31st Street and Grand Boulevard, in 1928. She then joined the Johnson Gospel Singers, which toured storefront churches. Although Jackson cut her first record for Decca in 1937, she didn't gain national recognition until the release of Rev. W. Herbert Brewster's "Move On Up a Little Higher" on the Apollo label in 1947, the first gospel record to sell a million copies. Her follow-up, "Even Me, Lord," fared equally well so that by 1949 she had closed her beauty shop to pursue singing full time. Around this time music was finally becoming accepted as a legitimate part of church services—further proof that gospel had finally arrived.

Jackson made her first appearance in New York's Carnegie Hall in 1950 to a sold-out crowd. "Think of it, me—a washwoman—standing there singing where such persons as Lily Pons and Caruso stood. I've never gotten over it," she once recalled in a newspaper interview. Four years later she hosted her own radio show, *Mahalia,* on Sunday evenings and signed a record contract with Columbia. In the 1960s she became involved in the civil rights movement and performed at many demonstrations.

Listeners were often overwhelmed by the power and raw honesty of Jackson's singing, falling to their knees and weeping. She sang songs about the black experience and about being black in white America. Jackson combined the soulful singing of Bessie Smith with Baptist hymns and spirituals.

After suffering a heart attack in 1964, Jackson's health continued to deteriorate. She died in 1972 at the age of sixty in Evergreen Park, Illinois. She is buried in a suburb of New Orleans.

Jackson recorded more than thirty albums during her career, most of them on the Columbia label. Among the best and more recent compilations of her work are *Gospels, Spirituals, and Hymns* (1991), which contains many of her classic 1950s and 1960s songs at Columbia, and *The Essential Mahalia Jackson* (2004).

Mahalia Jackson had two dreams that remained unfulfilled at the time of her death—to establish a church and to found a school of African American music. A musical based on her life, *Mahalia,* opened on Broadway in 1984.

See also: Nat King Cole, Sam Cooke, Thomas A. Dorsey
Further reading: Lorraine Goreau, *Just Mahalia, Baby* (1975); Mahalia Jackson and E. M. Wylie, *Movin' On Up: The Mahalia Jackson Story* (1966).

William Le Baron Jenney

Architect

BORN: September 25, 1832
Fairhaven, Massachusetts

DIED: June 15, 1907
Los Angeles, California

Called the "father of the skyscraper," William Le Baron Jenney designed such pioneering buildings as the Leiter Building, the Fair department store, the Manhattan Building, the Sears Building at State and Van Buren, the Montgomery Ward Building at State and Adams, and the Home Insurance Building, the world's first skyscraper. Virtually every major Chicago architect worked in Jenney's architectural firm, including Louis Sullivan, Daniel H. Burnham, William Holabird, Martin Roche, and Howard Van Doren Shaw.

Shortly after turning eighteen, Jenney traveled to California by way of clipper ship to join in the gold rush. Finding no easy fortune, he spent some time in the Philippines. Upon his return to the United States, he attended Harvard University and in 1853 enrolled as an engineering student at the École Centrale des Arts et Manufactures in Paris, where he shared rooms with the English writer George du Maurier and the American painter James McNeill Whistler.

In 1857 Jenney was appointed a chief engineer on the Isthmus of Tehuantepec, Mexico. During the Civil War, he was assigned to the staff of Gen. Ulysses S. Grant and then served under Gen. William T. Sherman. Jenney acted as the chief engineer of the 15th Corps at the Battle of Vicksburg and later served as the army's chief engineer. He attained the rank of major in March 1865 and resigned in May 1866. In the late 1860s, he and his wife, Elizabeth H. Cobb, settled in Riverside, Illinois, a suburb laid out by noted landscape architects Frederick Law Olmsted and Calvert Vaux.

Jenney developed steel-frame construction, which replaced the burdensome masonry-bearing wall of architecture made famous by the Monadnock Building. In the steel-frame method, the exterior wall was reduced to a curtain supported by interior framing, a technological breakthrough that made possible the development of the modern skyscraper. Architectural critic Carl W. Condit called it "the first adequate solution to the problem of large-scale urban construction." He claimed further that skeletal construction "completed the most radical transformation in the structural art since the development of the Gothic system of construction in the twelfth century." Jenney's innovative method was quickly adopted across the country.

Jenney's twelve-story Home Insurance Building, constructed in 1884–1885 at the northeast corner of LaSalle and Adams Streets, is credited with being the world's first skyscraper, and it was reportedly the first structure to use steel as a building material. Unfortunately, despite its historical significance, it was razed in 1931.

Jenney entered into several partnerships during his career. In February 1891, he formed a partnership with William B. Mundie. Later E. C. Jensen joined and the firm was known as Jenney, Mundie, and Jensen. Jenney was elected Fellow of the American Institute of Architects (AIA) in 1872 and also served as president of the Illinois chapter of the AIA. He retired in 1905 and moved to California, where he died in 1907. His body was returned to Chicago, and his ashes were scattered next to his wife's grave in Graceland Cemetery.

See also: Daniel H. Burnham, William Holabird, Howard Van Doren Shaw, Louis Sullivan

Further reading: Carl W. Condit, *The Chicago School of Architecture: A History of Commercial and Public Building in the Chicago Area, 1875–1925* (1964).

Jens Jensen
Landscape Architect

BORN: September 13, 1860
Near Dybbøl, Denmark

DIED: October 1, 1951
Ellison Bay, Wisconsin

Jens Jensen is considered the dean of the Prairie style of landscape architecture as well as a leader of the Midwestern conservation movement. He designed Lincoln Park, Douglas Park, and Columbus Park and was instrumental in the preservation of the Indiana dunes. He used native plants and indigenous materials in his work and popularized their use in gardens. He organized the early conservation movements that would eventually lead to the creation of the Forest Preserve District of Cook County, the Illinois state park system, and the Indiana Dunes State Park and National Lakeshore, creating a distinctively Midwestern style of maintaining parks and gardens that became known as the Prairie style of landscape architecture.

Born in Denmark to a wealthy farming family, Jensen attended the Tune Agricultural School in Jutland. He underwent mandatory service in the Prussian army (Prussia had invaded his hometown when he was a boy and annexed the land). In 1884 he immigrated to the United States with his fiancée, Anne Marie Hansen.

Jensen attended Luther College in Decorah, Iowa, before moving to Chicago, where he took a job as a laborer for the West Park Commission. Before long he was promoted to foreman. In 1888 he designed and planted a garden of exotic flowers in Union Park. When the garden withered he transplanted native wildflowers. In this way he created what came to be known as the American Garden.

In 1895 Jensen was appointed superintendent of the 200-acre Humboldt Park. By the late 1890s the West Park Commission was embroiled in various corruption scandals. But Jensen, maintaining his distance, refused to get involved. In 1900, he was fired by the park commission board for not playing along. Eventually he was reinstated, but by the time Jensen was selected as chief landscape architect and general superintendent of the West Park System in 1905, many of the city's parks had deteriorated.

In addition to redesigning existing parks Jensen created new small parks in such inner-city neighborhoods as Humboldt Park, where he extended the lagoon, planted native grasses, and recreated a garden with native flowers. He designed a "prairie river" with native grasses and combined the performing arts and nature by including a "players' green," that is, a slightly elevated stage for outdoor theatrical performances such as masques to educate people about nature and conservation.

Columbus Park is considered his masterpiece. Jensen himself thought of it as his greatest achievement. He designed berms ("reminiscent of glacial ridges," says Chicago Park District historian Julia Bachrach) and created a lagoon using two waterfalls made of stonework that were meant to represent the source of the waterway. In 1907 he built the Garfield Park Conservatory, one of the largest conservatories in the world. The Garfield Park Conservatory was considered revolutionary in its day: Jensen installed horizontal stonework that resembled the natural landscapes of the Midwest. In addition, he designed the Shakespeare Garden at Northwestern University in Evanston, which featured plants, herbs, and flowers mentioned in Shakespeare's works. He also designed parks in Racine and Madison, Wisconsin; Dubuque, Iowa; and Springfield, Illinois.

In 1908 Jensen began a series of Saturday afternoon walking trips, outings to natural areas in the Chicago area. He often led the groups himself. These walks inspired the formation of the Prairie Club, which sponsored walking trips to the Indiana dunes and other areas of natural beauty that were threatened by industrial and commercial development. According to Julia Bachrach, the club built a beach house on the dunes at Tremont, Indiana, in 1913, and to celebrate it they produced and performed a masque entitled "The Spirit of the Dunes." Jensen was also the inspiration behind Friends of Our Native Landscape, founded in 1913. Both the Friends and the Prairie Club fought to save the Indiana dunes. Eventually, in 1926, 2,250 acres were set aside as the Indiana Dunes State Park.

As an appointee to the Special Park Commission, Jensen used his deep knowledge of landscape and nature to study Chicago's open spaces, create playgrounds in the most densely populated neighborhoods, and develop a plan for parks and other recreational areas throughout the metropolitan area. Jensen and the renowned Prairie school architect Dwight Perkins conducted the study, recommending the creation of new parks and playgrounds in the inner city as well as the protection of thousands of acres of land. They also recommended that a belt of natural lands be created around the perimeter of the city and suggested a new system of boulevards that would link the nature preserves with the existing parks and boulevards. What's more, they asked for Daniel Burnham's support. He in turn incorporated their ideas into his 1909 *Plan of Chicago*.

In 1920 Jensen retired from the park system and started his own landscape architecture practice. He worked on private estates and municipal parks throughout the United States, including the Henry Ford Hospital, the Henry Ford Museum, and the Ford pavilion at the 1933 Chicago Century of Progress Exposition. He also designed hundreds of parks, golf courses, and landscapes for schools, hospitals, hotels, and resorts as well as the private residences of Henry and Edsel Ford, Harold Florsheim, and Ogden Armour, among others.

When his wife passed away in 1934 Jensen moved to his summer home in Ellison Bay in Door County, Wisconsin, and in 1935 he established the Clearing, "a school of the soil." Influenced by the folk schools of his native Denmark, the Clearing is non-competitive—there are no credits and no grades. The method of teaching is based on a combination of discussion, conversation, the study of nature, and hands-on work.

Jensen died in Ellison Bay in 1951 at the age of ninety-one.

The Jens Jensen Legacy Project, a joint effort of the Chicago Department of Cultural Affairs and Chicago Park District, is intended to educate and inform the general public about the legacy and vision of Jensen.

Jensen Boulevard is named in his honor.

Further reading: Julia S. Bachrach, *The City in a Garden: A Photographic History of Chicago Parks*, 2nd ed. (2011) and "Jens Jensen," *Chicago Wilderness*, Spring 2001; Leonard K. Eaton, *Landscape Artists in America: The Life and Work of Jens Jensen* (1964); Robert E. Grese, *Jens Jensen: Maker of Natural Parks and Gardens* (1998); Jens Jensen, *Siftings* (1990); Cathy Jean Maloney, *The Gardener's Cottage in Riverside, Illinois* (2010).

Other resources: The Clearing, www.theclearing.org; Jens Jensen Legacy Project, www.jensjensen.org.

Jack Johnson

Boxer

BORN: March 31, 1878
Galveston, Texas

DIED: June 10, 1946
Raleigh, North Carolina

John Arthur Johnson was not only the first black heavyweight champion of the world, he was also one of the greatest fighters in the history of boxing.

Johnson quit school in Galveston, Texas, after the fifth grade. Endowed with lightning speed, he learned to box at a neighborhood gym. He traveled the country on freight trains and was frequently arrested for vagrancy. In Galveston, a local boxer offered the princely sum of $5 to anyone who could stay on his feet in the ring with him for four rounds. Johnson accepted the challenge and defeated his astonished foe handily. Shortly afterward Johnson was offered a match at the Galveston Athletic Club. After a few more semiprofessional bouts, Johnson went back to traveling on freight trains again, making his way to St. Louis, then to Florida, and finally to Chicago, where he got a job as a sparring partner for the West Indian welterweight Joe Walcott.

Johnson then went to California where he found work as a sparring partner with "Kid" Carter. He began winning match after match, always against black men. His earnings grew, but he spent his money as quickly as he made it. A natural showman, Johnson also performed on the vaudeville stage demonstrating basic boxing movements, warbling a few songs, dancing, and playing the harmonica and bass fiddle.

In 1905 Johnson fought a white boxer, Marvin Hart, in San Francisco. Although observers agreed that Johnson was the clear winner, the referee thought otherwise and gave the decision to Hart. This devastating loss set Johnson's goal of attaining a championship back several years. Worse, many white fighters, including the reigning world champion at the time, James J. Jeffries, refused to fight him. Johnson continued to win, however. His victory over another white boxer, Tommy Burns (who was at that point the world champion), on December 26, 1908, in Sydney, Australia, led to pandemonium. Blacks celebrated as angry whites took to the streets. Even after the win over Burns, stubborn whites refused to accept Johnson as the world champion because Jeffries had retired undefeated. Finally, Jeffries agreed to come out of retirement to meet Johnson in what was billed the "fight of the century." When Johnson beat Jeffries on July 4, 1910, in Reno, Nevada, he was finally declared the undisputed heavyweight champion of the world. Johnson's victory triggered race riots throughout the country.

Johnson lived well out of the ring, wearing impeccably tailored suits and driving fancy cars. The boxer chose to keep company with white, usually blond, women, many of whom were prostitutes. Three of Johnson's four marriages were to white women, which didn't go over well with the boxing establishment or with the general public, who preferred their heroes to be monogamous and to maintain the color line. But Johnson paid his critics no heed and flouted conventional morality. His flamboyant lifestyle was criticized not only by whites but also by conservative blacks, who found his conduct deeply offensive. Johnson's notoriety inspired the state legislatures of Wisconsin, Iowa, Kansas, Minnesota, New Jersey, Michigan, and New York to introduce bills outlawing interracial marriages. The bulk of the African American community, however, still felt a source of pride in Johnson's achievements—if not his controversial exploits. Significantly, the *Chicago Defender*, the city's black newspaper, staunchly supported Johnson.

In 1911 Johnson opened his own café, the Café de Champion, at 42 West 31st Street, just south of Chicago's red-light district. Then a series of personal tragedies ensued. Johnson's second wife committed suicide, and one of his employees, Adah Banks, shot the boxer in the foot during a dispute over the attentions of a young white girl, Lucille Cameron. Cameron worked as a bookkeeper and secretary at Johnson's café. Her mother, who resented her daughter's independent spirit, accused Johnson of abducting her. "Jack Johnson," she insisted, "has hypnotic powers, and he has exercised them on my little girl." But Cameron refused to cooperate. Responding to public pressure, the city council passed a resolution denouncing Johnson and urged the revocation of his café license. The state of Illinois closed the café down shortly thereafter. After the tumult subsided, Jack Johnson and Lucille Cameron were married.

In 1912 Johnson was convicted of violating the Mann Act, which prohibited the transportation of women across state lines for immoral purposes. Johnson allegedly sent money to Belle Schreiber, a former prostitute at the infamous Everleigh Club, so she could return to Chicago from Pittsburgh. Convicted and sentenced to one year and a day in the Joliet penitentiary, he jumped bail and sailed for France.

His flight caused a sensation, and Johnson became the world's most famous fugitive. He resumed his fighting career abroad. In 1915 he fought Jess Willard in Cuba and won by a knockout in the twenty-sixth round. Johnson later claimed that he had thrown the fight but then repudiated that story.

For the next four or five years Johnson lived the life of a hobo, moving from country to country. He traveled to Barcelona and talked of starting an advertising agency and then made his debut as a professional matador in July 1916. In 1919 he moved to Mexico, where he planned to open a saloon and promote prizefights. Unable to bear the thought of spending the rest of his life in exile, though, Johnson returned to the United States, surrendering to federal agents in San Diego on July 20, 1920. He was ordered to serve out his term at Leavenworth, Kansas.

After his release ten months later, Johnson returned to the vaudeville circuit, although with less success. In his mid-forties, he reentered the ring, fighting Homer Smith in Montreal and winning in ten rounds. In his later years he appeared at exhibition bouts, but his chief source of income was as a circus attraction. In 1936 he made his operatic debut in a cameo role as a captured general in *Aida* at New York's Hippodrome.

Johnson died in an automobile accident near Raleigh, North Carolina, in 1946. His body was returned to Chicago and buried in Graceland Cemetery.

In 1968 Johnson's colorful life was dramatized in Howard Sackler's popular Broadway play, *The Great White Hope,* starring James Earl Jones in the role of Jack Jefferson, a persecuted black heavyweight champion modeled after Johnson. Jones won the 1969 Tony for best actor. The following year, Jones received an Oscar nomination for his performance in the film version. In 2005 filmmaker Ken Burns produced a two-part documentary for PBS about Johnson entitled *Unforgivable Blackness: The Rise and Fall of Jack Johnson,* based on the book by Geoffrey C. Ward. In 2010 Charles R. Smith Jr. published *Black Jack: The Ballad of Jack Johnson,* a children's book for ages five through eight.

Johnson was inducted into boxing's Hall of Fame in 1954.

Further reading: Finis Farr, *Black Champion: The Life and Times of Jack Johnson* (1964); Jack Johnson, *Jack Johnson Is a Dandy: An Autobiography* (1969; published posthumously); Geoffrey C. Ward, *Unforgivable Blackness: The Rise and Fall of Jack Johnson* (2004).

John H. Johnson

Publisher

BORN: January 19, 1918
Arkansas City, Arkansas

DIED: August 8, 2005
Chicago, Illinois

Publisher, chairman, and CEO of the largest African American publishing company in the world, John H. Johnson once said, "I don't see, never did see, failure as an option." He helped corporate America realize the vast purchasing power of the African American consumer and, in the process, virtually invented the black consumer market.

Johnson was born in Arkansas in 1918, the grandson of slaves. His father died when he was six. In 1933 he moved to Chicago with his widowed mother. He attended DuSable High School, where his classmates included Nat King Cole and Redd Foxx, and he was student council president and editor of the school newspaper and class yearbook. After he graduated in 1936, he worked part-time as an office clerk at the black-owned Supreme Liberty Life Insurance Company. Within two years he was promoted to assistant to the company's president, Harry Pace. As part of his job, Johnson researched newspapers and magazines and prepared a digest of events, news, and profiles in the black community for Pace. By 1942 he had his own idea of condensing African American articles into a monthly magazine that would cater to the black population—essentially an African American version of *Reader's Digest.*

Johnson's mother borrowed $500 and used her furniture as collateral in order to support her son's dream of starting his own magazine. When Johnson mailed a charter subscription offer to Supreme Life customers, some 3,000 people responded, each sending $2. With that money he had enough funds to publish the first issue of *Negro Digest.* Its content consisted of African American history, literature, arts, and culture. He used the same technique to expand into other cities. Within a year *Negro Digest* had sold 50,000 copies a month. Several years later he changed the name from *Negro Digest* to *Black World.*

Johnson had bigger dreams. By November 1945 he was ready to release the first issue of *Ebony* magazine, which was modeled on the success of the mainstream *Life* magazine. Johnson made the deliberate decision with *Ebony* to publish only profiles of successful black men and women as well as articles on civil rights legislation, freedom rides and marches, segregation, and discrimination. Initially, selling this idea to advertisers was difficult. But after he convinced Eugene McDonald, the head of Zenith Radio Corporation, to advertise in the magazine, others followed suit. Magazine distributor Joseph Levy, who was also impressed with Johnson's hard work and determination, offered some valuable marketing tips and even helped with the distribution to newsstands in urban areas. Buoyed by the positive reception, in 1951 Johnson founded the weekly news digest *Jet,* an offshoot of *Ebony.* In September 1955, *Jet* published an open-coffin photograph of Emmett Till, the Chicago teenager who was murdered in Mississippi and whose death set off a social and political furor.

Johnson's other magazines included *Tan,* which was similar to *True Confessions; African American Stars;* and *Ebony Jr.,* a children's magazine. In addition to his publishing activities, he also developed a line of cosmetics, purchased three radio stations, and started a book publishing company and a television production company.

At its height in 2004, *Ebony* had a paid circulation of 1.7 million. The company headquarters has been at 820 South Michigan Avenue since December 1971.

Johnson had attended the University of Chicago and Northwestern University. Although he didn't graduate from either school he was later awarded an impressive thirty-one honorary doctoral degrees from such schools as Harvard University, Carnegie Mellon University, and Wayne State University. He gave generously to many causes, including $4 million to Howard University in Washington, D.C. The university named its communications school after him. In 1996, President Bill Clinton awarded Johnson the Presidential Medal of Freedom.

Among his many firsts, Johnson was the first African American businessman to have his own building on Michigan Avenue and the first African American to appear on *Forbes* magazine's list of the 400 wealthiest Americans.

Johnson died of congestive heart failure at Northwestern Memorial Hospital in Chicago at the age of eighty-seven in August 2005. His wife, Eunice W. Johnson, was an influential name herself. For nearly fifty years she presented the Ebony Fashion Fair, considered a showcase for the world's top designers around the world, to predominantly black audiences in the United States and abroad. She also chose the name of the magazine, selecting the word "ebony" to reflect what she considered the mystique of that black wood. She died on January 3, 2010, of renal failure.

In 2010, Desiree Rogers, a former White House social secretary for the Obama administration, took over as chief executive of Johnson Publishing.

Further reading: John H. Johnson and Lerone Bennett Jr., *Succeeding Against the Odds: The Autobiography of a Great American Businessman* (1992).

John Jones

Politician

BORN: Circa 1816
Greene County, North Carolina

DIED: May 27, 1879
Chicago, Illinois

The most eminent African American of his day, John Jones was the first black person to hold elected office in Cook County and in the state of Illinois. Jones began his career as a tailor and eventually gained prominence as a civil rights leader and abolitionist in early Chicago.

Jones was born in North Carolina, the son of a freed slave woman and a German man named Bromfield. Jones learned the craft of tailoring from a Mississippian named Richard Clere. He married Mary Richardson in Alton, Illinois, before moving to Chicago in 1845 with a total savings of $3.50. The couple rented a one-room cottage at the corner of Madison and Wells, and Jones opened a small tailor shop a few blocks away. Jones, who taught himself to read and write, prospered making clothes for wealthy white Chicagoans.

Jones often entertained fellow abolitionists, such as Allan Pinkerton, John Brown, and Frederick Douglass, in his home. His shop functioned as one of the stops along the Underground Railroad, that secret network of farmers, merchants, and clergy, among others, who shepherded thousands of slaves to safety in the North.

Jones also waged an effective campaign against Illinois's notorious Black Laws, which deprived African Americans of the right to testify in courts and forbade them to purchase property, among other restrictions. Moreover, an Illinois law prohibited free blacks from settling in the state. In response, Jones wrote a sixteen-page pamphlet in 1864 entitled *The Black Laws of Illinois and a Few Reasons Why They Should Be Repealed*. He made speeches and lobbied the state legislature until these statutes were finally revoked in 1865.

By 1871 Jones earned the distinction of being the wealthiest African American in the Midwest and one of the most affluent in the country. The Chicago Fire, however, reduced his income considerably, although he continued to enjoy a comfortable standard of living.

In 1872 Jones was elected to the Cook County Board of Commissioners for a three-year term, winning with significant white support. He was defeated three years later, however.

Jones died in 1879 after a long illness. He was buried in Graceland Cemetery in Chicago.

See also: Oscar De Priest, Allan Pinkerton

Further reading: Arna Bontemps and Jack Conroy, *Anyplace But Here* (1966); Harold F. Gosnell, *Negro Politicians: The Rise of Negro Politics in Chicago* (1935); Rayford W. Logan and Michael R. Winston, eds., *Dictionary of American Negro Biography* (1982); Wilbur Henry Siebert, *The Underground Railroad from Slavery to Freedom* (1967); Allan H. Spear, *Black Chicago: The Making of a Negro Ghetto, 1890–1920* (1967); Dempsey J. Travis, *An Autobiography of Black Chicago* (1981).

Stuart M. Kaminsky
Author

BORN: September 29, 1934
Chicago, Illinois

DIED: October 9, 2009
St. Louis, Missouri

Film historian, college professor, biographer, and author, Stuart Kaminsky is best known for his crime novels. His four detective series were set in Chicago, Los Angeles, Moscow, and Florida; each series is very different in style, voice, and place. During a career that spanned many decades, the prolific Kaminsky wrote more than seventy novels. In 2006 the Mystery Writers of America named him a Grand Master. His most popular character, Toby Peters, was the opposite of Philip Marlowe, the wise-cracking, hard-drinking private eye created by Raymond Chandler. Peters was neither handsome nor particularly smart and certainly not cool: more like David Janssen's weary, downtrodden television character Harry Orwell than James Garner's laid-back Jim Rockford.

A native of Chicago's West Side, Kaminsky graduated from Marshall High School. He received a B.A. in journalism in 1957 and an M.A. in English literature in 1959, both from the University of Illinois at Urbana-Champaign. Also during the 1950s he served as an army medic in France, where he contracted hepatitis C. Later, he worked as a photographer with a Milwaukee newspaper, did some university public relations work, and labored for various trade publications.

After receiving his doctorate in film studies from Northwestern University in 1972—his dissertation was on the work of filmmaker Don Siegel—Kaminsky joined the faculty of his alma mater and taught in the radio, television, and film program until 1989. He left Northwestern to become the first director of the Graduate Film Conservatory at Florida State University. He retired from teaching altogether in 1994 to devote himself to writing full time.

Kaminsky's first novel, *Bullet for a Star* (1977), was a lighthearted twist on the hard-boiled American detective fiction epitomized by Raymond Chandler. It introduced the character of Toby Peters (née Pevsner), a divorced and taco-loving former security guard with Warner Brothers who had been fired in 1936 and turned to private-eye work. Kaminsky often used historical figures in his work, and each title in the Toby Peters series features a particular celebrity. For example, in *Bullet*, the actor Errol Flynn hires Peters to retrieve a compromising photo, Albert Einstein appears in *Smart Moves* (1986), and Joan Crawford turns up in *Mildred Pierced* (2003).

Death of a Dissident (1981) marked the debut of the Moscow police inspector Porfiry Rostnikov, a man in his fifties who distrusts his superiors and the KGB. One of the titles in the series, *A Cold Red Sunrise* (1988), won the 1989 Edgar Award for best novel from the Mystery Writers of America. Another series featured Abe Lieberman, a sixty-something Chicago police detective who partners with a younger Irish American cop named Bill Hanrahan. Still another series starred the character of Lew Fonesca, a fortyish former process server with the Cook County state's attorney's office who operates as a private eye in Sarasota.

In addition to fiction, Kaminsky also wrote biographies of the film directors Don Siegel, Ingmar Bergman, and John Huston, and of actor-director Clint Eastwood. Other nonfiction titles include *American Film Genres: Approaches to a Critical Theory of Popular Film* (1974) and, with Dana H. Hodgdon, *Basic Filmmaking* (1981). He also supplied English dialogue for Sergio Leone's epic *Once Upon a Time in America* (1984), wrote novelized versions of the television shows *The Rockford Files* and *CSI: New York,* and worked as a screenwriter on an episode of *A Nero Wolfe Mystery.*

Kaminsky supported the work of other writers. In the autumn of 1979 Sara Paretsky attended one of his classes, "Writing Detective Fiction for Publication," at Northwestern. He encouraged her to set her novels in a milieu that she knew well—in her case, the financial world. "I don't think it's an overstatement to say I owe my career to him," Paretsky, author of more than a dozen novels featuring female private investigator V. I. Warshawski, once said. She wrote *Indemnity Only* (1982) during the writing course. Kaminsky went beyond just offering advice though. He also prepared the book for publication and even got her an agent.

Kaminsky employed a distinctive set of research techniques for his period works of fiction that included reading biographies, perusing the pages of the *New York Times* and the *Los Angeles Times,* watching period movies of the era he was writing about, and listening to radio show broadcasts of the time. The plot points of his novels often paralleled the lives of the celebrity characters. In one of his works, Judy Garland hires Toby Peters to solve the murder of a Munchkin on the MGM lot. In another, echoing a pivotal scene in Hitchcock's *North by Northwest,* Cary Grant tries to save Peters from falling off a cliff. Kaminsky also used structural and plot references from old movies in his non-series Hollywood novels.

"I write the books for myself, but am very happy that others like them," Kaminsky said.

Kaminsky also acted as a publisher. Under the name Mystery Vault, he reprinted out-of-print books and quality trade paperbacks. The eclectic list of titles included novels by Dorothy Salisbury Davis, John Lutz, Max Allan Collins, Mickey Spillane, and Don Westlake. In 2009 he edited *On a Raven's Wing* in celebration of Edgar Allan

Poe's bicentennial, with new works by authors influenced by Poe.

In March 2009, Kaminsky moved to St. Louis to await a liver transplant to treat the hepatitis that he contracted while serving in the military. He suffered a stroke two days after his arrival. He died on October 9, 2009, at the age of seventy-five from hepatitis and complications from a stroke in Barnes-Jewish Hospital in St. Louis.

In early 2010, Kaminsky's last novel, *A Whisper to the Living,* in the Rostnikov series, was published.

Florence Kelley
Social Reformer

BORN: September 12, 1859
Philadelphia, Pennsylvania

DIED: February 17, 1932
Philadelphia, Pennsylvania

Florence Kelley led the struggle for the passage of pioneering social and labor laws, helped women organize unions, coordinated the campaign to abolish child labor, and fought to secure minimum-wage laws in the United States. Labeled a political radical by her enemies, Kelley was a combative intellectual who used her talents to remedy social ills. She especially focused her reform efforts on helping women and children. Although she lived in Chicago only eight years, Kelley left an indelible imprint on the city and its institutions.

Kelley came from a prominent Philadelphia family of Quakers. Her father, a judge and congressman, was also one of the founders of the Republican Party in Pennsylvania. A sickly child, Kelley devoured the English and American classics of literature that lined her father's library shelves. She studied at Cornell University at a time when very few women attended college. Denied permission to enter the School of Law at the University of Pennsylvania, Kelley instead established an evening school for working women in Philadelphia. Later she studied in Leipzig, but again not being allowed to graduate, she enrolled at the Law School of Zurich. There, exposure to Marxist theory led her to become an ardent socialist and prompted her to translate into English Friedrich Engels's *The Condition of the Working Class in England in 1844* (1887).

After marrying a young Polish-Russian-Jewish physician, Lazare Wischnewetzky, the couple moved to New York in 1886 with their infant son. Another son and a daughter were born soon after. Several years later, Kelley divorced her husband and moved with her three children to Chicago, determined to meet Jane Addams and visit the famous house on Halsted Street.

Kelley arrived at Hull House "on a snowy morning between Christmas 1891 and New Year's 1892 . . . a little before breakfast time," she recalled. Addams put her to work as head of Hull House Bureau of Labor, a placement service for young girls. She stayed for seven years. In her first year at the settlement house, Kelley canvassed the area and was appalled to find the neighborhood surrounded by unventilated, foul-smelling sweatshops and dimly lit, drab tenements. "Shops over sheds or stables, in basements or on upper floors of tenement houses," she wrote, "are not fit working places for men, women, and children."

From this study emerged *Hull-House Maps and Papers* (1895), a devastating piece of investigative reporting that exposed the horrors of the sweatshops to the general public. Kelley's work resulted in the passage of the first factory law in Illinois, which prohibited employment of children under the age of fourteen in the factories. On July 12, 1893, Governor John Peter Altgeld appointed her chief factory inspector, with a staff of twelve. Around this time she registered at Northwestern University's law school. She graduated in 1894 and was admitted to the Illinois bar. She chose not to practice law, however.

Kelley left Chicago in 1899 to become the general secretary of the National Consumers League in New York, which, under her leadership, became the single most important lobbying group in the nation for social and labor reform. In 1909 she presented the idea of a minimum wage at the league's annual meeting. By 1913 it had become a national issue. It wasn't until 1938, however, that Congress passed the Fair Labor Standards Act, which established both a national minimum wage and an eight-hour day. Kelley was also vice president of the National Woman Suffrage Association for many years and served with many important national organizations, including the U.S. Children's Bureau, the National Child Labor Committee, and the General Federation of Women's Clubs.

Because of her belief in socialism, Kelley was the subject of various FBI probes. She died in 1932 at the age of seventy-two before seeing many of her ideals come to fruition. Concepts that once seemed radical—such as the minimum wage and the eight-hour day—are now taken for granted. Through Kelley's pioneering efforts, the dehumanizing effects of industrial capitalism were alleviated.

See also: Grace Abbott, Jane Addams, John Peter Altgeld, Alice Hamilton, Henry Demarest Lloyd, Ellen Gates Starr

Further reading: Jane Addams, *Twenty Years at Hull-House* (1910); Dorothy Rose Blumberg, *Florence Kelley: The Making of a Social Pioneer* (1966); Mari Jo Buhle, *Women and American Socialism* (1979); Mina Carson, *Settlement Folk: Social Thought and the American Settlement Movement 1885–1930* (1990); Allen F. Davis and Mary Lynn McCree, eds., *Eighty Years at Hull-House* (1969); Josephine Goldmark, *Impatient Crusader: Florence Kelley's Life Story* (1953); William Preston Jr., *Aliens and Dissenters: Federal Suppression of Radicals, 1903–1933* (1963); Kathryn Kish Sklar, ed., *The Autobiography of Florence Kelley: Notes of Sixty Years* (1986).

Edward J. Kelly

Politician

BORN: May 1, 1876
Chicago, Illinois

DIED: October 20, 1950
Chicago, Illinois

Edward Joseph Kelly served as mayor of Chicago for fourteen years, and with Pat Nash, his right-hand man, he ran the most powerful political machine in the nation. Stubborn and outspoken with a fierce Irish temper, Kelly was a popular mayor, and with his plush accommodations on the Gold Coast and his elegant wardrobe, he looked and acted the part.

Kelly dropped out of school in the fifth grade to work full time. At the age of eighteen, this second-generation Irishman from Bridgeport got a job with the Chicago Sanitary District, where he worked for thirty-nine years. He started humbly enough, chopping down trees on canal banks, but he eventually rose to the post of chief engineer.

Kelly also served as president of the South Park Board. Many major civic improvements occurred during his term: the beautification of Grant Park; the construction of the Shedd Aquarium, the Adler Planetarium, Buckingham Fountain, and Soldier Field; and the renovation of the Museum of Science and Industry. Although situated on the periphery of Chicago politics, Kelly counted a number of influential and high-ranking politicians among his friends, including Twenty-Eighth Ward alderman Patrick A. Nash.

When Mayor Anton J. Cermak was killed by an assassin's bullet in 1933, Cook County Democratic Chairman Nash chose Kelly as the perfect successor. Although Kelly had never held elected office before, Nash viewed this as an advantage. The new mayor would have executive ability without any political liabilities. Kelly's administration benefited enormously from New Deal programs. According to historian Michael F. Funchion, "Federal funds allowed the city to build [the State Street] subway and new highways, improve roads and sewage systems, enlarge its airport and construct ten housing projects." More importantly, Kelly sought early in his term to trim the city's bloated budget, starting with the public schools. The Great Depression hit the troubled school system especially hard. For months teachers did not receive any pay. There was even talk of closing down the

schools. Determined to keep them open, Kelly embarked on a program of severe belt tightening. He removed all physical education and home economics courses from elementary schools, increased teacher workloads, shortened the school year by one month, slashed teacher's salaries by almost 25 percent, and closed all special schools and departments. Kelly insisted that such drastic action was unfortunate but, short of closing the schools altogether, necessary.

Kelly turned the city into a smooth, efficiently run machine and was reelected in 1935 in a landslide. Such efficiency, however, came at a high price. Money was needed to run the city, to provide the services, and to maintain the quality of life. For this, according to historian Roger Biles, Kelly and the Democratic machine turned to the seemingly unlimited resources of organized crime. Indeed, according to some estimates, the city received approximately $20 million a year in illegal revenue, much of it from gambling. Another source of financial assistance came from the Roosevelt White House. Roosevelt not only admired Kelly's political astuteness, he also enjoyed his company and invited him to luncheons and social gatherings.

Kelly lured a large share of black voters away from the Republican Party. He ceased the police harassment of black gambling operations that was so prevalent during Cermak's term in office, and, according to Funchion, "he appointed some blacks to influential positions in city government, and he dispensed patronage jobs to them in greater numbers than any previous Chicago mayor." Kelly's courting of the black vote was not simply politics. He took several unpopular stands, such as advocating school integration and open housing, which angered many white voters. "The time is not far away when we shall forget the color of a man's skin and see him only in the light of intelligence of his mind and soul," he said.

Kelly was reelected in 1939 and 1943, but the death of his friend and colleague Pat Nash in 1943 came as a devastating blow. The affable Nash had acted as a peacemaker. Without his diplomatic skills, dissension ran unchecked in the city council. Kelly's fierce temper and occasional high-handedness further exacerbated matters.

A series of scandals, erratic garbage collection and street cleaning, police corruption, and high taxes brought down the once-popular mayor, but Biles suggests that it was Kelly's stubborn commitment to open housing (a housing situation in which people of all races and creeds live in the neighborhoods of their choice) that galvanized the city's ethnic groups against him and guaranteed his political demise. Top Democrats, unhappy with Kelly's choice of candidates for the 1946 election, chose former Twenty-Fourth Ward alderman Jacob Arvey as the new party leader. They convinced Kelly to resign in favor of another Bridge-port Irishman, Martin H. Kennelly.

When Kennelly won the mayoral election, Kelly retired from public life altogether, content to play the role of elder statesman. In 1950, during a routine examination in his doctor's office, Kelly suffered a fatal heart attack. He was buried in Calvary Cemetery in Evanston.

Kelly expanded the power and influence of the Democratic machine, attracting into its fold groups that had been ignored or taken for granted by earlier administrations. Kelly laid the foundation for the broad-based support and success of the administrations of both Richard J. Daley and his son Richard M. Daley.

See also: Jacob Arvey, Anton J. Cermak, Richard J. Daley

Further reading: Roger Biles, *Big City Boss in Depression and War: Mayor Edward J. Kelly of Chicago* (1984); Michael F. Funchion, "Political and Nationalist Dimensions" in *The Irish in Chicago* (1987), Lawrence McCaffrey et al., eds.; Edward M. Levine, *The Irish and Irish Politicians* (1966).

Michael "Hinky Dink" Kenna

Politician

BORN: August 20, 1857
Chicago, Illinois

DIED: October 19, 1946
Chicago, Illinois

For more than four decades Michael "Hinky Dink" Kenna, the tight-lipped Democratic boss of the First Ward, controlled the purse strings of a segregated area of brothels and saloons just south of the Loop known as the Levee. His aldermanic partner in vice, "Bathhouse John" Coughlin, may have received most of the attention, but Kenna quietly ran the show.

Michael Kenna was born in a frame shack at the edge of an Irish neighborhood, commonly referred to as Conley's Patch, which ran from 12th to 16th Streets and from Michigan Avenue to the lake. He left school at the age of ten and began hawking newspapers on State Street, running errands for saloonkeepers, and striking up friendships with madams and hostesses. Already quite an aggressive entrepreneur, he purchased a newsstand at Monroe and Dearborn Streets at age twelve.

Kenna was a loner who thirsted for adventure. In 1880 he made his way to Leadville, Colorado, which had earned a reputation as wild and untamed. Carrying a letter of recommendation from *Chicago Tribune* publisher Joseph Medill, Kenna landed a position as circulation manager of the *Lake County Reveille*. He stayed in Leadville for two years, but the continual violence—shootings and street brawls were commonplace—persuaded him to return to Chicago.

Back in town, he opened a saloon, the Workingmen's Exchange, at Clark and Van Buren Streets, and became something of a political operator, working quietly behind the scenes and making his presence felt. He dutifully supported John Coughlin for First Ward alderman. With the twilight of Mike McDonald, Chicago's first underworld kingpin, Kenna saw his opportunity. All he needed was a friend in the city council; Coughlin was his man.

It was a strange match—the brash, loud, outspoken Coughlin and the morose, distant, and somber Kenna. Kenna was a devout teetotaler and was regarded as an exemplary husband, while Coughlin, although no philanderer, did enjoy an occasional nip from the bottle. Despite their differences both men seemed to need each other. Kenna laid the groundwork for a political organization that would be built on graft, corruption, and thievery, whose membership included a network of pimps, gamblers, saloonkeepers, and brothel owners. In return for protection against police raids, Kenna demanded their loyalty and, most importantly, their votes. Kenna also gained the votes of the First Ward homeless and residents of boarding houses. It was a foolproof plan, and it worked beautifully.

Kenna soon itched for a seat of his own in the city council. He lost in 1895, but his next attempt was more successful. He trounced the Republican incumbent of the First Ward, Francis "Paddy" Gleason in 1897. Kenna's saloon at Clark and Van Buren Streets was the real seat of First Ward politics. Here he would hang out with "the boys," conducting business and plotting schemes. Upstairs was a boarding house that was always full—it reportedly could hold as many as 300 people. On one side of Kenna's barroom stood a table heaped with free food, which his customers consumed appreciatively. The "free lunch" bought a lot of votes in its day. As Prohibition took hold, however, Kenna's famous saloon was shut down and transformed into a combination candy, sandwich, and cigar store.

When an ordinance was passed providing for one alderman per ward in 1923, Kenna agreed to step down and left "Bathhouse John" Coughlin to take care of business. He did, however, retain his title of Democratic ward committeeman, and he continued to wield his power until Coughlin's death in 1938, although in a diminished capacity, for as early as the mid-1920s a violent pall characterized First Ward politics as people like Johnny Torrio and Al Capone began to take over.

With his partner gone, Kenna was persuaded, although he was over eighty, to run for Coughlin's old seat in 1939. Kenna ran and won. For a while he dutifully attended sessions at city hall until, one day, he stopped coming altogether. In his place, he sent his secretary. Kenna retired from active political life in 1943 and spent the last years of his life in seclusion in various downtown hotels. He died at the age of eighty-nine in the Blackstone Hotel.

See also: Mathias "Paddy" Bauler, Al Capone, "Bathhouse John" Coughlin, Ada and Minna Everleigh, Carter Harrison I, Carter Harrison II

Further reading: Herman Kogan and Lloyd Wendt, *Lords of the Levee: The Story of Bathhouse John and Hinky Dink* (1943).

Robert Kennicott

Naturalist

BORN: November 13, 1835
New Orleans, Louisiana

DIED: May 13, 1866
Fort Nulato, Alaska

An early pioneer and naturalist, Robert Kennicott founded the Academy of Sciences.

Born in New Orleans, Robert Kennicott was raised in West Northfield, Northfield Township, now Glenview, Illinois. He was among the first settlers. The Kennicott property included an oak and hickory grove surrounded by mostly tall-grass prairie. Despite having little in the way of formal education—Kennicott was largely self-taught in natural history—at the age of twenty he made a comprehensive survey of southern Illinois for the Illinois Central Railroad, and the following year he helped establish the Academy of Sciences in Chicago. By the time he was twenty-two he established a natural history museum at Northwestern University.

In 1853 Kennicott began collecting and cataloging natural history items for the Smithsonian Institution in Washington, D.C. At that time he began a correspondence with Spencer Fullerton Baird, an ornithologist and assistant secretary at the Smithsonian, and William Stimpson, a scientist and marine biologist, also at the Smithsonian.

In the late 1850s, Kennicott joined the Smithsonian as an explorer and cataloger, traveling through British North America, now Canada, and reaching as far north as Fort Yukon. Later he embarked on an expedition to collect natural history specimens in northwestern Canada in what are now the Mackenzie and Yukon river valleys. On his journeys he also encountered fur traders from the Hudson's Bay Company and encouraged them to collect natural history artifacts to forward to the Smithsonian. In 1862 he returned to Washington, D.C., where he became a member of the Megatherium Club, a group of young naturalists whose founder was William Stimpson.

In 1864 Kennicott became a member of the Western Union Telegraph Expedition, whose purpose was to find a telegraph line between North America and Russia by way of the Bering Sea. He also explored the Alaska territory. His expeditions contributed to the eventual purchase of Alaska by the United States in 1867.

Unfortunately, Kennicott died of a heart attack at Fort Nulato, Alaska, while on the expedition. He was only thirty-one.

The family homestead, the Kennicott house in Glenview, Illinois, still stands, a natural landscape surrounded by the din of street traffic. The 123-acre site at 1421 Milwaukee Avenue, known as The Grove, is a national historic landmark and is owned by the Glenview Park District.

The Robert Kennicott Papers are housed at Northwestern University in Evanston, Illinois.

See also: Donald Culross Peattie

Otto Kerner Jr.

Politician

BORN: August 15, 1908
Chicago, Illinois

DIED: May 9, 1976
Chicago, Illinois

Otto Kerner Jr. was a popular Chicago politician and judge who came from a prominent Chicago family—his father was also a judge. Kerner graduated from Brown University in Rhode Island, studied at Cambridge University in England, and graduated from Northwestern University Law School. After passing the Illinois bar in 1934, he began to practice law in Chicago. During World War II he joined the Illinois National Guard as a private and resigned with the rank of major general after serving in Africa, Sicily, and the Pacific.

In 1947 President Harry S. Truman named Kerner to the position of U.S. attorney for northern Illinois. In 1954 Kerner secured the influential position of county judge of Cook County. In 1960 Kerner was elected governor of Illinois and won reelection to a second term in 1964. He resigned, however, in 1968 to accept an appointment to the U.S. Court of Appeals for the Seventh Circuit.

Kerner's career ended on a somber note when he was sentenced to three years in prison after a 1973 conviction for income-tax evasion and conspiracy stemming from a racetrack stock scandal. He became the first sitting judge of a U.S. court of appeals to be convicted.

Kerner suffered a fatal heart attack in the Edgewater Beach Hotel in 1976, shortly after his release from prison. He was sixty-eight.

Charles H. Kerr

Publisher

BORN: April 23, 1860
LaGrange, Georgia

DIED: June 1, 1944
Los Angeles, California

Charles Hope Kerr published socialist and pro-labor books, novels, magazines, and pamphlets in Chicago, which by the late nineteenth century had earned the reputation as the center of leftist publishing in the English-speaking world. Today the company he founded in 1886 is the oldest pro-labor publishing house in the United States.

Kerr was the son of Congregational liberals. His father, Alexander Kerr, was born in Scotland, immigrated with his family to Illinois in 1838, and eventually found work as a schoolteacher in Georgia. Following the outbreak of the Civil War, the elder Kerr, a dedicated abolitionist, fled with his wife and his infant son, Charles, along the Underground Railroad, a secret network that carried runaway slaves and sympathizers to safety in the North.

Charles Kerr grew up in Rockford, Illinois, and Madison, Wisconsin, where his father was chairman of the classics department at the University of Wisconsin. He graduated from the University of Wisconsin at Madison in 1881 with a degree in Romance languages. He then settled in Chicago.

Kerr began his career as a clerk in the independent publishing firm of James Colegrove, which specialized in Unitarian books and tracts and published *Unity,* a socialist magazine. In 1883 Kerr began working on the magazine. When the Colegrove company dissolved in 1886, Kerr established his own firm, Charles H. Kerr and Company, and took over *Unity.* Growing disillusioned and wanting more control over his life and career, he left the magazine in 1893 to become the publisher of a radical Unitarian magazine, *New Occasions.* In 1894 Kerr published *The Pullman Strike,* Rev. William H. Carwardine's classic inside account of the Pullman strike and its devastating effect on both the neighborhood and the labor movement.

In 1899 Kerr allied himself with the burgeoning socialist movement, joining the Chicago branch of the Socialist Party of America in 1901. Around this time, the Kerr Company began billing itself as a "Socialist Cooperative Publishing House." Kerr helped establish a socialist school, Ruskin College (named after a workingmen's college in Oxford, England) in Glen Ellyn, Illinois. In 1900 Kerr launched a new monthly, the *International Socialist Review.* The *Review,* promised Kerr, sought "to counteract the sentimental Utopianism that has so long characterized the American movement." The concept of utopianism, which took its name from the title of Sir Thomas More's futuristic work *Utopia,* refers to the belief that humankind can learn to live in an ideal state. The *Review* soon became the leading socialist journal in the country. The *Review*'s top-flight contributors included Eugene Debs, Elizabeth Gurley Flynn, Mary Harris "Mother" Jones, folksinger Joe Hill, Helen Keller, John Reed, and its most prominent names, Jack London and Carl Sandburg.

In 1899 Kerr began publishing his "pocket library of socialism," including Clarence Darrow's *Realism in Literature and Art* (1899), Jack London's *The Scab* (1915), and Upton Sinclair's *Our Bourgeois Literature: The Reason and the Remedy* (1905). The company also published the works of Mother Jones, Mary E. Marcy, and William "Big

Bill" Haywood and issued the English-language edition of Karl Marx's *Das Kapital* as well as the writings of Lenin, Trotsky, and Irish labor leader James Connolly. Yet Kerr didn't publish only socialist tracts. The company also released alternative titles, including books on animal rights, the first book in the United States on the Baha'i faith, and a fair number of utopian, science-fiction, and fantasy novels.

Impatient with the methodical and overly cautious tactics of the socialists' agenda, Kerr turned his support to the Industrial Workers of the World, which, like him, vehemently opposed America's participation in World War I. Such so-called treasonous talk prompted the postmaster general to refuse to send the *International Socialist Review* through the mails in adherence to the Espionage Act, which forbade any materials inciting "treason, insurrection, or forcible resistance to any law of the United States." It was censorship at its most effective, and it for all intents and purposes shut down the magazine.

Growing increasingly frustrated with the conservatism of the socialist movement, Kerr left Chicago, and the company he founded, in 1928. That year Scots-born John Keracher, head of the Proletarian Party, assumed control of the company. Kerr retired to Los Angeles, where he died in June 1944 at the age of eighty-four.

In 1986 the Charles H. Kerr Company celebrated its centennial, publishing eleven new titles, including *The Haymarket Scrapbook*. Although one of its owners, the inestimable Franklin Rosemont, died from an aneurism in 2009 at the age of sixty-five, the company continues to reissue old radical classics and publish new works from its headquarters at 1726 West Jarvis Avenue in Rogers Park.

See also: John Peter Altgeld, Clarence Darrow, Eugene Debs, Henry Demarest Lloyd, Lucy and Albert Parsons, Allan Pinkerton, George Pullman, Carl Sandburg

Further reading: Alan Maass, "The Little Red Book House," *Chicago Reader*, October 17, 1986; Dave Roediger and Franklin Rosemont, eds., *Haymarket Scrapbook* (1986); Allen M. Ruff, "Socialist Publishing in Illinois: Charles H. Kerr & Company of Chicago, 1886–1928," *Illinois Historical Journal*, Spring 1986.

Johnny "Red" Kerr

Basketball Player and Broadcaster

BORN: July 17, 1932
Chicago, Illinois

DIED: February 26, 2009
Riverwoods, Illinois

Considered the dean of Bulls basketball, Johnny "Red" Kerr was associated with the Chicago Bulls franchise for nearly forty years as a player, a coach, and a broadcaster. A pioneer of Chicago Bulls basketball, he was the first coach in the team's franchise history. He won the NBA Coach of the Year award for leading the Bulls to the playoffs during their first season in 1966–67.

Kerr was the son of a Scottish immigrant. His father died when Kerr was three; his mother worked for the War Department and later Continental Can. Kerr's first love was soccer—his father was a soccer player. Thus he didn't play basketball at Tilden High School until his senior year when his coach, impressed by his height, persuaded him to join the team. The 6'9" Kerr played center.

At Tilden, Kerr led his basketball team to the 1950 Chicago Public League title. After high school, he attended the University of Illinois where he helped the Fighting Illini win the Big Ten championship and advance to the NCAA Final Four. In 1954 the Syracuse Nationals drafted Kerr. During his first season he helped the team win their first NBA Championship. He was an All-Star three times with the Nationals: in 1956, 1959, and 1963. In 1963 the Nationals moved to Philadelphia and changed their name to the 76ers. Two years later Kerr was traded to the Baltimore Bullets.

Altogether, Kerr played twelve seasons in the NBA: for the Syracuse Nationals, the Philadelphia 76ers, and the Baltimore Bullets. As a player, Kerr held the NBA record for the most consecutive games played—844—a record that was held until Randy Smith broke it in 1983. As head coach of the Bulls Kerr led the team to a record of 62–101.

Kerr returned to Chicago in 1965 when the expansion Chicago Bulls selected him as their first head coach. Under his leadership, the Bulls became the first expansion team to win a playoff spot during its first season. For his efforts, Kerr won the NBA Coach of the Year award in 1966–67. Although they earned another playoff spot the following year, team owner Dick Klein forced Kerr to leave the Bulls and sign with the Phoenix Suns, another expansion team. After his coaching days were over, he returned to Chicago as a broadcaster and became known as the dean of Chicago basketball.

He finished his playing career with more than 10,000 points and over 10,000 rebounds. In sum, he appeared in 905 NBA games. For his achievements as a player, coach, administrator, and broadcaster he received the 2009 John W. Bunn Lifetime Achievement Award from the Naismith Memorial Basketball Hall of Fame.

In addition to basketball, Kerr was president of Kerr Financial Services, an insurance investment company.

Kerr died in late February 2009 at the age of seventy-six after a long battle with prostate cancer. Earlier that month, on February 10, he had attended a retirement ceremony at the United Center held in his honor. The tribute included a taped recording by President Barack Obama. On the day he died, members of the Chicago Bulls were given a tour of the White House by President Obama. A sculpture in Kerr's likeness was erected at the Madison Street concourse of the United Center.

Further reading: Johnny Kerr, *Bull Session* (1989).

John Kinzie

Pioneer

BORN: Circa 1763
Quebec

DIED: January 6, 1828
Chicago, Illinois

At one point called the "Father of Chicago" (Jean Baptiste Point du Sable now holds that distinction), John Kinzie was Chicago's first permanent white settler. A trader by profession, he was a man respected by both his fellow whites and the Indians.

Born in Quebec, Kinzie was the son of John McKenzie (also spelled McKinzie), a British army surgeon. Shortly after Kinzie's birth, his parents moved to Detroit, where his father died. As a young boy, Kinzie ran away and made his way back to Quebec, where he became an apprentice to a silversmith. He roamed the forests and developed a friendly relationship with the Indians, trapping and trading and producing buckles and bracelets. He mastered their language and earned a reputation among them as fair and trustworthy.

Kinzie established business connections in Sandusky and Maumee, Ohio, and as far west as St. Joseph, Michigan, and he later became an Indian trader in Detroit. He arrived in Chicago in 1804 and almost immediately established friendly relations with the native population. Indeed, the Kinzie family became the outpost's leading citizens. Jacqueline Peterson in *Ethnic Chicago* (1984) refers to Kinzie as "unquestionably the most powerful man" in Chicago from 1804 to 1812.

Kinzie sold supplies to the soldiers at Fort Dearborn and bought furs from the Indians, but squabbles among the traders did occur. Kinzie was on bad terms, for example, with the Indian interpreter Jean La Lime. During a confrontation in April 1812, Lalime reportedly shot Kinzie in the shoulder. Kinzie retaliated by fatally stabbing Lalime. One theory is that Lalime attacked Kinzie in a fit of jealousy over the trader's success. Another argued that Kinzie was the aggressor. Whatever the truth, an inquiry was held and Kinzie was acquitted.

On August 9, 1812, instructions from Detroit reached Captain Nathan Heald, the commander at Fort Dearborn, to evacuate the garrison, which had come under threat of a possible Indian attack, and to proceed to Fort Wayne, Indiana. Kinzie argued against evacuation, maintaining that it was safer to remain in the fort rather than risk journeying through hostile Indian territory. Captain William Wells, a noted Indian scout, arrived with twenty-seven Miami Indians as escorts for the journey.

Concerned for his family's safety, Kinzie placed his wife and four children on a boat. He, however, accompanied Captain Wells and the rest of the party headed for Fort Wayne. On August 15, 1812, one of the most tragic episodes in Chicago history occurred. Five hundred Indians—mostly Potawatomi—attacked the procession less than two miles from the fort and near what is now 1600 South Indiana Avenue. Twenty-six soldiers (although some sources say twenty-eight), including Wells, twelve children, and two women were slain.

Theories as to the reason for the attack vary. Historian Allan Eckert argues that the Indians attacked for military purposes. The War of 1812 had just begun, and the Indians were allies of the British; Fort Dearborn was an important, strategically located base and, therefore, an obvious military target.

After the fighting, Kinzie's wife, Eleanor, returned to her house with the children and hid under feather mattresses. When Kinzie returned, unharmed, the Indians threatened to kill him until Billy Caldwell—the half-Potawatomi, half-Irish chief—interceded. After the fighting subsided, Kinzie and his family fled by boat to the safety of Detroit. Kinzie returned to Chicago in 1816 and resumed his Indian business, partly on his own and partly as an employee of the American Fur Company. He never regained his former status, however. He died in Chicago in January 1828 at age sixty-five.

Subsequent generations of Kinzies exerted considerable influence in the city so that by 1832, notes historian

Peterson, "Kinzie was once again the foremost name in Chicago."

Kinzie Street is named in his honor and Marion Court in honor of his daughter, Ellen Marion Kinzie, the first white child born in Chicago.

See also: Gurdon S. Hubbard, Jean Baptiste Point du Sable
Further reading: A. T. Andreas, *History of Chicago from the Earliest Period to the Present Time*, 3 vols. (1884–1886); Josiah Seymour Currey, *The Story of Old Fort Dearborn* (1912); Ulrich Danckers and Jane Meredith, *Early Chicago: A Compendium of the Early History of Chicago to the Year 1835 When the Indians Left* (2000), with John F. Swenson, contributing editor, and a contribution by Helen H. Tanner; Juliette A. Kinzie, *Wau Bun, the "Early Days" of the Northwest* (1901); Jacqueline Peterson, "The Founding Fathers: The Absorption of French-Indian Chicago 1816–1837" in *Ethnic Chicago* (1984), Melvin G. Holli and Peter d'A. Jones, eds.; Bessie Louise Pierce, *A History of Chicago*, 3 vols. (1937–1957); Milo Quaife, *Chicago and the Old Northwest, 1673–1835* (1913, 2001).

Herman Kogan
Journalist and Historian

BORN: November 6, 1914
Chicago, Illinois

DIED: March 8, 1989
New Buffalo, Michigan

Newsman and historian, Herman Kogan was one of Chicago's most prolific—and respected—editors and writers.

Kogan started his journalism career in 1930 as a copy boy with the *Chicago Daily News* and the *Chicago Evening Post*. While still attending the University of Chicago, he worked as a police reporter for the City News Bureau. The *Chicago Tribune* then hired him as a rewrite man and reporter. Kogan also worked for the *Chicago Sun* before enlisting in the Marine Corps. After completing his military duty, he returned to the paper, which by that time had changed its name to the *Chicago Sun-Times*. In 1961 he created and edited the weekend magazine *Panorama* for the *Chicago Daily News*. After serving as general manager of WFLD-TV, he returned to the *Sun-Times,* where he edited the paper's *Book Week* and *Show* sections.

With Lloyd Wendt, Kogan coauthored several classics of Chicago history, including *Lords of the Levee* (1943), a biography of the infamous First Ward aldermen "Bathhouse John" Coughlin and Michael "Hinky Dink" Kenna; *Give the Lady What She Wants* (1952), a history of Marshall Field and Company; and *Big Bill of Chicago* (1953), a biography of Mayor William Hale Thompson. Other books include *A Continuing Marvel* (1973), a history of the Museum of Science and Industry, and *The First Century: The Chicago Bar Association, 1874–1974* (1974).

Generous with his time and talent, Kogan was quick to offer advice and friendly encouragement to other writers. He died of a heart attack while walking near his home in Michigan at the age of seventy-five.

Heinz Kohut
Psychoanalyst

BORN: May 3, 1913
Vienna, Austria

DIED: October 8, 1981
Chicago, Illinois

Heinz Kohut, a longtime professor at the University of Chicago, was one of the twentieth century's most important post-Freudian psychoanalysts and the creator of the seminal theory and practice of self-psychology.

Kohut's theory of self-psychology is the most revolutionary theory since Freud's drive theory in the field of psychoanalysis. Although Kohut's theory complemented Freud's drive theory, which placed sex and aggression as the focus of psychoanalysis, Kohut believed these sexual and aggressive drives were observable and symptomatic only when the Self was in a state of disequilibrium. Thus, Kohut's self-psychology is a deficit theory that is centered on restoring the fragmenting Self to a healthy cohesive state free from chronic anxieties, depression, addictive behaviors, and vulnerabilities to personal slights, rather than emphasizing the taming of the drives. His method introduced the pivotal use of empathy and vicarious introspection as both a means for understanding patients as well as therapeutic tools. Although initially controversial, self-psychology now not only ranks among the leading theories in psychoanalysis internationally but also has infiltrated popular culture; for example, the term "mirroring" was coined by Kohut.

Born and raised in an upper-middle-class Viennese family, Kohut studied classical literature and biology at the Doblinger Gymnasium. He grew up attending opera several times a week and was a keen admirer of literature and painting. As a medical student at the University of Vienna, he became interested in Freud's theories. After graduating in 1938, he underwent psychoanalysis by one of Freud's disciples, August Aichhorn.

When Adolf Hitler took over Austria during World War II, Kohut decided to leave Vienna for England. He stayed there one year before immigrating to the United States in early 1940. He had all of $25 in his pocket and settled in Chicago, where his childhood friend, Siegmund Levarie, lived. He did his residency in neurology and psychiatry at the University of Chicago. From the early to mid-1940s he underwent a painstaking analysis with Ruth Eissler and, in 1946, began coursework at the Chicago Institute for Psychoanalysis. After graduating in 1950, he joined the faculty, lecturing in psychiatry while also working as a psychoanalyst.

Kohut's early practice concentrated largely on neurology and neuropathology. Only later did his interests shift to psychoanalysis. In addition to his books, he published widely in professional journals, including articles on applied psychoanalysis as well as the psychology of music. He was a visiting professor at the University of Cincinnati, president of the American Psychoanalytic Association in 1964, and vice president of the International Psychoanalytic Association from 1965 to 1973.

His analysis of patients who were not responding to traditional psychoanalysis—and therefore not developing the predictable oedipal transferences underlying neurotic disorders—led Kohut to his theory of the Self, and its subsequent treatment. He argued that those suffering from "self disorders"—what he originally called narcissistic personality and behavior disorders with profound deficits in the core of the Self, typically manifested by chronic states of depression, anxiety, and low self-esteem—developed instead "self-object" transferences of childhood yearnings for admiration, validation, or succor, all of which he considered "psychological oxygen." His theory was unprecedented and resulted in massive criticism among colleagues as well as divisiveness within analytic circles. Initially, critics did not consider Kohut's treatment to be psychoanalysis. But over time Kohut's influence transformed the way psychoanalysts thought about narcissism, transferences, aggression, sexual behaviors, and dreams.

Kohut's books include *The Search for the Self* (1978), three volumes of papers predating his groundbreaking work *The Analysis of the Self: A Systematic Analysis of the Treatment of the Narcissistic Personality Disorder* (1971); *The Restoration of the Self* (1977); and *How Does Analysis Cure* (1984): all are now required reading in the field of psychoanalysis.

Other edited volumes of his writings include *Self Psychology and the Humanities* (1985), *The Curve of Life: Correspondence of Heinz Kohut, 1923–1981* (1994), and *Heinz Kohut: The Chicago Institute Lectures* (1996).

In 1971 Kohut received a diagnosis of lymphoma, an illness that he kept a secret except from his family and very close friends. He lingered for many years before dying of congestive heart failure at Billings Hospital in Chicago at the age of sixty-eight.

Kohut always insisted that his theories complemented Freud's; they did not replace them. "I'm very fond of Freud's model," he once said, "but I think the shift in emphasis is an important one."

Further reading: Allen Siegel, *Heinz Kohut and the Psychology of the Self* (1996, Makers of Modern Psychotherapy series); Charles B. Strozier, *Heinz Kohut: The Making of a Psychoanalyst* (2001).

James L. Kraft

Entrepreneur

BORN: December 11, 1874
Fort Erie, Ontario

DIED: February 16, 1953
Chicago, Illinois

James Lewis Kraft, a Canadian immigrant, revolutionized the packaging and merchandising of cheese and cheese products. He experimented until the Kraft Company produced an item that had a longer shelf life, a more uniform flavor, and a taste that appealed to millions of consumers.

The son of Minerva and George Franklin Kraft, Kraft attended school in Ontario, Canada. At age sixteen he left home to earn money for his financially strapped family, peddling eggs in hotels and retail shops across the border in Buffalo, New York. In Buffalo he attended a business class, walking the twelve miles from the school to his home in Ontario. When he was eighteen, Kraft found work at a grocery shop in Fort Erie and saved enough money to establish his own ice business. It collapsed, however. He then invested in a Buffalo cheese company and moved to

Chicago in 1903 to manage the regional branch. When his partners phased him out, Kraft, with only $65 of capital to his name, rented a wagon and a horse named Paddy and bought a supply of cheese from a wholesaler and resold it. By the end of his first year, Kraft was $3,000 in debt. "In those days people didn't care very much for cheese," Kraft said in 1931. "Our national per capita consumption was less than one pound a year. And that was easy to understand for American-made cheese of that day was an uncertain commodity. You bought it in chunks—and no chunk was ever like another." Despite these early difficulties, Kraft continued working as a cheese retailer and the business slowly began to prosper.

In 1909 the business was incorporated as J. L. Kraft and Brothers Company, and in 1911 Kraft became an American citizen. In 1916, Kraft acquired a patent to make a pasteurized processed cheese, a product that could be shipped long distances without spoilage. During World War I, the United States government ordered more than six million tons of Kraft cheese to feed its hungry, war-weary soldiers on the front. The cheese business boomed.

In 1924 the first Kraft test kitchen was established. Four years later, the company merged with the Phenix Cheese Corporation, makers of Philadelphia cream cheese. By the end of 1929, the company owned more than fifty subsidiaries with operations in Canada, Australia, England, and Germany. In 1930 Kraft became a subsidiary of the National Dairy Products Corporation, and Kraft became chairman of the board in 1943. Two years later, the company name became Kraft Foods Company. In 1986 Dart and Kraft, a multinational food, consumer, and commercial products company, split into two companies—Kraft and Premark International, and in 1988 Kraft became a subsidiary of Philip Morris Companies. Kraft produced a diverse line of products. The company introduced Miracle Whip salad dressing in 1933, Kraft macaroni and cheese dinners in 1936, and Parkay margarine in 1937. The company also manufactured caramels, marshmallows, and ice cream toppings.

Kraft used innovative advertising methods to sell his products. He was among the first businessmen to advertise in consumer journals; for example, he was an early promoter of full-color advertisements in national magazines such as *Ladies Home Journal* and *Good Housekeeping*. In 1933 the company entered showbiz when it sponsored a two-hour musical and variety radio program, the *Kraft Musical Revue*, which eventually became *Kraft Music Hall*. In 1948 the *Kraft Television Theatre* premiered on the NBC television network.

A devout Baptist and an active member of the North Shore Baptist Church at 5244 North Lakewood Avenue, Kraft was the president and treasurer of the International Council of Religious Education and chairman of the organization committee of the Council's Crusade for Christian Education. Over the years Kraft accumulated an impressive collection of carved Chinese jade pieces. In the process, he became quite an expert on the subject and wrote a book about it, *Adventure in Jade*, in 1947.

Kraft died at the age of seventy-eight in February 1953.

In 1972 the company moved its corporate offices to northwest suburban Glenview, Illinois, and subsequently to Northfield, Illinois. As of 2009, Kraft Foods, Inc. was the world's second-largest packaged-food company (behind Mars), although it remains the world's largest producer of cookies and crackers—Oreo and Chips Ahoy cookies are among their most durable products. In 2010 Kraft Foods purchased the England-based confectioner Cadbury for $19 billion in cash and stock. As a result of the buyout, Kraft became the world's second largest confectionary operation, after Switzerland-based Nestlé. Kraft's other well-known brands include Oscar Mayer meats and Ritz crackers.

See also: Oscar Mayer, William Wrigley

Further reading: Kenan Heise and Michael Edgerton, *Chicago: Center for Enterprise*, 2 vols. (1982).

Ardis Krainik

Arts Executive

BORN: March 8, 1929
Manitowoc, Wisconsin

DIED: January 18, 1997
Chicago, Illinois

As general director of the Lyric Opera of Chicago, Ardis Krainik rescued the institution from near financial ruin. But she also made international headlines in 1989 when she announced that Luciano Pavarotti was no longer welcome at the Lyric—he had cancelled an appearance in *Tosca* on a mere three weeks' notice. Her swift decision was indicative of both her personality and her management style: resolute, fair-minded, and decisive.

Krainik was the personification of the Lyric Opera. She joined the company, then called the Lyric Theatre, as a singer and as a secretary to its founder, Carol Fox, during its first season in 1954 and spent her entire career there. A mezzo-soprano, she sang small parts during her first five years at the Lyric, but by the time she became assistant manager in 1960 she set aside her singing career altogether. Later she advanced to the position of artistic administrator. When Fox resigned in 1981, Krainik took over. At the time the company was on the edge of financial ruin. Endowments had dried up and cost overruns on overly ambitious productions had taken their monetary toll, leaving the company with a hefty $1.2 million deficit. In response, she restructured the company's operations and cut $500,000 from its budget. She also cut back on orchestra rehearsals, began to recycle products, and borrowed stage sets instead of designing them. In other words, she cut to the bare essentials.

It paid off. By 1993 Krainik raised the money needed for a $100 million project to purchase and restore the Civic Opera House. Artistically, she made a firm commitment to modern opera, announcing "Toward the 21st Century," a decade-long series that included two twentieth-century operas every season (one by an American composer, one by a European composer) as well as newly commissioned works. Among the works presented were William Bolcom's *McTeague,* Bruce Saylor's *Orpheus Descending,* and Shulamit Ran's *Between Two Worlds,* as well as Samuel Barber's *Antony and Cleopatra,* John Corigliano's *Ghosts of Versailles,* and Carlisle Floyd's *Susannah.*

As general director, Krainik usually presented seven productions each season, from Handel through Wagner's entire *Ring* cycle. She hired fashionable directors and designers, including David Hockney for Puccini's *Turandot,* Robert Wilson for Gluck's *Alceste,* and Peter Sellars for Wagner's *Tannhauser.* Among the singers who performed during her tenure were Maria Callas, Marilyn Horne, Placido Domingo, Jessye Norman, Kiri Te Kanawa, Samuel Ramey, and Renée Fleming.

Krainik died in her Lake Shore Drive home in January 1997 at the age of sixty-seven.

In 1996 the main auditorium of the Civic Opera House was renamed the Ardis Krainik Theatre in honor of her service.

Ray Kroc

Entrepreneur

BORN: October 5, 1902
Chicago, Illinois

DIED: January 14, 1984
La Jolla, California

Ray Albert Kroc, a high school dropout and former paper cup salesman, sold billions of hamburgers in more than thirty countries during his lifetime and, in so doing, helped change the eating habits of the American public. "McDonald's is not a restaurant. It's a hamburger business. It's a religion," he used to say. The secret of success, suggested Kroc, is not intelligence, education, or even talent, but self-discipline. Oak Brook, Illinois–based McDonald's, the world's largest restaurant chain, now operates more than 31,000 outlets in 119 countries.

Kroc always considered himself a regular guy. "I've never liked codfish aristocrats or society," he said. Once described as the service sector's equivalent of Henry Ford, Kroc was the son of a real estate agent. He dropped out of Oak Park–River Forest High School when he was fifteen

and served with the Red Cross Ambulance Corps in France during World War I. Fellow Chicagoan and friend Walt Disney was in the same unit.

A music lover, Kroc spent a brief time playing jazz piano professionally. When he was nineteen, he joined the vaudeville circuit with his partner, Harry Sosnick. It was a short-lived but lucrative relationship, bringing in $150 a week. At the age of twenty, Kroc turned away from the arts, married, and got a respectable job selling paper cups. It didn't last long. He soon quit and got a job as musical director of Chicago radio station WGES. He then moved to Florida to sell real estate and lost everything. "I was stone broke. I didn't have an overcoat, a topcoat, or a pair of gloves," he recalled. In 1926 Kroc returned to Chicago and went back to selling cups for the Lily Tulip Cup Company.

By the late 1930s, Kroc had become the sole distributor of a soda fountain machine, called the Multimixer, which was able to mix five milkshakes simultaneously. A short-order restaurant in San Bernardino, California, owned by Dick and Mac McDonald, had purchased eight of Kroc's machines—an unusually high number, Kroc thought. Curious about this, Kroc decided to visit the restaurant himself. He was impressed with what he saw. "They had people standing in line, clamoring for more," he recalled. Kroc tried to talk the brothers into opening a chain of hamburger stands so he could supply them with his milkshake makers. They balked at the suggestion but agreed to allow Kroc to franchise the restaurant and their small chain of hamburger stands for 0.5 percent of the gross.

On April 15, 1955, Kroc opened the first McDonald's franchise at 400 Lee Street in Des Plaines, Illinois. It was a tiny red-and-white tiled building without seats or bathrooms. In those days hamburgers sold for fifteen cents each and an order of French fries was ten cents. Six years later, in 1961, Kroc founded the McDonald's Corporation and bought out the McDonald brothers for $2.7 million. The first year the company grossed $6 million. By 1969 it had leapfrogged to $266 million. In 1961 Hamburger University, the McDonald's training school, opened in Elk Grove Village, Illinois (it is now in Oak Brook); fourteen students graduated in its first class. Since then, more than 5,000 students attend the "university" each year.

Kroc's populist policies made the McDonald's Corporation one of the most progressive businesses in the country. His door, he insisted, was always open. "He liked being treated like one of the boys," said Fred Turner, a McDonald's corporate executive and the founder of Hamburger University.

McDonald's changed the leisure habits of the average American by making eating out inexpensive, fast, and enjoyable. Kroc did not invent the fast-food business—there were other fast-food franchises already in existence in the mid-1950s such as Burger King, Kentucky Fried Chicken, and Chicken Delight—but McDonald's dominated the industry to such an extent that the "Golden Arches" has become an integral part of American popular culture. "Slightly more than half of the U.S. population lives within a three-minute drive to a McDonald's unit," John F. Love wrote in his book *McDonald's Behind the Arches* (1986). By insisting upon uniform standards of cleanliness, quality, and quick service, Kroc revolutionized the food industry. With few exceptions, a McDonald's restaurant in Portland, Maine, is virtually indistinguishable from a McDonald's restaurant in Portland, Oregon.

In 1974 Kroc bought the San Diego Padres, after his attempt to buy his favorite baseball team, the Chicago Cubs, failed. Kroc was a controversial owner. Tempestuous and hot-tempered, he scolded his players over the public address system on opening day of his first home game for "putting on a lousy show . . . (with) the most stupid baseball playing I've ever seen." He later apologized. In 1976 Kroc bought the San Diego Mariners hockey team but sold them one year later.

Kroc donated generously to charities through the Kroc Foundation. He received the Horatio Alger Award in 1972. One of the charitable programs that Kroc helped found is the Ronald McDonald House, which provides free or low-cost lodging near hospitals for families with children requiring extended care. The first Ronald McDonald House opened in Philadelphia in 1974. There are two in Chicago—622 West Deming Place on the North Side, which opened in 1977, and 5736 South Drexel Avenue on the South Side, which opened in 1986. As of 2007, there were 271 Ronald McDonald Houses in 31 countries.

Since the early 1970s McDonald's has successfully exported its brand of Americana overseas, with thousands of "Golden Arches" operating in countries around the world.

Kroc died in his La Jolla, California, home at the age of eighty-one in 1984. Only seven weeks after his death, the original McDonald's at 400 North Lee Street in Des Plaines—too small to accommodate seating or the requisite drive-through window—closed. It is now a museum (open for limited hours only during the summer months). A new and bigger McDonald's was built directly across the street.

"I can tell you I have never worked a day in my life," Kroc said in 1973. "Work is something you hate to do. To do what you love is not work."

Further reading: Ray Kroc with Robert Anderson, *Grinding It Out: The Making of McDonald's* (1977).

Gene Krupa
Musician

BORN: June 15, 1909
Chicago, Illinois

DIED: October 16, 1973
Yonkers, New York

A pioneering jazz drummer, Gene Krupa epitomized the Chicago style of jazz with his relentless beat and showy stage personality. Krupa's frenetic drumming never failed to stir the audience.

Of German and Polish ancestry, Krupa grew up on Chicago's South Side around 88th Street and Commercial Avenue. One night in 1925 his older sister took him to meet drummer Roy C. Knapp, a studio musician and highly respected music teacher, at the Capitol Theater at 7941 South Halsted Street. Krupa wanted to learn timpani "but I talked him into studying drums," recalled Knapp years later. Krupa studied with Knapp for several years.

"Chicago was a real training ground," Krupa noted. "Great drummers like Baby Dodds, George Wettling, Zutty Singleton, Tubby Hall, and Davey Tough were playing all around at clubs like the Sunset or the Grand Terrace or Kelly's Stables." Krupa was particularly influenced by Dave Tough. Krupa was asked to join the legendary Austin High Gang (a group of jazz musicians who attended Austin High School on the West Side and modeled their intense style of playing after Louis Armstrong and Joe "King" Oliver) even though he attended a different school, Bowen High on the South Side.

In December 1927, Krupa, along with Frank Teschemacher, Jimmy McPartland, Bud Freeman, Joe Sullivan, Jim Lannigan, and Eddie Condon, recorded four tunes—"Liza," "Nobody's Sweetheart," "China Boy," and "Sugar"—that are considered the epitome of what came to be called the Chicago style of jazz, an energetic, highly rhythmic music that, in the jargon of the day, could really "swing."

In 1929 Krupa moved to New York to work with trumpet player and bandleader Red Nichols and then began to gig and record with the likes of Benny Goodman and Bix Beiderbecke. In 1936 Krupa appeared with Goodman, pianist Teddy Wilson, and vibraphonist Lionel Hampton at the Congress Hotel in what is considered the first performance by a racially integrated group in a downtown Chicago hotel. "We didn't worry about what would happen," Krupa confided to jazz critic Harriet Choice in 1973. "A guy was either a good musician or a bad one, and we just got out there and played." Krupa formed his own outfit in 1938. Backed by singer Anita O'Day and trumpeter Roy Eldridge, Krupa's group became one of the most popular swing bands of its day.

In 1943 Krupa was arrested and sentenced to ninety days in San Quentin prison for contributing to the delinquency of a minor. Accounts of the episode vary. According to newspaper reports, Krupa had sent his valet, still a minor, to fetch his marijuana cigarettes. Another account asserts that Krupa, tipped off by a friend of an imminent police search, warned his valet to dispose of any marijuana. Instead the valet retained possession of what he had found. Others say it was a setup; that Krupa had refused to pay off crooked cops. Whatever the exact circumstances, the incident damaged Krupa's career, soiled his reputation among his fans, and caused severe financial strain. Benny Goodman extended his full support, and Krupa, uncertain of the long-term effect of the episode on his career, accepted Goodman's gracious offer to rejoin the band. After touring with Goodman and later with Tommy Dorsey's orchestra, Krupa formed his own big band in 1944. He led several combos sporadically throughout the 1950s. In 1960 Krupa suffered a heart attack but continued to play throughout the 1960s and early 1970s. In 1959 a Hollywood film was made of his life, *The Gene Krupa Story*, starring Sal Mineo in the title role.

To borrow a jazz term, Krupa was a "hot" drummer. Krupa's aggressive style evolved from the music of New Orleans marching bands, especially the drumming of Zutty Singleton and Warren "Baby" Dodds, musicians who had moved to Chicago and played in South Side clubs. Music historian Donald Clarke calls him the "original model" of today's rock drummer. Krupa's hair-flying, arms-flailing, gum-chewing performances made a tremendous impact on audiences. Some critics felt that his showy style—booming bass and noisy snares—was too overbearing and complained that his loud and frenzied drumming tended to drown out other instruments. He is credited, however, with focusing public attention on the drum as a solo instrument. Benny Goodman himself once called Krupa "without doubt" his favorite drummer.

Krupa died from leukemia in 1973 at the age of sixty-four. Several days after his death his body was flown back to Chicago where a High Mass was held at the Immaculate Conception Church, 2944 East 88th Street, in his old neighborhood. He was buried at the family plot in Holy Cross Cemetery in Calumet City, Illinois.

See also: Bud Freeman, Benny Goodman

Further reading: Samuel B. Charters and Leonard Kunstadt, *Jazz: A History of the New York Scene* (1981); Donald Clarke, *The Penguin Encyclopedia of Popular Music* (1989); James Lincoln Collier, *Benny Goodman and the Swing Era* (1989).

Irv Kupcinet

Newspaper Columnist

BORN: July 31, 1912
Chicago, Illinois

DIED: November 10, 2003
Chicago, Illinois

Known to everyone as Kup, Irv Kupcinet was as famous, and often more so, than the people he covered in his daily column. He was the last of a breed and a contemporary of such legendary columnists as Walter Winchell and Hedda Hopper. More than just a gossip columnist, he was an institution in his own right and a longtime chronicler of Chicago's nightlife. Indeed, his column was the longest-running newspaper column written by the same writer in the United States, a relic of a time when celebrities and politicians passed through Chicago, usually by train, on the way to New York or Los Angeles. He was a friend to one and all and treated everyone he met with kindness and courtesy, whether president of the United States or busboy.

Born in 1912, Irving Kupcinet was the son of Max Kupcinet, a truck driver for a bakery, and Olga, the youngest of four children of Russian immigrants. He grew up in the predominantly Jewish North Lawndale neighborhood and lived in a small apartment at 16th Street and Kedzie Avenue over a grocery store. He attended Harrison High School where he played football. But once he took a journalism class, he was hooked. He edited the school paper and was president of his senior class. Still, his athletic prowess earned him a football scholarship to Northwestern University. After a short time there he transferred to the University of North Dakota at Grand Forks, where he played on an all-star college football team with the future president Gerald Ford.

After college Kupcinet was drafted as a reserve player for the Philadelphia Eagles but left after suffering a shoulder injury. Returning to his journalism background, he found work in 1935, initially as a reporter, at the *Chicago Times* at $32.50 a week. This led to his stint as a sports columnist; his column always ended with a short "people" section. By then the paper had decided it wanted a gossip column and "Kup's Column" was born. His column started at the *Chicago Times* on January 18, 1943. Five years later that paper merged with the *Chicago Sun* to become the *Chicago Sun-Times*. It would remain Kupcinet's newspaper home until the day he died in 2003.

Although Kupcinet loved celebrities, he was neither jaded nor a pushover. He seemed to know everyone as he table-hopped, barhopped, and generally hobnobbed at such now long-defunct clubs as Chez Paree, the London House, the Black Orchid, Club Alabam, and Fritzel's with the likes of Frank Sinatra, Ava Gardner, and Bob Hope. The place where he was most at home was Booth One, his table at the Pump Room in the Ambassador East Hotel. At the Pump

Room waiters wore tuxedos and offered all kinds of food wagons: pastry wagons, roast wagons, cheese wagons, fruit wagons. Kup, usually accompanied by his wife, Essee, held center court at Booth One for so many years that his presence there became as much a part of the hotel as the actual staff members. Guests included Elizabeth Taylor, Janet Leigh and Tony Curtis, Jane Wyman and Ronald Reagan, Robert Wagner and Natalie Wood, Salvador Dalí (who drew a picture on the tablecloth), and a drunken John Barrymore as well as Humphrey Bogart and Lauren Bacall, Paul Newman, Marilyn Monroe, Mickey Rooney, Jack Benny, Mel Brooks, Richard Pryor, and Warren Beatty. Sonny Bono was the first man in Pump Room history allowed to take off his sport coat at Booth One, while John Belushi, living up to his Everyman image, ate caviar with his fingers.

Kupcinet wrote six columns a week of approximately 1,000 words each. He always thought of himself as a reporter first. Despite his fame, he was serious about his role as a journalist. He cultivated sources everywhere, from publicity agents, head waiters, and cabbies to lawyers and even gangsters. Among his more unusual sources was someone who went by the name of "Ivan Bunny." Bunny was in fact two brothers, Jimmy and Ivan Colitz. The eponymous Ivan was an auto parts supervisor. Kup worked the telephone, double-checking every detail and following up on every lead. He prided himself on his scoops, of which there were many. He was the first to report President Harry S. Truman's decision not to run in 1952. And even as late as the 1990s it was Kup who got the scoop that Michael Jordan was retiring (the first time around).

Kupcinet's career was not confined to the newspaper industry. In 1953, he began broadcasting Chicago Bears football games on the radio with Jack Brickhouse, a position that he held for twenty-four years, providing the color commentary. Kupcinet was also a pioneering talk show host. He started in the early 1950s on a WGN-TV variety show; then, until 1957, he was on a late night news and interview show on WBBM before becoming the Chicago anchor for NBC's *America After Dark,* a precursor to *The Tonight Show.* In 1959 he was the host of *At Random* on WBBM until it moved to WMAQ, then WLS, and finally to WTTW. Through his show he met popes, presidents, comedians, and actors. The program later changed its name to *Kup's Show. Kup's Show,* which ended its long run in 1986, featured "the art of lively conversation," as Kupcinet put it. At its peak, *Kup's Show* was syndicated to seventy stations around the country.

Taking advantage of his fame, Kupcinet made cameo appearances in two movies, *Anatomy of a Murder* in 1959 and *Advise and Consent* in 1962. He lived with his family in a nine-room apartment at 442 West Wellington Avenue. Later, in the late 1960s, he and his wife moved into the Carlyle, at 1040 North Lake Shore Drive.

During the later years his column was written by his longtime assistant, Stella Foster, and appeared twice a week. His wife of sixty-two years, Essee Kupcinet, died in 2001.

In 1982 he was elected to Chicago's Journalism Hall of Fame. In 1986 the Wabash Avenue Bridge was renamed the Irv Kupcinet Bridge, and there is even a salad named in his honor, the Irv Kupcinet chicken chopped salad, at Petterino's at the corner of Dearborn and Randolph. The restaurant itself is an homage to Kup's era and is named after Arturo Petterino, the longtime maître d' of the Pump Room.

Kupcinet died at the age of ninety-one in November 2003 from respiratory complications with pneumonia at Northwestern Memorial Hospital. His last column ran a few days before. Always a snappy dresser, he was buried in a Pucci navy-blue pinstripe suit.

Further reading: Carol Felsenthal, "The Lost World of Kup," *Chicago Magazine*, June 2004; Rick Kogan, *Sabers & Suites: The Story of Chicago's Ambassador East* (1983); Irv Kupcinet, *Kup: A Man, an Era, a City* (1988).

Ann Landers

Advice Columnist

BORN: July 4, 1918
Sioux City, Iowa

DIED: June 22, 2002
Chicago, Illinois

*Forty lashes with a
wet noodle.*

—Ann Landers

Born Esther Pauline Friedman, she became known around the world as Ann Landers, the wise and wisecracking advice columnist who transformed herself into a national institution and a cultural icon. Her opinion made an impact, leading to legislation, conversation, and occasionally even changing social habits.

Landers grew up as Eppie Friedman in Sioux City, Iowa, with her twin sister, Pauline Esther, or Popo, as she was known. They were born seventeen minutes apart. Their father, Abraham Friedman, was a Russian Jewish immigrant who sold chickens from a wagon when he first came to the United States but eventually owned movie theaters and burlesque houses.

The twins were exceedingly close growing up. They shared the same interests, attended the same high school, and enrolled at—and dropped out of—the same college (Morningside College in Sioux City). They even had a double wedding in a Sioux City synagogue on July 2, 1938, complete with matching gowns and veils and a double honeymoon spent at the Edgewater Beach Hotel. Eppie dropped out of college to marry Jules W. Lederer, a chain-smoking workaholic hat salesman from Detroit who later created Budget Rent-a-Car. The couple lived in New Orleans for a time before moving to Eau Claire, Wisconsin, where she became active in Democratic politics and even won the county party chairmanship. By then, she had already made influential contacts. She also had a knack for being in the right place at the right time.

The couple moved to Chicago in 1954, settling into an apartment at 1000 North Lake Shore Drive. In a prophetic gesture, she contacted an executive friend at the *Chicago Sun-Times* and volunteered to help sort the letters for the paper's advice columnist, "Ann Landers." As it turned out, they were searching for a replacement since the original "Ann Landers"—Ruth Crowley, a registered nurse—had recently passed away. (Crowley had used the name of a friend, Fran Landers, as her pseudonym.) Twenty-seven candidates vied for the job; they were all given the same sample letters to reply to but, unlike her competition, Eppie drew on the advice of real experts for her answers.

The persona that Eppie adopted—that of the plainspoken, blunt, and witty confidante—was an expression of her own larger-than-life personality. When Eppie Lederer became the new Ann Landers, the column had already existed for a dozen years. But it didn't take her long to put her own indelible stamp on it.

Landers offered hard-nosed, incisive, down-to-earth, and witty advice, giving her opinions and words of wisdom to millions of readers on everything from acne to alcoholism to AIDS. She drew on experts from all fields in her column. As always, her identical twin sister was in competition with her. She wrote her own advice column, initially in the *San Francisco Chronicle*, and called herself Abigail Van Buren or "Dear Abby."

Landers's first column appeared on October 16, 1955, in the *Chicago Sun-Times*. She remained at the *Sun-Times* until March 1987 when she moved to the *Chicago Tribune*. By 1993, the apex of her career, Landers was the world's most widely syndicated—and read—columnist. Her column appeared in more than 1,200 newspapers around the globe with some ninety million daily readers. She was among the country's most influential women, adviser to popes and presidents as well as ordinary men and women. Her friends included the rich and mighty: Walter Cronkite, Barbara Walters, Kirk Douglas, Helen Hayes, and Roger Ebert, while presidents from Ronald Reagan to Bill Clinton consulted her.

Landers lived in a fourteen-room, 5,599-square foot co-op at 209 East Lake Shore Drive, with its unobstructed views of Lake Michigan. Eventually she did most of her work from home. Her driver would pick up the letters at the paper, drop them off, and she would read them, often, and most famously, in the bathtub: she once said she could read through 800 letters during two hours in the tub. She would then send the completed columns, which she wrote on her IBM Selectric typewriter, back with her driver. "A fax machine was as high tech as Eppie ever got; she never used a computer or a cell phone," writes journalist Carol Felsenthal. Her preferred working hours typically were from 11 P.M. or midnight until 3:30 or 4 A.M. "She would seldom wake before 11," notes Felsenthal.

Landers was not afraid to address controversial issues such as homosexuality or AIDS but occasionally she had to explain her own behavior to her readership, such as when she admitted in 1982 that she had recycled old material in her columns or when she called Pope John Paul II a "Polack." But the biggest embarrassment occurred in 1975, when her husband left her for another woman. She admitted in her column that she was getting a divorce—and received some 30,000 sympathetic letters in response.

Landers died at the age of eighty-three of multiple myeloma, a cancer of the bone marrow, on a Saturday afternoon in her master bedroom with her hired caretaker, Carolina Miranda, by her side.

In 2005 David Rambo's one-woman play based on Landers, *The Lady with All the Answers,* premiered at the Old Globe Theatre in San Diego. Three years later it made its Chicago-area premiere at the Northlight Theatre in Skokie. The production was revived in 2008 at the Pasadena Playhouse and the following year, in 2009, it ran at the Cherry Lane Theatre in Greenwich Village with Judith Ivey in the title role.

Further reading: Carol Felsenthal, "Dear Ann," *Chicago Magazine,* February 2003; Rick Kogan, *America's Mom: The Life, Lessons, and Legacy of Ann Landers* (2005).

Kenesaw Mountain Landis

Judge and Baseball Commissioner

BORN: November 20, 1866
Millville, Ohio

DIED: November 25, 1944
Chicago, Illinois

Some thought he was baseball's worst commissioner, others thought he was the best. Whatever the opinion, Judge Kenesaw Mountain Landis couldn't be ignored. Baseball commissioner from 1921 until his death in 1944, Landis was called a bully, a buffoon, a flamboyant publicity seeker, and a man in love with his own name and reputation. No one could deny, however, that he was baseball's greatest fan.

Landis was born of Swiss and German ancestry on an Ohio farm. His father, Dr. Abraham Landis, had served as a surgeon in the Union army and named his newborn son after the Battle of Kennesaw Mountain (the second "n" was dropped in his son's name), which took place in northwestern Georgia on June 27, 1864. The family moved to Indiana when Landis was eight. As a young man he got a job on a local newspaper and also played amateur and semipro baseball. A self-starter intrigued by the legal profession, he taught himself the new art of shorthand and secured a position as an official court reporter for the Cass County Circuit Court. He enrolled in the YMCA Law School of Cincinnati, completed his degree at the Union Law School in Chicago in 1891, and was admitted to the Illinois bar in the same year. The eager lawyer opened his own practice shortly thereafter. Landis received a big career boost in 1892 when he was chosen as secretary to Judge Walter Q. Gresham, then secretary of state in the administration of President Grover Cleveland. He returned to Chicago after Gresham died in 1895 and resumed his law practice.

Landis always expressed an interest in politics. He managed the unsuccessful gubernatorial campaign of Frank O. Lowden in 1904. Even though Lowden didn't win, Landis's work attracted the attention of Theodore Roosevelt. In 1905 Roosevelt appointed the thirty-eight-year-old Landis to the United States District Court for the Northern District of Illinois. As a judge, Landis often stood squarely on the side

of conservatism—albeit a conservatism tempered with his own idiosyncratic streaks of defiance. He advocated firing squads for German spies caught in America. He sentenced Wobblie (a nickname for Industrial Workers of the World, the influential labor organization founded in Chicago in 1905) William "Big Bill" Haywood to twenty years in prison for condemning the nation's war effort during World War I, but then he angered the business community by fining the Standard Oil Company a whopping $29,240,000 in 1907 for violations in a freight-rebate case. The Supreme Court later reversed this decision.

Landis earned a reputation as an outspoken magistrate whose outrageous behavior on the bench raised eyebrows among the more sedate members of the profession. He blurted out whatever came into his head. Indeed, his courtroom etiquette was far from what was considered proper. When an elderly offender protested that his sentence was too severe by saying, "I'm a sick man. I can't do five years," Landis, with little sympathy, rebutted, "Well, you can try, can't you?"

The shocking circumstances surrounding baseball's 1919 Black Sox Scandal resulted in efforts to "clean up" the game and renew public confidence in the national sport. Landis was elected baseball's first commissioner in 1920—he took office in 1921—to serve a period of seven years. He refused to relinquish his judgeship, but when threatened with impeachment for holding both the position of federal judge and the position of baseball commissioner, he resigned from the bench.

From the start, Landis was a controversial figure. He banned the eight White Sox players associated with the Black Sox Scandal from baseball, even though they had been acquitted in a court of law. "Regardless of the verdict of juries, no player that throws a ball game . . . will ever play professional baseball!" declared an angry Landis. He made many enemies and received many threats, but he remained fearless. "I have no yellow streak," he boasted. Throughout his tenure, though, he remained a devout baseball fan. Two days before the 1944 World Series, Landis entered St. Luke's Hospital for a general checkup. He was too ill to attend the games, the first World Series he had missed since taking office in 1921. A little more than a week after he was reelected to his final seven-year term, Landis died.

See also: Charles A. Comiskey
Further reading: J. G. Taylor Spink, *Judge Landis and Twenty-Five Years of Baseball* (1947).

Ring Lardner
Humorist and Journalist

BORN: March 6, 1885
Niles, Michigan

DIED: September 25, 1933
East Hampton, New York

A prolific sportswriter, Ringgold Wilmer Lardner wrote darkly sardonic stories in the American vernacular. He had a good ear for the way people talked as well. He usually composed in the first person and adopted the idiom of the common folk, accurately reflecting the dialect of everyday speech. His baseball stories won him a national following and along with George Ade and Finley Peter Dunne, he ranks as one of Chicago's great humorists.

Lardner received a wealthy upbringing in Niles, Michigan, five miles north of the Indiana border. After graduating from high school, Ring (he never went by Ringgold) held a series of inconsequential jobs. His father, concerned that young Lardner would become an incorrigible roustabout, sent him off to the Armour Institute of Technology in Chicago to study mechanical engineering.

Lardner displayed no talent for nor had any interest in engineering, and he returned to Niles in 1905, landing a job as a sportswriter for the *South Bend Times*. Lardner covered baseball during its infancy, when the game wasn't very respectable, populated as it was, claims biographer Jonathan Yardley, by crude, unsophisticated men who drank too much but had the good fortune to be able to throw, catch, or hit a ball. To Lardner and thousands of other young men and boys of his generation—as Yardley points out, there were very few women in the ballpark stands in those days—the players were heroes just the same.

When Lardner entered journalism, sportswriting was a dull, usually anonymous occupation (he received no byline during his early years with the *South Bend Times*). He injected life into the characters and portrayed the game he loved so dearly as "clean, honorable, ordered, subtle, intricate, beautiful, somehow natural," according to Yardley. Lardner's peripatetic career in journalism included many stops in many towns on many papers. He worked briefly in Chicago for the *Inter-Ocean* and the *Chicago Examiner* before coming to the *Chicago Tribune* in 1909. In December 1910, he joined *Sporting News* in St. Louis as editor, then jumped to the *Boston American* as baseball correspondent in February 1911 before returning to Chicago and accepting a desk job on the *Chicago American*. He became a baseball reporter for the *Chicago Examiner* in 1912, and finally, from 1913 to 1919, he wrote the sports column for the *Chicago Tribune*, "In the Wake of the News," that made him famous.

Lardner was only twenty-eight when he took over "In the Wake of the News" from the late Hugh E. Keough. It was a popular feature of the paper, and Lardner did his best to live up to his predecessor's high standards. During the first four years, he turned out a column seven days a week. In 1914 a series of letters from "Jack Keefe," a fictitious pitcher for the Chicago White Sox, was published in the *Saturday Evening Post*. The series later appeared in *You Know Me, Al* in 1916. The book was so popular that Lardner followed it up with more collections, *Treat 'Em Rough* in 1918 and *The Real Dope* in 1919.

Disillusioned with baseball after the Black Sox Scandal of 1919, Lardner wrote a devilishly wicked parody of the song "I'm Forever Blowing Bubbles":

> *I'm forever throwing ball games*
> *Pretty ball games in the air*
> *I come from Chi*
> *I hardly try—*
> *Just go to bat and fade and die.*

In 1919 Lardner left the *Tribune* and moved to the East Coast, settling in Greenwich, Connecticut. He began writing the nationally syndicated "Ring Lardner's Weekly Letter." He enjoyed tremendous freedom to write about whatever he wanted—his family, his travels, life among the rich and famous, politics—but he almost never wrote about sports. In 1922, however, he agreed to work on a comic-strip version of *You Know Me, Al* for the Bell Syndicate in New York. Even after moving to New York, Lardner often wrote variations of the Chicago characters and situations that had made him famous. Instead of satirizing big city mores, however, he mocked the hypocrisy of small-town America.

In 1928, Lardner wrote a four-times-a-week column for the *New York Morning Telegraph* called "Ring's Side." By this time, though, he was physically and psychologically spent, and the heavy drinking he had done most of his life was beginning to show. The magic was gone and the strain proved too much. Even so, in 1931 Lardner accepted another offer, this time from the Bell Syndicate and the Chicago Tribune–New York Daily News Syndicate, to write a one hundred-word essay six times a week, "Night Letter from Ring Lardner," for the then princely sum of $750 per week. The first installment appeared February 1, 1931, and the last one, not quite three months later, on April 24. His last major writing assignment was as a radio critic for the *New Yorker*. For many years, Lardner had alternated between heavy drinking and abstinence. His health declined. He contracted tuberculosis and on September 25, 1933, he suffered a fatal heart attack at the age of forty-eight.

Lardner's best-known short story is "Champion," about an ambitious boxer who alienates his family and friends on his way to the top. The movie *Champion* appeared in 1949, starring Kirk Douglas as boxer Midge Kelly. Lardner's other works of fiction include *Gullible's Travels* (1917), *Own Your Own Home* (1919), *The Big Town* (1921), *How To Write Short Stories* (1924), *What of It?* (1925), and *The Love Nest and Other Stories* (1926). He collaborated with George M. Cohan on the play *Elmer the Great* (1928) and with George S. Kaufman on the play *June Moon* (1929).

The independent filmmaker, novelist, and short story writer John Sayles portrayed Lardner in his 1988 film about the Black Sox Scandal, *Eight Men Out*.

See also: George Ade, Finley Peter Dunne
Further reading: Jerry DeMuth, *Small Town Chicago: The Comic Perspective of Finley Peter Dunne, George Ade, Ring Lardner* (1980); Donald Elder, *Ring Lardner* (1956); Ring Lardner, *The Best Short Stories of Ring Lardner* (1988); Jonathan Yardley, *Ring: A Biography of Ring Lardner* (1977).

Victor Lawson

Publisher

BORN: September 9, 1850
Chicago, Illinois

DIED: August 19, 1925
Chicago, Illinois

Victor Fremont Lawson helped establish the *Chicago Daily News* with Melville E. Stone and was president of the Associated Press. Under Lawson's leadership, the *Daily News* became the most prominent evening newspaper in the United States.

Lawson was the son of a frugal Norwegian immigrant, Iver Larson Bo, who joined the Norwegian community that had settled in the Fox River Valley of Illinois and changed his name to Lawson. Iver Lawson soon moved to Chicago, opened a small clothing store, and began investing in real estate.

Victor Lawson was born in his parents' home on Superior Street on September 9, 1850. His first job was in the circulation department of the *Chicago Journal*. He attended Phillips Academy in Andover, Massachusetts, and then enrolled at Harvard University. Although a hardworking and bright student, Lawson suffered from poor eyesight and ill health. Several trips to Minnesota for hunting and fishing improved his condition tremendously.

In 1866 Iver Lawson and a fellow Norwegian, John Anderson, founded the *Skandinaven* newspaper. When his father died, Victor Lawson returned to Chicago and became the publisher of the paper—the only daily newspaper in the Norwegian language in the United States.

In 1876 Lawson purchased shares in the *Chicago Daily News,* which was struggling financially at the time, and helped Melville Stone and the staff regain their footing. Lawson assumed the title of publisher in August 1876 and teamed up with Stone: Stone handled the editorial chores while Lawson took care of business matters. The *Daily News,* promised Stone, would carry "pure news only." By the end of the 1870s, the *Daily News* had established itself as the leading newspaper in the city and remained so until the turn of the century. The list of illustrious names who worked under Lawson and Stone was considerable, including Eugene Field, Ben Hecht, George Ade, John T. McCutcheon, and James Weber Linn.

Lawson was notoriously tight when it came to paying his reporters but could also be extremely generous, as when he offered free lectures and language courses to immigrants and sponsored special health-care programs for the city's poor children. Children held a special place in his heart. He built a "Newsboys' Hall" overlooking Calhoun Place, on Wells Street near Madison and Washington Streets, which contained a stage, a clubroom, a gymnasium, a restaurant, and a drill hall where the members of the *Daily News* Newsboys' Band practiced. Among the street urchins who got their start hawking Lawson's paper were Michael "Hinky Dink" Kenna and James C. Petrillo of the Musicians Union.

Lawson was a pioneer in many ways. He was the first publisher to print a paper's circulation figures. He introduced the idea of using children as news hawkers, a policy that reformers eventually campaigned against. Lawson's was the first paper to run full-page ads, the first to utilize the new Mergenthaler linotype machine, and the first to publish a daily newspaper column in the country—Eugene Field's "Sharps and Flats."

A deeply religious man, Lawson forbade liquor advertisements in the paper, yet he employed staffers who were known to partake of the bottle frequently. Hiring competent reporters to cover the news, especially foreign news, was Lawson's overriding concern. He trained his correspondents thoroughly before they ventured overseas. Lawson didn't neglect the arts either. After World War I he introduced an innovative book section and hired Henry B. Sell as its editor.

In 1890 Lawson established the Chicago City Press Association, a forerunner of the City News Bureau, a local newsgathering operation that supplied material to Chicago newspapers. He served as president of the Associated Press—originally established in 1848 by seven newspapers in New York as the New York Associated Press—from 1894 to 1900 and as a member of the board of directors from 1893 to 1925. In addition to his newspaper duties, Lawson was also prominent in civic affairs and served as a member of the Chicago Commission on Race Relations in 1920.

Lawson died in 1925 of a heart attack. His memory is commemorated by sculptor Lorado Taft's imposing figure of a medieval knight, entitled *The Crusader,* in Graceland Cemetery.

Lawson was universally admired for his integrity, his forthrightness, and for the highly developed social conscience he brought to journalism. Fellow journalist Ben Hecht called Lawson "the fairest mind American journalism has produced."

The Victor Lawson Papers are housed in Chicago's Newberry Library.

See also: George Ade, William Bross, Eugene Field, Henry Demarest Lloyd, John T. McCutcheon, Melville E. Stone

Further reading: Charles H. Dennis, *Victor Lawson: His Time and His Work* (1935).

Meyer Levin

Novelist

BORN: October 8, 1905
Chicago, Illinois

DIED: July 9, 1981
Jerusalem, Israel

Much of Meyer Levin's fiction revolves around Jewish American themes or is based on historical incidents from Chicago's past. *The Old Bunch* (1937) was Levin's first attempt to portray Jewish American life and culture. *Citizens* (1940) is set during the violent clash that occurred between police and workers at the Republic Steel plant in 1937, and *Compulsion* (1956) is a fictionalized account of the infamous Leopold-Loeb murder case.

Born near Maxwell Street, Meyer Levin was the son of Jewish immigrants. He loved to read, and as a youngster he would check out books from the Jewish People's Institute on nearby Taylor Street. His first story, about a Jewish boy who tries to hide his humble Maxwell Street origins from his gentile girlfriend, was published when he was fifteen in a magazine called *Ten Story Book*. At sixteen, he entered the University of Chicago and graduated two years later. Levin started his career as a reporter with the *Chicago Daily News* in 1924. He had sent a sketch of a short story to his idol, and *Daily News* staffer, Ben Hecht, who replied with a terse but encouraging, "You can write." That was all Levin needed. "In those days," recalled Levin in his autobiography, "one didn't apply for a newspaper job in order to become a journalist. One applied in order to become an author."

Levin's most compelling childhood memory was of "fear and shame at being a Jew." Racine Avenue, where he grew up, was the dividing line between Jews and Italians. The Italian children would bully and taunt the bookish Levin. These experiences were so traumatic that for many years, Levin confessed in his autobiography, he hid his Jewish heritage.

His early novels—*Reporter* in 1929 and *Frankie and Johnny* in 1930—deliberately avoided Jewish themes altogether. Yet his early short stories were primarily concerned with Jewish subjects. "Molasses Tide" is a portrait of Jews along Roosevelt Road. In "Chewing Gum," he wrote about an old Jewish immigrant who peddles gum for a living. "A Seder" returns to a theme popular with Jewish authors at that time: the alienation between Old World Jews and the younger, secular generation of Americanized Jews. In 1931 Levin wrote his first novel with a Jewish theme, *Yehudah,* based on his six-month experience on a kibbutz in Haifa in 1927.

Although he visited Palestine three times as a young man, it wasn't until he served as a war correspondent during World War II for the Jewish Telegraphic Agency and the Overseas News Agency that he was able to fully accept and come to terms with his Jewish identity. Only then was he able "to recover my feeling of free and full identification as a Jew. For through my war experiences I came to recognize the . . . indestructibility of the Jewish quality," he explained in his autobiography *In Search* (1950). At that point confronting and writing about his Jewishness almost became an obsession. In 1947 he worked with the Jewish underground to illegally transport Jewish emigrants to Palestine, the future state of Israel. These Israeli themes cropped up years later in two novels about Zionist pioneers, *The Settlers* (1972) and *The Harvest* (1978).

In 1956 Levin wrote his best-selling book, *Compulsion,* based on the true story of Richard Loeb and Nathan Leopold, sons of wealthy German Jews, who kidnapped and killed fourteen-year-old Bobby Franks, a neighbor's son, for "kicks." The book zoomed up the best-seller charts, and the heretofore-obscure Levin found himself "a celebrity, an authority." John Logan's remarkable play about the murder, *Never the Sinner,* premiered in 1985 at the Stormfield Theatre in Chicago.

Levin's works were frequently the subject of lawsuits. In 1964 Leopold, after serving a thirty-three-year prison sentence, sued Levin and fifty-six other defendants, including publisher Simon & Schuster and film producer Darryl F. Zanuck, for $1,405,000 in damages, on the grounds that the book and the subsequent movie version of *Compulsion* (1959) invaded his privacy. Leopold ultimately lost.

In 1954 Levin became embroiled in yet another ugly legal battle involving the play based on the diary of concentration camp victim Anne Frank. Levin had discovered the diary while on assignment in Europe and translated it into English. Originally, Otto Frank, Anne's father, agreed that Levin would write a Broadway play based on the diary. In 1954 Levin sued Frank and two Broadway producers, Kermit Bloomgarden and Cheryl Crawford, for fraud and plagiarism. Levin had already written the play only to be told by Bloomgarden that his effort was "unstageworthy." When Crawford reportedly hired two non-Jewish writers to complete the stage adaptation, Levin became convinced that the work was rejected because it was, in his words, "too Jewish." According to biographer Steven J. Rubin, the stage adaptation was almost identical to Levin's original. "The main difference between the two versions was that they left out the Jewish character and concentrated on the schmaltz," said Levin, who was later awarded $50,000 in damages.

During his later years, Levin divided his time between New York and Israel. He died in Jerusalem in 1981 at the age of seventy-five.

Levin wrote more than twenty books, including two autobiographies, *In Search* (1950) and *The Obsession* (1973).

His last novel, *The Architect* (1981), loosely based on the life of Frank Lloyd Wright, features a cast of prominent Chicago historical figures, including Dankmar Adler, Louis Sullivan, Clarence Darrow, Jane Addams, Theodore Dreiser, and Harriet Monroe.

See also: Clarence Darrow

Further reading: Ira Berkow, *Maxwell Street: Survival in a Bazaar* (1977); John Logan, *Never the Sinner: The Leopold and Loeb Story* (1999); Steven J. Rubin, *Meyer Levin* (1982).

Vachel Lindsay

Poet

BORN: November 10, 1879
Springfield, Illinois

DIED: December 5, 1931
Springfield, Illinois

Although hailing from downstate Illinois, Nicholas Vachel Lindsay studied in Chicago, was a considerable presence on the local literary scene for several years, and was the first member of the so-called poetry revivalists to become famous. Lindsay attempted to reform American poetry. Poet Edgar Lee Masters described him as a latter-day Johnny Appleseed, planting the seeds of literary mysticism with whoever would listen and dreaming of rescuing America—through the spoken word—from the clutches of the commercialism that it had so wholeheartedly embraced. Lindsay was given many epithets: ascetic, visionary, mystic, and puritan. In him dwelt the soaring and restless spirit of a Walt Whitman or William Blake.

Vachel Lindsay was born in Springfield, Illinois, in 1879, the son of a country doctor. Lindsay was especially close to his mother. A fragile child, he avoided the rough and tumble of boys' games in favor of reciting stories. The Lindsays were devout Christians, followers of Alexander Campbell, who had established a religious society in 1812 called the Disciples of Christ. Dr. Lindsay was an elder of Springfield's First Christian Church, and Mrs. Lindsay taught the adult Sunday school class. Lindsay was encouraged to follow in his father's footsteps. As a dutiful son, he enrolled at Hiram College, a Campbellite institution in Ohio, but he did miserably in all his medical courses.

Lindsay's attitude brightened when he was accepted as a student at the Art Institute of Chicago. He wished to become an illustrator or a cartoonist although he had a natural talent for writing and kept a diary of his activities and thoughts. Lindsay arrived in Chicago on January 2, 1901, and rented an apartment on South Paulina Street. He registered for night classes and subsisted on a diet of milk and pastries. Lindsay detested alcohol, didn't smoke, and believed in pursuing a chaste life. Indeed, his greatest vice was his weakness for sweets. He attended church regularly and began reading the poems of the English mystic poet William Blake. He then moved to Kenwood Avenue and

50th Street on the South Side and found a job in the toy department at Marshall Field's sorting boxes. More importantly, he began to write poetry.

From 1904 to 1905 Lindsay lived in New York City and continued his art studies at the New York School of Art while also lecturing against alcohol and other vices. The Chicago-based *Poetry* magazine virtually launched Lindsay's career when it published "General William Booth Enters into Heaven," an arresting tribute to the founder of the Salvation Army. It was also the title of his first poetry book, published in 1913. Critics hailed Lindsay as a major new figure on the poetry scene and praised his work as a masterpiece. William Dean Howells called it "this fine brave poem that makes the heart leap." "It is perhaps the most remarkable poem of a decade," said another critic.

In 1912 Lindsay took to the road, a Christ-like figure traversing the countryside, living the life of the vagabond and preaching his gospel of peace and beauty. His pockets were empty. Beggary, he insisted, was "the noblest occupation of man." In return for money, lodging, and a meal, he exchanged booklets and recited poetry. He made his first national lecturing tour in 1920 and began to attract a large and devoted following. That same year he became the first American poet invited to recite at Oxford.

Strongly attached to his mother, who died in 1922, and, according to Edgar Lee Masters, "not attractive to women," Lindsay did not wed until May 1925, when at forty-five he married Elizabeth Conner. They had two children and resided in Spokane, Washington, until 1929, when they returned to Springfield. In December 1931, exhausted and debt-ridden from family obligations and the renovation of his home, he committed suicide as his wife and children slept.

The highly rhythmic musical quality of Lindsay's work contains elements of ragtime, evangelical hymns, and marching bands. Popular or cult heroes—Abraham Lincoln, William Jennings Bryan, Ralph Waldo Emerson, Charles Darwin—are the subjects of many of his poems. Many consider Lindsay a true visionary, a misunderstood troubadour trapped in the wrong century. Some of Lindsay's important poems include "The Congo," "Bryan, Bryan, Bryan, Bryan," "Abraham Lincoln Walks at Midnight," "The Santa Fe Trail," and "The Eagle That Is Forgotten," the last a tribute to Illinois governor John Peter Altgeld.

See also: Edgar Lee Masters, Harriet Monroe

Further reading: Dale Kramer, *Chicago Renaissance: The Literary Life of the Midwest 1900–1930* (1966); Edgar Lee Masters, *Vachel Lindsay: A Poet in America* (1935).

Little Walter

Musician

BORN: May 1, 1930
Marksville, Louisana

DIED: February 15, 1968
Chicago, Illinois

Considered the greatest blues harmonica player ever, Little Walter was famous for his pioneering use of the microphone as well as his natural skill on an instrument that, until his arrival, had never been taken seriously. He was the first musician to electrify the harmonica and, with his fresh and dazzling approach and radical innovations, his blues had almost a jazz sensibility. "By running his harmonica through an amplifier, Walter changed the sound of the Blues and helped invent Rock & Roll," writes Rich Cohen. Before he arrived on the scene, no one took the harmonica seriously. Afterward, says Cohen, "whole songs were built around it."

Born Marion Walter Jacobs in a small Louisiana town, Little Walter was a French-speaking Creole who was raised in Alexandria, Louisiana. He took up the blues harmonica, or harp, as a child, playing polkas and waltzes. At the age of twelve he quit school and started playing harmonica as a street musician in both big cities (New Orleans) and small (Monroe). Rich Cohen has described him as one of those New Orleans street urchins "you see around Jackson Square, working the grift."

When Little Walter was fourteen he moved to Helena, Arkansas, where he listened to and absorbed the music of such prominent bluesmen as Rice Miller (better known as Sonny Boy Williamson II), Big Walter Horton, Robert Junior Lockwood, and Robert Nighthawk. Slowly he built a following in the clubs. He had a good ear and a natural skill and played the harp like a horn. Eventually he began to imitate the jump blues style of sax player Louis Jordan but as played on a harmonica. Still a young teenager, Little Walter hosted a radio show in Helena in 1945 and occasionally made brief trips to Chicago to sample the music scene there.

Within a year or so, he decided to move to Chicago with his friend Honeyboy Edwards. On their first day in the city they went to Maxwell Street and played their music for spare change. In 1947 he made his recording debut ("I Just Keep Loving Her") on the tiny Ora-Nelle label, which operated out of the back room of Bernard Abrams's Maxwell Radio and Records Store in the neighborhood. He also began playing as part of a trio that included Jimmy Rogers and Muddy Waters, recording with Waters on the Chess label. Five years later, on May 12, 1952, he recorded an instrumental that Waters and his band had been using as a set closer. Called "Juke," it was released under Little Walter's own name. Following its success, he formed his own band even as he continued to record with Waters.

"Juke," which was recorded at the end of a Muddy Waters session, is the only harmonica instrumental to reach the top of the R&B charts. Another big hit was his recording of "My Babe," Willie Dixon's secular version of the gospel classic "This Train." From 1952 to 1958 Little Walter had fourteen Top Ten R&B hits, including "Sad Hours," "Mean Old World," "Tell Me Mama," "Off the Wall," "Blues with a Feeling," "You're So Fine," "You Better Watch Yourself," and "Last Night." He also appeared as a harmonica sideman on records by Jimmy Rogers, Memphis Minnie, Johnny Shines, Bo Diddley, Otis Rush, and Robert Nighthawk, among others. In 1964 he toured with the Rolling Stones, but by then his acute alcohol abuse had taken a devastating toll on his once-good looks and now-ravaged body.

Little Walter's revolutionary techniques have been compared to Charlie Parker and Jimi Hendrix. When the harmonica was drowned out by electric guitarists in the Chicago blues clubs that he played he devised a new method to assure that he could be heard above the din: he cupped a small microphone in his hands and plugged it into a public address system or guitar amplifier and used the amplification to develop new timbres and sonic effects that were unheard of on the instrument at the time. It has been said that he was the first musician to use electronic distortion.

Little Walter had a well-deserved reputation as a heavy drinker with a short fuse. On February 14, 1968, he was playing dice out on the street when an argument broke out. He grabbed the dice money and then someone hit him on the head with a pipe. He died in his sleep at his girlfriend's apartment at 209 East 54th Street the next day, only three months shy of his thirty-eighth birthday. He is buried at St. Mary's Cemetery in Evergreen Park, Illinois.

In 2008 Little Walter was inducted into the Rock and Roll Hall of Fame in its sideman category. The role of Little Walter was played by Columbus Short in the 2008 film *Cadillac Records*.

See also: Leonard Chess, Willie Dixon, Howlin' Wolf, Muddy Waters

Further reading: Rich Cohen, *Machers and Rockers: Chess Records and the Business of Rock & Roll* (2004); Tony Glover, Scott Dirks, and Ward Gaines, *Blues with a Feeling: The Little Walter Story* (2002).

Discography: *The Blues World of Little Walter* (1993); *His Best: Chess 50th Anniversary Collection* (1998); *Best of Little Walter* (2007); *The Complete Chess Masters: 1950–1967* (2009).

Mary Livermore

Suffragist and Social Reformer

BORN: December 19, 1820
Boston, Massachusetts

DIED: May 23, 1905
Melrose, Massachusetts

Mary Ashton Rice Livermore was involved in many reform movements during the nineteenth century, from suffrage to temperance to the abolition of slavery. And like other reformers of her day, she turned her back on a life of comfort to seek ways to better the human race.

Mary Rice grew up in Boston and attended public school there. As a teenager she enrolled in the Female Seminary in Charleston, Massachusetts, where she taught after graduating. In 1845 she married Daniel Parker Livermore, a Universalist minister. The couple moved to Chicago in 1857. Livermore contributed her time to various charitable groups such as the Chicago Home of the Friendless. In addition, she cofounded the Home for Aged Women and the Hospital for Women and Children. She and her husband also edited a Unitarian periodical called the *New Covenant*. She became convinced that the key to social reform—the way to improve the status of women in particular and society in general—was to support woman suffrage.

During the Civil War, Livermore, along with Jane Hoge, became associate manager of the Chicago branch of the United States Sanitary Commission, a volunteer organization run by civilians. The organization inspected camps, raised money, and stored and dispatched supplies to Union soldiers. According to historians J. Christopher Schnell and Jeanne Madeline Weimann, during the Battle of Vicksburg, Livermore carried more than 3,000 supply boxes down the Mississippi River.

As casualties mounted and additional food and supplies were desperately needed, the commission became strapped for cash. In the autumn of 1863, Livermore and Hoge came up with the idea of sponsoring the Great Northwestern Sanitary Fair as a fund-raising venture. War mementos and souvenirs were sold to the highest bidder, a series of dinners prepared by an all-volunteer staff were served, and in the evenings guests attended concerts, pantomimes, and

lectures. It was a great success, bringing in an estimated $86,000, and it became the prototype for similar fairs around the country in New York, Philadelphia, Cleveland, Pittsburgh, and St. Louis.

Livermore next turned her attention to the woman suffrage movement and organized the first suffrage convention in Chicago in 1868. Speakers included such famous suffragists as Elizabeth Cady Stanton and Susan B. Anthony. Livermore was elected president of the Illinois Woman Suffrage Association. In 1869 she founded the city's first woman suffrage publication, *The Agitator*. The following year *The Agitator* merged with the Boston-based *Woman's Journal*, and Livermore moved to the Boston suburb of Melrose to take over the editorial duties of the journal, becoming active in the suffragist movement in Massachusetts. In 1872 she joined the lecture circuit, promoting the education of women and challenging the liquor laws.

Livermore wrote two autobiographies, *My Story of the War: A Woman's Narrative of Four Years' Personal Experience,* in 1887, and *The Story of My Life, or, The Sunshine and Shadow of Seventy Years,* in 1897. Along with Frances Willard, president of the Woman's Christian Temperance Union, she edited *A Woman of the Century,* a biographical dictionary of prominent women that appeared in 1893.

Livermore died at her home in Melrose of bronchitis and a heart condition at the age of eighty-four.

A *Chicago Tribune* editorial of May 24, 1905, said, "During all her long life her influence and her ability to its utmost were used quietly, persistently and effectively, for the advancement of the individual and national life, and for the betterment of woman's condition."

See also: Frances E. Willard

Further reading: J. Christopher Schnell, "Mary Livermore and the Great Northwestern Fair," *Chicago History,* Spring 1975; Jeanne Madeline Weimann, *The Fair Women* (1981).

Henry Demarest Lloyd

Social Reformer and Journalist

BORN: May 1, 1847
New York, New York
DIED: September 28, 1903
Chicago, Illinois

The first of the great journalistic muckrakers, Henry Demarest Lloyd spent a lifetime trying to right society's evils. He advocated the principle of direct democracy—the belief that people should be able to manage their own community affairs as much as possible—and believed in the oneness of the human race.

Born in New York City, Henry Demarest Lloyd was the son of a Calvinist minister of the Dutch Reformed Church. He graduated from Columbia College in 1867 and later from the Columbia Law School. In 1869 he was admitted to the New York bar. Active in the local reform movement, he campaigned against New York's corrupt political machine boss, William "Boss" Tweed. He contributed articles to the *New York Post* and edited two monthlies, *People's Pictorial Tax-Payer* and *Free-Trader*.

In 1872 Lloyd moved to Chicago to join the staff of the *Chicago Tribune* as financial and literary editor. He conducted numerous investigations into corporate misdoings. He directed his most vehement criticism toward monopolies, especially the Standard Oil Company, which he described as "the greatest, wisest, meanest monopoly in history." In 1873 he married Jessie Bross, daughter of *Chicago Tribune* publisher William Bross. In 1885 Lloyd left the *Tribune* to pursue his reform agenda further. He wrote several books on labor problems, including *Wealth Against Commonwealth* (1894), a defiant denunciation of the Standard Oil Company. His brand of adversarial politics was too militant for many, and he was defeated in his bids for the United States Congress in 1888 and 1894.

Lloyd stood by his convictions no matter how unpopular the cause. During the hysteria that came in the wake of the Haymarket Riot of 1886, he asked Governor John Peter Altgeld to grant executive clemency to the Haymarket martyrs. This led his father-in-law to prevent both Lloyd and his wife from inheriting *Tribune* stock. Lloyd supported Eugene Debs during the Pullman Strike of 1894 and was on the side of the miners during the 1902 Pennsylvania coal strike.

Lloyd experimented in unconventional living arrangements. Various generations of his family lived in his Wayside mansion in Wilmette, just north of Chicago, along with honored guests. At various times, these guests included Jane Addams, Eugene Debs, Florence Kelley, and Booker T. Washington. Young factory workers and other laborers were also welcome at the Lloyd residence.

Lloyd was a leading force in Wilmette community life. He was village treasurer in 1886 and served as a member of the school and village boards. The Wayside mansion still stands at Lloyd Place and Sheridan Road. A statue designed by Charles Haag commemorates him.

During his later years, Lloyd traveled extensively in England, Ireland, Switzerland, and New Zealand, where he studied different methods used to cope with labor problems. From these travels emerged two books, *Labour Copartnership* (1898) and *A Country Without Strikes* (1900).

Lloyd succumbed to pneumonia in 1903 while campaigning for public ownership of public transportation in Chicago.

See also: Jane Addams, John Peter Altgeld, William Bross, Eugene Debs

Further reading: Chester McArthur Destler, *Henry Demarest Lloyd and the Empire of Reform* (1963); Michael H. Ebner, *Creating Chicago's North Shore: A Suburban History* (1988); John L. Thomas, *Alternative America: Henry George, Edward Bellamy, Henry Demarest Lloyd and the Adversary Tradition* (1983).

Rudy Lozano

Community Organizer

BORN: July 17, 1951
Harlingen, Texas
DIED: June 8, 1983
Chicago, Illinois

Rudy Lozano dedicated his brief life to improving the quality of life in Chicago's Latino community. As a member of Mayor Harold Washington's transition team, he made aggressive efforts to unite African American and Latino interests. Lozano was a trade union official, community activist, organizer, and Midwest regional director of the International Ladies' Garment Workers' Union (ILGWU).

Born in South Texas, Lozano moved with his family to Chicago in the early 1950s and settled in the largely Mexican Pilsen community. He was an active student at Harrison High School. Later, when he enrolled at the University of Illinois at Chicago, he helped create the Latin American Recruitment Program. As Midwest regional director at ILGWU, he organized factory workers at Del Rey Tortilleria.

In 1982 Lozano worked hard to register Latino voters in the Twentieth District in order to elect Juan Soliz as state representative. When Soliz lost to incumbent Marco Domico, Lozano and Soliz joined forces and organized the Near West Side branch of the Independent Political Organization (IPO), a group that functioned as an alternative to the regular Democratic machine. In 1983 Lozano ran against incumbent Frank Stemberk for alderman of the Twenty-Second Ward; he lost in a close race.

On June 8, 1983, Lozano was shot to death in his Pilsen apartment at 4035 West 25th Street. He was thirty-one.

In 1984 an eighteen-year-old gang member, Gregory Escobar, was convicted of Lozano's murder and sentenced to forty years in prison. Motives for the slaying ranged from an argument over a possible drug deal gone bad to charges that Lozano employed rival gang members during his aldermanic campaign. Family and friends of the slain activist, however, called the murder "a political assassination" ordered by anti-union businessmen.

In 1989 the Rudy Lozano branch of the Chicago Public Library opened at 1805 South Loomis Street. The Rudy Lozano Leadership Academy at 2570 South Blue Island Avenue, an alternative high school serving youth from the predominantly Latino neighborhoods of Pilsen, Little Village, and Back of the Yards, is also named after him.

Sid Luckman

Football Player

BORN: November 21, 1916
Brooklyn, New York

DIED: July 5, 1998
Aventura, Florida

Sid Luckman, considered the first T-formation quarterback, was the greatest long-range passer of his era. He turned the T-formation into a formidable weapon. During his twelve seasons as the quarterback of the Chicago Bears, from 1939 to 1950, he led the team to four National Football League (NFL) championships.

The son of German Jewish immigrants, Luckman grew up in the Flatbush section of Brooklyn, playing football, stickball, and baseball on the city streets. He played both baseball and football at Erasmus Hall High School and football as a single-wing tailback at Columbia University. Since the university offered no football scholarship, he made ends meet by dishwashing, babysitting, and working for a messenger delivery service. He finished third in the 1938 Heisman Trophy voting.

Despite the overall mediocrity of the Columbia team, Luckman's efforts and talents caught the eye of football scouts around the country, particularly George Halas, coach of the Chicago Bears. At the time, the Bears had introduced a version of the T-formation offense that emphasized passion and speed over brute strength. Although the T-formation was not new, it needed a versatile athlete to make it successful on the field. Luckman was that athlete, and Halas knew it.

The T-formation was so innovative because both college and professional teams at the time relied on running the ball with only occasional passing—the quarterback hardly touched the ball. Instead the quarterback's function was to act mostly as a blocker for the running backs. Most of the time the tailback passed the ball, not the quarterback. Essentially the T-formation liberated the quarterback and, in the process, revolutionized football: the T-formation became the foundation of most modern professional football offenses.

Ironically, Luckman had no intention to turn professional, but Halas's persistence changed his mind. Halas offered the reluctant footballer $5,500—a considerable amount at the time—and even brought the contract along to their meeting so Luckman could sign it. And Luckman did. After an initial season where he learned the ins and outs of the formation, he blossomed. He memorized the team's complex offense. In 1940, the Bears won the NFL championship game by smashing the Washington Redskins, 73–0.

Luckman won three other championship titles for the Bears, in 1941, 1943, and 1946. What's more, he led the league in touchdown passes three times, in 1944, 1945, and 1946. In 1943, during a game between the Bears and the New York Giants, he passed for 453 yards, the first time a quarterback had thrown for more than 400 yards in a game. The Bears won that game 56–7. From 1940 to 1946, the Bears played in five championship games, and in 1942 they had a perfect season of 11–0, although they lost the championship game to the Redskins.

Luckman was named to the All-Pro team five times and was chosen most valuable player during the 1943 season. After a dozen seasons with the Bears, he retired in 1950. But he did not give up football entirely. He took his skills with him and tutored college coaches at Notre Dame, Pittsburgh, Holy Cross, and his alma mater, Columbia, where he helped initiate the T-formation.

After his football career ended, Luckman became a businessman and headed a Chicago cellophane company called Cellu-Craft Products. He died at Aventura Hospital and Medical Center in Florida in 1998 at the age of eighty-one.

In 1965 Luckman was inducted into the Pro Football Hall of Fame.

See also: George Halas, Walter Payton

Charles Blair Macdonald

Golfer

BORN: November 14, 1855
Niagara Falls, Ontario

DIED: April 21, 1939

The essence of the game is inequality, as it is in humanity.

—Charles Blair Macdonald

Golf pioneer Charles Blair Macdonald introduced golf to the Midwest, mastered the art of golf course architecture, and built the Chicago Golf Club in Wheaton, Illinois, considered one of the best golf courses in the world. For these reasons, Macdonald has been called the father of American golf architecture and the father of American golf.

Raised in Chicago, Macdonald was born into wealth. His Scottish ancestors owned vast land holdings in the Mohawk Valley, an area of upstate New York settled by Scottish immigrants in the eighteenth century. When he was sixteen, he spent two years at the University of St. Andrews, the home of golf. At the time, Macdonald had never even seen a golf ball never mind played a round of golf. Golf courses did not yet exist in the United States. He was not impressed by his introduction to the game, accustomed as he was to the rough and tumble of American sports. "It seemed to me a form of tiddle-de-winks, stupid and silly," he said.

Macdonald's grandfather was a member of the Royal and Ancient Golf Club of St. Andrews, and it was this grandfather who turned his reluctant grandson over to the resident golf pro, the now-famous Tom Morris, better known as Old Tom Morris. Old Tom taught Macdonald the fundamentals of the game and then he handed him over to his own son, Young Tom. Despite his initial reservations, Macdonald fell in love with the game.

In 1874 Macdonald returned to Chicago. Most of the city had been destroyed by the fire in 1871. But Macdonald soon went to work as a broker. He contrasted Chicago's bustling atmosphere—the residents were trying their best to overcome the tragedy of the fire—to the calm, leisurely life that he savored so much in St. Andrews. To Macdonald Chicago seemed uncivilized and barbaric even, a rough, uncultured city that had little time or patience for leisure.

By the early 1890s, though, the city had had a change of heart. Much of it was linked to the 1893 World's Columbian Exposition, that great fair where Chicago invited the world to visit. Before the fair opened, a group of Englishmen visited the city. They complained to Hobart Chatfield-Taylor, their host, that there was no place to play golf in "the West." Fortunately, Chatfield-Taylor had connections. His father-in-law, Senator Charles B. Farwell, owned an estate in Lake Forest. He asked Macdonald, a friend of his, to "lay out some holes." Thus, in 1892 Macdonald finished his first golf course. But it was hardly more than a "seven-hole pitch-and-putt" on Farwell's lawn. It had stakes rather than holes. Still, this rough attempt would eventually lead to what is today called the Onwentsia Club. Most people at the time, though, didn't pay the game much heed.

Undaunted (and now a full-fledged convert to the game), Macdonald was determined to build a genuine golf course. He raised several hundred dollars, the equivalent of $5,000 today, and laid out nine holes on a farm in Belmont, now Downers Grove. Subsequently, he added nine more holes. Thus, on July 18, 1893, the Chicago Golf Club was formally chartered: the first eighteen-hole golf club in the United States. A nine-hole course is still there and is operated by the Downers Grove Park District.

The following year he was determined to create a course comparable to the golf course at St. Andrews—in other words, a Scottish links. With this in mind, he bought a 200-acre farm near the train station in Wheaton for $140 an acre ($2,900 in today's money).

Typically, Scottish links golf refers to sand dunes that separate the ocean from tillable land. Of course, in Wheaton the landscape was far different from Scotland—no sea, mountains, or dunes. Thus, Macdonald was forced to come up with an alternative: to invent his own version of a Scots links course in America; and he made sure that the same code of conduct observed in Britain made it over the Atlantic to the United States.

When the Chicago Golf Club opened, it was a huge success. Members of the city's business community gravitated toward it, including Marshall Field, Potter Palmer, and George Pullman. Within a short period of time, ordinary Chicagoans wanted to try their hand at this new sport, too. Golf courses and country clubs began opening throughout the entire Chicagoland region. In the meantime, Macdonald continued his golf advocacy, promoting the game wherever and whenever the opportunity arose. He was the founding vice president of the United States Golf Association and a cochairman of the association's first rules committee.

In 1900 he moved to New York with the idea of building the perfect golf course, one that would combine Scottish design principles with a local flavor. In 1911 the National Golf Links of America opened, his prototypical course and the course that subsequent generations of golf course architects would turn to for inspiration.

Macdonald wrote his memoir, *Scotland's Gift: How America Discovered Golf*, in 1928. He died in 1939 at the age of eighty-three.

Further reading: George Bahto, *The Evangelist of Golf: The Story of Charles Blair Macdonald* (2002); Charles Blair Macdonald, *Scotland's Gift: How America Discovered Golf* (1928); Jim Noyes, "Fore! Father," *Chicago*, August 2005.

Norman Maclean
Writer and Professor

BORN: December 23, 1902
Clarinda, Iowa

DIED: August 2, 1990
Chicago, Illinois

Fly-fishing . . . is truly an art. . . . To do it right you need not only skill but the imagination to think like a fish. . . . There is no clear distinction between it and religion.

—Wallace Stegner

I am haunted by waters.

—Norman Maclean

After enjoying a long and fruitful career as an English professor at the University of Chicago, Norman Maclean published his first collection of stories at the mature age of 73 in 1976. It proved to be an auspicious debut. Largely through word of mouth, the elegiac *A River Runs Through It,* after an initial print run of 5,000, went on to sell more than 400,000 copies. It was also the first time that the University of Chicago Press published a work of original fiction. Maclean writes with a love and affection for people no longer here, although his eponymous long tale is, ostensibly, about fly-fishing. But it is also about so much more. Fly-fishing provides meaning and gives shape to the story; in the Maclean mindset it is considered not a mere form of recreation but rather an art that reflects and even transcends life itself.

Norman Maclean was born in Clarinda, Iowa, on December 23, 1902. When he was seven, the family moved to Missoula, Montana, where he and his younger brother, Paul, grew up. They were educated at home by their father, who was a Canadian Scots Presbyterian minister. Maclean lived, to borrow another literary reference, a Jekyll-and-Hyde existence: the strict, sacred environment at home contrasted sharply with the rough, profane streets of Missoula. Maclean has referred to himself during this period as a "tough choirboy" and a "tough flower girl" coming from a "schizophrenic" background. At the time, Missoula was still very much a Wild West kind of town where cowboys and miners, lumberjacks and prostitutes mingled on the main street. Train robberies and public hangings were commonplace.

Maclean's father, the Rev. John Norman Maclean, born in Dalhousie, New Brunswick, was a faith-filled man with a literary bent who believed fly-fishing and religion to be all but inseparable. In both, one could find grace. Thus, Norman and Paul learned to cast "Presbyterian-style" on a four-count beat by using their mother's metronome.

The Reverend Maclean enjoyed quoting the poetry of John Milton, Robert Burns, and William Wordsworth, but especially the words contained in the Bible. He also never tired of reminding his children that Christ's disciples were fishermen. The Reverend Maclean was an excellent fly fisherman himself. It was he who passed this passion along to his two sons. "To him," wrote Norman, "all good things—trout as well as eternal salvation—come by grace and grace comes by art and art does not come easy." The siblings often fished in cold, rough waters, their boots soaked through while their lower limbs turned numb and blue. It was all part and parcel of the Maclean family ritual.

Paul was an excellent fly fisherman, better than both his father and his older brother. In 1938, at age thirty-three, he was beaten to death with the butt of a revolver and his lifeless body dumped in an alley in Chicago. The family never learned the details surrounding his death—only that he had put up a valiant fight. The Macleans were haunted by the uncertainty of his death for the remainder of their lives.

As a teenager, Maclean worked in logging camps and for the U.S. Forest Service, standing watch and fighting forest fires. He received his B.A. in Latin from Dartmouth in 1924, where he taught briefly before doing graduate work at the University of Chicago. Maclean spent nearly all of his adult working life at the University of Chicago teaching English literature, with an emphasis on Shakespeare and the Romantic poets. During the last decade of his tenure there he earned the title of William Rainey Harper Professor of English. A popular and ubiquitous figure on campus, Maclean was known for being tough but fair. He retired in 1973. Maclean's life in Chicago was largely confined to Hyde Park and the University of Chicago campus with occasional forays outside the neighborhood. He was particularly taken, for example, by what he called the "kind of industrial beauty" of the Calumet River ("You have to forget how it smells, but, you know, the Post-Impressionists would have loved it"), reveling in the rough juxtaposition of decay and replenishment.

It took many decades for Norman Maclean to make a name for himself outside academic circles. Only after retirement did he begin to write down the stories he used to recite to his children, Jean and John, when they were small. Essentially, *A River Runs Through It* is a re-imagining of these stories—"Western stories," he called them. The collection consists of three stories: the title tale, "Logging and Pimping and 'Your Pal, Jim,'" and "USFS 1919: The Ranger, the Cook, and a Hole in the Sky." Now considered one of the classic American stories of the twentieth century, "A River Runs Through It" concerns many things—at its most basic level, it is about fly-fishing in Montana. But it is also about family and faith—specifically, about the death of a beloved brother and the oftentimes unspoken love that exists between siblings and parents. "In our Scottish family," Maclean once wrote, as a way of explanation, "the family and religion were the center of the universe, and, like Scots, we did not believe we should praise each other but should always love and be ready to help each other."

"A River Runs Through It" is also a mature work written from the perspective of an older Maclean as he looks back on his own life and the life of his family; the parts of the river echo the stages of time, the ebb and flow of life itself. In Maclean's words—and it is contained in his craftsmanship—the act of fly-fishing becomes a metaphor for the meaning of life, its cyclical nature, its uncertainty, its unpredictable ups and downs. "The past is everywhere around me," he observes. "Now nearly all those I loved and did not understand when I was young are dead, but I still reach out to them." The story is written in a laconic style that is reminiscent partly of the work of another Westerner, Ivan Doig, and partly of the Cape Bretoner, Alistair Macleod, both of Scots descent. Annie Proulx has called it an allegory, a requiem, and a memoir: "It is one of the rare truly great stories in American literature." It concludes with an ending just as lyrical and poignant as the famous last paragraphs of James Joyce's "The Dead."

Maclean died on August 2, 1990, in Chicago. He was eighty-two. A residence hall at the University of Chicago campus is named in his honor. Two years after his death the movie adaptation of *A River Runs Through It*, directed by Robert Redford, was released. Maclean's other works include *Young Men and Fire*, an investigation into the Mann Gulch wildfire of 1949, which the University of Chicago Press published posthumously in 1992.

Further reading: Richard Friedenberg, *A River Runs Through It: Bringing a Classic to the Screen* (1992), with an introduction by Robert Redford; William Kittredge and Annick Smith, "The Two Worlds of Norman Maclean: Interviews in Montana and Chicago," *TriQuarterly*, Spring/Summer 1984; Norman Maclean, *A River Runs Through It and Other Stories, Twenty-Fifth Anniversary Edition* (2001), with a new foreword by Annie Proulx; Ron McFarland and Hugh Nichols, eds., *Norman Maclean* (1988); Wallace Stegner, "Haunted by Waters" in *Where the Bluebird Sings to the Lemonade Springs: Living and Writing in the West* (1992); O. Alan Weltzien, ed., *The Norman Maclean Reader* (2008).

George W. Maher

Architect

BORN: December 25, 1864
Mill Creek, West Virginia

DIED: September 12, 1926
Douglas, Michigan

Like Louis Sullivan and John Wellborn Root, George Washington Maher advocated indigenous American architecture. He laid out the villages of Kenilworth—including his own home at 424 Warwick Road—and Glencoe, Illinois, and built numerous mansions along the North Shore.

Born in West Virginia, Maher moved with his family to New Albany, Indiana, in the late 1860s. When he was still a young boy his family settled in Chicago. Maher served as an apprentice at the architectural firm of Bauer and Hill, but after a short stay moved to the office of Joseph L. Silsbee. There he received most of his architectural training, and he also met and worked with both George Grant Elmslie, a Scots-born architect who adopted the Prairie style of architecture, and Frank Lloyd Wright. In 1888 Maher opened his own firm, where he practiced what he called the "motif rhythm theory." Essentially it was a system that used harmony to pull together the interior and exterior of houses through decorative details to create an organic whole. He first used this method in 1897 for the John Farson House in Oak Park, Illinois.

Maher specialized in residential architecture and town planning. In the early 1890s he designed houses in the Edgewater community. Among his other commissions were the Patten Gymnasium at Northwestern University on its Evanston campus, and the home of E. J. Magerstadt, at 4930 South Greenwood Avenue in Kenwood on the South Side.

In failing health, Maher committed suicide at his summer home in Michigan in 1926. He was sixty-two.

See also: Frank Lloyd Wright
Further reading: Judith A. Barter, ed., *Apostles of Beauty: Arts and Crafts from Britain to Chicago* (2009).

Jacques Marquette

Missionary

BORN: June 10, 1637
Laon, France

DIED: May 18, 1675
Ludington, Michigan

In 1673 Father Jacques Marquette left St. Ignace, Michigan, on a long and treacherous journey that took him through the wild Illinois prairie to a desolate spot near Lake Michigan that the Indians called Checagou.

The previous year Governor Frontenac of New France, in what is now the province of Quebec in Canada, commissioned a twenty-eight-year-old cartographer named Louis Jolliet to locate a great river that lay somewhere in the West. Marquette was chosen to accompany Jolliet on the expedition. Determining that the Mississippi River flowed into the Gulf of Mexico, Marquette and Jolliet traveled up the Illinois River, stopping at the Indian village of Kaskaskia, near present-day Utica, Illinois. Marquette promised the Indians that he would return one day to preach the Gospel. Journeying up the Des Plaines River, Marquette and his party floated down the south branch of the Chicago River to Lake Michigan before finally reaching Green Bay in the fall of 1673. Remembering his promise to the Illinois Indians, Marquette embarked on another journey.

On December 4, 1674, Marquette reached the mouth of the Chicago River. Too sick to continue—he was suffering from severe dysentery and chronic fever—he settled in a cabin at what is now Damen Avenue and the south branch of the Chicago River. Thus Marquette, along with his two French companions, became the first white men on record to live in Chicago.

Marquette spent a blustery winter on the prairie before returning to Kaskaskia, where he was received by the Illinois Indians, according to his diary, like "an angel from heaven." His health rapidly deteriorating, Marquette died near Ludington, Michigan, on the return journey back to the mission at St. Ignace.

Marquette Avenue, Marquette Drive, and Marquette Road are all named in his honor.

Further reading: Milo Quaife, *Chicago and the Old Northwest* (2001).

Vito Marzullo

Politician

BORN: September 10, 1897
Senerchia, Italy

DIED: March 5, 1990
Chicago, Illinois

Vito Marzullo, the Italian immigrant who became the undisputed dean of the city council for over thirty years, epitomized Chicago politics of the old school where "who you knew" was more important than "what you knew." And sometimes it seemed that Marzullo ran the Twenty-Fifth Ward on the Near West Side as if it was his own personal fiefdom and the residents his subjects. Yet the garrulous Marzullo was more of a benevolent monarch than a ruthless despot.

Young Vito came to the United States from Italy in 1910 with his family. After receiving only a fourth-grade education, he trained as a machinist at the Lewis Institute, then located at Madison Street and Damen Avenue. His initial attempt to enter politics was not encouraging—he was defeated in his effort to become a Democratic precinct captain. His first political job was as a clerk in the county treasurer's office.

In 1939 Marzullo was elected to the Illinois state legislature, while, at the same time, holding the position of ward superintendent in the Department of Streets and Sanitation. In 1953 he won his first term as alderman of the Twenty-Fifth Ward. He also served as Democratic ward committeeman in the Twenty-Fifth Ward from 1956 until 1984. Imbued with a fierce independent streak, Marzullo frequently defied the organization. Although a longtime admirer of Richard J. Daley, Marzullo broke with the mayor when he refused to back the Democratic presidential hopeful, George S. McGovern, in 1972. He supported the Republican candidate, Richard M. Nixon, instead. "I'd rather drop dead (than support McGovern)," he offered as an explanation. He went his way again in 1983 when he backed Republican mayoral candidate Bernard Epton over the Democratic choice, Harold Washington. Why the party switch again? "He says he don't want no Machine," said Marzullo, referring to Washington's reform agenda.

In 1983 Marzullo stepped down as the Twenty-Fifth Ward's Democratic committeeman. Two years later the federal court redrew the map of his ward, to reflect the change in population makeup to a largely African American and Latino base. Marzullo decided to retire. "The intellectuals, the millionaires, the obstructionists, they messed it up," he grumbled. "They redrew my ward and they used cats and dogs and mouses and counted them as people."

They say you only live once, but Marzullo had the rare experience of reading about his own death in the morning paper. In April 1989, over a bowl of cornflakes, he read his obituary in the pages of the *Chicago Tribune*. Momentarily stunned, the politician merely complained later that the premature report of his demise ruined his breakfast.

Marzullo came out on top in more than twenty-three elections, most of them unopposed. "Nineteen times nobody filed against me, even for public nuisance!" said Marzullo, according to author Milton Rakove. He survived so long in the notoriously treacherous world of politics because he knew how to play the game, and, most important, he knew how to please the people that mattered the most—his constituency. Marzullo was aided by an army of precinct captains—"foot soldiers," he called them—who functioned as his eyes and ears on the street. These public servants would canvass the neighborhood, listening to the needs and complaints of the residents—which ranged from providing free legal service to repairing broken street lights—then report back to their boss. Considered a genuine relic of old-style Chicago politics, Marzullo was often asked to speak at prestigious universities around the country about clout, vice, and other infamous Windy City peculiarities. Some of his words of wisdom include "Those who know the least speak the most" and "Do good and forget; do bad and remember."

Marzullo died of pneumonia at Rush Presbyterian–St. Luke's Hospital in 1990 at the age of ninety-two. He was buried in Mount Carmel Cemetery in Hillside, Illinois.

See also: Richard J. Daley

Further reading: David K. Fremon, *Chicago Politics Ward by Ward* (1988); Milton Rakove, *Don't Make No Waves—Don't Back No Losers: An Insider's Analysis of the Daley Machine* (1975) and *We Don't Want Nobody Nobody Sent: An Oral History of the Daley Years* (1979).

Edgar Lee Masters

Poet

BORN: August 23, 1869
Garnett, Kansas

DIED: March 5, 1950
Philadelphia, Pennsylvania

Edgar Lee Masters was one of the leading figures of the Chicago Renaissance literary movement of the early twentieth century. For over twenty years, Masters toiled in literary obscurity. It wasn't until the publication of *Spoon River Anthology* (1915) that Masters received any real recognition. *Spoon River* became the most widely read book of American poetry in its day, and with its plain, straightforward verse, it influenced the direction of modern poetry.

Born in Garnett, Kansas, Edgar Lee Masters moved with his family to Lewistown, Illinois, as a young child. He studied the great works of British and American literature—Emerson, Dickens, Scott, Thackeray, Byron, and Shakespeare. When he was old enough, he secured a position on the local newspaper and occasionally submitted poetry. His father thought he should receive a proper education and encouraged him to pursue a "respectable" calling. Consequently, Masters enrolled at Knox College in Galesburg, Illinois, to study law. He was admitted to the Illinois bar in 1891 and moved to Chicago in 1892.

Masters rented a room in a boarding house two blocks away from the Levee, Chicago's infamous red-light district.

He got a job with the Edison Company as a bill collector and sometime lawyer and in 1893 found work at a downtown law firm. According to literary historian Dale Kramer, Masters was terrible in the courtroom—he was a poor speaker with no flair for the dramatic—but he did prepare excellent drafts, briefs, and contracts. After working long hours at the office, Masters went home and continued to toil late into the night on his own writing. In his spare time he wrote political essays for the *Chicago Chronicle* and organized and acted as president of the Jefferson Club, a social club that sponsored banquets in honor of the charismatic Democratic leader William Jennings Bryan. In 1903 Clarence Darrow invited Masters to join his firm. (The two men had known each other for several years.) Masters managed the office and handled the civil litigation cases. Although his salary increased considerably, he took no pleasure in his legal career. He concentrated further on his writing.

In 1914 Masters published poetry in *Reedy's Mirror*, a St. Louis literary paper, under the pseudonym of Webster Ford (he felt that using his real name might damage the firm's credibility). The poems consist of monologues by the deceased residents of a fictitious Illinois town called Spoon River. The Spoon River poems explore the restrictions and desperation of small-town life. Published in book form in 1915 as *Spoon River Anthology,* the poems caused a literary sensation. By 1940 the book had been published in seventy editions and translated into several languages. Masters's literary reputation rests largely on *Spoon River.*

Eventually Masters moved to New York. Although a prolific writer, none of his other works were as successful. They include *Domesday Book* (1920), *The New Spoon River* (1924), and *The Sangamon* (1942). Masters also was an accomplished biographer. His biography *Vachel Lindsay: A Poet in America* was awarded the Mark Twain Medal in 1935. He also wrote biographies of Mark Twain, Abraham Lincoln, and Walt Whitman. In 1936 he published his autobiography, *Across Spoon River.*

By 1943 Masters, in poor health as a result of pneumonia and malnutrition, was living alone in New York's Chelsea Hotel. Although reports circulated that he was broke, Masters always denied being poor. Upon learning of Masters's fate, members of Manhattan's literary circle were both acutely embarrassed and startled that one of their own was living under such dire conditions. As a result, the Academy of American Poets awarded Masters a $5,000 fellowship.

Masters died at the age of eighty in a Philadelphia convalescent home in 1950.

The Spoon River Anthology continues to resonate with contemporary audiences: in June 2011, Tom Andolora, a New York vocal coach, turned Masters's masterpiece into an ambitious theater piece with music. *The Spoon River Project,* as he calls it, was held in an outdoor production at the historic Green-Wood Cemetery in Brooklyn.

See also: Clarence Darrow, Vachel Lindsay, Harriet Monroe

Further reading: Dale Kramer, *Chicago Renaissance: The Literary Life of the Midwest 1900–1930* (1966); Herbert K. Russell, *Edgar Lee Masters: A Biography* (2001).

William Maxwell

Writer and Editor

BORN: August 16, 1908
Lincoln, Illinois

DIED: July 31, 2000
New York, New York

As fiction editor at the *New Yorker,* William Maxwell edited some of the best-known writers of the twentieth century, including John Updike, John Cheever, John O'Hara, J. D. Salinger, Mary McCarthy, Eudora Welty, Isaac Bashevis Singer, and Frank O'Connor. Maxwell was an editor's editor. But he was also a highly respected novelist and short story writer in his own right. Although he lived and worked in New York for more than half of his adult life, it was the Midwest that forged his identity and that he returned to again and again in his own work.

William Keepers Maxwell Jr. was born in downstate Lincoln, Illinois, on August 16, 1908, a descendant of Scottish pioneers, and the son of William Keepers Maxwell, an insurance executive, and Eva Blossom Blinn. When he was ten, his beloved mother died from the devastating 1918–19 Spanish flu epidemic that swept the globe, and his world literally collapsed overnight. The epidemic killed over thirty million people in a single year; in Chicago, nearly 11,000 people died, disproportionately pregnant women. He wrote about the epidemic and his mother's death in his third novel, *They Came like Swallows* (1937). Indeed, much of the material that formed the foundation of his fiction was inspired by his time in the Midwest. After his mother died, he went to live with his aunt and uncle in nearby Bloomington.

Eventually, though, his father remarried and he and the family moved to Chicago, living in the Rogers Park neighborhood, where Maxwell attended Senn High School.

The move from small-town Illinois to a big-city high school in Chicago had a profound, and positive, influence on Maxwell. Indeed, he called his experiences in Chicago "a stroke of fortune." He wrote for a student literary magazine called the *Forum* and took art classes. He worked odd jobs for his father at his downtown office during the school holidays. After his junior year at Senn, he took a job on a farm called Bonnie Oaks outside the town of Portage, Wisconsin. Bonnie Oaks was an artists' colony of sorts in a bucolic setting. It was there where he met the writer Zona Gale, who became one of his literary mentors. He returned to Senn during his senior year and then attended the University of Illinois at Urbana-Champaign, where he earned a bachelor's degree. He earned his master's degree at Harvard, then taught in Illinois schools for two years.

Like many a Midwestern young man, Maxwell moved to New York with literary stars in his eyes. (He once said, "After I left Illinois, I was always a tourist, wherever I was.") His dreams came true when he interviewed for a staff position with the *New Yorker,* and the magazine's founding editor, Katharine White, hired him in 1937. He remained there until his retirement as fiction editor some four decades later. From 1969 to 1972 he was president of the National Institute of Arts and Letters.

Maxwell enjoyed a prestigious career, and yet, at heart, he remained a humble and private man. Maxwell felt the editor's role was to be unobtrusive. "As a writer I don't very much enjoy being edited. As an editor I tried to work so slightly on the manuscript that ten years later the writer would read his story and not be aware that anybody was involved but him."

In addition to his position at the *New Yorker*, Maxwell was a prolific writer himself. His first novel, *Bright Center of Heaven,* was published in 1934. Included among his many other works are the story collections *Billie Dyer and Other Stories* (1992) and *Over by the River and Other Tales* (1966), as well as the highly acclaimed novel *So Long, See You Tomorrow* (1980), which won the American Book Award. Maxwell's fiction often revolved around particular and recurring themes: the fragility of life, the uncertainty of the world, the loss of innocence, the crushing of a child's dreams.

Much of his fiction is taken from his own life or his Illinois surroundings and is in some form or another autobiographical. Through his writing, he immortalized his mother. *They Came like Swallows,* for example, draws heavily on the death of his mother in 1918. In *The Folded Leaf* (1945) his mother is a shadowy figure in the background. In *So Long, See You Tomorrow,* it is her absence that is the thrust of the story. In the luminous *Ancestors: A Family History* (1972) the chapters about the happiness of his early family life were his form of "testifying." As he got older, he allowed her to be "less than perfect . . . more as if I had become Isherwood's camera and were photographing her in this or that moment."

Writes Edward Hirsch, "When he talked about the past, it was vividly, even painfully, present to him. It was as if at any moment he could close his eyes and slip through a thin membrane in time. I once asked him if he missed the past. He looked at me with some surprise and replied that he didn't miss the past because he was never separated from it. He said, 'I have a huge set of memories, which I carry around like a packed suitcase.'"

Maxwell was a great stylist and elegant composer of words. *Ancestors* is perhaps his most heartfelt work. In it he captures a vanished world as he retraces the history of his family from pioneers to itinerant preachers to small-town businessmen. This American of Scottish ancestry assembles a genealogical detective story, piecing together bits and pieces until some kind of picture, although a fragmented one, comes into view. Maxwell wanted characters in his fiction to sound like real people, and so he peppered his writing with the speech and idiom of the Midwest.

The stories of the older Maxwell that appear in *Billie Dyer* or *All the Days and Nights* (1995), as well as the novel *So Long, See You Tomorrow,* are not the stuff of high drama or complicated plots. Instead they focus on the internal lives of his characters, the small things and moments that are important to them but inconsequential to the outside world, like the unexpected passing of two boys in a school hallway and the guilt that one of them feels for having failed to acknowledge the presence of his friend. Small moments, but profound and universal emotions.

For forty years he worked seven days a week. Four days at writing and three days at the office—editing and writing. He had described the experience of losing his mother as the worst thing that could ever happen to him. Then he kept going on. To Alec Wilkinson, he was a product of the nineteenth century and the country people—the Scots pioneers—who came before him.

Maxwell also wrote the novel *Time Will Darken It* (1948) and another short story collection, *The Old Man at the Railroad Crossing and Other Tales* (1966). A collection of essays, *The Outermost Dreams,* was published in 1989. In sum, Maxwell wrote six novels, three collections of short stories, a volume of essays, fantasies for children, and a memoir. He was elected to the American Academy of Arts and Letters in 1963.

Maxwell died on July 31, 2000, at his Manhattan home at the age of ninety-one.

Further reading: Barbara Burkhardt, *William Maxwell: A Literary Life* (2005).

Oscar F. Mayer

Businessman

BORN: March 29, 1859
Kaesingen, Germany

DIED: March 11, 1955
Chicago, Illinois

Oscar F. Mayer founded and acted as chairman of the board of the Oscar Mayer company, the giant meatpacking firm. Today his name is virtually synonymous with "hot dog."

The Mayers were an old Bavarian family of ministers and foresters. Mayer's father died in 1870, forcing the young Oscar to leave school to support the family. He left his home in Bavaria to travel to Munich to work for a cousin, John M. Schroll, who owned a grocery store. The business failed, and Schroll decided to move with his family to America in 1873. Oscar asked his mother's permission to accompany his cousin. She agreed. They originally settled in Detroit where Mayer, then fourteen, found work at a butcher shop.

In 1876 the young immigrants moved to Chicago. Mayer got a job as an apprentice at the Armour meatpacking company while Schroll opened a drugstore on North Avenue near Larrabee Street. Mayer then found work in Kohlhammer's meat market on Clark Street, which served the wealthy Gold Coast neighborhood, learning the retail meat business. He stayed for three years. In 1880 Mayer wrote home to his brother Gottfried suggesting that he study sausage-making in Nuremburg and then come to Chicago. Gottfried agreed and he and another brother, Max, immigrated to the United States. Mayer and his brothers rented Kolling Meat Market, a small butcher and sausage-making shop in a predominantly German neighborhood on Sedgwick Street on the North Side. The shop, which he called Oscar Mayer and Brothers Company, specialized in homemade sausages and wieners.

The business prospered and Mayer built a two-story building several blocks away at 1241 North Sedgwick Street. On the first floor he established his business. The second floor he used as living quarters for his family—by this time he had a wife and infant son—and his two brothers. Gottfried managed the production department and Max ran the bookkeeping department. In 1883 Mayer founded Oscar Mayer and Company. The combination of masterful salesmanship and excellent products dictated success. Company salesmen traveled throughout the city and suburbs by horse and wagon making deliveries. By the turn of the century, the company employed forty-three workers, which included, according to one veteran, "five wagon salesmen, one pig-head-and-feet cleaner and cooker, and two stablemen."

Mayer began to add new products and experiment with innovative marketing techniques. By 1924 packaged sliced bacon appeared on the market. By 1928 fifteen varieties of sausages were being sold, and by 1929 Oscar Mayer became the first company to adopt brand identification. Every fourth wiener was wrapped in a yellow paper ring, which carried the company name and an official U.S. government inspection stamp.

In 1936 the company introduced Little Oscar. For many Chicagoans of a certain age, Little Oscar—the little person who dressed in white, wore an oversize chef's hat, and traveled across the country in the Wienermobile—came to personalize Oscar Mayer and Company. Later a cartoon image of Little Oscar appeared in television commercials, in newspaper advertisements, and on billboards. The Wienermobiles—there are six of them altogether—continue to make appearances throughout the United States.

In 1919 the company relocated its national headquarters to Madison, Wisconsin, while retaining its Chicago plant at 1241 North Sedgwick Street. Although Mayer maintained an active interest in the company, he had no problem delegating authority. From 1928 to 1955 he served as chairman of the board.

Mayer, who lived at 5727 North Sheridan Road for over forty years, died in 1955 at the age of ninety-five after a brief illness. Upon his death, his son Oscar G. Mayer was elected chairman of the board while Oscar G. Mayer Jr., the founder's grandson, became president. Oscar Mayer is now a division of Kraft Foods.

In early 2010 the company spent more than $50 million on a new print, television, and online advertising campaign that featured all of its products: bacon, premade sandwiches, bologna, sliced package meats, and, of course, hot dogs. The iconic Oscar Mayer wiener jingle is still a part of the campaign.

See also: James Kraft

Curtis Mayfield
Musician

BORN: June 3, 1942
Chicago, Illinois

DIED: December 26, 1999
Roswell, Georgia

As lead singer of the Impressions, Curtis Mayfield revolutionized rhythm and blues with his voice and funky sound—but his message of social justice inspired later generations of musicians, including hip-hop artists. He was not only among the first African American R&B and soul artists to include social commentary in their work, his music is among the most sampled by contemporary rappers. The Impressions became one of the most popular soul bands of the 1960s and 1970s.

Born on July 3, 1942, in the Cabrini-Green housing project on Chicago's North Side, Curtis Mayfield was the son of Kenneth Mayfield and Marion Washington. His father abandoned the family when Mayfield was just five. Two years later, at the tender age of seven, Mayfield began singing at his grandmother's Traveling Soul Spiritualists' Church. By the time he was in his teens he had taught himself how to play guitar, tuning the instrument to the black keys of the piano, which gave it a unique and quite distinctive sound.

At sixteen, Mayfield dropped out of Wells High School to form a five-piece band called the Roosters, which he would later change to the Impressions. Jerry Butler was the lead singer (he had been a member of Mayfield's grandmother's congregation). In 1958 the Impressions had a national hit with "For Your Precious Love" with Butler on the lead vocals. After its success, Butler left the group, leaving the vocals to Mayfield and his instantly recognizable falsetto. (Butler, who had a Top Ten hit of his own with "Only the Strong Survive" in 1968, among other hits, is a Cook County Board commissioner.)

In 1964, during the height of the civil rights era, Mayfield wrote one of the defining songs of the movement, "Keep on Pushing." Considered a bona fide civil rights anthem—it was reportedly a favorite of Dr. Martin Luther King Jr.—it indicated the direction his music was taking. A Top Ten R&B and pop hit, it inspired other musicians to explore social justice issues in their music. Another song, the durable "People Get Ready," and perhaps his best-known composition, served as further inspiration to the movement. Like many of Mayfield's recordings, it was neither strident nor preachy. Instead, it conveyed its (serious) message while wrapped in a dazzling package of soulful harmonies and gorgeous instrumentation.

By the early 1970s, Mayfield had left the Impressions and stretched out a bit to explore the movie industry, serving as the writer, performer, and producer of the soundtrack for *Super Fly* (1972), one of the many so-called blaxploitation films; that is, popular films that explored the African American experience and that were usually written by or featured African Americans and appealed to largely African American audiences. The title track and the antidrug song "Freddie's Dead" are among his most popular works. Indeed, the soundtrack is considered one of the most influential albums in African American history. Mayfield also appeared in a scene in *Super Fly* with his band, the Curtis Mayfield Experience. Mayfield contributed to other motion picture soundtracks, including *Claudine* (1974), *Sparkle* (1976), *A Piece of the Action* (1977), and *Short Eyes* (1977). As a member of the Impressions, he is featured on the song "Amen," an updated version of an old gospel track, which appeared in *Lilies of the Field* (1963) starring Sidney Poitier.

Mayfield also started his own label, Curtom Records, as well as the Mayfield and Windy C labels, and produced the work of other artists, including Mavis Staples, Aretha Franklin, and Gladys Knight and the Pips.

On August 13, 1990, Mayfield was conducting a sound check for an outdoor concert at Wingate Field in the Flatbush neighborhood of Brooklyn when high winds caused stage lighting equipment to collapse on top of him. Although he survived, he was seriously injured: his spine was crushed in three places, effectively paralyzing him from the neck down. Still, he eventually returned to the recording studio, releasing his final album, *New World Order,* in 1996. The circumstances for recording the album were unusual, though: his vocals were recorded while he was lying on his back.

After a decade of poor health—in 1998 his right leg was amputated due to complications from diabetes—Mayfield died the day after Christmas 1999 in Roswell, Georgia.

In 1991 the Impressions were inducted into the Rock and Roll Hall of Fame. In 1999 Mayfield was inducted as a solo artist.

See also: Nat King Cole, Sam Cooke

Further reading: Peter Burns, *Curtis Mayfield* (2003); Craig Werner, *Higher Ground: Stevie Wonder, Aretha Franklin, Curtis Mayfield, and the Rise and Fall of American Soul* (1995).

Aloysius A. Mazewski

Community Organizer

BORN: January 5, 1916
North Chicago, Illinois

DIED: August 3, 1988
Portage, Wisconsin

Aloysius A. Mazewski was one of the most influential figures in the Polish American community for over thirty years. As president of both the Polish National Alliance and the Polish American Congress, his clout spread far beyond Chicago's borders. Mazewski was the voice of Polonia in Washington, D.C., and he had the ear of every president from Lyndon Johnson to Ronald Reagan on matters concerning the Polish American community.

Aloysius Mazewski's father came to the United States at the age of fourteen. Aloysius was born in the suburb of North Chicago but lived at 5805 West Cullom Avenue in Portage Park on the Northwest Side for most of his life. He attended Lane Technical High School, where he was president of the Polish Students' Club and organized Polish American activities. After graduating from DePaul University Law School, Mazewski served as an army administrator during World War II. He left the service in 1946 with the rank of major, became active in ward politics, and started a successful law practice. In September 1967 Mazewski was elected president of the Polish National Alliance (PNA), and the following year he became president of the Polish American Congress (PAC).

The PNA is a fraternal insurance organization founded in Philadelphia in 1880. Its aims were several but none were more important than to lay the "proper foundation for the construction of institutions dedicated to the material and moral advancement of the Polish immigration in America." These institutions consisted of Polish settlement houses, schools, educational facilities, shelters, and businesses in the Polish community. By the end of 1880, the alliance established its headquarters in Chicago. In its early years, the PNA moved from rented office to rented office—338 South Clark Street, 26 West Washington Street, 60 West Noble Street, 112 West Division Street, and 547 West Noble Street—until it built its first permanent office at 1404 West Division Street in 1896. Polish fraternal groups were first organized in America during the 1860s to provide burial insurance and illness benefits for Polish immigrants. Eventually they acquired more of a patriotic flavor. The PNA, in particular, staunchly advocated Polish independence and promoted ethnic pride. Mazewski modernized the PNA's antiquated insurance program by offering a variety of plans to meet the needs of its diverse membership. In June 1977, the PNA moved into its spacious new quarters at 6100 North Cicero Avenue on the Far Northwest Side.

Mazewski was a tireless campaigner for human rights in Poland and was an early supporter of that country's Solidarity movement. In 1981 the alliance, under his leadership, organized a food drive for Poland at a time when the country was experiencing severe food shortages. The Polish American Congress Charitable Foundation, which he founded, raised $150 million for Poland during the Solidarity strikes of 1980.

In 1970 Mazewski became the first Polish American special delegate to the United Nations General Assembly. Among his other accomplishments, he was a member of the International Human Rights Conference in Madrid in 1980, and he served on the Federal Ethnic Studies Commission, which helped create the Ethnic Heritage Studies Act of 1972. In 1980 he was named to the United States Holocaust Commission. Along with Illinois Congressman Frank Annunzio, Mazewski was responsible for the passage of the Polish Veterans' Act of 1976, which provided medical benefits to Polish war veterans living in the United States who fought on the Allied side during World War II.

Mazewski suffered a fatal heart attack in 1988 at the age of seventy-two while playing golf near his summer cottage in Wisconsin. An estimated 10,000 mourners filed through St. Hyacinth Catholic Church at 3636 West Wolfram Street as he lay in state for two days.

Further reading: Victor Greene, *For God and Country: The Rise of Polish and Lithuanian Ethnic Consciousness in America* (1975); Melvin G. Holli and Peter d'A. Jones, eds., *Ethnic Chicago* (1984); Edward Kantowicz, *Polish American Politics in Chicago* (1972); Donald E. Pienkos, *P.N.A.: A Centennial History of the Polish National Alliance of the United States of North America* (1984).

Cyrus H. McCormick

Entrepreneur

BORN: February 15, 1809
Rockbridge County, Virginia

DIED: May 13, 1884
Chicago, Illinois

Cyrus Hall McCormick revolutionized farming and played an important role in the industrialization of Chicago. Before the invention of the horse-drawn McCormick reaper, farming consisted of crude tools and primitive techniques. Afterward, neither farming nor McCormick would ever be the same. McCormick became a household word throughout the world.

Cyrus McCormick received little formal education. His father, Robert McCormick, was also an inventor and had tried to invent his own reaper years earlier. Where he failed, his son succeeded. With the help of Jo Anderson, a slave, the twenty-two-year-old McCormick built his reaper in six weeks in the smithy of his father's farm in Virginia. Unknown to McCormick, there were forty-seven other patents for reapers at the time.

Although McCormick is credited with inventing the reaper in 1831, it was not marketed until the early 1840s. He obtained a patent in 1834. The first sales did not occur, however, until 1840 when he sold his invention for $100. For several years he kept the reaper off the market while he made additional improvements and even waged several legal battles over patent violations. One of the lawyers who represented him in court was Abraham Lincoln from Springfield, Illinois.

The first McCormick reaper could reportedly harvest as much as ten acres of wheat per day—a vast improvement over the two acres that a farm laborer could harvest. McCormick's reaper liberated the farmer from the land and was the first step on the road to farm mechanization. McCormick scouted locations for a manufacturing plant. In 1847 he chose Chicago, formed a partnership with businessman Charles M. Gray, bought land on the North Branch of the Chicago River, and built a factory there. His

brothers, Leander J. McCormick and William Sanderson McCormick, joined him, and together they began the mass production of the original reaper. In the first year McCormick's factory produced 500 machines. At the time of the Chicago Fire in 1871, production had grown to 10,000 reapers a year. By the turn of the century, 214,000 reapers were produced annually in the McCormick works, which by that time had relocated to the corner of Blue Island and Western Avenues. McCormick traveled around the world promoting his invention and expanding his network of dealers. One of his important innovations in marketing was the extension of liberal credit to the farmer.

In his later years, McCormick contributed funds to what became the McCormick Theological Seminary. In 1859 he started the *Chicago Times* newspaper, the leading antiwar paper in the North. Indeed, McCormick, the Virginian, was a vocal advocate of the "Copperheads," Northerners sympathetic to the Southern cause. McCormick became active in Democratic politics in Illinois and ran unsuccessfully for Congress in 1864.

McCormick was supposed to be happiest when working. According to Chicago folklore, the last words he uttered in his brownstone mansion at 675 North Rush Street were, appropriately enough, "Work, work!"

After McCormick's death, his wife, Nettie Fowler McCormick, took over the business. In 1902 the firm merged with the Deering Harvester Company to form International Harvester Company.

See also: Robert R. McCormick, Joseph Medill, John S. Wright
Further reading: Herbert N. Cassin, *Cyrus Hall McCormick* (1909); William Cronon, *Nature's Metropolis: Chicago and the Great West* (1992).

Robert R. McCormick

Publisher

BORN: July 30, 1880
Chicago, Illinois

DIED: April 1, 1955
Wheaton, Illinois

Robert Rutherford McCormick bore a famous name and came from an old established family, but with his aristocratic bearing and his penchant for English clothing, the eccentric McCormick was hardly a typical Midwesterner. For more than forty-five years as editor and publisher of the *Chicago Tribune*, he determined all of the newspaper's policy, and he ran the newspaper the way he saw fit. The *Tribune* was his newspaper. And in effect, it was his life, too.

Solemn, reserved, and aloof, Robert R. McCormick boasted an impressive pedigree. He was the son of Katherine Medill and Robert S. McCormick, the grandson of Joseph Medill, and the nephew of Cyrus H. McCormick. He attended the prestigious Ludgrove School in Middlesex, England, for three years and then enrolled at Groton Preparatory School in Massachusetts. After graduating from Yale in 1903, he entered the Northwestern University Law School and was admitted to the Illinois bar in 1908.

After law school McCormick entered into a short-lived partnership with his Northwestern classmate Samuel E. Thomason before turning to politics. From 1904 to 1906 he held the Republican aldermanic seat from Chicago's Twenty-First Ward on the Far South Side. In late 1905 he became president of the Board of Trustees of the Chicago Sanitary District. Torn between politics and journalism, McCormick ultimately chose the latter, declining the Republican nomination to the United States Congress in 1912.

When *Tribune* editor Robert W. Patterson died suddenly in 1910, McCormick became coeditor of the paper with his cousin, and Robert Patterson's son, Joseph Medill Patterson. McCormick handled the business side, while Patterson concentrated on the editorial functions. In 1911 McCormick became president of the Tribune Company. In 1915 McCormick served as a war correspondent in Europe, and one year later he became a major in the First Cavalry of the Illinois National Guard. From 1917 to 1918 he acted as an artillery officer with the American Expeditionary Force in France. He left with the rank of colonel. It was a title that he grew to cherish. Some people downplay their military past; McCormick emphasized it and became known as "the Colonel."

In 1921 McCormick became one of the founders of the Medill School of Journalism at Northwestern University. Four years later he became the sole editor and publisher of the *Tribune,* while his cousin Joe became editor of the *New York Daily News.* In 1922, in honor of the *Tribune*'s seventy-fifth anniversary, McCormick announced a $100,000 world competition for the design of a new office tower. Raymond Hood, a little known architect from New York, won the honors.

In 1924 McCormick purchased radio station WGN (the call letters refer to the *Tribune*'s then self-proclaimed title of the "World's Greatest Newspaper"). In 1939 he began broadcasting his own weekly radio show, "Chicago Theatre of the Air," where he talked at length about whatever was on his mind. These weekly ramblings amounted to an oral history of his life. He reminisced about incidents from his past or discussed his personal heroes—from General Douglas MacArthur to Sir Walter Scott to Thomas Jefferson.

Unlike other newspaper editors, McCormick had no problem with delegating authority. "The task of the editor cannot be handled by one man, no matter how remarkable he might be," he admitted. But he still had definite ideas as to what made a great newspaper. The paper, he said, must answer to the needs, hopes, and fears of its readers. "When the editor is sympathetic with the interests of every honest person, from ditch-digger to multimillionaire, his paper will be truly great."

McCormick held some strong opinions and was not afraid to express them. He staunchly advocated freedom of the press, considered himself a friend of big business, and supported nationalism. As an isolationist, he opposed the United States' entry into both world wars. He denounced labor unions, criticized the New Deal policies of President Franklin D. Roosevelt, and condemned the progressive stance of social reformer Jane Addams.

Circulation of the *Tribune* soared during his tenure, from 200,000 when he first arrived to almost 900,000 at his death. He expanded the Tribune Company holdings, buying paper mills and forests in Canada, shipping companies, radio and television stations, and publishing houses. He was also chairman of the board of the *New York Daily News,* which he and Patterson had founded in 1919. In 1951 he assumed the position of editor and publisher of the *Washington Times-Herald.* Several years later it was sold to the *Washington Post.*

In 1953 McCormick caught pneumonia, which was complicated by cirrhosis of the liver and circulatory problems. Two years later he died in his sleep at his Wheaton estate of Cantigny, the former home of his grandfather, Joseph Medill. McCormick was seventy-four.

See also: Victor Lawson, Cyrus H. McCormick, Joseph Medill

Further reading: Gwen Morgan and Arthur Veysey, *Poor Little Rich Boy (and How He Made Good)* (1985); John W. Tebbel, *An American Dynasty: The Story of the McCormicks, Medills and Pattersons* (1947); Frank C. Waldrop, *McCormick of Chicago: An Unconventional Portrait of a Controversial Figure* (1966); Lloyd Wendt, *"Chicago Tribune": The Rise of a Great American Newspaper* (1979).

John T. McCutcheon

Cartoonist

BORN: May 6, 1870
Near South Raub, Indiana

DIED: June 10, 1949
Lake Forest, Illinois

John Tinney McCutcheon, war correspondent, author, and dean of American cartoonists, turned his memories of a Hoosier boyhood and a talent for drawing into some of the best-loved and most warmly remembered cartoons in American journalism. McCutcheon, whose work reflected his own good humor and tolerance of human foibles, is perhaps best known for the charming "Injun Summer" cartoon, which debuted in the *Chicago Tribune* in 1907. Combining whimsy and unabashed sentimentality, McCutcheon's magic pen transformed shocks of corn into Indian teepees. Today the cartoon's imagery and period vernacular has led to some controversy about what some consider its patronizing treatment of Native Americans. During its day, though, it was but one of the highlights of his long and distinguished career in which he created more than 15,000 cartoons.

Ironically, John McCutcheon had no desire to become a cartoonist. "He wanted to be an illustrator," once recalled his good friend and colleague, George Ade. "He was a realist and simply wanted to picture people as he saw them. Later he found that people liked some of his quaint cartoons, and he began developing them slowly, by adding such features as the little dog in the corner, the little boy in another."

McCutcheon spent his early years on the family farm in Indiana and then moved with his family to Lafayette, Indiana, when he was six. He attended Purdue University, where he met fellow Hoosier George Ade. After graduating in 1889, McCutcheon moved to Chicago and got a job in the art department of the morning edition of the *Chicago News* (which became the *Chicago Record* and later the *Chicago Record-Herald*). Ade joined McCutcheon in Chicago. They proved to be an enthusiastic team. Ade provided the stories and McCutcheon illustrated them. Between 1873 and 1897, their feature, "Stories of the Streets and of the Town," ran in the *Chicago Record*. For three years, they roomed together in a tiny, furnished apartment near Michigan Avenue. McCutcheon created his first political cartoons during the 1896 presidential campaign, which pitted William Jennings Bryan against William McKinley. Between 1903 and 1904, he created a series of one-panel cartoons in the *Chicago Record-Herald and Tribune,* depicting the lives of residents of the town, which he called Bird Center. The cartoons, published as the book *Bird Center Cartoons: A Chronicle of Social Happenings at Bird Center, Illinois* in 1904, became a national sensation. Many people held *Bird Center* parties where people would portray the various characters. Even card games were created, each

card an original drawing by McCutcheon himself and printed in colors on heavy ivory-enameled cardboard. In the same year, a theatrical adaptation of *Bird Center* was mounted at the Majestic Theatre in New York. (It closed after a disappointing thirteen-week run.)

McCutcheon began his long career with the *Chicago Tribune* on July 1, 1903. Following the death of Pope Leo XIII a few weeks later, McCutcheon created what many consider to be one of his finest cartoons. Bearing no caption, it consisted of a globe wrapped in a black bow. The public reaction was immediate. People were profoundly moved by the cartoon's powerful simplicity—it was reproduced by newspapers and magazines all over the world.

McCutcheon filed his cartoons and dispatches from far, out-of-the-way places. He witnessed the Battle of Manila Bay during the Spanish-American War, toured China and Japan in 1899, and journeyed to South Africa at the turn of the century to cover the Boer War. His other adventures include big-game hunting with Teddy Roosevelt in 1909, covering the Mexican Revolution in 1914, and serving as a war correspondent in Europe from 1915 to 1916. In 1932 he received the Pulitzer Prize for journalistic excellence for his now eerily prophetic cartoon, "A Wise Economist Asks a Question," in which a well-dressed man wearing a shirt, tie, and hat smokes a pipe while sitting on a bench. A sign indicates that he is a "victim of bank failure." A curious squirrel asks him, "But why didn't you save some money for the future when times were good?" The man replies, "I did."

McCutcheon's kindness and humor endeared him to millions. Perhaps because he understood human frailties so well, his brand of political satire was never vicious. Instead, he gently poked fun at world leaders, from Pancho Villa to Teddy Roosevelt. He deliberately tugged at the heartstrings of his readers. "Mail Call," a cartoon published during the height of World War II, depicted a soldier, head in hands, sitting dejectedly on the steps of an army barracks because he didn't receive a letter from home.

McCutcheon had a distinctive drawing style and was considered a master of the ink-drawn line. He used a variety of pen tips and brushes to create visual effects through lines of various widths. Instead of shading his drawings with random cross-hatching, as many cartoonists of his era did, he chose to use closely spaced parallel lines to create both depth and motion.

His cartoons were collected in several anthologies from 1905 to 1928, including *Cartoons by McCutcheon; Bird Center Cartoons; The Mysterious Stranger and Other Cartoons; Congressman Pumphrey, the People's Friend; In Africa; T. R.*

in Cartoons; Dawson '11, Fortune Hunter; The Restless Age; An Heir at Large; and *Crossed Wires and the Master of the World.* In addition to illustrating George Ade's *Chicago Stories,* McCutcheon also illustrated Ade's *Artie, Pink Marsh, Doc Horne, Fables in Slang,* and *More Fables in Slang.*

In 1917 McCutcheon married Evelyn Wells Shaw, daughter of architect Howard Van Doren Shaw. He retired from newspaper work in 1945 and died four years later in his Lake Forest home.

McCutcheon served as a mentor for many younger cartoonists, including Chester Gould, the creator of *Dick Tracy,* and Frank King, the creator of *Gasoline Alley.*

McCutcheon Terrace is named in his honor.

See also: George Ade, John Fischetti
Further reading: John T. McCutcheon, *Drawn from Memory, Containing Many of the Author's Famous Cartoons and Sketches* (1950).

Mary McDowell

Social Reformer

BORN: November 30, 1854
Cincinnati, Ohio

DIED: October 14, 1936
Chicago, Illinois

Mary McDowell was a pioneering social reformer. As founder of the University of Chicago settlement house, she attempted to break down ethnic barriers in order to promote a universal brother- and sisterhood. It didn't always work, and she made some enemies along the way, but to the vast number of residents of the South Side community she became a familiar and cherished friend. "I've always been interested in unpopular causes," she once said.

Born in Cincinnati, Ohio, Mary McDowell entered the field of social work at the age of twenty. She came to Chicago to study at Hull House and began working as an associate of Jane Addams. Addams recommended McDowell to head the University of Chicago settlement house (later renamed in her honor). McDowell was also one of the founders of the Northwestern University Settlement. During the spring of 1893, graduate students at the University of Chicago canvassed an area north of the stockyards, a neighborhood teeming with immigrants. The University of Chicago settlement house was established in 1894 by the philanthropic committee of the Christian Union of the university and incorporated with its own board of directors in 1898. McDowell was named head resident. The first house was located in a small flat near 47th Street and Ashland Avenue. Here she was given the sobriquet "Angel of the Stockyards."

The settlement grew slowly. McDowell opened a kindergarten for area children. In 1896 four flats and an adjacent shop were rented to accommodate clubs, classrooms, lectures, and concerts. The following year, McDowell purchased four lots on Gross Avenue (later changed to McDowell Avenue.) The settlement house served the needs of the changing community and adopted a good-neighbor policy. McDowell became affectionately known as the "Settlement Lady." As the organization developed and its reputation grew, prominent citizens from outside the neighborhood visited, including Thomas G. Masaryk, the first president of Czechoslovakia; Senator Medill McCormick; educator Booker T. Washington; and author Upton Sinclair, who was in town gathering information for his novel *The Jungle.* The settlement house provided many essential services. Immigrants received English lessons and classes in nutrition and hygiene. In addition, they had access to a public bathhouse, neighborhood playgrounds, and vocational schools.

McDowell was a doer. She frequently harassed the local alderman to "clean up the neighborhood" and made trips abroad to study methods of garbage disposal. In 1914 she became the Progressive Party's candidate for county commissioner and in 1923 Mayor William E. Dever appointed her public welfare commissioner. McDowell was also quite vocal on other matters, including the passage of legislation insuring an eight-hour workday. The economic plight of women especially concerned her. McDowell founded the Woman's City Club and was the first president of the Illinois Women's Trade Union League. After the 1919 race riots in Chicago, she organized the first interracial committee of women. She also acted as executive of the Chicago branch of the National Association for the Advancement of Colored People (NAACP) and was a member of the Chicago Urban League's executive committee. Moreover, McDowell was a member of the Illinois Equal Suffrage Association, and she later became chairman of the National League of Women Voters' committee on International Cooperation to Prevent War. She also served as director of the Chicago Immigrants' Protective League.

"We believe that God hath made of one blood all nations of men and that we are His children, brothers and sisters of all," McDowell wrote.

McDowell died in October 1936 at the age of eighty-one in the home of her brother at 5345 South Ellis Avenue.

In 1967 the Mary McDowell Settlement House merged with the Chicago Commons Association. Today the Chicago Commons, from its West Humboldt Park headquarters, continues work begun more than a hundred years ago, with its diverse programs for both youth and seniors and its partnerships with residents, schools, other social service agencies, and community organizations.

See also: Jane Addams, William Rainey Harper, Graham Taylor
Further reading: Mina Carson, *Settlement Folk: Social Thought and the American Settlement Movement 1885–1930* (1990); Robert A. Slayton, *Back of the Yards: The Making of a Local Democracy* (1986); Howard Eugene Wilson, *Mary McDowell, Neighbor* (1928).

Joseph Medill

Publisher and Politician

BORN: April 6, 1823
Saint John, New Brunswick

DIED: March 16, 1899
San Antonio, Texas

Joseph Meharry Medill was a pioneer in the development of modern journalism. His paper, the *Chicago Tribune*, reflected, for better or worse, the man himself. Persistent, opinionated, and determined, Medill played a crucial role in the growth of the Republican Party in Illinois and served as mayor of Chicago (from 1871 to 1873) during two of the most chaotic years of the city's history.

Joseph Medill was born to a family of shipbuilders in the Canadian maritime province of New Brunswick. His parents had emigrated from Ulster in 1819. The family moved to Stark County, Ohio, when Joseph was nine. He later studied law in Massillon, Ohio, and was admitted to the Ohio bar in 1846. He formed a partnership with George McIlvaine but later decided to change careers to enter the world of journalism. With his three younger brothers, he purchased the *Coshocton* (Ohio) *Whig*, which he renamed the *Republican*. After moving to Cleveland in 1851 he established the *Daily Forest City* and renamed it the *Cleveland Leader*.

In 1855 Medill and an associate, Dr. Charles Ray of Galena, Illinois, purchased an interest in the *Chicago Tribune*, with Medill assuming the title of business manager and managing editor. From the beginning the *Tribune* was a controversial paper. In 1859 Medill advocated the nomination of Abraham Lincoln for president. Some historians contend that without the *Tribune's* vociferous support, Lincoln would never have received the nomination, much less won the presidency. During the Civil War the Republican *Tribune* competed against Cyrus McCormick's equally strident antiwar paper, the *Chicago Times*, battling for the hearts and minds of the city's readers. Ironically, the two families came to a mutual understanding when Medill's daughter married McCormick's nephew and a newspaper dynasty was born.

Medill was a man of strong opinions. He detested gambling. An avowed teetotaler, he staunchly supported the temperance movement. The somber and aloof Medill also harbored some rather unusual and contradictory beliefs. An outspoken abolitionist and one of the first journalists to oppose slavery, he was also blatantly racist and anti-Catholic. He held little sympathy for the unemployed and, according to historian David L. Protess, especially loathed strikers, whom he called the "scum and filth of the city." Indeed, in one particularly cruel editorial, he proposed placing "a little strychnine or arsenic" in their food.

In 1869 Medill was elected to the Illinois constitutional convention. Shortly after the Great Fire of 1871, he was elected mayor of Chicago on a platform that called for strict fireproofing regulations. He was an effective administrator. He convinced the Illinois legislature to grant the mayoral office more power, supervised the rebuilding of the city, established Chicago's first public library, and reformed the police and fire departments. During his first year in office he rescued the city from virtual bankruptcy through frugal and sound management practices. Succumbing to pressure from Protestant ministers, Medill enforced the Sunday closing laws that shut down taverns on the Sabbath. He never recovered politically from this very unpopular decision.

In ill-health and exasperated by the daily grind of city government, Medill asked the city council for a leave of absence for the remainder of his term. He designated Alderman Lester L. Bond of the Tenth Ward as acting mayor. He toured Europe, regained his strength, and returned to Chicago in 1874, not as mayor but as editor-in-chief of the *Tribune*. As editor, he promoted business interests and criticized the burgeoning labor movement. During the days leading up to the Spanish-American War, Medill published defiantly jingoistic editorials.

Medill died in San Antonio, Texas, in 1899 at the age of seventy-five.

That same year Medill's son-in-law, Robert W. Patterson, assumed the position of editor-in-chief at the *Tribune*. When Patterson died in 1910, Joseph and his son Robert R. McCormick took over. On October 19, 1925, the Tribune Company authorized funding for the Medill School of Journalism at Northwestern University—the school had existed since 1921—in honor of Medill's considerable contribution to the world of journalism.

See also: William Bross, Robert R. McCormick, Wilbur F. Storey
Further reading: Megan McKinney, *The Magnificent Medills* (2011); David L. Protess, "Joseph Medill: Chicago's First Modern Mayor" in *The Mayors: The Chicago Political Tradition* (1987), Paul M. Green and Melvin G. Holli, eds.; Lloyd Wendt, *"Chicago Tribune": The Rise of a Great American Newspaper* (1979).

Charles E. Merriam

Educator and Politician

BORN: November 15, 1874
Hopkinton, Iowa

DIED: January 8, 1953
Rockville, Maryland

Charles E. Merriam was one of the foremost economists in the United States. As an alderman, he strived to adapt scientific principles to the tumultuous world of Chicago politics. As political science professor at the University of Chicago, he taught a liberal—some would say radical—brand of political theory to generations of college students.

Merriam received his education in the Iowa public school system, at Lenox College, and at the University of Iowa. He received his doctorate in political science from Columbia University in 1900. He also studied at the universities of Paris and Berlin. Merriam came to Chicago in 1900 to join the faculty of the University of Chicago. Eleven years later he became chairman of the political science department. In 1909 he turned theory into practice when he was elected alderman from the Seventh Ward on the Far South Side. In 1911 he ran as the Republican candidate for mayor, but was narrowly defeated by Carter Harrison II. The next year he was reelected to his aldermanic seat and remained in office until 1917. Two years later he opposed William Hale Thompson in the Republican primary of the mayoral election, but again he was defeated.

Merriam was the darling of the city's reform element. He called for the streamlining of local government, advocated an end to political patronage, and suggested improvements in the civil service system. Moreover, he urged the consolidation of the police, health, fire, water, drainage, recreational, and judicial services of both city and county governments. Merriam was at his most unorthodox when he advocated "city-state" or "home rule" status for Chicago that would allow the city to enact legislation different from that in effect elsewhere in Illinois.

As a leading member of the Chicago Charter Convention during the first decade of the twentieth century, Merriam called for the adoption of a special city charter, reiterated the necessity of controlling local finances through tax collection, and recommended a municipal court system to replace the antiquated justice of the peace courts. Further, Merriam maintained that Chicago had the right to manage its own affairs without first seeking approval from Springfield.

During World War I, Merriam served as a captain in the United States Army Signal Corps. He traveled to Italy in 1918 as a member of the American Commission on Public Information, for which the Italian government decorated him with the rank of Commander of the Order of the Royal Crown of Italy. He served as vice-chairman of President Herbert Hoover's Commission on Social Trends, and he was appointed a member of President Franklin Roosevelt's National Planning Board. He was instrumental in the planning of Roosevelt's monumental Social Security program and helped organize the Social Science Research Council, a national clearinghouse. He was elected president of that council in 1924. In that same year he assumed the presidency of the American Political Science Association.

A prolific writer, among his many books are *A History of American Political Ideas* (1920), *New Aspects of Politics* (1925), *The Role of Politics in Social Change* (1936), *The New Democracy and the New Despotism* (1939), and *Systematic Politics* (1945).

Merriam, who lived at 6041 South University Avenue, retired from the faculty of the University of Chicago in 1940. In March 1952, he suffered a stroke. He died in January 1953 in Rockville, Maryland. Two years later, his son Robert Merriam ran for mayor but was defeated by Richard J. Daley.

See also: Richard J. Daley, Carter Harrison II, William Hale Thompson
Further reading: Barry D. Karl, *Charles E. Merriam and the Study of Politics* (1974).

Ralph Metcalfe

Politician

BORN: May 30, 1910
Atlanta, Georgia

DIED: October 10, 1978
Chicago, Illinois

Ralph H. Metcalfe, a former Olympic track star, rose through the ranks of the Cook County Democratic organization to emerge as a powerful alderman and congressman in the African American community. For most of his political life, he was a solid and silent member of Richard J. Daley's team—until late in his career when Metcalfe asserted his independence and broke with the mayor. The Daley camp branded Metcalfe a turncoat, but in the eyes of the African American community, he was a hero.

Born in Atlanta, Georgia, Ralph Metcalfe moved with his family to Chicago, where he grew up at 3409 South Calumet Avenue and attended the public schools. He became a track star at Tilden Technical High School. At Marquette University in Milwaukee, Wisconsin, Metcalfe became captain of the college track team and emerged as a national collegiate champion in the 100- and 220-yard dashes. A member of the United States Olympic track team in 1932 and 1936, he won silver medals both times, finishing second to Jesse Owens and sharing a gold medal in the 400-meter relay in 1936. During World War II he served in the army as a lieutenant.

After the war Metcalfe returned to Chicago and entered politics. In 1949 he became the first African American appointed to the Illinois State Athletic Commission and served as an administrative assistant to the Board of Examiners under Mayor Martin Kennelly. Metcalfe was a protégé of United States representative William L. Dawson, a powerful black politician who ran his South Side district with an iron fist. With Dawson's backing, Metcalfe replaced state senator C. C. Wimbish in 1952 as Democratic committeeman of the Third Ward. In 1955 he supported Richard J. Daley's bid for mayor and won his first term as alderman of the Third Ward. When Dawson retired in 1970, Daley supported Metcalfe's bid to take over Dawson's First Congressional District seat. Metcalfe won reelection three times.

In 1969 Metcalfe became the first African American elected to the post of president pro tempore of the city council. As a member of the Black Congressional Congress, Metcalfe grew increasingly critical of the Daley administration. When several close friends complained of police harassment, he openly advocated police reform. Finally, in 1972, Metcalfe broke rank with Daley over the sensitive issue of police brutality.

In 1974 influential members of the African American community formed a committee to elect an African American mayor. When Daley made it clear that he would run again, however, Metcalfe dropped his candidacy—he didn't think he had a chance—and instead endorsed independent hopeful Alderman William S. Singer. Metcalfe received a great deal of criticism for supporting Singer, a white man, over the only black candidate, state senator Richard Newhouse. Metcalfe countered that his decision was a matter of politics, not race. He did not agree with Newhouse on several important issues, he explained, including Newhouse's lack of support for the Equal Rights Amendment (ERA).

In 1976 Daley and the Democratic Party refused to support Metcalfe for reelection. Instead, Daley chose aide Erwin France to challenge Metcalfe in the Democratic primary for Congress. Metcalfe won easily. It was the first time in Chicago history, declares historian Dempsey Travis, that any politician—black or white—had defeated the machine in a congressional primary or general election.

Metcalfe founded the Ralph H. Metcalfe Youth Foundation, which sponsored health, athletic, and educational programs in the African American community. A popular figure among his constituency, he never lost his base of support, even in 1972 when he was investigated by the IRS concerning allegations that he took zoning bribes while he was a member of the city council. The charges were later dropped.

Metcalfe died of a heart attack in his third-floor apartment at 4530 South Michigan Avenue in 1978. He was sixty-eight.

In 1981 the West Pullman–Nansen Area School, located at 12339 South Normal Avenue, was renamed in his honor.

See also: Richard J. Daley, Harold Washington

Further reading: William J. Grimshaw, *Bitter Fruit: Black Politics and the Chicago Machine, 1931–1991* (1995); Dempsey J. Travis, *An Autobiography of Black Chicago* (1981) and *An Autobiography of Black Politics* (1987).

Ray Meyer

College Basketball Coach

BORN: December 18, 1913
Chicago, Illinois

DIED: March 17, 2006
Wheeling, Illinois

Ray Meyer coached the DePaul University basketball team from 1942 to 1984, compiling an impressive 724–354 record, stretched over forty-two seasons. He was also among the most beloved of college coaches in Illinois history. His gap-toothed smile was a fixture on the Chicago basketball scene for decades.

Born in Chicago, the son of a candy wholesaler and the youngest of ten children, Meyer played basketball at Quigley Prep and St. Patrick's High School, both in Chicago. He was cocaptain at Notre Dame University in South Bend, Indiana. At Notre Dame, he was forward from 1936 to 1938 and captain for the 1937–38 season. He served as an assistant coach at Notre Dame from 1940 to 1942 and was named head coach at DePaul University in Chicago from 1942 until his retirement in 1984. He coached the DePaul Blue Demons team to twenty-one postseason appearances.

During his long basketball coaching career, he won 724 games with a .671 winning percentage. He had thirty-seven winning seasons and twelve seasons where his team won more than twenty games. Two of his teams reached the Final Four, in 1943 and 1979, and in 1945 his team captured the National Invitation Tournament. In addition, he coached a college all-star team that played against the Harlem Globetrotters for nearly a dozen years.

Meyer received numerous coaching accolades over the years. In 1979 Meyer was named coach of the year by the National Association of Basketball Coaches. The previous year, in 1978, he was elected to the Basketball Hall of Fame. When he retired from coaching, his record of 724–354 earned him a ranking of number five among college coaches.

The gregarious Meyer also provided color commentary for DePaul University games when his son, Joey, coached the team. Meyer retired from coaching in 1984, although he stayed on at DePaul as special assistant to the president until September 1997, performing fundraising and ambassadorial functions for the university. However, he left under unfortunate circumstances, resigning as a protest to the firing of his son in April 1997 after a disastrous 3–23 season.

Among the many excellent athletes that Meyer had on his teams were such former NBA players as Dave Corzine, Mark Aguirre, and Terry Cummings.

Meyer died in March 2006 at an assisted-living facility in Wheeling, Illinois, at the age of ninety-two.

In 1999 DePaul dedicated the Ray Meyer Fitness and Recreation Center on its Lincoln Park campus in his honor. In addition, a portion of Belden Avenue near the center was renamed Ray Meyer Drive. On December 14, 2003, the floor at the Allstate Arena in suburban Rosemont, Illinois, where the Blue Demons play their home games, was dedicated as the Ray and Marge Meyer court.

See also: Johnny "Red" Kerr
Further reading: Ray Meyer with Ray Sons, *Coach* (1987).

Mezz Mezzrow

Musician

BORN: November 9, 1899
Chicago, Illinois

DIED: August 5, 1972
Paris, France

Clarinetist and sax man, Milton Mezzrow founded one of the first interracial jazz bands. Mezzrow, a young white Jewish boy from a wealthy Chicago family, found sustenance in African American culture. He survived prison and drug addiction to become an important figure in local, national, and international jazz circles. To some he was a sycophant and hanger-on and a mediocre musician at best, but others saw in him a touch of genius. "If you want to play real jazz," he wrote in his autobiography, *Really the Blues*, "go live close to the Negro, see through his eyes, laugh and cry with him, soak up his spirit."

A high-strung kid with a great deal of nervous energy, Mezzrow turned to crime out of boredom. "Don't get the idea I was born a criminal," he wrote in his autobiography. "My family was as respectable as Sunday morning, loaded with doctors, lawyers, dentists, and pharmacists, and they all worked hard to make a solid citizen out of me. They almost did it, too." Mezzrow observed, "The law didn't catch up with me until I was sixteen years old."

Mezzrow first picked up a musical instrument, the saxophone, at the Pontiac Reformatory in Michigan while serving a jail sentence for stealing a car. Following his release in 1917, he played clubs in and around Chicago. He turned professional in 1923 and played occasionally with members of the famous Austin High Gang of the 1920s, including Bud Freeman, Jimmy McPartland, Gene Krupa, and Frank Teschemacher. He also played with Irving Rothschild in 1925 and Husk O'Hare's Wolverines in 1926. Two years later, in 1928, Mezzrow recorded with the

Jungle Kings and the Chicago Rhythm Kings, and in the same year he served as the leader of the short-lived Purple Grackle Orchestra.

As many Chicago musicians did, Mezzrow moved to New York in 1928 to further his career, subbing for Gil Rodin in Ben Pollack's Band. In October 1928, he recorded with Eddie Condon. The following March he sailed for Europe and led his own band in Paris. By April 1929, he was back in New York. He later worked as a freelance musician in New York during the 1930s and 1940s.

In 1937 his interracial band, the Disciples of Swing, played the Harlem Uproar House and the Savoy Ballroom. During the early 1940s, he worked with fellow Chicagoan Art Hodes. Later, Mezzrow formed his own record company, King Jazz. In the late 1940s and early 1950s, he toured Europe before settling again in Paris, where he worked as a self-proclaimed entrepreneur and jazz promoter, organizing touring bands. During the 1950s he formed several all-star bands, which featured such top-notch musicians as Lee Collins, Zutty Singleton, and Buck Clayton.

Mezzrow is known not so much because of his music—which most critics find lacking in both execution and substance—but due to his sensational autobiography, *Really the Blues* (1946), which he cowrote with Bernard Wolfe. *Really the Blues* met with great literary success. Despite the recognition the book brought to Mezzrow, he truly deserves a place in the annals of jazz for organizing many important recording sessions with the great masters, especially those with clarinetist and saxophonist Sidney Bechet and trumpeter Tommy Ladnier.

Mezzrow set his own rules and lived life the way he saw fit. Tenor saxophonist Bud Freeman, who used to visit Mezzrow in his cramped Rogers Park apartment, recalls in his autobiography that Mezzrow "was the first white man I ever knew to move to Harlem and marry a black woman and have a child by a black. I had to love that about him because we lived in a time when prejudice was unbelievable. Mezz . . . knew things about the black people, their way of thinking and their music, that very few white people did." Mezzrow adopted black music and culture to such an extent that, according to coauthor Bernard Wolfe, he believed he actually was black.

Mezzrow continued to make appearances at festivals in Europe during the 1960s. During his last years, however, he rarely performed in public. Like many of the African Americans he idolized, Mezzrow died in Paris, in self-exile, in 1972.

See also: Bud Freeman, Benny Goodman, Art Hodes, Gene Krupa
Further reading: John Chilton, *Who's Who of Jazz: Storyville to Swing Street* (1978); Bud Freeman, as told to Robert Wolf, *Crazeology: The Autobiography of a Chicago Jazzman* (1989); Barry Kernfield, ed., *The New Grove Dictionary of Jazz*, vol. 2 (1988).

Albert A. Michelson

Physicist

BORN: December 19, 1852
Strelno, Prussia (now Strzelno, Poland)

DIED: May 9, 1931
Pasadena, California

Albert Abraham Michelson is regarded as one of the great minds of the twentieth century. He strove for absolute accuracy in his pioneering experiments to determine the speed of light, and this work, which he completed at the University of Chicago, paved the way for Einstein's theory of relativity.

Michelson's mother, Rosalie Pruzlubsk, the daughter of a physician, married Samuel Michelson, proprietor of a dry goods store in Prussia. The family immigrated to the United States when Michelson was two. He grew up in Virginia City, Nevada, and in San Francisco. He graduated from the United States Naval Academy in Annapolis, Maryland, in 1873. After two years of duty, Michelson returned to the academy to teach chemistry and physics. In 1878, while an instructor at Annapolis, he conducted preliminary experiments measuring the speed of light—the most precise measurements at that time—using a makeshift instrument that he constructed himself. In 1881 he resigned from the navy to concentrate further on his own scientific work.

In 1883 Michelson became professor of physics at Case School of Applied Science (now Case Western Reserve University). Six years later he moved to Clark University in Ohio. In 1892 he was appointed head of the physics department at the recently established University of Chicago. When he arrived in Chicago, Michelson was already a famous man. He continued to devote a large part of his research to measuring the speed of light. In 1880 he had invented the interferometer, a highly sensitive instrument that measured light rays and determined distances that even the most powerful telescope couldn't determine. In 1887 Michelson and Edward W. Morley ran two beams

of light against each other from opposite directions and proved that the speed of light is a constant. At that time the scientific community was grappling with the problems of measuring absolute motion (as opposed to relative motion). The concept of "ether" (an elastic medium in space through which motion occurs) helped to resolve certain fundamental theoretical difficulties of electricity and magnetism. Michelson and Morley demonstrated the absence of ether. The results of their experiments were not explained by classical Newtonian physics, and therefore formed the foundation of Albert Einstein's theory of relativity. In 1920, by using the interferometer, Michelson was able to measure the diameter of the star Betelgeuse, which allowed scientists to obtain a more accurate picture of the size of the universe. In 1927, after flashing light beams from Mount Wilson to another nearby peak, he calculated the speed of light at 186,284 miles per second. He spent his last years producing a more precise figure.

In 1907 Michelson was the first American to be awarded the Nobel Prize in Physics, for his work in meteorology and spectroscopy, which he had studied in Lake Geneva, Wisconsin. He was appointed head of the physics department at the University of Chicago in 1892 and remained on the faculty until he announced his retirement in 1930. In 1925 Michelson became the first Distinguished Service Professor at the University of Chicago.

Michelson wrote several books, including *Velocity of Light* (1902), *Light Waves and Their Uses* (1903), and *Studies in Optics* (1927).

Michelson was one of the most respected scientists in the world. Among the universities that awarded him honorary degrees were Cambridge, Yale, Princeton, Leipzig, McGill, Western Reserve, and Pennsylvania. He died in Pasadena, California, in 1931. He was seventy-eight.

See also: William Rainey Harper
Further reading: Dorothy Michelson Livingston, *The Master of Light: A Biography of Albert A. Michelson* (1973).

Ludwig Mies van der Rohe

Architect

BORN: March 27, 1886
Aachen, Germany

DIED: August 19, 1969
Chicago, Illinois

One of the founding fathers of modern architecture, Ludwig Mies van der Rohe created designs that were deceptively simple. To critics his work was cold, austere, and sterile; to admirers, it was bold, breathtaking, and innovative. Eventually, Mies van der Rohe came to epitomize modern architecture. By the time of his death, every major city in the Western world, wrote noted art critic Franz Schulze, bore Mies van der Rohe's indelible stamp.

Born Ludwig Mies in the German city of Aachen (in 1921, he added his mother's name, Rohe, with "van der" as the connecting bridge), Mies studied at a local trades school. He worked as an architectural draftsman until he moved to Berlin in 1905, where he was apprenticed to a furniture designer. At twenty-one, he designed the residence of a prominent client, which brought him to the attention of Germany's premier architect, Peter Behrens. After working with Behrens for three years, Mies established his own practice.

Fascinated by the aesthetic possibilities of glass, Mies was one of the first architects to design glass skyscrapers. By the early 1920s he had become a leading figure of modern architecture. In 1927 Mies, Walter Gropius, Behrens, and others constructed a housing estate, the Weissenhof settlement, on a hill overlooking the city of Stuttgart. The settlement, designed as a contemporary living space for the urban dweller, shocked the architectural establishment from their complacency. Weissenhof was such a radical departure from historic architectural norms—consisting as it did of low, box-like structures—that though designed with the ordinary citizen in mind it soon became the favored living quarters of journalists, actors, and intellectuals. Mies's stock rose even higher. It wasn't until 1929, however, with the completion of the German Pavilion at the Barcelona International Exposition—critics referred to it as Mies's European masterpiece—that the architect finally emerged as a world-class artist.

In 1930 Mies was appointed director of the Bauhaus, the influential German school of design. Yet three short years later, Mies shut down the school as Hitler and Nazism spread throughout the country. In 1936 Mies received a letter from John A. Holabird of the Chicago architectural firm of Holabird and Root. Holabird headed a search committee to locate a director of the architecture school at the Armour Institute of Technology (now the Illinois Institute of Technology). Mies expressed interest. In 1938, with conditions in Germany rapidly deteriorating, he accepted the offer. He stayed for twenty years. The following year the administration asked him to draw up a master plan for the school's one-hundred-acre campus.

Mies's spare, functional glass towers changed the Chicago landscape. Whereas the skyscrapers of the late nineteenth to early twentieth century used traditional materials such as stone and brick decorated with classical columns and motifs, Mies preferred a simpler, angular design with little or no ornamentation. Some critics would later condemn Miesian architecture for its sterility and lack of humanity. Mies, however, argued that architecture should mirror its particular culture and milieu. Thus his work, in large part, reflected the twentieth-century obsession with technology and industry.

Some of his most important buildings in Chicago include the Promontory Apartments at 5530 South Shore Drive (1949); the twin apartment buildings at 860–880 North Lake Shore Drive, among the first glass-and-steel high-rises in the world (1952); Crown Hall on the Illinois Institute of Technology campus on South State Street between 31st and 35th Streets (1956); and the Federal Center at Jackson, Dearborn, Adams, and Clark Streets (1965). The last building he designed was the fifty-two-story IBM building, completed in 1971. Among his famous international commissions are the New National Gallery in Berlin (1967) and the Dominion Centre in Toronto (1969).

In 1944 Mies became an American citizen. Although a man of means in his later years, he never lived a luxurious lifestyle. His apartment at 200 East Pearson Street was simply furnished. He reportedly preferred to live there rather than in a building that he designed for he feared that tenants might complain to him personally, notes Schulze.

In 1958 Mies retired from IIT. During the last decade of his life, arthritis confined him to a wheelchair, but he kept working. In 1966 he contracted cancer of the esophagus and died three years later from pneumonia at the age of eighty-three. His body was cremated and his ashes buried in Graceland Cemetery in Chicago near the graves of two other prominent Chicago architects, Daniel H. Burnham and Louis Sullivan.

Following Mies's death, there was a pronounced movement away from modernism. Postmodernists such as Michael Graves, Philip Johnson, and Thomas Beebe bemoaned the numbing sameness of high-rise boxes that dotted the urban skylines. In recent years, though, Mies's accomplishments have been reevaluated and his stature as one of the great architects of the twentieth century seems secure.

After his death such Miesian disciples as Joseph Fujikawa, Dirk Lohan, and Helmut Jahn carried on his legacy, as did the firms of C. F. Murphy and Associates and the prolific Skidmore, Owings, and Merrill. Several prominent examples of Miesian-influenced architecture include the Richard J. Daley Center at Washington and Dearborn Streets (1965); the CNA Building at Jackson Boulevard and Wabash Avenue (1972); the Willis Tower (formerly named the Sears Tower) at Adams and Franklin Streets (1974); Illinois Center at North Michigan Avenue and East Randolph Drive (1975); and the Federal Building at 77 West Jackson Boulevard (1991), which complements Mies's Federal Center a few blocks north.

In 1986 several institutions, including the Illinois Institute of Technology and the Art Institute of Chicago, sponsored major exhibitions of his life and work in honor of the centennial of his birth.

See also: Daniel H. Burnham, Louis Sullivan, Frank Lloyd Wright
Further reading: Mary Alice Molloy, *Chicago Since the Sears Tower: A Guide to New Downtown Buildings* (1990); Pauline A. Saliga, ed., *The Sky's the Limit: A Century of Chicago Skyscrapers* (1990); Franz Schulze, *Mies van der Rohe: A Critical Biography* (1985).

Edgar Miller

Artist

BORN: Circa 1899
Idaho Falls, Idaho

DIED: June 1, 1993
Evanston, Illinois

Edgar Miller believed that old houses could be turned into works of art. Miller, the American equivalent of England's William Morris, the founder of the arts and crafts movement, created four artists' studios on the North Side in the 1920s and 1930s, recycling ordinary materials—brick, stone, tile, glass, steel, and wood—often from Maxwell Street. And like Morris, he celebrated craftsmanship and rejected the sterile technology of the machine age.

"Miller's recycled houses," observes Richard Cahan, "point to a new architecture, but it has taken us decades to fully understand them." Ahead of his time, Miller, says Cahan, found "beauty and utility in reusing material." Miller and his colleague, Sol Kogen, are credited with starting the vernacular architecture movement in Chicago, referring to buildings that have been rehabbed by their owners rather than by architects.

Miller argued that humanity should respect and learn from nature. The son of James Edgar Miller, a beekeeper, and Hester Elizabeth Gibson Martin, Miller grew up in Idaho and loved the ruggedness of the West. At a young age, he displayed a natural talent at drawing and illustration. When he was four, he saw a painting of General George Armstrong Custer's last stand at Little Big Horn and announced to his family that he wanted to become an artist. Seven years later he served as an apprentice with a local architectural firm.

In November 1913 Miller's father took Edgar and his brother to Australia to raise bees near Melbourne. In Australia Miller took classes in basic drawing, dropped out of art school, and had a brief stint at a lithography firm. He then returned to high school in Idaho Falls, where his cartoons earned sufficient notice to allow him to attend the School of the Art Institute in Chicago.

Arriving in Chicago in January 1917, Miller found a room at Jane Addams's Hull House on the Near West Side. His teachers at the Art Institute included the muralist John W. Norton, the illustrator and publisher Ralph Fletcher Seymour, and the sculptor Albin Polasek. George Bellows, a guest instructor, had a major influence on Miller; Bellows's lecture on American artist Jay Hambidge's theory of dynamic symmetry initially made an impact on Miller (though he would later dismiss it). The theory, which was based on mathematical laws inspired by proportion and symmetry in Greek architecture and sculpture, essentially reduced all things to geometric forms and patterns. Either way, Bellows helped Miller look at art in an entirely different way. "I learned how to look at a line and see its significant direction of movement," Miller observed. Still, Miller was frustrated by the overall instruction at the school; instructors encouraged him to become a specialist, whereas he wanted to learn more about the techniques of many art forms. In 1919, along with other students, Miller left the school over a dispute with the administration.

Miller's first job after leaving the Art Institute was as an apprentice in the studio of the versatile sculptor, metalworker, and commercial designer Alfonso Ianelli. The lesson that Miller took away from his five years there was to create art that could be applied to everyday life. Thus, he designed books, murals, posters, and stained glass. He worked also with the studio's clients, which included many of the city's major businesses: Marshall Field and Company, the architect Barry Byrne, and the architectural firm of Holabird and Root.

By the time Miller left Ianelli, he had established an estimable reputation in the city's art world. In the early 1920s he opened his own art gallery on Pearson Street. Along with other modernists, he exhibited work at the House at the End of the Street. In addition, he helped run a gallery on the top floor of the Dil Pickle Club in the bohemian neighborhood called Towertown, located west of the historic Water Tower. He continued to work as a commercial artist, accepting as many assignments as he could handle, from woodcut illustrations for advertisements to pen-and-ink illustrations for ads and magazine covers. In the mid-1920s he turned increasingly toward interior design. The renowned architect Howard Van Doren Shaw hired Miller to design stained glass windows for three buildings, including an office at the Lakeside Press Building in Printer's Row, where he created windows that depicted the history of the printing press, from William Caxton to William Morris's Kelmscott Press.

In 1927 his former Art Institute classmate Sol Kogen approached Miller with the idea of building an artists' colony in Old Town. Kogen had spent some time in Paris and was inspired by that city's bohemian Montmartre neighborhood; he dreamed of recreating it in Chicago. Miller and Kogen rehabbed old houses such as the Victorian house at 155 West Carl Street, later to be known as the Carl Street Studios (in 1936 Carl Street was changed to Burton Place); a complex of artists' studios at 1734 North Wells Street; and the R. W. Glasner Studio in the rear of the Wells Street building. The Wells Street and Glasner studios came to be known collectively as the "Kogen-Miller colony." The buildings are houses designed by artists for artists.

Miller's other works include the Walter Guest apartments at 2150 North Cleveland Avenue; stained glass windows at Kelvyn Park High School, 4343 West Wrightwood Avenue; and the "Love Through the Ages" mural at the Tavern Club, 333 North Michigan Avenue. He was also commissioned by restaurants and hotels, such as the Palmer House, to create murals. In addition, he created glass doors and murals for the Standard Club; leaded glass windows at the Lawson YMCA Chapel at 30 West Chicago Avenue; and stained glass windows at the Medinah Athletic Club, 505 North Michigan Avenue (now the InterContinental Chicago hotel). In the late 1930s, he worked alongside Andy Rebori on various commercial projects, including the Frank F. Fisher Apartments at 1209 North State Parkway.

In the early 1950s, Miller and his wife Dorothy moved to an eighteen-room mansion at 5754 North Sheridan Road. More than two years later, he moved to Florida and then to San Francisco before returning to Chicago in the mid-1980s, living in the Carl (Burton Place) and Wells Street studios that he had designed years earlier. In 1987 he was declared as one of the founders of Old Town. Two years later the Graham Foundation for Advanced Studies in the Fine Arts presented an exhibition of his work.

In 1991 Miller injured himself at the Carl Street Studios, falling on the stairs in his apartment. Increasingly frail and suffering from dementia, he died at St. Francis Hospital in Evanston in June 1993.

Until recently, Miller's unique genius has been largely overlooked, partly because his work was displayed in private homes or in public buildings that took some effort to find rather than in more easily accessible museums.

Fortunately, that has changed and now he is recognized as one of the city's most respected, and unique, artists.

See also: Howard Van Doren Shaw, Lambert Tree

Further reading: Shirley Baugher, *Our Old Town: The History of a Neighborhood* (2001); Richard Cahan and Michael Williams, *Edgar Miller and the Handmade Home: Chicago's Forgotten Renaissance Man* (2009); Nick J. Matsoukas, "The Kogen-Miller Studios," *Western Architect,* December 1930; Christine Newman, "An Old Town Odyssey," *Chicago,* October 2000; Sue Ann Prince, ed., *The Old Guard and the Avant-garde: Modernism in Chicago, 1910–1940* (1990); Toni Schlesinger, "Old Town's Mad Masterpiece," *Chicago,* May 1988.

Harriet Monroe
Poet and Publisher

BORN: December 23, 1860
Chicago, Illinois

DIED: September 26, 1936
Arequipa, Peru

Poet, journalist, and essayist, Harriet Monroe is best remembered as the guiding spirit behind *Poetry,* the magazine that she founded in 1912. Not only did *Poetry* form the heart and soul of the Chicago literary renaissance, it was the only magazine in the United States at that time devoted exclusively to poetry.

Monroe's father, Henry Monroe, a lawyer, arrived in Chicago in 1852. Monroe was born in 1860 in the family's rented house at Twelfth Street (now Roosevelt Road) and Wabash Avenue. A lonely child, she found solace in the books that lined her father's library. According to historian Geoffrey Johnson she was unusually sensitive, and even at ten years old she had considered suicide to relieve her from her inner demons. Social historian Dale Kramer wrote that Monroe's emotional attachments were toward "the arts and to countries and to mountains. Harriet dedicated herself to a poet's life."

In 1877 Monroe enrolled at Visitation Convent, a genteel girls' boarding school in Georgetown. Most of her classmates were there to learn how to become perfect wives. Monroe had other ideas. After graduation, she began planning her future. As she states in her autobiography, she wanted her life to have purpose, to accomplish a great good, for "to die without leaving some memorable record" was, in her mind, a great tragedy. "My career was to be rich and all-embracing."

Monroe supported herself with freelance articles, lectures, and teaching. At two different periods in her life, she served as the art critic for the *Chicago Tribune.* In 1891 she convinced members of the World's Columbian Exposition

committee that a poem commemorating the fair was not only appropriate but essential. The committee commissioned Monroe, at her suggestion, and she submitted her first draft in May 1893. Influential committee members rejected the poem, which honored the United States and its heroes, as too long and too staid. Even so, Monroe insisted on her fee of $1,000. After much heated discussion, the poem was used. In December 1894, Monroe became embroiled in a legal battle when the *New York World* published "Columbian Ode" without her permission. In a bold, precedent-setting move, she sued for infringement of copyright and was awarded $5,000 in punitive damages.

Monroe continued to write sporadically for the *Tribune* as well as publish literary and travel essays in the *Atlantic,* the *Century,* and London's *Fortnightly Review.* She also supplemented her income with teaching and lecturing. In 1910 she took off on one of her frequent journeys, traveling across Siberia from Moscow en route to visit her sister in Peking. After much thought, she returned to Chicago in 1911, determined to create a market for poetry. "The poets needed a magazine, an organ of their own, and I would start one for them!" she declared.

It was a bold move. No magazine of its kind existed in the United States. With the financial help of Hobart C. Chatfield-Taylor, a wealthy Chicago socialite, Monroe pushed ahead with her plans. She was able to convince one hundred prominent people to pledge $50 a year for five years toward the fledgling magazine. The list of contributors included a veritable who's who of Chicago's elite at the time: Potter Palmer; businessman Martin Ryerson; George Pullman; businessman John Glessner; Daniel H.

Burnham; Samuel Insull; Charles L. Hutchinson, president of the Art Institute; Edith Rockefeller McCormick; Charles H. Swift; Rev. F. W. Gunsaulus, president of the Armour Institute of Technology; Herman H. Kohlsaat, editor of the *Chicago Record-Herald;* Victor Lawson, editor and publisher of the *Chicago Daily News;* Howard Van Doren Shaw; Clarence Darrow; and Harriet Moody, widow of the poet William Vaughn Moody. Next, she began recruiting poets, gambling on the young and untried. One of those poets was Ezra Pound, a self-imposed American exile who had become the literary sensation of London and Paris.

Pound was instrumental in the success of Monroe's new magazine, which she simply called *Poetry.* He introduced the work of William Butler Yeats, Robert Frost, Richard Aldington, James Joyce, Ford Madox Ford, D. H. Lawrence, William Carlos Williams, and an American student of philosophy at Oxford, Thomas Stearns Eliot. It was Pound who sent Monroe a copy of Eliot's "The Love Song of J. Alfred Prufrock."

Monroe worked diligently on the day-to-day chores of putting out a magazine. Among her editorial assistants were Chatfield-Taylor, Edith Wyatt, and Henry Blake Fuller. The first issue was published on September 23, 1912, and included an essay by Monroe, a poem by William Vaughn Moody, and contributions from Pound and others.

Poetry became the talk of the literary set. The city's poets and authors—including Carl Sandburg, Vachel Lindsay, and Edgar Lee Masters—stopped by the magazine headquarters at 543 North Cass Street (now Wabash Avenue). Monroe herself became a close friend and confidant to the city's literary folk and distinguished guests—Glenway Wescott, Marianne Moore, Robert Graves, Malcolm Cowley, Eunice Tietjens, and many others. She published the early works of Lindsay and Masters. The local press was generally supportive of the magazine, and Chicago newspapers, including the *Tribune* and the *Friday Literary Review,* were generous in their praise.

Monroe's collected verse, *Chosen Poems,* was published in 1935. She also wrote a biography of her famous brother-in-law (he was married to her sister, Dora), architect John Wellborn Root. She began to write her autobiography when she was invited in 1936 to represent Chicago for a convention of PEN (International Association of Poets, Playwrights, Editors, Essayists, and Novelists) in Buenos Aires. Taking advantage of the South American locale, she decided to take a side trip to Chile and Peru. The journey proved too strenuous for her—she was seventy-five—and she died on September 26, 1936, in the Peruvian village of Arequipa and was buried there.

In 2002 *Poetry* magazine received a $200 million grant from the estate of Ruth Lilly, the American heiress and great-granddaughter of Eli Lilly, founder of the pharmaceutical firm that bears his name. In 2007 the Chicago-based John Ronan Architects was hired to build a new home for *Poetry* magazine and the Poetry Foundation, in an environmentally sustainable building at the southwest corner of Dearborn and Superior Streets. The first permanent home in the history of *Poetry,* the $21.5 million, two-story, 22,000-square-foot space houses a 30,000-volume noncirculating library, a public garden, and a 125-seat multipurpose room that is acoustically designed for the spoken word. It opened in June 2011.

See also: Margaret C. Anderson, Henry Blake Fuller, Vachel Lindsay, Edgar Lee Masters, John Wellborn Root

Further reading: Geoffrey Johnson, "Little Captain of the Ragged, the Mad Army of Poets," *Chicago Reader,* September 6, 1985; Dale Kramer, *Chicago Renaissance: The Literary Life of the Midwest, 1900–1903* (1966); Harriet Monroe, *A Poet's Life: Seventy Years in a Changing World* (1938); Joseph Parisi and Stephen Young, eds., *Between the Lines: A History of "Poetry" in Letters, 1962–2002* (2006), *Dear Editor: A History of "Poetry" in Letters Part I: 1912–1962* (2002), and *The "Poetry" Anthology, 1912–2002: Ninety Years of America's Most Distinguished Verse Magazine* (2002); Alson J. Smith, *Chicago's Left Bank* (1953); Ellen Williams, *Harriet Monroe and the Poetry Renaissance: The First Ten Years of "Poetry," 1912–22* (1977).

Dwight L. Moody

Evangelist

BORN: February 5, 1837
Northfield, Massachusetts

DIED: December 22, 1899
Northfield, Massachusetts

Although not ordained, Dwight Lyman Moody was an influential evangelist whose wildly successful campaigns predated a later generation of preachers from Billy Sunday to Billy Graham, Jimmy Swaggart to Ted Haggard. Not so much concerned with social sins—smoking, card playing, drinking, gambling—Moody chose to emphasize the spiritual well-being of his congregation. "Character," he once said, "is what a man is in the dark." Moody has been credited with pioneering a brand of Christianity that has transcended denominations, laying the groundwork for such modern phenomena as megachurches and the Promise Keepers.

The sixth child of Edwin and Betsy Holton Moody, Dwight Moody attended school in Northfield, Massachusetts, until he was thirteen and then moved to Boston at seventeen to work in his uncle's shoe store. His employment, however, was on the condition that he attend the Mount Vernon Congregational Church. Moody began participating in the Sunday school classes at the church, taught by Edward Kimball. In April 1855 Kimball converted Moody to evangelical Christianity. The following year Moody moved to Chicago and found work as a shoe salesman. He spent more time, however, with pursuits more spiritual then selling shoes.

Moody started a Sunday school for slum children in 1858 at Chicago Avenue and Wells Street. Then he moved the Sunday school to an abandoned saloon on the north side of the Chicago River in a rough part of town. He persuaded the local street urchins to find God in his Sunday school, enticing them with pennies or maple-sugar candy.

With attendance overflowing capacity, he used the upstairs room in North Market Hall on Hubbard Street for his school, reportedly recruiting students by pulling orphans off the street. In February 1864 he opened the Illinois Street Church. When this was destroyed in the Chicago Fire in 1871, he rebuilt the church and called it the North Side Tabernacle. The name was changed again to the Chicago Avenue Church, located at Chicago Avenue and LaSalle Street, predecessor of today's structure at LaSalle Street and North Avenue.

Moody was a familiar figure on Chicago streets. He went about the business of selling God to thousands of apathetic Chicagoans. He ventured into saloons and brothels, accosting thieves, liars, and beggars, and demanded to know if they were Christian. If not, he would ask why not. "Come to my church. Be saved!" he would exclaim. Journalists called him "Brother Moody." Others, less kind, dismissed him as "Crazy Moody." During the Civil War, Moody conducted missionary services among the Union soldiers at Camp Douglas on the South Side. When the war ended he became president of the Chicago branch of the Young Men's Christian Association (YMCA). From 1873 to 1875 he embarked with organist Ira D. Sankey on tours through Scotland, England, and Ireland, where he spread the expansive spirit of evangelism. He returned to the United States a famous man. Deciding to leave Chicago, he returned to his hometown in Massachusetts to establish the Northfield School for Girls and, several years later, the Northfield School for Boys. He made another successful tour of Great Britain from 1881 to 1883, and a final one from 1891 to 1892.

During his prolonged absence from Chicago, Moody's work was continued by Emma Dryer, a teacher at Illinois State Normal University, whom he first met in 1870. In 1886 Moody returned to Chicago to deliver a lecture calling for the establishment of a permanent ministry training school. The following year the Chicago Evangelization Society was organized, and on September 26, 1889, the Chicago Bible Institute, a coeducational missionary school, officially opened. The goal of the organization was "to educate, direct, and maintain Christian workers as Bible readers, teachers, and evangelists."

Moody purportedly reached more people than any church-sanctioned clergyman. He achieved this by preaching a simple brand of Christianity that millions of ordinary folk found immensely appealing. Contemporary accounts describe Moody's campaigns as the spiritual equivalent of business conventions. With Ira D. Sankey, Moody published several popular collections of hymns, including *Sacred Songs and Solos* (1873) and *Gospel Hymns* (1875–1891). Although Sankey wrote only a handful of hymns himself (and the tone-deaf Moody didn't write any), he is credited with popularizing the gospel hymn among the white community.

The growth of the Chicago Bible Institute coincided with Chicago's rapid escalation as a great commercial center. Moody's aggressive recruiting methods, as well as his insistence on a quality teaching staff, helped transform his humble Sunday school into a top-notch institution. Indeed, throughout its long history, the Moody Bible Institute (the Chicago Bible Institute was renamed the Moody Bible Institute of Chicago after Moody's death) has enjoyed a stellar reputation as a world-class evangelical training center. The institute combines theological education with biblical training and offers programs leading to B.A., B.S., and M.A. degrees. More than one hundred years after its founding, the school continues to spread the word.

In December 1899, Moody died in his native Massachusetts of a heart attack at the age of sixty-two. The Moody Church, dedicated in 1925 at North Avenue and LaSalle

Street, serves as a memorial to this remarkable evangelist. In 1999 the Moody Church celebrated the centenary of his death with a program honoring his life and work. As part of the celebration, the Moody Bible Institute introduced an interactive D. L. Moody Museum on its campus.

Moody Avenue is named in his honor.

See also: Billy Sunday, David Swing

Further reading: Richard K. Curtis, *They Called Him Mister Moody* (1962); Lyle W. Dorsett, *A Passion for Souls: The Life of D. L. Moody* (2003); Gene A. Getz, *MBI: The Story of the Moody Bible Institute* (1969); Paul D. Moody, *My Father: An Intimate Portrait of Dwight Moody* (1938); John C. Pollock, *Moody: A Biographical Portrait of the Pacesetter in Modern Mass Evangelism* (1963).

Joy Morton

Entrepreneur

BORN: September 27, 1855
Near Nebraska City,
Nebraska Territory

DIED: May 10, 1934
Lisle, Illinois

Joy Morton founded the Morton Salt Company and established the Morton Arboretum in west suburban Lisle, Illinois.

Morton's parents were among the early settlers of the Nebraska Territory. His mother, Caroline, was an artist and musician. His father, Julius Sterling Morton, was a prominent politician who served as secretary of agriculture during President Grover Cleveland's second term in office. In 1872, Julius Morton founded Arbor Day.

Joy Morton attended the Helmuth Institute in London, Ontario, for a short time before enrolling at the University of Michigan. He then transferred to Mayhew Commercial College in Detroit. Morton then worked for a bank in Nebraska City and for a railroad company in Aurora, Illinois, before he finally settled in Chicago. In 1880 Morton accepted the offer of a partnership in the firm of E. I. Wheeler and Company, a Chicago agent for the Michigan Salt Association. He was so successful that he was able to acquire a half interest in the company by 1885. When Wheeler died the same year, Morton reorganized the firm as Joy Morton and Company. Salt was in great demand at the time. Chicago's meatpacking industry alone consumed massive quantities of salt.

As the company prospered, Morton expanded into other areas. In 1889 he became a stockholder and director in the American Trust and Savings Bank of Chicago and in the Nebraska City National Bank. He also invested heavily in Chicago real estate. In addition, he expanded the salt company and acquired warehouses in cities throughout the Midwest. In 1910, in an effort to promote its new moisture-proof salt container, the company created the now familiar image of a young girl coyly holding an umbrella, accompanied by the catchy slogan "When It Rains, It Pours."

Morton also chaired the Commercial Club of Chicago's railway terminus committee for Daniel Burnham and Edward Bennett's 1909 *Plan of Chicago*. He served on the Chicago Plan Commission for twenty-five years.

Morton purchased a farm in west suburban Lisle, Illinois, and in 1922 established the Morton Arboretum on 178 acres of land for scientific research in horticulture and agriculture. Today, at 1,700 acres, the Morton Arboretum remains a popular spot for nature lovers throughout Chicagoland.

See also: Daniel Burnham

Further reading: James Ballowe, *A Man of Salt and Trees: The Life of Joy Morton* (2009).

Archibald J. Motley Jr.

Painter

BORN: October 7, 1891
New Orleans, Louisiana

DIED: January 16, 1981
Chicago, Illinois

Archibald John Motley Jr., the brother of novelist Willard Motley, was the first American painter who devoted his career exclusively to African American subject matter and was one of the first successful black artists in the twentieth century. Motley's candid depictions attempted to portray African American life as accurately as possible.

Born in New Orleans of Creole and African American ancestry, Archibald Motley Jr. moved to Chicago with his family in 1894. Motley's upbringing instilled a strong sense of pride in his African heritage. His father was a Pullman porter who played an important role in the founding of the Brotherhood of Sleeping Car Porters, and his mother was a schoolteacher.

Motley was the only male in his Englewood High School art class. Through his position as a railroad porter, Motley's father met Rev. Frank W. Gunsaulus, president of the Armour Institute of Technology. Gunsaulus offered Motley a full scholarship to study architecture at the Armour Institute. Flattered but determined to become a painter, Motley turned him down. Gunsaulus, in turn, was impressed by the young man's persistence and offered to pay for one year of study at the Art Institute. Motley agreed, and he enrolled in 1914. Four years later he graduated with honors, "one of the few Chicago blacks," says Elaine D. Woodall in *Chicago History*, "to have completed the full four-year course."

Unable to secure employment as a commercial artist at advertising agencies because of his race, Motley found work as a dining car waiter, a steamfitter in the Union Stockyards, and a plumber, while continuing to paint in the evenings. In 1920, at the urging of friends, he submitted *Portrait of My Mother* to the Art Institute for its Annual Exhibition by Artists of Chicago and the Vicinity. During the next few years *Portrait* and four other works were accepted. This recognition was a major turning point in Motley's career.

In 1928 Motley's paintings were exhibited at the New Gallery in New York. Motley was one of the first African American artists to have a solo exhibition at a commercial gallery. Woodall refers to this exhibition as "the unrivaled hit of the season." The following year Motley won a Guggenheim Fellowship to study art in Paris for one year. That same year he became one of twelve African Americans to receive a Harmon Foundation award for his painting *Octaroon Girl* (1925). The Harmon Foundation, founded by a wealthy white businessman named William E. Harmon, was a philanthropic organization that mounted traveling exhibitions of African American art from 1928 to 1933. The foundation's exhibitions revealed an aspect of African American life that few white Americans knew existed.

Motley portrayed a wide spectrum of contemporary African American life. He painted African Americans at play in dance halls, in pool halls, and at family picnics and other family gatherings; he painted aristocrats and criminals; and occasionally, he depicted historical scenes. Portraiture was his forte. *Portrait of My Mother*, which Woodall calls one of the first realistic portrayals of an African American by an African American, is considered a landmark in African American art.

Motley's frank representation of black life offended certain members of the African American community. One of the most outspoken critics was William Farrow, president of the Chicago Arts League, an African American arts organization. Farrow objected to Motley's depiction of what Farrow considered "low-life" situations—cabarets and dance halls—and which Farrow believed only reinforced negative stereotypes of the race.

Motley returned to the United States from Paris as the country faced the economic hardship of the Great Depression. Private funding for the arts consequently withered, and Motley, like other artists, could only find work through the government-sponsored arts program. From 1935 to 1939 Motley worked for the mural division of the Illinois Federal Arts Project. In 1935 Motley taught as artist-in-residence at Howard University in Washington, D.C.

Among Motley's major pieces are *A Mulattress* (1924), *Mending Socks* (1924), *Syncopation* (1924), *Black Belt* (1934), *Dans la rue, Paris* (1929), *Blues* (1929), *Playing Poker* (1930), *The Plotters* (1933), *Picnic* (1936), *The Liar* (1936), and *Gettin' Religion* (1948).

Motley's work, among the work of other African American artists, was featured in August 1990 in *Against the Odds: African-American Artists and the Harmon Foundation* at the Chicago Public Library Cultural Center. In October 1991, the Chicago Historical Society (now renamed the Chicago History Museum) sponsored *The Art of Archibald J. Motley Jr.*, a major retrospective of his career.

Motley did not consider himself an "African American artist"—he found that expression too limiting—but rather an American painter of African American art. It is ironic then that he is remembered as one of the first members of his race to achieve success in the art world. "I feel my work is peculiarly American, a sincere personal expression of the age, and I hope a contribution to society," he said. "The Negro is part of America and the Negro is part of our great American art."

Motley painted only sporadically during the last thirty years of his life. He lived at 350 West 60th Street for many years, but later moved to 1809 North Lincoln Park West, where he died at the age of eighty-nine.

See also: Willard Motley

Further reading: Elizabeth Kennedy, ed., *Chicago Modern 1893–1945: Pursuit of the New* (2004); Gary A. Reynolds and Beryl J. Wright, *Against the Odds: African-American Artists and the Harmon Foundation* (1989); Elaine D. Woodall, *Archibald J. Motley, Jr.: American Artist of the Afro-American People, 1891–1928* (1977) and "Looking Backwards: Archibald J. Motley and the Art Institute of Chicago, 1914–1930," *Chicago History*, Spring 1979.

Willard Motley

Novelist

BORN: July 14, 1912
Chicago, Illinois

DIED: March 4, 1965
Mexico City

A disciple of the realism school of writing, Willard Motley wrote about the dark side of urban life. Although African American, his books were populated with characters named Romano and Kosinski who lived out their sad, empty lives on Chicago's desolate streets and back alleys.

The Motleys were the only African American family in the all-white Englewood neighborhood on Chicago's South Side. With the notable exception of the race riots that swept through the South Side in the summer of 1919, Willard Motley's youth was mostly free from racial strife.

Motley decided at an early age to be a writer. His literary career began in 1922 when he wrote a children's column for the *Chicago Defender*. After graduating from Englewood High School in 1929, he searched for work, but with the country in the middle of the Great Depression he gave up the struggle. Instead, he decided to take advantage of the free time and bicycled to New York. This trip and other travels formed the raw material for much of his fiction. Upon his return to Chicago, Motley held a series of blue-collar jobs that allowed him to observe life directly through the eyes of society's working poor. He was an order-filler for the Rock Island Railroad, a dishwasher, a short-order cook, a waiter, and a janitor. In 1937 he gathered his meager savings, bought an old car, and headed for the West Coast. He traveled extensively in California, Colorado, and the Pacific Northwest.

In 1940 Motley submitted a story to the *New Anvil*, a leftist publication edited by Jack Conroy and Nelson Algren. Although the piece was rejected, Conroy and Algren invited Motley to come down to their offices to talk. They introduced Motley to the Chicago literary scene. He then found work with the Works Projects Administration (WPA) Federal Writers' Project, conducting interviews and gathering case histories. His beat was the West Side slums, where he talked to as many people as he could—from police officers to social workers to judges and lawyers.

In the early 1940s Motley sold his first short stories to *Commonwealth* magazine. The following year he moved to a converted sweatshop on Maxwell Street and conducted extensive research on the West Madison Street skid row area. He prowled the streets and alleys, the bars and juke joints, diners and flophouses, gospel missions and run-down hotels, always asking questions and jotting down observations in his notebook.

His first novel, *Knock on Any Door* (1947), centered around the life of a young Italian American named Nick Romano, a former altar boy turned cop killer who was executed in the electric chair. His motto: "Live fast, die young,

and have a good-looking corpse." Motley spent eight years researching and writing the book. With a draft at 2,100 pages and 600,000 words, it was a monumental first effort. After extensive editing, however, Motley emerged with a best seller on his hands. It was later made into a movie starring John Derek as Romano and Humphrey Bogart as his lawyer.

Motley's next novel, *We Fished All Night* (1951), was set in postwar Chicago and told the tale of three veterans and their rise to the top of local politics. Motley made extensive use of Chicago locations, from the Gold Coast to Bughouse Square, Soldier Field to Riverview Park. *Let No Man Write My Epitaph* (1958) was set on skid row and continued the story of the Romano family, focusing on Nick Romano Jr., the illegitimate son of the lead character from *Knock on Any Door*. Although reviews were mixed, the book did attract the attention of Hollywood, and in 1960 it was turned into a movie starring James Darren and Shelley Winters.

From 1944 to 1945 Motley worked on a three-act play, *You Lovely People,* about the bohemians of Chicago's Near North Side. It was never completed. He moved to Mexico in September 1951 and died in a Mexico City clinic from gangrene in 1965. He was only fifty-two. At the time of his death Motley was working on another book, *My House Is Your House* (he also considered calling it *Tourist Town*), about an influx of visitors into a small Mexican village. It was edited and retitled *Let Noon Be Fair* and was published posthumously in 1966.

Race was never a central issue in Motley's work. Unlike Richard Wright, who chronicled the African American experience exclusively, Motley wrote mostly about ethnic whites. Nelson Algren once called Motley a white writer. "He wrote about white people for white people," he insisted. Neither Motley nor his brother, painter Archibald J. Motley Jr., wanted to be considered "African American artists." Not until he was older did Motley address racial concerns, and that was primarily in the form of newspaper articles and essays.

See also: Nelson Algren, Jack Conroy, James T. Farrell, Archibald J. Motley Jr., Richard Wright

Further reading: Jerome Klinkowitz, *The Diaries of Willard Motley* (1978).

Elijah Muhammad

Religious and Community Leader

BORN: October 7, 1897
Near Sandersville, Georgia

DIED: February 24, 1975
Chicago, Illinois

Elijah Muhammad—born Elijah Poole—was a day laborer who rose to become the millionaire leader of the Nation of Islam, also known as the Black Muslims, with national headquarters located on the South Side of Chicago. Muhammad promulgated the philosophy of black self-help and black self-determination with the ultimate goal of black nationhood. As spiritual leader of the Black Muslim movement, he was one of the most powerful religious figures of twentieth-century America.

Elijah Poole's father was a former slave and Baptist preacher in rural Georgia. As a boy, young Poole worked as a sawmill helper and field hand. He attended school through the fifth grade and left home at sixteen. He moved to Atlanta where he married, and then moved with his wife and children to Detroit in 1923. He worked at odd jobs in Detroit and for a brief spell was a Baptist minister.

In 1931 Poole met Wallace Fard (or Wali Farad), a former Detroit silk peddler and leader of a small religious sect. "I recognized him," Muhammad later recalled, "to be the person the Bible predicted would come 2,000 years after Jesus' death." Fard denounced Christianity as the white man's way of keeping blacks enslaved. Poole converted, abandoned his "slave" name, adopted a Muslim name, and became Fard's chief assistant. Fard had already founded Temple No. 1 of the Nation of Islam in 1931 in Detroit. Under Fard's direction, Temple No. 2 was established in Chicago in 1934. Fard mysteriously disappeared that same year and Muhammad assumed the leadership role. When his succession was disputed, Muhammad moved the base of operations from Detroit to Chicago, organized his own movement, and deified Fard as the incarnation of Allah.

Muhammad frequently clashed with both local and national authorities. In 1934 he was arrested on charges of contributing to the delinquency of a minor because he refused to enter his son into the Detroit public school system, preferring to enroll him in a Muslim parochial school instead. During World War II he was convicted of evading selective service and accused of supporting the enemy (Muhammad supported Japan because it was a nonwhite country). Although he forbade participation in the American armed forces it wasn't because he abhorred violence but because he didn't want his followers to participate in "Caucasian wars." Muhammad served a four-year sentence in a Michigan federal prison but continued to act as leader of the Black Muslims from his cell.

One of his best-known converts was heavyweight boxing champion Cassius Clay, who later changed his name to Muhammad Ali. Ali refused to serve in the armed forces in 1967 on the grounds that he was a practicing Muslim minister. For this act he was stripped of his boxing title, although the U.S. Supreme Court overturned his draft evasion conviction in 1971. Ali's well-publicized conversion brought the organization to the attention of the American public and gave it a legitimacy that it had not previously had.

In the mainstream press, Muhammad was criticized for being antiwhite. The Black Muslims, in contrast to the civil rights movement, which called for integration, sought a complete break from the "white devils" that controlled the country. Furthermore, Muhammad made other demands: freedom for all Black Muslim prisoners, an end to police brutality, equal employment opportunity for blacks, exemption from taxation, the banning of interracial marriages, and total racial unity and religious conformity. But in 1974 the Muslim leader softened his criticism of the white power structure, exhorting his followers to "stop putting the blame on the slave owner. You have only yourself to blame."

The Black Muslim financial empire was built on a network of black-owned businesses across the country that included clothing stores, restaurants, farms, banks, grocery stores, import businesses, and food processing plants. As the Black Muslim membership grew, so did conflicts within the movement itself. In 1972 reports of a power struggle emerged when four people were killed in Baton Rouge, Louisiana. Probably the most controversial incident during Muhammad's years in power occurred when one of his protégés, Malcolm X (born Malcolm Little), who had started his own nationalist movement, was assassinated in New York in 1965.

The father of eight children, Muhammad reportedly fathered an additional thirteen out of wedlock. In 1982 circuit court judge Henry Budzinski ruled in favor of three of Muhammad's illegitimate children and five of his legitimate children to recover assets previously given to the sect.

Muhammad died in February 1975 at the age of seventy-seven in Chicago's Mercy Hospital. At the time of his death he was living in a large Middle Eastern–style mansion at 4847 South Woodlawn Avenue. He was buried in Mount Glenwood Cemetery in Glenwood, Illinois, twenty-five miles south of Chicago.

Following the death of his father, Wallace D. Muhammad (he later changed his first name to Warith) took over the Nation of Islam and shortly thereafter repudiated his father's separatist teachings and embraced orthodox Islam. "We believe that Jews, Christians, and Muslims share an affinity. We believe in one and the same God. We represent one humanity," the younger Muhammad said. In 1980 he changed the name of the organization from the World Community of Al-Islam in the West to the simpler American Muslim Mission, with its local headquarters at 4855 South Woodlawn Avenue.

In 1978 Louis Farrakhan, a former calypso singer from Boston who became a Black Muslim in 1955, revived the Nation of Islam and, with a core of several thousand followers, established an office in a former funeral parlor at 734 West 79th Street. Despite talk of a possible reconciliation between the two organizations, Farrakhan continues to carry on Muhammad's black nationalist legacy.

Further reading: Edwin Black, "Louis Farrakhan—Would You Buy a Toothpaste from This Man?" *Chicago Reader,* April 11, 1986; C. Eric Lincoln, *The Black Muslims in America* (1961).

James Mulligan
Army Officer

BORN: June 25, 1830
Utica, New York

DIED: July 26, 1864
Kernstown, Virginia

James Adelbert Mulligan commanded one of Chicago's most celebrated units during the Civil War. Not only did he emerge as a local hero, he also won recognition throughout the North.

Born in New York State, James Mulligan came to Chicago with his Irish immigrant parents when he was six years old. After graduating from St. Mary of the Lake University in 1850, he accompanied John L. Stevens, a noted traveler of the day, to South America. Upon returning to Chicago, Mulligan worked in the law office of Arnold, Larned and Lay. In 1854 he edited a Catholic weekly, the *Western Tablet.* The following year he was admitted to the Illinois bar.

When the Shields' Guards, an Irish military group, was formed in 1854, Mulligan was chosen to be its first lieutenant. Later he became secretary and then captain. In 1857 President James Buchanan appointed him to a clerkship in the Interior Department in Washington, D.C. Mulligan then returned to Chicago and formed a partnership with lawyer Henry S. Fitch, United States Attorney for the Chicago District.

After the fall of Fort Sumter, South Carolina, to Confederate forces in April 1861, Mulligan placed an advertisement in a local newspaper exhorting all men of Irish extraction to fight "for the honor of the Old Land and for the defense of the New." Several Irish military units already existed in Chicago, including the Montgomery Guards and the Emmet Guards. There was some fear among native politicians that the solidly Democratic Irish would refuse to support the Union cause and the Republican president. Their concern was unjustified. According to historian A. T. Andreas, 325 men signed up within an hour and a half. By the end of the week, the number had grown to more than 1,000. Mulligan was elected colonel of the new unit, which earned the nickname of "Mulligan's Brigade."

By this time, however, Illinois had already met its military quota. Despite the setback, the brigade voted to remain together and continue to drill and prepare for battle. A determined Colonel Mulligan traveled to Washington and persuaded the War Department in May 1861 to accept his regiment into the Union army. On June 5, 1861, Mulligan's Irish Brigade became the first independent Illinois regiment. Its official name was the Twenty-Third Illinois Infantry.

Upon Mulligan's return to Chicago, the preparation for war began in earnest. The company obtained permission to use the grounds of Kane's Brewery on West Polk Street between Blue Island and Archer Avenues and renamed it "Fontenoy Barracks." The newly formed regiment was ordered to report to St. Louis, Missouri, to be equipped with artillery. By the end of August 1861, the brigade, stationed in Lexington, Missouri, was given the task of holding the city against an attack by Confederate General Sterling Price. After continuous fighting, the city fell in late September. The brigade suffered severe casualties—more than one hundred men died—and the lack of water and ammunition made matters worse. Among the many wounded was Mulligan himself, who, at the insistence of his commanding officer, reluctantly surrendered. He was later released in exchange for a captured Confederate officer. The battle-scarred Irishman, who received a Congressional citation for his efforts, returned to Chicago to a hero's welcome. He then traveled to Washington to ask President Lincoln to resurrect the Irish Brigade.

In December 1861, Major General George McClellan ordered the brigade restored, with company headquarters based at Camp Douglas on the South Side. The regiment patrolled the camp until June 1862. The Mulligan battery was then attached to the Illinois Light Artillery and saw action in Virginia in the Shenandoah Valley campaigns before being ordered to Annapolis, Maryland. In July 1863, Mulligan was placed in command of all federal troops at Hancock, Maryland. At Petersburg, Virginia, he established Fort Mulligan. In April 1864, the Twenty-Third Illinois Infantry returned to Chicago to recoup. Its weary soldiers, reduced from 800 to 300, prepared themselves for another long campaign. Returning to Virginia, the brigade formed a part of the First Infantry Division, again under Mulligan, and was ordered to occupy Leetown.

On July 24, 1864, at the Battle of Kernstown, Virginia, Mulligan was mortally wounded. As he fell off his horse, he saw the colors of the Irish Brigade waving above him. "Lay me down," he reportedly told his men, "and save the flag." He was carried to a nearby farmhouse and died two days later. His body was returned to Chicago and was buried in Cavalry Cemetery, Evanston.

Mulligan Avenue is named in his honor.

See also: Elmer E. Ellsworth, Philip Sheridan

Further reading: A. T. Andreas, *History of Chicago from the Earliest Period to the Present Time*, 3 vols. (1884–86); Bessie Louise Pierce, *A History of Chicago*, 3 vols. (1937–57).

George Mundelein

Priest

BORN: July 2, 1872
New York, New York

DIED: October 2, 1939
Mundelein, Illinois

In 1916, at the remarkably young age of forty-three, George William Mundelein became archbishop of Chicago. During his twenty-four years in office, Mundelein emerged as an influential figure in both national and international church affairs.

One of nine children, George Mundelein was a third-generation German American. His maternal grandfather fought for the Union at Fort Sumter during the Civil War. Mundelein grew up poor on the streets of New York. He received his education at the Christian Brothers' De La Salle Institute, and at seventeen he graduated with a bachelor of arts degree from Manhattan College. Around this time he chose to enter the priesthood and won a scholarship to begin his ecclesiastical studies at St. Vincent's Seminary in Latrobe, Pennsylvania. An energetic and bright student, Mundelein earned an outstanding academic record before he went on to study further in Rome.

After he was ordained in 1895, Mundelein returned to Brooklyn, where he became assistant secretary to the bishop. On weekends he served a Lithuanian congregation. Two years later he was made chancellor of the Brooklyn diocese. In 1906 Mundelein became the nation's youngest monsignor, and three years later, its youngest auxiliary bishop. When James Quigley, Archbishop of Chicago, died in 1915, Mundelein was chosen to succeed him. He was installed as archbishop on February 9, 1916. Unlike his congenial predecessor, Mundelein projected a harsher, more businesslike image. He would tolerate no insubordination.

Mundelein was a thorough and efficient administrator, and his term was one of the most productive in Chicago ecclesiastical history. He authorized the construction of more than 200 new churches, according to historian Edward R. Kantowicz. In addition, several important institutions were erected during his term: Quigley Preparatory Seminary in 1918 (originally established in 1905 by Archbishop Quigley as Cathedral College preparatory school); Rosary College in west suburban River Forest in 1922; and Mundelein College, a women's commuter college, in 1930. In 1918 he purchased land in Area, Illinois, forty-five miles northwest of Chicago, and founded a seminary—St. Mary of the Lake—whose goal was to train priests for the Chicago diocese. The town was later renamed Mundelein in his honor. Furthermore, the archbishop devoted a good share of his time and efforts to philanthropic activities. He created the Associated Catholic Charities, founded homes for wayward boys and girls, and supported the Big Brother organization.

Mundelein advocated a strong central authority. Not surprisingly, his methodical approach to management did not always win converts. Indeed, some fellow clergy criticized him for running the archdiocese like a "German meat market." Mundelein tried to "Americanize" the Catholic Church by emphasizing cultural homogeneity and downplaying cultural pluralism. To this end, he directed that English be used as the chief language of instruction in parochial schools and that a uniform curriculum be implemented throughout. In essence, he sought to mold a peculiarly American brand of Catholicism. He didn't, for example, believe in "hyphenated" Americans, since he thought divided loyalty among the citizenry would only diminish national identity. People, he once said in a *Chicago Tribune* interview, could not serve two nations simultaneously. While he recognized the existence of national parishes—that is, parishes dominated by a particular ethnic group—he attempted to restrict the creation of new ones.

On March 24, 1924, Mundelein became a cardinal. Two years later, he and Chicago hosted the International Eucharistic Congress, the first ever held in the United States. A resounding success, the event attracted millions of Roman Catholics from around the world. Mundelein counted Franklin Delano Roosevelt among his many influential friends. He fervently supported the president's New Deal policies, and Roosevelt, in turn, reciprocated by appointing Catholics to high-ranking positions in his administration.

The cardinal died in October 1939 at the age of sixty-seven in his home at St. Mary of the Lake Seminary in Mundelein, Illinois.

See also: Joseph Bernardin, Arnold Damen, James Quigley
Further reading: Edward R. Kantowicz, *Corporation Sole: Cardinal Mundelein and Chicago Catholicism* (1983); Charles Shanabruch, *Chicago's Catholics: The Evolution of an American Identity* (1981).

Paul Muni
Actor

BORN: September 22, 1895
Lemberg, Austria

DIED: August 25, 1967
Santa Barbara, California

Actor of a thousand faces, Paul Muni was one of the most respected thespians of his generation. From Al Capone to Louis Pasteur to Emile Zola to Benito Juarez, Muni didn't just play a part, he lived it.

Born in Austria but brought to the United States as a child, Muni Weisenfreund (his full birth name was Meshilem Meier Weisenfreund) got his start on the stage of the Yiddish theater. Muni came from a theatrical family, which settled in New York, then Cleveland, and finally Chicago. He originally had ambitions of becoming a violinist. When his parents needed an actor to play the role of an old man and no one else was available, they turned to their young son. His parents owned their own theater, the Weisenfreund Theater, on 12th Street near Halsted. Here in the back rooms and dusty stages of the Maxwell Street neighborhood, Muni quickly mastered the tricks of the trade, playing a wide range of roles.

Muni moved to Philadelphia, where he joined a burlesque company and then signed up with Molly Picon's troupe in Boston. In 1918 he joined the Yiddish Art Theater Company in New York City and toured the country. He made his Broadway debut in *We Americans* in 1926 at the age of thirty-one. The following year Muni landed the role of the gangster in *Four Walls,* which led to a major part in *The Dybbuk* in London.

In 1928 Muni arrived in Hollywood. It proved to be a humbling experience for him. Twentieth Century Fox changed his name to the more manageable Paul Muni. And when he was signed up to appear in *The Valiant* in 1929, his film debut, studio officials were not impressed. "Who hired that actor?" one executive reportedly asked. "He has no sex appeal. Girls won't be interested in him."

Surprisingly, his role in *The Valiant* earned him his first Academy Award nomination for best actor. Muni's second film, *Seven Faces* (1929), flopped, but the actor made a comeback with back-to-back successes, both in 1932: *Scarface* and *I Am a Fugitive from a Chain Gang.* The latter earned him his second best actor nomination. Muni won his first Oscar for his performance as the French scientist in *The Story of Louis Pasteur* (1936). In the following year, *The Life of Emile Zola* won the best picture award, and Muni garnered his fourth best actor nomination. In 1956 he won a Tony for *Inherit the Wind.*

Muni took his profession seriously. He labored for months on a characterization—he spent six months alone preparing for the role of Emile Zola before even going in front of the camera—and he thoroughly researched his roles. A proudly defiant actor, Muni refused to be typecast and even refused to sign any long-term contracts. He simply would not compromise when it came to quality, even if it meant rejecting a role that he felt was not right for him. In 1940 he canceled an $800,000 contract in a gangster movie because he didn't like his part. The movie was *High Sierra* and the actor who replaced him was Humphrey Bogart. "The movies," he said in an interview with the *Chicago Tribune,* "are, really, no place for an actor. Everyone in a studio must, of necessity, be dependent on everyone else. On the stage, I am on my own—entirely dependent on myself."

A private man who had no interest in the Hollywood lifestyle, Muni once stated that he openly disdained applause "because no actor should come out of his role to take bows." He disapproved, too, of the star system and refused to bow to its pressures. Unlike most screen actors, he would not make more than two films a year, which allowed him to accept stage work.

In 1959 Muni appeared in *The Last Angry Man* and received his fifth, and last, Oscar nomination. His health deteriorated and he died from a heart attack in his Santa Barbara home in 1967. He was seventy-one.

Some of Muni's other movies include *The Good Earth* (1937), *Juarez* (1939), *Hudson's Bay* (1940), *A Song to Remember* (1944), and *Angel on My Shoulder* (1946).

Further reading: Ira Berkow, *Maxwell Street: Survival in a Bazaar* (1977); Jerome Lawrence, *Actor: The Life and Times of Paul Muni* (1974).

Bronko Nagurski

Football Player

BORN: November 3, 1908
Rainy River, Ontario

DIED: January 7, 1990
International Falls, Minnesota

Maybe it's the name that sounds bigger than life. At six-foot-two and 235 pounds, Bronko Nagurski was often called the strongest man to play the game of football. He was also the sport's most versatile player—he was able to play most positions. The highlight of his football career came during his years with the Chicago Bears. More than any other player, Nagurski's exploits on the field and his aggressive playing style earned the Bears the nickname "Monsters of the Midway."

Bronko Nagurski's hulking frame looked intimidating both on and off the gridiron. "I assure you that you will not see a more remarkable physical specimen anywhere," Bears coach George Halas once observed. Indeed, Nagurski's brute strength is the stuff of sports legend—how he knocked over burly linebacker after burly linebacker as if they were human bowling pins, and how he scrambled forty-five yards for a touchdown, sent two linebackers reeling in opposite directions, ran over a defensive back, and straight-armed the safety before careening off the goalposts and smashing into a brick wall.

Born in Ontario, Bronislaw Nagurski was raised across the American border in International Falls, Minnesota. He played every position on his high school football team. Minnesota coach Clarence Spears recruited him after seeing the strapping lad plowing a field—without a horse. Nagurski enrolled at the University of Minnesota in 1926 and became the star of the team, playing tackle on both defense and offense. In 1929 he became the only player in college football history to be named All-American at two positions: tackle and fullback.

In 1930 Nagurski joined the Chicago Bears of the National Football League at those positions and turned the team into a contender. He played with the Bears until age twenty-nine, when arthritis forced him to retire. During his nine seasons with the Bears, Nagurski gained more than 4,031 yards running in 872 carries and scored nineteen touchdowns, according to newspaper accounts. He made All-Pro three times and led the Bears in rushing in 1933 and again in 1936. He is eighth on the club's all-time rushing list.

In 1943, with so many young men away at war, Nagurski was persuaded to come back to play one final season with his old team as tackle. During the NFL title game on December 26 against the Washington Redskins at Wrigley Field—then the Bears' home—he agreed to run with the ball. In the last quarter he scored the last touchdown of his career, an easy three-yard romp to the goal line. The Bears won 41–21. Nagurski retired permanently from football in 1943 and devoted his time to farming. For a brief period he was the backfield coach at UCLA. In 1945 he turned to professional wrestling, which he had first tried in 1933. In 1939 he won the National Wrestling Alliance championship. He retired from the wrestling mat in 1960 to become a wrestling referee. Three years later he became a charter member of the Pro Football Hall of Fame.

Nagurski shied away from publicity of any kind. He operated a gas station in International Falls up until 1968. Occasionally he would grant an interview, as in 1985 when his old team battled for the Super Bowl championship, but generally he preferred to stay out of the limelight. Most of Nagurski's football career took place during the height of the Great Depression. Unlike today's players, for whom multimillion dollar contracts have become the norm, Nagurski reportedly never earned more than $5,000 a year.

Nagurski died of natural causes in January 1990 at Falls Memorial Hospital in International Falls, Minnesota. He was eighty-one.

See also: Red Grange, George Halas, Sid Luckman, Walter Payton
Further reading: George Vass, *George Halas and the Chicago Bears* (1971).

Agnes Nestor

Labor Activist

BORN: June 24, 1880
Grand Rapids, Michigan

DIED: December 28, 1948
Chicago, Illinois

Agnes Nestor rose from lowly worker in a glove factory to a position of power in the Glove Workers Union to the presidency of the Chicago Women's Trade Union League (WTUL) at a time when there were few women labor leaders. She sought better working conditions for working women and championed woman suffrage.

Born in Michigan, Agnes Nestor came to Chicago when still a teenager and found work at the Eisendrath Glove Factory as a glove-maker. By the time she was in her early twenties, she had developed into a quietly effective labor activist. In 1902 Nestor led a successful ten-day strike against the factory. Among her demands were an end to rental of machinery and payment for supplies from the employees' pockets and the formation of a union shop. The same year she became president of the Local 2 of the International Glove Workers Union (IGWU). In 1904 Nestor joined the Chicago WTUL. The purpose of the league was to organize all women workers throughout the country in an effort to secure better working conditions, reduce working hours, and win a decent living wage. In 1906 Nestor was elected secretary-treasurer of the IGWU. She served in that capacity until 1913.

In 1909 Nestor and fellow labor activist Elizabeth Maloney introduced a bill in the Illinois legislature that attempted to reduce the number of working hours for women in the state. Opposition to the bill was fierce. Merchants, manufacturers, and small businesses vigorously fought for its defeat. In 1909 the Illinois ten-hour-day law was passed, which reduced the number of working hours for women from twelve to ten. On several occasions, the league attempted to pass the eight-hour-day law through the Illinois legislature. Not until 1937—more than twenty-five years after it was introduced—did that bill finally succeed.

Following the resignation of Margaret Dreier Robins, Nestor was elected president of the Chicago WTUL in 1913. President Woodrow Wilson, impressed with her accomplishments and determination, appointed her a member of a national commission to investigate vocational education. In the autumn of 1915 Nestor was elected president of the International Glove Workers Union.

During World War I she was a member of the Council of National Defense and was the only woman on the advisory council to the secretary of labor. She was also the American labor representative to conferences in Britain, France, and Austria. In addition, she served as director of the National Women's Trade Union League of America and was a member of the World's Fair Commission.

In 1930 Nestor was appointed the only woman member of the Commission on Unemployment and Relief, a group launched to raise millions for the city's jobless poor. The commission conducted surveys in order to discover the number of unemployed people who were not on relief. It was replaced, in February 1932, by the Illinois Emergency Relief Commission. At that time, the Chicago WTUL established its own Unemployment Relief Committee to deal with the special problems of unemployed women members of the league.

Nestor broke barriers. Not only did she and the union improve working conditions for countless working women, she also served as a role model for many young girls. During her lifetime, Nestor witnessed a dramatic change in the number of women employed in the workforce. Following World War II, women entered fields that were traditionally not open to them. "In my mother's day," she recalls in her autobiography, "less than two million women were employed in the industry. In 1897, when I first went to work, there were five million women employed in industry. Today, there are twenty-odd million working women, and industry is constantly looking to hire more."

In 1942 Nestor authored *Brief History of the International Glove Workers Union of America*. In 1948 she wrote her autobiography, *Woman's Labor Leader*. The *Chicago Journal* called her "the biggest little woman in Chicago." Upon her death in December 1948, the labor press remarked "the woman who works has lost her best friend."

See also: Jane Addams, Margaret Haley, Alice Hamilton, Florence Kelley, Mary McDowell, Ellen Gates Starr

Further reading: June Sochen, *Movers and Shakers: American Women Thinkers and Activists, 1900–1970* (1973).

Walter A. Netsch Jr.

Architect

BORN: February 23, 1920
Chicago, Illinois

DIED: June 15, 2008
Chicago, Illinois

Plainspoken Walter Netsch Jr. was a maverick Chicago architect whose idiosyncratic, geometric buildings departed from standard architectural styles. He was known for his individualistic, bold, and defiantly modernist designs. He spent virtually his entire career at the prestigious architectural firm of Skidmore, Owings & Merrill.

Born in Chicago, Walter Netsch was the son of a father who was an executive with a meatpacking plant in the Stockyards neighborhood. He grew up in a household where art was appreciated: his mother enrolled him in art classes and took him to the opera. He received his degree in architecture at the Massachusetts Institute of Technology in 1943 and then served in the U.S. Army Corps of Engineers in Alaska's Aleutian Islands during World War II. After his discharge, he joined Skidmore, Owings & Merrill (SOM) in 1947.

His first assignment at SOM was to help design Oak Ridge, Tennessee, which was being built by the U.S. Atomic Energy Commission. He moved to the Chicago office of SOM in 1954 and became a general partner the following year. Netsch's first assignment in Chicago was the Inland Steel Building at 30 West Monroe Street in 1958, which was the first office building erected in the Loop since the Great Depression. An innovative building and an important early example of modernism, it had column-free office floors and an adjoining tower for elevators. Years later the noted architect Frank Gehry said that the building inspired him to visualize his famous Guggenheim museum in Bilbao, Spain.

In 1960 SOM was commissioned to design the soaring Air Force Academy in Colorado, both then and now a daring and imaginative piece of work. Made of aluminum, it consists of seventeen silver spires—tetrahedrons, or elongated triangles—swept upward like a modernist version of the great cathedrals of Europe. It became a tourist attraction in its own right. In 2004, on its fiftieth anniversary, the academy was designated a National Historic Landmark.

During the 1960s Netsch developed field theory, an architectural aesthetic unique to him. *Chicago Tribune* architecture critic Blair Kamin has defined the theory as a "shifting of square shapes into a geometrically complex series of skewed grids." Netsch used this theory to design such buildings as the University of Illinois's Architecture and Art Building at 845 West Harrison Street with its mazelike floors and intentionally confusing floor plans.

Soon after working on the Air Force Academy, Netsch began running his own design operation within SOM. His works included the design of the University of Illinois–Chicago (UIC) campus. Using a combination of concrete, granite, and brick, the geometric complex was connected by elevated pedestrian walkways. His master plan and buildings for UIC were often criticized as being not user friendly. Cars were banned, resulting in a garrison-like effect. It was a controversial move—critics referred to it as Fortress Illini—and by the mid-1990s, over Netsch's strenuous objections, the campus was demolished and replaced with a traditional college quadrangle. Netsch called the redesign "a suburban mall revision."

Netsch also designed the main library and the Lindheimer Astronomical Research Center at Northwestern University; the Regenstein Library at the University of Chicago, the east wing of the Art Institute of Chicago, and Hermann Hall at the Illinois Institute of Technology. In addition, he designed numerous libraries and academic buildings throughout the United States, including at Grinnell College and at Miami University in Ohio.

Although his work was often controversial, he did win awards from the American Institute of Architects. Netsch broke from the Miesian boxes of the 1950s and 1960s and, Blair Kamin contends, "anticipated the unorthodox, computer-generated shapes" of Frank Gehry.

Netsch retired from SOM in 1979 but continued to be a consultant at the firm until 1981. After Harold Washington became mayor two years later, Netsch was named president of the Chicago Park District. As president, he issued a plan to decentralize the system into smaller units. But political disagreements led him to resign from the board in 1987.

Netsch died from pneumonia at his home in Chicago in June 2008. He was eighty-eight.

See also: Bruce Graham, Ludwig Mies van der Rohe

Danny Newman

Press Agent

BORN: January 24, 1919
Chicago, Illinois

DIED: December 1, 2007
Lincolnwood, Illinois

A longtime press agent for Lyric Opera and an arts and entertainment promoter, Danny Newman was considered one of the greatest arts patrons of the last half of the twentieth century. He helped not only Lyric Opera but also theater companies, symphonies, ballet companies, and opera companies across North America. His most important achievement, though, was the impact he had on how nonprofit arts groups built their audience bases. A pioneer in arts marketing, he was responsible for the now almost universal use of subscription ticket sales in the performing arts. What's more, his book *Subscribe Now!* (1977) has been used in thirty-one countries and printed in ten editions and has become a textbook in many graduate schools of arts management.

A self-proclaimed press agent, Newman believed that the only way that an arts company could survive was to build a loyal base of subscribers. With this in mind, he launched Lyric Opera's first subscription campaign in 1955. To him it was the most cost-effective and efficient way to solve the problem of attracting customers to performances. The future depended on turning the usual fickle, single-ticket buyers into committed subscribers. As a result of his marketing initiatives, tickets to Lyric Opera performances became among the hardest tickets to obtain in town. With his outgoing personality and never-say-never approach to sales, Newman was an indefatigable supporter of the arts, an impresario. *Chicago Tribune* classical music critic John von Rhein called him "part P. T. Barnum, part Billy Sunday."

The son of a tobacconist, Newman was raised in Rogers Park. He began selling subscriptions door-to-door at the age of fourteen and then joined an acting troupe called the Mummers of Chicago. But he soon turned from acting to behind-the-scenes activities, becoming a press agent and promoting a variety of vaudeville acts, from lion tamers and ventriloquists to acrobats and strippers.

During World War II, Newman served in the U.S. Army, seeing action at the Battle of the Bulge, where he was wounded twice and subsequently was awarded the Purple Heart and Bronze Star. After the war, he returned to Chicago. In 1948 he married his first wife, the stage and movie actress Dina Halpern.

Over the years, Newman served as a manager, actor, screenwriter, and manager. As a consultant for the Ford Foundation and the Theater Communications Group, Newman, beginning in 1961, helped launch subscription campaigns at more than 500 arts organizations on five continents, from Finland to the Philippines. "He invented the method that allowed theaters to prosper across the country," said Roche Schulfer, executive director of the Goodman Theatre. From 1946 to 1951 he coproduced the celebrity radio show *Famous Names,* which was hosted by the then-unknown Mike Wallace. He also promoted concerts and recitals for the Allied Arts Corporation and was executive producer for the Chicago Yiddish Theatre Association.

He received many honors during his long life. Among them was a knighthood from Italy and a Gold Baton Award of the American Symphony Orchestra League. The Vancouver Symphony commissioned a symphonic work in his honor and he held honorary degrees from DePaul University and Roosevelt University. In addition to *Subscribe Now!* he wrote *Tales of a Theatrical Guru* (2006).

On his eighty-eighth birthday, Lyric Opera named its box office in his honor and even placed his motto, "Subscribe Now!" on the wall.

In 2001 Newman retired as the public relations officer of the Lyric Opera, the only remaining member of Lyric's original administrative staff from 1954 when it was founded. He died of pulmonary fibrosis at his home in Lincolnwood, Illinois, at the age of eighty-eight.

See also: Dina Halpern, Ardis Krainik
Further reading: John von Rhein, "Legendary Promoter of Lyric, the Arts," *Chicago Tribune,* December 3, 2007.

Ralph G. Newman

Bookstore Owner and Lincoln Scholar

BORN: November 3, 1911
Chicago, Illinois

DIED: July 23, 1998
Chicago, Illinois

A self-made man, Ralph G. Newman was an Abraham Lincoln scholar and owner of the Abraham Lincoln Book Shop in Chicago as well as an expert in Civil War manuscripts and related paraphernalia. His shop even became a tourist attraction among Civil War aficionados. A college dropout, Newman wrote or edited more than a dozen historical books, including *The American Iliad* (1974) and *Lincoln for the Ages* (1959).

Newman was an accidental bookman. His father operated a cigar store on the West Side. After graduating from high school in 1929, he attended Crane Junior College for a year before dropping out to work in a bank. He also spent a year at Northwestern University before deciding once and for all that the college life was not for him. During this time he even played minor league baseball for teams in Tucson, Arizona, and Wichita, Kansas.

In 1932, during the height of the Great Depression and with no particular plans in mind, he came across a used bookstore that was going out of business. When he was told that he could buy the entire stock for $10,000, Newman saw an opportunity. Despite being a college dropout with little interest in reading or books, he decided to buy the store, persuading some of his former bank colleagues to lend him money. He called it Home of Books. When he started discounting books—an unheard of practice at the time—as much as seventy-five percent, he was able to not only repay the loan but he felt confident enough to move the shop to a more prominent location in the Chicago Daily News building.

Because of its location and his own gregariousness, Newman soon befriended many of the *Daily News*'s staff, including Lloyd Lewis, the paper's managing editor, Ben Hecht, and Carl Sandburg, who, at the time, was a former *Daily News* reporter and columnist. Sandburg had already published the first two volumes of his Lincoln biography while Lewis had written about Lincoln and the Civil War general William Tecumseh Sherman.

Lewis and Sandburg urged Newman to change from a general stock to Civil War titles that would attract a more specialized clientele. Newman, the astute businessman, considered it a good business move. In 1940 he renamed his bookstore the Abraham Lincoln Book Shop. After attending a dinner and presentation on Stonewall Jackson at the former Bismarck Hotel, Newman, along with fifteen other avid Civil War buffs, established the Civil War Round Table, the first of about two hundred around the world. As Lewis and Sandburg pounded the pavement, operating essentially as volunteer publicists for the shop, word

of mouth spread throughout the community of Civil War aficionados. Newman not only sold Lincoln and Civil War books, he also sold Lincoln autographs and papers. Before long, he was recognized as an authority both on Lincoln and on the Civil War. In 1962, he was among the founders of the Ulysses S. Grant Association.

In addition to the bookstore, Newman also acted as an appraiser of historic documents, including the presidential papers of Harry S. Truman, Lyndon B. Johnson, and Richard Nixon. It was the last that led to his indictment in 1975 on charges of preparing a false affidavit that allowed Nixon to obtain an illegal tax break on the papers he had donated to Newman. Newman was convicted in November 1975 and fined $10,000.

But the conviction did not seem to affect his business. The subsequent publicity, in fact, tripled his business.

Newman also served as president of the Chicago Public Library Board, chairman of the Illinois Sesquicentennial Commission in 1968, and chairman of the Illinois Pavilion at the 1964–65 New York World's Fair.

In 1971 Daniel Weinberg became a partner with Newman and in 1984 Weinberg purchased Newman's interest to become the sole proprietor. The shop, located at 357 West Chicago Avenue, continues to specialize in Lincolniana and material related to the Civil War and offers appraisal services for libraries, museums, banks, insurance companies, and private collectors. In addition, the shop operates a publishing wing, Americana House, which reprints major historic works that are out of print.

Newman died in July 1998 at the age of eighty-six.

Further reading: Barbara Hughett, *The Civil War Round Table: Fifty Years of Scholarship and Fellowship* (1995).

Richard Nickel

Photographer

BORN: May 31, 1928
Chicago, Illinois

DIED: May 9, 1972
Chicago, Illinois

*Great architecture has
only two natural enemies:
water and stupid men.*

*Why do they always wreck
the finest buildings?*
　　　　　—Richard Nickel

The 1960 campaign to save the Garrick Theater not only sparked Chicago's modern preservation movement. It also raised questions about the obligation that government and the citizenry had to safeguard the architectural legacy of cities. And it demonstrated how the new movement called preservation shaped the city and its destiny. A major figure in this new preservation movement was Richard Nickel.

Nickel was raised in Polish neighborhoods on the Northwest Side of Chicago, first at 4327 West Haddon Avenue, then at 4329 West Crystal Street, and finally at 2457 North Rockwell Street. He served in the army after World War II ended. When he returned to Chicago after his military service in 1948, not quite sure what to do with his life, he took advantage of the GI Bill and enrolled at the Institute of Design—an offshoot of the German Bauhaus movement—to study commercial photography. Essentially, students were taught to think for themselves. They were also encouraged to believe that they could change the world through art.

Nickel was fortunate to have two masters of photography as his mentors: Harry Callahan and Aaron Siskind. Callahan taught Nickel about the technological aspects of photography while Siskind persuaded Nickel to see the world with fresh eyes through the lens of a view camera. To both Callahan and Siskind, photography was a means of self-expression.

The assignment that would change Nickel's life was the class that Siskind taught on the architecture of Louis Sullivan. Siskind assigned his students, including Nickel, to shoot all of the one hundred or so Sullivan-designed buildings across the country then in existence. Nickel was placed in charge of the ambitious project. He coordinated an Institute of Design exhibition on Sullivan in 1954, and was assigned to work on a book on Sullivan and his partner Dankmar Adler to be called *The Complete Architecture of Adler and Sullivan*. It was finally published in 2010.

Nickel not only photographed Adler and Sullivan buildings in Chicago, he also took cross-country trips to shoot the firm's buildings around the country. Through his prodigious research, he uncovered thirty-eight Adler and Sullivan buildings but he also watched as more and more of the architects' buildings were being razed to make way for new construction. Alarmed at the wanton destruction of these historic structures, he became, essentially, an accidental preservationist. "He was one of the first people in America to protest the razing of a building solely because of its architectural significance," wrote his biographer Richard Cahan.

In addition to the work of Adler and Sullivan, Nickel photographed the demolition of many historic buildings, including Henry Ives Cobb's Federal Building on Dearborn Street between Adams and Jackson, Burnham and Root's First Regimental Infantry at Michigan Avenue and 16th Street, the Grand Central train station at 201 West Harrison Street, and Holabird and Roche's Republic Building at 209 South State Street. But he also photographed the construction of new buildings, such as Mies van der Rohe's Federal Office Building and Bertrand Goldberg's Marina City.

Cahan has called Nickel "an urban legend of sorts." Nickel was fearless in his quest to document as many doomed Chicago buildings as possible. He would go to great lengths to take photographs that would do justice to his subjects. But he not only took photographs, he salvaged as much of the buildings—bits and pieces, fragments, ornaments—as he could and even enlisted the help of friends, colleagues, and family members. In April 1963, for example, Nickel and architect Philip Gardner were arrested when they were caught rescuing leaded-glass windows from the Oscar Steffens house, a Frank Lloyd Wright–designed building at 7600 North Sheridan Road in Rogers Park that was under demolition. When a police officer asked the men what they were doing, Nickel replied forthrightly, "I'm saving these Frank Lloyd Wright windows." "Who's Frank Lloyd Wright?" the clueless officer asked. Nickel knew that salvaging was risky and dangerous work, and, ultimately, he would pay dearly for it. He is remembered for his courage and his prophetic zeal—the preservation movement had not caught on yet when he started his lonely campaign—as much as for the photographs he left behind.

Few buildings are as closely associated with Nickel as Adler and Sullivan's seventeen-story Garrick Theater, erected in 1892 at 64 West Randolph Street. Originally called the Schiller Theater and built for Chicago's German opera company, it later functioned as a vaudeville theater where the likes of Mary Pickford, Al Jolson, Lionel Barrymore, Sophie Tucker, Jimmy Durante, Eddie Cantor, and Bob Hope, among others, performed. Between World War I and the Great Depression, the Garrick, home to sheet-music publishers, served as Chicago's equivalent of Tin Pan Alley—such famous songs as "Let Me Call You Sweetheart" and "Yes, Sir, That's My Baby" were written there. Later, it became the CBS television studio and, during its last dire days, a movie theater.

By 1960, then, the once dignified building had fallen on hard times. Worse, many of Sullivan's exterior details were missing, covered over in slapdash fashion, or simply neglected. Formerly a handsome light brown terra cotta, it had turned to a funereal black, caked with layers of dirt and soot. In truth, the Garrick was a run-down eyesore of a building, a shell of its former glorious self. When the city announced plans to build a civic center across the street, the owners of the building thought that a parking garage would be more profitable than a down-on-its-heels movie theater.

The pending demolition of the Garrick haunted Nickel. He and others appealed to Mayor Richard J. Daley for assistance. He solicited letters from critics, historians, and famous architects (Le Corbusier and Philip Johnson voiced their support). He wrote letters to the local newspapers, and he did his best to shame Daley to do the right thing by salvaging the building. In a letter to the mayor, Nickel wrote that saving the Garrick "would be evidence that Chicago has a cultural conscience—and a heart and a soul which is above the singular money interest of a conventional city."

On June 8, 1960, Nickel and twenty other supporters picketed the theater. Along with Thomas Stauffer, a blustery Hyde Park resident with clout, Nickel organized four days of picketing in front of the building, carrying a placard that read: "DO WE DARE SQUANDER CHICAGO'S GREAT ARCHITECTURAL HERITAGE?" The group gathered some 3,300 signatures. Even cartoonists got involved. On June 23, *Chicago Sun-Times* cartoonist Jacob Burck published a drawing of two middle-aged tourists pointing to the ruins of the Acropolis in Greece. "If we had this in Chicago," one of them observes, "we'd knock it down and make a parking lot."

Responding to the ongoing pressure, Daley eventually appointed a committee to look into the matter. But it was all in vain. Ultimately, the committee concluded that it would cost the city at least $3 million, and possibly as high as $5 million, to purchase and restore the building. A court decision concurred: the economic cost of maintaining the theater outweighed the city's right to preserve it. In the meantime, Nickel salvaged what he could, including hundreds of fragments from the building. These fragments ended up in museums, institutions, and in private collections. Some were incorporated into the façade of the Second City on North Wells Street in Old Town.

Outrage over the demolition of the Garrick Theater and other historic buildings led Congress to pass the National Historic Preservation Act in 1966. This, in turn, led to the creation of the National Register of Historic Places, as well as to various local historic preservation societies. In addition, the battle to save another building, Sullivan's thirteen-story Chicago Stock Exchange at 30 North LaSalle Street, resulted in the founding of Landmarks Illinois, the statewide preservation advocacy group whose logo, appropriately enough, depicts the entry arch of the Stock Exchange. The salvaging of the Stock Exchange building became Nickel's last heroic stand. It was a structure that he would return to again and again.

Nickel's obsession with his work left little time for his personal life. A marriage at an early age to Adrienne Dembo led to divorce. Many years later, in 1972, Nickel pursued another serious relationship when he became engaged to Carol Ruth Sutter, a thirty-two-year-old social worker at Lutheran General Hospital in Park Ridge. He promised her he would finish the Adler and Sullivan book and stop his dangerous work. But first he had to return to the Stock Exchange Building one more time.

Nickel was salvaging ornaments and fragments from the building on April 13, 1972, when a portion of the then half-demolished structure collapsed and killed him. It is unclear if he was killed while in the Trading Room or in a basement beneath the room. Either way, his body was not found until some twenty-eight days later when, on the afternoon of May 9, heavy equipment operator Ray Beinlich saw Nickel's shoulder protruding from the rubble. Ironically, it was noted that on his last day, Richard Nickel did not have his camera with him.

Nickel was buried at Graceland Cemetery, not far from the grave of his hero, Louis Sullivan. In 1977, the Stock Exchange's Trading Room, the room where Nickel probably died, was restored and recreated at the Art Institute. To Nickel, the Trading Room held special significance. "I think it is sort of a holy room," he said, during its demolition. "The more you're here, the more you're in awe of it."

In 1973, the Art Institute of Chicago presented a one-man exhibition of one hundred of Nickel's photographs. Nearly thirty years later, in 2001, Lookingglass Theater presented *They All Fall Down: The Richard Nickel Story*, an adaptation by Laura Eason and Jessica Thebus of Richard Cahan's biography of Nickel, with Chicago actor Larry Neuman Jr. in the role of the photographer. The Richard Nickel Committee, a nonprofit organization, administers the Richard Nickel Archive and helps preserve Nickel's work. In late 2010, Nickel's archives were donated to the Ryerson and Burnham Libraries at the Art Institute of Chicago.

In June 2010, the Chicago City Council designated the Richard Nickel Studio, at 1810 West Cortland Street in Lincoln Park, an official landmark. Nickel owned the two-story structure from 1969 to 1972.

See also: Louis Sullivan, Frank Lloyd Wright

Further reading: Richard Cahan, *They All Fall Down: Richard Nickel's Struggle to Save America's Architecture* (1995); Richard Cahan and Michael Williams, *Richard Nickel's Chicago: Photographs of a Lost City* (2006); Richard Nickel and Aaron Siskind with John Vinci and Ward Miller, *The Complete Architecture of Adler & Sullivan* (2010).

William Butler Ogden

Politician and Entrepreneur

BORN: June 15, 1805
Walton, New York

DIED: August 8, 1877
Fordham Heights, New York

An early Chicago booster, William Butler Ogden was Chicago's first mayor (1837–1838) and helped to write the city charter. "I was born close to a sawmill, was early left an orphan, graduated from a long schoolhouse and at 14 fancied I could do anything I turned my hand to," he once wrote. Ogden was a popular and influential figure in Chicago's salad days.

Ogden planned to study law, but the sudden death of his father forced him to take over the family business—his father was a real estate developer—while he was still a teenager. Although Ogden enjoyed a successful career in real estate, he felt that politics was the nobler profession. In 1834 he was elected to the New York legislature. The following year he moved to Chicago to try to salvage an investment of his brother-in-law.

In 1835 Chicago was still a frontier village of swamp and prairie, not a very encouraging sight for a transplanted Easterner. Despite the bleak setting, Ogden had great faith in the future of the town and decided to stay. Within several years, Ogden had made a fortune in real estate, becoming one of the richest men in the city. The panic of 1837, which plunged the country into a recession, brought Ogden his share of hard times, but he managed to weather the storm. That year he was elected Chicago's first mayor when the population was slightly over 4,000 people. As mayor, Ogden is credited with keeping the city solvent and, by refusing to panic, preventing it from falling deeper into debt. By the early 1840s, Chicago was back on its feet again. After completing his one-year term as mayor, Ogden was ready to serve the city in other ways. In 1840 he was elected alderman of the Sixth Ward and, in 1847, alderman of the Ninth Ward.

The railroad brought phenomenal growth to the city and virtually guaranteed it a promising and vital future. Ogden, more than anyone, understood this. The rails brought the world to Chicago and Chicago to the world. In 1848 Ogden introduced the first railroad to the city, the Galena and Chicago Union Railroad, which linked the prosperous mining town of Galena in western Illinois with the then small town of Chicago. Due to its central location and proximity to water transport, Chicago quickly became the railroad capital of the country and a great commercial center.

Unhappy with management policy, Ogden quit the Galena and Chicago Union and founded another railway, the Chicago and North Western Railroad, which later acquired the Galena and Chicago Union line. From 1859 to 1868 he served as president of the Chicago and North Western. In 1862 he was elected the first president of the Union Pacific. But less than a year into his term, he left.

In 1857 Ogden became one of the founders of the Chicago Dock and Canal Company, which he and two associates, Van H. Higgins and Stanley H. Fleetwood, established to develop an industrial area on the north bank of the Chicago River. Today this area at McClurg Court and Illinois Street, called the Ogden Slip, is the home to the River East Art Center (REAC), formerly known as the North Pier Terminal.

Ogden was also the first president of Rush Medical College and president of the Board of Trustees of the University of Chicago. Above all these other activities, Ogden was a builder. He was instrumental in the construction of nearly one hundred miles of city streets, erected the first swinging bridge over the Chicago River, and donated land for churches and schools.

Although a lifelong Democrat, Ogden opposed slavery and felt compelled to switch to the Republican Party. In 1860 he ran for the Illinois Senate. Two years later, he bolted from the party as a result of a dispute with President Lincoln over the Emancipation Proclamation—he felt the proclamation was premature. Ogden then retired from politics altogether.

Ogden purchased property in Fordham Heights, New York, in 1866. He died there in 1877.

The Ogden School at 24 West Walton Street, part of the Chicago public school system, is built on the former site of his brother's home. Now called the Ogden International School of Chicago, a new building, which features several green roofs, opened in August 2011. A quotation from one of Ogden's favorite poets, Sir Walter Scott, is carved on the wall: "Breathes there the man with soul so dead who never to himself hath said this is my own, my native land."

Ogden Avenue is named in his honor.

Further reading: Robert J. Casey and W. A. S. Douglas, *Pioneer Railroad: The Story of the Chicago and North Western System* (1948); Jack Harpster, *The Railroad Tycoon Who Built Chicago: A Biography of William B. Ogden* (2009); Frederick F. Rex, *The Mayors of the City of Chicago* (1934).

Joe "King" Oliver

Musician

BORN: May 11, 1885
New Orleans, Louisiana

DIED: April 10, 1938
Savannah, Georgia

Joseph "King" Oliver, an early exponent of jazz, spread New Orleans–style jazz to Chicago and inspired a young musician, Louis Armstrong, to take it in altogether new directions. Oliver's Creole Jazz Band "set an accepted standard of ensemble improvisation which has seldom been equaled," wrote Walter C. Allen and Brian A. L. Rust in *King Joe Oliver* (1955).

Joe Oliver joined a brass band as a youngster in New Orleans. He earned his nickname during a gig at the Adabie Cabaret where his brilliant cornet playing upstaged his colleagues. When Storyville, the sprawling New Orleans red-light district, was shut down in November 1917 by orders of the U.S. Navy, scores of jazz musicians fled north to the wide-open city of Chicago, hoping to re-create a little bit of Louisiana on the shores of Lake Michigan. Oliver found gigs at the Dreamland Café at 35th and State Streets and at the notorious Pekin Cabaret, a gangland favorite, on State near 27th Street, among many other clubs.

In January 1920, Oliver formed his own band at the Dreamland. After spending some time in California, Oliver returned to Chicago in 1922 to open at the Lincoln Gardens at 459 East 31st Street under the name of King Oliver's Creole Jazz Band. In mid-1922 he decided to add a second cornet to the band and sent a telegram to Louis Armstrong, a young protégé of his from New Orleans, and asked him to come to Chicago. Armstrong wasted no time in joining his New Orleans colleague up north. The band toured the Midwest on a series of one-night stands, playing to enthusiastic crowds. In 1923 they made their first recording on the Gennett label. Successive record deals followed on Okeh, Paramount, and Columbia. Other members of this seminal Chicago band included Honore Dutrey on trombone, Johnny Dodds on clarinet, Lil Hardin on piano, and Baby Dodds on drums.

Soon after the studio sessions, Armstrong left to pursue his own career. Meanwhile Oliver found work at the Plantation Café before spending several years in New York. He returned to Chicago in 1928 and in early 1931 he went back into the studio. These Brunswick and Vocalion sessions were Oliver's last known recordings. Dental trouble in the early 1930s forced Oliver to cut back on gigs. In 1937 he moved to Savannah, Georgia. He died there the following year of a cerebral hemorrhage at the age of fifty-two.

Oliver composed many jazz standards, including "Dipper Mouth," "West End Blues," "Snag It," "Dixieland Blues," "High Society," and "Doctor Jazz." Jazz critics often refer to Oliver's Creole Jazz Band as the epitome of New Orleans–style jazz and consider Oliver an early musical pioneer. Indeed, music writer Donald Clarke has called Oliver "one of the founding fathers of American music."

See also: Louis Armstrong

Further reading: Donald Clarke, *The Penguin Encyclopedia of Popular Music* (1989); Dempsey J. Travis, *An Autobiography of Black Jazz* (1983).

Francis O'Neill

Musician and Police Superintendent

BORN: August 25, 1849
Tralibane, Ireland

DIED: January 28, 1936
Chicago, Illinois

Chief of the Chicago Police Department from 1901 to 1905, Francis J. O'Neill is best remembered as a great authority on traditional Irish folk music. He wrote seven books on the subject and rescued many old tunes from certain oblivion. O'Neill preserved traditional Irish music for future generations. To this day, O'Neill's collections remain the definitive reference source for musicians, scholars, and students of Irish music.

O'Neill came from a prosperous farming family in Tralibane, three miles southeast of the seaport of Bantry in West Cork. He was the son of John O'Neill and Catherine O'Mahony. He studied Latin, Greek, and mathematics. He learned to love the music of his native Cork from his neighbors, which included a lively group of psalm singers, flutists, and pipers who gathered in the home of his grandfather.

He left home in 1865 at the age of sixteen to become a cabin boy, sailed to Australia, to the Black Sea, and around Cape Horn, and survived a shipwreck in the Pacific. After a brief sojourn in San Francisco, he worked as a shepherd, a schoolteacher, and a railway clerk at various places throughout the country before settling in Chicago in 1873.

His first job in Chicago was as an unskilled laborer dressing hogs and pounding ice for $1.75 a day. He found work in the Chicago and Alton Railroad as a laborer in a freight house and then in the shipping department of John V. Farwell and Company. Unhappy, he sought a more challenging profession. Like many Irishmen before and since, he joined the police department. He remained there for

O'Neill's was the greatest influence on the evolution of Irish traditional dance music in the twentieth century.

—Nicholas Carolan

thirty-two years, until his retirement in 1905. One month after joining, O'Neill was shot in the back by a burglar at Clark and Monroe Streets on August 17, 1873.

He survived the attack and moved up through the ranks, becoming a desk sergeant in 1887 at the Deering Street station at 2913 South Loomis Street in Bridgeport. He rose to the rank of lieutenant in 1890, and in 1894 was promoted to captain of the eighth district, which included the Union Stockyards. In July of that year he was credited with helping to quell potentially violent strikes at the yards. On April 29, 1901, Mayor Carter Harrison II appointed O'Neill chief of police. He was reappointed for a second term in 1903.

An accomplished flute player, O'Neill went wherever there was hope of finding a tune. And in perhaps the most unusual kind of patronage in the city's history, he made it a practice to hire as many Irish musicians to the force as possible. Even when he was chief of police, he would not let the duties of his office interrupt his search for music. One day when no one could find O'Neill, rumors began circulating that he had been assassinated. In a near panic, a contingent of officers was dispatched to locate the missing police chief. After searching unsuccessfully, a policeman who knew O'Neill's love for music suggested a visit to the Brighton Park neighborhood, where a fiddler friend of O'Neill's lived. When the officers arrived they found the two musicians in the living room, the chief with his flute and the friend with his fiddle.

O'Neill carried his tin whistle around with him at all times. On his travels to discover Irish music in the city, O'Neill was often accompanied by Sergeant James O'Neill (no relation) from Belfast, who wrote down the tunes. (Francis O'Neill could not read music—in fact, he had more than fifty musical collaborators; James O'Neill was the best known.) Impromptu Irish music sessions often took place in James O'Neill's house at 3522 South Washtenaw Avenue in the Brighton Park neighborhood.

Francis O'Neill collected tunes from local Irish immigrants as well as from noted Irish musicians who passed through town. By 1903 he had spent close to three decades collecting tunes, sifting through material, and discoursing with musicians. That year he published, at his own expense, *O'Neill's Music of Ireland*, a monumental work that contained 1,850 pieces of music, including dance tunes, airs, and compositions by the famous blind Irish harper Turlough O'Carolan. In 1905 he resigned from the police force to devote the rest of his life to the study of Irish music, collecting lyrics and compiling tunes. More volumes followed: *The Dance Music of Ireland* (1907), *Irish Folk Music: A Fascinating Hobby* (1910), and *Irish Minstrels and Musicians* (1913), among others.

O'Neill was an advocate for Irish music on and off the police force. He supported the Feis, a celebration of Irish music and dance that was held on August 3, 1913, at Comiskey Park and organized by the Gaelic League of Ireland and the Chicago Gaelic Society. In 1934 O'Neill contributed arrangements to *The Pageant of the Celt*, a musical dramatization of Irish history, which was staged at Soldier Field.

In January 1936, O'Neill died in his home at 5448 South Drexel Boulevard from a heart ailment. He was eighty-six. A funeral mass was held at Saint Thomas the Apostle Church. He personally designed the family mausoleum in Mount Olivet Cemetery where he is buried with his wife, Anna, and son, Rogers. Two monuments in O'Neill's hometown of Tralibane in County Cork have been erected in his honor: a plaque at the traditional Irish crossroads and a statue overlooking a valley.

During the past few decades there has been a revival of interest in traditional Irish music both in Ireland and in the United States. Musicians from the Chieftains to the Pogues to Chicago's own champion button accordionist Jimmy Keane and fiddler Liz Carroll owe a large debt to the work of Francis J. O'Neill.

O'Neill was an avid collector of Irish music throughout his entire life. By 1898 he had enough material to fill 1,500 volumes, considered the largest private collection of Irish literature in the United States. In 1931 he donated his collection to the University of Notre Dame.

Chief O'Neill's Pub & Restaurant at 3471 North Elston Avenue takes its name and inspiration from the chief. It hosts Irish music sessions on Tuesday and Sunday evenings.

See also: Terence Teahan

Further reading: Nicholas Carolan, *A Harvest Saved: Francis O'Neill and Irish Music in Chicago* (1997); Charles Ffrench, ed., *Biographical History of the American Irish in Chicago* (1897); Miles Krassen and Larry McCullough, liner notes to *Irish Traditional Instrumental Music from Chicago, Volume II* (1978); Lawrence E. McCullough, *Irish Music in Chicago: An Ethnomusicological Study*, Ph.D. diss. (1978); Ellen Skerrett and Mary Lesch, eds., *Francis O'Neill: Chief O'Neill's Sketchy Recollections of an Eventful Life in Chicago* (2008).

James O'Reilly

Actor and Director

BORN: January 11, 1927
Chicago, Illinois

DIED: May 19, 1990
Naperville, Illinois

James O'Reilly left an indelible mark on Chicago theater as both an actor and as a director. He served as artistic director for two of the leading off-Loop theater companies in town—the Court Theatre in Hyde Park from 1964 to 1970 and the Body Politic Theatre in Lincoln Park from 1980 to 1986—and he gave some of the most powerful and heartfelt performances ever to grace Chicago stages.

A Chicago native, James O'Reilly was raised in the Norwood Park neighborhood on the Far Northwest Side and spent his freshman year at Taft High School. While still a teenager he moved with his father to Texas and finished high school in a small town near Brownsville. After his father's death in the early 1940s, O'Reilly returned to Chicago and enrolled at Loyola University to study chemistry. A brief stint in the army toward the end of World War II interrupted his studies, but after the war he returned to Chicago and resumed his education at Loyola. At the same time he worked at the *Chicago Daily News,* first on the loading dock and later in the mailroom. Despite his success in the theater, O'Reilly worked in the *Daily News* mailroom well into the early 1970s.

O'Reilly caught the acting bug at Loyola. In those days local theater consisted of little more than stock companies, community groups, suburban theater, and college productions. Although there were several attempts to create a uniquely Chicago theatrical community in the 1950s, it wasn't until the late 1960s and early 1970s that contemporary off-Loop professional theater really blossomed.

O'Reilly continued to live two lives. By day he worked in the *Daily News* mailroom; in the evening he pursued his love of the theater, acting in and directing as many productions as he could handle. In 1964 he became artistic director of the Court Theatre in Hyde Park. After three decades in Chicago theater, O'Reilly felt he was ready for a change. In 1970 he resigned from the Court Theatre and left the city. He acted for a short time in the Meadowbrook Theater in Rochester Hills, Michigan, and then served as director for two seasons at the Cohoes Music Hall in upstate New York. By the time he returned in the mid-1970s, Chicago was in the middle of a theatrical renaissance. Young fledgling companies with names such as Steppenwolf and the now-defunct Wisdom Bridge were making the city an exciting place to work.

O'Reilly started all over again. He began to find work as a freelance actor and director. He returned to his old home, the Court Theatre, and appeared in such plays as George Bernard Shaw's *Mrs. Warren's Profession,* Henrik Ibsen's *A Doll's House,* and, most successfully, in Sean O'Casey's classic *Juno and the Paycock* as the blustery Captain Jack Boyle. In 1979 O'Reilly directed two short plays by South African playwright Athol Fugard at a new theater company, the financially struggling Body Politic Theatre. The theater was, at that time, searching for a new artistic director. O'Reilly offered his services and was immediately accepted.

Under O'Reilly's leadership, the Body Politic presented fresh interpretations of Shakespearean classics as well as vibrant productions of contemporary Irish and English drama. The Body Politic quickly earned a reputation as the premier presenter of finely crafted Anglo-Irish drama in the city. O'Reilly developed and nurtured an ensemble company. He is credited with turning the Body Politic around—artistically if not financially. It was he who suggested that the Body Politic pool resources and share space with the adjacent Victory Gardens Theater to cut costs. Now such arrangements are commonplace. Even so, the theater struggled before finally closing in 1996.

O'Reilly portrayed a wide range of characters during his theatrical career. His more notable performances included Hugh, the old schoolmaster, in Brian Friel's *Translations* in 1982, which he also directed; the worldly barkeep in John Millington Synge's *Playboy of the Western World* in 1983; the aging actor in *The Dresser* in 1983; the cynical civil servant in Hugh Leonard's *A Life* in 1984; Shylock in Shakespeare's *The Merchant of Venice* in 1984; and the weary London police inspector in *The Rat and the Skull* in 1985. In the same year O'Reilly directed Bob Gibson's *The Courtship of Carl Sandburg* at the Northlight Theater in Evanston and at the Apollo Theater in Chicago, for which he received popular and critical acclaim.

O'Reilly made his last appearance on a Chicago stage in 1989 in *King Lear.* Meanwhile he continued to teach theater classes at Loyola University and at Northern Illinois University in DeKalb, Illinois. O'Reilly also appeared in several motion pictures, including *Class* (1983) and *The Killing Floor* (1985).

In May 1990, O'Reilly collapsed at a friend's house and died shortly afterward at Edward Hospital in Naperville, Illinois. At the time of his death, he was planning to direct and act in three plays, including an adaptation of *Macbeth* for the Pendragon Theatre Company in Lakeside, Michigan.

See also: Kenneth Sawyer Goodman

Further reading: Richard Christiansen, *A Theater of Our Own: A History and a Memoir of 1,001 Nights in Chicago* (2004); Special Collections Department of the Chicago Public Library, *Resetting the Stage: Theater Beyond the Loop 1960–1990* (1990).

Ruth Page

Dancer and Choreographer

BORN: March 22, 1899
Indianapolis, Indiana

DIED: April 7, 1991
Chicago, Illinois

Ruth Page was a pioneer of American dance, and for more than seven decades she was a formidable presence on the Chicago dance scene. At a time when the best dance was almost exclusively associated with foreign countries, Page departed from tradition and dared to choreograph ballets with peculiarly American themes. She worked with virtually every Chicago opera company at one time or another. Further, she created a new art form by turning operas into ballets, which she did with *La Traviata, Carmen,* and *Americans in Paris.*

Ruth Page was the daughter of a prominent Indianapolis family. Her father was a surgeon and her mother was a professional pianist and one of the founders of the Indianapolis Symphony Orchestra. Page decided at the age of five to be a dancer when her mother took her to see the famous Russian ballerina Anna Pavlova in Indianapolis. As a teenager Page took summer ballet classes in Chicago with Anna Pavlova's Company. Then, still a teenager, she joined the company and toured Latin America, accompanied by her mother. Upon returning to the United States, she attended a girls' boarding school in New York and studied ballet with the Belgian dancer Adolph Bolm.

In 1914 Page became a soloist for the Metropolitan Opera Ballet in New York. Several years later, in 1919, she made her Chicago debut with the Chicago Grand Opera Company in a production of Bolm's *The Birthday of the Infanta,* based on a story by Oscar Wilde. She continued as a member of the Bolm's Ballet Intime company for several years. In 1924 Page became the principal ballerina of the Chicago Allied Arts, an experimental group, and choreographed *Oak Street Beach,* which was inspired by the Chicago beach of the same name. The following year she became the first American dancer to perform with Sergei Diaghilev's Ballets Russes. She returned to Chicago in 1926 to become the premier dancer of the Ravinia Opera Company in Highland Park, Illinois. From 1934 to 1937 she served as the chief dancer and ballet director of the Chicago Opera Company.

Page was determined to build an indigenous dance repertoire in a country with little or no dance roots. She earned a reputation for creating unconventional ballet. *Americans in Paris* (1936) featured tap dancing. *Hear Ye! Hear Ye!* (1934), with music by noted American composer Aaron Copland, was set during a murder trial. *La Guiablesse* (1933), based on a legend from Martinique, was performed at the Century of Progress Exposition in 1933 in Chicago with a virtually all-black cast, including Talley Beatty and Katherine Dunham, then an anthropology student at the University of Chicago. In 1938 Page and Bentley Stone established the Page-Stone Ballet Company and spent several years touring the United States and Latin America. That year they presented their celebrated production of *Frankie and Johnny,* a ballet based on the American folk ballad. It has since become a modern ballet classic.

Page believed that opera, with its broad emotions and intense passions, could be successfully translated into the language of dance. In 1939 she transformed the opera *Carmen* by Bizet into the ballet *Guns and Castanets,* and set it in the Spanish Civil War of the 1930s. Other examples of her work include *Camille,* a dance version of Verdi's *La Traviata,* and *Revenge,* based on Verdi's *Il Trovatore.* One of her most unique ballets, *Billy Sunday* (1946), based on the sermons of the famous Chicago revivalist and Bible thumper, incorporated spoken word with dancing.

Despite her periodic absences from the city, Page continued to exert considerable influence on the Chicago dance scene. From 1942 to 1943 and again in 1945 she served as ballet director and premiere dancer with the Chicago Opera Company. In 1954 she became ballet director of the Chicago Lyric Opera and two years later she became ballet director and choreographer with the Chicago Opera Ballet, which attracted such international guest artists as Maria Tallchief and Mia Slavenska.

Throughout her long career Page never relinquished her dream of establishing a resident, professional ballet company in the city. In 1974 she formed Ballet Chicago. But even her indomitable presence was not enough. The troupe folded four years later due to lack of funding, inadequate community support, and insufficient theater space.

From 1962 until her death Page served as director and choreographer for the annual *Nutcracker* production at the Arie Crown Theatre in McCormick Place. It has since grown into a cherished Christmas tradition. In 1970 Page founded the Ruth Page Foundation and School of Dance in a former Moose lodge at 1016 North Dearborn Parkway. The school continues to offer classes in dance to adults and children and also houses the Chicago Repertory Dance Ensemble, one of the leading modern dance troupes in the city.

Outspoken and always entertaining, Page was quick to offer an opinion on most subjects. She said of theater critics, "The professional critic, he is a strange beast, and we would probably be better off if he were banished from the theater." She opined about architects, "Sometimes I think I would like to line up all the architects who have designed theaters in this country and shoot them." As for Chicago itself, Page observed, "I have learned from long experience that Chicago is the most difficult city in the world to get things going in. Chicagoans are timid and don't trust their own taste, and they must be sure that what they are getting has been approved every place else before they can accept it."

In 1986 the Chicago Dance Arts Coalition, an arts organization and professional association for dance founded in 1981, presented the first Ruth Page Awards for excellence in dance. In 1989 Delaware Place between Dearborn and Clark was renamed Ruth Page Place.

Page died of heart failure in April 1991 at her North Lake Shore Drive apartment. She was ninety-two. She is buried in Graceland Cemetery.

The Ruth Page Nutcracker Papers, 1965–1997, are held at the Newberry Library.

See also: Gerald Arpino, Ann Barzel, Mary Garden, Joseph Holmes
Further reading: Ronald L. David, *Opera in Chicago* (1966); John Martin, *Ruth Page: An Intimate Biography* (1977); Ruth Page, *Page to Page* (1978), Andrew Mark Wentick, ed.

William S. Paley

Broadcaster

BORN: September 28, 1901
Chicago, Illinois

DIED: October 26, 1990
New York, New York

One of the giants of the American broadcast industry, William Samuel Paley controlled the Columbia Broadcasting System (CBS) for almost fifty years in one capacity or another.

Paley, the son of Ukrainian Jews, was born in an apartment in the rear of his father's storefront cigar shop at 1767 Ogden Avenue in the Maxwell Street neighborhood on the city's Near West Side. After graduating from Schurz High School on the Northwest Side, he enrolled at the Western Military Academy in Alton, Illinois, for college prep work. He attended the University of Chicago for one year but quit to move to Philadelphia to enter the family cigar manufacturing business, which by that time had grown into a successful company. After graduating from the Wharton School of Finance in 1922, Paley served as the company's advertising director.

During the late 1920s, he saw tremendous potential for the fledgling radio broadcast industry that had grown up almost overnight. In 1928 he purchased a small network of radio stations from a friend, left the cigar business altogether, and moved to New York. By September of that year, he became the president of the Columbia Broadcasting System. Paley made some bold moves in those early years. He hired Bing Crosby, then an untested singer with an unreliable reputation, and lured Jack Benny away from rival NBC. Regular television broadcasts were introduced in 1939.

At first unsure of the new medium, Paley, an innovative programmer, turned CBS into one of the country's three major television networks by deliberately appealing to a mass audience. His reign at CBS was characterized, noted a colleague, by "creativity, energy, integrity, style, wit and an enormous sense of the public interest." Among the CBS programs that earned the network both critical raves and audience popularity during the Paley years were *The Ed Sullivan Show, The Jackie Gleason Show, I Love Lucy, The Mary Tyler Moore Show, All in the Family,* and *M*A*S*H*.

In 1983 an unsuccessful hostile takeover attempt by cable television king Ted Turner forced Paley to retire. Lawrence Tisch of Loews Corporation, one of CBS's biggest stockholders, assumed control. Three years later, however, Paley returned and was reelected chairman of the board.

Paley died in his Manhattan home of a heart attack. He was eighty-nine.

Bertha Honore Palmer

Philanthropist

BORN: May 22, 1849
Louisville, Kentucky

DIED: May 5, 1918
Sarasota, Florida

For many years, Bertha Honore Palmer held the title of the Nation's Hostess. Overseas, she became an unofficial goodwill ambassador for the United States. At home, she entertained politicians, labor leaders, and ordinary folk. Like another wealthy socialite, Louise DeKoven Bowen, Palmer used her riches to relieve the suffering that existed all around her.

Bertha Honore led a charmed life. She was the daughter of a prominent family from the West Side. Her father, real estate developer Henry M. Honore, brought his family to Chicago from Louisville, Kentucky, in 1855. Bertha attended the best schools—St. Xavier's Academy and the Dearborn Seminary. In August 1870 Honore, at the age of twenty-one, married Potter Palmer, a diligent, somber-faced Yankee from Massachusetts, who was twenty-three years her senior.

The Chicago Fire of 1871 destroyed the couples' considerable fortunes. Their magnificent buildings burned to the ground; the Grand Pacific Hotel, the Sherman House, Crosby's Opera House, and the Palmer House all were reduced to rubble and ash. But Potter Palmer was not only determined to build a bigger and better hotel, he was also determined to erect a luxurious mansion far away from the Prairie Avenue district where the elite of the city then lived. In 1882 he commissioned Henry Ives Cobb and Charles S. Frost to design a three-story castle along 3,000 feet of marshland, which later became part of Lake Shore Drive. The castle contained a great hall, an eighty-foot tower, marble mosaic floors, and a grand oak staircase.

The Palmer castle ushered in a new era in Chicago hospitality. Here, in this fantastic testament to Chicago's burgeoning strength as an industrial capital, Bertha Palmer entertained princes, statesmen, politicians, actors, labor leaders, artists, opera stars, and even presidents. She also welcomed factory girls and millinery workers to her home (the Women's Trade Union League met there). She became an avid collector of American and French impressionist paintings and was considered somewhat of a trendsetter in her day. Palmer never backed away from a cause that she believed in. She championed the rights of working women and lobbied for the improvement of the status of women, including the novel notion of equal pay for equal work. It was neither "unfeminine nor monstrous" to compete with men, she believed. Palmer spoke frequently about social abuses, poor wages, and the inadequate educational opportunities for women.

Palmer was also a leading figure on the women's-club scene, belonging to both the Fortnightly Club and the Chicago Woman's Club. She helped push for protective legislation and supported the causes of women reformers, including Jane Addams, Mary McDowell, and Louise DeKoven Bowen. She was also a familiar sight at Hull House. Moreover, she was vice president of the Civic Federation, a group of prominent Chicagoans who organized to fight vice and corruption. In 1893 Chicago hosted the World's Columbian Exposition, which Palmer saw as a great opportunity to advance women's rights. In addition to proposing the general plan of the interior of the Women's Building, she also played hostess to many of the distinguished visitors who came from around the world.

Her husband, Potter, died on May 4, 1902, at age seventy-five. Shaken but determined to carry on, Bertha moved to Sarasota, Florida, in 1910 at age sixty-one. She farmed and tended to her new estate until she died of breast cancer in 1918. She was buried in a mausoleum at Graceland Cemetery next to her husband and close to her parents and brothers.

See also: Jane Addams, Louise DeKoven Bowen, Potter Palmer
Further reading: Sally Sexton Kalmbach, *The Jewel of the Gold Coast: Mrs. Potter Palmer's Chicago* (2009); Ishbel Ross, *Silhouette in Diamond: The Life of Mrs. Potter Palmer* (1960); Rima Lunin Schultz and Adele Hast, eds. *Women Building Chicago 1790–1990: A Biographical Dictionary* (2001).

Potter Palmer
Merchant

BORN: May 20, 1826
Potter's Hollow, New York

DIED: May 4, 1902
Chicago, Illinois

A quiet, self-educated man, Potter Palmer revolutionized merchandising in Chicago—some would say throughout the country—thus earning the title of the first merchant prince of Chicago.

Potter Palmer's grandparents were Quakers who moved to New York from the whaling town of New Bedford, Massachusetts. At eighteen, Palmer obtained a job at a general store in Durham, New York, as a clerk. In 1847 he opened his own dry goods store in Oneida, New York, and later opened one in Lockport, New York. Searching for a larger market, he moved to Chicago in 1852 and opened a dry goods store, P. Palmer and Company, on Lake Street. His little shop grew, and sales steadily increased. A shrewd businessman, Palmer invested in vast amounts of real estate, which contributed greatly to his wealth.

In 1856 Palmer hired a hard-working assistant from Massachusetts named Marshall Field. The New Englander believed personable service and quality goods equaled success. Palmer watched him closely. Within a few months, Palmer promoted Field to head salesman. In 1867 an exhausted Palmer, weary of the retail business, retired altogether and sold his share of the business to his partners, Marshall Field and Levi Z. Leiter. He then proceeded to buy property along State Street. After persuading the city council to widen the street, he made plans to erect an opulent hotel that would lure customers away from Lake Street, at that time the retail center of the city. Further, he agreed to build his former colleagues—then operating under the name of Field, Leiter and Company—a spanking new store at State and Washington Streets. The elegant six-story structure opened in October 1868.

The first Palmer House, designed by Chicago's pioneer architect, John Van Osdel, opened on September 26, 1870, at the corner of State and Quincy Streets, only to perish in the Chicago Fire in October 1871. Rather than giving up, the fire only served to goad Palmer into even more furious activity. He built a bigger and better Palmer House a few blocks north at State and Monroe streets. This post-fire Palmer House claimed to be the world's first fireproof hotel and the first equipped with electricity, telephones, and elevators. It was demolished in 1925 to make way for the present Palmer House.

The city's elite lived along elegant Prairie Avenue on the near South Side. Marshall Field had settled there, as did George Pullman and businessman John Glessner, among many others. Palmer, breaking from tradition, decided to build an extravagant mansion on Lake Shore Drive between Banks and Schiller Streets. It was a prophetic and, truth be told, bold move—the area was little more than a marshy wilderness at the time.

Palmer purchased the land and hired a pair of famous architects, Henry Ives Cobb and Charles S. Frost, to build him a new home at 1350 North Lake Shore Drive. Made of Ohio limestone and Wisconsin granite, the pseudo-Gothic Palmer castle ultimately cost more than $1 million—an unbelievably vast sum in those days. Some of the city's most splendid balls and dances were held in the ballroom of the massive mansion, hosted by his gracious wife, Bertha Palmer. Soon, like-minded affluent Chicagoans abandoned Prairie Avenue to follow the State Street merchant to the North Side. By the turn of the century so many affluent families had moved to Lake Shore Drive and adjacent streets that the area soon earned the sobriquet of the "Gold Coast." Sadly, Palmer's castle became yet another victim of the wrecker's ball when it was unceremoniously demolished in 1950 to make way for a high-rise apartment building.

As a retailer, Palmer introduced many innovations. He allowed customers to examine merchandise in their homes and then return it if they were not satisfied or to exchange it, after it was bought, for other items. He advertised heavily. Above all, Palmer treated his customers—no matter what their economic status—with courtesy and respect. Potter Palmer based his successful career on pleasing his patrons. It was a lesson that others emulated, most notably, his protégé Marshall Field.

Palmer died in Chicago in May 1902, several weeks shy of his seventy-sixth birthday.

Over the years Chicago's central shopping district has shifted from State Street to Michigan Avenue as many of the big department stores such as Goldblatt's and Montgomery Ward went out of business. Despite these changes, the Palmer House, now a Hilton hotel, remains a Loop landmark. One of the last great downtown hotels, the Palmer House continues to invite guests from around the world to come to its State and Monroe address.

Palmer Street is named in his honor.

See also: Marshall Field, Bertha Honore Palmer, Richard Sears, Aaron Montgomery Ward

Further reading: Kenan Heise and Michael Edgerton, *Chicago Center for Enterprise*, 2 vols. (1982); Harold M. Mayer and Richard C. Wade, *Chicago: Growth of a Metropolis* (1969); Donald L. Miller, *City of the Century: The Epic of Chicago and the Making of America* (1996); Lloyd Wendt and Herman Kogan, *Give the Lady What She Wants! The Story of Marshall Field and Co.* (1952).

Francis W. Parker

Educator

BORN: October 9, 1837
Bedford, New Hampshire

DIED: March 2, 1902
Pass Christian, Mississippi

Called the "father of progressive education," Francis Wayland Parker founded the Chicago Institute, which eventually merged with the University of Chicago, and earned a reputation as an indefatigable advocate of progressive teaching methods.

The son of a cabinet maker, Francis Parker was orphaned when still a small child and raised by a farmer. At age thirteen he enrolled at Mt. Vernon Academy in New Hampshire, and at sixteen he began to teach. Parker taught in several New Hampshire schools until 1853, when he was appointed principal of a one-room frontier school in Carrollton, Illinois. He remained there until the outbreak of the Civil War. Parker then returned to New Hampshire and joined the Fourth New Hampshire Volunteers as a lieutenant. Soon thereafter he was promoted to colonel and was taken prisoner by Confederate troops and incarcerated in a military camp in Greensburg, North Carolina.

After the war, Parker resumed his teaching career. In 1869 he was appointed principal of the Dayton, Ohio, school system. Following his wife's death in 1871, Parker resumed his own education, studying in Germany and observing the teaching methods of such progressive pioneers as Friedrich Froebel and J. N. Pestalozzi. In 1875 he was appointed superintendent of schools in Quincy, Massachusetts.

Parker began experimenting with new methods of teaching. Influenced by the principles of E. A. Sheldon, he broke all the traditional rules. At that time, students learned via the rote method. They memorized facts and figures and regurgitated the statistics at the appropriate time. Parker's method was different. He demanded that his pupils actually think for themselves and learn to gain enough confidence to express themselves. Each child, he argued, was a unique individual, and each child learned at his or her own rate. He advocated a curriculum that emphasized observation, recommended field trips, and preached that the moral development of a child was just as important as—if not more important than—the act of learning.

Parker came to Chicago in 1883 and was appointed principal of the Cook County Normal School, a training school for elementary and high school teachers, then located in the village of Englewood, Illinois. Englewood was annexed to Chicago in 1889 and the renamed Chicago Normal School was incorporated under the aegis of the Chicago Board of Education in 1896. Much criticism was directed at Parker's controversial ideas. He resigned in 1899 to head an experimental school, the Chicago Institute, devoted to unconventional teaching methods. The institute consisted of a training school for teachers, a kindergarten, an elementary school, and another school—the Francis W. Parker School—located on the North Side near Lincoln Park. In 1901 the Chicago Institute was incorporated into the University of Chicago as the School of Education. John Dewey became the director after Parker's death. Dewey resigned in 1904 to accept a position at Columbia University. Francis W. Parker school, a private institution, continues to serve the Lincoln Park community and, through its extensive adult education evening classes, the greater Chicago area. Parker alumni include the actress Celeste Holm, the cinematographer Haskell Wexler, and the playwright and writer David Mamet.

Truth be told, Parker was a bit of a tyrant. "He roared, he growled, he stormed, he banged . . . he scared the wits out of students, and he terrified teachers," wrote one of his supporters, union leader Margaret Haley. But, as Haley also admitted, he proved to be an inspiring role model. Among his books are *Talks on Pedagogics* (1894) and *Talks on Teaching* (1896).

Parker died in 1902 in Mississippi at the age of sixty-four.

See also: Margaret Haley, William Rainey Harper, Ella Flagg Young

Further reading: Jack K. Campbell, *Colonel Francis W. Parker: The Children's Crusader* (1967); Ida Cassa Heffron, *Francis Wayland Parker: An Interpretative Biography* (1934).

Albert Parsons

Labor Activist

BORN: Circa 1848
Montgomery, Alabama

DIED: November 11, 1887
Chicago, Illinois

Lucy Parsons

Labor Activist

BORN: Circa March 1853
Johnson County, Texas

DIED: March 7, 1942
Chicago, Illinois

Lucy Ella and Albert R. Parsons were influential leaders in the Chicago labor movement of the late nineteenth century. An eloquent and fiery orator, Lucy marched and protested in the name of economic freedom and spoke frequently about labor unrest, anarchism, industrial unionism, women's rights, and civil rights. Albert, an apprentice printer, served in the Confederate army during the Civil War. After the war he edited the *Waco* (Texas) *Spectator* and from 1869 to 1871 he worked as assistant assessor for the Internal Revenue Service. He is best remembered as one of the Haymarket Eight.

Lucy Parson's personal background is rather sketchy. Born Lucy Gatherings, she was thought to be a former slave of mixed African American, Indian, and Mexican ancestry. She married Albert Parsons in 1872. The couple settled in Chicago in late 1873 at a time when the city was in great economic and social turmoil. Albert joined the Social Democratic Party of North America and cofounded the first Knights of Labor Assembly in Chicago. He also ran for alderman of the Fifteenth Ward on the North Side. At that time, the Parsons lived near Larrabee Street and North Avenue.

City officials viewed both Lucy and Albert Parsons with nervous suspicion. In 1878 Albert founded the Traders and Labor Assembly of Chicago and was elected secretary of the Chicago Eight Hour League. He edited two radical publications, the *Socialist* and, with Lizzie Swank, the *Alarm,* the publication of the International Working People's Association.

Lucy was every bit as radical as her husband. A major foe of capitalism, she compared the American businessman with members of the European aristocracy, believing that wage workers were not much higher on the social scale than slaves, and she advocated nothing less than the destruction of the existing ruling class. Parsons championed the establishment of a fair and equitable society based upon the principle of cooperation rather than competition and promoted equal rights for all, regardless of sex or race. Parsons argued that the social evils of society are a result of economic injustice, and thus concluded that the abolition of capitalism would produce racial and sexual equality.

A clash between workers and police at the McCormick Harvesting Machine Company on May 3, 1886, led to a protest meeting on Desplaines Street near Haymarket Square the following evening. The events that unfolded that evening became known as the Haymarket Riot. Albert Parsons was one of the speakers who addressed the crowd that rain-soaked night. Mayor Carter Harrison I also attended the meeting but returned to his Ashland Avenue mansion, certain that all was well. Before retiring for the evening he stopped at the Desplaines Street police station and told Captain John Bonfield to send his officers home. For reasons still unclear, Bonfield defied the mayor's wishes, marched to Haymarket Square, and ordered the crowd to disperse. In the tumult that followed, an unidentified figure hurled a bomb. Albert and Lucy Parsons, who by this time had walked to nearby Zepf's Hall at 630 West Lake Street to escape the rain, heard the commotion outside. When the uproar subsided, Lucy returned home and Albert traveled to stay at a friend's house in far western Geneva, Illinois.

At the insistence of Lucy, who feared for his safety, Albert fled to Waukesha, Wisconsin, to escape possible prosecution. However, he surrendered several weeks later on June 21, 1886. On August 20, a jury returned a guilty verdict against eight men for the murder of police officer Mathias Degan and conspiracy to start a police riot: George Engel, Samuel Fielden, Adolph Fischer, Louis Lingg, Oscar Neebe, Albert Parsons, Michael Schwab, and August Spies. Ultimately, seven (Louis Lingg died in prison under mysterious circumstances), including Albert Parsons, were sentenced to death. Lucy crisscrossed the country proclaiming her husband's innocence and explaining the wretched conditions that led to the Haymarket Riot and the rise of the eight-hour-day movement. During her crusade, she spoke to an estimated 200,000 people in some sixteen states. Her efforts were not sufficient to prevent the executions of four of the Haymarket Eight—Parsons, Spies, Fischer, and Engel—who were hanged at noon on November 11, 1887, a day that came to be known around the world as "Black Friday." Two days later, the funeral procession began at the house of August Spies, one of the Haymarket martyrs, at 2132 West Potomac Avenue in Wicker Park. The procession traveled south along Milwaukee Avenue and down Wells Street to the Grand Central railroad station. The bodies were then taken by train to Waldheim Cemetery in Forest Park, Illinois—the only cemetery willing to accept their remains.

On June 26, 1893, Governor John Peter Altgeld pardoned the surviving defendants—Oscar Neebe, Samuel Fielden, and Michael Schwab. Lucy Parsons carried on. In 1891, she and Lizzie Holmes edited *Freedom, A Revolutionary Anarchist-Communist Monthly* and from 1905 to 1906, Parsons edited *The Liberator*. She became involved in Eugene Debs's Social Democratic Party and was a seminal figure in the founding of the Industrial Workers of the World.

Parsons was a featured speaker at various anarchist forums in Chicago and was known to drop in at the city's foremost bohemian hangout, the Dil Pickle Club on the Near North Side. As late as the 1930s, she traveled and lectured across the country in defense of free speech and fair working conditions. In 1889, she wrote a biography of her late husband, *Life of Albert R. Parsons, with Brief History of the Labor Movement in America.*

In March 1942, Parsons and a companion died when her wood stove caught fire at her home at 3130 North Troy Street. She was buried next to the grave of the Haymarket Martyrs in Waldheim Cemetery.

The identity of the bomb thrower who caused the Haymarket Riot remains a mystery. Novelist Frank Harris, in his fictional account of the Haymarket Affair, *The Bomb* (1908), claimed it may have been Rudolph Schnaubelt, Michael Schwab's brother-in-law. Others contend that the bomb thrower was George Schwab, a German shoemaker, or George Meng, a German anarchist. But there is no conclusive evidence.

In 2011, the Museum of Contemporary Art commissioned the Scottish sound artist Susan Philipsz's *We Shall All Be,* a site-specific installation that drew on history, literature, and pop and folk music. More specifically, the installation included Phillipsz singing the Scots ballad "Annie Laurie" a cappella. Albert Parsons reportedly sang "Annie Laurie" the night before he was executed. On April 30, 2011, local and national labor leaders commemorated the 125th anniversary of the Haymarket Affair with a re-enactment in Haymarket Square that featured artists and musicians dressed in period costume, including Chicago actress Alma Washington as Lucy Parsons.

See also: John Peter Altgeld, Eugene Debs, William "Big Bill" Haywood, Carter Harrison I, Ben Reitman

Further reading: William J. Adelman, *Haymarket Revisited,* 2nd ed. (1986); Carolyn Ashbaugh, *Lucy Parsons, American Revolutionary* (1976); Paul Avrich, *The Haymarket Tragedy* (1984); Alan Calmer, *Labor Agitator: The Story of Albert R. Parsons* (1937); Philip Foner, ed., *Autobiographies of the Haymarket Martyrs* (1976); James Green, *Death in the Haymarket: A Story of Chicago, the First Labor Movement, and the Bombing That Divided Gilded Age America* (2007); Frank Harris, *The Bomb* (1963); Dave Roediger and Franklin Rosemont, eds., *Haymarket Scrapbook* (1986); Carl Smith, *Urban Disorder and the Shape of Belief: The Great Chicago Fire, the Haymarket Bomb, and the Model Town of Pullman* (1995).

Ed Paschke

Artist

BORN: June 22, 1939
Chicago, Illinois

DIED: November 25, 2004
Chicago, Illinois

One of the most celebrated Chicago-born painters of the twentieth century, Ed Paschke is often associated with the Chicago Imagists school of art, a group of artists who borrowed from pop culture, outsider art, and surrealism to create their own distinctive style. Although influenced by the work of Andy Warhol and especially by comic book art, Paschke, ultimately, went his own way.

Edward Francis Paschke Jr. was born in 1939 at St. Elizabeth's Hospital in Chicago, the second son of Waldrine and Edward Stanley Paschke, a bakery truck driver. Of Polish descent, he grew up on the Northwest Side near Central Park and Diversey Avenues and then in a neighborhood further north near Belmont and Milwaukee Avenues. In the late 1940s, the family moved to a 160-acre farm in Lyndon Station, Wisconsin, ten miles north of the Wisconsin Dells, before returning to Chicago and settling on the Far Northwest Side near Addison and Harlem Avenues.

Among Paschke's earliest and most enduring influences were comic strips and comic books. He was a loyal and avid reader of the Sunday comics in both the *Chicago Tribune* and *Chicago Sun-Times* and had a particular fondness for the drawing style of *Tarzan of the Apes.* He began to draw his own comics and then moved on to other subjects, including horses and chickens, and contributed cartoons to his high school paper.

Paschke earned a bachelor of fine arts degree from the Art Institute of Chicago in 1961 and a master's of fine arts from the same institution in 1970. *Playboy* magazine hired him as an illustrator of their fiction and nonfiction articles; he contributed illustrations to the magazine off and on until as late as 1989.

His early paintings concentrated on movie stars, wrestlers, and circus freaks: he was called the Weegee of the art world. He was especially known for his idiosyncratic portraits of everyone from George Washington and Adolf Hitler to Elvis Presley and Osama bin Laden. He depicted Marilyn Monroe, for example, as a green-faced accordion player, and the film actress Claudette Colbert as a tattooed lady.

Paschke had his first solo show at the Deson-Zaks Gallery in Chicago in 1970 and his first New York exhibit at

Hundred Acres in Soho the following year. From 1977 to 1996 he exhibited regularly at the Phyllis Kind Gallery in Chicago. The first retrospective of his work was held at the Pompidou Center in Paris in 1989. In the same year a comprehensive retrospective was also held at his alma mater, the Art Institute. He taught at Northwestern University in the Department of Art Theory and Practice from 1976 until his death.

Paschke was generous with his time and offered moral support to other artists. He gained a level of local celebrity that was unusual for artists, as famous in his own field as, say, the basketball icon Michael Jordan was in his. In fact, at one point, Paschke and Jordan shared the same fifty-foot billboard for a Bigsby and Kruthers clothing store advertisement, their visages greeting drivers along one of Chicago's busy expressways.

Paschke died in his sleep at his North Side Chicago home of heart failure on Thanksgiving morning 2004. He was sixty-five.

See also: Roger Brown
Further reading: Neal Benezra, *Ed Paschke* (1996).

Walter Payton
Football Player

BORN: July 25, 1954
Columbia, Mississippi

DIED: November 1, 1999
South Barrington, Illinois

His nickname was "Sweetness." On the football field he ran with a combination of grace and grit unparalleled in Chicago football history. The late general manager of the Bears, Jim Finks, called Payton "a complete football player, better than Jim Brown, better than O. J. Simpson." He remains the National Football League's second all-time rusher.

Born in Columbia, Mississippi, Walter Jerry Payton was one of three children of Edward, a factory worker, and Alyne Payton. Since his older brother, Eddie, was already a running back at the all-black John J. Jefferson High School, Payton wanted to avoid playing football altogether. But after Eddie graduated, the football coach asked Walter, by then a sophomore, to try out for the team. An avid drummer in the school band, he agreed to join the team only if the coach allowed him to follow both pursuits. During his junior year his high school merged with the integrated Columbia High.

After graduating, Payton followed Eddie to Jackson State College (now Jackson State University) in Jackson, Mississippi, where he excelled on the gridiron, finishing fourth in the Heisman Trophy voting. He graduated with a bachelor's degree in communications and began work on a master's in education for the deaf.

In 1975 Payton was the fourth pick in the National Football League (NFL) draft when the Chicago Bears selected him as a running back. His first game during the 1975 season began rather inauspiciously: he carried the ball only eight times for a net yardage of zero. In the season finale, though, he ran the ball for 134 years on 20 carries, the best rushing performance for a Bear since Gale Sayers played for the team. Payton finished his rookie year with 679 yards and seven touchdowns, the lowest numbers of his pro football career.

During the 1976 season, Payton gained 1,390 yards and scored 13 touchdowns. In a game in 1977, Payton rushed for 275 yards, the best single-game performance in NFL history until it was surpassed in 2000. Payton won the NFL rushing title in 1977 and was voted the league's Most Valuable Player that year. From 1976 to 1981, he rushed for more than 1,000 yards during every season and, in 1979, earned the National Football Conference (NFC) rushing crown.

When Mike Ditka was hired in 1982 as the Bears head coach, Payton's career switched into high gear. Payton was now surrounded by high-quality players on both offense and defense, including quarterback Jim McMahon, receivers Willie Gault and Dennis McKinnon, and defensive players Richard Dent, the late Dave Duerson, and Wilber Marshall as well as Dan Hampton and Mike Singletary. And when the defensive lineman William "the Refrigerator" Perry arrived in 1985, the lineup of that year's Super Bowl team was complete.

In 1984 the Bears finished the season with a 10–6 record. More importantly, they won their first postseason game since defeating the Washington Redskins in 1963. In the following season Payton set the NFL record for the most consecutive one-hundred-yard games (eleven). On January 26, 1986, the Bears defeated the New England Patriots in the Super Bowl by a score of 46–10: Payton rushed 22 times for 61 yards. Before the team's legendary run through the playoffs, Payton starred with his fellow teammates in the popular "Super Bowl Shuffle" video and recording. The recording achieved gold status.

During his last season as a Bear, in 1987, Payton shared his position with Neal Anderson. That same year he announced his retirement. The following year he joined the Chicago Bears Board of Directors. He attempted to buy a new NFL franchise—he held a fifteen percent interest in a group that tried to secure an NFL expansion franchise in St. Louis—but the deal fell through.

In total, Payton played with the Bears from 1975 to 1987. He retired with 16,726 rushing yards; 3,838 rushing attempts; combined rushing, receiving, and returning yardage of 21,803; seventy-seven 100-yard rushing games; and ten 1,000-yard rushing seasons. At various times, Payton held numerous NFL records: career rushing yards (16,726), most yards in a single game (275), most career 100-yard games (77), and most seasons with 1,000 or more rushing yards (10). In addition, he was named to the Pro Bowl nine times, received the NFL Player of the Year awards in 1977 and 1985, was Offensive Player of the Year in 1977, and was the *Sporting News* NFC Player of the Year in 1976–77. In 2000, the NFL Man of the Year Award was renamed the Walter Payton NFL Man of the Year Award.

After retiring, Payton devoted his time and energy to Walter Payton Inc., a company that he had founded during his playing days that dealt primarily in real estate, restaurants, timberland, travel, and nursing homes. At one time he was a partner in twenty restaurants and nightclubs. He also raced cars and boats and was co-owner of Dale Coyne Racing in the CART IndyCar World Series.

In 1995 he and his partners Mark Alberts and Scott and Pam Ascher bought a Chicago, Burlington, and Quincy Railroad roadhouse in Aurora, Illinois, and changed the name to Walter Payton's Roadhouse. It consisted of a restaurant, brewery, meeting facilities, and museum. A beer, Walter Payton Pilsner, was named after him. In 2011, the Warrenville, Illinois-based brewery, Two Brothers Brewing Company, bought the historic roundhouse building and renamed it Two Brothers Roundhouse.

In early 1999 Payton announced that he was suffering from PSC (primary sclerosing cholangitis), a rare condition where the bile ducts are closed. While waiting for a donor liver, he passed away on November 1, 1999, of a form of bile duct cancer. He was only forty-five. A few days later, on November 6, 1999, a public memorial service was held in his honor at Soldier Field.

His wife, Connie Payton, operates the Walter and Connie Payton Foundation (WCPF), a foundation that helps abused, neglected, and underprivileged children in Illinois. In 2000 the Walter Payton College Preparatory High School in Lincoln Park opened. Its curriculum consists entirely of honors and advanced placement classes. In 2002 the Payton family established the Walter Payton Cancer Fund and in September 2007 the University of Illinois at Chicago Medical Center opened the Walter Payton Liver Center.

Payton was elected to the Pro Football Hall of Fame in 1993 and to the College Football Hall of Fame in 1996. On February 20, 2010, he was inducted into the Black College Hall of Fame in Atlanta, Georgia.

See also: Red Grange, George Halas, Sid Luckman, Bronko Nagurski

Further reading: Walter Payton and Don Yaeger, *Never Die Easy* (2001); Jeff Pearlman, *Sweetness* (2011).

James C. Petrillo
Labor Activist

BORN: March 16, 1892
Chicago, Illinois

DIED: October 23, 1984
Chicago, Illinois

James Caesar Petrillo, president of both the American Federation of Musicians (AFM) and the Chicago local of the AFM, was one of the most powerful and controversial labor leaders of his day. His rough, combative, and often confrontational style earned him the nickname "Little Caesar." Although extreme in his tactics, no one doubted his sincerity or questioned his honesty. It was understood he merely wanted the best for "his boys."

The son of an immigrant Italian sewer cleaner, James Petrillo grew up in the Little Italy neighborhood around the vicinity of Halsted and Taylor Streets. He had a difficult time in school. Indeed, he felt a perverse pride in revealing just how bad a student he was. "I was in the third grade three times. Finally, after the third year, they told me, 'You're impossible. Get out of here.' And I did. It was the best thing that ever happened to me."

He quit school and hit the streets, picking up any kind of work he could find. He ran an elevator, sold newspapers, and drove a horse and cart. At Hull House, Jane Addams instilled in him a love of the cornet—he looked like a musician, she said. At fourteen, he formed his own four-piece band, playing at picnics and at Polish and Italian weddings. He secured his first union job as a $10-a-week sergeant-at-arms of the American Musicians Union (AMU). His duty was to maintain order in the union hall. In 1914, at age twenty-two, he was elected president of the AMU, but he lost the position three years later. "They threw me out," he said. "They said I was too rough—the way I talked and hollered." In retaliation he jumped to the rival Chicago Federation of Musicians Local 10 of the American Federation of Musicians (AFM). In 1919 he was elected vice president of Local 10, and in 1922 he became president, a post that he retained for forty years. In the early days, the union struggled to stay on its feet, but when the mob began intimidating the musicians and actually threatened to take over, Petrillo held firm. With each year, his power and influence increased. In 1931 he became vice president of the national AFM.

Working conditions for Chicago musicians were never easy. Many changes occurred in the entertainment field during the first few decades of the twentieth century. The decline of vaudeville and burlesque and the gradual disappearance of live music in the theater adversely affected the employment opportunities for musicians. What's more, technological advances, what Petrillo called "canned music," threatened the livelihood of the live performer. In *The Musicians and Petrillo* (1953), Robert D. Leiter estimates that 2,000 musicians were employed in Chicago theaters during the silent film era, providing music accompaniment to the images on the screen. The introduction of sound drastically curtailed the need for live musicians, forcing them to find other means of support. Many couldn't. The number of unemployed musicians during the 1930s skyrocketed. In order to provide them with work, Petrillo initiated a series of concerts in Grant Park during the Great Depression that ran from 1935 through 1943 under the joint sponsorship of the union local and the Chicago Park District.

In 1940 Petrillo was elected national president of the AFM. One of the first things he did upon assuming office was to require radio stations to pay musicians who performed on radio programs. (Previously they had played for free publicity.) Although Petrillo ultimately prevailed, radio stations surreptitiously circumvented the measure by substituting phonographic records and thus misleading the public into believing that what they were hearing were live performances. On August 1, 1942, Petrillo directly confronted the problem of recorded music when he forbade the 133,000 union members to record or use electrical transcriptions or any other mechanical means of reproducing music. This drastic action effectively ended any recording for twenty-seven months.

In June 1944, the War Labor Board ordered the union to end the ban. Petrillo held his ground and refused. Even the personal request of President Franklin D. Roosevelt couldn't change his mind. Two federal court suits, a War Labor Board hearing, and a Senate investigation followed, yet Petrillo remained intractable. In actuality Petrillo permitted the recording industry to produce records but only for enjoyment in the home and for armed forces use. Consequently many young musicians who were just coming into their own at that time—such as Earl Hines, Billy Eckstine, and Woody Herman, to name just a few—were denied the opportunity to record during this crucial stage in their careers. Records were still being released, however. Manufacturers, aware of Petrillo's intention, simply released reissues or relied on their backlogs in order to survive. When the controversy finally ended in November 1944, record companies agreed to pay royalties to the union treasury for every record produced, to be placed into a special Music Performance Trust Fund for unemployed musicians. Petrillo and the union had achieved a major victory. Even so, four years later, Petrillo announced a second ban, which did not have as much of an impact.

In 1948 Petrillo resigned from the presidency of the AFM although he retained his hold on the local chapter until 1962. That year, in one of the biggest upsets in local union history, dissident members defeated his bid for reelection of the presidency of Local 10 by a margin of less than one hundred votes. In 1964 Petrillo accepted the chairmanship of a newly created civil rights department within the union. At that time, over thirty cities had dual musician locals—one black and one white. Although Petrillo traveled across the country until 1971, ostensibly promoting the integration of the segregated music unions, several historians have recently questioned his sincerity. Petrillo, insists Clark D. Halker, a musician and former history professor at North Central College in Naperville, Illinois, did virtually nothing to end discrimination against African Americans in local unions. The musicians had to do it themselves.

The controversial labor leader died of cancer in October 1984 in St. Joseph Hospital. He was ninety-two.

Further reading: Clark D. Halker, "Banding Together," *Chicago History*, September 1989; Robert D. Leiter, *The Musicians and Petrill* (1953).

Wally Phillips

Broadcaster

BORN: July 7, 1925
Portsmouth, Ohio

DIED: March 27, 2008
Naples, Florida

Wally Phillips was the king of morning radio in Chicago for two decades on WGN radio, dominating morning radio in a way that is unimaginable today. He has been called one of the founding fathers of morning radio.

Phillips had an enduring and emotional bond with his audience, a rarity then and even more so now. He ruled the airwaves from the 1968 Democratic National Convention to the death of Elvis Presley to the election of Ronald Reagan. At the peak of his popularity, nearly 1.5 million listeners, or about half of the listening audience in his time slot, tuned into his program.

Phillips was born in Portsmouth, Ohio, in 1925. His father died when Phillips was a young boy of six and the family then moved to Cincinnati. Phillips dropped out of high school to join the army during World War II. He did not see combat, however; he spent the war years in Georgia. When the war ended Phillips attended drama school and then secured a job as a deejay in Grand Rapids, Michigan. He returned to Cincinnati a year later. There he began to develop his signature style: of remixing prerecorded interviews for their humorous effect. Sometimes, though, he would get carried away. He was fired when he inserted a bogus story into a newscast.

In 1956 Phillips moved to Chicago to work at WGN. Bob Bell, who would later become famous in his own right as Bozo the Clown, also started that year. Both were introduced to Chicago audiences as "comedians from Cincinnati."

Phillips developed an altogether different style of broadcasting: he was a performer, newsman, moderator, comedian, and friend all rolled into one oversized personality. He was just as comfortable talking to heads of state and celebrities as to the ordinary man and woman on the street. He had a fondness for prank calls and tongue-in-cheek advertising that included taped sound bites and sound effects. He once called the city of Ipanema, Brazil, to see if there was a young girl there who was, as the lyrics of the song say, "tall and tan and young and lovely."

Phillips was a friendly voice on the radio. He was a masterful storyteller but also an expert at the breaking news story, juggling news reports from the field while talking to experts and seamlessly relaying information to listeners. He offered information, but, most importantly, he offered companionship. He had a smooth delivery and handled phone calls from listeners with grace and facility. All he did was talk—and talk he did from 6 A.M. to 10 A.M. He enjoyed huge ratings not only in Chicago but throughout the Midwest.

In 1965, after three years at the station in the 9 A.M. to noon slot, he assumed WGN's 6 A.M. to 10 A.M. show. He left the morning show in the spring of 1987. His competition came not from other deejays—for two decades no one came close to him in the ratings—but in societal change: in a new type of music (rock and roll) and a new type of deejay (such rock jocks as Larry Lujack and Dick Biondi competed against each other for the burgeoning rock audience). Black radio also began to grow. By the 1970s the FM format was taking a significant portion of the audience away from AM stations. In addition, the rise of so-called shock jocks, such as Steve Dahl and Kevin Matthews, who ridiculed Phillips mercilessly as boring and behind the times, reflected the changing times.

After leaving the morning shift in 1986, Phillips held the afternoon and weekend spots at WGN until he retired in 1998. During his so-called retirement years he continued to host a weekly two-hour weekend show on WAIT-AM for four years. In 1993 he was inducted into the Radio Hall of Fame.

In 1969 he started the Neediest Kids Fund to buy holiday gifts for children. It is now a year-round program maintained through the McCormick Tribune Foundation.

Phillips died at his home in Florida at the age of eighty-two. He had suffered from Alzheimer's.

See also: Bob Bell

Allan Pinkerton

Detective

BORN: August 25, 1819
Glasgow, Scotland

DIED: July 1, 1884
Chicago, Illinois

The motto of the Pinkerton Detective Agency was "The eye that never sleeps." Diligent sleuth, romantic loner, loyal patriot—those were the images of the Pinkerton detective that founder Allan Pinkerton so carefully nurtured and presented to the world. Pinkertons scoured the country in search of outlaws, robbers, and thieves, and the Pinkerton name became known and feared throughout the land.

The son of a Glasgow police sergeant, Allan Pinkerton was a cooper by trade. As a young man, he joined the Chartists, a working-class movement that was sweeping across Britain, demanding rights for the common laborer. In order to avoid being sent to a penal colony for his radical activities, Pinkerton and his wife immigrated to America in 1842. He spent his first year in Chicago, working at Lill's Brewery, then opened a cooper's shop in the Scottish settlement of Dundee, forty miles west of the city, where he made barrels and casks. Pinkerton was introduced to detective work by accident when he came across the hideout of a gang of counterfeiters and helped capture them. He was elected deputy sheriff of Kane County in the late 1840s. An avowed abolitionist, he converted his shop into one of the stops on the Underground Railroad.

In 1850 Pinkerton opened his own detective agency, the Pinkerton National Detective Agency. Its original purpose was to help runaway slaves escape to Canada, but quickly Pinkerton's one-man operation began to pursue small-time crooks that passed bogus checks. At the same time, Pinkerton also acted as a special agent for the post office, investigating mail robberies and verifying the honesty of employees. He returned to Chicago in the early 1850s, was appointed a deputy sheriff of Cook County in 1852, and, by 1860, had become prominent in abolitionist circles.

Pinkerton's detective agency supplied a much-needed service—protection of the citizenry. Organized law enforcement was slow to get off the ground in many U.S. cities. Chicagoans, like other Americans who were distrustful of authority, feared a centralized police system. Instead, private citizens maintained their own vigil against crime. In the evening night watchmen patrolled the streets. Such an overtaxed system was woefully inadequate to meet the security needs of the growing metropolis, however.

Despite his working-class origins, Pinkerton felt little sympathy towards unions. Strikes were, he thought, unnecessary evils, and unions nothing more than hotbeds of anarchy. Pinkerton agents infiltrated labor unions and passed on whatever they learned to the employers. "Between 1933 and 1935," writes Pinkerton historian Frank T.

Morn, "the agency had 1,228 operatives . . . in practically every union in the country." Pinkerton firmly believed that workers who applied the Protestant ethic of hard work and perseverance would be amply rewarded in the end.

Pinkerton's reputation spread far beyond the boundaries of Chicago. During the Civil War, President Abraham Lincoln chose Pinkerton to run the United States Secret Service for the Union army. Two of his chief functions were to investigate Union spies and to gather information behind Confederate lines. In addition, he investigated various plots against the government, including an alleged assassination attempt against Lincoln in Baltimore in 1861. In the early days of the firm, Pinkerton would go undercover himself, often donning various disguises and rounding up some of the country's most notorious outlaws, including the infamous Reno brothers of Indiana.

Pinkerton undercover agents were almost as famous as the criminals they sought. Frank Dimaio, for example, pursued Butch Cassidy and the Sundance Kid's "Hole in the Wall" Gang, successfully tracing them all the way to Argentina. Another Pinkerton in the 1890s was Tom Horn, a gunman, army scout, and veteran of military campaigns against Native Americans. Detective writer Dashiel Hammett was a Pinkerton from 1913 to 1918, and for a brief time in the 1920s he worked on the Fatty Arbuckle case in Hollywood. One of the most determined Pinkertons was Charles Siringo. Siringo, who had used sheriff Pat Garrett's name as a reference while applying for the job and whose first assignment was to prevent jury tampering during the Haymarket trial in 1887, also spent some time pursuing Butch Cassidy and his gang. Indeed, he claimed to having logged 25,000 miles in search of the elusive outlaws.

Probably the most celebrated detective on staff was James McParlan (sometimes spelled McParland) who infiltrated the Pennsylvania coal mines in the late 1800s and was largely responsible for the crushing of the Irish labor organization, the Molly Maguires. In 1970, a movie based on McParlan's exploits, called *The Molly Maguires,* starring Sean Connery with Richard Harris playing McParlan, was released.

Pinkerton complained that dime novels, lurid and sensational as they were with simple-minded plots and cardboard characters, demeaned his profession. As early as 1871 he considered writing stories, based on actual Pinkerton cases, to combat the frivolous image of the detective as portrayed in the dime novels. His first book, *The Expressman and the Detective* (1875), was a great success, selling a brisk 15,000 thousand copies within sixty days of its publication, notes Morn. Between 1874 and 1884 Pinkerton published—although he did not actually write them—sixteen detective books, including *The Molly Maguires and the Detectives* (1877); *Strikers, Communists, Tramps, and Detectives* (1878); *The Spy of the Rebellion* (1883); and *Thirty Years a Detective* (1884).

After Pinkerton suffered a slight stroke in 1869, his two sons, William and Robert, assumed control of the agency. Pinkerton died in July 1884 in Chicago. He was buried in Graceland Cemetery. In 1999, the Pinkerton Detective Agency—by that time its name had changed to Pinkerton Consulting and Investigations—merged with the William J. Burns Detective Agency under Securitas AB, a Swedish-based security company.

Further reading: John J. Flinn, *History of the Chicago Police from the Settlement of the Community to the Present Time* (1887); James D. Horan, *The Pinkertons: The Detective Dynasty That Made History* (1967); Richard Lindberg, *To Serve and Collect: Chicago Politics and Police Corruption from the Lager Beer Riot to the Summerdale Scandal* (1991); Frank T. Morn, *The Eye That Never Sleeps: A History of the Pinkerton National Detective Agency* (1982); Ernest Poole, *Giants Gone: Men Who Made Chicago* (1943).

Jean Baptiste Point du Sable
Fur Trader and Pioneer

BORN: Unknown

DIED: August 28, 1818
St. Charles, Missouri

Jean Baptiste Point du Sable, an enigmatic figure in Chicago history, is credited with being the first permanent resident of Chicago as well as its first black resident. He also started the city's first commercial enterprise: a farm and trading post at the mouth of the Chicago River. He is known as the Father of Chicago.

For many years, Point du Sable, of West African and French ancestry, was thought to have been born in what is now Haiti. Most historians today discredit that notion. On the other hand, Juliette Kinzie, the wife of John H. Kinzie and the author of the 1856 memoir *Wau-bun, the "Early Day" in the North-west*, claimed that he was a native of Santo Domingo (now the Dominican Republic), but other scholars, including the historian Milo Quaife, considered such claims unsubstantiated. Instead, Quaife suggested that Point du Sable might have been born in Quebec. Indeed, independent scholar John F. Swenson, who has done extensive research on Point du Sable, says that it is very possible that he might have been born at Vaudreuil, near Montreal, some time before 1750 (historically, his birth date has been given as 1745).

His name is also a bone of contention. Long known to the general public as Du Sable, historians insist that it is more accurate to refer to him as Point du Sable (some, like Swenson and Dominic Pacyga, spell it as de Sable). According to Swenson, his name means "sand point" in French. Unlike earlier published reports, where he was described as a well-educated man, Swenson maintains that, in fact, he was illiterate.

In the late 1770s Point du Sable operated a successful fur trading business at the mouth of the Rivière du Chemin, or Trail Creek, in what is now Michigan City, Indiana. In August 1779, he was arrested at Trail Creek by British authorities and imprisoned at Fort Michilimackinac in what is now St. Clair, Michigan, allegedly on suspicion of harboring American and French sympathies. Once the British determined that he was not, in fact, a traitor to the crown, he was released from prison. In the summer of 1780, the British Lieutenant-Governor Patrick Sinclair hired him to manage a tract of land called the Pinery located on the St. Clair River in eastern Michigan until roughly May 1784.

Some time in the 1780s, probably around 1784 or 1785, Point du Sable settled on the north bank of the Chicago River near the site of what is now the Tribune Tower. Certainly, by 1790, Pacyga theorized, he was "well established." By that time, too, he had married a Potawatomi woman by the name of Catherine; they had two children.

Once settled in Chicago (or Checagou, as it was then spelled), Point du Sable traded with both Indians and Europeans in what was essentially a barter economy. Living in a log cabin filled with handsome furniture and paintings, he became a man of property: he owned a barn, a working mill, a bakehouse, a poultry house, a dairy, a smokehouse, and two stables. He set aside tracts of land and grew wheat, corn, hay, and alfalfa, and raised dairy and beef cattle, which allowed him to supply meat and dairy products to clients in Detroit.

In 1800, he sold his property to Jean La Lime, a French Canadian trapper who worked for John Kinzie. Pacgya suggests that his dark skin may have made him feel out of place as more and more white people moved to the burgeoning settlement. In addition, his "probable" allegiance to Britain also complicated matters. Point du Sable moved to St. Charles, Missouri, where he bought a house and acquired several tracts of land. Unfortunately, he became entangled in various real estate transactions that fell through. He died, destitute, in 1818.

Several institutions and sites in Chicago today bear his name. DuSable High School in the Bronzeville neighborhood is named in his honor. In addition, Jean Avenue and De Saible Street, a private street on the South Side, are also named in his honor. In 1961, Dr. Margaret Burroughs, a prominent African American artist and writer who taught at DuSable for more than two decades, cofounded, along with her husband Charles Burroughs, the DuSable Museum of African American History. (Burroughs died in November 2010.)

In 1965, the area that was built on the site of his original homestead was named Pioneer Court. In 1976, the Jean Baptiste Point du Sable Homesite was officially recognized as a National Historic Landmark. In October 2009, a bronze bust and plaque were dedicated in his memory on Michigan Avenue at the Chicago River, and in October 2010, the Michigan Avenue Bridge was renamed the DuSable Bridge.

See also: Gurdon S. Hubbard, John Kinzie, Jacques Marquette

Further reading: Ulrich Danckers and Jane Meredith, *Early Chicago: A Compendium of the Early History of Chicago to the Year 1835 When the Indians Left* (2000), with John F. Swenson, contributing editor, and a contribution by Helen H. Tanner; Dominic A. Pacyga, *Chicago: A Biography* (2009); Milo Quaife, *Chicago and the Old Northwest, 1673–1835: A Study of the Northwestern Frontier Together with a History of Fort Dearborn* (reprint, 2001); Christopher Robert Reed, *Black Chicago's First Century, 1833–1900* (2005).

George Pullman

Industrialist

BORN: March 3, 1831
Brocton, New York

DIED: October 19, 1897
Chicago, Illinois

George Mortimer Pullman revolutionized rail travel. Prior to the invention of the Pullman sleeping car, passengers had to endure interminable, uncomfortable, and oftentimes unbearable rail journeys. A practical businessman, Pullman founded the company town of Pullman on the shore of Lake Calumet so that his employees could work and live in a peaceful setting, far removed from the corrupting influence of urban living or labor strife. Visitors came from all over the world to see it. Pullman, however, was hardly a benevolent boss, and the community he created was hardly a workers' paradise.

One of ten children, George Pullman left school at fourteen to become a sales clerk and apprentice cabinetmaker. In the early 1850s he moved to Rochester, New York, where he invented an innovative system of raising entire city blocks from their muddy foundations to a higher street level by placing thousands of giant jackscrews under the buildings and, with the help of a few hundred able-bodied men, turning the screws. In 1855 Pullman moved to Chicago and continued the lucrative business of street raising. A busy downtown hotel, the Tremont, located at the corner of Lake and Dearborn Streets, was slowly falling into a quagmire of mud. Pullman insisted he could raise it without breaking a window or even disturbing a single guest. And in 1858, he did just that.

For a while Pullman had been considering the idea of building railroad cars with sleeping facilities. In 1858 he contracted with the Chicago and Alton Railroad to design sleeping berths. Passengers loved the comfortable new arrangements, but the railroads were skeptical. Pullman had made the car one foot wider and two and one half feet higher than the usual standards. If the railroads wished to use his sleeping cars they would have to widen their bridges and station platforms. Some called the new invention "Pullman's Folly."

Impatient and tired of waiting for a reply, Pullman moved to Colorado in 1859 to seek his fortune among the gold mines. He devoted most of his time, though, to improving the sleeping car's design. He returned to Chicago in 1865 and introduced the first Pullman car: the Pioneer. In 1867, he founded the Pullman Palace Car Company and completed the first combination sleeping and dining car, followed by the first dining car one year later. Shortly thereafter, he opened his first manufacturing plant in Palmyra, New York, then moved it to Detroit and added additional plants in St. Louis, Missouri; Elmira, New York; Wilmington, Delaware; and San Francisco.

In 1880 the Pullman Company bought four thousand acres on the western shore of Lake Calumet, then miles south of Chicago, and established the town of Pullman, Illinois. By creating a controlled environment, he thought

Pullman would be an effective means of reducing labor unrest. Historian William C. Adelman suggests that the industrialist modeled the community of Pullman after the northern English town of Saltaire. Pullman also bore some resemblance to the planned community of New Lanark, Scotland. Pullman was intended to be an antidote to crowded slums.

Pullman hired a twenty-six year old architect from New York, Solomon S. Beman, to design the community, the nation's first planned industrial town (other planned towns, such as Vandergrift, Pennsylvania, would follow Pullman's example). Most of the residential units, which were to be inhabited by skilled workers, consisted of row houses, but there were also apartments and some single-family homes. Unskilled workers, though, lived in shabby tenements or in wooden shanties. The town had its own newspaper, church, schools, and hospital. Pullman himself selected the plays that ran in the theaters. The Hotel Florence, named in honor of Pullman's daughter, faced the park. Alcohol was sold to visitors there but not to the actual workers. A miniature lake was created, and schooling was free through the eighth grade. The Arcade, a sort of precursor to today's shopping malls, contained a theater, a library, a post office, a YMCA, a bank, and approximately thirty shops.

Despite the apparent concern for his employees, Pullman was, above all, a businessman; and the company town of Pullman was in the business of making money. During the depression of 1893, company profits fell drastically. Pullman announced layoffs, reduced hours, and slashed wages, yet rents remained the same. In 1894 the workers went on strike in one of the ugliest clashes between capital and labor in Chicago history, and indeed, labor history. They were soon joined by Eugene Debs's American Railway Union, which then boycotted Pullman cars, against the initial advice of Debs, who sought arbitration. When Pullman refused to compromise, Debs endorsed the strike.

By the end of June, the strike reached national proportions as workers refused to handle Pullman cars and the country's railroads screeched to a halt. In response, President Grover Cleveland dispatched troops from nearby Fort Sheridan to the town to restore order and to have Debs arrested. The strike ended in July and the Pullman plant reopened in early August. Pullman had made no concessions.

Pullman had little in common with his employees and either could not or would not sympathize with their plight. His policies—wage reductions while maintaining high rents—created a community populated by angry, bitter people. "We are born in a Pullman house, taught in the Pullman school, catechized in the Pullman church, and when we die we shall be buried in the Pullman cemetery and go to the Pullman hell," observed one resident. Although Pullman emerged victorious, his victory rang hollow, for he died in 1897 a bitter man, despised by labor and criticized by members of his own family, who disagreed with his cavalier treatment of Pullman employees. He was buried in Graceland Cemetery under tons of asphalt, safe from the wrath of angry workers.

The town of Pullman was annexed to Chicago in 1889 despite the Pullman family's objections. In 1908 the Illinois Supreme Court ordered the company to sell its property. The South Pullman District, between 111th and 115th streets and Cottage Grove and Langley Avenues, was designated a national landmark in 1971 and a Chicago landmark on October 16, 1972.

In 1991 playwright Jeffrey Sweet's *American Enterprise*, a theatrical portrait of Pullman's life and times, enjoyed a successful run at the Organic Theater in Chicago.

See also: John Peter Altgeld, Clarence Darrow, Eugene Debs

Further reading: William C. Adelman, *Touring Pullman* (1972); Stanley Buder, *Pullman: An Experiment in Industrial Order and Community Planning, 1880–1930* (1967); William H. Carwardine, *The Pullman Strike* (1973); Hardy Green, *The Company Town: The Industrial Edens and Satanic Mills That Shaped the American Economy* (2010); Carroll Rede Harding, *George M. Pullman 1831–1897 and the Pullman Company* (1951); Dominic A. Pacyga and Ellen Skerrett, *Chicago: City of Neighborhoods* (1986).

James Quigley

Priest

BORN: October 15, 1854
Oshawa, Ontario

DIED: July 10, 1915
Rochester, New York

As Chicago's second archbishop, James Edward Quigley sought to bring together the city's multiethnic Catholics. Quigley believed that Catholicism did not end when the church door swung closed. Rather, he felt "that Catholicism must extend to all aspects of life," noted historian Charles Shanabruch. Quigley encouraged the establishment of national parishes within the Chicago archdiocese as the best possible way of maintaining church ties with the city's burgeoning immigrant population. Quigley respected the uniqueness of all nationalities.

Born in Canada of Irish immigrant parents, James Quigley moved with his family to Lima, New York, before settling in Rochester. When he was ten, the Quigleys moved again, this time to Buffalo. Here he studied with the Christian Brothers at St. Joseph's College, graduating in 1872. When he was still a teenager Quigley was accepted at West Point. His mother, however, had hoped that her eldest son would join the priesthood. Bowing to her wishes, Quigley enrolled at the Vincentian seminary of Our Lady of the Angels in Buffalo and then continued his studies at the University of Innsbruck in Austria. In 1879 he earned a doctor of theology degree from the College of the Propaganda in Rome. Ordained shortly after, Quigley was assigned to a parish in Attica, New York. In 1884 he was chosen as rector of the Buffalo cathedral and, in February 1897, Quigley was consecrated bishop of Buffalo.

In December 1902 Quigley was chosen to succeed the late Patrick Feehan, Chicago's first archbishop, as head of the Chicago diocese. The new archbishop arrived in the city in March of the following year. In his first speech to his constituency he proclaimed, "I shall seek the counsel of others and in the multitude of counsel may find the right, but I must decide for myself. Whatever I do, I shall do in justice and charity. Having done it, I will be ready to bear the consequences, if I shall make a mistake."

Quigley's twelve-year term as archbishop of Chicago was a fruitful one. He built parochial schools, organized Catholic charities, and encouraged the Jesuits to establish what would later become Loyola University and the Vincentians to organize DePaul University. In 1904 he founded Cathedral College, a Catholic preparatory school for boys. Continuing the policy of his predecessor, Quigley formed national parishes to appeal to the city's various immigrant groups. Quigley, however, was especially interested in reaching the poor and the disadvantaged, to make the church less intimidating, and to make it a regular part of the daily life of his parishioners. The church under Quigley, asserts historian Shanabruch, attempted to answer the spiritual—as well as social and financial—needs of its diverse flock.

Archbishop Quigley died unexpectedly on July 10, 1915, at the age of sixty in his brother's home in Rochester, New York. His body was returned to Chicago, and he was buried in Mount Carmel cemetery in Hillside, Illinois.

See also: Joseph Bernardin, Arnold Damen, George Mundelein
Further reading: Rev. Msgr. Harry C. Koenig, S.T.D., *A History of the Parishes of the Archdiocese of Chicago*, 2 vols. (1980); Charles Shanabruch, *Chicago's Catholics: The Evolution of an American Identity* (1981).

Ray Rayner

Television Personality

BORN: July 23, 1919
New York, New York

DIED: January 21, 2004
Fort Meyers, Florida

Ray Rayner was an iconic figure in the history of children's television in Chicago. At one point, his eponymous morning show was watched by as much as seventy percent of the Chicago viewing audience.

Born Raymond M. Rahner in New York, Rayner was a navigator during World War II. His plane was shot down over France and for two and a half years he was a prisoner of war. It was there, of all places, where he caught the entertainment bug. When the Germans decided they wanted a theater and radio station, Rayner was persuaded to give it a try.

After serving in the army during World War II, he returned to New York. He attended Holy Cross College for one year before transferring to Fordham University, receiving a bachelor's degree in philosophy. Years later, in 1970, he earned a master's degree in humanities at the University of Chicago.

Rayner worked on a Long Island radio station and then at various radio and television stations in the Midwest: as a news director for a radio station in Dayton, Ohio; as a disc jockey in Grand Rapids, Michigan; and, finally, in 1953, in Chicago, where he was hired as a staff announcer at WBBM-TV. He worked on several television shows, including *The Little Show* and *Popeye's Firehouse*. In 1961, he moved to WGN-TV, where he appeared on *The Dick Tracy Show, Bozo's Circus, Rocket to Adventure,* and as the host of his own show. But he made his Chicago television debut on a morning variety show, *Rayner Shine*.

He began his WGN career as Sergeant Henry Pettibone on *The Dick Tracy Show*. Several months later he joined *Bozo's Circus* as Oliver O. Oliver, a clown with a Kentucky accent who acted as Bozo's foil. In 1962 he became host of *Breakfast with Bugs Bunny*. Two years later it was renamed *Ray Rayner and His Friends*.

His "friends" included Cuddley Dudley, an oversized orange-colored cocker spaniel dog (with the voice of Roy Brown). A live human also appeared on the show, Dr. Lester Fisher, then director of the Lincoln Park Zoo. But the most popular nonhuman was Chelveston the Duck. Rayner named the rowdy duck after the air force base in Chelveston, England, where he had been stationed during the war.

Rayner's persona was that of an eccentric, but beloved, figure: friendly, kind, and gentle with a whimsical sense of humor. He wore a jumpsuit that was covered with small pieces of paper. Ostensibly he wrote the things that he needed to do on the pieces during those pre-Post-it days, but actually they were blank.

In addition to his various television shows, Rayner also did voice-overs, commercials, and industrial films. In the 1970s he was a particular favorite at the Candlelight Dinner Playhouse in Summit and the adjacent Forum Theatre.

Rayner left *Bozo's Circus* in 1971 and retired from his morning show in December 1980. He moved to Albuquerque, New Mexico, where the restless Rayner did another morning show as well as the weather forecast for the CBS affiliate until 1989.

Rayner died on January 21, 2004, of respiratory failure in Fort Meyers, Florida, at the age of eighty-four.

See also: Bob Bell, Frazier Thomas

Further reading: Daniel Berger and Steve Jajkowski, eds., *Chicago Television* (2010).

Ben Reitman

Social Activist and Physician

BORN: Circa 1879
St. Paul, Minnesota

DIED: November 17, 1942
Chicago, Illinois

Outlandish in dress and shocking in behavior, Ben Reitman was one of the most colorful figures in Chicago history. But he wasn't all flash. Reitman contributed significantly to the social welfare of the poor and the homeless. Nicknamed the "King of the Hoboes," Reitman served as the director of the peripatetic Hobo College where the city's drifters, misfits, and malcontents gathered. As a young boy he succumbed to the excitement of a life on the road. It was a deeply ingrained habit that he would never outgrow.

Reitman's father, an itinerant peddler who moved to New York from Russia, abandoned his wife and two sons. For several months the family lived in Cleveland before moving to Chicago and settling in the red-light district on South Clark Street, shuttling in and out of cheap rooming houses. Some of Ben's earliest acquaintances were hookers, thieves, and bums. An inquisitive boy who loved adventure, he hopped the freight cars and quickly mastered the art of panhandling. Reitman made his mark all over the world. He worked for Buffalo Bill's Wild West show in Paris, was mistakenly arrested on a murder charge in Ireland, and was in San Francisco when the devastating earthquake of 1906 struck.

Reitman secured a job at the Polyclinic Laboratory in 1898 in Chicago, where he was encouraged to study medicine. A kindly doctor, Dr. Leo Loeb, offered to pay his tuition at the College of Physicians and Surgeons. Reitman gratefully accepted and, despite his lack of a formal education, enrolled at the college. In July 1901, he married May Schwartz, who was, according to Reitman's biographer Roger A. Bruns, an emotionally troubled student at the Chicago Musical College. During their European honeymoon, Reitman deserted his then pregnant wife—he could not handle the responsibility, suggests Bruns—and returned to Chicago in time to enroll for his sophomore year at the College of Physicians and Surgeons. He graduated in 1904, obtained a license, and opened an office at 39th Street and Cottage Grove Avenue.

In 1915 Reitman founded the Hobo College at 1118 West Madison Street. "The word hobo should be a badge of honor, like the name of any profession," declared Reitman. "We seek to make it so." Funded through the generosity of merchants and benefactors, the college attracted assorted denizens of skid row and visiting hoboes. The most notable benefactor was James Eads How, a wealthy eccentric from St. Louis who financed several hobo colleges across the country.

The college, which changed locations almost yearly, presented lectures, debates, and discussions on almost any subject—economics, health, religion, philosophy, as well as more practical matters such as the ins and outs of the vagrancy laws. The college once presented a course in panhandling "from the viewpoint of a scientist." It offered short courses in law, public speaking, and English composition in addition to amateur plays, debates, open forums, and musical programs.

Reitman's college attracted top-notch guest lecturers—professors from local universities, physicians, psychologists, lawyers, and reformers. Regular speakers included "Prof" Paddy Carroll, who lectured on "How to Live Without Eating," and "Yellow Kid" Weil, king of the con men. Several hobo speakers delivered lectures at University of Chicago sociology classes. The university and the Hobo College also held debates, and there were a few instances where the hoboes actually bested the allegedly superior Hyde Parkers—much to the chagrin and embarrassment of the university students. Reitman always made an effort to drop by the infamous Dil Pickle Club, Chicago's premier bohemian hangout. He delivered speeches, lined up speakers, and chaired meetings at the club.

Reitman and his lover, the radical Emma Goldman, gained national notoriety when they publicly advocated birth control, which had become a national issue by 1915. Reitman and Goldman circulated pamphlets in major cities across the country, including Chicago. In October of that year they were arrested in Portland, Oregon, for distributing the pamphlets, which, according to local law, violated an obscenity ordinance, and were fined $100 each. Later, Reitman was arrested in New York on the same charge and was sentenced to—and served—sixty days in the workhouse. In Cleveland he was sentenced to—and again served—six months and received a $1,000 fine. He was acquitted of charges in Rochester.

Despite the notoriety that surrounded Reitman, Dr. John Dill Robertson, commissioner of the city's Health Department, hired him in 1917 to work among Chicago's hobo population. Reitman did much to eradicate the spread of sexually transmitted diseases. He established the first municipal disease clinic in Chicago at the Iroquois Hospital that year. Later he inaugurated similar programs at the Cook County Jail and the Chicago House of Corrections before establishing his own organization, the Chicago Society for the Prevention of Venereal Disease. In 1937 the Chicago Syphilis Project hired Reitman to study vice and prostitution in the city's sprawling slums and especially in the areas around North Clark and West Van Buren Streets, along West Madison Street, and on South State Street between 31st and 35th Streets. During the project's first two years, notes Bruns, Reitman submitted over 300 reports. Further, he gave talks on the subject at YMCAs, labor organizations, and churches.

In 1932 Reitman wrote *The Second Oldest Profession*, a study of prostitution. In 1937 he published a second book, *Sister of the Road: The Autobiography of Box-Car Bertha*, which was made into a movie in 1972, starring Barbara Hershey and the late David Carradine. The movie is also notable for being the directorial debut of filmmaker Martin Scorsese.

In October 1939 Reitman suffered a stroke. Three years later he succumbed to a fatal heart attack at the age of sixty-three in his home at 6826 South Bishop Street in Chicago. He was buried in Waldheim Cemetery in Forest Park, Illinois.

See also: "Slim" Brundage, Albert and Lucy Parsons

Further reading: Roger A. Bruns, *The Damndest Radical: The Life and World of Ben Reitman, Chicago's Celebrated Social Reformer, Hobo King, and Whorehouse Physician* (1987); Jay Walljasper, "Those Vagabond Days." *Chicago Tribune Sunday Magazine*, August 15, 1982.

Carolyn Rodgers

Poet

BORN: December 14, 1940
Chicago, Illinois

DIED: April 2, 2010
Chicago, Illinois

Carolyn Rodgers was one of the leading members of the Black Arts Movement (BAM), an African American movement with strong political connotations that made its biggest impact in the 1960s and 1970s. Rodgers's work combined powerful elements of feminism, black power, spirituality, and black empowerment and self-identity.

Carolyn Marie Rodgers was born in December 1940 to Clarence Rodgers, a welder, and Bazella Rodgers, of Little Rock, Arkansas. She was the youngest of four children and the only one born in Chicago. She grew up in Hyde Park.

Rodgers was a student of Gwendolyn Brooks—Brooks often held workshops in her South Side home—and participated in the writing workshops of the Organization of Black American Culture (OBAC). In 1965 she earned a bachelor's degree from Roosevelt University and in 1980 a master's degree from the University of Chicago. Rodgers's early poems were often militant and experimental and were written from the perspective of an angry young black woman, incorporating slang and vernacular spellings as well as free verse and extensive street language. Some members of the black community took offense to her use of profanity in her work, finding it unbecoming for a poet of her stature.

Rodgers advocated the Black Arts Movement, which was created in the mid-1960s by the black poet Amiri Baraka. Followers of the movement believed that gaining political power went hand in hand with the growth of the black arts. As she matured, however, her writing turned inward, away from the black collective experience and toward a more individual and reflective perspective.

In addition to writing poetry, Rodgers also spoke and wrote extensively about the black aesthetic, the black point of view, in poetry. She wrote numerous essays on poetry and black culture and taught at several universities, including Malcolm X College, Fisk University, Emory University, the University of Washington, Indiana University, Harold Washington College, and Columbia College. In 1967 she helped Haki Madhubuti and Johari Amini establish the Third World Press, an African American publishing house that has become one of Chicago's most important cultural institutions as well as one of the country's oldest black-owned book publishers. In addition, she started her own publishing company, Eden Press.

Rodgers wrote nine books. Her best-known book is *how i got ovah: new and selected poems* (1975), which was a finalist for the National Book Award in 1976. In the early 1980s her play *Love* was produced off Broadway at the New Federal Theater. Her other poetry collections include *Blackbird in a Cage* (1967), *Paper Soul* (1968), *2 Love Raps* (1969), *Songs of a Blackbird* (1969), *A Statistic Trying to Make It Home* (1969), *The Heart as Evergreen* (1978), *Eden and Other Poems* (1983), *Finite Forms* (1985), *Morning Glory* (1989), and two chapbooks from her own press, *We're Only Human Poems* (1996) and *A Train Called Judah* (1998). She also wrote a novel and numerous short stories, essays, and criticism. In 2006 she wrote the foreword to *Black Writing from Chicago*, an anthology of African American writing.

In 2009 she was inducted into the International Hall of Fame for Writers of African Descent at Chicago State University's Gwendolyn Brooks Center for Black Literature and Creative Writing.

She died of cancer while in hospice care at Mercy Hospital in Chicago. She was sixty-nine.

See also: Gwendolyn Brooks
Further reading: Richard R. Guzman, ed., *Black Writing from Chicago: In the World, Not of It?* (2006).

George F. Root

Composer and Music Publisher

BORN: August 20, 1820
Sheffield, Massachusetts

DIED: August 6, 1895
Bailey's Island, Maine

One of the most popular songwriters during the Civil War era was a frail-looking gentleman named George Frederick Root, whose most famous song, "The Battle Cry of Freedom," became the Union rallying cry and propelled him to national fame. "There was no song," wrote *Chicago Tribune* music critic George Upton, "that equaled 'The Battle Cry' in popularity and patriotic inspiration."

The first child of Sarah Flint and Frederick Ferdinand Root, George Frederick Root came from a musical family. In 1826 they moved to Willow Farm in North Reading, Massachusetts. Later, Root studied flute and voice at the Boston Academy of Music Chorus. After finishing school he accepted a position as a music teacher at Jacob Abbott's School for Young Ladies in New York. He also taught music at Rutgers Female Institute in New Jersey. In 1859 Root went to Paris to continue his studies in piano and singing. Years earlier, in 1851, he had written his first cantata, *The Flower Queen; or the Coronation of the Rose*.

In 1852, inspired by the success of Stephen Foster, Root began experimenting with popular compositions. Still not certain of public reaction, he published his first song, "Hazel Dell," under the pseudonym G. Friedrich Wurzel. Much to his happy surprise, it became a great success. Despite this good fortune he continued his association with "serious" music. In January 1853 he taught sacred music at the Union Theological Seminary in New York and, in the same year, helped establish the first Normal Musical Institute, also in New York City.

In 1858 George's brother, Ebenezer Towner Root, and Chauncey Marvin Cady formed the music publishing firm of Root and Cady in Chicago at 95 Clark Street. George joined the company two years later and settled in Hyde Park at Cornell and Lake Park Avenues. Root and Cady quickly became one of the city's leading publishers of sheet music.

The attack on Fort Sumter on April 12, 1861, that started the Civil War inspired Root's first war song, "The First Gun Is Fired! May God Protect the Right!" A quick three days later it was published. The American sheet-music industry capitalized on the outbreak of war. Topical and patriotic songs were in great demand by the public and sold briskly. The inspiration for "The Battle Cry of Freedom," probably Root's best-loved composition, came one day in 1862 when President Lincoln had issued a second call for Northern troops. "We must rally for the Union," Root agreed. The next morning, he wrote these words at his desk:

> *Yes, we'll rally round the flag,*
> *boys, we'll rally once again.*
> *Shouting the battle cry of Freedom;*
>
> *We'll rally from the hillside,*
> *We'll gather from the plain,*
> *Shouting the battle cry of Freedom*

As he finished writing the song, Jules and Frank Lumbard, two of Chicago's best singers of war songs, walked into his office asking if he had any new material. A war meeting was to be held outside the courthouse and the brothers needed something stirring to appease the crowd. Root handed them the manuscript of "The Battle Cry of Freedom." The crowd loved it and joined in singing the chorus.

Before long the North was singing along to Root's song; recruiting figures skyrocketed. Root, it was said, had accomplished more with one song than a battalion of general's enlistment speeches could ever do. And the song boosted morale in the Union trenches, too. A young soldier wrote: "The tune put as much spirit and cheer into the army as a splendid victory. Day and night you could hear it by every campfire and in every tent."

Root wrote many other war songs, including "Just Before the Battle, Mother" (1864), "Tramp, Tramp, Tramp" (1864), and "The Vacant Chair" (1862). Root's most popular sentimental ballad was "Rosalie, the Prairie Flower," published in 1855. He also wrote gospel hymns. Popular evangelists Dwight Moody and Ira Sankey frequently used Root's compositions in their services. The firm also published music books and issued a monthly magazine, *The Song Messenger of the Northwest.*

Like many Chicagoans, Root lost much of his wealth in the Chicago Fire of 1871 when his office was destroyed. In 1872, the University of Chicago awarded him the degree of doctor of music. In 1891, Root penned his autobiography, *The Story of a Musical Life.* He died at his summer home in Maine in August 1895. He was seventy-four.

See also: Dwight L. Moody

Further reading: Richard Crawford, *The Civil War Songbook* (1977); Dena J. Epstein, *Music Publishing in Chicago Before 1871: The Firm of Root & Cady* (1969); Irwin Silber, ed., *Songs of the Civil War* (1960); Sigmund Spaeth, *History of Popular Music in America* (1948).

John Wellborn Root

Architect

BORN: January 10, 1850
Lumpkin, Georgia

DIED: January 15, 1891
Chicago, Illinois

With the possible exception of Dankmar Adler and Louis Sullivan, the partnership of Daniel H. Burnham and John Wellborn Root constituted the most important architectural affiliation in the city. Architecture, Root felt, must reflect its age and environment. "Now, in America, we are free of artistic traditions," he once wrote. "A new spirit of beauty is being developed and perfected, and even now its first achievements are beginning to delight us. This is old things made over; it is new. It springs out of the past, but it is not tied to it; it studies the traditions, but it is not enslaved by them."

John Wellborn Root came from proud Southern stock. His family fled from their native Georgia when General William T. Sherman's army ransacked the town during the Civil War. Root spent nearly two years abroad near

Liverpool, England, where he studied music and architecture. He returned to the United States and entered New York University, graduating with a civil engineering degree in 1869. For a short time, he worked in New York as a draftsman under James Renwick, the architect who designed St. Patrick's Cathedral. In 1871 Root moved to Chicago to take a job as a draftsman at the firm of Carter, Drake, and Wight. It was here that he first met Daniel H. Burnham, another young man on the rise in the city's architectural world.

In 1873 Burnham and Root established their own company. After struggling for several years, they made a name for themselves as an innovative firm that welcomed challenge and diversity. Their first important work was in 1874 when they were commissioned to design the Prairie Avenue house of John B. Sherman, nicknamed "the father of the Stockyards." Important commercial assignments followed—the Montauk Building at 64 West Monroe Street (1882); the Rookery at 209 South LaSalle Street (1886); St. Gabriel's Church at 4501 South Lowe (1888); and the Monadnock Building at 53 West Jackson Boulevard (1891). Another building, the Montauk, which was demolished in 1902, revolutionized building construction. The base of the Montauk rested on what Root called a "floating raft," a slab of concrete reinforced with steel rails, which helped distribute weight throughout the structure.

Even more significant was the Monadnock. Generally considered Root's masterwork, it was nothing less than a pioneering feat that broke completely with traditional styles of architecture and used the most advanced design techniques then known. Six-foot-thick walls at the base supported a sixteen-story building, which indicated that it was not possible to erect a structure taller than the Monadnock using traditional masonry construction. Taller buildings required the skeleton construction method. Robert D. Andrews, president of the Boston Architectural Club, applauded Root's "prodigious courage" and called the building an achievement that he found "unsurpassed in the architectural history of our country."

In 1892 the firm designed the twenty-two-story Masonic Temple at the northeast corner of State and Randolph Streets, at the time the tallest building in the world. One of Root's last major works was for the headquarters of the Women's Christian Temperance Union (1892) at the southwest corner of LaSalle and Monroe Streets. Known as the Woman's Temple, it was demolished in 1926.

Root was a popular figure in Chicago. His standing in the artistic community grew when he married the sister of Harriet Monroe, the founder of *Poetry* magazine. Monroe,

also an able biographer, wrote a well-received study of her brother-in-law in 1896.

The famed Chicago school of architecture celebrated American design. Although several of the Chicago school architects, including Louis Sullivan, were trained in Europe, they looked to America for inspiration and found their most distinctive identity in the form of the skyscraper. Root, in particular, had no desire to slavishly emulate old models. "He wished to offer to the older nations," notes Monroe, "a proof of new forces, new ideals, not yet developed and completed, but full of power and prophetic of charm."

Root served on the planning commission for the World's Columbian Exposition of 1893. It was he who recommended the area around Jackson Park as the best possible site. At first it seemed a curious choice. A semi-wild patch of marshland, Root pronounced it perfect for his vision of "a Venetian effect of palaces and lagoons against the lake's beautiful open spaces." He drew a plan that called for a classically influenced structure, the Court of Honor, to be situated around a basin that contrasted with a series of modern buildings fronting the lagoons. Root envisioned a shimmering city of many colors, shades, and hues that reflected the innovative Chicago school and expressed the vibrant architecture of the American heartland.

Root's conception of an exuberant, playful, modern American exposition was never realized. On the blustery evening of January 11, 1891, he escorted several guests to their carriage from his Astor Street home. The next day he contracted pneumonia. He died a few days later, on January 15, at the age of forty-one.

See also: Daniel H. Burnham, Harriet Monroe, Louis Sullivan

Further reading: R. Reid Badger, *The Great American Fair: The World's Columbian Exposition and American Culture* (1979); David F. Burg, *Chicago's White City of 1893* (1976); Carl W. Condit, *The Chicago School of Architecture: A History of Commercial and Public Buildings in the Chicago Area, 1875–1925* (1964) and *The Rise of the Skyscraper* (1952); Donald Hoffman, *The Architecture of John Wellborn Root* (1973); Erik Larson, *Devil in the White City* (2003); Harriet Monroe, *John Wellborn Root, A Study of His Life and Work* (1966).

Julius Rosenwald

Entrepreneur and Philanthropist

BORN: August 12, 1862
Springfield, Illinois

DIED: January 6, 1932
Chicago, Illinois

An imaginative businessman and generous philanthropist, Julius Rosenwald derived his greatest enjoyment from helping others. "Charity is the one pleasure that never wears out," he said. He founded the Museum of Science and Industry, contributed considerably to African American and Jewish charities, and, as president of Sears, Roebuck and Company, ran one of the biggest mail-order firms in the country. He was, in the words of his biographer Morris R. Werner, a "practical humanitarian."

Julius Rosenwald's father, Samuel, emigrated from Germany in the 1850s and settled in Springfield, Illinois, where he established himself as a leading clothing merchant. Rosenwald attended public schools in Springfield. In 1879 he moved to New York to work in his uncle's clothing firm, Hammerslough Brothers, as a stock boy for $5 a week. In 1884 he and his brother, Morris, started their own store, J. Rosenwald and Brothers. One year later, he settled in Chicago, and with his cousin, Julius E. Weil, he established Rosenwald and Weil, a clothing outfit, in the Farwell Block at 185 Market Street (now Wacker Drive). Among his customers was the fledgling firm of Sears, Roebuck and Company. Rosenwald and his brother-in-law, Aaron Nusbaum, bought shares in the company. In 1895 Rosenwald advanced to vice president. Richard Sears retired in late 1908 partly due to ill-health and partly due to minor business differences with Rosenwald. There were no hard feelings, however, and the two men parted amicably. According to company historian Lorin Sorensen, Rosenwald became president of Sears in 1908 and chairman of the board in 1924.

Initially, Sears catered primarily to farmers and isolated homesteaders who had little or no access to affordable goods. Within a matter of years, though, the firm expanded its customer base to include an increasing number of urban dwellers. Under Rosenwald's innovative and progressive management, the company experienced phenomenal growth. He improved the quality of goods and services, insisted on accurate catalog descriptions, established a laboratory to set and maintain standards, and developed an efficient and fast system of processing orders. When he initiated the innovative money-back guarantee, sales skyrocketed. Further, he opened retail stores and established mail-order branches throughout the country. In February 1925, the first retail outlet opened in a corner of Sears's mail-order plant at Homan Avenue and Arthington Street. Eight months later, the first Sears retail department store opened in Evansville, Indiana.

Establishing better working conditions for his employees was a priority to Rosenwald. He introduced generous health benefits, offered paid vacations, and built athletic fields and tennis courts for the enjoyment of his employees. As business thrived and his personal fortune grew, Rosenwald felt obligated to share his good fortune with society. "I really felt ashamed to have so much money," he confessed in his later years. Rosenwald abhorred waste and extravagance and believed that "unselfish effort" gave his life purpose. Prior to his death, he provided over $60 million to civic causes. In 1917 he established the Julius Rosenwald Foundation and made sizable contributions to the building of YMCAs and YWCAs, including a YMCA for African Americans on Wabash Avenue.

Rosenwald was impressed with Booker T. Washington's *Up from Slavery* as well as a biography of the white railroad magnate William H. Baldwin; Baldwin had befriended Washington and raised money for educational programs. He came to believe African Americans and Jews had much in common. Both, he thought, suffered greatly from years of discrimination. Consequently, Rosenwald contributed to the construction of more than 5,300 public schools for black children in the South. He also supported black colleges and universities—including Howard, Fisk, and Dillard—and donated money to the National Association for the Advancement of Colored People (NAACP) and the Chicago Urban League, two historic African American institutions. "To Rosenwald, racial prejudice was simply out-of-date and un-American," writes Rebecca Janowitz.

In addition to his great support of education, Rosenwald subsidized the construction of recreational and residential centers for African Americans in more than two dozen northern communities. He acquired a tract of land between 46th and 47th Streets and Michigan and Wabash Avenues to provide low-income housing facilities for some of the city's African Americans. The five-story Michigan Boulevard Garden Apartments at 4638 South Michigan Avenue were completed in 1929 and, unlike today's public housing units, included a mixture of professionals and working-class tenants.

In 1928 he established a foundation called the Rosenwald Fund, which included a fellowship program that lasted from 1928 to 1948. Its purpose was to support and encourage black achievement. Fellowships were given to 587 blacks and 278 white Southerners for study and research. Among the recipients of the fund were Marian Anderson, Zora Neale Hurston, Langston Hughes, and James Baldwin.

Rosenwald was also concerned for the welfare of the Jewish community. In 1908 he donated $75,000 toward the construction of the Chicago Hebrew Institute, a cultural and educational center on Taylor Street; he served as president of the Associated Jewish Charities of Chicago; and he contributed to various other Jewish charities.

Impressed with industrial museums in Munich and Vienna, Rosenwald promoted the idea of one in Chicago and, indeed, actually purchased material for the museum exhibits. He did not live long enough to see his work completed. The Museum of Science and Industry opened more than a year after Rosenwald's death. In later years, Rosenwald suffered from bone disease and a weak heart. Despite his poor health, he never officially retired. He did, however, reduce his workload. In May 1929, Rosenwald's wife Augusta died. The Rosenwalds had been married thirty-nine years. Rosenwald remarried on January 8, 1930. Two years later he died in his sleep on January 6, 1932. He was buried in Rosehill Cemetery beside the graves of his mother and his first wife.

The advent of the automobile brought drastic changes to the mail-order business. As patrons became less and less dependent on the Sears catalog, the company opened more retail stores. Anticipating the popularity of the automobile, Rosenwald's successor, Robert E. Wood, who became president in 1928, introduced a policy to locate retail stores in the suburbs, where there was plenty of free parking.

See also: Richard Sears, Aaron Montgomery Ward

Further reading: Peter Ascoli, *Julius Rosenwald: The Man Who Built Sears, Roebuck and Advanced the Cause of Black Education in the American South* (2006); Philip P. Bregstone, *Chicago and Its Jews: A Cultural History* (1933); Leon Harris, *Merchant Princes: An Intimate History of Jewish Families Who Built Great Department Stores* (1979); Rebecca Janowitz, *Culture of Opportunity: Obama's Chicago; The People, Politics, and Ideas of Hyde Park* (2010); John E. Jeuck and Boris Emmet, *Catalogues and Counters: A History of Sears, Roebuck & Co.* (1950); Donald R. Katz, *The Big Store: Inside the Crisis and Revolution at Sears* (1987); Herman Kogan, *A Continuing Marvel: The Story of the Museum of Science and Industry* (1973); Lorin Sorensen, *Sears, Roebuck and Co. 100th Anniversary 1886–1986* (1985); Morris R. Werner, *Julius Rosenwald: The Life of a Practical Humanitarian* (1939).

Barney Ross

Boxer

BORN: December 23, 1909
New York, New York

DIED: January 18, 1967
Chicago, Illinois

Barnet David Rasofsky, the Maxwell Street boy who held boxing's lightweight, junior welterweight, and welterweight crowns during the 1930s, was a graduate of the school of hard knocks. Yet the easygoing Ross took whatever life dished out to him in stride. Ross is considered one of the top ten welterweights in boxing history.

Though born in New York, Ross and his family moved to Chicago when he was an infant. His father, a Russian Jewish immigrant, opened a grocery store in the Maxwell Street neighborhood. Barney was a sickly child, suffering from a lung ailment and arthritis. In 1924 tragedy struck when his father was killed in his store on Jefferson Street during a robbery attempt.

Ross quit school at fourteen and began hanging out with a rough crowd, joined a gang, and even ran errands for Al Capone. He learned how to take and throw punches. "You had to," he said later. "The Jews and Italians (on the Near West Side) were always at war. Many a night I would come home cut and bruised and get another licking at home for fighting." During the Great Depression, Chicago produced many Jewish boxers, including welterweight champ Jackie Fields and heavyweight contender King Levinsky, a former fish peddler also from Maxwell Street. Ross, a street fighter in his own right, thought maybe he, too, had the makings of a boxer. He began working out in gyms and, with an eye toward turning professional, changed his name to the more "American-sounding" Ross.

At the age of eighteen, he fought amateur bouts. In 1929 he won both the Chicago and Intercity Golden Gloves featherweight championships. He turned pro, he once said, because he wanted to earn enough money to get his two younger brothers out of the orphanage, in which they were placed when Ross's mother moved to Connecticut to take care of her late husband's blind mother. In 1933 Ross beat Tony Canzoneri in a ten-round decision at the Chicago Stadium to win both the lightweight and junior welterweight titles. He won a rematch later that year. In 1934 Ross captured the welterweight championship in New York against Jimmy McLarnin. He lost the title but regained it in 1935. Ross remained unbeaten until 1938, when he lost by decision to Henry Armstrong.

After eighty-two bouts with no knockouts, Ross retired from the ring. For a time, he operated a cocktail lounge in Chicago. When World War II broke out, he joined the marines and saw action at Guadalcanal, where he was hit by shrapnel and contracted malaria. During the battle, he was credited with killing twenty-two Japanese soldiers. Promoted to corporal and then sergeant, he was awarded the Silver Star for his acts of gallantry. But Ross's injuries required extensive hospitalization. To relieve the pain, doctors injected him with morphine, which led to an addiction problem.

On September 11, 1946, Ross confessed he was a drug addict and entered the United States public health hospital in Lexington, Kentucky. At one point, he estimated he had spent $250,000 on his habit. His wife, Catherine, then divorced him. But Ross persevered, kicked the habit, and remarried his wife. When the movie *Monkey on My Back* (1957) was made about his drug problems without his consent, Ross filed suit against the producers of the film, asking for $5 million in damages and claiming that advertisements for the movie ruined his reputation. Subsequently, he lectured frequently and traveled across the country talking about the evils of narcotics.

In 1947 Ross became the secretary-treasurer in charge of labor relations for the Eureka Shipbuilding Corporation in Newburgh, New York. The following year, he joined the George Washington legion, an organization of American volunteers recruited to fight for the Jewish state in Palestine.

With Martin Abramson, Ross wrote his autobiography, *No Man Stands Alone: The True Story of Barney Ross,* in 1957.

In January 1967, Ross died at the age of fifty-seven of throat cancer in his Lake Shore Drive apartment.

Further reading: Ira Berkow, *Maxwell Street: Survival in a Bazaar* (1977); Douglas Century, *Barney Ross: The Life of a Jewish Fighter* (2006).

Dan Rostenkowski

Politician

BORN: January 2, 1928
Chicago, Illinois

DIED: August 11, 2010
Benedict Lake, Wisconsin

Dan Rostenkowski went from dealmaker to political anachronism in his lifetime. Despite his sudden fall from grace, he still was considered among the most effective and influential leaders in Congress during the twentieth century. He was a workhorse: he served eighteen terms in Congress. And yet despite his considerable clout, he fell victim to corruption charges. His imprisonment came to symbolize the excesses of power and an old-fashioned way of doing business. The times may have changed, but Rostenkowski didn't. He paid the price for it.

A child of Polish politicians, Daniel David Rostenkowski was the grandson of Polish immigrants and the only son and youngest of three children. His grandfather Peter was active in Polish fraternal organizations—from 1913 to 1918 he was national president of the Polish Roman Catholic Union of America (PRCU)—and served as a delegate to the 1912 Democratic National Convention in Baltimore. His father, Joe, was alderman of the Thirty-Second Ward from 1933 to 1955 and later served in Congress.

Rostenkowski grew up around St. Stanislaus Kostka Catholic Church on Noble Street near Division Street in a house built by his grandfather, a three-flat residence at 1372 North Evergreen Avenue. St. Stanislaus Kostka was Chicago's first Polish Catholic church. He attended St. John's Military Academy in Delafield, Wisconsin, where he played three sports. Baseball legend Connie Mack invited him to try out for the Philadelphia Athletics baseball team but he turned down the offer to follow in his father's political footsteps. It was around this time, too, that he shortened his name to Rosten. "Lopping syllables off your ethnic surname to speed assimilation in America was a common practice," notes one of Rostenkowski's biographers, Jim Merriner. But the new name didn't last long. Rostenkowski "reclaimed" his original name, notes Richard Cohen, when he decided to go into politics in 1952. After serving in the army in Korea with the Seventh Infantry Division, he attended night classes part-time at Loyola University, then called Loyola College. On the side, he took real estate classes at Pearson Real Estate School.

Because of his many connections, Rostenkowski secured an investigator's job in the city's corporation counsel office. In 1952 he ran for his father's old seat in the state legislature. After one term as a state representative and two terms as a state senator, he ran for the Eighth Congressional District seat, beating his Republican challenger William Schmidt. His time in Illinois state politics served him well. There he learned the fine Illinois art of horse-trading, something that he would put to good use when he went to Washington. In 1952 he ran for, and won, a seat in the Illinois House of Representatives. A few years later, he was elected to the U.S. House of Representatives in 1958 at the age of 30. For many years he was its youngest member. Five years later he earned a seat on the prestigious—and powerful—House Ways and Means Committee. Assuming the chairmanship in 1981, he held that post until 1994.

Rostenkowski's accomplishments were many: he steered massive amounts of federal cash to metropolitan Chicago for repaving the Kennedy Expressway, expanding the Chicago Transit Authority, and building the Deep Tunnel flood relief program. In addition, he played a major role in the revamping of Social Security and helped pass legislation that simplified federal income tax laws. He served on the House Ways and Means Committee for nearly 40 years; 13 years as its chairman, from 1981 to 1994. He was a major player in shaping congressional tax policy. He helped create the legislation that created Medicare in 1966 and helped fashion laws on taxes, trade, and welfare. In 1983 he brokered a deal that helped to maintain the solvency of the Social Security system. He helped to create a bill that led to the 1986 tax reform act, a major rewriting of the federal tax code that reduced tax rates and eliminated loopholes.

Rostenkowski's legal troubles began with, of all things, postage stamps, as a 1992 grand jury investigation looked into criminal activities at the House post office. Merriner calls the HPO "a Democratic patronage sink." The grand jury charged that Rostenkowski had bought $22,000 in stamps with public monies and then converted it to cash for his own personal use. Essentially, Rostenkowski and several other legislators were accused of abusing congressional postal privileges; of using the perks of his office to make money. Two years later he was indicted on seventeen counts, ranging from mail and wire fraud to obstruction of justice. But that wasn't all. In addition, he was accused of hiring ghost payrollers, maintaining office slush funds,

and giving gifts to political supporters and friends (from furniture to fine china to crystal)—all seemingly minor infractions that, in an earlier era, were considered the usual way of doing business. But times had changed, and Rostenkowski didn't, or refused to, keep up with the times.

Despite the charges hanging over his head, Rostenkowski ran for reelection in the 1994 midterm elections when Republicans won back control of both the House and the Senate. But his heart didn't seem in it. He lost to a political novice, Michael Patrick Flanagan, who served just one term.

In 1996 Rostenkowski pleaded guilty to two felony counts of mail fraud for misusing taxpayer money. He was sentenced to seventeen months in federal prisons; he served two months short of his full sentence by spending time in a Salvation Army halfway house in Chicago and paying a $100,000 fine. In December 2000 President Bill Clinton issued a pardon, expunging Rostenkowski's criminal record.

Rostenkowski biographer Richard Cohen claims that the prosecutors "never proved that Rostenkowski took a penny for himself." Merriner is not so sure. He calls a January 12, 1998, *Newsweek* article in which the magazine says there was no evidence that he had lined his own pockets "a stretch."

Rostenkowski died at the age of 82 from lung cancer at his Wisconsin summer home.

Further reading: Richard E. Cohen, *Rostenkowski: The Pursuit of Power and the End of the Old Politics* (1999); James L. Merriner, *Mr. Chairman: Power in Dan Rostenkowski's America* (1999); "Rosty's Difficult Winter," *Newsweek*, January 12, 1998.

Mike Royko

Newspaper Columnist

BORN: September 19, 1932
Chicago, Illinois

DIED: April 29, 1997
Chicago, Illinois

Mike Royko was the quintessential Chicago newsman from the old school: a grumpy contrarian who wrote what he thought, not what others wanted to hear. For more than three decades he wrote a remarkable 7,500 daily columns, first for the *Chicago Daily News*, then the *Chicago Sun-Times*, and, finally, the *Chicago Tribune*. He was the voice of the Everyman.

He was born in Chicago, the son of Michael Royko Sr., a Ukrainian immigrant and saloonkeeper, and Helen Royko, a Polish homemaker. Growing up in the heart of Nelson

Algren territory in Humboldt Park on the Northwest Side, he held various jobs before turning to journalism. He set bowling pins, worked as part of a landscaping crew, labored in a machine shop and in a lamp factory, and pushed carts around a department store.

Royko attended Wright Junior College, the University of Illinois, and Northwestern University. He dropped out of college in 1952 to enlist in the air force. He started his journalism career while serving in the air force during the Korean War as a columnist for the newspaper of the Glenview Naval Air Station. He talked his way into editing the

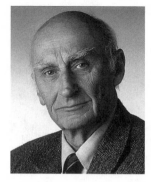

base's newspaper, a skill he picked up, according to the *New York Times,* from a journalism textbook—the night before he offered to edit it. If that was not enough, he lied and said he had worked for the *Daily News.*

In 1956 Royko applied to the City News Bureau and then the *Lincoln-Belmont Booster,* a neighborhood newspaper, before securing a position at the *Chicago Daily News* in 1959 as a night beat police reporter and then as a political reporter, covering Cook County politics in a weekly political column called "The County Beat." His success led to a daily column, which began in 1964. When the *Daily News* folded in 1978, Royko moved his column to the *Chicago Sun-Times.* But when the Australian media mogul Rupert Murdoch bought the paper in 1984, Royko bolted across the street to the *Chicago Tribune,* explaining in typical Royko fashion that no journalist worth his or her salt would work for such a man, or, as he so colorfully put it, "No self-respecting fish would be wrapped in a Murdoch paper." Royko referred to Murdoch disparagingly as "the alien."

Royko was the unofficial spokesman for the little guy and gal. For more than thirty years he wrote 900 words five or six times a week. When, in 1992, he was cut back to four times a week, the workaholic Royko thought it a sign of weakness. At his peak, his columns were syndicated nationwide to more than 600 newspapers.

Royko celebrated the corner tavern and the corner store, the customs and rituals of the neighborhood. Like his fellow columnist of an earlier era, Finley Peter Dunne, Royko created an alter ego as his mouthpiece. Slats Grobnik epitomized the working-class Chicago of Eastern European heritage. In the Grobnik columns, two men conversed in a bar in a Polish neighborhood, offering their world-weary and skeptical observations on the state of the world. The columns were collected in *Slats Grobnik and Some Other Friends* (1973). Another popular character was *Dr. I. M.*

Kookie, who enabled Royko to deliver tongue-in-cheek criticism of popular culture and poke mischievous fun at what he thought was its overly introspective, navel-gazing obsessiveness.

Royko's favorite watering hole was the Billy Goat Tavern, the underground pub located across the street from the Tribune Tower on Lower Wacker Drive and made famous by John Belushi on *Saturday Night Live.* Appropriately, Belushi paid homage to Royko in his movie *Continental Divide,* where he played a grizzled Chicago columnist clearly modeled after Royko.

In 1971 Royko wrote an unauthorized, and not very flattering, biography of Richard J. Daley. *Boss* (1971) was an unsparingly honest portrait of the mayor as a corrupt and greedy autocrat. A rousing success, it spent twenty-six weeks on the *New York Times* best-seller list.

Royko's columns were gathered into numerous collections, including *Up Against It* (1967), *I May Be Wrong, But I Doubt It* (1968), *Sez Who? Sez Me* (1983), *Like I Was Sayin'* (1985), *Dr. Kookie, You're Right* (1989), *One More Time: The Best of Mike Royko* (2000), and *For the Love of Mike: More of the Best of Mike Royko* (2001). In 2010 the University of Chicago Press reprinted *Up Against It* as *Early Royko: Up Against It in Chicago* with a foreword by Rick Kogan.

In 1972 Royko won the Pulitzer Prize for commentary and in 1990 the National Press Lifetime Achievement Award.

Royko died at the age of sixty-four at Northwestern Memorial Hospital of a brain aneurysm. He was buried in Acacia Park Cemetery on the Northwest Side of Chicago.

The Mike Royko Papers are housed at the Newberry Library.

See also: John Belushi, Finley Peter Dunne
Further reading: Rick Kogan, *A Chicago Tavern: A Goat, a Curse, and the American Dream* (2006).

Arthur Rubloff

Real Estate Developer

BORN: June 25, 1902
Duluth, Minnesota

DIED: May 24, 1986
Chicago, Illinois

One of the leading real estate figures of the Midwest, Arthur Rubloff coined the term "Magnificent Mile" and helped to develop North Michigan Avenue, among other projects.

Born in Minnesota, the son of a Russian Jewish immigrant, Arthur Rubloff dropped out of grade school and left home to find work as a galley boy on a Great Lakes

ore boat. He then spent several years in a Cincinnati furniture store and picked up a few other odd jobs until he moved to Chicago in 1917, where his father had set up a clothing factory. A year after his arrival, his father's plant burned down. The tragedy effectively put the elder Rubloff out of business. Good fortune surfaced, however, when Arthur met a Chicago realtor who, impressed with the young man's vigor, persuaded him to enter the realty business. In

1921, Rubloff joined Robert White and Company, where he stayed until 1930, when he left to establish his own firm, Arthur Rubloff and Company.

Like that other famous Chicagoan, Daniel H. Burnham, Rubloff dreamed big. In 1945 he conceived the idea of Evergreen Plaza on the South Side, one of the first enclosed malls in the country. "It took nine years to get off the ground and I almost went broke because the concept was so new that it was very difficult to generate interest," he recalled. In 1947 Rubloff, together with John Root of the architectural firm of Holabird and Root, unveiled a $200 million plan for the development of upper Michigan Avenue from the Chicago River to Oak Street that promised to turn the boulevard into the "most modern mile in the world."

Initially the idea met with a cool reception. "I'd spent $50,000 preparing the plans and I was called all kinds of names," recalled Rubloff. "Some people thought I was trying to steal the town." Despite this initial trouble the North Michigan Avenue Association ultimately gave their approval to the proposal. By 1949 the association sponsored the planting of trees along the street; property owners and retailers echoed their support.

Rubloff was also instrumental in the development and revitalization of other Chicago neighborhoods, such as Old Town and Sandburg Village. Sandburg Village, built on the former site of a housing project, was completed in 1966 and attracted to the area thousands of predominantly young white men and women. He also promoted a plan to renovate fourteen and a half acres in the North Loop. Mayor Richard J. Daley expressed interest in the idea, but succeeding administrations—especially Michael J. Bilandic's and Jane Byrne's—rejected the plan as too costly and outmoded.

Rubloff, whose worth was estimated at $100 million when he died in 1986, donated $6 million to the Art Institute in 1984, reportedly the largest single contribution made to the institution until that time. Substantial gifts were also given to Northwestern University, the University of Chicago, Michael Reese Hospital, the Lincoln Park Zoo, and the Chicago Historical Society (now the Chicago History Museum) as well as the United Negro College Fund, Lewis University, Hull House, and the United Way.

Rubloff was a master at blowing his own horn. He took hyperbole to new heights. "I did North Michigan Avenue's Magnificent Mile. I built Sandburg Village. Saved the Near North Side, that's what I did. Everyone was against it," he once remarked to a local writer. Rubloff's critics, however, were not quite as generous. Many contended that such projects would have eventually been developed—with or without his help. As far back as 1913, the Bowes Realty Company, a successful brokerage firm, began to buy and sell property along the street from the Michigan Avenue Bridge to Chicago Avenue and leased space to a number of elegant shops, which started a trend that continues to this day. Frederic Bowes, the president of the firm, reportedly convinced property owners not to allow "undesirable" businesses—such as gas stations and saloons—to locate there.

It was Rubloff, however, who aggressively promoted the beautification of North Michigan Avenue and envisioned the thoroughfare as Chicago's showpiece, comparable to Fifth Avenue in New York or the Champs Elysees in Paris. Nelson Forrest, executive director of the Greater North Michigan Avenue Association, called Rubloff a "promotional pioneer. He sparked the momentum for the area to become a private-enterprise development."

Rubloff died in his Lake Shore Drive high-rise in May 1986 at the age of eighty-three. At the time of his death he was affiliated with Arthur Rubloff and Company in an advisory capacity only.

Carl Sandburg

Poet

BORN: January 6, 1878
Galesburg, Illinois

DIED: July 22, 1967
Flat Rock, North Carolina

Carl Sandburg was a quintessentially American poet and one of the most loved poets of the twentieth century. But he was more than a poet. He was a crusading journalist, a teller of children's tales, a historian of Abraham Lincoln, an idealistic socialist, and a traveling troubadour who sang and collected the folk songs of his native land.

Carl August Sandburg was the son of Swedish immigrants, August and Clara Johnson, who had settled in Galesburg, Illinois. According to historian Dale Kramer, his father changed the family name to Sandburg before Carl was born. As a youth, he preferred to be called Charlie—he felt it sounded more American. He started to work at fourteen, driving a milk wagon. Then he held a series of jobs: dishwasher, porter at a barber shop, potato digger, window washer, and manual laborer in the harvest fields.

During the Spanish-American War of 1898, Sandburg enlisted in Company C Sixth Infantry Regiment of the

Illinois Volunteers in the army and served eight months in Puerto Rico. Upon his return to Illinois, he enrolled at Lombard College in Galesburg. In 1899 he applied to West Point, but he failed to pass the entrance exam. At Lombard, he edited the college monthly, served as a correspondent for a Galesburg newspaper, and captained the basketball team. He printed his first book of poetry there, *In Reckless Ecstasy* (1904), using a printing press owned by his former professor.

Sandburg dropped out of college in 1902 and continued his habit of working at whatever came his way. For a period of time he sold stereoscopic photographs. In 1907 he settled in Milwaukee, where he became a socialist organizer and later an advertising manager for a department store. He also recruited members for the Social Democratic Party and worked on several Milwaukee newspapers until the city's socialist mayor, Emil Seidel, asked him to serve as his secretary. Sandburg accepted and stayed there for two years.

In 1908 Sandburg married Lillian Steichen, sister of the noted photographer Edward Steichen. In 1912 the couple moved to Chicago, where Sandburg had friends, and settled down into the second-floor apartment of a frame house at 4646 North Hermitage Avenue in the Ravenswood neighborhood. Sandburg then decided to try his hand at journalism, which he felt offered more job opportunities. He began working on the *Chicago World,* and later switched to an experimental tabloid, *Day-Book,* at 500 South Peoria Street, that accepted no advertising. In 1917 Sandburg joined the *Chicago Daily News,* where he covered the labor beat. Later he reviewed movies. Sandburg remained on the staff until 1927.

Sandburg had poetry published as early as 1904 in obscure journals, but it wasn't until his work appeared in *Poetry* magazine in 1914 that his career took off. Poems like "Fog," or his most famous, "Chicago," attracted the lion's share of attention. His free verse, liberally scattered with slang and street-corner colloquialisms, caught the literary world off guard and ushered in a new era of what some critics referred to as poetic modernism. Two years later his collection of poetry, *Chicago Poems,* received mostly favorable reviews. Some of his other poetry volumes include *Cornhuskers* (1918), *Smoke and Steel* (1920), and *Slabs of the Sunburnt West* (1922).

Sandburg also proved to be an astute and compassionate reporter. In 1919 he wrote *The Chicago Race Riots,* a penetrating analysis of the riots that ravaged the city's Black Belt during the hot summer of that year. In addition, Sandburg was a biographer. His monumental six-volume

biography of Lincoln was composed of *Abraham Lincoln: The Prairie Years* (two volumes, 1926) and *Abraham Lincoln: The War Years* (four volumes, 1939). The latter set of volumes earned Sandburg the Pulitzer Prize for history in 1940.

In 1936 he compiled *The People, Yes,* a history of the common folk told in poetry. Sandburg preserved songs that otherwise may have been lost, collecting material from people "who sing because they must," he wrote. He scoured the country with guitar in hand, collecting and singing the songs of the cowboy, the hobo, and the railroad worker. Collections of his songs include *The American Songbag* (1927) and *New American Songbag* (1951). He also wrote several children's books, including *Rootabaga Stories* (1922) and *Potato Face* (1930). His last works include *Remembrance Rock* (1948), a novel—his first—that begins at Plymouth Rock and continues through World War II; *Complete Poems* (1950), which won him a second Pulitzer Prize in 1951; the autobiographical *Always the Young Stranger* (1952), a reminiscence of his youth in Galesburg; and *Honey and Salt* (1962).

In 1962 Governor Otto Kerner Jr. designated Sandburg the poet laureate of Illinois. In 1985 contemporary folksinger Bob Gibson produced a musical play, *The Courtship of Carl Sandburg,* which incorporated the writer's letters, poetry, children's tales, and stories. Schools across the country are named in Sandburg's honor.

Sandburg was a rarity, a critically acclaimed poet who also appealed to a broad audience. Called one of America's natural resources, he was often compared to another American icon, Mark Twain. He died at his North Carolina home in July 1967 at the age of eighty-nine.

See also: Floyd Dell, Eugene Field, Ben Hecht, Harriet Monroe

Further reading: Arnie Bernstein, ed., *"The Movies Are": Carl Sandburg's Film Reviews and Essays, 1920–1928* (2000), with an introduction by Roger Ebert; Harry Golden, *Carl Sandburg* (1961); Dale Kramer, *Chicago Renaissance: The Literary Life of the Midwest, 1900–1930* (1966); Carl Sandburg, *Poems for the People,* edited by George and Willene Hendrick (2001); Alson J. Smith, *Chicago's Left Bank* (1953).

Other resources: *The Day Carl Sandburg Died* (Bonesteel Films, 2011).

Ron Santo

Baseball Player

BORN: February 25, 1940
Seattle, Washington

DIED: December 3, 2010
Scottsdale, Arizona

Ron Santo was the consummate Chicago Cub. Not only was he considered one of the finest baseball players to don a Cubs uniform, he was also among the team's biggest fans. Ebullient both on and off the field, he was known for his famous heel clicks (whenever the Cubs did particularly well on the field, he would jump in the air and click his heels together) as well as for his cheers and groans in the broadcast booth. Despite being considered among baseball's all-time great third basemen, he never was elected into the Baseball Hall of Fame during his lifetime.

Ronald Edward Santo was born in Seattle, Washington. He signed as a free agent with the Cubs after high school, in 1959, and made his debut at Wrigley Field on June 26, 1960. By the following year, he had gained a reputation as a skilled fielder who also happened to be a powerful right-handed batter.

Santo played for the Chicago Cubs for most of his career, from 1960 to 1973. The following year, his final season, he moved to the South Side to play for the rival Chicago White Sox as a designated hitter (he couldn't play his regular position because the Sox already had a third baseman, Bill Melton, on the roster). During his long career, he hit 342 home runs and won five Gold Glove awards for fielding every season from 1964 to 1968. In addition, he was named to the All-Star team nine times. In December 2011, he was finally rewarded for his considerable achievements on the baseball field by being posthumously elected to the Baseball Hall of Fame.

Santo was a major reason for the success of the 1969 Cubs team that, for most of the season, led the Eastern Division of the National League and seemed destined to play in the World Series. During that frustrating and, ultimately (for Cubs fans), disappointing season, the Cubs squandered the wide lead that they had held over the New York Mets in the National League East (the Mets went onto win the pennant and the World Series that year).

At the age of eighteen, Santo learned that he had juvenile diabetes, a revelation that he kept secret until he was named to his first All-Star team in 1963. He feared that letting the secret out would jeopardize his career. When he retired from baseball, he would spend a great deal of his time and effort raising millions of dollars for diabetes research. But the disease did exact a heavy toll on his health over the years, contributing to several heart attacks as well as the amputation of both legs: the right one in 2001, the left one in 2002. After fifteen seasons with the Cubs, he retired with a career batting average of .277; his other statistics were impressive, too: 342 home runs, 2,254 hits, and 1,331 runs batted in.

In 1990, Santo began working as a Cubs color commentator on WGN. Occasionally he even shared the broadcast booth with another Chicago sports icon, the legendary broadcaster Harry Caray. Like Caray, Santo was plainspoken and known for his unintentionally humorous malapropisms and off-the-cuff comments: he mangled names and sometimes seemed to lose track of what was taking place on the field. But no matter, the fans loved him anyway. Nor did he make any effort to hide his disgust at Cubs players when they performed poorly—but he also displayed great pleasure when they did well. Although he also worked with Steve Stone, Thom Brennaman, and Bob Brenly, for most of his broadcasting career he shared the booth with play-by-play announcer Pat Hughes.

In September 2003, the Cubs retired Santo's number 10 jersey at Wrigley Field. In 2004, Santo's son, Jeff, wrote, coproduced, and directed *This Old Cub*, a documentary about the elder Santo's battle with diabetes.

Santo died at the age of 70 in Arizona due to complications from bladder cancer and diabetes. His funeral was held at Holy Name Cathedral on the Near North Side; his casket was carried by several of his former Cub teammates, including Ernie Banks, Ferguson Jenkins, Randy Hundley, Glenn Beckert, and Billy Williams. Following the service, the funeral procession circled his beloved Wrigley Field. Santo was later cremated and his ashes were scattered there.

See also: Harry Caray

Abe Saperstein

Basketball Coach

BORN: July 4, 1902
London, England

DIED: March 15, 1966
Chicago, Illinois

That truly American sports institution, the Harlem Globetrotters, was founded by a native of London's Whitechapel district, Abe Saperstein. For nearly forty years, he led his team to glory in countries all over the world, while such gifted athletes as Meadowlark Lemon, Goose Tatum, and Wilt Chamberlain provided hilarious comedy routines and displayed breathtaking ball-handling techniques. Saperstein championed African American athletes long before it was fashionable to do so.

Abe Saperstein moved to Chicago from England with his family as a youngster. He attended Lakeview High School on the North Side and later the University of Illinois. Although small in stature—he was an inch or so under five feet—Saperstein excelled in sports. When he realized he was too short to make the college basketball squad, he decided to try his hand at coaching.

Saperstein began his coaching career at Welles Park at Western and Montrose Avenues. Then he began coaching the Armour Post American Legion team. Saperstein recruited African American players from the South Side to play at the Boys' Brotherhood Republic, a Jewish youth center founded in the Maxwell Street neighborhood. In 1927 he was hired to coach an African American semipro team in Chicago, the Giles Post American Legion Quintet. The following year the team played twice a week at the Savoy Ballroom. After the engagement at the Savoy ended, several of the players, who were having so much fun, vowed to continue to play.

Saperstein had wanted a colorful, descriptive name for his team, something catchy and easy to remember. Since they were a traveling unit, he coined the term "Globetrotters," and since they were all an all-black outfit, he referred to them as the "Harlem" Globetrotters. In those days the team consisted of only five or six players, though sometimes Saperstein himself donned a uniform. The number of players increased as the team grew in popularity. Saperstein did virtually everything. In addition to his coaching duties, he acted as the team chauffeur—driving his players from town to town in a Model T Ford—booked and arranged games, and scouted. The Globetrotters played anybody. Sometimes it was for a straight guarantee up front, other times for a percentage of the box office.

Occasionally they played two games a night. Saperstein suggested that the players relieve the tension of life on the road by doing tricks with the ball—rolling it up and down their arm, for example. At first they balked at such a suggestion, believing it would demean the game they loved so well. Finally, one day in Newton, Iowa, they decided to give the coach's idea a workout. They spun the ball on their fingers and drop-kicked it through the hoop. The crowd, after they got over the novelty of the impromptu performance, roared with delight. Under Abe Saperstein, the Globetrotters became the world's most watched—and most watchable—basketball team and their exploits were reported in the pages of the daily press.

In the summer of 1961 Saperstein founded the American Basketball League with eight teams—including the Chicago entry, the Chicago Majors—after being denied a franchise in the rival National Basketball Association. He also served as commissioner of the ill-fated league. Saperstein's name, however, attracted more attention than any of his players. Basketball posters advertised "Abe Saperstein's Chicago Majors." Taking advantage of his fame and his association with the Harlem Globetrotters, Saperstein began featuring entertainment such as bicycle acts, ping-pong champions, and jazz bands during halftime. Even the Globetrotters made an occasional appearance. Yet the crowds didn't come. By December 1962, the team had folded.

Saperstein died of a heart attack in 1966 at Weiss Memorial Hospital in Chicago. He was sixty-three.

"Abe Saperstein adopted the United States and did more for his nation than most other men in sports," wrote *Chicago Tribune* sports columnist Dave Condon, following the coach's death. "Abe Saperstein reduced the globe to the size of a basketball. From behind the Iron Curtain to the tip of South America, he displayed America's Negro athlete with a dignity that was the best advertisement that democracy ever knew."

Saperstein was inducted into the National Basketball Hall of Fame in 1971. Today a new generation of Harlem Globetrotters continues to entertain both here and abroad.

Florence Scala

Community Activist and Restaurant Owner

BORN: September 17, 1918
Chicago, Illinois

DIED: August 28, 2007
Chicago, Illinois

*We were indispensable. . . .
They were out to demolish
the whole community.*

—Florence Scala after
learning that the city
of Chicago planned to
build a branch of the
University of Illinois
in the Taylor Street
neighborhood

In the early 1960s, Florence Scala fought City Hall to preserve the Little Italy neighborhood after Mayor Richard J. Daley announced his plan to construct the University of Illinois's Chicago Circle campus at Harrison and Halsted Streets. Despite creating the Harrison-Halsted Community Group, protesting in front of City Hall, and even filing a lawsuit in both state and federal courts, Scala's bid ultimately failed. Still, she chose to live in the neighborhood she tried to protect until her death.

She was born Florence Giovangelo in 1918 in the Taylor Street neighborhood on Chicago's Near West Side, the daughter of Italian immigrant parents, Alex and Teresa Giovangelo. From 1934 to 1954 she was a volunteer at Hull House, the social settlement founded by Jane Addams, where she had been educated. "My father was a tailor," she told Studs Terkel, "and we were just getting along in a very poor neighborhood. He never had any money to send us to school. When one of the teachers suggested that our mother send us to Hull House, life began to open up." From 1949 to 1958, she served as secretary and treasurer of the Near West Side Planning Board, and from 1957 to 1959 as secretary of the Near West Side Conservation Community Council.

In 1961 Scala became co-chair of the Harrison-Halsted Community Group and even waged an unsuccessful run to become alderman of the First Ward as an independent candidate. It was, by all accounts, an ugly campaign: she endured taunts, threats, and several bombing attempts.

When Mayor Richard J. Daley announced plans to demolish a good chunk of her Italian neighborhood to make way for the University of Illinois at Chicago campus, Scala, along with longtime Hull House resident Jessie Binford, mounted a vigorous, if unsuccessful, campaign to thwart

his plans and preserve the community. On March 5, 1963, the trustees of Hull House accepted an $875,000 settlement from the city, which prompted Scala and Binford to sue the board. Scala and Binford took their fight all the way to the Supreme Court. The court, though, decided in favor of the university: ultimately, more than 800 houses and 200 businesses were razed to make way for the campus. The Hull House Settlement itself closed on March 28, 1963. Scala, though, did receive a pyrrhic victory of sorts when the original Hull House building on South Halsted Street was saved and turned into a museum.

In addition to her work as an activist, Scala was also a picture editor at Encyclopaedia Britannica and a volunteer coordinator for the Illinois Department of Mental Health. She is famous for another reason: in 1980, along with her brother, Mario, she opened a popular Italian restaurant, Florence, at 1030 West Taylor Street, housed in the same building where she grew up. She closed the restaurant in 1990. She was, she said at the time, tired of working six days a week; her husband, Charles Scala, had died five years earlier.

Scala died of colon cancer on August 28, 2007, in the same Taylor Street apartment where she had grown up. "She was my heroine," Studs Terkel said after learning of her death. Syndicated columnist Georgie Anne Geyer—a former *Chicago Daily News* reporter—referred to Scala as "the Rosa Parks of the Italian-American neighborhood."

See also: Studs Terkel

Further reading: Kathy Catrambone, *Taylor Street: Chicago's Little Italy* (2007); Carolyn Eastwood, *Near West Side Stories: Struggles for Community in Chicago's Maxwell Street Neighborhood* (2002); Humbert Nelli, *Italians in Chicago, 1880–1930: A Study in Ethnic Mobility* (1973); Studs Terkel, *Division Street: America* (1967).

Richard W. Sears

Merchant

BORN: December 7, 1863
Stewartville, Minnesota

DIED: September 28, 1914
Waukesha, Wisconsin

Richard Warren Sears was an affable Minnesota farm boy with a knack for business who founded the "Cheapest Supply House on Earth." The mail order firm of Sears, Roebuck and Company prospered due to high-quality goods and personal service. The firm that he cofounded became one of the largest department store chains in the country; the Sears name still is one of the most recognizable in Chicago.

Richard Sears began his career at the Minneapolis and St. Louis Railway as a station agent in North Redwood, Minnesota. In 1886 he received an offer from manufacturers to sell a shipment of pocket watches that had been refused by a local merchant and left at the station. At the bargain rate Sears was offering, the watches sold quickly. This first flush of success convinced him that there was more money to be made in the big city. He left the railway in 1886 and

established his own firm, the R. W. Sears Watch Company, in Minneapolis.

The following year he set up headquarters in Chicago near Dearborn and Randolph Streets, which at that time was experiencing rapid growth and offered ample business opportunities. He placed a small ad in the *Chicago Daily News* for a watchmaker, hiring a young Hoosier named Alvah Roebuck, who had been working for a Hammond, Indiana, jeweler, to repair the watches. In 1888 Sears opened a branch office in Toronto and issued his first mail-order catalog. In 1889, tired of the mail-order business, he sold his interest to Roebuck and moved to Iowa, where he entered banking. Rural life, he discovered, was not to his liking, so in 1892 he resumed his business relationship with Roebuck, and started another mail-order venture. In 1893 the firm changed its name to Sears, Roebuck and Company and rented a large building on West Van Buren Street. By this time, Sears had begun adding other merchandise to the catalog, from silverware to revolvers.

Sears was always on the lookout for new products to sell. Gradually he began adding more merchandise—baby carriages, bicycles, even ready-to-assemble houses. Occasionally, he got carried away, advertising items that he didn't yet have in stock, but this oversight had more to do with his good-natured enthusiasm than any deliberate attempt to cheat his customers, according to Lorin Sorensen. On the contrary, Sears promised quality goods at inexpensive prices, and he delivered. For those who still remained skeptical, he boldly offered the revolutionary "send no money" policy—goods were payable on inspection. It was risky but it worked. "All but a small fraction," notes Sorensen, "paid promptly and most sent in new orders." Despite stiff competition from an already established mail-order firm, Montgomery Ward and Company, sales zoomed.

The company's chief selling point was the bulky Sears, Roebuck and Company catalog. Sears, who did most of the writing, composed homespun passages in a folksy, familiar manner that appealed to his predominantly rural readers. By 1894 the book had grown to a hefty five hundred pages and was as much a part of the American household as the Bible. With sales booming, construction began in January 1905 on a larger plant at Homan and Arthington Streets on the West Side. When completed in 1906, the nine-story building contained its own printing plant and dining halls, and was surrounded by landscaped parks.

In 1895 Roebuck left the firm. Julius Rosenwald, who ran a clothing factory and supplied suits to the firm, bought shares in the company and became vice president.

In November 1908 Sears resigned over a dispute with Rosenwald regarding company policy. Sears wanted to offer discounts and promote popular items to encourage sales. Rosenwald recommended waiting until the economy, which had taken a slight downturn, improved. Sears chose to retire to his Wisconsin farm in early 1909. The parting of ways, however, was amicable. Rosenwald then succeeded Sears as president.

Sears died on September 28, 1914, in Waukesha, Wisconsin, at the age of fifty. He left behind an estate worth $25 million and a name that is still one of the most widely recognized in the retail business.

One of the world's tallest buildings, the Sears Tower, at Franklin and Adams Streets, built in 1974, honored the founder of the firm. At that time, with approximately 350,000 employees, the company was the largest retailer in the world. In 1989 Sears, Roebuck and Company announced that it planned to move its headquarters from downtown Chicago to northwest suburban Hoffman Estates. In 2009, the Sears Tower changed its name to the Willis Tower. The London-based insurance broker Willis Group Holdings earned the right to rename the building.

See also: Julius Rosenwald, Aaron Montgomery Ward

Further reading: John E. Jeuck and Boris Emmet, *Catalogues and Counters: A History of Sears, Roebuck & Co.* (1950); Donald R. Katz, *The Big Store: Inside the Crisis & Revolution at Sears* (1987); Lorin Sorensen, *Sears, Roebuck and Co., 100th Anniversary 1886–1986* (1985).

Ike Sewell

Restaurant Owner

BORN: September 9, 1903
Wills Point, Texas.

DIED: August 20, 1990
Chicago, Illinois

Ric Riccardo

Restaurant Owner

BORN: Italy
DIED: 1954

Ike Sewell is credited with inventing one of Chicago's most popular exports—the deep-dish pizza. Sewell first achieved fame as an All-America football player at the University of Texas at Austin. During the 1920s he worked for American Airlines and moved to Chicago in 1936 as a liquor salesman. Frequent visits to the city's restaurants and taverns led to a friendship with Ric Riccardo Sr., owner of the popular Riccardo's restaurant on North Rush Street, for many years a favorite of local journalists. Sewell proposed opening a Mexican restaurant as a sideline business. Riccardo, who did not particularly like Mexican food, compromised and suggested a pizzeria instead. After some experimenting, they came up with the idea of a pizza that consisted of layers of cheese topped with a thick crust and then baked in a skillet.

In 1943 Sewell and Riccardo opened Pizzeria Uno at 29 East Ohio Street. It met with such success that the pair opened a second pizzeria, Pizzeria Due, at 619 North Wabash Avenue, in 1955. In 1979 Sewell franchised the deep-dish pizza concept.

In 1963 Sewell finally did open that Mexican restaurant he had dreamed about for decades earlier, Su Casa, at 49 East Ontario Street.

Sewell died of leukemia in 1990 in Chicago at the age of eighty-seven.

In January 2010, the parent company of Pizzeria Uno filed for bankruptcy. Its restaurants, including the original Pizzeria Uno location at Ohio Street and Wabash Avenue, remained open.

Born Riccardo Novaretti in Italy around the turn of the last century, Ric Riccardo was a bit of a Renaissance man.

After traveling around the world as a ship's mate, he got married in New Orleans and then brought his new wife, Mimi, to Chicago in the 1920s. There Riccardo opened a restaurant on South Oakley Avenue. In addition to being a chef he was also a dancer, musician, and artist—Riccardo also contributed work for the Works Progress Administration (WPA) Federal Art Project in Illinois.

In 1935, he bought a former speakeasy on Rush Street and opened a restaurant and gallery space, which he called, at the time, Riccardo Restaurant and Gallery. In 1947, he expanded into the adjacent buildings. It was in this new and larger space where he put his famous bar that was shaped like an artist's palette. Mounted on the wall behind the bar were seven paintings, which Riccardo called "The Seven Lively Arts." The murals depicted allegorical scenes of the fine arts, and several were created by prominent artists: *Architecture* by Aaron Bohrod, *Drama (Mephistopheles)* by Ivan Albright, *Literature* by Rudolph Weisenborn, *Music* by William Schwartz, *Painting* by Vincent D'Agostino, *Sculpture* by Malvin Marr Albright (Ivan Albright's twin brother), and *Dance* by Riccardo himself.

Riccardo died in 1954 at the age of fifty-one. His son, Rick, took over the tavern but sold it in 1974 to Nick and Bill Angelos. The Angelos brothers closed it in the mid-1990s but not before hosting a big farewell party on August 25, 1995.

See also: Ivan Albright
Further reading: Jeff Huebner, "The Return of the Magnificent Seven," *Chicago Reader*, September 5, 2002; Rick Kogan, "Last Call at Ric's: A Final Toast to the Watering Hole Ric Riccardo Left Chicago," *Chicago Tribune*, September 15, 1995.

Ralph Shapey

Composer

BORN: March 12, 1921
Philadelphia, Pennsylvania

DIED: June 13, 2002
Chicago, Illinois

Ralph Shapey was an avant-garde composer known for his unconventional chamber works and oftentimes quirky sense of humor. He wrote compositions of great complexity, atonal and dissonant, as well as compositions of enormous power that were highly influenced by abstract expressionism. He was called a "radical traditionalist"—his music was paradoxical, combining radical language with a romantic sensibility. "A great work of art," he once said, "transcends the immediate moment into a world of infinity." Shapey believed that music must speak for itself.

Born in Philadelphia, Shapey began studying the violin at the age of seven. A precocious student, he continued his violin studies as a teenager under Emanuel Zeitlin and composition studies with German composer Stefan Wolpe and was selected as the conductor of the Philadelphia National Youth Symphony Orchestra. At the youthful age of twenty-one, he was a guest conductor at the Philadelphia Symphony Orchestra.

During World War II Shapey served in the U.S. Army. After the war he moved to New York, where he worked as a freelance violinist, composer, conductor, and teacher. In

1955 he wrote his first major orchestral work, *Challenge: The Family of Man.* He spent from 1955 to 1959 at the MacDowell arts colony, where he created other works, including *Ontogeny* in 1958, *Invocation* in 1959, and *Rituals,* also in 1959. Another piece, *Incantations for Soprano and Ten Instruments* (1961), was written for soprano and ten instruments; the *New York Times* described it as "terrifying" as well as "altogether extraordinary."

In 1963 Shapey commuted to his native Philadelphia to conduct the Philadelphia Symphony Orchestra and to conduct the chorus at the University of Pennsylvania. The following year he joined the composition faculty as a professor of music at the University of Chicago. He also founded the Contemporary Chamber Players, a professional new music ensemble that concentrated on twentieth-century works and became known for its high performance standards and diverse repertoire. He not only served as the music director and conductor for the Players for nearly three decades, he also mentored many young composers, including the Pulitzer Prize–winning Shulamit Ran.

Shapey won numerous awards and honors over his career. In 1951 he won the George Gershwin Award. Years later, in 1982, he won a MacArthur "genius" grant and the Friedman Award from the Kennedy Center in 1990. He also received commissions from various prominent foundations and organizations, including the Fromm Foundation, the Library of Congress's Elizabeth Sprague Coolidge Foundation, the National Endowment for the Arts, the Philadelphia Orchestra, and the Chicago Symphony Orchestra. In 1989 he was elected to the American Academy and Institute of Arts and Letters and in 1994 to the American Academy of Arts and Sciences. In addition, he was distinguished professor of music at Queens College in New York City in 1985. As a conductor, Shapey led the New York Philharmonic Chamber Music Society, as well as the symphony orchestras of Chicago, London, Philadelphia, and Jerusalem. He also conducted the London Sinfonietta, for whom he recorded *Rituals for Symphony Orchestra* (2007).

Over his long career, Shapey wrote more than 200 compositions, from solo pieces to pieces for duos, trios, and string quartets. He also wrote chamber works for woodwinds, percussion, and piano as well as longer works for chorus and orchestra in all genres with the exception of opera.

His works include "Etchings" (1945), an early work for solo violin; "Movements" (1960), and "Five" (1960). He was a master at writing unconventional chamber works, such as "Concerto for Clarinet" and "Chamber Group" for violin, French horn, piano, and percussion in 1954; "Interchange" in 1966, a four-movement suite; and "Three for Six" in 1979, a chamber work. Among his other major works are "Praise" (1976), an hour-long oratorio for bass baritone solo, double chorus, and chamber group on the crisis of faith; and "The Covenant" (1978) for soprano and sixteen players, which he dedicated to the state of Israel on the thirtieth anniversary of its founding.

Shapey's style was steeped in Romanticism and characterized by irony, passion, and vitality, as well as the sweeping gesture and the dramatic arc. In addition to abstract expressionism, his other influences included the work of the French American composer Edgard Varèse. Although both critics and listeners have often described his music as atonal, Shapey himself strongly disagreed. On the contrary, he thought of himself as a tonal composer.

In 1992 the Pulitzer Prize for Music jury selected Shapey's "Concerto Fantastique," commissioned in honor of the joint centenaries of the University of Chicago and the Chicago Symphony Orchestra, but the Pulitzer Board withdrew the award at the last moment in favor of the jury's second choice, Wayne Peterson.

Shapey retired from the University of Chicago in 1991, although he continued to conduct the Contemporary Chamber Players until 1994. In addition, he recorded for the CRI, Opus One, and New World labels, and in 2002 published a textbook, *A Basic Course in Music Composition.* His works have been catalogued by Patrick D. Finley as *A Catalogue of the Works of Ralph Shapey* (1997).

Shapey died in Chicago in June 2002 at the age of eighty-one.

Howard Van Doren Shaw

Architect

BORN: May 7, 1869
Chicago, Illinois

DIED: May 7, 1926
Baltimore, Maryland

Howard Van Doren Shaw was the preferred architect of Chicago's commercial and industrial elite. The Ryersons, the Swifts, and the Donnelleys all turned to him to design their substantial homes. According to his biographer Thomas Tallmadge, Shaw was "probably the most highly regarded architect in the sphere of domestic, ecclesiastical, and non-commercial architecture in the Middle West."

A Midwesterner taught at Ivy League schools, Howard Van Doren Shaw belonged to the privileged class. He attended the Harvard School, a private prep school in Chicago and, in 1890, graduated from Yale University. Three years later he received his degree from the Massachusetts Institute of Technology. Shaw then traveled extensively in Europe. Shaw returned to Chicago and apprenticed under William Le Baron Jenney, the designer of the world's first skyscraper. After a year or two, Shaw set up his own practice in the attic of his father's home on South Calumet Avenue. In 1895 he moved into an office downtown.

Shaw's architecture was not midwestern in the sense that the Prairie school style of Frank Lloyd Wright was midwestern. Rather the eclectic Shaw borrowed freely from a variety of sources and was greatly influenced, in particular, by the English arts and crafts movement of the nineteenth century. Many of his private homes feature that movement's characteristic high-gabled and half-timbered look. Although he preferred English-based designs, Shaw also adopted French and Italian elements when it suited his purpose.

Shaw was a zealous worker. His wife noted that "he wished to do every detail himself." Even when he was at his most successful, his staff never consisted of more than twenty members. Shaw moved to north suburban Lake Forest in 1897 and designed homes along the North Shore for Chicago's wealthy industrial and commercial elite, who desired suburban retreats far removed from the bustle of the city and who, like Shaw, admired the classicism of European architecture. Shaw's greatest achievement was Market Square, the architectural showpiece of Lake Forest, often called the first planned suburban shopping center in America. Constructed between 1912 and 1916, Market Square consisted of a group of two-story buildings surrounding a square that "invoked the setting of a Tudor market town with elements borrowed from Flanders and northern Germany of the fifteenth and sixteenth centuries," notes historian Michael H. Ebner.

Shaw was made a fellow of the American Institute of Architects in 1907. In 1926 the federal government appointed him a member of a small architectural committee to design and build war memorials in Europe—a memorial chapel at Flanders Field in Belgium, and a naval war monument at Brest, France. In the same year, Shaw received the Gold Medal of the American Institute of Architects.

Among his most important commercial works are the Second Presbyterian Church at 1936 South Michigan Avenue, which he remodeled extensively in 1901 after a fire gutted the building the previous year; the Lakeside Press Building at 731 South Plymouth Court (1897), his first non-residential design; the Mentor Building at the corner of Monroe and State streets (1906); the now demolished Nyberg Automobile Works, 2435–37 South Michigan Avenue (1907), the heart of what was then "Automobile Row"; the R. R. Donnelley and Sons Company building at 350 East 22nd Street (1912); the Fourth Presbyterian Church at 125 East Chestnut Street (1912); the Quadrangle Club at the University of Chicago (1921); Marktown (1917), a planned industrial community designed as an English-style village in East Chicago, Indiana; and the original location of the Goodman Theatre (1925), his last work. In addition to many large single-family homes in the Hyde Park and Kenwood neighborhoods, Shaw also designed a number of high-rises, including the nine-story 1130 North Lake Shore Drive building (1910), the first luxury apartment building in the city constructed in the Tudor style. Shaw was the designer and one of the owners as well as a resident.

Ragdale, Shaw's Lake Forest estate completed in 1898, is a writer's retreat today and the only artists' colony in the Midwest that operates throughout the year. Shaw borrowed the name from a Tudor house that he had seen one summer in England. It suggested, he thought, a kind of "cultivated shabbiness."

Shaw died in 1926 in a sanitarium in Baltimore of pernicious anemia on his fifty-seventh birthday. He was buried in Graceland Cemetery.

See also: Daniel H. Burnham, R. R. Donnelley, William Le Baron Jenney, John Wellborn Root, Frank Lloyd Wright

Further reading: Jean F. Block, *Hyde Park Houses: An Informal History, 1856–1910* (1978); Carl W. Condit, *The Chicago School of Architecture: A History of Commercial and Public Building in the Chicago Area, 1875–1925* (1964); Susan Dart, *Evelyn Shaw McCutcheon and Ragdale* (1980); Leonard K. Eaton, *Two Chicago Architects and Their Clients: Frank Lloyd Wright and Howard Van Doren Shaw* (1969); Michael H. Ebner, *Creating Chicago's North Shore: A Suburban History* (1988); Alice Hayes and Susan Moon, *Ragdale: A History and Guide* (1990); Pauline A. Saliga, ed., *The Sky's the Limit: A Century of Chicago Skyscrapers* (1990).

John G. Shedd

Entrepreneur and Philanthropist

BORN: July 20, 1850
Alstead, New Hampshire

DIED: October 22, 1926
Chicago, Illinois

Financier, merchant, and philanthropist, John Graves Shedd was the millionaire Chairman of the Board of Marshall Field and Company. During his term as president, over 19,000 men and women were in his employ, prompting him to boast that "the sun never sets on Marshall Field's." Despite his importance in the business world, Shedd is best known today as the man who financed the great aquarium that bears his name.

Born on a farm in New Hampshire, John Shedd was the youngest son of a family of eight. When not quite seventeen, the ambitious lad announced he was "going to find something better than farming." Poorly educated by today's standards—his entire schooling consisted of nothing more than attending country schools "off and on during winters"—Shedd found work at several grocery and dry goods stores in Vermont and New Hampshire.

Feeling restrained by small-town life, Shedd decided to start over again in the West. He arrived in Chicago after the great fire of 1871, determined to work for "the biggest store in town." Within a year he was offered a job as a $10-a-week stockroom clerk at Field and Leiter's store. The hardworking Shedd caught Marshall Field's attention. He rose quickly through the ranks from stockboy to salesman to department head to merchandise manager. In 1893 he was made a partner, and finally, in 1901, a vice president. When Field died in 1906, Shedd succeeded him as president.

Shedd celebrated his success by moving from his brick home in the South Lawndale neighborhood to a newly built twenty-two room Gothic mansion at 4515 South Drexel Boulevard in Kenwood, one of Chicago's most fashionable neighborhoods during the 1890s. Throughout his life Shedd stressed character building as the road to a long and successful career. At the dedication of the YMCA Hotel, Shedd said:

"Anything that stands for right living and right thinking—for purity and truth—is just as necessary to the development of character in the young as sunlight and pure air are to the development of plant life. In building character, I place plain straightforward truthfulness first." Like fellow businessman Julius Rosenwald, Shedd gave generously to various causes and groups. Among his gifts were $125,000 to the YMCA, $50,000 to the Art Institute, and $50,000 to the YWCA.

In 1922 Shedd retired from the presidency of Field's to become chairman of the board of directors. Even so, he maintained a full and busy schedule. For many years, the South Park Board had contemplated building an aquarium that would add significantly to Chicago's stature as a world-class city. Shedd made an offer to assist in its financing during a meeting at the architectural offices of Graham, Anderson, Probst, and White in 1924. As a gift to the city of Chicago, Shedd donated $3 million to the board for the construction of an aquarium in Grant Park, to be located just east of the Field Museum. Construction began in the autumn of 1927. The doors opened to the public on June 1, 1930.

Unfortunately, Shedd didn't live long enough to see the aquarium that bears his name. He died in 1926 due to complications from appendicitis at the age of seventy-six.

On April 27, 1991, a new $43 million oceanarium opened at the Shedd Aquarium. The oceanarium was the first addition to the aquarium since it opened in 1930. The 170,000-square-foot pavilion recreates a Pacific Northwest rain forest and houses aquatic mammals and birds, including beluga whales, white-sided dolphins, seals, sea otters, and penguins.

See also: Marshall Field, Potter Palmer, Julius Rosenwald
Further reading: Lloyd Wendt and Herman Kogan, *Give the Lady What She Wants! The Story of Marshall Field and Co.* (1952).

Philip Sheridan

Army General

BORN: March 6, 1831
Albany, New York

DIED: August 5, 1888
Nonquitt, Massachusetts

Philip Henry Sheridan, for whom Sheridan Road and Fort Sheridan are named, was one of the most competent generals in the Civil War, respected by both northern and southern forces. A great tactician, he was also a great leader of men and earned a reputation as the Union army's best cavalry soldier.

The third of six children of John and Mary Sheridan, Irish immigrants from County Cavan, Philip Sheridan grew up in Somerset, Ohio. As a teenager he found employment in a country store. In 1848, he entered West Point. His graduation was delayed until 1853 due to an altercation with a cadet officer whom the hotheaded Sheridan attempted to attack with a bayonet.

Sheridan earned a reputation as a brave and fearless leader in battle, known to rout the enemy when other, less daring commanders would choose to stand back. His courageous—some would say foolhardy—derring-do won the

admiration of no less than the laconic General Ulysses S. Grant. "No man ever had such a faculty of finding things out as Sheridan," wrote Grant. So impressed was the general that he made Sheridan commander of the cavalry of the Army of the Potomac during the Civil War.

Sheridan was involved in several key Civil War battles, including Chickamauga, Chattanooga, Wilderness, and Spotsylvania Courthouse, and he participated in the Richmond raid against General J. E. B. Stuart. In 1864 he was placed in command of the Union army at Shenandoah. On the morning of October 19, he heard the roar of cannon fire and turned a near disaster into victory when he rallied his confused troops and successfully routed the army of General Jubal A. Early. Sheridan's famous ride from Winchester to Cedar Creek, Virginia, resulted in his promotion to major general of the regular army.

After the war, Sheridan was appointed as military governor of Louisiana and Texas. In the winter of 1868–69, he participated in raids against the Cheyenne Indians. He then spent a year in Europe during the Franco-Prussian War, and returned to the United States in 1871 to settle in Chicago, where he was placed in charge of army headquarters. As founder and first president of the Washington Park Club, which opened in 1884 at 61st Street and South Park Avenue, Sheridan cut a dashing figure on the city's social scene. Not only was he a fine dancer, according to contemporary newspaper accounts, but his charm was especially popular with the ladies.

Soon after Sheridan's arrival in 1871, the Chicago Fire erupted. Reacting quickly, Sheridan ordered buildings on South Wabash Avenue near Congress Street blown up to check the fire from spreading further south—a tactic that saved lives and property. The city was placed under martial law and federal troops were brought in to preserve order.

Sheridan dispatched to Mayor Roswell B. Mason this optimistic report: "I am happy to state that no case of outbreak of disorder has been reported. No authenticated case of incendiarism has reached me and the people of the city are calm, quiet and well-disposed."

In 1884 Sheridan succeeded General William T. Sherman as commander in chief of the army, and in 1888 Congress granted him the rank of full general. In May 1886, the city's business community became alarmed when violence erupted during the tragic Haymarket Affair. The Commercial Club of Chicago and the Board of Trade pledged to sell the 600-acre tract of land along the Lake Michigan shoreline nearly thirty miles north of the city for $10 if the government agreed to construct a fort on the site. On March 3, 1887, the government consented. One year later General Sheridan visited the site, then called Fort Highwood. When Sheridan died in 1888, the fort was renamed in his honor.

Sheridan died in Nonquitt, Massachusetts, in August 1888 at age fifty-seven, three days after completing his memoirs.

On July 16, 1924, General Sheridan's daughter, Mary Sheridan, unveiled a bronze statue of her father at the intersection of Belmont Avenue and Sheridan Road as an estimated 100,000 people looked on. The piece, designed by the noted Belgian sculptor Gutzon Borglum, captured the general in a characteristically energetic pose—mounted on a horse and ready for battle as he rode through the Shenandoah Valley.

See also: Elmer E. Ellsworth, James Mulligan

Further reading: Michael H. Ebner, *Creating Chicago's North Shore: A Suburban History* (1988); Richard O'Connor, *Sheridan the Inevitable* (1953).

Paul Sills

Director

BORN: November 18, 1927
Chicago, Illinois

DIED: June 2, 2008
Baileys Harbor, Wisconsin

Paul Sills was the founding father of improvisational theater and, hence, the unofficial creator of the Second City, *SCTV, Saturday Night Live, 30 Rock,* and other television shows that either directly or indirectly demonstrate his influence. The Second City has been described as a comedy farm, a comedic finishing school, and, said George Wendt, the "Harvard of humor." Sills was the unsung hero of the Second City and he preferred it that way, feeling much more comfortable behind the scenes than on the stage.

Sills was born Paul Silverberg in Chicago on November 18, 1927. His mother, Viola Spolin, was a drama teacher for the Chicago branch of the Works Progress Administration's Recreational Project. Spolin developed a series of theater games as a way to foster creative expression. When his parents separated, he and his mother moved to California in 1943, but Sills returned to Chicago to finish high school. After graduating he joined both the merchant marine and the army and then enrolled at the University of

Chicago. He began directing at venues such as the Playwrights Theater Club. In 1955 he and fellow classmate David Shepherd created the Compass Players.

The short-lived Compass is credited as being the first theater company to use improvisational techniques to create live theater. The format is now a familiar one—newsy, sketch-comedy routines performed by actors who had to be fast on their feet as well as agile of mind—but at the time it was revolutionary. The Compass ensemble featured figures that would later become household names, such as the then husband-and-wife team of Mike Nichols and Elaine May, and Barbara Harris. After the Compass collapsed, Sills, along with Bernard Sahlins and Howard Alk, dusted it off to try again. This time they came up with the idea of the Second City (Nichols and May chose to decamp to Broadway).

The Second City opened on December 16, 1959. Its first home was located in a storefront at 1842 North Wells Street that was once a Chinese laundry, Wong Cleaners. It then moved to its now-familiar space at 1616 North Wells Street in 1967. The Second City presented a cabaret-style revue of topical sketches that was acerbic, witty, and entertaining. In addition to Alk, the first cast consisted of Eugene Troobnick, Severn Darden, Mina Kolb, Barbara Harris, Roger Bowen, and Andrew Duncan. Essentially they were a bunch of misfits and outsiders from the University of Chicago.

Opening night could hardly have been less encouraging. It consisted of an audience of barely one hundred people. The only props were bentwood chairs. But as word of mouth grew and the public became accustomed to this new brand of comedy, its popularity blossomed. When the Second City started American comedy consisted largely of stand-up comics. The Second City, on the other hand, emphasized ensemble work, improvisation, and sketches instead of jokes. It was subtly intellectual rather than broadly slapstick. To be a successful part of the Second City ensemble the performers had to trust their fellow performers to make one another look good. It was collaborative in the best and broadest sense of the word. The Second City, in other words, changed the comedy landscape in the United States forever.

Second City shows are tightly scripted. Co-founder Bernard Sahlins told Chicago Tribune theater critic Chris Jones, "We use improv as a tool, not a performance form. Material rises out of improvisation, but it has been written, tried out and tested before it goes into the show as a finished piece. The improvisation is basically public rehearsals."

Essentially, the Second City hired young (read: cheap), smart, and funny men and women, then held on to them for a relatively short period of time (say, two to three years)

before encouraging them to see for themselves what they could do in the broader comedy world. Significantly, though, the Second City retained control of the material created on the stage. It was a comedy theater but also an education, a comedy university.

And Sills provided the foundation. He developed and expanded his mother's techniques to create what he called story theater, where a character steps out of the story to serve as a third-person narrator. His writing and workshops influenced everything from Broadway shows to the early plays of David Mamet (he once swept the floors there), to the theatrical adaptations by the Chicago theater companies Lookingglass and the Chicago Shakespeare Theater, to such earlier companies as the Organic and Body Politic.

Further, Sills wielded a considerable influence over the development of American comedy in the twentieth century. Playwright Jeffrey Sweet called Sills "the Orson Welles of improv." Such contemporary comedies as Larry David's Curb Your Enthusiasm employ a Second City sensibility. Even David's co-stars, Jeff Garlin and Shelley Berman, came out of the Second City. Today the Second City boasts $30 million in annual revenue.

But Sills had moved on. In the 1970s, he relocated to Door County, Wisconsin, where he worked as a writer and teacher, performing with local community theater groups while making occasional forays back to Chicago. In 1988, Sills, Mike Nichols, and George Morrison created the New Actors Workshop of New York; its productions were based on Sills's idea of story theater.

Sills died of complications from pneumonia at his home and studio in Baileys Harbor, Wisconsin. He was eighty years old.

In 2009 the Second City celebrated its fiftieth anniversary with an SCTV reunion and a one-night only event of Second City alumni, as well as an entire weekend of improv shows, panel discussions, performances, and documentaries. In December 2009, Second City CEO Andrew Alexander announced plans to build a new venue for the Second City a few hundred yards from its original location.

See also: John Belushi, Del Close, Viola Spolin

Further reading: Janet Coleman, The Compass: The Improvisational Theatre That Revolutionized American Comedy (1991); Chris Jones, "50 Years of Constant Funny," Chicago Tribune, December 6, 2009; Sheldon Patinkin, The Second City: Backstage at the World's Greatest Comedy Theater (2000); Bernard Sahlins, Days and Nights at the Second City: A Memoir, with Notes on Staging Review Theatre (2001); Jeffrey Sweet, Something Wonderful Right Away (1986); Mike Thomas, The Second City Unscripted: Revolution and Revelation at the World-Famous Comedy Theater (2009).

Shel Silverstein

Poet, Songwriter, and Cartoonist

BORN: September 25, 1930
Chicago, Illinois

DIED: May 10, 1999
Key West, Florida

Shel Silverstein wore many hats during his long career: poet, singer-songwriter, musician, composer, cartoonist, screenwriter, and author of children's books. Translated into twenty languages, his books have sold more than 20 million copies. But to the general public, he is perhaps best known as the man who wrote Johnny Cash's uncharacteristically goofy hit, "A Boy Named Sue."

Sheldon Allan Silverstein was born in Chicago and grew up in the Logan Square neighborhood. Inspired by the cartoons of Al Capp, he began drawing at the age of twelve. After graduating from Roosevelt High School, he attended the University of Illinois at Chicago, the Chicago Academy of Fine Arts, and, finally, Roosevelt University. His work was first published in Roosevelt's student newspaper, the *Roosevelt Torch*. In 1953, he was drafted into the army and served overseas in Japan and Korea. It was then that he began drawing cartoons for the *Stars and Stripes* military publication. When he returned to the United States, he began submitting his cartoons—in between gigs selling hot dogs at Chicago sports venues—to various magazines, including *Look* and *Sports Illustrated*. In 1957 he began contributing his cartoons to the Chicago-based *Playboy* magazine; he would continue his association with *Playboy* through the mid-1970s.

Despite his success as a cartoonist, Silverstein met even greater acclaim as a children's author and illustrator. In 1963 he published his first children's book, *Uncle Shelby's Story of Lafcadio, the Lion Who Shot Back*. It was only a modest success. He had better luck, though, with a subsequent effort, *The Giving Tree* (1964), which, through word of mouth, eventually sold millions and became a children's classic.

Silverstein's first collection of poems, *Where the Sidewalk Ends: The Poems and Drawings of Shel Silverstein,* was published in 1974 and became an instant best seller. It was followed by *A Light in the Attic* in 1981 and *Falling Up* in 1996; both ostensibly children's poetry but with an adult mindset. Although often compared to Dr. Seuss, A. A. Milne, and Edward Lear, Silverstein was uniquely himself. Laid-back and conversational in style, his work contained elements of silliness with a touch of sophistication, especially evident in his use of imaginative word play along with an ample display of equal parts irreverence, wit, and whimsy.

Perhaps his most surprising success was in songwriting, for in addition to drawing cartoons and writing children's books, he also wrote songs, often in the country and western genre. In 1969, the Man in Black himself, Johnny Cash, had a huge hit with Silverstein's tongue-in-cheek "A Boy Named Sue." But Silverstein wrote for, or had hits by, other musicians, too, including the quirky "The Cover of the Rolling Stone" and "Sylvia's Mother," both for Dr. Hook & the Medicine Show; as well as the novelty "Unicorn Song," a huge hit for the Irish Rovers in 1967, an adaptation of Silverstein's poem that appears in *Where the Sidewalk Ends*. He also wrote songs for Loretta Lynn, Bobby Bare, Mel Tillis, Jerry Reed, and Waylon Jennings. In 1984, he won a Grammy Award for Best Children's Album for *Where the Sidewalk Ends*. In addition, he wrote "I'm Checking Out" for the film *Postcards from the Edge* starring Meryl Streep, which was nominated for an Academy Award in 1991.

Silverstein also wrote nine plays. In 1988 several of his plays were adapted into *Wild Life* and produced at the Vanguard Theater in New York. In 2001, a number of his short sketches were produced as *An Adult Evening with Shel Silverstein* at the Atlantic Theater Company, also in New York.

His other books include *Take Ten* (1955); *Grab Your Socks!* (1956); *Now Here's My Plan: A Book of Futilities* (1960), his first collection of cartoons that appeared in American magazines; *Uncle Shelby's ABZ Book* (1961), his first book of original material for adults; *A Giraffe and a Half* (1964); *The Missing Piece* (1976); *Different Dances* (1979); *Draw a Skinny Elephant* (1998); *Runny Babbit* (2005); and *Don't Bump the Glump! And Other Fantasies* (2008).

His recordings include *Hairy Jazz* (1959); *Inside Folk Songs* (1962); *I'm So Good that I Don't Have to Brag* (1965); *A Boy Named Sue and Other Country Songs* (1969); the soundtrack to the Dustin Hoffman film *Who Is Harry Kellerman and Why Is He Saying Those Terrible Things about Me?* (1971); *Freakin' at the Freakers Ball* (1972); *Songs & Stories* (1978); *The Great Conch Train Robbery* (1980); with Pat Dailey, *Underwater Land* (2002); and *The Best of Shel Silverstein: His Words His Songs His Friends* (2005).

In 2007, *Playboy's Silverstein Around the World*, a collection of his illustrated travel essays that originally appeared in *Playboy*, was published. In 2010, Sugar Hill Records released *Twistable, Turnable Man: A Musical Tribute to the Songs of Shel Silverstein,* featuring interpretations of Silverstein songs by John Prine, Kris Kristofferson, Lucinda Williams, Nanci Griffith, Andrew Bird, and My Morning Jacket, among others. And in 2011, HarperCollins released *Every Thing On It: Poems and Drawings,* which contained more than 130 of Silverstein's previously unpublished poems and illustrations.

Silverstein died in 1999 in his Key West home of a heart attack. He is buried at Westlawn Cemetery in Norridge, Illinois.

Further reading: Lisa Rogak, *A Boy Named Shel: The Life and Times of Shel Silverstein* (2007).

Gene Siskel

Movie Critic

BORN: January 26, 1946
Chicago, Illinois

DIED: February 20, 1999
Evanston, Illinois

With his television partner and fellow critic Roger Ebert, Gene Siskel cohosted the popular and long-running syndicated television program *At the Movies.* He was also the film critic of the *Chicago Tribune.* Siskel and Ebert's influence on the moviegoing public and the movie industry was considerable and long lasting. Their opinions could make the difference between the success or failure of a film. *Spy Magazine* declared the two men the country's most influential film critics; they also made *Entertainment Weekly*'s "Most Powerful People in Hollywood" lists, even though they chose to remain removed from the West Coast.

Born in Chicago in 1946, Eugene Kal Siskel was raised by his aunt and uncle in in the North Shore suburb of Glencoe, Illinois, after both parents died when he was nine. He had a love of cinema from an early age. The Nortown Theatre on the Far North Side was his favorite movie theater when he was growing up. Two films in particular, *A Star Is Born* and *A Streetcar Named Desire,* made significant impressions on him.

Siskel attended Culver Military Academy, an independent college preparatory boarding school in Culver, Indiana. He then enrolled at Yale, graduating with a major in philosophy in 1967 (the late Chicago television sportscaster Tim Weigel was his roommate). After college he joined the Army Reserve, where he was assigned to the U.S. Department of Defense Information School and wrote press releases. His contacts at Yale—he studied under author John Hersey—helped get him a job at the *Chicago Tribune* in 1969 as a neighborhood reporter. A few months after his arrival, the *Tribune's* film critic Cliff Terry took a yearlong sabbatical to attend Harvard University. Seeing an opportunity, Siskel wrote a memo to the paper's Sunday editor explaining why he would be the right candidate to replace Terry. The young reporter made the persuasive case that the popularity of such seminal 1970s film directors as Francis Ford Coppola, Martin Scorsese, Robert Altman, Steven Spielberg, and George Lucas indicated that the mainstream daily press should take the movies seriously and hire a full-time film critic. The next day the editor asked Siskel to come in for an interview and shortly thereafter he was offered the job.

In 1974 Siskel began providing movie reviews and features for WBBM-TV, the CBS affiliate in Chicago. Over at WTTW, the PBS affiliate, producer Eliot Wald came up with the idea to team Siskel up with Roger Ebert, the film critic of the rival *Chicago Sun-Times,* to host a local film program, *Opening Soon at a Theater Near You.* The two men reluctantly agreed to the experiment, but before long they developed a natural on-air chemistry with each other. As the show grew in sophistication, so did its audience. Eventually it evolved into *Sneak Previews,* which gained national attention when PBS started broadcasting it in 1978.

Three years later Siskel and Ebert left PBS and signed a contract with Tribune Entertainment, the parent company of the *Chicago Tribune* and WGN-TV. *At the Movies* went into national syndication in 1982. In 1986 they left Tribune Entertainment to move to Disney's Buena Vista Television. The show was renamed *Siskel & Ebert at the Movies* and then simply *Siskel & Ebert.* After Siskel jumped ship to the Disney channel, *Tribune* editor Jim Squires made the unpopular decision to relieve Siskel of his duties as chief film critic, essentially demoting him to the role of syndicated movie columnist and author of the weekly "Flick Picks" as well as the annual "Beat Siskel" Oscar contest. From 1987 to 1992, Siskel was a correspondent for *CBS This Morning* and from 1996 to 1999 for *Good Morning America.* He also wrote for numerous publications, including *Sports Illustrated* and *TV Guide.*

In May 1998 Siskel had surgery to remove a cancerous growth from his brain. He had returned to work shortly after the surgery before taking some time off to recuperate. In February 1999, he died from complications. He was only fifty-three. He was buried in Westlawn Cemetery in Chicago.

On the tenth anniversary of his death, Ebert commented on the special on-air chemistry that they had. "We just had it, because from the day the *Chicago Tribune* made Gene its film critic, we were professional enemies."

Siskel was inducted into the Chicago Journalism Hall of Fame in 1997 and in 2001 into the Illinois Broadcasters Hall of Fame. Following his death, the Film Center of the School of the Art Institute changed its name to the Gene Siskel Film Center.

Other resources: Roger Ebert, "Remembering Gene," Roger Ebert's Journal web site, www.rogerebert.com.

John M. Smyth

Merchant and Politician

BORN: July 5, 1843
Off Newfoundland

DIED: November 4, 1909
Chicago, Illinois

Pioneer Chicago furniture dealer John M. Smyth was one of the city's most influential businessmen. Retail stores selling furniture made by the company that he founded in 1867 were a familiar sight on Chicago streets for many decades.

Born at sea off the shore of Newfoundland in 1843, Smyth came to Chicago with his parents, Irish immigrants Michael and Bridget, in 1848 after having originally settled in Montreal. At thirteen Smyth found work at a printing office to help support his recently widowed mother and sibling. He held other jobs too—news carrier, clerk, and advertising salesman for several Chicago newspapers. Using $250 of his savings, Smyth formed a partnership with Thomas Mitchell and, in 1867, opened a small furniture store at 92 West Madison Street. Within a year he bought Mitchell out.

The first Smyth furniture store was a modest effort. A mere secondhand shop, it nevertheless upheld policies that were, for that time, revolutionary. For one thing, Smyth generously offered credit to newlyweds and to all those who had lost everything in the Chicago Fire. A rapid population growth, access to raw materials, and an increased demand for comfortable domestic furniture helped to make Chicago the furniture capital of the United States by the turn of the century. In 1895, notes historian Sharon Darling, there were 276 furniture manufacturing companies in the city that employed over 28,000 workers. Taking advantage of Chicago's booming market, Smyth was able to move to larger headquarters at 12 North Michigan Avenue in 1889. Unfortunately, that building suffered a ruinous fire in April 1891. Seven months later, he was ready to start over again, erecting an eight-story building on the same site.

Smyth was also actively involved in local politics. A lifelong Republican, he served as a Chicago alderman from 1878 to 1882. He managed various political campaigns on the county and national levels. In 1892 Mayor Hempstead Washburne appointed him to the library board, but he resigned three years later. He was chairman of the Republican County Central Committee for several years, and he was considered by many to be an exemplary mayoral candidate. Smyth, although flattered, declined to run for mayor.

Smyth succumbed to pneumonia in Chicago at the age of sixty-six in November 1909.

In 1983 the John M. Smyth Company closed seven of its furniture stores due to escalating operating costs. Other retailers that specialized in furniture and furniture-related accessories, such as Colby's and Pier I Imports, helped fill the void.

The corporate offices of John M. Smyth Company—and its chain of Homemakers outlets—was located at 1013 Butterfield Road in Downers Grove, Illinois, until the company declared bankruptcy in 2005.

Further reading: Sharon Darling, *Chicago Furniture Art, Craft, & Industry 1833–1983* (1984).

Georg Solti

Conductor

BORN: October 21, 1912
Budapest, Hungary

DIED: September 5, 1997
Antibes, France

The Grammy-award winning Georg Solti was one of the most successful and highly respected conductors of the twentieth century.

Born Gyorgy Stern in Budapest to a Jewish family, Georg Solti was the son of Móricz Stern and Teréz Rosenbaum. His father later changed the name from Stern to Solti to avoid any threat of antisemitism (Solti's cousin is the painter and photographer, László Moholy-Nagy). Solti studied piano and composition with Ernst von Dohnanyi, Zoltan Kodaly, Béla Bartók, and Leó Weiner at the Franz Liszt Academy in his native Budapest. He gave his first concert at the age of twelve. Six years later he became an assistant at the Budapest Opera. During the summers of 1936 and 1937 he was an assistant to Arturo Toscanini at the prestigious Salzburg Festival.

Solti made his debut as a conductor at the Budapest Opera on March 11, 1938, with Mozart's *The Marriage of Figaro*. But that was also the day when Hitler annexed Austria to the Third Reich. Subsequently, Solti's status as a Jew proved to be untenable in his native Hungary, especially under the oppressive regime of Miklos Horthy. So, when World War II broke out, he immigrated to Zurich, Switzerland, where he resumed his career as a pianist, even winning the Geneva International Piano Competition.

After the war, though, Solti went back to conducting operas. He was chief musical director of the Munich Opera from 1947 to 1951 and of the Frankfurt Opera from 1952

to 1961. He was also musical director of the Royal Opera House in London's Covent Garden from 1961 to 1971. In 1960 he signed a three-year contract to be music director of the Los Angeles Philharmonic but, unbeknownst to him, management had appointed Zubin Mehta as assistant conductor. Consequently, he resigned without actually taking the post. In 1969 he assumed his best-known position, that of director of the Chicago Symphony Orchestra (CSO), where he remained until 1991. In addition to his CSO responsibilities, he also was director of the Orchestre de Paris from 1972 to 1975, and from 1979 to 1983 director of the London Philharmonic Orchestra. From 1992 to 1994, Solti was artistic director of the Salzburg Easter

Festival. In 1983 he conducted Richard Wagner's Ring Cycle at Bayreuth. For the fiftieth anniversary of the United Nations, he formed the World Orchestra for Peace.

Solti died suddenly of a heart attack on September 5, 1997, in Antibes, France. His *Memoirs,* cowritten with Harvey Sachs, were published a month after his death. In September 2007, a tribute recording of his last concert was released on the Decca label.

See also: Margaret Hillis

Albert G. Spalding

*Baseball Player
and Manager*

BORN: September 2, 1850
Byron, Illinois

DIED: September 9, 1915
Point Loma, California

As one of its founding fathers, Albert Goodwill Spalding contributed greatly to the rise of baseball as an American institution, and more importantly, notes historian Peter Levine, "as respectable entertainment for the urban middle class." Spalding cofounded the National League, managed and owned the Chicago White Stockings (which later became the Chicago Cubs), and founded a successful sporting goods business that still bears his name. Sports, he said, built character. It was Spalding who molded baseball into the game we know today.

Born to Harriet and James Spalding in 1850 in the farming town of Byron, Illinois, Albert Spalding's happy family life was shattered when his father died at forty-six. His mother sent her grieving son to school in the neighboring town of Rockford. There, miserable and lonely, young Spalding fell in love with the game of baseball. Baseball instilled in the forlorn youth a confidence and self-assurance that he had never experienced before.

In 1865 members of Rockford's business community asked Spalding to join their new baseball club, the Forest Citys, as a pitcher. The new team played in various regional tournaments, including one held against the highly respected Washington Nationals, then billed as the best team in the country. In one of the great moments of the young athlete's life, Spalding's team edged the mighty Nationals 29-23. Impressed by the victory and by Spalding's pitching arm, the Chicago Excelsiors asked him to join their team. He accepted the offer and moved to Chicago in September 1867.

In 1871 Spalding signed with the Boston Red Stockings. He led his team to a second-place finish that year and to four consecutive league championships from 1872 to 1875. Spalding became a local hero. In the summer of 1875, the president of the Chicago White Stockings, William A. Hulbert, persuaded Spalding to return to the Midwest and signed him to the team as captain, manager, and pitcher; Spalding started playing for the White Stockings the following season. It was a fortuitous event both for Spalding and for the team because he managed to turn the White Stockings into the sport's most successful club, and at the same time he transformed what once was a lowly sport into a respectable pastime for all of middle-class America. He was instrumental, with Hulbert, in establishing a new professional league, the National League of Professional Baseball Clubs, in 1876.

In their quest for middle-class respectability, managers like Spalding, Cap Anson, and Charles A. Comiskey went to great lengths to impress upon their players the importance of good moral behavior and used whatever means necessary—admonishments, fines, even dismissal—to curb their excesses. Spalding banned Sunday ball, for example, in order not to offend churchgoers, and he built comfortable and attractive ballparks throughout the city.

Spalding led the White Stockings all the way to the new league's pennant in its inaugural 1876 season. After the 1877 season, however, he retired from active play, serving instead as the team's secretary. When Hulbert died in 1882, Spalding became club president and owner. Under Spalding, the White Stockings grew in popularity. In 1895 the team played at the Congress Street Grounds on the West Side in "an attractive middle-class neighborhood," writes historian Steven A. Reiss in *City Games*. In 1891 Spalding moved the team to the 35th Street Grounds and several years later to the West Side Park near 12th (now Roosevelt Road) and Taylor Streets.

Spalding's White Stockings dominated baseball for the next decade, winning pennants in 1882, 1885, and 1886. Leading the team to victory after victory was first baseman Cap Anson. Other outstanding athletes during those golden years included third baseman Ned Williamson, shortstop Tommy Burns, second baseman Fred Pfeffer, catcher Frank Flint, and the great right fielder Mike "King" Kelly. Yet baseball players, observes Reiss, still had "little social prestige—baseball players were placed on the same unfavorable social level as actors and prize fighters." It wasn't until after the turn of the century, when club owners began to charge higher admission prices and increase players' salaries, that the game began to attract an appreciable middle-class clientele. Further, the growth of cities created an interest in recreational activity. Spalding and others tapped into this growing segment of the population. The rise in mass transit also allowed increased access to public sporting events, so by 1920 baseball, for these and other reasons, had become the national pastime.

Meanwhile, capitalizing on his reputation and good name and clearly sensing the palpable interest that the sport was creating across the country, Spalding opened a sporting goods store in Chicago in 1876. In addition to the usual bats and balls, Spalding provided a full line of sporting goods equipment. Business boomed. In the 1880s Spalding published the National League's annual official play book, *Spalding's Official Baseball Guide,* and in 1892 he formed a separate division within the sporting goods firm, the American Sport Publishing Company. Always looking for additional ways to advertise his wares, he provided the National League teams with baseballs—all bearing, of course, the Spalding insignia. In order to cash in on the bicycle craze then sweeping the country, Spalding began, in 1894, to manufacture his own line of bicycles. In addition, he organized baseball tours around the world.

In September 1915, Spalding suffered a minor stroke. Shortly thereafter he succumbed to another more devastating attack and died at the age of sixty-five.

Baseball, Spalding declared, served as a good training ground for life beyond the diamond. Spalding not only shaped the leisure activities of America in the late nineteenth century, he also, concludes historian Levine, helped turn—through his roles as athlete, manager, publisher, and promoter—a simple sandlot game into a national sport and a much beloved national pastime.

In 1939 the Baseball Hall of Fame inducted Spalding posthumously into its membership.

Although Spalding is credited with declaring that baseball was strictly American in origin—invented by Abner Doubleday in 1839—such contemporary scholars as Beth Hise disagree. Hise, co-curator of the exhibit "Swinging Away: How Cricket and Baseball Connect," contends that baseball originated in England during the first decades of the eighteenth century, perhaps even earlier, and was brought over by English immigrants to the New World in the nineteenth century.

See also: Cap Anson, Charles A. Comiskey

Further reading: Arthur Charles Bartlett, *Baseball and Mr. Spalding* (1951); John F. Burns, "A Playing Field of England Celebrates Two Games," *New York Times,* July 15, 2010; Sam Coombs and Bob West, eds., *America's National Game* (1991); Beth Hise, *Swinging Away: How Cricket and Baseball Connect* (2010); Peter Levine, *A. G. Spalding and the Rise of Baseball: The Promise of American Sport* (1985); Larry D. Names, *Bury My Heart at Wrigley Field: The History of the Chicago Cubs—When the Cubs Were the White Sox* (1990); Steven A. Reiss, *City Games: The Evolution of American Urban Society and the Rise of Sports* (1989).

George K. Spoor

Filmmaker

BORN: December 18, 1871
Highland Park, Illinois

DIED: November 24, 1953
Chicago, Illinois

Gilbert M. "Broncho Billy" Anderson

Actor and Director

BORN: March 21, 1880
Little Rock, Arkansas

DIED: January 20, 1971
Woodland Hills, California

In early 1907, film producer George K. Spoor and actor and director Gilbert M. Anderson, better known as "Broncho Billy," established a movie studio that they called Essanay (the name was taken from the initials of each man's surname), a 72,000-square-foot studio in the Uptown neighborhood. It was the beginning of a short-lived era in Chicago history. From 1907 to 1917 Chicago was the film capital of the world.

During the early years of the twentieth century, Chicago flourished as a center for motion picture production, fueled in part by the countless nickelodeon theaters that opened throughout the city. The operators of these venues charged 5 cents and usually operated out of storefronts. Typically the action on the screen was accompanied by a piano player who played the popular tunes of the day.

In 1895, George Kirke Spoor was a Chicago newspaper vendor who owned and operated a stand at the Chicago and Northwestern station at Kinzie Avenue and Wells Street—but he was also the box office manager at the Waukegan Opera House in the northern suburb. Along with Edward Amet, Spoor developed an early movie projector called the Magniscope. His partner, Amet, though, didn't think there was much of a future in motion pictures and sold his interest in the invention exclusively to Spoor. Spoor then established the National Film Renting Company with offices at 62 North Clark Street. The company distributed projectors and films to motion picture theaters nationwide. (Two of Spoor's employees, Donald Bell and Albert Howell, would later start their own movie projector company, Bell & Howell.)

Anderson was born Max Aronson in Arkansas. He got his start in vaudeville and, in 1903, appeared in Edwin S. Porter's seminal *The Great Train Robbery*, considered the first narrative movie. Anderson moved to Chicago and worked for a short time at the Selig Polyscope movie studio, producing, directing, and starring in a series of Westerns, which earned him the sobriquet of "Broncho Billy." By 1907, though, Anderson was ready for a move. He left Selig to join Spoor at Essanay. Initially, Anderson and Spoor formed the Peerless Film Manufacturing Company, but, in August 1907, they renamed it Essanay.

Anderson appeared, wrote, and directed in more than 300 short films for Essanay, but he was especially known for his Westerns: he was the movies' first cowboy star. While Spoor stayed in Chicago running the studio, Anderson was away on location. Many of the Essanay films were shot in the small Alameda County, California, town of Niles.

Despite Anderson's association with Westerns, Essanay concentrated largely on slapstick and other styles of comedy. The studio's first movie, a one-reel comedy called *An Awful Skate, or The Hobo on Rollers* (1907), starred the cross-eyed actor Ben Turpin. Increasingly, the studio went on location, either in Chicago itself or elsewhere. In 1908 Anderson directed *The James Boys in Missouri*, using Riverview Park and Scottdale, in Michigan, as settings. But, because of Chicago's bleak winters, most of the movies were shot out West. Essanay made a remarkable 2,000 movies, of which about 215 survive today. According to film historian David Kiehn, Essanay shot 1,500 films in Chicago and an additional 500 on the West Coast. Spoor and Anderson even opened a western branch in Niles Canyon, outside of Oakland. Many of the films burned in a studio vault fire in 1916; others were lost forever when Spoor sold the Uptown building in 1932.

Essanay attracted the biggest names in the fledgling motion picture industry. In addition to Ben Turpin, it featured films starring Gloria Swanson (who was born at 341 West Grace Street in the Lakeview neighborhood), Wallace Beery, and Francis X. Bushman, the reigning matinee idol of his day. But no one was bigger than a young Englishman by the name of Charlie Chaplin. Anderson lured Chaplin away from Mack Sennett's Keystone Studios to Essanay with a promise of $1,250 a week plus a signing bonus. Chaplin didn't spend much time in Chicago—it was too cold for his tastes, for one thing and it was too much of a backwater town to suit his towering ambition, for another. Instead, Chaplin longed for the world stage. When he did stay in Chicago, he spent some time either at a small hotel on Wabash Avenue or lodged with Anderson and his wife, Mollie, at their apartment at 1027 West Lawrence Avenue, a few blocks from the studio. But his presence did help put Essanay on the map. When his contract came up for renewal, Chaplin demanded the princely sum of $10,000 a week. Spoor refused, and Chaplin bolted to the Mutual Film studio when they offered him a better deal.

During its heyday, Essanay's Uptown complex housed three studios, a carpentry shop, prop and wardrobe storage, a film processing room, a publicity department, and dressing rooms. Its screenwriters included Ring Lardner Sr., George Ade, and Hobart Chatfield-Taylor. A young woman from downstate Freeport by the name of Louella Parsons, ran the scenario department, where she sifted through hundreds of screenplays. Katherine Anne Porter worked as an extra. Essanay published its own newspaper, a four-page weekly called the *Essanay News* that reported the news of the industry to the movie community.

But the fledgling motion picture industry in Chicago was facing legal problems: in 1908 Essanay, Selig, and seven other production companies formed the Motion Picture Patent Company as well as the General Film Company in an attempt to control all aspects of motion picture distribution. In 1915 the Supreme Court ruled that his amalgamation violated the Sherman Antitrust Act. Both companies were ordered to disband, essentially breaking up their monopoly. This decision, as well as the departure of many of the studio's leading actors to California, combined with the Spanish flu epidemic, World War I, and mounting financial difficulties, led to their ultimate decline. Meanwhile, Essanay's competitor, Selig, shut down operations in 1918.

Spoor stayed on in the movie business. In the early 1930s, he introduced "Natural Vision," an early version of the widescreen, 3-D film process. But it never caught on. Ironically, he continued to live near his former studio, at 908 West Argyle Street. After he shut down Essanay, he sold the facilities to his former employees, Bell and Howell. In 1973 they donated part of the Essanay complex to WTTW. The buildings later became the headquarters of the Essanay Stage and Lighting Company, one of the city's premier rental houses for industrial film and commercial production.

In 1947 Spoor received a Special Academy Award for his contributions to the motion picture industry. He remained in Chicago until his death in 1953.

In 1916 Anderson sold his interest in Essanay and returned to New York, retiring from acting. He briefly returned to the industry as a producer, working with Stan Laurel and Oliver Hardy, before leaving the business for good in the early 1920s. In 1958 he received an Honorary Academy Award as a "motion picture pioneer." He died in 1971 at the age of ninety at the Motion Picture & Television Country House and Hospital in Woodland Hills, California. In 2002 he was inducted into the Western Performers Hall of Fame at the National Cowboy & Western Heritage Museum in Oklahoma City, Oklahoma. An annual Broncho Billy Silent Film Festival is held every year in Niles, California. The Niles Essanay Silent Film Museum is located in Fremont, California, near Oakland.

Essanay studio was located at 1333–45 West Argyle Street, just west of Broadway. Now St. Augustine College, it consisted of two red brick buildings. At the main entrance letters still spell out ESSANAY. The doorways are flanked by terra cotta Indians wearing traditional headdresses. One of the former soundstages is housed in the building at the 1343 address (it is now the Charlie Chaplin auditorium and is adorned with a poster for *The Kid,* Chaplin's 1921 film that he made after he left Essanay). Before Essanay moved to Uptown, its offices were located at 501 N. Wells Street (1360 N. Wells today). In 1996 the Argyle Street building was granted landmark status by the Commission of Chicago Landmarks.

In 2007 the world premiere of Paul Peditto's play *Sounds of Silents (The Essanay Years)* was staged at the Prop Theatre at 3502 North Elston Avenue.

Further reading: Arnie Bernstein, *Hollywood on Lake Michigan: 100 Years of Chicago and the Movies* (1998); Charles A. Jahant, "Chicago: Center of the Silent Film Industry," *Chicago History* 3, no. 1, Spring/Summer 1974; David Kiehn, *Broncho Billy and the Essanay Film Company* (2003); Robert Loerzel, "Reel Chicago," *Chicago,* May 2007; Paul Peditto, *Sounds of Silents (The Essanay Years)* (2002); Michael Phillips, "When Chicago Created Hollywood," *Chicago Tribune,* July 22, 2007.

Amos Alonzo Stagg

Football Coach

BORN: August 16, 1862
West Orange, New Jersey

DIED: March 17, 1965
Stockton, California

The career of Amos Alonzo Stagg paralleled the development of intercollegiate football. As the coach at the University of Chicago, he gave the city six Big Ten conference titles and five unbeaten seasons. He contributed greatly to the strategy of football. But more than this, he viewed sports as a great moral force and football, in particular, as the greatest of character builders. He fought vigorously against the professionalizing of sports. Stagg felt that athletes should play sports not for profit but for enjoyment.

Stagg's father, a cobbler, always worked to better himself and passed this ethic down to his son. Stagg toiled his way through high school tending furnaces, lawns, and gardens. Since the nearest high school was several miles away in Orange, New Jersey, he was forced to pay a nonresident tuition. Determined to complete his education, Stagg didn't finish high school until he was twenty-one. He spent one year at Phillips-Exeter Academy in New Hampshire and lived a miserable existence in dire poverty.

Stagg entered Yale in the fall of 1884. The star pitcher on their baseball team, he led the squad to five successive championships. He was called the greatest pitcher of his day and received many offers from professional baseball teams while still a student. He turned them all down in

order to finish school—and because he preferred what he considered the honesty of the college game, where he felt the sport remained pure, unscathed by the influence of money. But Stagg was a talented football player at Yale as well. He played as tight end and was selected to the first College Football All-America team in 1889. In 1951 he was inducted into the College Football Hall of Fame as both a player and a coach.

In 1888 Stagg received his bachelor's degree. He then studied for two more years at divinity school with the intent of becoming a preacher. There was, however, one major stumbling block: he was a terrible public speaker. "I sized myself up and decided I wasn't cut out to be a pulpit man. My goal, though, remained the same—to guide and train youth."

In 1890 Stagg accepted a coaching job with the YMCA College in Springfield, Massachusetts. Two years later he met with William Rainey Harper, one of his professors at Yale, in New York. Harper told Stagg that millionaire John D. Rockefeller was building a university in Chicago that would be unlike any college institution in the country. He encouraged Stagg to come aboard and offered him the position of director of the athletic department. Stagg was the first coach to be given academic status. Like many coaches at that time, Stagg also played on the team.

Stagg insisted that a stadium be built for his players. Marshall Field, the wealthy merchant, donated ten acres of land in an area just north of the campus. Initially called Marshall Field, the stadium was renamed Stagg Field in the late 1890s. Stagg pioneered many changes during his forty-year-plus career. One of the most important was the forward pass, which allowed the ball to be moved up and down the field more quickly—previously football had been primarily a running game. President Theodore Roosevelt had expressed alarm at the number of football casualties. Coaches at that time employed a dangerous blocking technique called the "flying wedge," in which players formed a V-shaped phalanx around their team's ball carrier, locked arms, and moved down the field, protecting the ball carrier by beating back the opposing team's tacklers. During the 1905 college season alone, three athletes died on the playing field and almost ninety sustained serious injuries. Concerned critics of the game recommended rule changes. Stagg agreed. He helped organize the National Collegiate Athletic Association and served on the National Football Rules Committee. He also advocated the forward pass. Its full acceptance from collegiate football officials changed the essential character of the game. Since more points could be scored faster, it allowed for a more exciting game.

In addition, Stagg created the game's first tackling dummy; introduced knee pads, the huddle, and the short punt formation; and pioneered the T-formation, the fake pass, and the onside kick. He was the first to award varsity letters to deserving athletes and the first to use numbers on football player jerseys for the convenience of both spectators and the press.

In 1932, at age seventy, Stagg was forced to retire due to the university's mandatory retirement clause. As a way of making amends, the administration offered the coach a post in the public relations department at a higher salary. Stagg refused and, instead, accepted the head coaching position the next season at the College of the Pacific in Stockton, California. He stayed for fourteen years, resigning in December of 1946 to join his son, the director of athletics at Susquehanna University in Selinsgrove, Pennsylvania. In 1953 he became advisory head coach at Stockton Junior College in Stockton, California.

In 1927 Stagg wrote a memoir called, appropriately, *Touchdown*. He was a five-time member of the United States Olympic Committee—he coached the 400- and 800-meter runs and the 1600-meter relay in the 1924 Olympics in Paris. At age eighty-one he was named coach of the year at the College of the Pacific.

When he turned ninety-five, Stagg admitted that age was finally beginning to catch up with him. "I slipped a little. I stopped running," he said. By the time he retired at age ninety-eight, he was suffering from Parkinson's disease. Stagg, the "grand old man of the Midway" died in 1965 at a Stockton, California, nursing home at age 102.

At the end of the 1939 season, the University of Chicago dropped intercollegiate football altogether at the insistence of university president Robert Maynard Hutchins, who felt that team sports distracted students from the business of learning. Years later, in May 1969, varsity football returned to the Hyde Park campus. In 1966 Stagg Field was demolished. A new 1,500-seat Stagg Field, located at East 56th Street and Cottage Grove Avenue, replaced the original stadium that had stood at East 57th Street and Ellis Avenue—the site of the world's first controlled nuclear reaction on December 2, 1942.

See also: Marshall Field, Red Grange, George Halas, William Rainey Harper, Robert Maynard Hutchins

Further reading: Thomas Wakefield Goodspeed, *The Story of the University of Chicago, 1890–1925* (1925); Robin Lester, *Stagg's University: The Rise, Decline, and Fall of Big-Time Football at Chicago* (1999); Ellis Lucia, *Mr. Football, Amos Alonzo Stagg* (1970); Amos Alonzo Stagg, as told to Wesley Winans Stout, *Touchdown* (1927); Richard J. Storr, *Harper's University: The Beginnings* (1966).

Ellen Gates Starr
Social Reformer

BORN: March 19, 1859
Laona, Illinois

DIED: February 10, 1940
Suffern, New York

Ellen Gates Starr, along with Jane Addams, cofounded Hull House, the pioneering settlement institution located at 800 South Halsted Street.

Starr met Addams in 1877 at Rockford Female Seminary. One year later Starr left to accept a teaching position at a country school in Mount Morris, Illinois. The following year she moved to Chicago to teach English and art appreciation at the Kirkland School, a wealthy girls' school on the North Side. Addams and Starr maintained their friendship through correspondence and occasional visits. A journey to Toynbee Hall, a settlement house located in the working-class Whitechapel section of London, in 1888, inspired Addams to establish a similar institution in Chicago. She asked Starr to join her in the new venture.

In September 1889 they moved into an old mansion at what is now Halsted and Polk Streets. The neighborhood consisted of a mix of Irish, Italians, Germans, and Eastern European Jews who toiled in the nearby sweatshops and factories. Starr and Addams did not regard themselves as missionaries or as morally superior social reformers who lived and worked among the poor, but as neighbors and colleagues who brightened their own lives and the lives of others through art, music, and literature.

Starr's early years at Hull House were spent organizing reading classes, reading clubs, and art classes and teaching book-binding, a craft she learned in England. But as she aged, she grew more passionate and her political beliefs assumed a more radical nature. The pursuit of beauty—a lifelong interest—was accompanied by an intense desire for social justice. She defended organized labor and supported the unionization of women. It wasn't unusual to see the frail-looking Starr marching in picket lines. Gradually she embraced socialism and, in 1916, she ran unsuccessfully as the Socialist candidate for alderman of the Nineteenth Ward.

Starr retired from Hull House in 1930. Raised in a Unitarian household, she converted to Catholicism in her later years.

Starr died at the age of eighty in the Convent of the Holy Child in Suffern, New York.

See also: Grace Abbott, Jane Addams, Alice Hamilton, Florence Kelley

Further reading: Suellen Hoy, *Ellen Gates Starr: Her Later Years* (2010); Rima Lunin Schultz and Adele Hast, eds., *Women Building Chicago 1790–1990: A Biographical Dictionary* (2001).

Melville E. Stone
Newspaper Editor

BORN: August 22, 1848
Hudson, Illinois

DIED: February 15, 1929
New York, New York

Melville Elijah Stone opposed the "yellow journalism" that was so prevalent in the newspaper business during his lifetime. He thought newspapers could be objective and fair and didn't need to resort to sensationalism. During his tenure as its editor, the *Chicago Daily News* grew. He had a sense of what the people wanted, and he delivered it. A man of high integrity, he insisted that the newspaper not only be entertaining but also informative and, most of all, reliable. He wanted a paper that rivaled the *Chicago Tribune*. Uncertain of his own talents, Stone surrounded himself with one of the finest staffs of any American newspaper.

Melville Stone was the son of a Methodist minister. His family lived in several Illinois towns, including DeKalb and Naperville, before settling in Chicago in 1860. While still a student, Stone did some reporting for the *Chicago Tribune*. In 1868 he became the sole proprietor of a promising iron foundry and machine shop, the Lake Shore Iron Works at 371–77 Illinois Street, but lost everything in the Chicago Fire of 1871. After the loss, Stone turned once again to journalism. He became managing editor of the *Republican*, which soon changed its name to the *Chicago Inter-Ocean*, for which he served as city editor. The *Inter-Ocean*'s motto, which history later showed to be a dubious one, proclaimed: "Republican in everything, independent in nothing."

In June 1873, Stone jumped to the *Evening Mail*, which later merged with the *Chicago Evening Post*, where he rose to the position of managing editor. Stone then quit and moved east to Washington, D.C., and became a correspondent for several New York and St. Louis newspapers. He returned to Chicago in 1875 with the idea of launching an independent paper. He was able to do so with reporter William E. Dougherty and a wealthy Englishman, Percy Meggy, who provided the necessary $5,000 cash. Together, they started the *Chicago Daily News*, the city's first penny newspaper. The following year Victor Lawson bought

Meggy and Dougherty's shares. Stone handled the editorial duties and Lawson the business functions.

With Stone's consent, Lawson took over as publisher in 1876. Lawson owned the building where the newspaper was published and was the editor-publisher of the daily *Skandinaven* located on the ground floor. The *News*'s biggest rival was the afternoon paper, the *Evening Post*, run by Jim and Dave McMullen. It was a bitter rivalry. The *Daily News* claimed that the *Post* was stealing their material, and Stone devised a mischievously clever scheme to prove it. One day the *News* published a dispatch allegedly from a Belgrade, Yugoslavia, correspondent who reported that the Serbs were starving. "Er us siht la Etsll iws nel lum cmeht," followed by the alleged translation. Sure enough, it appeared in the next edition of the *Post*—verbatim. The cryptic message simply read, "The McMullens will steal this sure"—spelled backward. From then on, the circulation of the maverick *News* zoomed and the *Post,* the laughingstock of the city, nosedived. In a final coup, the *Daily News* purchased the *Evening Post* in 1878. In 1881 Stone and Lawson started a morning newspaper, the *Chicago Morning News*.

Stone made a conscious effort to recruit the best writers in the business. He hired John Ballantyne, formerly of the *Chicago Herald,* as managing editor and Slason Thompson as chief editorial writer. Borrowing a practice from the august London *Times,* he had on call a score of scholars who were able to file reports whenever necessary. He also brought on board some of the finest columnists and cartoonists to grace the page of a daily newspaper, including John T. McCutcheon, George Ade, and Eugene Field.

Despite his considerable success in journalism, Stone felt woefully inadequate in his position as editor. An editor of a major American newspaper, he maintained, should be worldly and well educated. "I had a staff of unequalled capacity," he wrote in his autobiography, *Fifty Years a Journalist* (1921). "But I alone was unequipped. I was prematurely prominent." In 1888 Stone decided to leave the *Daily News* and sold his interest to Lawson. To avoid competition Lawson agreed to pay Stone $10,000 a year for ten years to stay out of the newspaper business in Chicago. Stone traveled to Europe and returned to Chicago several years later to become vice president and eventually president of the Globe National Bank. He held that position until the bank merged with the Continental Bank in 1898.

In 1893 Stone assumed the management of the Chicago office of the Associated Press (AP) of Illinois. Under his leadership, the AP earned a reputation as an astute observer of the international scene. Various special interest groups, however, asserted that the AP, which dispatched correspondents all over the globe, held a monopoly on the news and insisted that the operation was not as objective as it claimed. Trade unionists, for example, appeared before a congressional inquiry and denounced the AP as "unfriendly to their cause." When the wire service reported the death of Pope Leo XIII in 1903, several Methodist ministers accused Stone of being Catholic or at least of harboring Vatican sympathies. The monopoly issue was finally resolved in 1918 when the U.S. Supreme Court declared that news is a commodity "of such high public need that any one dealing in it is charged with a public duty to furnish it to any one demanding it and ready to pay the price."

Stone retired from the AP in 1921 and moved to New York City. He died there in 1929 at the age of eighty. Dwindling circulation caused the *Chicago Daily News* to cease publication on March 4, 1978.

See also: George Ade, Eugene Field, Victor Lawson, Robert R. McCormick, John T. McCutcheon, Joseph Medill, Wilbur F. Storey

Further reading: Charles H. Dennis, *Victor Lawson: His Time and His Work* (1935).

Wilbur F. Storey

Editor and Publisher

BORN: December 18, 1819
Salisbury, Vermont

DIED: October 27, 1884
Chicago, Illinois

As the unorthodox and controversial editor of the *Chicago Times,* Wilbur Fisk Storey earned the dubious title of "father of sensational journalism" years before William Randolph Hearst arrived on the scene. He was many things during his life—most of them negative. Though a chauvinist, nationalist, and unabashed racist, Storey knew what made the news, and he transformed the lowly *Times* into a newspaper of national importance. He did his job exceedingly well—at one point the *Chicago Times* enjoyed the largest circulation of a daily in Chicago. Perhaps the paper's motto, "To print the news and raise hell!" best sums up both Storey's life and profession.

Wilbur Storey was born on a farm near Salisbury, Vermont. When he was ten, his father moved to Middlebury. Two years later, young Storey learned the printer's trade in the offices of the *Middlebury Free Press*. In 1836 he went to New York and secured a position as a compositor on the *Journal of Commerce*. With ambitions of becoming a journalist, Storey moved to LaPorte, Indiana, where he founded the *LaPorte Herald*. He also established newspapers in Mishawaka, Indiana, and Jackson, Michigan. In 1854 he purchased an interest in the *Detroit Free Press*.

In 1861 Storey settled in Chicago and purchased the *Chicago Times* from Cyrus H. McCormick. Storey's lurid sheet printed tales of murder, robbery, and scandal. Many of the reports consisted of bald-faced lies and wild fabrications. Anything and everything was grist for the mill. The paper found a ready market. Storey was constantly being sued—in one period, twenty-one libel suits and three criminal indictments were leveled against the *Times*. And, in a highly publicized incident, Storey was soundly horsewhipped in public by Lydia Thompson, a burlesque performer, in February 1870, when the editor dared to publish an editorial casting doubts on her morals. "You dirty old scoundrel," she cried out in indignation. Storey pressed charges and appeared in court the next day. Thompson was fined $100, but the judge suspended the fine.

A firm believer in states' rights, Storey originally opposed the nomination of Abraham Lincoln for president. Once Lincoln won, however, and war was declared, he supported the new administration's attempt to save the union. Like many citizens, he saw no contradiction in supporting the war while opposing abolition. After the issuance of the Emancipation Proclamation in 1862, everything changed. Storey believed the president had gone too far. He would back Lincoln as long as the Illinoisan made no effort to free the slaves. An unabashed racist, Storey firmly believed that African Americans and Asian Americans—indeed, any non-Caucasian—had no place in the American nation. He venomously attacked all who were not of Anglo-Saxon stock and even advocated returning the black people to Africa. While he admitted that slavery was "a great evil," he felt an even greater danger lay in allowing slaves to remain in the country. But at the same time, he defended the natural and civil rights of the American Indian, whom he called the "original Americans."

The most feared editor of his day, Storey didn't care whom he offended. His enemies were legion—temperance reformers, abolitionists, Republicans, fellow editors, and even Union generals. On June 2, 1863, General Ambrose Burnside charged Storey with sedition and issued an order to suppress the newspaper. Federal troops swooped down in the largely Democratic city of Chicago, taking possession of the *Times* office. In turn, a mob of pro-Storey demonstrators threatened to burn down the rival and pro-Republican paper, the *Chicago Tribune*. On June 5, President Lincoln revoked the order and the *Times* resumed publication.

By 1871 the *Chicago Times* was the premier newspaper in the Midwest. But the paper's popularity couldn't stop a natural disaster when the building that housed the paper was destroyed during the Chicago Fire. At first devastated, Storey vowed to return. He rented a shack at 105 West Randolph Street and on October 18, 1871—ten days after the fire had raged through the city—the *Times* was back in business.

But Storey was not just any rabble-rousing publisher. Despite the controversy he inspired, he was a pioneer in the field of journalism. According to his biographer, Justin E. Walsh, Storey introduced the first Sunday newspaper in the Midwest devoted to "entertainment" journalism, and he refined the craft of newspaper feature writing.

In 1863 Storey had contracted paresis, a partial paralysis brought on by syphilis. As his emotional and mental state deteriorated, Storey's behavior became even more erratic and unpredictable until he finally descended into periods of madness, fluctuating back and forth between incoherence and lucidness. Despite his illness, in 1876 Storey established the short-lived *Chicago Evening Telegraph,* an afternoon newspaper. But the interest and readership simply weren't sufficient to sustain its survival beyond a brief three months. The following year he formed an overseas branch of the *Times*—the first foreign office of a Midwestern newspaper in Europe.

In May 1882 a stroke—his third—left Storey totally paralyzed. He died two years later and was buried in Rosehill Cemetery. In 1876 Storey, who supervised every detail of his inflammatory paper, had said: "I don't wish to perpetuate my newspaper. I am the paper! I wish it to die with me so that the world may know I was the *Times*!" Ultimately Storey received his wish. Without Storey, the paper lost its spirit. In 1891 Carter Harrison I—then considering a run for mayor again—purchased the *Times* and established it as a Democratic mouthpiece. On March 3, 1895, the publication that Storey founded died. Erratic circulation persuaded the Harrison family to sell the paper to Herman H. Kohlsaat, who merged it with his own daily, the *Chicago Herald,* and renamed it the *Times-Herald.*

Further reading: Justin E. Walsh, *To Print the News and Raise Hell: A Biography of Wilbur F. Storey* (1968).

Louis Sullivan

Architect

BORN: September 3, 1856
Boston, Massachusetts

DIED: April 14, 1924
Chicago, Illinois

Chief theorist of the Chicago school of architecture, Louis Henri Sullivan was called the greatest architect of his day. Indeed, many consider him the father of modern architecture, although, as *Chicago Tribune* architecture critic Blair Kamin notes, that label is misleading and oversimplified. Sullivan attempted to create an authentically American style of architecture rooted in American values and aligned very closely to nature. Along with Daniel H. Burnham, John Wellborn Root, and Frank Lloyd Wright, he epitomized the famed Chicago school and promulgated the theory that architecture should respond to the particular milieu of a period and not slavishly copy European models. "Form follows function," he declared. It was a characteristically simple statement and it became the basis for the Chicago style and, some would argue, the foundation for much of contemporary design.

When Louis Sullivan first arrived in Chicago at the age of seventeen in 1873, he looked around him from the platform of a railroad station and said to himself, "This is the place." If difficult to prove, it is, nevertheless, a way to begin Sullivan's sojourn in Chicago. Sullivan had studied briefly at the Massachusetts Institute of Technology (MIT) before moving to Chicago two years after the Chicago Fire. He found work as a draftsman in architect William Le Baron Jenney's office—Jenney is credited with building the first skyscraper—under the watch of foreman John H. Edelmann. The unsung Edelmann had a formidable influence on the young Sullivan. Edelmann believed that the human race was an integral part of the natural order. It was a lesson Sullivan remembered as he matured and was later reflected in Sullivan's merging of architectural and natural forms.

But Sullivan was growing restless. After less than six months in Chicago, he applied at the École des Beaux Arts in Paris where he studied for a year. Returning to Chicago, he began working with Dankmar Adler, forming a partnership two years later. Adler was a brilliant engineer while Sullivan was an unsurpassed designer. Their firm gained international recognition with the completion of the architecturally significant Auditorium Theatre at Michigan Avenue and Congress Parkway, which was dedicated with much fanfare on December 9, 1889. A young apprentice by the name of Frank Lloyd Wright was the one who had turned Sullivan's rough sketches into blueprints. The Auditorium took three and a half years to complete and cost $3.2 million—the most expensive building in the city at that time. Many called the Auditorium the finest structure in the city—perhaps even in the country.

Sullivan and Adler were famous. They turned away from residential assignments, which had been their bread and butter, to concentrate on commercial work, including the Getty Tomb in Graceland Cemetery (1890), Holy Trinity Cathedral at 1121 North Leavitt Street (1900), and the Schlesinger and Mayer Store (later Carson Pirie Scott and Company and now the Sullivan Center) at State and Madison Streets (1904). In 1885 Sullivan helped organize the Illinois State Association of Architects.

The World's Columbian Exposition of 1893 was supposed to showcase the best of Chicago architecture. Instead, fair director Daniel H. Burnham, who took over following the death of his partner John Wellborn Root in 1891, transformed the exposition into a celebration of the Beaux-Arts style, a classical form based on European models. Sullivan referred to the fair as "an appalling calamity" in *The Autobiography of an Idea* (1924). "The damage wrought" by the World's Fair, he observed, "will last for half a century." The firm of Adler and Sullivan contributed one of the few departures from the classical motif—their Transportation Building.

In 1895 Adler quit the partnership over a misunderstanding with Sullivan. Sullivan, alone at the helm and in the middle of an economic recession, experienced severe financial difficulties. What's more, he refused to compromise his architectural vision. Clients either had to agree to his terms or he wouldn't work with them at all. As a result, business floundered. Finally, in 1909, he was forced to sell everything he owned, even his most cherished possessions, which included, according to biographer Robert Twombly, his jade collection and his copy of Walt Whitman's *Leaves of Grass,* to make ends meet.

By 1910 Sullivan was suffering from insomnia and exhibited suicidal tendencies brought on by poverty and constant worry. His heavy drinking only aggravated the situation. Although he designed a number of buildings in his last years, none were major, and he never regained his former stature. The times passed him by and changes in architecture took place; he was barely able to keep his head above water. Conditions became so bad that in 1917 he considered accepting a civil service position with the government. His last project, in 1922, was the Krause Music Store façade on Lincoln Avenue.

Sullivan was devoted to modernism, especially in the form of the skyscraper. His far-thinking designs were not fully appreciated in his lifetime. He believed in a purely American brand of architecture based on forms that reflected their time periods. Yet his work, as many critics have pointed out, was not merely lines and drawings.

Rather, he succeeded in finding a warm poetic touch—with such ornamental flourishes as rounded arches, terra cotta panels, and floral decoration—in the steel, brick, and mortar. What mattered most to him was how the materials could be shaped to create a cohesive whole. Indeed, Sullivan left behind an indelible personal legacy in architecture, the most public of arts.

By the early 1920s, Sullivan was a broken man. Unable to find work, he relied more and more on the kindness of friends and advocates—he was a poor man with few possessions and little capital. Shortly after completing *The Autobiography of an Idea* in 1924, Sullivan, the dean of American architects, died of kidney and heart trouble in the back room of a run-down Chicago hotel at the age of sixty-seven. He was buried next to his parents in Graceland Cemetery.

Some other notable Sullivan and Adler works in Chicago include the Standard Club (1887); the Martin Ryerson tomb in Graceland Cemetery (1887); and the James Charnley residence at 1365 North Astor Street (1891), which featured the work of Frank Lloyd Wright.

Unfortunately, many other Adler and Sullivan buildings have been lost. The Chicago Stock Exchange Building, at 30 North LaSalle Street, was demolished in 1972 and replaced by a nondescript modern office building. The Stock Exchange's Trading Room, though, was rebuilt within the Art Institute while its entrance arch was reconstructed outside the museum's Columbus Drive and Monroe Street entrance. The seventeen-story Garrick Theater building, at 64 West Randolph Street, was demolished in 1961 to make way for a parking garage. In 2006 a fire seriously damaged the Pilgrim Baptist Church at 3301 South Indiana Avenue in the Bronzeville neighborhood (in April 2011, rebuilding efforts were announced to begin in the summer of 2011).

Sullivan is hardly forgotten today, however. On the contrary, a renewed appreciation of his special genius exists among contemporary critics and architects who see in his heartland vision the democratic spirit of America. In March 2010, Mark Richard Smith's documentary *Louis Sullivan: The Struggle for American Architecture* was screened at the Gene Siskel Film Center. Later that year, two major institutions sponsored Sullivan exhibits: the Art Institute's *Looking after Louis Sullivan* and the Chicago Cultural Center's *Louis Sullivan's Idea*. In 2010, Sullivan served as an inspiration for the upscale restaurant, called Henri, at 18 South Michigan Avenue. In 2011, Target, the retail giant, announced that it would be opening a store in the landmark Sullivan Center, formerly known as the Carson Pirie Scott building.

See also: Daniel H. Burnham, William Le Baron Jenney, Richard Nickel, John Wellborn Root, Frank Lloyd Wright

Further reading: Hugh Dalziel Duncan, *Culture and Democracy: The Struggle for Form in Society and Architecture in Chicago and the Middle West During the Life and Times of Louis H. Sullivan* (1989); Blair Kamin, "Touched by Genius," *Chicago Tribune*, July 11, 2010; Richard Nickel and Aaron Siskind with John Vinci and Ward Miller, *The Complete Architecture of Adler & Sullivan* (2010); James F. O'Gorman, *Three American Architects: Richardson, Sullivan, and Wright, 1865–1915* (1991); Joseph Siry, *Carson Pirie Scott, Louis Sullivan and the Chicago Department Store* (1988); Robert C. Twombly, *Louis Sullivan, His Life and Work* (1986).

Billy Sunday

Evangelist

BORN: November 19, 1862
Ames, Iowa

DIED: November 6, 1935
Chicago, Illinois

By denouncing scientists, radicals, and liberals and cloaking his xenophobic, narrow-minded speeches under the mantle of patriotism, the flamboyant preacher William Ashley Sunday gained an enormous following, especially in rural America, during the late nineteenth and early twentieth centuries. A former baseball player from the cornfields of Iowa, Sunday venerated hard work and clean living. His sermons, peppered with common slang and everyday speech, combined the euphoria of frontier camp meetings with the cautious morality of small-town life. Sunday touched a raw nerve. Battered by economic recessions, strikes, and political corruption, the nation looked for easy answers to its woes. Sunday supplied the cure—an old-fashioned return to the "good old days" of God-fearing, Christian morality. Sunday, a master manipulator, told his followers, who included a large segment of the American public, what they wanted to hear. During his prime years, between 1896 and 1918, Billy Sunday was the most popular preacher on the evangelist circuit.

Sunday's father was the son of German immigrants—Sontag ("Sunday" in German) was the original family name. He died of pneumonia one month after his son was born. Sunday endured a poverty-ridden childhood. After high school, he held a series of casual jobs. He was working as an undertaker's assistant when Cap Anson, manager of the Chicago White Stockings baseball team, discovered him. Sunday, it seems, was an extremely fast runner and his speed-demon feet led him to a career in baseball. He joined the White Stockings in 1883. Sunday played professional baseball for a total of eight years for teams in Chicago, Pittsburgh, and Philadelphia. His lightning speed proved an asset—he stole ninety-five bases in one season—but he was no hitter. Still, he was a dedicated athlete and Anson rewarded his hard work by making him business manager of the team.

In 1886 Sunday underwent a religious conversion. While sitting with his teammates outside a tavern in Chicago, he began listening to an evangelist group from the Pacific Garden Mission that was singing gospel hymns. He returned many times until one night he "publicly accepted Christ as [his] Savior." He was ordained in the Presbyterian Church in 1903.

In 1891 Sunday began working with the Young Men's Christian Association and then served as an assistant to evangelist J. Wilbur Chapman, described by fellow preacher Dwight Moody as "the greatest evangelist in the country." By 1896, Sunday started to preach on his own, meeting in churches and tents and eventually graduating to the much larger tabernacles—makeshift wooden structures that could shelter thousands of people—in major cities. His enthusiastic style, unassuming folksiness, and sheer magnetic personality were a hit from the start. In 1900 he hired a popular white gospel singer, Fred Fischer, to sing such crowd-pleasing hymns as "In the Sweet Bye and Bye" and "We Will Gather by the River."

As his popularity grew, Sunday's demands increased. He insisted, according to historian William G. McLoughlin Jr., that no preaching take place by local ministers and all regular church services be discontinued while he was in town. The ministers, cognizant of his popularity, invariably complied. He had no need to fear competition, however. For many years, it seemed that he had none. He drew thousands upon thousands to his revival meetings and sensationalized a style of preaching that predated the likes of Billy Graham, Jimmy Swaggart, and Jim Bakker. Entertaining and controversial, Sunday used whatever it took to persuade customers to fill his increasingly large tabernacles. And, in tune with public attitudes, he denounced the abuse of wealth, attacked the consumption of liquor, and vilified the sinful wickedness of America's big cities, encouraging his followers to return to simpler times. Further, he castigated birth control advocates as "the devil's mouthpiece" and warned decent young ladies to avoid movies that were "too suggestive." Smokers and drinkers, saloonkeepers and immigrants, hobos and the unemployed, nonconformists and rebels, atheists and sinners—none of these people had a place in Sunday's pantheon. Indeed, he easily dismissed all of them as pawns of Satan.

During his later years, Sunday was the subject of numerous scandals and lawsuits. The times had changed—the youth of the "Roaring Twenties" expressed little interest in evangelical reform—but Sunday refused to change with it. Further, the twenties witnessed a rapid growth among more moderate Catholics and mainline Protestants in urban settings. Sunday lost touch with the public and, more and more, began to symbolize the beliefs and values of an older, nineteenth-century America.

In 1935, at his brother-in-law's house in Chicago, Sunday suffered a heart attack—his third—that proved to be fatal.

See also: Cap Anson, Dwight L. Moody, David Swing

Further reading: Elijah Brown, *The Real Billy Sunday* (1914); Roger A. Bruns, *Preacher Billy Sunday and Big-Time American Evangelism* (1992); Lyle W. Dorsett, *Billy Sunday and the Redemption of Urban America* (2004); W. T. Ellis, *Billy Sunday: The Man and His Message* (1936); Robert F. Martin, *Hero of the Heartland: Billy Sunday and the Transformation of American Society, 1862–1935* (2002); William G. McLoughlin Jr., *Billy Sunday Was His Real Name* (1955).

Gustavus F. Swift

Industrialist

BORN: June 24, 1839
Sandwich, Massachusetts

DIED: March 29, 1903
Chicago, Illinois

Gustavus Franklin Swift, founder of Swift & Company, was one of the great figures of the business world in nineteenth-century Chicago. Like many business leaders of that era, he exhibited initiative, self-reliance, and a burning ambition. "He talked little and accomplished much and let the results talk for him," said newspaper accounts.

A native of New England, Swift was brought up on a farm, the ninth child of a family of twelve, and educated in the local public schools. At fourteen, he joined his brother in the meat business. In 1859 he opened a butcher shop in the village of Eastham, Massachusetts, with $20 in capital from his father. With this, he bought a heifer, which he slaughtered and dressed and sold. Already an astute

businessman, he began experimenting with different packaging methods to make the products look attractive. He opened meat businesses in several Massachusetts towns, traveling in meat wagons to market directly to the customers, but the buying and selling of cattle became his most profitable venture.

In 1872 Swift formed a partnership with James A. Hathaway in Boston and later expanded the business to Albany and then to Buffalo, New York. Sensing that the real center of the cattle market lay in the Midwest, Swift decided to move his base to Chicago in 1874. In the same year, another cattleman, Philip Danforth Armour, had also settled in the city.

Swift acted as a cattle buyer before he turned to meatpacking. In order to avoid paying freight costs, he conceived the idea of slaughtering the cattle in Chicago and shipping the dressed beef—instead of live cattle—to Eastern cities. Some, not convinced of the viability of such a method, called him "that crazy man Swift." Uncertain, too, was Hathaway, who sold his share of the business. Meanwhile, Swift introduced a refrigerator car to prevent meat from spoiling while in transit and sent his first refrigerated shipment to Boston in 1877. It quickly became the accepted mode of transporting highly perishable goods.

As early as 1861, Chicago had earned the unofficial title "Porkopolis" of the Midwest. With the opening of the Union Stock Yards in December 1865, the business of buying, selling, and distributing livestock took place in one location. Railroads delivered the animals to Chicago while more and more packing facilities were built and plants were enlarged. As the industry grew, so did the city, until by the end of the 1870s, reports historian Louise Carroll Wade, more than seventy livestock firms were doing business in Chicago.

When Swift moved his base of operations to Chicago in 1875, the city was primarily known for its pork curing and packing. Although he didn't invent the refrigerated car—it was a gradual process—he is credited with being the first packer to fully understand its significance. The quick acceptance of refrigerated transportation in the 1880s not only allowed the packing houses to operate year-round, it also made possible a tremendous increase in chilled beef shipments. Other meat packers followed suit. Faced with stiff competition, Swift transformed the beef by-products into such highly profitable items as margarine, glue, soap, and fertilizer. In 1885 Swift & Company incorporated with branch packing houses established in Kansas City, Omaha, and St. Louis. He also opened offices in Britain and the Far East.

Swift, like most meatpackers of his day, felt he had the right to hire and dismiss whomever he pleased and conduct business as he saw fit. Wade points out that he hired nonunion workers from as far away as Baltimore, Philadelphia, and New York to break strikes. Many of these strikebreakers were Polish, Bohemian, and German immigrants as well as African Americans from the South. Swift was concerned with every detail of the business and expected his workers to be also. He did not tolerate any mistakes. Swift believed in awarding good work not with words but with a raise in pay and greater responsibility. Although a wealthy man, he cared little for money or the extravagances that it could bring. He had two chief interests in life besides his business—his family and his church.

Swift and his wife attended services regularly at the Union Avenue Methodist Church. Meetings of the church's board of trustees frequently took place in the living room of his home on South Emerald Avenue, which was just three blocks away. Swift was such a fixture at the institution that it came to be known as "Swift's Church."

By the time Swift died in 1903 at age sixty-three, Swift & Company employed over 20,000 workers and sales had grown to $200 million. After his death, the company expanded beyond its meatpacking base into the processing of poultry, dairy products, and such specialty items as Brown 'N' Serve sausage, Butterball turkeys, and Hostess Ham. Esmark, a Chicago-based holding company founded in 1973, divested Swift Independent Packing Company in 1980 and established in its place Swift Fresh Meat Company. In 1984 Esmark was sold to Beatrice Companies. Today, Swift & Company is based in Greeley, Colorado.

See also: Philip Danforth Armour

Further reading: Louis F. Swift, with Arthur Van Vlissingen Jr., *The Yankee of the Yards: The Biography of Gustavus Franklin Swift* (1927); Louise Carroll Wade, *Chicago's Pride: The Stockyards, Packingtown, and Environs in the Nineteenth Century* (1987).

David Swing

Minister

BORN: August 18, 1830
Cincinnati, Ohio

DIED: October 3, 1894
Chicago, Illinois

David Swing was a controversial yet popular figure in the Chicago religious community for almost three decades, and was one of the most famous preachers of his generation. Like another outspoken minister, Preston Bradley, Swing challenged established church doctrine.

David Swing studied classical literature at Miami University in Oxford, Ohio. After graduating in 1852, he decided to study theology at the Old School Seminary in Cincinnati. Only one year later, he was offered—and accepted—a position to teach Greek and Latin at his alma mater. He taught there for twelve years. At the same time, he began to preach in the area and soon accepted other preaching assignments at churches throughout southern Ohio. In 1886 he agreed to become pastor at the Westminster Presbyterian Church in Chicago.

A forceful and articulate speaker, Swing quickly began to attract a large and devoted following. His sermons were published weekly in local newspapers. In 1871 the Westminster Presbyterian Church and the North Presbyterian Church united to form the Fourth Presbyterian Church at Grand and Wabash Avenues. Shortly after the merger, however, the church was destroyed in the Chicago Fire. The congregation met temporarily in the Standard Hall at 13th Street and Michigan Avenue, but the hall's small size necessitated a move to the larger space of the McVicker Theatre on West Madison Street. The congregation finally moved into their new, permanent home at Rush and Superior streets in January 1874.

Swing was an unconventional minister during a time when a wave of religious skepticism was sweeping the country. The Presbyterian Church, in particular, had come under attack in some quarters for failing to address the spiritual needs of its congregations. Swing, one of the most vociferous critics, attempted to personalize the church, to update church teachings, and to make the church relevant to the daily lives of his congregation. In 1873 Swing became chief writer for the *Alliance,* a nondenominational weekly with a liberal bent. The publication helped spread the preacher's beliefs.

Not everyone agreed with Swing's brand of liberal Presbyterianism, however. In 1874 Rev. Dr. Francis L. Patton, editor of the *Interior,* a Presbyterian journal, accused Swing of teaching heresy and filed charges against him before the Chicago Presbytery. Swing, Patton insisted, had failed to faithfully teach the essence of the gospel in his role as Presbyterian minister and had advocated doctrines contrary to Presbyterian theory. The trial, held in the lecture room of the First Presbyterian Church at Indiana Avenue and 21st Street, held the city's attention for weeks and even gained national exposure. Swing was ultimately acquitted of all charges. Nevertheless Patton promised to appeal to the Synod of Northern Illinois, the governing church body. Despite support from his congregation and the ministry of the Fourth Presbyterian Church, who requested that he continue his work, Swing chose to resign rather than endure the ordeal again and in order to avoid any further damage to the reputation of the church.

Friends of Rev. Swing decided to contribute $1,000 each for three years to establish a new, independent church. The Central Church opened in 1879 at the corner of State and Randolph streets. Swing preached there until his death in October 1894 in his Lake Shore Drive home. He was sixty-four.

The Fourth Presbyterian Church, located at Michigan Avenue and Chestnut Street since 1914, continues to serve the citizens of Chicago—from Gold Coast residents to the working poor—through service and ministry. The church's outreach programs, counseling centers, and tutoring classes guarantee that its considerable influence stretches far beyond its North Michigan Avenue location. Further, the eloquent tradition begun by Rev. Swing has been maintained by succeeding generations of preachers from Harrison Ray Anderson, pastor from 1928 to 1961, and Elam Davies, pastor from 1961 to 1984, to John M. Buchanan, the current pastor.

See also: Preston Bradley, Dwight L. Moody, Billy Sunday

Further reading: Marilee Munger Scroggs, *A Light in the City: The Fourth Presbyterian Church of Chicago* (1990).

Lorado Taft
Sculptor

BORN: April 29, 1860
Elmwood, Illinois

DIED: October 30, 1936
Chicago, Illinois

Lorado Zadoc Taft was the first Chicago sculptor to receive widespread recognition. Several of his works, including *Fountain of Time* (1922) in Washington Park, are scattered throughout the city. Taft, it was said, attempted to create work that hinted of eternity. "I cannot think of art as a mere adornment of life—a frill on human existence—but as life itself," he once said.

Born in Elmwood, Illinois, Lorado Taft and his family moved to Champaign in 1871, where Lorado's father secured a position teaching geology at the University of Illinois. Taft graduated from the University of Illinois in 1879 and studied sculpture at the École des Beaux-Arts in Paris for three years. In 1886 he opened a studio in Chicago and from 1886 to 1907 taught at the Art Institute. In 1919 Taft returned to the University of Illinois as a nonresident professor of art.

In 1906 Taft moved from the Loop to a brick coach house at 60th Street and Ellis Avenue in Hyde Park and founded Midway Studio, an artists' colony where ideas were exchanged and visions realized. Taft enjoyed playing the role of mentor. He furnished emotional sustenance, provided housing, and found work for his budding artists. In 1929 the studio moved one block away to 6016 South Ingleside Avenue. With a few friends, Taft established another artists' colony at Eagle's Nest in western Illinois in the late 1890s as a summer refuge for novelists, architects, musicians, and poets, including Henry Blake Fuller, Hamlin Garland, and Harriet Monroe, as well as such prominent visitors as physicist Albert A. Michelson and cartoonist John T. McCutcheon.

Taft first came to prominence with his sculpture for the Horticulture Building at the World's Columbian Exposition in 1893. In 1911 he achieved even greater recognition with his magnificent sculpture of the Indian chief Black Hawk in Oregon, Illinois. Examples of Taft's finest sculpture are scattered throughout Chicago. Outside the Art Institute is *The Fountain of the Great Lakes* (1913), while inside stands *The Solitude of the Soul* (1911); *Seated Woman with Children* (1915) is in the Belden Triangle; *Pastoral* and *Idyll* (both 1913) in the Garfield Park Conservatory; and two impressive portraits are in the Graceland Cemetery—*Eternal Silence: Dexter Graves Monument* (1909) and *The Crusader: Victor Lawson Monument* (1931).

By far his most acclaimed work, though, is the massive *Fountain of Time* at the west end of the Midway Plaisance in Washington Park near the University of Chicago. Dedicated in 1922, its weathered patina still manages to convey both a sad beauty and a haunting timelessness. Based on a poem, "The Paradox of Time," by Austin Dobson ("Time goes, you say? Ah, no, / Alas, time stays: we go"), Taft envisioned the *Fountain of Time* as a teeming wave of humanity—men, women, and children—rushing toward an invisible goal in the figure of Father Time. The sculpture took fourteen years to complete.

Fountain of Time was part of Taft's grand scheme to turn the Midway Plaisance into a sculpture park. A canal would run down the center, flanked on both sides by statuary of the world's greatest thinkers. At the east end of the mile-long parkway, Taft planned to construct a companion piece, *Fountain of Creation*, based on the Greek myth of Deucalion and his wife, Pyrrha. Taft devoted many years to this project but, due to a lack of funds, it remained a dream unfulfilled. Another vision that never came to fruition was his plan for a "dream museum," a hall of sculpture consisting of chronologically arranged miniature plaster models of the great sculpture of civilization.

Taft wrote articles, lectured extensively, served on fine arts commissions, and wrote several books, including *The History of American Sculpture* (1903) and *Modern Tendencies in Sculpture* (1921). A staunch classicist, he attacked modern art as a capricious flight of fancy, unable to withstand the test of time. Taft loved discussing art, but he did more than just talk. He actually demonstrated the artistic process to his students, by using modeling clay.

In October 1936 Taft suffered a stroke in his Ingleside studio. He died at the age of seventy-six. In 1946 his widow, Ada Bartlett Taft, wrote a biography of her husband, *Lorado Taft: Sculptor and Citizen*.

Further reading: Ira J. Bach and Mary Lackritz Gray, *A Guide to Chicago's Public Sculpture* (1983); Perry R. Duis and Glen E. Holt, "Escape to Eagle's Nest," *Chicago History*, September 1982; Patrick Reynolds, "'Fra Lorado,' Chicago's Master Sculptor," *Chicago History*, Summer 1985; James L. Riedy, *Chicago Sculpture* (1981); Allen Weller, *Lorado in Paris: The Letters of Lorado Taft, 1880–1885* (1985).

Graham Taylor

Social Reformer

BORN: May 2, 1851
Schenectady, New York

DIED: September 26, 1938
Ravinia, Illinois

As founder of the Chicago Commons settlement house, Graham Taylor promoted understanding between different classes, races, and faiths through championing social Christianity. Taylor believed that the power of the word could quell, if not resolve, society's ills. Taylor stands with Jane Addams and Mary McDowell as one of Chicago's great social pioneers.

Graham Taylor came from a long line of ministers of the Dutch Reformed Church. His father, William Taylor, moved to Philadelphia shortly after Graham's birth in 1851 and remarried when Graham's mother died. The family worshipped together daily. To young Graham, Sunday was "the gladdest time of the week . . . because in the afternoon and early evening play and merriment mingled with instruction, story-telling, vesper hymns, and dear home-companionship." In 1866 he enrolled at Rutgers College in New Jersey to study theology. Disturbed by the harshness and severity of the Dutch Reformed Church— he remembered the pulpit as an ominous place presided over by stern-faced preachers—Taylor found solace in the gentle faith of his father, but he credited his Sunday school teacher with teaching him "what religion had to do with life"—that the church could have a positive impact on the daily activities of the community.

In 1873 Taylor, while still a theology student at the Reformed Theological Seminary in New Brunswick, New Jersey, accepted an invitation to preach at the Dutch Reformed Church in Hopewell, New York. Shortly thereafter, he was ordained on July 1, 1873. In 1880 the Fourth Congregational Church in Hartford, Connecticut, hired Taylor as their new pastor. Eight years later he was appointed to the faculty of the Hartford Theological Seminary, and his reputation grew.

In 1892 Taylor agreed to head the Department of Christian Sociology at the Chicago Theological Seminary. There he advocated a brand of social Christianity that emphasized the natural kinship of the human family. This kinship was possible for everyone to attain, said the social reformer, by applying Christian principles to everyday life. Taylor was a popular and influential lecturer. Taylor was also a frequent visitor to Jane Addams's Hull House, the legendary settlement house on the Near West Side. He felt that Chicago needed "a multiplication of Hull House all over the city."

In 1894 Taylor established the Chicago Commons settlement house, which was modeled very closely after Hull House, and moved his family into a dilapidated brick dwelling on the West Side at the corner of Union Street and Milwaukee Avenue. The Commons was located in a working-class neighborhood populated by mostly German, Scandinavian, and Irish immigrants. The Chicago Commons offered classes, operated a nursery school, sponsored social clubs, and arranged picnics in the park and outings at country camps. It promoted cultural activities, too, in the form of a library, music lessons, concerts, and theater. From October to June, the Commons presented weekly lectures on everything from child labor to "Tolstoy and the Russian Peasant." Guest speakers there included Clarence Darrow, Emma Goldman, and Lucy Parsons.

From 1896 to 1905, Taylor published a small magazine, the *Commons,* which later merged with *Charities* and, in 1909, became a bimonthly called the *Survey.* The magazine contained news and activities of the Commons and enjoyed a national and foreign readership. Taylor also wrote a weekly column for the *Chicago Daily News* from 1902 until 1938.

From 1903 to 1906, Taylor taught at the Chicago Theological Seminary and lectured at the University of Chicago's Department of Sociology and Anthropology. In 1908 Taylor established the Chicago School of Civics and Philanthropy, which was absorbed by the University of Chicago in 1920 and became the School of Social Service Administration (SSA). Although Taylor was not on the faculty, the curriculum continued to reflect his influence. In 1923 the SSA attained status as a fully-fledged graduate school within the university.

Despite not being a trailblazer in the manner of Jane Addams, Taylor was a devoted and energetic spokesman for the Social Gospel movement, a movement that applied the teachings of Jesus to an urban setting and whose followers included Addams, McDowell, Henry Demarest Lloyd, and John Dewey. Taylor never intended for the Chicago Commons to replace the influence of the church, as some theologians had suggested. Rather, he felt the Commons and other settlement houses could supplement and support the work of the ministries.

In 1913 Taylor authored *Religion in Social Action.* In 1930 he completed his autobiography, *Pioneering on Social Frontiers,* and in 1936 he wrote about his settlement house experiences in *Chicago Commons Through Forty Years.*

Taylor died quietly in his sleep in September 1938 at his home in Ravinia. He was eighty-seven.

See also: Jane Addams, John Dewey, Henry Demarest Lloyd, Mary McDowell, Dwight L. Moody, David Swing

Further reading: Mina Carson, *Settlement Folk: Social Thought and the American Settlement Movement 1885–1930* (1990); Louise Carroll Wade, *Graham Taylor, Pioneer for Social Justice 1851–1938* (1964).

Koko Taylor

Blues Musician

BORN: September 28, 1928
Bartlett, Tennessee

DIED: June 3, 2009
Chicago, Illinois

The undisputed queen of Chicago blues, Koko Taylor was a force of nature. She broke down barriers in a musical genre largely dominated by male singers and was still performing well into her seventies. With her gap-toothed smile and powerful vocals, Taylor was an original.

Koko Taylor was born Cora Walton in Tennessee and grew up on a sharecropper's farm just outside Memphis. (She received her nickname "Koko" from her childhood love of chocolate.) She lived a quintessential blues existence straight out of a Hollywood biopic; she and her siblings lived in a shotgun shack with no running water or electricity. By the time she was eleven both of her parents had died. To survive, she did what many other African Americans of her time and place did—she picked cotton. Taylor's music was deeply rooted in the American South. A devout churchgoer, she grew up singing in the southern Baptist tradition but she also had an affinity for the blues and a brash vocal style to match.

In 1952 she moved to Chicago to be with her future husband, Robert "Pops" Taylor, and found work scrubbing floors for wealthy families along the North Shore by day while trolling the clubs with her husband at night. With her husband's encouragement, she asked performers if she could sit in. It was at one of those sessions, in 1962, where Willie Dixon, a talent scout and producer at Chess Records, first saw her perform. He had never heard a woman sing the blues the way she sang the blues. He wrote "Wang Dang Doodle" for her. "I didn't know Willie Dixon from Adam's house cat," Taylor told the *Chicago Tribune*. The 1965 recording of "Wang Dang Doodle" (with a then unknown Buddy Guy on guitar) on Chess Records not only launched her career—it also became her signature song.

Taylor remained at Chess until 1972 until she moved to the Chicago-based Alligator Records. Her Alligator debut, *I Got What It Takes,* was released in 1975. At that time, Alligator was a fledgling record label dominated mostly by male guitarists. (In 2011 Alligator celebrated its 40th anniversary.) Founder Bruce Iglauer had never recorded a female vocalist before but he was impressed with Taylor's voice and larger-than-life persona. She continued to play the clubs. She was a fixture at the Wise Fools Pub on North Lincoln Avenue.

Taylor won a Grammy Award in 1984 for her work on *Blues Explosion,* a compilation album on Atlantic Records, and she was nominated eight other times, mostly for her Alligator recordings. Her other recordings included *Koko Taylor* (1969), which features her signature version of Willie Dixon's "Wang Dang Doodle"; *Basic Soul* (1972); *The Earthshaker* (1978), which includes "Hey Bartender" and "I'm a Woman," the latter her ribald response to Muddy Waters's "Mannish Boy"; *From the Heart of a Woman* (1981); *Queen of the Blues* (1985); *Force of Nature* (1993); *Royal Blue* (2000); and *Deluxe Edition* (2002). She recorded her final album, *Old School,* in 2007.

Taylor also won the Blues Music Award nearly thirty times, more than any other performer. Between 1999 and 2001, she owned her own club, simply called Koko Taylor's, at 1233 South Wabash Avenue, before the South Loop became gentrified. It is now the Wabash Tap, a neighborhood bar.

She died of complications from gastrointestinal surgery at Northwestern Memorial Hospital in Chicago in June 2009, less than four weeks after performing at the Blues Music Awards in Memphis, Tennessee. She was eighty years old.

On June 11, 2009, some 1,000 mourners gathered at the RAINBOW/PUSH Coalition headquarters at 930 East 50th Street on the South Side. At this music-filled wake, Taylor was dressed in an off-white silk brocade dress, gloves, and a tiara—clothes befitting a queen. The Reverend Jesse Jackson delivered the eulogy at her funeral the next day.

The Koko Taylor Celebrity Aid Foundation (www .kokotaylor.com/foundation.html) assists destitute blues performers and provides social services to the arts and entertainment industry.

See also: Willie Dixon, Howlin' Wolf, Muddy Waters

Terence Teahan
Musician

BORN: August 17, 1905
Castleisland, Ireland

DIED: April 19, 1989
Chicago, Illinois

Terence P. Teahan, or "Cuz," as he was affectionately called, was one of the last great links between indigenous Irish music and Irish American music. A gifted musician and a natural storyteller, Teahan contributed greatly to the city's rich Irish American musical heritage.

A native of County Kerry, Ireland, Terence Teahan used to listen to music at the local ceilidhs (informal dances) or at the homes of the area's fiddle, flute, and concertina players. He began to play the concertina when he was a small boy and studied for two years under the legendary fiddler, Padraig O'Keefe. Teahan didn't pick up the instrument again until nearly thirty years later when he had immigrated to the United States, yet a large portion of his repertoire consisted of tunes learned under the great master. "There was no radio or television or even records to distract you then," explained Teahan. "When you heard a tune at a dance, there was nothing in the world to knock it out of your head unless maybe the birds or the wind. Once you had a tune, you had it."

Teahan initially came to Chicago in 1928 and found work with Sears, Roebuck and Company and Western Electric. He went back home to Ireland in 1931 for several years, then returned to Chicago in 1933. In 1936 the Illinois Central Railroad hired Teahan as a laborer in its freight yards. He stayed at the railroad until his retirement in 1970.

Despite his rich musical background, Teahan didn't perform for many years. However, he did enjoy attending dances at Gaelic Park, then located at 47th Street and California Avenue. In 1940 an acquaintance entered his name for an amateur contest on the "Morris B. Sachs Radio Hour." Borrowing a battered accordion, Teahan performed "Miss McLeod's Reel" and beat the competition hands down. Teahan played at dances, taverns, and dancing schools, at weddings, benefits, and various Irish community functions around Chicago and the Midwest. He earned a reputation as a patient and generous teacher and as a wonderful storyteller. He was always there to encourage or offer a kindly word of advice to younger musicians. Teahan was not only a collector—and discoverer—of old Irish tunes, he was also a prolific composer as well. He penned Irish polkas, slides, jigs, hornpipes, and reels. With Josh Dunson he coauthored the book *The Road to Glountane,* a collection of original compositions and poetry.

A great preservationist of Kerry music, Teahan composed many tunes in the Kerry style—generally known for its strong rhythmic quality—and in the grand Irish tradition, named them for family members, friends, and occasionally for acquaintances. He was also known to compose a nod to himself ("Cuz from Castleisland") or his native soil ("The Road to Glountane" refers to the road he took to get to his home in Castleisland). Like virtually all traditional Irish musicians, Teahan owed a considerable debt to the great collector of Irish tunes Francis O'Neill, and Teahan included in his repertoire many tunes that O'Neill had collected decades earlier.

Teahan's recordings include *Old Time Irish Music in America* (1997), recorded with accordion player Gene Kelly. He is also featured on *Irish Traditional Music in America: Chicago* (2001). His compositions have been recorded by some of the best talent on the Irish music scene today, including the Chieftains and Chicago's Liz Carroll.

Teahan died in April 1989 at the age of eighty-three.

See also: Francis O'Neill

Further reading: Terence Teahan and Josh Dunson, *The Road to Glountane* (1980).

Other resources: Miles Krassen and Larry McCullough, liner notes to *Irish Traditional Instrumental Music from Chicago, Volume II* (1978); *Hidden Treasures: Irish Music in Chicago* (2000).

Studs Terkel
Author

BORN: May 16, 1912
New York, New York

DIED: October 31, 2008
Chicago, Illinois

Although born in New York City, Studs Terkel has come to personify Chicago in a way that few, if any, had done before. He came to embody the essence of Chicago and at the same time gained recognition as a national figure. His uniform never changed, either: red checked shirt, red knit tie—loose at the collar—gray trousers, and blue blazer. To his critics, he was a sentimental populist with simplistic views, but many others credited him with transforming the previously arcane practice of oral history into a popular literary form. A gifted interviewer, he often elicited profound insights and revelations from even the most reluctant of interviewees. He was old-fashioned in another way, too. He never drove a car nor did he even possess a driver's license. He saw no need for it. A chronicler and larger-than-life character in his own right, he eventually became famous just for being himself.

Louis "Studs" Terkel was born in the Bronx borough of New York, the third son of Samuel Terkel, a tailor, and the former Anna Finkel, who had emigrated from Poland. "I came up the year the *Titanic* went down," Terkel liked to joke. In 1921 he moved with his family to Chicago. His parents had bought the Wells-Grand Hotel, a rooming house at 531 North Wells Street on the Near North Side, and it was here where he did his real growing up—in Room 18.

Then he got an official education. Terkel earned philosophy and law degrees from the University of Chicago, although he never actually practiced law (he failed the bar exam). Instead, he took a job doing statistical research on unemployment in Omaha, Nebraska, with the Federal Rehabilitation Administration. He also worked in Washington, D.C., counting bonds for the Department of the Treasury.

He returned to Chicago in the mid-1930s and joined the Federal Writers' Project with the Works Progress Administration, writing scripts for WGN radio. He also did some acting, making his debut in 1935 in Clifford Odets's *Waiting for Lefty* at the Chicago Repertory Group. That was when he dropped his given name and borrowed his now-famous sobriquet from James T. Farrell's character, Studs Lonigan. *Lefty* led to other acting gigs in such television soap operas as *Ma Perkins* and *Road of Life,* usually playing villains and various heavies. "I would always say the same thing and either get killed or sent to Sing Sing," said Terkel.

During World War II, he spent a year writing speeches and shows in the special services of the army air force in 1942 and 1943. He was discharged because of perforated eardrums that resulted from childhood surgeries. Returning to Chicago, he found work doing news, sports, and commentary for various radio stations, including *The Wax Museum,* an eclectic program where he primarily played jazz but also some country, folk, opera, and gospel. In some ways, it was a groundbreaking show: he was among the first radio broadcasters to promote Mahalia Jackson, Pete Seeger, Woody Guthrie, Big Bill Broonzy, and Burl Ives; that is, among the first to present to mainstream America such controversial figures.

In the early 1950s, Terkel created and hosted *Studs' Place,* one of the early examples of the so-called Chicago school of television. It starred Terkel in the role of the proprietor of a neighborhood diner. Among the cast members was Win Stracke, who would later cofound the Old Town School of Folk Music. Others in the genre included *The Dave Garroway Show* and *Kukla, Fran, and Ollie.* What made the Chicago school unique was the down-to-earth quality of its stars, its lack of pretense, and its use of an authentic and naturalistic kind of programming that many

found appealing. *Studs' Place* was set in a restaurant where Terkel did what he did best: he talked and he listened, he listened and he talked. He didn't interview people. He engaged in conversations with them.

His television career was short-lived, though. NBC had picked up *Studs' Place* for national distribution but then, shortly thereafter, because of the omnipresence of McCarthyism, the executives decided to cancel it. Terkel was an outspoken figure; his presence made the NBC brass uncomfortable. Terkel believed he was blacklisted because of his liberal opinions and outspokenness. With his television and radio careers in limbo, he switched to the theater, appearing in a national touring show of *Detective Story,* as well as in other plays.

Ironically, in the 1930s he had applied for a job in the fingerprints division of the FBI. But rather than hiring him the agency began, in 1945, collecting a dossier on him, which eventually amounted to 259 pages in length: the FBI reportedly spent 45 years, from 1945 until 1990, tracking Terkel as a suspected Communist and essentially questioning his loyalty to the United States.

Eventually Terkel got on his feet again and was hired by a new fine arts station called WFMT. WFMT was a natural fit for him: he played jazz and folk music and talked. Essentially he was hired to be himself. Years later, his official title at the station became, fittingly, "free spirit." Terkel was a fixture at the station from 1952 to 1997. During his long tenure there he talked to everyone who was anyone, from Georg Solti to Toni Morrison, from Aaron Copland to Oliver Sacks, from Bob Dylan to Leonard Bernstein, from Rosa Parks to Dr. Martin Luther King Jr.

By the mid-1960s Terkel was ready to tackle another career, as oral historian of the voiceless. When New York book publisher Andre Schiffrin of Pantheon Books was looking for someone who would be the American equivalent of Jan Myrdal (whose book, *Report from a Chinese Village,* consisted of a collection of interviews about ordinary Chinese people), he turned to Terkel. Schiffrin contacted him and persuaded him to write a book compiled from interviews with ordinary Chicagoans. Although Terkel had already written *Giants of Jazz,* a collection of biographies, in 1957, he still thought Schiffrin was "out of his mind"—but he proceeded with the project anyway. The result was *Division Street: America* (1967). It received rave reviews and turned Terkel into the unofficial oral historian not only of Chicago but of the United States. Indeed, Chicago's Division Street became a prototype for the rest of America. What's more, the fifty-something Terkel had become an instant overnight sensation.

When Schiffrin was forced out as head of Pantheon, Terkel, always the loyalist, followed him to the New Press, where he continued to churn out book after book. In sum, he published eighteen books, several of them considered modern classics.

Terkel's other books include *Hard Times: An Oral History of the Great Depression* (1970); *Working: People Talk About What They Do All Day and How They Feel About What They Do* (1974); *Talking to Myself: A Memoir of My Times* (1977), his own memoir; *American Dreams: Lost and Found* (1980), which consisted of interviews of police officers, convicts, nurses, former slaves, and former KKK members; *"The Good War": An Oral History of World War II* (1984), a remembrance of World War II, for which he won the Pulitzer Prize in 1985; and *The Great Divide: Second Thoughts on the American Dream* (1988). Terkel also wrote *Race: What Blacks and Whites Think and Feel About the American Obsession* (1992); *Coming of Age: The Story of Our Century by Those Who've Lived It* (1995); *My American Century* (1997); *The Spectator: Talk About Movies and Plays with Those Who Make Them* (1999); *Will the Circle Be Unbroken?: Reflections of Death, Rebirth, and Hunger for Faith* (2001); *Hope Dies Last: Keeping the Faith in Difficult Times* (2003); *And They All Sang: Adventures of an Eclectic Disc Jockey* (2005); and *Touch and Go: A Memoir* (2007). *Chicago* (1986) was a rambling essay on his adopted city. Several of his books were adapted for the stage. *Talking to Myself* and *Race* were produced at the Victory Gardens and Lookingglass theaters, respectively.

Even after he had found a second career as an oral historian, Terkel still did some acting. In 1988 he portrayed the reporter Hugh Fullerton in John Sayles's film *Eight Men Out* about the infamous Black Sox Scandal of 1919.

Over the years Terkel accumulated accolade after accolade. In 1980 Terkel won a Peabody Award for excellence in journalism. In 1989 WTTW broadcast a documentary about him simply called *Studs*. In honor of his 80th birthday the city of Chicago named the Division Street Bridge after him. In 1997 he received the National Humanities Medal and the National Medal of Arts. He was the only white writer to be inducted into the International Literary Hall of Fame for Writers of African Descent at Chicago State University.

Terkel died in his North Side home on October 31, 2008, at the age of ninety-six.

His last book, *P.S.: Further Thoughts from a Lifetime of Listening,* a collection of radio show transcripts, short essays, and other writings, was published shortly after his death in November 2008.

Several weeks after his death, Steppenwolf Theatre presented *A Tribute to Studs Terkel: Will the Circle Be Unbroken?,* a staged reading of Derek Goldman's adaptation of Terkel's book of the same name, which the company had staged twice before. Participants included David Schwimmer, K. Todd Freeman, and Joyce Piven. In January 2011, pianist Josh Moshier performed the world premiere of his "Studs Terkel Project" at the Chicago Cultural Center. Accompanied by the Moshier-Lebrun Collective, the piece is an extended suite for jazz quintet that was inspired by Terkel's work.

Before he died, Terkel donated nearly 6,000 hours of interviews and broadcasts that he conducted for WFMT radio from 1952 to 1997 to the Chicago History Museum. In May 2010, the Library of Congress agreed to digitally preserve the tapes and make them accessible online. While the Library of Congress will create the Studs Terkel Oral History Archive, the Chicago History Museum will retain ownership of the tapes and the copyright to the content. The museum sponsors a website, Studs Terkel: Conversations with America, at www.studsterkel.org.

Frazier Thomas

Television Entertainer

BORN: June 3, 1918
Rushville, Indiana

DIED: April 3, 1985
Chicago, Illinois

For thirty years Frazier Thomas hosted children's programs on WGN television. Generations of Chicago-area youngsters grew up watching the big, gentle man and the beloved puppet character he created, Garfield Goose.

Frazier Thomas worked as a summer replacement and later as a staff announcer on radio station WLW in Cincinnati. In the late 1940s he appeared on Cincinnati's WLW-TV, an experimental television station where he began developing the character of a goose named Garfield. Although the name *Garfield* was formed from the first three numbers of WLW's telephone exchange, the idea of making the character a goose was inspired by an incident from Thomas's childhood. A Catholic church that stood across the street from his house held many bazaars and church socials. On one occasion the nuns used a goose puppet to exchange prizes for a nickel. Thomas, in turn, remembered the goose when he needed a gimmick to give birthday prizes away on a Cincinnati children's show.

When he came to WBBM-TV in Chicago in 1952, Thomas built the show around the Garfield character and developed it further with the help of Ivan Hill, a Chicago advertising executive. "Hill was an amateur psychologist," noted Thomas in 1959. "Together we would outline and build the goose's character, taking great care to make his reactions as normal as possible." Two years later, Thomas moved to WGN, taking the goose with him.

Thomas, an ex-magician, wrote, produced, and hosted *Garfield Goose and Friends*. Garfield was the mad goose that referred to himself as "king of the United States" while Thomas, the same host, acted as the "prime minister"— dressed, appropriately, in a military uniform. Telecast Monday through Friday after school, it also featured Beauregard Burnsides III, sort of a canine Sherlock Holmes, who diligently tracked down the elusive Romberg Rabbit. "Actually a goose is ideal for a puppet character, if you know geese," Thomas said in a newspaper article in 1957. "A goose will take over a farm. Get a couple of geese on a farm and they run the place. It's only natural for Gar to think he's king of the United States."

Thomas once described Garfield as "rather human." Although he couldn't talk, he did display distinctly human tendencies. "He's boastful, selfish and sometimes even greedy and stubborn," said Thomas. "Giving emotions to a goose helps a youngster to see his own mistakes. Seeing a goose goof may help a youngster understand his own world better."

Garfield Goose wasn't the only program that Thomas produced. He also started *Family Classics* in the early 1960s, which presented movies suitable for the entire family. He himself screened and, when necessary, edited the films. "The matter of what is in good taste and what is not is a very personal thing; it differs from family to family," he once explained. "I know I can't possibly please everyone, but at the same time I try to keep every film I show within the boundaries of good taste as I see it."

The avuncular Thomas never talked down to his audience. Perhaps this quality accounted for his phenomenal success and longevity. *Garfield Goose* was not so much a pioneering show as an extremely popular one. There was an especially strong connection between Thomas and the audience. "Children like to pretend," he said, "but there is a limit to what they'll accept. We knew they wouldn't believe a goose could talk, but it was just barely conceivable a goose could be trained to punch typewriter keys with his beak."

In 1976 the *Garfield Goose* show went off the air and was incorporated into a segment of WGN-TV's long running *Bozo's Circus*. When Thomas succeeded Ned Locke as host and circus master of the popular children's program, the Garfield Goose character was included in the show. The segment was discontinued in 1981 when *Bozo's Circus* changed its format. Garfield Goose made his last appearance on Chicago television in January 1981.

Thomas died in April 1985 in Ravenswood Hospital at the age of sixty-six.

See also: Fran Allison, Bob Bell, Ray Rayner, Burr Tillstrom

Theodore Thomas

Conductor

BORN: October 11, 1835
Esens, Germany

DIED: January 4, 1905
Chicago, Illinois

Theodore Christian Friedrich Thomas, founder and conductor of the Chicago Symphony Orchestra, brought symphonic music to the general public. He turned the Chicago orchestra into one of the best in the world and helped raise the musical tastes of the rough-hewn city on the prairie.

Theodore Thomas was trained by his father, also a musician. He made his violin debut in Germany at the age of ten. In 1845 his family immigrated to the United States and settled in New York City. At fifteen, Thomas went on his own as a violinist and toured the South. For the next several years he performed solo and with various orchestras in New York. In 1854 he met the pianist William Mason, the son of a prominent Boston composer. Mason invited Thomas to join a new chamber group. The Mason-Thomas ensemble performed a popular series of concerts in New York. By the end of the decade, Thomas was serving as the guest conductor of the house orchestra at the Academy of Music, a theater in New York City that presented various companies. He quickly became its regular conductor.

In 1864 Thomas founded the New York–based Theodore Thomas Orchestra. In 1866 he was appointed musical director of the Brooklyn Philharmonic. Two years later the Theodore Thomas Orchestra began a series of evening concerts at the Central Park Gardens, a popular restaurant and open-air beer garden. The concerts attracted a large and loyal following. The next year Thomas, encouraged by the audience response, decided the time was right to tour the country. In 1876 Thomas was invited to become conductor of the New York Philharmonic and two years later he accepted the position of musical director at the newly established Cincinnati College of Music, while still associated with the Brooklyn and New York orchestras. Finally, in 1891 Thomas accepted an offer to take over the Chicago Orchestra, as it was originally called. During his early years with the Chicago Orchestra, Thomas toured regularly, mostly to Midwestern cities, but he also made forays into the South and to the West Coast.

Thomas had yearned to settle down in one location and conduct his own permanent orchestra. Chicago, with its gruff image and large ethnic working-class population, offered the conductor his greatest challenge. Although early programs were criticized for being too long and too highbrow, the city eventually warmed to the stern perfectionist. Thomas did his best to reach out to the citizenry, and he frequently arranged a series of concerts for the city's working-class population. The first of a series of three "workingmen's" or "people's" concerts was held in the Auditorium Theatre on January 20, 1893, notes historian Philo Adams Otis. The audience, according to contemporary *Chicago Tribune* accounts, listened intently. Thomas also encouraged the city's industrialists to take a break from their moneymaking ventures to attend concerts.

Shortly after settling in Chicago, Thomas was asked to be the musical director of the World's Columbian Exposition of 1893. He found the experience rather disappointing—Chicagoans flocked to the free early afternoon concerts, which featured lighter fare, but avoided the more serious evening performances. Still, the exposition did showcase the considerable talents of the members of Thomas's orchestra as well as thirty musicians from other American and international cities.

Thomas was a risk taker. To get people into the seats, he presented Beethoven and Wagner, but once he knew that the audience was his, he experimented with more adventuresome programming such as the Chicago premiere of Antonin Dvořák's symphony *From the New World* (1893) and Richard Strauss's *Death and Transfiguration* (1889). There were so few qualified musicians in Chicago during the 1890s, however, that Thomas had to import players from New York—quite a difficult task, since many musicians were reluctant to move to a city with such a sparse cultural life.

Furthermore, Thomas was unhappy with the massive size of the Auditorium Theatre—it took more than excellent acoustics to fill the empty seats, he noted. With a seating capacity of more than 4,800, it was much too large for symphony concerts. What's more, Thomas grew weary of the constant abuse heaped on him by the local press, who criticized his programming for not including more American composers. Under such conditions, the short-tempered Thomas threatened to resign.

A fund-raising campaign to finance the construction of a new—and smaller—home for the orchestra helped change Thomas's mind. Music lovers from throughout the city contributed a total of $750,000 toward the structure. On December 14, 1904, Orchestra Hall—a few blocks north of the Auditorium Theatre—was dedicated in a program that featured Handel, Beethoven, Wagner, and Strauss. Unfortunately, Thomas didn't have the opportunity to enjoy his new home. Three weeks after the dedication ceremonies, which he had conducted, he died of pneumonia in his home at 43 East Bellevue Place. He was succeeded by his former assistant, thirty-two-year-old Frederick Stock.

From 1905 until 1913 the orchestra was referred to as the Theodore Thomas Orchestra. In 1913, it was named the Chicago Symphony Orchestra (CSO).

Thomas, the most celebrated American conductor of the late nineteenth century, laid the foundation for the current world-renowned CSO. The orchestra began to develop an international reputation under Budapest-born Fritz Reiner, who conducted from 1953 to 1963. Fellow Hungarian Georg Solti continued the grand tradition with his appointment as music director in 1969. The CSO's 1990–91 season was historically significant for two reasons—the one hundredth anniversary of the CSO and the farewell appearance of Solti. Solti was succeeded by Daniel Barenboim. And in 2008 the Italian-born Riccardo Muti was appointed music director, beginning with the 2010–11 season.

See also: Georg Solti

Further reading: Rudolph A. Hofmeister, *The Germans of Chicago* (1976); Philo Adams Otis, *The Chicago Symphony Orchestra: Its Organization, Growth, and Development 1891–1924* (1924); Ezra Schabas, *Theodore Thomas, America's Conductor and Builder of Orchestras, 1835–1905* (1989); George P. Upton, ed., *Theodore Thomas: A Musical Autobiography* (1964).

Mary Harris Thompson

Physician

BORN: April 15, 1829
Fort Ann, New York

DIED: May 21, 1895
Chicago, Illinois

In 1865 Dr. Mary Harris Thompson founded the Chicago Hospital for Women and Children at 49 Rush Street as a haven for indigent and pregnant women, Civil War widows, and orphans who would otherwise be forced to rely on the run-down and overcrowded Cook County Hospital. Mary Thompson is credited with being Chicago's first woman surgeon. She worked passionately to change society's attitude toward women in medicine. Her goal was to create a hospital solely staffed by women to minister to the welfare of women and children.

Born in New York State of English parents, Mary Thompson grew up on a farm and received her education at a country school. Her parents then sent her to Fort Edward Institute at Fort Edward, New York, and later to West Poultney School in Vermont. An instructor at West Poultney who was impressed with Thompson's intelligence persuaded her to attend the New England Female Medical College in Boston. At first she studied to become a teacher of physiology, anatomy, and hygiene, but she changed her mind and decided to become a physician. After one year at the New York Infirmary for Women and Children, she returned to Boston to graduate and chose to seek the road virtually no woman—or at least very few women—had dared travel.

Thompson began practicing medicine in Chicago in July 1863 at the age of thirty-four. Despite her competence, she had to endure many frustrating years in the medical profession. She was not allowed to perform surgery, for example, without a male surgeon present. In 1865 she rented a large frame house at Rush and Indiana Streets and began taking care of indigent women and children as patients. Thompson's hospital had fourteen beds. In 1866 the hospital moved to 212 Ohio Street, and four years later to a large wooden structure at 402 North State Street.

According to the accepted wisdom of the time, women were "mentally unsuited" to practice medicine. It was considered "unladylike," and those who had such ambitions were viewed with suspicion. Thompson established her own hospital because she was unwelcome in Chicago medical schools and because she particularly wished to help women and children—especially Civil War widows and their offspring—in need of medical treatment.

In 1865 Thompson approached Dr. William Heath Byford, an influential staff member of the Chicago Medical College, requesting that women be allowed to attend lectures at the college. While managing the Chicago Hospital for Women and Children, Thompson applied to several Chicago medical schools in order to further her education, but was rejected. Dr. Byford supported her proposal. In 1869

Thompson was selected as one of four women admitted to the Chicago Medical College during its one-year experiment to admit women. Thompson graduated at the end of that year although some faculty members continued to question the wisdom of granting a degree to a woman. Consequently the program was discontinued the following year.

In 1870 Byford suggested the establishment of a separate college—the Woman's Hospital Medical College—that would prepare women for a career in the medical profession. Thompson was hired as a teacher. Lectures were held at the Chicago Hospital for Women and Children. Declining enrollment, however, convinced committee members to reorganize in 1877. Thompson, for reasons unclear, refused to accept a position on the faculty. The Chicago Hospital for Women and Children and the college were destroyed during the Chicago Fire of 1871. Several temporary homes were utilized until 1885, when a new hospital was constructed at Paulina and Adams Streets at a cost of $64,000. The Relief and Aid Society, a charitable organization, helped raise much of the funding.

Thompson's hospital pioneered a number of medical firsts, many after the founder herself died. In 1871 it established the first women's medical college in the Midwest. The hospital established Chicago's first nursing school in 1874, installed the Midwest's first cancer detection clinic in 1943, and established the first mental hygiene clinic for working women in 1946.

The Chicago Hospital for Women and Children was managed and staffed by women; men began to be admitted as patients in the 1890s. Among the physicians on its staff were Drs. Lucy Waite, Frances Dickinson, Marie J. Mergler, Sara Hackett Stevenson, and Julia H. Smith, the first woman admitted to the American Medical Association.

Thompson died in May 1895. By that time she was a well-respected physician, known throughout the country, whose achievements helped rid opposition to women in the medical profession. In 1892 Northwestern University made the Woman's Hospital Medical College a department of the university. Financial difficulties led to its closing in 1902. On June 27, 1895, the Board of Trustees voted to change the name of the Chicago Hospital for Women and Children to the Mary Thompson Hospital. It operated at 140 North Ashland Avenue from 1928 until 1988, when economic problems forced it to close.

Further reading: Thomas Neville Bonner, *Medicine in Chicago 1850–1950: A Chapter in the Social and Scientific Development of a City* (1957); Carter Lucas, *History of Medicine and Surgery and Physicians and Surgeons of Chicago* (1922).

William Hale Thompson

Politician

BORN: May 14, 1867
Boston, Massachusetts

DIED: March 19, 1944
Chicago, Illinois

Few political careers in Chicago have been as controversial, as colorful, and as flamboyantly outrageous as that of William "Big Bill" Thompson. He has been called a buffoon, a charlatan, a rogue, and many other less-than-flattering names. Despite these epithets, there is no denying his considerable popularity—he was elected mayor of Chicago three times—and his rough charm. There was something irresistibly appealing about Thompson. Though he made his share of empty and asinine campaign promises ("If I am elected mayor, I will protect the fair womanhood of Chicago!"), he usually spoke his mind—even if it was from both sides of his mouth—and kept the city entertained for a good many years. Thompson was a great showman, if an abysmal statesman.

Contrary to his lowbrow, man-on-the-street image, William Hale Thompson was, in fact, a child of wealth. His father, a real estate developer, brought the family to Chicago when Thompson was an infant. As a young man, in a stab at independence, Thompson worked out West as a brakeman for the Union Pacific Railroad and as a cook on a cattle ranch in New Mexico. After his father's death in 1891, he returned to Chicago to take over the family business.

Thompson joined the Chicago Athletic Association and within a year became captain of the water polo team as well as captain of the Chicago Athletic Association football team. A big, handsome young man, he was considered prime political property. "The worst you can say of him is that he's stupid," said an insider. In 1900 Thompson entered politics as the Republican aldermanic candidate from the Second Ward and defeated the Democratic incumbent, candy manufacturer Charles F. Gunther. From 1902 to 1904 Thompson was a member of the county board. In 1915 he won the mayoral seat for the first time. Three years later he made an unsuccessful attempt against Representative Medill McCormick for a seat in the U.S. Senate. In 1919, he was reelected mayor.

Thompson enjoyed a tight relationship with Chicago's gangsters. Al Capone and Johnny Torrio reportedly contributed large sums of money toward his campaign war chest, and he paid back the favor. Thompson, of course, denied that he and the Capone element were in cahoots. Thus, when Judge John H. Lyle accused him of bowing to the orders of thugs and criminals, Thompson blew up. "I don't care about name-calling, but he has attacked my integrity and I'd like to knock this loony judge down, kick him in the face and kick hell out of him!"

In 1917 the United States declared war on Germany, but Thompson would have none of it. Partly to appease the half a million people of German descent in the city, the mayor vociferously opposed America's entry into the war under the jingoistic banner of "America First." Critics dubbed him "Kaiser Bill." By 1923, however, Thompson's scandal-racked administration had lost all credibility. Thompson, who at one time had high hopes of climbing to the presidency, knew he couldn't even win back the mayor's seat. He decided to sit out the 1923 election. Anti-Thompson factions in the Republican Party nominated instead the perfectly respectable, if rather dull (compared to Thompson, though, any candidate would have appeared dull) postmaster, Arthur C. Lueder. Lueder, in turn, lost to reform candidate William E. Dever.

From his early days in politics, Thompson had always attracted a considerable African American vote. He openly courted the black constituency, attending civic functions, rallies, and funerals on the South Side and appointing black politicians like Edward Wright and Archibald Carey to high positions in city government. Consequently, Thompson was hailed as a loyal friend in the African American community. However, one of the worst race riots in Chicago history occurred during his term in 1919. Thompson stood idly by for several days, refusing to summon the state militia—although state troops did eventually play a major role in quelling white violence—while the South Side burned.

Thompson's 1927 campaign against Dever was one of the wildest in Chicago mayoral history. Dever had shut down countless taverns during his term in office in obedience to Prohibition laws. Thompson promised to reopen them and to return the city to the wide-open town status of the old days. "When I'm elected we will not only reopen places these people have closed, but we'll open 10,000 new ones." His campaign strategy worked and he was elected for the third time. During this, his final term, Thompson lost control of the city to the mob. Racketeering became the biggest business in Chicago. When critics blasted Thompson for his close ties with crime figures, he simply ignored them, instead introducing bogus issues. One such issue was his quest to oust school superintendent William McAndrew—who had been appointed by Dever. Thompson accused McAndrew of being a pawn of the British government, promising to rid the schools of any subversive British influence, and, if necessary, to "punch King George in the snoot." As Chicagoans shook their head in dismay, the rest of the country barely stifled a disbelieving laugh.

But he did do some good. Thompson's most enduring legacy is that of "Big Bill the Builder." During the Thompson years, several major beautification projects got off the ground, including the construction of play lots and bridges as well as the improvement of city streets and sewers. In 1931, his career on the ropes again, Thompson won the Republican mayoral nomination but was overwhelmingly defeated by Anton J. Cermak. Undaunted, he sought a fourth term. He couldn't muster the votes.

In 1936 Thompson stubbornly returned to politics by forming the short-lived Union Progressive Party to run for governor. He was ignominiously defeated by Henry Horner. In 1939 he threw his hat into the Republican mayoral primary ring one last time against Dwight H. Green. He lost again. Green was defeated by incumbent mayor Edward J. Kelly in the general election.

In February 1944, Thompson caught a bad cold and lapsed into a coma. He died in his suite at the Blackstone Hotel at age seventy-six on March 19.

See also: Al Capone, Anton J. Cermak, William E. Dever, Edward J. Kelly

Further reading: Douglas Bukowski, *Big Bill Thompson, Chicago, and the Politics of Image* (1997); Virgil W. Peterson, *Barbarians in Our Midst: A History of Chicago Crime and Politics* (1952); Frederick F. Rex, *The Mayors of the City of Chicago* (1934); Lloyd Wendt and Herman Kogan, *Big Bill of Chicago* (2005).

Emmett Till

Civil Rights Martyr

BORN: July 25, 1941
Chicago, Illinois

DIED: August 28, 1955
Money, Mississippi

I never wanted Emmett to be a martyr. I only wanted him to be a good son.

—Mamie Till-Mobley

Death earned young Emmett Till immortality.

The murder of fourteen-year-old Till, a black teenager from Chicago, by two white men in Mississippi in 1955, acted as an impetus for the fledgling civil rights movement and served as a defining moment in the lives of many figures from the civil rights era. Since then, his short life and tragic death have been commemorated in song, poetry, plays, and documentaries.

Emmett Till was the son of Mamie and Louis Till. The couple separated in 1942, a year after their son was born (Louis Till, a private in the army, was court-martialed on murder and rape charges and executed in 1945). When he was six, Emmett was diagnosed with polio, which left him with a slight speech defect—he stuttered. After spending some years in south suburban Argo, Mamie and Emmett moved to the second floor of a building that her mother owned at 6427 South St. Lawrence Avenue. Emmett grew up to be hardworking and gregarious, a fastidious boy who cared greatly about his appearance. His mother instilled in him a strong feeling of self-confidence and quiet pride. He also had the gift of the gab—he thought he could talk his way out of most anything.

In August 1955, Mamie's uncle, Mose Wright, or Papa Mose as he was known, visited Chicago to attend a funeral. When Emmett learned that his cousin Wheeler Parker was going down to Mississippi with Papa Mose and that another cousin, Curtis Jones, was planning to join them, he begged his mother to let him go too. Despite having some reservations about the visit—Emmett had never been down South before—Mamie eventually relented and granted her son permission. Before he left, Mamie warned him to "mind his manners" with white people even if it meant "to get on your knees and bow when a white person goes past." She also gave him a memento to take with him—a silver ring belonging to his late father that bore the initials LT and the date May 25, 1943. Emmett wore it on the middle finger of his right hand.

On Saturday, August 20, Emmett and Mamie arrived at the Englewood train station at 63rd Street and Woodlawn Avenue. The diesel-powered City of New Orleans that would carry Emmett away was already waiting at the platform. Mamie barely had time to give her son a proper send-off. After she waved goodbye to him, the train disappeared over the horizon. Mamie, of course, had no idea that that would be the last time she saw her son.

Emmett stayed at the four-bedroom house of his great-uncle Papa Mose and great-aunt Lizzy along with his cousins Wheeler, Curtis, Maurice, Robert, and Simeon. Even though Emmett was on vacation, he was expected to pitch in with the chores, which included picking cotton. On his first day he picked about twenty-five pounds of cotton—not much for a Mississippi boy but to Emmett it was more than he could handle. He was exhausted by the end of the day. When not picking cotton, he helped his aunt with the washing or lent a hand picking vegetables in the garden for dinner. But it was not all work. Emmett and his cousins also found time to swim in a nearby lake, walk through the woods by the Tallahatchie River, or fish for bass and catfish. In the evening everyone would gather around the Philco radio, listening to such programs as *The Lone Ranger, Mr. and Mrs. North,* or *Gunsmoke.*

On the evening of August 28, Emmett and Curtis drove to Bryant's Grocery and Meat Market in the nearby town of Money to buy a few items, things like bubble gum, ice cream, and soft drinks. Even though Bryant's was owned by Roy and Carolyn Bryant, a white couple, its clientele was primarily black, mostly sharecroppers and their children. The boys were hot and dirty after a day of picking cotton. Twenty-one-year-old Carolyn was working the checkout counter by herself; Emmett and his cousins went into the store one at a time. Emmett paid two cents for bubblegum and left.

It is not clear exactly what happened next.

Carolyn Bryant later testified in court that a black man with "a northern brogue" grabbed her by the waist and said, "How about a date, baby?" It was when she ran out to get a pistol from her car that she heard the wolf whistle. Emmett tended to make a whistling sound whenever he got stuck on a word. Emmett and his cousins got into their Ford and drove away from Money as fast as they could.

Around two in the morning that same night, Roy Bryant, accompanied by his half-brother, J. W. Milam, pounded on the door of the Wright home. Bryant told Mose they had come to get the boy from Chicago. They awakened Emmett from his sleep and told him to get dressed. Once outside they asked Carolyn if he was the boy she had seen inside the store. "Yeah," she said. "That's the one."

Three days later, a white teenage fisherman found Emmett Till's badly beaten body in the Tallahatchie River, a dozen miles downstream from Money and just two miles from Mamie's birthplace of Webb. A seventy-pound gin fan had been crudely tied around his neck with barbed wire. His face was unrecognizable. He had been shot in the head with a Colt .45 automatic pistol. It was the ring on his right finger that gave him away. Bryant and Milam were arrested on kidnapping charges. They admitted to kidnapping Emmett—ostensibly to teach him a lesson—but denied that they had killed him, insisting instead that they had simply let him go.

Against the wishes of the state of Mississippi, Mamie demanded that Emmett's body be brought back to Chicago and insisted that the casket be open so all the world could see what had been done to her son. The open-casket visitation of Emmett Till was held at Roberts Temple Church of God in Christ at 40th and State Streets. Bishop Louis Henry Ford, the noted preacher, presided over the funeral, reading a passage from Matthew 18:6. Photographs of Till's mutilated body lying in the open casket were published in *Jet* magazine and the *Chicago Defender,* Chicago's premier African American newspaper. Some 2,000 people waited outside the church during the funeral services while more than 40,000 viewed his body that day and night. The response was so high that visitation was extended to four days. And on the day Emmett was buried—September 6—a grand jury indicted Bryant and Milam for murder.

The trial began on September 19. Many journalists who would later become famous covered the proceedings, including television reporter John Chancellor, Murray Kempton of the *New York Post,* and David Halberstam. It was Halberstam who would later call the trial "the first great media event of the civil rights movement." Mose Wright identified in open court two white men as being Emmett's abductors. The defense built its case though on the identity of the body, claiming that no one could accurately identify it as being Emmett Till. Despite death threats, Mamie testified, insisting that the body pulled from the Tallahatchie River was indeed that of her son. Even so, the all-white jury was not convinced. Instead it took them just sixty-seven minutes to return a verdict of not guilty.

The reaction to the verdict was swift and powerful. Protest rallies occurred in cities throughout the United States and even as far away as Paris, where the African American jazz singer Josephine Baker led a demonstration. Newspaper editorials roundly condemned it, too. And in the January 24, 1956, issue of *Look* magazine Bryant and Milam freely admitted their guilt, knowing full well that the double jeopardy provision of the law prevented them from being retried.

Over the years, there has been conflicting information about the case. In 1996, for example, filmmaker Keith Beauchamp, in the documentary *The Untold Story of Emmett Till,* asserted that as many as fourteen people may have been involved in the crime, prompting the National Association for the Advancement of Colored People (NAACP) to request that the case be reopened. Subsequently, in May 2004, the U.S. Justice Department conducted its own investigation. Till's body was exhumed and an autopsy performed. Ultimately, the FBI concluded that the official cause of death was a gunshot wound to the head and, further, that the statute of limitations prevented federal charges from being filed. Hence, the case was officially closed. In 2007, a grand jury in Leflore County, Mississippi, refused to indict Carolyn Bryant—by this time a seventy-three-year-old woman—on charges of manslaughter, due to insufficient evidence.

Emmett Till's life has been commemorated in many ways. In 1991, a seven-mile portion of 71st Street on Chicago's South Side was renamed Emmett Till Road. In 2005 the Roberts Temple Church achieved landmark status. "The spark that changed America happened in that building," said Jonathan Fine, president of Preservation Chicago. In addition, Till's death has inspired countless poems (including "Mississippi—1955" by Langston Hughes, "The Last Quatrain of the Ballad of Emmett Till" by Gwendolyn Brooks, and "Mississippi Griot" by Sterling Plumpp), songs ("The Death of Emmett Till" by Bob Dylan), plays (James Baldwin's *Blues for Mister Charlie*, Toni Morrison's *Dreaming Emmett*), and novels (Bebe Moore Campbell's *Your Blues Ain't Like Mine*, Lewis Nordan's *Wolf Whistle*, and Richard Powers's *The Time of Our Singing*). Mamie Till-Mobley and playwright David Barr collaborated on *The State of Mississippi v. Emmett Till*, which the Pegasus Players debuted on September 7, 1999 (Barr later changed its name to *The Face of Emmett Till*). Before her death, Mamie Till-Mobley founded the Emmett Till Foundation, a Chicago-based nonprofit organization dedicated to the memory of Emmett Till, which helps raise money for college scholarships, among other purposes.

Till's story continues to resonate on the Chicago cultural scene, too. In January 2008, poet Kharu B and composer Ernest Dawkins and his Chicago 12 ensemble performed the world premiere of "UnTill Emmett Till," a jazz, gospel, and blues suite, at the Velvet Lounge at 67 East Cermak Road—with vocalist Dee Alexander singing the part of Till's mother—and again in early December 2009 at Hamilton Park on 72nd Street, blocks away from Till's childhood home. In April 2008, Chicago playwright Ifa Bayeza's *The Ballad of Emmett Till*, based on interviews with survivors of the tragedy, received its world premiere at the Goodman Theatre.

Emmett Till is buried in Burr Oak Cemetery in Alsip, Illinois. In July 2009, the cemetery received national press when it was discovered that several employees dug up old graves in an alleged grave-reselling scam. During the controversy, the alleged perpetrators moved the casket that held Till's body to a damp shed on the grounds of the cemetery. In August 2009, it was announced that the original coffin that held the body of Till was donated to the National Museum of African American History and Culture, scheduled to begin construction in 2012 and to open in 2015 in Washington, D.C. In response to the scandal, poet Cornelius Eddy composed "Emmett Till's Glass-Top Casket," which appeared in the April 5, 2010, issue of the *New Yorker*.

Mamie Till-Mobley died at the age of eighty-one on January 6, 2003, the same year that her autobiography, *Death of Innocence*, was published. She is buried next to her son.

In August 2010, several events marked the fifty-fifth anniversary of Till's murder, including a gala, "A Time of Reflection and Remembrance," held at the Smart Museum in Hyde Park; the launching of the "Never Again" campaign at the "Hands Across Emmett Till Memorial Bridge" at 71st Street and Wentworth Avenue; and a wreath-laying ceremony at the gravesites of Till and his mother at Burr Oak Cemetery.

The famous photograph of a swollen-faced and battered Till lying in his open coffin at his funeral hangs in the Hall of Shame, a series of similarly grisly images at the International Civil Rights Center and Museum, which opened in February 2010 in Greensboro, North Carolina.

See also: Gwendolyn Brooks

Further reading: Gwendolyn Brooks, *Selected Poems* (1963); Christopher Metress, ed., *The Lynching of Emmett Till: A Documentary Narrative* (2002); Sterling D. Plumpp, "Mississippi Griot" in *Blues: The Story Always Untold* (1989); Harriet Pollack and Christopher Metress, eds., *Emmett Till in Literary Memory and Imagination* (2008); Mamie Till-Mobley, with Christopher Benson, *Death of Innocence: The Story of the Hate Crime That Changed America* (2003); Stephen J. Whitfield, *A Death in the Delta: The Story of Emmett Till* (1988); Juan Williams, *Eyes on the Prize: America's Civil Rights Years, 1954–1955* (1987).

Other resources: *The Murder of Emmett Till* (2003), a documentary by Stanley Nelson; Emmett Till Legacy Foundation, www.emmetttilllegacyfoundation.com.

Burr Tillstrom

Television Entertainer

BORN: October 13, 1917
Chicago, Illinois

DIED: December 6, 1985
Palm Springs, California

From 1947 to 1957, *Kukla, Fran, and Ollie* reigned as one of the most popular children's programs on television. It was unscripted and spontaneous television at its best. Created by Burr Tillstrom, the hand puppets of *Kukla, Fran, and Ollie* were as human as any fictional character—perhaps more so. Along with Dave Garroway and Studs Terkel, Tillstrom and his Kuklapolitans epitomized the best of Chicago television from the late 1950s, which was characterized by locally produced shows noted for their low-key, no-frills approach to programming. Sophisticated, witty, and intended for both children and adults, the show, which was completely ad-libbed, had a major influence on later generations of puppeteers, including Jim Henson, creator of *The Muppets*.

A generation of children grew up watching the antics of *Kukla, Fran, and Ollie*. Hal Boyle, an Associated Press columnist, once said that the Kuklapolitans had done more for Chicago than Mrs. O'Leary's cow. Tillstrom's opinion of his achievements was more humble. His creativity and his life were fueled by one key ingredient—humor. "Being able to laugh at yourself is the only thing that will save the world," he once remarked. "It has to start with you."

A native North Sider, Burr Tillstrom attended Senn High School. In 1935 he worked for a puppet theater under the auspices of the Works Progress Administration (WPA) at the Chicago Park District. He gave up a partial scholarship in puppetry at the University of Chicago to work at it for a living. When he attended the first American Puppet Festival in Detroit in 1936, he was further convinced that he had made the right decision. "I went back to basic cloth construction that I knew, and I made a clown. I used to stuff him in my oversize pocket." For six months Tillstrom's new creation had no name, until he went backstage one night to the dressing room of a ballerina, Tamara Toumanova, who was appearing at the Auditorium Theatre. As she pulled the puppet from his pocket, Toumanova exclaimed, "Ah, Kukla!," a term of endearment in Russian and Greek meaning "doll." The name stuck and, to Tillstrom's wonder and delight, a star was born.

Kukla, Fran, and Ollie premiered on Chicago television in 1947 on the ABC affiliate WBKB before moving to the NBC network in early 1949. The human element of the show was Fran Allison. In 1952, NBC curtailed the highly respected show to fifteen minutes a day and then trimmed it further to a half-hour Sunday broadcast. *Kukla, Fran, and Ollie* then moved back to ABC, where it remained on the air until 1957. With nothing more than his hands, his imagination, and his remarkable voice, Tillstrom created a diverse set of most believable characters. There was Kukla, the wistful Everyman with the sad eyes and bulbous nose; Ollie, the sharp-witted, one-toothed dragon; the garrulous Madame Oglepuss, whom Tillstrom created because of his fondness "for buxom babes who sing in opera"; and the bluntly honest Beulah Witch, who never hesitated to speak her mind. Other tightly drawn personalities included Col. Cracky, Fletcher Rabbit, Mercedes, Clara Coo Coo, and Cecil Bill. "The puppeteer's world is different from any other," explained Tillstrom. "You can express things that happen only in the imagination. You can make up and tell stories, fairy tales that nobody else can touch, and you can poke fun without being cruel."

In addition to *Kukla, Fran, and Ollie,* Tillstrom did some solo work, appearing regularly on *That Was the Week That Was*. One segment of this show, a "hand ballet" that represented a couple separated by the Berlin Wall, earned him an Emmy. Tillstrom returned to Chicago in 1967 when the Kuklapolitans joined Channel 32 (WFLD-TV) as "news commentators." They appeared three times a week and gently poked fun at current events. "No matter how bad the shape of the world," said Tillstrom, "I think humor can save us all."

At the height of *Kukla, Fran, and Ollie*'s popularity—from 1948 to 1957—the cast received 15,000 letters a day, and the monthly *Kuklapolitan Courier,* enjoyed a circulation of 22,000. In 1954 Oliver J. Dragon himself made his debut at the Lyric Opera House with the Boston Pops Orchestra for the Midwest performance of *St. George and the Dragon,* written by Tillstrom and *Kukla, Fran, and Ollie*'s music director, Jack Fascinato. A generation later, in 1970, the Kuklapolitans briefly resurfaced on public television.

Tillstrom won three Emmys and two Peabody Awards during his career. He died in December 1985 at the age of sixty-eight in Palm Springs, California. In his will, Tillstrom donated the puppets to the Chicago History Museum.

See also: Fran Allison, Dave Garroway, Studs Terkel

310

Dempsey Travis

Businessman and Realtor

BORN: February 25, 1920
Chicago, Illinois

DIED: July 2, 2009
Chicago, Illinois

Dempsey Travis was a self-made millionaire who helped revitalize African American neighborhoods on the South Side.

The only child of a laborer, Travis wore many hats in his lifetime: businessman, jazz musician, realtor, author, historian, civil rights activist. He straddled the worlds of business and politics with aplomb. At various times, Travis was president and CEO of Travis Realty Company as well as president of the South Side chapter of the National Association for the Advancement of Colored People (NAACP). He held board positions on the Chicago Historical Society (now the Chicago History Museum), the Museum of Broadcast Communications, the New Regal Theater Foundation, and Northwestern Memorial Hospital, and he served as president of the Society of Midland Authors.

Travis was born in Chicago's historic Black Belt, traditionally the area between Roosevelt Road and 79th Street and Wentworth and Cottage Grove Avenues. He graduated from DuSable High School in 1939 (his classmates included Nat King Cole, publisher John H. Johnson, and comedian Redd Foxx). His original ambition was to be a jazz pianist, and jazz was a major influence throughout his life. During World War II, he was drafted into the army and served four years in a segregated unit. It was during his military service that an ugly racial incident occurred. At Camp Shenango in Pennsylvania white military police shot at a group of black soldiers. Travis himself was injured in the melee—he was shot three times in the back. He survived, but one of his comrades was killed.

After his army stint, Travis attended Roosevelt University, graduating in 1949. Among his fellow students were Harold Washington, the future mayor of Chicago, and Gus Savage, the future congressman. That same year Travis founded Travis Realty Company and, later, Sivart Mortgage Corporation, selling properties to African Americans after white flight to the suburbs. His status as president of the Dearborn Real Estate Board, an association of African American realtors, and his prominence in the black community, however, "provided no immunity from discrimination by the insurance industry," he realized. Feeling compelled to do something about it, he started a campaign against redlining, the practice of withholding loans from risky neighborhoods.

A friend and colleague of Harold Washington, Travis was a staunch supporter of Washington's historic run for mayor of Chicago.

Travis wrote twenty-one books, many of them on jazz, and published them through his own publishing house, Urban Research Press. His African American trilogy—*Autobiography of Black Chicago* (1989), *An Autobiography of Black Politics* (1987), and *An Autobiography of Black Jazz* (1983)—chronicled not only his own life but also the struggles and triumphs of Chicago's African American community. The title of his autobiography *I Refuse to Learn to Fail* (1992) sums up his philosophy. His last book, *Obama's Race to the White House,* was published in late 2008 before Obama's historic win.

Travis died at eighty-nine in his South Side home.

See also: Harold Washington

Lambert Tree

Judge and Philanthropist

BORN: November 29, 1832
Washington, D.C.

DIED: October 9, 1910

All my life I have dreamed of living at the Tree Studios.
—Studs Terkel

Lambert Tree was a circuit court judge, ambassador, and, above all, a patron of the arts. As a judge he presided over the indictment, trial, and conviction of corrupt members of the Chicago City Council. But he is mostly remembered as the man who created the Tree Studios, for many years the oldest artists' colony in the United States. The buildings still bear his name and his likeness: the faces of Tree and his wife look over the doorways at the north and south entrances on Ontario and Ohio Streets.

Born in Washington, D.C., Lambert Tree was the son of a post office clerk. He was educated at private schools in the District of Columbia; attended the University of Virginia, where he read law; and was admitted to the bar in 1855. That same year he moved to Chicago to become a junior partner in the law firm of Clarkson and Tree. The firm prospered. In 1859 he married Anna J. Magie, the daughter of a Chicago pioneer.

In 1864 Tree became president of the Chicago Law Institute, and in 1870 he was elected to the Cook County circuit court bench. On the bench he took a principled stand against corruption and was encouraged to run for mayor, but he decided against it. A staunch Democrat, he ran for elective office several times, including in 1884 against the popular Civil War general John Logan for a U.S. Senate seat, which he lost by only one vote. In 1885,

President Grover Cleveland appointed Tree minister to Belgium. He worked in Brussels for three years before being promoted to minister to Russia, a short-lived assignment because the election of a Republican president, Benjamin Harrison, led to Tree's resignation. From 1892 to 1895 he was the president of the Illinois State Historical Library Board, and from 1892 to 1910 he was a trustee of the Newberry Library. He was also one of the incorporators of the American Red Cross.

Because of Tree's pristine reputation, Mayor Carter H. Harrison joined with him in 1887 to establish the Lambert Tree Award and the Carter H. Harrison Award. These civilian awards—the highest honors granted by the city—are given annually to a member of the police and fire departments for outstanding bravery in the line of duty. The award presentations alternate from year to year between the two awards, with either the Tree Award or the Harrison Award having been presented annually since 1887, with the exception of 1890–96.

Tree died from a heart attack on October 9, 1910, while returning from a trip overseas. But his crowning legacy, the Tree Studios, remains, albeit in a different form.

In 1894, Tree and his wife, Anna, created the Tree Studios, a low-rent housing haven for artists located at 603–21 North State Street. Two wings, at Ohio and Ontario Streets, were added in 1912 and 1913. The State Street building was designated a Chicago landmark on February 26, 1997, and the Ohio and Ontario annexes and courtyard received landmark status on June 27, 2001. The original State Street building was designed in a Queen Anne style while the annexes were designed in the English Arts and Crafts style.

Although a reformer and a progressive thinker, Tree was also a pragmatist. The Tree Studios were designed to be not only artists' havens but also a commercial enterprise. Hence, the rents from the shops on the ground floor were intended to underwrite the modest rents from the studios above. Tree created a legal trust: only artists could live at the Studios. That clause remained in effect until 1959, when the complex was sold to the Medinah Temple. Developer Albert Friedman purchased the property in 2001.

Lambert and Anna Tree believed in artists and the importance of art to the community. What's more, they believed art had a moral purpose. The Trees had visited and been impressed with the Montmartre neighborhood in Paris. The Tree Studios may have had its precedents— the Tenth Street Studio in Greenwich Village (now demolished) and Grundmann Studios in Boston (also demolished). Still, it was unique in that it was in continuous use from 1894 until 2001 as a residential and work space specifically designed for creative artists.

Many artists had come to Chicago in 1893 to attend the World's Columbian Exposition as exhibitors, decorators, and visitors. Tree, an art lover, wanted them to stay. But lack of appropriate housing and work space made it difficult to attract artists to the city. Tree Studios was intended as a motivation for them to stay. The units were designed specifically for the needs of the working artist in mind. Thus, all the skylights had northern exposure. Doors connected all the studios so that artists could view one another's work and visit one another, thus instilling a sense of community and camaraderie. Bathrooms down the hall were located on the second floor; nude models in the corridors were a common sight. Consequently, a sign was posted: "In consideration of visitors, all models are required to wear a garment when leaving the studio to walk to the washroom." Early leases warned that no foul-smelling foods (such as cabbage) were to be cooked at any time, and no piano or loud music was to be played after 6 P.M.

It was a difficult to become a tenant: prospective tenants had to prove that they were artists with an art portfolio. In addition they had to be recommended by at least two artists already in residence. For a short period of time, applicants even had to be approved by the Art Institute of Chicago— many of the school's instructors already lived there.

The possibility of demolition hung over the Tree Studios numerous times over the course of its existence, even as far back as the early 1920s. In 1999, developer Steven Fifield threatened to raze a portion of the Tree Studios to make way for a parking garage and an apartment tower. In response, on September 22, 2000, a rally, candlelight vigil, and 1960s-style demonstration was held outside the Tree Studios to protest the threat of its demolition. Flyers insisted, "If it can stop a war in Vietnam, it can stop a wrecking ball."

In 2000 Richard M. Daley's administration agreed to salvage the Tree Studios (and the Medinah Temple) by thwarting the Fifield proposal and accepting competing developer Albert Friedman's plan instead. The former temple now houses Bloomingdale's home-furnishing store, and the Studios were rehabbed and opened to shops and arts-related businesses. The end result was that Friedman's plan forced out the remaining artists who lived there.

More than 500 artists have lived in the Tree Studios over the years, including sculptors Albin Polasek and John Storrs, the latter best known for his statue of Ceres, the goddess of grain, on top of the Chicago Board of Trade

Building; illustrator J. Allen St. John, who illustrated Edgar Rice Burroughs's Tarzan and Mars book series; muralist John Warner Norton, who painted the murals in the former *Chicago Daily News* building; painters Ruth Van Sickle Ford, Pauline Palmer, and Rowena Fry; actors Peter Falk and Burgess Meredith; and architect Andrew Rebori. More recent residents have included Ellen Lanyon, whose tiled mural along the Chicago Riverwalk depicts the history of the city, as well as courtroom artist Verna Sadock, art and antique dealer Jim Romano, and artist and collector Barton Faist.

In 1999 an exhibition on the Tree Studios, "Capturing Sunlight: The Art of Tree Studios," was presented at the Chicago Cultural Center.

The Lambert Tree Papers are housed at the Newberry Library.

Further reading: Carrie Golus, Patrick Welch, and Annie Morse, *Capturing Sunlight: The Art of Tree Studios* (1999); Jeff Huebner, "City Without Art," *Chicago Reader,* November 2, 2001; Blair Kamin, "Disaster Averted, but . . . Ouch," *Chicago Tribune,* September 12, 2000; Anne Keegan, "Artists in Residence," *Chicago Tribune Sunday Magazine,* March 7, 1993.

Bill Veeck

Baseball Club Owner

BORN: February 9, 1914
Hinsdale, Illinois

DIED: January 2, 1986
Chicago, Illinois

William Louis Veeck Jr. was one of the most controversial sports figures in the business; to this outgoing, wisecracking, maverick promoter, baseball was entertainment. Some argued that by injecting humor into the game—such as sending a midget, to use his parlance, to the plate—he demeaned the sport. Others credited him with saving the game, insisting that his cartoon-like antics actually helped boost attendance figures. Bill Veeck, often described as the "Barnum of baseball," was one of a kind.

Bill Veeck was the son of William Veeck, a Chicago sportswriter who later became president of the Chicago Cubs. Veeck grew up in Hinsdale and attended Hinsdale High School before transferring to Phillips Academy in Andover, Massachusetts, for a brief eight weeks. He finally ended up at the Ranch School in Los Alamos, New Mexico. When his father died in 1933, Veeck dropped out of Kenyon College in Ohio to work for the Chicago Cubs, toiling at various positions. By the early 1940s he had advanced to treasurer. More than anything else, Veeck wanted to own a baseball club, but with Philip K. Wrigley firmly ensconced at the top, that didn't seem likely with the Cubs.

In 1941 Veeck and Charley Grimm purchased the Milwaukee Brewers, a Cub farm team in the American Association, transforming the once-lowly team from last place to winners of three consecutive American Association pennants. Veeck enjoyed turning losing teams into winners. In 1945 he sold his interest in the Milwaukee Brewers, and the following year he became part owner of the Cleveland Indians of the American League, making him, at age thirty-two, the youngest chief executive in baseball. By 1948 his team had won the World Series. In 1951 Veeck bought the

St. Louis Browns of the American League, but the results were something less than spectacular. He left after two disappointing seasons.

Many club owners didn't like Veeck's unconventional tactics. When he signed the American League's first African American player, Larry Doby, to the Cleveland Indians in 1947, he reportedly received thousands of hate letters in the mail. The following year he signed the legendary African American pitcher Satchel Paige to the Cleveland Indians. In Milwaukee during World War II, he introduced early morning baseball for the night-shift workers, and he even served coffee and donuts. On one occasion, in 1949, he drove a hearse around the baseball diamond to indicate the death of his team's pennant chances. In 1960 he introduced an exploding scoreboard at Comiskey Park that went off whenever a White Sox player hit a home run.

The most notorious incident of Veeck's career occurred in August 1951 in St. Louis when he signed Eddie Gaedel—at three feet seven inches and sixty-five pounds—and sent him to pinch-hit in the second game of a doubleheader. The fans loved it, but the top brass didn't. The next day Will Harridge, president of the American League, barred Gaedel from baseball, a move that Veeck called discriminatory against "little people."

In 1959 Veeck bought the Chicago White Sox. With Veeck in charge, the team won its first American League pennant in forty years. The glory days, however, did not last long. In ill health, Veeck left the Sox in 1961 and, in obedience to his doctor's orders, he slowed down, took it easy, and lived a leisurely life in Easton, Maryland. From 1968 to 1970 he served as president of Suffolk Downs racetrack near Boston.

In 1975 Veeck learned that the White Sox were about to be sold and the club moved to Toronto or Seattle. He feverishly put together enough money to make a bid to keep the team in Chicago. Although he met the financial obligations, Veeck's offer was turned down due to his reputation as a showman with questionable judgment. Detroit Tigers owner John Fetzer intervened and convinced the league that in all fairness to Veeck another vote should be taken. This time his bid was accepted. Veeck, however, had not changed his ways. In 1977, strapped for cash and in dire need of good people, he came upon the novel idea of "renting" a player for a short-term lease. The free-agent system, which gave athletes the right to negotiate with other teams for the most lucrative contract, had priced quality players out of his range.

Veeck signed thirteen ballplayers, each to a one-year contract, including such power hitters as Richie Zisk, Oscar Gamble, and Eric Soderholm. The "South Side Hit Men," as they were invariably called, hit home run after home run—a total of 192, in fact. They didn't win a pennant that year, but they did create a lot of excitement in the city, especially on the South Side. In 1979 a Veeck gimmick—Disco Demolition Night—turned into an unmitigated disaster; the on-field melee forced the White Sox to forfeit the second half of a doubleheader to the Detroit Tigers. He had offered reduced admission to anyone who brought a disco record into the stadium. The records, part of the anti-disco movement that was particularly strong that year, were then collected and destroyed. But despite personal appeals from Veeck himself, the fans went wild, burning the records and running onto the field. It was one of the most embarrassing moments in Veeck's professional career. He had had enough of baseball, and, it seems, baseball had had enough of him.

In 1980 Veeck attempted to sell the team to Edward DeBartolo Sr., a multimillionaire and Ohio businessman with racetrack holdings, when baseball commissioner Bowie Kuhn thwarted the deal. Veeck then sold the team in early 1981 to the current owners, Jerry Reinsdorf and Eddie Einhorn. When Einhorn publicly slighted Veeck's management ability, the offended Veeck switched his allegiance to Wrigley Field. He did not attend a game at Comiskey Park for five years.

Veeck wrote four books, including *Veeck—as in Wreck: The Autobiography of Bill Veeck* (1962). For a short time he served as president of Samuel and Veeck, a Cleveland public relations firm. In October 1984 Veeck underwent surgery to remove a malignant lung tumor. He died in January 1986 at the age of seventy-one.

During a memorial service held two days after his death, 800 fans, family, and friends gathered at St. Thomas the Apostle Church at 5472 South Kimbark Avenue in Hyde Park to honor his life and celebrate his spirit. The Reverend Thomas Fitzgerald delivered a moving and eloquent eulogy to the uncommon man with the common touch. "You are a prince in all the good senses of the word," he stated. "A prince without pretensions."

See also: Cap Anson, Harry Caray, Charles A. Comiskey, William Wrigley Jr.

Further reading: Gerald Eskenazi, *Bill Veeck: A Baseball Legend* (1987).

Charles H. Wacker

Entrepreneur and Civic Leader

BORN: August 29, 1856
Chicago, Illinois

DIED: October 31, 1929
Lake Geneva, Illinois

Charles H. Wacker made his fortune in the beer-brewing business, but he is best remembered as a prominent civic leader who led the movement to beautify Chicago; he was chairman of the influential Chicago Plan Commission. He was largely responsible for the two-level thoroughfare along the Chicago River that bears his name.

The son of German immigrants, Charles Wacker attended public school in Chicago and Lake Forest Academy. He studied music in Stuttgart, Germany, and attended lectures at the University of Geneva in Switzerland. Wacker began his career as an office boy in the grain commodities firm of Moeller and Company. In 1880 he formed a partnership with his father to establish F. Wacker and Son, a malting business. In 1882 he joined the firm of Wacker and Birk Brewing and Malting Company as secretary and treasurer, with his father as president. In 1884 his father died and Wacker became president. In 1888 Wacker was nominated for treasurer of the state of Illinois, but he chose to avoid public office. In 1893 he served as one of the principal stockholders and directors of the World's Columbian Exposition, which celebrated the 400th anniversary of Columbus's journey to America and announced to the world Chicago's arrival as a great city.

The success of the exposition, and the sense of beauty and harmony it brought to the city, led architect and urban planner Daniel H. Burnham to create the *Plan of Chicago*, coauthored with Edward Bennett and published in 1909. The Chicago Plan Commission was formed to carry out the Burnham Plan, which the city adopted in 1910. Wacker was appointed chairman of the Chicago Plan Commission, a position he held from 1909 to 1926.

The plan called for, among other things, the beautification of the lakefront, the expansion of the park system, and the widening of major north-south arteries into the city's downtown district. As chairman of the Chicago Plan Commission, Wacker promoted and helped achieve Burnham's vision. He recommended removing the South Water Street market—the city's major produce district—from the south branch of the Chicago River to relieve traffic congestion, and replacing it with a modern, double-decker thoroughfare.

James Simpson, president of Marshall Field and Company, was one of the first prominent citizens to recommend that South Water Street be changed to Wacker Drive when the market was moved. The proposal was introduced in the city council in 1924. "Every village which has a town pump has a Water Street," noted Alderman A. A. McCormick. "I urge you to give this great new improvement a name that will mean something. I want to see Mr. Wacker honored while he is still alive." The city council passed the ordinance with only one dissenting vote. The South Water Street market was relocated to the Southwest Side two years later in 1926.

The construction of Wacker Drive and the opening of the North Michigan Avenue Bridge in 1920 changed the essential character of Michigan Avenue north of the river. By making that area more accessible to the Loop, it assured the future of the boulevard and its adjacent streets as an important commercial and retail district.

Wacker was president of the Chicago Relief and Aid Society, president of the United Charities of Chicago, and a director of the Chicago chapter of the American Red Cross. In addition to his many civic interests, Wacker exerted a strong influence on German American activities in the city. He was treasurer of the German Opera House Company, a director of the German Old People's Home, and a member of several German singing societies. A longtime resident of the North Side, Wacker lived at 2340 North Commonwealth Avenue. His boyhood home at 1838 North Lincoln Park West is still standing.

Wacker died in October 1929 in his Lake Geneva home. He was seventy-three.

See also: Daniel H. Burnham

Further reading: Carl W. Condit, *Chicago 1910–29: Building, Planning, and Urban Technology* (1973); Dominic A. Pacyga and Ellen Skerrett, *Chicago: City of Neighborhoods* (1986).

Charles Walgreen

Entrepreneur

BORN: October 9, 1873
Rio, Illinois

DIED: December 11, 1939
Chicago, Illinois

Charles Rudolph Walgreen turned the corner pharmacy into a multimillion-dollar business and, in the process, popularized the drugstore soda fountain and lunch counter.

Born a few miles outside of Galesburg, Illinois, Charles Walgreen was the son of immigrant Swedes. In 1887 Walgreen moved with his family to Dixon, Illinois. He enrolled at Dixon Business College for one year and then found a job as a bookkeeper in the town's largest general store. He left that position to do piecework at the Henderson Shoe Factory.

Although apprehensive about waiting on the public, Walgreen took a job as a $4-a-week apprentice at a neighborhood drugstore. When the town was hit by a severe snowstorm, the owner ordered Walgreen to shovel the snow off the sidewalk. Unfortunately, Walgreen became so engrossed with a conversation with several friends who had dropped by that he simply forgot. Needless to say, his boss was not pleased, and young Walgreen left on a bad note. It proved an important move because he then decided to leave Dixon altogether. He borrowed $20 from his sister and caught the train to Chicago.

Walgreen held jobs in a number of downtown, North Side, and South Side pharmacies. In 1897 he passed the Illinois State Board of Pharmacy. During the Spanish-American War, Walgreen enlisted in the Illinois National Guard and was shipped off to Cuba. He saw no action but was assigned to handle the pharmaceutical chores at Siboney Hospital. Using savings borrowed from his father, Walgreen purchased his first store at 4134 South Cottage Grove Avenue in 1901. The store was typical of small drugstores at that time, both in design and merchandise. It sold such products as tooth powder, soaps, vegetable tonics, perfumes, pills, and tablets. Determined to make his establishment stand out from the crowd, Walgreen devised an ingenious system for attracting neighborhood customers. Whenever a customer telephoned for nonprescription items, he would loudly and clearly repeat the caller's name and address and the articles ordered so that his assistant, standing nearby, could collect and wrap the items and deliver the order to the caller's home before the caller hung up. It was great public relations and it worked. Word got out that Walgreen's was a good place to do business. In 1909 he opened his second store at Cottage Grove Avenue and 39th Street.

Walgreen devoted more and more time to the appearance of his stores. He displayed attractive products in the windows while, inside, customers were charmed by the pleasant aroma of toiletries and perfume bottles. An important part of Walgreen's success was the soda fountain, always popular with customers. As soon as the first hint of winter arrived, however, business plummeted so badly that Walgreen was forced to shut down the fountain from mid-October to mid-May. Alarmed at the loss of clientele, Walgreen began introducing sandwiches, desserts, and hot fare. Curiously, Walgreen worried that the heady mixture of food and toiletries would clash and, perhaps, offend some of his sensitive customers. "For a long time Dad wouldn't sell toasted sandwiches," admitted his son, Charles R. Walgreen Jr., in 1959 to the *Chicago Tribune*, "because he thought the odor would interfere with the sale of perfume."

In 1921 Walgreen opened a store in the Venetian Building at 17 East Washington Street in the heart of the busy downtown retail district and only two blocks from Sargent's, the city's oldest pharmacy. This bold move deviated sharply from the previous and successful practice of locating outlets in densely populated residential neighborhoods. The following year, in 1922, a Walgreens employee, Ivar Coulson, made history when he added a few scoops of vanilla ice cream to the company's watery malted drinks of milk, chocolate syrup, and malt powder. Then he added a generous dollop of whipped cream and capped it with a bright cherry. Before long, eager customers were lining up three and four deep for a taste of Walgreens double-rich chocolate malted milk.

By 1916 Walgreens consisted of nine stores and by the mid-1920s, more than sixty. There were ninety-two stores in the Chicago area alone by 1926, in addition to outlets in Hammond and Gary, Indiana; Milwaukee, Wisconsin;

and Joliet, Illinois. The company's first store in New York opened the following year. In 1931 there were 446 stores separated into eighteen divisions and stretching from Minneapolis to Houston. By the time Walgreen retired in 1934, there were more than 500 stores across the country.

Through successful marketing techniques, aggressive promotion, and knowledgeable service, Walgreens developed from a neighborhood store into the nation's largest drugstore chain. In 1949 the company moved from its South Side headquarters into new corporate offices at 4300 West Peterson Avenue. In 1975 Walgreens relocated to the northern suburb of Deerfield, Illinois.

On September 6, 1984, Walgreens celebrated the opening of its 1,000th store. The following year the firm was chosen by Dun's *Business Month* as one of the nation's five best-run companies. In February 2010, Walgreens bought the New York-based Duane Reade drugstore chain for $618 million in a deal valued at $1.1 billion.

For years Walgreen had lived in a mansion at 116th Street and Longwood Drive in the Morgan Park/Beverly neighborhood on the South Side. In 1946 the house became part of the Cenacle retreat house. It is now part of the Mercy Mission, a girls' school.

Walgreen died of cancer two weeks before Christmas in 1939 at the age of sixty-six.

See also: Marshall Field, Potter Palmer

Further reading: Sandra M. Jones and Bruce Jepsen, "Walgreens' Big Apple Buy," *Chicago Tribune*, February 18, 2010; Herman Kogan and Rick Kogan, *Pharmacist to the Nation: A History of Walgreen Co.* (1989); Myrtle R. Walgreen and Marguerite Harmon Bro, *Never a Dull Day* (1963).

Aaron Montgomery Ward

Merchant

BORN: February 17, 1844
Chatham, New Jersey

DIED: December 7, 1913
Highland Park, Illinois

Aaron Montgomery Ward was a self-made man who established the world's first mail-order business and later one of the largest department stores in Chicago. More significant, though, was his determination to maintain and expand Chicago's front yard. For this reason, Ward earned the title "watchdog of the lakefront."

Born in New Jersey, Montgomery Ward attended grade school in Niles, Michigan. At age eleven he started working in a barrel factory, at fourteen in a brickyard. He worked for various dry-goods firms in St. Louis, Missouri, and St. Joseph, Michigan, before coming to Chicago after the Civil War. There he found work as a clerk at Field, Palmer, and Leiter. He stayed for several years before becoming a traveling salesman who sold goods to general stores. It proved a valuable experience.

Ward observed the ways of rural life. Farmers, he soon learned, often exchanged news and indulged in a little gossip at the country store. He heard the farmers' complaints that prices were too high and selections too limited. Ward had a novel idea. Why not sell directly to the farmers via the mail? No one had ever done it before, but he felt it was worth the risk. By avoiding the cost of a middleman, he would be able to save money that, in turn, he could pass along to the customers in the form of lower prices.

In 1872 Ward opened a small mail-order dry-goods business on North Clark Street and, within two years, issued his first catalog. His enlightened policies—a return of goods was allowed—virtually ensured success. The business expanded and the catalog grew. By 1890 the company moved into a building at the corner of Michigan and Madison that, says historian Nina Baker, became "the showplace of Michigan Avenue." Chicagoans flocked downtown to see its six steam elevators and gleaming marble lobby. In 1899 the structure was enlarged with the addition of a tower, capped by the "Spirit of Progress," a weathervane in the form of a seventeen-foot statue of a young girl that came to symbolize the company. In 1908 a new home was built at Chicago and Larrabee Avenues. By World War I, Montgomery Ward and Company had established itself as an American institution.

Unlike its chief competitor, Sears, Roebuck and Company, Montgomery Ward was slow to enter the retail market. Management opened retail outlets initially in small to mid-sized cities. It was not until much later that the company felt confident to compete with the large department stores in the big cities. Montgomery Ward did not open a store on State Street, for example, until 1957.

Ward bought property on Michigan Avenue. From his office he could see Grant Park, which in those days was used primarily as a dumping ground, littered as it was with squatters' shacks, railroad sheds, freight cars, and assorted debris. Incensed, Ward waged a one-man campaign to protect the lakefront from commercial development. Increasingly, Ward devoted less and less time to his business, although he still acted as president of the company. His utmost priority was maintaining an unobstructed lakefront by keeping Grant Park between Randolph and 11th Streets clear of structures. Ward often took matters into his own hands—literally. If he saw someone lugging debris into the lakefront area, he would send his lawyers down to the scene immediately.

Eventually Ward took his battle against developers into the courts—at his own expense and frequently requesting court injunctions—in an effort to preserve the lakefront for the people of Chicago. Many citizens, however, did not agree with his methods or honor his quest. In a rare interview Ward told a newspaper reporter, "I think there is not another man in Chicago who would have spent the money I have spent in this fight. . . . I fought for the poor people of Chicago—not the millionaires."

In 1897 the Supreme Court declared that no building, with the exception of the Art Institute, could be erected on the strip of land between Michigan Avenue and the lake.

Ward retired in 1901. In 1907 he bequeathed $8 million toward the construction of what would later become the Field Museum of Natural History. Following his death, Ward's wife endowed $9 million to Northwestern University for the establishment of a medical and a dental school.

Ward died in 1913 of pneumonia in Highland Park, Illinois. He was buried in Rosehill Cemetery.

Montgomery Ward, the department store chain, went out of business in 2001. All that remains today is an online and catalog version of the once-popular bricks-and-mortar retailer.

See also: Marshall Field, Potter Palmer, Richard W. Sears
Further reading: Nina Baker, *Big Catalogue: The Life of Aaron Montgomery Ward* (1956); Daniel J. Boorstin, "A. Montgomery Ward's Mail-Order Business," *Chicago History,* Spring/Summer 1983; Frank B. Latham, *A Century of Serving Customers: The Story of Montgomery Ward* (1972); Lois Wille, *Forever Open, Clear, and Free: The Historic Struggle for Chicago's Lakefront* (1991).

Harold Washington

Politician

BORN: April 15, 1922
Chicago, Illinois

DIED: November 25, 1987
Chicago, Illinois

The election of Harold Washington in 1983 as Chicago's first black mayor united the disparate elements of the black population into a collective whole. Washington's appeal was monolithic and cut across economic and social lines, from ghetto street children to middle-class professionals. Within the African American community—and indeed, even outside it—Washington was a genuine folk hero.

Harold Washington was born in Cook County Hospital in 1922, the fourth child of Roy and Bertha Washington. He once described his father, a lawyer and minister, as his "one and only hero in life." Roy Washington attended law school at night and worked full time in the Union Stockyards, and he instilled in his inquisitive son a love of learning. Washington started reading before he was four years old. He spent his formative years at a number of South Side addresses in the heart of the Black Belt: 3936 South Grand Boulevard, across the street from the famous Grand Terrace nightclub; 3936 South Parkway; 4507 South Vincennes Avenue; 4444 South Indiana Avenue; and 111 East 44th Street.

Washington attended DuSable High School. At DuSable he was profoundly influenced by his teacher, Mary Herrick, a social reformer in the tradition of Jane Addams. He dropped out in his senior year and served in a segregated unit of the U.S. Army Air Forces in the Philippines during World War II, building runways since, as an African American, he was not considered fit for combat duty. In 1946 Washington enrolled at Roosevelt College, a new institution that boasted open enrollment for blacks. In 1948 Washington was unanimously elected president of his class. In 1952 he graduated from Northwestern University Law School and was admitted to the Illinois bar the following year.

Washington learned about politics from his father, a former precinct captain. In 1954 he joined the Third Ward democratic organization as corporation counsel. The new ward committeeman, Ralph Metcalfe, gave Washington a chance to revive an organization called the Young Democrats, whose purpose was to attract young professionals into machine politics. Within a few months Washington developed the Young Democrats into the largest minority political organization in town.

In 1964 Washington was elected to the Illinois House of Representatives. During those years he straddled the fence on several key issues, trying to step gingerly between independent action and party loyalty. He sponsored or co-sponsored bills that forbade realtors, banks, and savings and loan associations from discrimination on the basis of race, creed, or color. In 1969, one year after the assassination of Dr. Martin Luther King Jr., Washington introduced legislation to celebrate the fallen civil rights leader's birthday in Illinois. Governor Dan Walker finally signed the bill into law in 1973.

The rise of the civil rights movement in the 1960s, coupled with years of benign neglect under the regular Democratic organization—white leaders took black voters for granted—led to anger and resentment in the African American community. For the first time, black leaders thought the unthinkable—that a black candidate, under proper circumstances, could actually defeat the Democratic machine. The African American community faced its first test when Mayor Richard J. Daley died on December 20, 1976. Alderman Wilson Frost, an African American ally of Daley and president pro tempore of the city council, declared that he was—adhering to the chain of command—the acting mayor of the city. But Daley supporters refused to accept Frost. Instead they locked the door to the late mayor's city hall office and installed guards outside to discourage intruders. When the city council convened the next day, the members elected a white alderman, Michael J. Bilandic of the Eleventh Ward, by a lopsided vote of 45–2. Outraged at the treatment of Frost, the Committee for a Black Mayor—which included Rev. Jesse Jackson, Ralph Metcalfe, and Cecil Partee—assembled a list of potential candidates. Among those considered were Roland Burris, Erwin France, Frost, Jackson, Metcalfe, Washington, and Partee. After a serious deliberation, the committee made their choice: Harold Washington.

During the special mayoral election held in April 1977, Washington only received 11 percent of the vote—African Americans didn't support him because they didn't think he could win a general election, and whites simply didn't know who he was. Washington realized that his candidacy was little more than a symbolic protest against the policies of city hall rather than a serious attempt to win the mayor's seat. That attempt would have to wait for another day; meanwhile, the seeds of discontent had been assiduously planted.

The black community pulled further and further away from the regular Democratic organization. When Washington was slated for a vacant state senate seat in 1977, he won easily. In 1980 he defeated incumbent Bennett Stewart—long considered a yes man in the black community—for U.S. representative from the First Congressional District. He was reelected to a second term in 1982. By 1983, straw polls indicated that the African American community was ready to run a candidate for mayor again. Washington, who enjoyed his work in Congress and didn't think the time was right, reluctantly agreed to run. He defeated incumbent mayor Jane Byrne and state's attorney Richard M. Daley in the Democratic primary. But faced with the prospect of supporting a black candidate for mayor, many white Democrats bolted the party and voted for Bernard Epton, a white Republican from Hyde Park. In addition, Washington's conviction of failure to file federal income tax forms for four years—he served thirty-six days in Cook County Jail in 1972—made more than a few voters uneasy. Nevertheless, in April 1983, Harold Washington did what many thought was the impossible. He became the first African American mayor in Chicago history.

Washington's first term in office was marred by intraparty squabbles over such issues as maintaining city services and promoting affirmative action programs. The mayor's forces—the Washington 21—consisted of sixteen blacks and five whites, while the opposition—the Vrdolyak 29—consisted of twenty-eight whites, led by Tenth Ward alderman Edward Vrdolyak, and one Latino. Nicknamed "Council Wars" by Chicago comic Aaron Freeman, the struggle in the city council chambers severely compromised Washington's ability to govern. Even two years into Washington's term, the Vrdolyak 29 refused to confirm his nominees for various boards and committees.

In December 1982, U.S. District Judge Thomas R. McMillen ordered the city to draw a new map, creating new ward boundaries that would accommodate four additional wards—two black and two Latino. In May 1984 the U.S. Court of Appeals for the Seventh Circuit ruled that McMillen did not go far enough and ordered the redrawing of boundaries to properly reflect the black and Latino majorities by creating five wards. In December 1985, Judge Charles R. Norgle of the U.S. District Court ordered that a special election be held in March 1986. This election broke the stalemate, and Washington gained control of the city council.

In 1987 Washington ran for reelection. While not as vicious or racially hostile as the campaign four years earlier, the election did have its share of troubling racial overtones, augmented by a disconcerting amount of party switching. Nevertheless, Washington won a second term. But he didn't have much time to enjoy it. In November 1987 he was stricken with a massive heart attack while working in his office.

The body of the late mayor lay in state in the rotunda of city hall. Thousands of mourners waited outside in the rain to offer their last respects and thousands more packed into Christ Universal Temple, at 11901 South Ashland Avenue, for the funeral service on Monday, November 30. The funeral procession then weaved through South Side neighborhoods en route to the burial site in Oak Woods Cemetery, 1035 East 67th Street. From 119th Street to Vincennes Avenue, 71st Street to Cottage Grove Avenue, people waved, wept, and offered a silent prayer.

Washington served four years and seven months in office. During that time he savored many victories and endured many defeats. Among his triumphs were four years of a balanced budget, the institution of the city's first Ethics Ordinance, collective bargaining in city hiring, a renewed commitment to the neighborhoods, increased representation by women and minorities in city government, and construction of a new central library, at State and Van Buren Streets, named in his honor.

Yet there was much left to be done—the Chicago Housing Authority and school reform were also on the Washington agenda. Historians will be debating his accomplishments—and the exact meaning of the Washington legacy—for many years to come.

See also: Richard J. Daley, Ralph Metcalfe
Further reading: William J. Grimshaw, *Bitter Fruit: Black Politics and the Chicago Machine, 1931–1991* (1995) and "Harold Washington: The Enigma of the Black Political Tradition" in *The Mayors: The Chicago Political Tradition* (1987), Paul M. Green and Melvin G. Holli, eds.; Melvin G. Holli and Paul M. Green, *The Making of a Mayor, Chicago 1983: Harold Washington* (1983); Florence H. Levinsohn, *Harold Washington: A Political Biography* (1983); Alton Miller, *Harold Washington: The Mayor, The Man* (1989); Gary Rivlin, *Fire on the Prairie: Chicago's Harold Washington and the Politics of Race* (1992); Dempsey J. Travis, *An Autobiography of Black Politics* (1987) and *Harold—The People's Mayor: An Authorized Biography of Mayor Harold Washington* (1989).

Muddy Waters

Musician

BORN: April 4, 1915
Rolling Fork, Mississippi

DIED: April 30, 1983
Westmont, Illinois

When Muddy Waters added an electric guitar to the Mississippi Delta blues, he created a musical revolution whose reverberations are still being felt. An entire generation of young, white musicians—from the Rolling Stones to Rod Stewart—found inspiration in his raw, unpolished sounds. He helped create the Chicago blues style. To this day, he remains one of the most influential bluesmen of the twentieth century.

A sharecropper's son, Waters, whose given name was McKinley Morganfield, began playing harmonica and singing at family gatherings when he was still a young boy. He didn't take up guitar until he was seventeen, when he built one himself, learning to play by listening to the radio. He ordered his first real guitar from the Sears, Roebuck catalog—for $11. His early musical influences included such seminal bluesmen as Son House and Robert Johnson. According to musical legend, he received his famous sobriquet because he liked to play in a muddy creek near his home.

In the early 1940s, folklorists Alan Lomax and John Work traveled through the South making field recordings of traditional music for the Library of Congress. Waters was working on the plantation of Colonel William Stovall near Clarksdale, Mississippi, when the two researchers captured his raw blues on tape. In 1943 Waters headed to Chicago, joining the thousands of other African Americans who moved to the great cities of the North in search of a better life. But unlike his fellow migrants, Waters had every intention of becoming a professional musician.

Postwar Chicago had an active club scene, especially along South 43rd Street. Sonny Boy Williamson I, Lonnie Johnson, Roosevelt Sykes, Big Maceo, Tampa Red, Memphis Minnie, and Big Bill Broonzy attracted a substantial following, and older players like Arthur "Big Boy" Crudup, Sunnyland Slim (Albert Luandrew), and Robert Nighthawk (Robert McCollum) performed late into the night. Waters got a job during the day in the shipping department of a paper factory, loading and unloading trucks. In the evening, he played house parties around town. Soon, though, he moved up to the neighborhood dives, where he played with the likes of Sunnyland Slim, Jimmy Rogers, and Little Walter. At first Waters stayed with friends at 3652 South Calumet Avenue. At one point he lived with a cousin at 1857 West 13th Street on the West Side before finding his own place a few houses down at 1851 West 13th Street.

Waters made plenty of influential contacts. Broonzy took the young Mississippian under his wing, while Sunnyland Slim arranged a recording session with Chess's Aristocrat label. In April 1948, Waters recorded "Rollin' Stone," I Can't Be Satisfied," and "I Feel Like Going Home." In the 1950s, he had several R&B hits, including "I'm Your Hoochie Coochie Man," "Mannish Boy," and "Got My Mojo Working," songs that became part of his permanent performing repertoire. And he worked with some of the finest musicians in town, including Junior Wells, Buddy Guy, Otis Spann, James Cotton, Willie Dixon, Hubert Sumlin, Earl Hooker, and Big Walter Horton. The brash sound of Waters's brand of urban blues ensured that the music would thrive in Chicago's loud and raucous clubs. He pioneered the new electric blues in clubs like the Flame Club and the Checkerboard Lounge and formed the first "truly" electric band on the South Side.

White musicians discovered the blues in the late 1950s and early 1960s. In Chicago, Paul Butterfield and Mike Bloomfield began playing the blues, influenced partly by English musicians who had picked it up and partly by an older generation of black bluesmen. This blues revival revived the careers of many bluesmen, including Muddy Waters. Consequently, Waters made extensive tours in Europe, and in 1960 he appeared at the Newport Jazz Festival. He became an "overnight sensation" when he opened for the Rolling Stones.

"I always wanted to be great. I always wanted to be known cross-country, not like an ordinary person who just lives and dies," Waters said in 1981.

The bluesman had lived at 4339 South Lake Park Avenue for many years. After his wife died in the early 1970s, he moved with his children to a house in suburban Westmont on South Adams Street and spent the last ten years of his life there. In 1979 he even got married in the back yard of the Westmont home with Eric Clapton acting as best man. Clapton as well as B. B. King occasionally stopped by. Waters was fond of Westmont. He bragged about it whenever he had the opportunity and played occasional benefit concerts for his children's schools, including Westmont High.

Waters died of cancer at the age of sixty-eight in his Westmont home. He was buried in Restvale Cemetery in south suburban Alsip. In 2005 the village of Westmont renamed a section of its main street Honorary Muddy Waters Way.

In 1984 a musical biography, *Muddy Waters: The Hoochie Coochie Man,* by Jimmy Tillman and Jackie Taylor, enjoyed a successful run at the Jane Addams Center. In August 1985 the Chicago City Council named the stretch of South 43rd Street between Oakenwald Avenue and State Street Muddy Waters Drive.

See also: Big Bill Broonzy, Leonard Chess, Little Walter, Howlin' Wolf

Further reading: Samuel B. Charters, *The Bluesmen* (1967); Rich Cohen, *Machers and Rockers: Chess Records and the Business of Rock & Roll* (2004); Peter Guralnick, *Feel Like Going Home: Portraits in Blues and Rock 'n' Roll* (1981); Charles Keil, *Urban Blues* (1966); Robert Palmer, *Deep Blues* (1981); Mike Rowe, *Chicago Breakdown* (1975); Arnold Shaw, *Honkers and Shouters: The Golden Years of Rhythm and Blues* (1978).

Discography: *The Chess Box* (1989), a three-disc box set.

Harry Weese

Architect

BORN: June 30, 1915
Evanston, Illinois

DIED: October 29, 1998
Manteno, Illinois

The maverick architect and urban planner Harry Weese was among a handful of post–World War II architects who steered architecture away from the Miesian sterile glass boxes that so defined American architecture at the time to a more humanistic style. Weese was an advocate for contemporary architecture and urban life; he created architecture that respected humanity. Weese also had an outsized personality to match his vaulted ambition. His work was not like anyone else's.

Harry Mohr Weese was the son of Harry Weese Sr., the company treasurer at Harris Bank, and Marjorie Mohr, the daughter of a steel company executive. His father was both a staunch Republican and a devout Methodist. Weese Jr. was neither of these. As a child he exhibited an interest in nature, something that would follow him in his chosen profession.

After graduating from New Trier High School in Winnetka, Weese attended the Massachusetts Institute of Technology (MIT) and Yale University. He spent the summer of 1937 cycling across the northern European countryside and was especially impressed with the Scandinavian countries. After graduating from MIT in 1938 he received a fellowship in city planning at Cranbrook Academy in Bloomfield Hills, Michigan—it was a pivotal moment in his life. At Cranbrook, he made deep and lasting friendships with the future architects Eero Saarinen and I. M. Pei.

In 1939 Weese joined the architectural firm of Skidmore, Owings, and Merrill (SOM). During World War II he served in the U.S. Navy as an engineering officer. He returned to SOM briefly after the war before opening his own practice in 1947 with his brother-in-law and former Cranbrook classmate Benjamin Baldwin. His office was first at Michigan and Ohio and then later at 612 North Michigan Avenue. Weese lived with his family in various downtown apartment buildings before settling into a row house in Old Town that he designed himself. The family weekend getaway was in northwest suburban Barrington. It was an eccentric house—also designed by the architect—that consisted of a two-story building with asymmetrical wings that were connected by an interior suspension bridge.

Weese's output was prodigious. He designed nearly 1,000 buildings during his long career, everything from churches and single-family houses to schools and small-town buildings. His primary influences, in addition to his Cranbrook colleagues, were Louis Sullivan and Daniel Burnham. Weese's most significant works include the Time-Life Building (1969); the Upper School building on the campus of the Latin School of Chicago (1969); the Seventeenth Church of Christ, Scientist on Wacker Drive (1968); the Metropolitan Correctional Center (1975); an addition to the Newberry Library (1981); Fulton House, at 345 North Canal Street (1981); and River Cottages, four row houses with nautical themes (and each with its own private dock) at 357–365 North Canal Street (1990). Weese also undertook major restoration work on Louis Sullivan's Auditorium Theatre, the Field Museum, and Orchestra Hall. His firm also designed the all-glass, triangular Swissôtel and the Sterling Morton Library at the Morton Arboretum.

Not all of Weese's works received praise. The hulking Marriott Hotel on North Michigan Avenue was criticized for its bulkiness and inelegant design (ironically, Weese, his wife Kitty, and a friend Jody Kingrey had founded Baldwin Kingrey, the city's first modernist design store, on this site). *Chicago Tribune* architecture critic Blair Kamin went so far as to call it "graceless." Still, during his peak decades of the 1960s and 1970s (in 1976 his firm employed about 250 associates with branches in Washington, D.C., Miami, and Los Angeles), he offered an alternative to the Miesian boxes and International Style that so dominated the city's skyline.

Weese was also a city planner. Since he was a young man Weese had wanted to complete what Daniel Burnham had left unfinished: his *Plan of Chicago*. Weese dreamed of creating a world's fair that would surpass the famous 1893 World's Columbian Exposition. It was in his role as a city planner that he created some of his most enduring work.

He helped preserve the buildings in Printer's Row, considered the city's first loft district, by buying the old printing buildings and reselling them as residential lofts, and he helped redevelop the downtown riverfront neighborhood as a residential and recreational area.

In 1978 the American Institute of Architects honored Weese's firm for outstanding achievements in architecture.

Unfortunately, the 1980s were Harry Weese's lost decade. During that decade, he endured a spectacular alcohol-fueled collapse and was in and out of rehabilitation centers more than a dozen times. During his last years the once-proud architect was committed to a veterans' hospital in downstate Illinois, a life largely spent confined to bed after suffering a series of strokes.

Weese retired in the 1980s and died at the age of eighty-three in 1998 at the Illinois Veterans Home in Manteno, Illinois.

See also: Daniel Burnham, Bruce Graham, Mies van der Rohe, Louis Sullivan

Further reading: Robert Bruegmann, *The Architecture of Harry Weese* (2010); Robert Sharoff, "Reconstructing Harry Weese," *Chicago*, July 2010; Kitty Baldwin Weese, *Harry Weese Houses* (1987).

Johnny Weissmuller

Swimmer and Actor

BORN: June 2, 1904
Windber, Pennsylvania

DIED: January 20, 1984
Acapulco, Mexico

Sportswriters often called Peter John Weissmuller the greatest swimmer of the twentieth century. During his career, Weissmuller set sixty-seven world records and won five Olympic gold medals. On the screen, he became internationally known as the man who played "Tarzan" and "Jungle Jim."

Shortly after Johnny Weissmuller was born in 1904 in Pennsylvania, his Austrian parents moved to Chicago. Weissmuller grew up on the North Side and lived at 1921 North Cleveland Avenue. He was an altar boy at St. Michael Church, at 458 West Eugenie Street in Old Town. When he contracted polio at age nine, doctors recommended swimming as therapy. At fifteen, Weissmuller attracted the attention of Bill Bachrach, swimming coach at the Illinois Athletic Club (IAC). Scouting for good swimmers one day, Bachrach saw the lithe Weissmuller with friends at Lake Michigan. Impressed, he invited him to swim a few laps in the IAC pool. Bachrach wasted no time in signing him up as a member and began offering him swimming lessons. The relationship apparently worked, for Bachrach became Weissmuller's coach, mentor, and friend. In August 1921, Weissmuller won the 50- and 220-yard national championships.

At the 1924 Olympics in Paris, Weissmuller set world records in the 100- and 400-meter freestyle events, and four years later, at the Olympic Games in Amsterdam, he won the 100-meter race. Weissmuller retired from swimming in 1929. By that time he held every world freestyle record. In 1930 Weissmuller was working out at a Hollywood Athletic Club pool when he was spotted by novelist Cyril Hume, who at the time was working on a screenplay adaptation of Edgar Rice Burroughs's *Tarzan*. Weissmuller passed the screen test, and a movie career was born. "I went to the back lot at MGM. They gave me a G-string and said, 'Can you climb a tree? Can you pick up that girl?' I could do all that," Weissmuller once recalled.

Although not the first, Weissmuller was the screen's most popular Tarzan. He made a dozen *Tarzan* movies over a dozen or so years, beginning with *Tarzan the Ape Man* in 1935 and ending with *Tarzan and the Mermaids* in 1948. Since the actor's lines amounted to little more than "Me Tarzan, you Jane," acting in front of the camera was hardly a challenge. The economic rewards were large, but he grew weary of portraying the monosyllabic, chest-beating, tree-climbing ape man. "I've been wearing animal skin scanties too long," he explained. Instead, he turned, in 1948, to another woodland character, Jungle Jim, only this time he was allowed to wear clothes. He made a number of Jungle Jim movies during the 1940s and 1950s, including *Jungle Jim* (1948) and *Jungle Jim in the Forbidden Land* (1952), until *Jungle Jim* moved to television in 1958.

When his television career subsided in 1968, Weissmuller promoted health-food stores and cocktail lounges. In the early 1960s, he returned to the Chicago area as vice president of public relations for the General Pool Corporation in Addison, Illinois. In 1950 the Associated Press rated Weissmuller the greatest swimmer of the last half century, and in October 1983 Weissmuller was inducted into the U.S. Olympic Hall of Fame.

Weissmuller, who had a history of heart trouble, suffered a series of strokes in 1977. An invalid since 1979,

Weissmuller died in Acapulco, Mexico, in 1984 at age seventy-nine. He was buried there. A memorial mass was held several days later at St. Michael Church, the Weissmuller family church.

See also: Edgar Rice Burroughs
Further reading: Johnny Weissmuller, *Water, World and Weissmuller* (1964).

Ida B. Wells
Social Reformer

BORN: July 16, 1862
Holly Springs, Mississippi

DIED: March 25, 1931
Chicago, Illinois

A proud and courageous woman, Ida B. Wells fought against discrimination in all guises and demanded equal justice for African Americans, often at great personal expense. Wells was a staunch suffragist, and she urged the then radical concept of integration as the best solution to the racial problem. Since she advocated so many causes, she came into close contact with many white reformers, including Jane Addams. A leading figure in the anti-lynching campaign, Wells traveled widely across the United States and throughout Great Britain. At one point, her outspokenness led federal authorities to describe her as being a far more dangerous agitator than Marcus Garvey, the black activist.

Wells was the daughter of slaves. Her father was a carpenter, her mother a homemaker who died from yellow fever when Wells was sixteen, which proved to be a turning point. A precocious young woman, Wells assumed control of the household and acted as the chief guardian of her younger siblings. She became a voracious reader (she loved Shakespeare).

Wells began teaching in a Mississippi country school before moving to Memphis in 1880. She demanded respect. Her uncompromising attitude often clashed with the social customs of the time. In 1884 she filed a lawsuit against the Chesapeake and Ohio Railroad when the conductor told her she would have to ride in the smoking car, the section set aside for African American passengers. Wells steadfastly refused to budge. She was then forcibly removed. She sued the railroad and won a $500 settlement on the grounds that the accommodations violated the separate but equal law. In 1887, however, the Supreme Court of Tennessee reversed the decision, declaring that the smoking car could be considered first-class accommodations—by "colored" standards.

Wells began writing for church papers when she was invited to join the staff of the African American weekly, the *Memphis Free Speech and Headlight.* Eventually she bought a one-third interest. An outspoken woman, she once publicly criticized the Memphis school system for its segregationist policies. As a result, she was dismissed from her teaching post in 1891. By this time, Wells had discovered the power of the press. She shortened the name of the Memphis newspaper to the *Free Speech* and continued to write against discrimination. In 1892, after three young African American businessmen—Thomas Moss, Calvin McDowell, and Lee Stewart—were lynched in Memphis, she initiated a newspaper campaign against the perpetrators and the white population that tacitly stood by in silence. She made many enemies in Memphis. When her newspaper office was burned to the ground, Wells moved to New York City, where she became a staff writer for the *New York Age,* an African American publication. She lectured throughout major American cities on the plight of the African American and made two visits to Great Britain.

In 1893 Wells visited Chicago to attend the World's Columbian Exposition. At that time the African American population of the city, according to historian Allan H. Spear, numbered less than 15,000. By 1915, however, the figure had risen to more than 50,000, and the first indications of a recognizable black community began to emerge on the South and West sides.

Wells campaigned vigorously during the fair for a pavilion to honor the accomplishments of African Americans. Her proposal was turned down. The rejection prompted Wells, along with Frederick Douglass, Ferdinand L. Barnett, and I. Garland Penn, to coauthor a scathing eighty-one-page booklet, called *Why the Colored American Is Not in the World's Columbian Exposition,* attacking city officials. Ten thousand copies were circulated at the fair.

In August 1894, Wells settled permanently in Chicago, and on June 27, 1895, she married Ferdinand L. Barnett, a Chicago lawyer and the first black Cook County assistant state's attorney. She contributed to the *Conservator,* her husband's newspaper and the first African American newspaper in the city. In 1895 she published *A Red Record: Tabulated Statistics and Alleged Causes of Lynchings in the United States, 1892–1893–1894.* In 1910 Wells founded and became president of the Negro Fellowship League, an organization with offices at 3005 South State Street that found employment, coordinated social services, and provided housing for African Americans, especially newly arrived migrants from the South. From 1913 to 1916, she was a probation officer of the Chicago municipal court.

When it came to justice, Wells refused to compromise. A critic of Booker T. Washington's "separate but equal" accommodation theory, Wells instead encouraged integration. For this reason, too, she attacked the policies of W. E. B. DuBois's Niagara Movement and of the National Association for the Advancement of Colored People (NAACP) as being too moderate. Unlike Washington and DuBois, Wells believed it would take more than economic improvement to eradicate racism. "We must educate the white people out of their 250 years of slave history," she wrote in her autobiography. In 1930 Wells became an independent candidate for state senator, running against Democrat Warren B. Douglas and Republican Adelbert H. Roberts. She placed a distant third.

Wells, who lived at 3624 South Parkway Boulevard (now King Drive) and later at 328 East Garfield Boulevard, died in Chicago of uremic poisoning in March 1931. She was sixty-eight. In December 1989, public television broadcast *Ida B. Wells: A Passion for Justice,* a critically acclaimed one-hour documentary of her life and work.

See also: Robert S. Abbott, Jane Addams
Further reading: Alfreda M. Duster, ed., *Crusade for Justice: The Autobiography of Ida B. Wells* (1970); Paula J. Giddings, *Ida: A Sword Among Lions* (2008); Allan H. Spear, *The Making of a Negro Ghetto 1890–1920* (1967); Mia Bay, *To Tell the Truth Freely* (2008).

William A. Wieboldt
Merchant

BORN: March 8, 1857
Near Cuxhaven, Germany

DIED: December 9, 1954
Evanston, Illinois

William A. Wieboldt founded the chain of department stores that bore his name. Wieboldt parted with tradition when he became one of the first Chicago merchants to establish his stores in neighborhoods away from the busy downtown shopping district. "My heart is in the neighborhood store," he once said. "Then I'm part of the community."

Wieboldt's father, a farmer near Cuxhaven, Germany, died when Wieboldt was two. As a youth, Wieboldt toiled long and hard on the farm, sometimes as much as fifteen hours a day. A letter from an uncle, W. R. Wieboldt, who had a store in Chicago, encouraged him to come to the New World to seek his fortune. He arrived in the United States in 1871 at the age of fourteen and found work at his uncle's store on Blue Island Avenue. Also employed in the store—in the millinery department—was another German-born youth, Anna Louisa Kruger. The couple courted and married in 1883.

Wieboldt's uncle then sent him to manage another store, in Sheboygan, Wisconsin. The venture failed and Wieboldt returned to Chicago. After working for his uncle for twelve years, Wieboldt felt it was time for him to strike out on his own. In 1883, with his wife as partner and $2,600 in savings, Wieboldt established a tiny general store—it was only twenty-five feet wide—on Indiana Avenue near Ashland Avenue and lived above the establishment in a small flat. The store turned a small profit during its first year. Encouraged, Wieboldt opened a larger store on Milwaukee Avenue at Paulina Street. That, too, prospered, and he established a chain of stores throughout Chicago, including a store at Lincoln and Belmont Avenues in 1912 and another outlet at Ashland Avenue and Monroe Street in 1925.

By locating stores in the neighborhoods, Wieboldt aimed to meet the needs of "the great middle millions of Chicagoland." Customers flocked to the full-service, budget-priced department stores. In 1921 he and his wife established the Wieboldt Foundation, a charitable, civic, and educational organization that dispensed benefits to charitable institutions. He retired from active management of the store in 1923 but continued to attend board meetings. His son, Werner, succeeded him as president.

Wieboldt died in 1954 in Evanston Hospital. He was ninety-seven.

In 1987, faced with mounting financial problems and a rapidly eroding customer base, Wieboldt Stores declared bankruptcy and closed its remaining thirteen stores, including its flagship State Street store. The Wieboldt Foundation is still in existence with offices at 53 West Jackson Boulevard.

See also: Marshall Field, Maurice Goldblatt, A. Montgomery Ward
Further reading: Dominic A. Pacyga and Ellen Skerrett, *Chicago: City of Neighborhoods* (1986).

Frances E. Willard

*Educator and
Social Reformer*

BORN: September 28, 1839
Churchville, New York

DIED: February 17, 1898
New York, New York

Frances Elizabeth Willard waged a lifelong battle against alcohol and its devastating effects. Alcohol, she said, weakened the fabric of society. Willard's vigorous campaigning as a prominent member of the Woman's Christian Temperance Union (WCTU) and founder of the World's Woman's Christian Temperance Union laid the groundwork that led to the eventual passage of the National Prohibition Act of 1919.

Willard taught school and traveled for several years before settling in Evanston. In 1871 she was named president of the Evanston College for Ladies and two years later became dean of women when the college became the Women's College of Northwestern University.

Willard resigned from the university in 1874 to become secretary of the national WCTU. Her new position gave her the opportunity to assume a prominent role in the national crusade against alcohol then sweeping the country. Five years later she was named president of the WCTU, a title she retained until her death. A powerful and forceful speaker, Willard toured the country speaking out against the evils of liquor. In addition, she promoted woman suffrage, insisted on stiffer penalties for sexual crimes against women, and advocated passage of the eight-hour workday.

Willard died in her sleep in a New York City hotel room in 1898 at the age of fifty-eight. In 1965 the Willard House at 1730 Chicago Avenue in Evanston, Illinois, was placed on the National Register of Historic Places.

Willard Court is named in her honor.

Further reading: Ruth Bordin, *Frances Willard* (2001).

Daniel Hale Williams

Physician

BORN: January 18, 1856
Hollidaysburg, Pennsylvania

DIED: August 4, 1931
Idlewild, Michigan

An eminent member of Chicago's African American community in the 1890s, Daniel Hale Williams was the best-known black physician in the country. Williams was also one of the founders of Provident Hospital in Chicago, the first interracial institution of its kind in the United States.

Williams grew up in Pennsylvania, Illinois, and Wisconsin. He was apprenticed to a shoemaker at the age of twelve and held odd jobs until 1878, when he took up the study of medicine. He came to Chicago in 1880. Three years later he graduated from the Chicago Medical College (now a part of Northwestern University) and opened a practice at Michigan Avenue and 31st Street in a racially mixed neighborhood on the South Side. The African American population then numbered only 10,000, according to Williams's biographer Helen Buckler. Williams treated both black and white patients.

At that time, black physicians were not permitted to work on the staffs of the city's hospitals, so Williams co-founded a black hospital, Provident. Pleased with the interracial emphasis, such well-known and wealthy Chicagoans as Philip Danforth Armour, Marshall Field, and George Pullman contributed money to its construction. On May 4, 1891, Provident Hospital opened in a three-story, twelve-bed building on South Dearborn Street between 27th and 29th Streets. Families from throughout the neighborhood brought supplies—sheets, linens, sugar, soap, even loaves of bread. In 1896 the hospital moved to a larger building—it had sixty-five beds—at 36th and Dearborn Streets.

Williams considered Provident Hospital to be a model, claims historian Allan H. Spear, "not of a Negro community institution, but of a venture in interracial cooperation." The advisory board consisted mostly of white Chicagoans, but the board of trustees and the hospital staff were predominantly African American. In addition, Provident established the first nursing school for black women in the United States.

The first successful suture of the human heart occurred at Provident in 1893. Although there were reports of a similar operation performed in St. Louis two years before and perhaps even earlier by another physician, Williams is credited with being the first surgeon to conduct such an operation. In July of that year, a laborer, James Cornish, was brought to the hospital with a severe knife wound in his chest. Using primitive equipment and without the benefit of X-rays, Williams courageously entered the chest cavity and delicately sewed the lining of the heart with fine catgut. The operation made headlines across the world.

A perfectionist, Williams insisted on the highest standards. Doctors and nurses were chosen solely on the basis of ability and included such outstanding physicians as Frank Billings and Christian Fenger, both white men. Unfortunately, this selectivity sometimes meant excluding African American physicians, which caused some resentment in the black community. As a light-skinned African American, Williams was sensitive to charges that Provident discriminated against darker-skinned blacks. Of mixed African American, American Indian, and European ancestry, the light-skinned, red-haired Williams could have passed for white "as some of his relatives and forebears had," notes biographer Helen Buckler. Even so, he chose not to. Still, he was never fully accepted by African Americans, and he never could explain to his critics' satisfaction why virtually all the staff appointments and nursing students were light-skinned. Provident physician and Williams's chief rival at the hospital, George Cleveland Hall, called Williams a "snob" who "doesn't seem to know what race he wants to belong to." Faced with mounting racial tension, white staff members gradually chose to leave, so that by 1916 all the nurses and most of the physicians were black. Williams himself, weary of the situation, resigned in 1912.

From 1894 to 1898, Williams served as surgeon-in-chief of Freedman's Hospital in Washington, D.C. There he established another school of nursing for African Americans, and in 1895 he founded the National Medical Association (NMA), an organization for African American physicians and, indeed, the only national organization that accepted black physicians. In 1898 Williams returned to Provident Hospital, where he became chief of surgery. He remained at Provident until 1912, when he was appointed attending staff surgeon at St. Luke's Hospital (now Rush Medical Center) until 1926. He was also an attending surgeon at Cook County Hospital in Chicago. Williams was the only black charter member of the American College of Surgeons. He was also a visiting professor of surgery at Meharry Medical College, a black institution, in Nashville, Tennessee.

Williams suffered a stroke in 1926. He died at his summer retreat in Idlewild, Michigan, in August 1931.

Williams Avenue on the South Side is named in his honor.

In 1929 Provident Hospital relocated to 51st Street and Vincennes Avenue. In 1974 the trustees of Provident announced that the hospital would become an outpost of Cook County Hospital. In September of 1990 the Cook County Board purchased the 300-bed hospital—shuttered since September 1987, soon after it filed for bankruptcy—for $1 from the United States Department of Housing and Urban Development. Provident Hospital reopened in 1993.

See also: Frank Billings
Further reading: Helen Buckler, *Doctor Dan: Pioneer in American Surgery* (1954); Allan H. Spear, *Black Chicago: The Making of a Negro Ghetto, 1890–1920* (1967).

Frank Lloyd Wright

Architect

BORN: June 8, 1867
Richland Center, Wisconsin

DIED: April 9, 1959
Phoenix, Arizona

Frank Lloyd Wright, one of the great names of architecture, created a whole new style of American architecture that bore little resemblance to European models. Wright sought to achieve a natural balance between the landscape and manufactured materials. He adapted buildings to their environment. To Wright, everything was connected.

The son of William Wright and Anna Lloyd Jones, Frank Lloyd Wright was raised by his mother, who instilled in him an appreciation of art. After spending two years as a civil engineering student at the University of Wisconsin, he moved to Chicago in 1887 to pursue a career in architecture, where he quickly found work as a draftsman at the architectural firm of Joseph Lyman Silsbee. He didn't stay long, though. Less than a year later, he became an apprentice with another great architectural firm, Adler and Sullivan (Wright worked with Louis Sullivan on the design of the Auditorium Theatre building).

In 1893 Wright opened his own practice, first in the Schiller Building, at 64 West Randolph Street (later called the Garrick Theatre) and then at the Steinway Hall Building, on West Van Buren Street near Michigan Avenue, in a loft-like space that was shared by other prominent

Chicago architects, including Dwight Perkins, the designer of Steinway Hall. Wright and his team, who were inspired not only by Louis Sullivan but also by the burgeoning arts and crafts movement started in England by William Morris, were working in this space when what became known as the Prairie school of architecture first came into being.

In 1898 Wright relocated his practice to west suburban Oak Park, Illinois (though he would later rent office space for a short period, 1910 to 1911, in Room 1020 of the Fine Arts Building at 410 South Michigan Avenue; he also designed a glass window that is still on display on the second floor of the building). His first project was the William H. Winslow house at 515 Auvergne Place in River Forest. Even then he utilized the innovative design that would make him famous. He used new materials—reinforced concrete, sheet metal, electric lighting, stucco—in a new and exciting way. Unlike the neoclassical style of the nineteenth century or the steel and glass of the twentieth century, Wright's style emphasized the organic foundation of architecture— the colors and textures of nature.

Wright developed a new type of architecture. His Prairie style, characterized by overhanging eaves and wide roofs on low-lying houses, blended in with the flat, horizontal landscape of the Midwest. The Prairie style produced a whole generation of architects. Among the most important Wright disciples are Walter Burley Griffin, George W. Maher, George C. Nimmons, George Grant Elmslie, and William Drummond.

In August 1914, while working on the Midway Gardens entertainment center in Chicago, Wright received news that a deranged servant had burned Taliesin, his Spring Green, Wisconsin, retreat, to the ground and killed seven guests, including Wright's mistress. In the aftermath of the tragedy, Wright found solace in his work. In 1915 he designed the Imperial Hotel in Tokyo, which was completed in 1922 and was the only major building to survive the earthquake of 1923. Other important Wright buildings include the Susan Lawrence Dana House (1903) in Springfield, Illinois; Fallingwater (1936), a private home in Bear Run, Pennsylvania; Taliesin West (1938) in Scottsdale, Arizona; the Johnson Wax Administration Building (1936) in Racine, Wisconsin; and the Solomon R. Guggenheim Museum (1956) in New York City, which opened after his death. Another significant work was Midway Gardens (1916), a combination concert hall, ballroom, supper club, and public garden built on the southern boundary of Hyde Park that was considered an important social and cultural innovation of its time. With its fusion of high and low culture, it hosted symphony orchestras that

appealed to both the city's elite and its middle and working classes, but it was not economically viable, and was thus demolished.

As early as the 1920s Wright argued that modern cities were becoming filthy and uninhabitable places. During his last years, he made increasingly more provocative remarks. "The modern city is a place for banking and prostitution and very little else," was a typical Wright comment of that period. While such contemporary colleagues as Daniel H. Burnham and John Wellborn Root found fame designing commercial structures, Wright preferred to concentrate on private homes and experiment with interior design. Often the interior of a Wright-designed home was just as striking as its exterior, featuring such design elements as the innovative concept of confining the living and sleeping areas to one floor—without any doors or partitions—or his highly stylized dining room chairs. One of the most famous and universally admired residences in the world is the Robie House (1909) at 5757 South Woodlawn Avenue in Hyde Park. With its broad overhanging roofs and long horizontal lines, the Robie House is considered the epitome of the Prairie style.

West suburban Oak Park contains the largest concentration of Wright-designed buildings in the world. The Frank Lloyd Wright Historic District features a collection of twenty-five structures designed by the architect between 1895 and 1915. The Frank Lloyd Wright Home and Studio at Forest and Chicago Avenues, founded in 1974, sponsors lectures and walking tours, presents exhibitions, and operates the Gingko Bookshop. (In late 2010, the administrative offices of the Home and Studio moved to Wright's Rookery Building at 209 South La Salle Street; the adjacent ShopWright gift shop opened in July 2011.) At Lake Street and Kenilworth Avenue is the Unity Temple (1908), the only public building designed by Wright in Oak Park. Some prominent Wright homes include the Edwin H. Cheney House (1904) at 520 North East Avenue in Oak Park and, in Chicago, the James Charnley House (1891) at 1365 North Astor Street, the Isadore Heller House (1896) at 5132 South Woodlawn Avenue, and the Emil Bach House (19159) at 7415 North Sheridan Road. In the early 1930s Wright and his wife, Milanov, founded the Taliesin Fellowship, a residential architectural school, at their 600-acre country estate in Spring Green, Wisconsin.

Wright died in 1959 at the age of ninety-one in Phoenix, Arizona. His work continues to inspire interest today. Reproductions of his tables and especially his tall-backed dining chairs remain popular, while jewelry and scarves decorated with his designs find a ready market.

Among Wright's many books are *An Organic Architecture* (1939) and *An American Architecture* (1955).

See also: Daniel H. Burnham, Walter Burley Griffin, George W. Maher, Ludwig Mies van der Rohe, John Wellborn Root, Howard Van Doren Shaw, Louis Sullivan

Further reading: Leonard K. Eaton, *Two Chicago Architects and Their Clients: Frank Lloyd Wright and Howard Van Doren Shaw* (1969); Finis Farr, *Frank Lloyd Wright: A Biography* (1961); Brendan Gill, *Many Masks: A Life of Frank Lloyd Wright* (1987); Donald Hoffman, *Frank Lloyd Wright's Robie House: The Illustrated Story of an Architectural Masterpiece* (1984); Ada Louise Huxtable, *Frank Lloyd Wright* (2005); James F. O'Gorman, *Three American Architects: Richardson, Sullivan, and Wright, 1865–1915* (1991); Paul E. Sprague, *Guide to Frank Lloyd Wright & Prairie School Architecture in Oak Park* (1986); Robert C. Twombly, *Frank Lloyd Wright: An Interpretive Biography* (1973); Frank Lloyd Wright, *An Autobiography* (1977).

John S. Wright

Pioneer

BORN: July 16, 1815
Sheffield, Massachusetts

DIED: September 26, 1874
Philadelphia, Pennsylvania

Called a visionary by his contemporaries, John Stephen Wright was an early Chicago booster. The city, he often wrote, was destined for greatness.

Born in Sheffield, Massachusetts, John Wright was a precocious child. By the age of twelve he was studying algebra, Greek, and Latin at a nearby academy. At fourteen he was sent to a private school. Wright first saw Chicago from the vantage point of a schooner when he and his father anchored near the mouth of the Chicago River in October 1832. The boy envisioned a future city in the muddy squalor. His father was less optimistic. He dismissed the frontier village—little more than a hamlet really—as a festering eyesore, and left it at that.

When the family eventually settled in the city, in 1833, the elder Wright built a general store and called it "The Prairie Store." Young Wright persuaded his father to let him buy several lots of land—forty-four acres south of 12th Street (now Roosevelt Road)—for $35,000, according to Wright biographer Lloyd Lewis. Nearly two years later he was offered $50,000 for less than half the land. By the end of 1836, Wright owned 7,000 acres, worth an estimated $200,000. Twenty years later it was worth a whopping $1.7 million. In 1836 he purchased a warehouse on South Water Street and engaged in the shipping business at the insistence of his father, who encouraged his son to acquire a proper vocation.

The winter of 1836–37 brought word from Eastern financial markets of a possible credit crunch. Hard times, it was said, were on the way. Despite the dire warnings, Wright forged ahead with his plans and opened the warehouse on South Water Street in May 1837. When the panic of 1837 struck with its full and devastating force, Wright, like many other Chicagoans, lost everything—his land, his business, and his newly acquired wealth.

In 1839 Wright formed the Union Agricultural Society "for the sole purpose of instruction and science, and improvements in scientific and practical agriculture and the mechanical arts in the counties of LaSalle, Will, Cook, McHenry, and Kane," and he embarked upon a career in public service. Wright encouraged the trustees of the society to establish a farmers' newspaper—nonpolitical and nonpartisan. He, in turn, became a reporter, an editor, and the publisher of the agricultural monthly. Wright also edited the weekly *Union Agriculturalist and Western Prairie Farmer,* which covered the usual farm news but also featured events and happenings in the city. Its slogan was "Farmers, Write for Your Paper." In 1843 the name was shortened to the *Prairie Farmer.* In 1870 Wright published his book, *Chicago: Past, Present, Future,* an early history of the city.

Wright was clearly a man ahead of his time. He campaigned for higher salaries for teachers—both male and female, an unusual position to take in his day. He was an early advocate for developing Chicago as a railroad hub, and he worked tirelessly to improve Chicago's schools. He not only predicted that Chicago would one day be a great meatpacking center, but he also prophesied in 1837 that the city would eventually surpass the population of Pittsburgh. In less than a decade, that prediction proved true. In 1861 he declared that Chicago's population would even surpass Philadelphia's before the turn of the century. Of course, Wright was correct again.

By the early 1850s Wright was looking for other economic opportunities. He saw a future in the reaper and became convinced that this was the business for him. He built a factory and began manufacturing reapers; in so doing he became the chief rival of Cyrus H. McCormick, the "reaper king." On the eve of the Civil War, Wright formed the Land Investment Company and resumed speculating in real estate. He felt the war would benefit the city greatly. "No earthly power," he wrote, "not even the dissolution of the Union, can divert from Chicago the business and the traffic of the great Northwest." Even the Chicago Fire of 1871 could not quench Wright's enthusiasm. "Nothing of the least consequence to the future of the city perished in the flames," he claimed. "Only buildings and perishable property to be at once replaced." His optimistic vision, however, was not shared by Eastern capitalists.

Frustrated by the cold shoulder he received from Eastern businessmen, Wright fell into a deep depression. By Christmas 1871 his mental condition had deteriorated so badly that he was placed in an asylum for the insane in Boston. Upon his release, he roamed around Boston—he refused to return to Chicago—preaching that a promised land lay in the Midwest to anyone who would listen. Few people did.

Wright spent his last days in and out of various insane asylums on the East Coast and in the Midwest. He died on September 26, 1874, in Philadelphia. His body was returned to Chicago and buried in Rosehill Cemetery.

Wrightwood Avenue is named in his honor.

See also: William Bross, Gurdon S. Hubbard, Cyrus H. McCormick

Further reading: Lloyd Lewis, *John S. Wright: Prophet of the Prairies* (1941).

Richard Wright

Novelist

BORN: September 4, 1908
Near Natchez, Mississippi

DIED: November 28, 1960
Paris, France

Richard Wright began his writing career in Chicago and set his best-known novel, *Native Son* (1940), in his adopted city. He believed that good writing could make a difference—that, in fact, it could change the world. From 1940 to 1960, Wright was the most famous African American writer in the world.

Richard Wright was born on a Mississippi cotton plantation. His grandfather was a slave, and his father an illiterate sharecropper. Wright endured a harsh, poverty-stricken childhood in the rural South. His father left when he was five, and his mother became an invalid when he was ten. Consequently, Wright was shuffled from orphanage to orphanage until he struck out on his own at fifteen and moved to Memphis. For several years he roamed the country. Disgusted with the Jim Crow racism that permeated the South, he decided to move north because he felt he would have a chance to live a better life there. When he arrived in Chicago in December 1927, he lived briefly with his aunt in a South Side rooming house. He found work as a clerk in the central post office, where he hauled and sorted mail, as a dishwasher at a North Side café, and as a porter at Michael Reese Hospital. He also attended writing classes and Communist Party functions, but most of all he dreamed. The North was not what he had expected. He felt disillusioned by the rampant racism he experienced in Chicago and was appalled by the segregation.

Wright joined the Chicago chapter of the John Reed Club, a leftist literary group, and he eventually became the club's secretary. The club provided the emotional support that he and other like-minded writers could not find elsewhere. In 1935 Wright wrote guidebooks for the Federal Writers' Project, and for several months in 1936 he worked as a publicist for the Federal Negro Theatre Project in Chicago. In 1937 he moved to New York. After World War II ended, he settled in Paris. "There is more freedom in one square block of Paris than in all of the United States," he declared.

His first book, *Uncle Tom's Children: Four Novellas*, published in 1938, launched his writing career. In 1939 Wright received a Guggenheim fellowship that enabled him to complete a full-length novel, *Native Son*, in 1940. The book—based partly on his own experiences and partly on the true case of Robert Nixon, a black man electrocuted in 1938 for the murder of a white girl—is a bitter indictment of racial injustice in America. It was acclaimed as an intense, heartfelt, and brutally honest portrayal of a young African American convicted of murder.

Native Son was an immediate success and the first novel by a black writer to be chosen as a Book-of-the-Month Club selection. Reactions to *Native Son* from the African American community were mixed, however. Although proud that a member of their race had met with literary success, a number of blacks chafed at Wright's decision to make such a violent figure of Bigger Thomas, the protagonist. They feared that the character's behavior not only confirmed—and fanned—the worst racial prejudice but also perpetuated the image of African Americans as brutes. The response from the white mainstream press was less harsh.

Fanny Butcher, literary critic of the *Chicago Tribune,* called *Native Son* "an astonishing piece of work."

The book spawned several stage and film versions. In 1941 a dramatization at New York's famous Mercury Theatre, produced by John Houseman and directed by Orson Welles, opened on Broadway. In 1950 Wright himself portrayed the lead character in the film version. Shot on location in Chicago in 1949 by a French director, the movie received poor distribution in the United States. When it finally played in Chicago two years later, it was panned as a well-intentioned but amateurish production. In 1978 the Goodman Theatre, under the direction of artistic director Gregory Mosher, presented a critically acclaimed interpretation of Wright's book, and in 1987 another movie version was released featuring a stellar cast, including Geraldine Page, Oprah Winfrey, Matt Dillon, and newcomer Victor Love as Bigger Thomas. Film exteriors were shot around 63rd Street and Greenwood Avenue.

The largely autobiographical *Black Boy,* published in 1945, further enhanced Wright's reputation as a major writer. But, like *Native Son,* it also inspired strong reactions. Among Wright's other works were *The Outsider* (1953); *The Long Dream* (1958); and *Eight Men* (1961), a posthumously released collection of short stories; and *Lawd Today* (1963), a novel about an African American postal worker in Chicago. Wright also wrote nonfiction, including *Twelve Million Black Voices* (1941), *Black Power* (1954), *The Color Curtain* (1956), *Pagan Spain* (1957), and *White Man, Listen!* (1957).

Wright lived a life of self-imposed exile on the periphery of society. Racial discrimination intensified his profound sense of isolation. Not only did he feel out of place within white mainstream society, he also felt alienated among his own people. An idealist at heart, he believed that somewhere on earth there was a land where men and women of all races and creeds lived together in peace and prosperity. Though he never found his utopia, he did find comfort in the permanence of the word and in his belief that the written word was the most powerful weapon of all because it could, in the right hands, effect social change. It was his sweet optimism that gave him hope and a sense of purpose even in his darkest moments.

Although Wright lived in Chicago for only ten years, the city shaped him and his work in ways both negative and positive. Wright died of a heart attack complicated by dysentery in November 1960 in Paris. He was fifty-two.

Wright's novels are still considered classics of American literature.

See also: Nelson Algren, Jack Conroy, Willard Motley

Further reading: Michel Fabre, *The Unfinished Quest of Richard Wright* (1973); Addison Gayle, *Richard Wright: Ordeal of a Native Son* (1980); Hazel Rowley, *Richard Wright: The Life and Times* (2001); Jennifer Jensen Wallach, *Richard Wright: From Black Boy to World Citizen* (2010); Jerry W. Ward Jr. and Robert J. Butler, *The Richard Wright Encyclopedia* (2008); Constance Webb, *Richard Wright: A Biography* (1968).

William Wrigley Jr.

Baseball Club Owner and Entrepreneur

BORN: September 30, 1861
Philadelphia, Pennsylvania

DIED: January 26, 1932
Phoenix, Arizona

William Wrigley Jr. founded a chewing-gum empire, bought the Chicago Cubs, and built Wrigley Field. A classic underachiever during his early years in Philadelphia— he dropped out of grammar school—Wrigley nevertheless had ambition, smarts, and determination. A tireless promoter, the extroverted Wrigley once said, "Anybody can make gum. Selling it is the problem."

William Wrigley ran away from home at age of eleven and got a job selling newspapers in New York before returning a few weeks later to his native Philadelphia. His father, a soap manufacturer, found him a job stirring a vat of soap in his factory at a salary of $1.50 a week. Although only thirteen, young Wrigley pleaded with his father to make him a traveling soap salesman. The older man reluctantly agreed.

Wrigley made a grand salesman—eager, aggressive, and hard working. In 1901 he moved to Chicago to open a branch of the family firm and expanded his line to include lamps, clocks, guns, fountain pens, cameras, safety razors, accident insurance, and baking powder. Soon the baking powder outsold everything else, and in 1892 Wrigley abandoned the soap line altogether. As an incentive, Wrigley offered two packs of chewing gum with each ten-cent can of baking powder. Encouraged by the positive response, Wrigley decided to discontinue the baking powder and began work on what would become a new empire: chewing gum.

Early brand names for the gum were Vassar, Lotta (as in "a lotta gum"), and Sweet Sixteen Orange. In 1893, operating out of a nondescript storeroom on East Kinzie Street, Wrigley introduced Juicy Fruit and Wrigley's Spearmint.

In 1898 he formed the William Wrigley Jr. Company. In 1911 Wrigley moved into an elegant mansion, originally built for a wealthy brewer named Joseph Theurer, at 2466 North Lakeview Avenue. Previously the family had lived in rather makeshift quarters—in the Plaza Hotel, located at the corner of North Avenue and Clark Street, and in a small apartment on North Dearborn Street near Burton Place. In 1921 Wrigley sold the house to his son, Philip. The Theurer/Wrigley house was designated a Chicago landmark in August 1979.

Wrigley was one of the first Chicago businessmen to advertise on a grand scale, using billboards, advertising space on streetcars, and ads in the major newspapers. The Wrigley ad campaign was deceptively simple, "Tell 'em quick and tell 'em often." He borrowed lavishly to fund his expensive campaign. Business eventually picked up, with Wrigley's Spearmint sales increasing to well over the $1 million mark the first year. By 1910 Wrigley's Spearmint was on its way to becoming America's favorite gum.

In 1912 Wrigley moved his plant to 35th Street and Ashland Avenue in the newly created Central Manufacturing District (CMD), a planned industrial community in the McKinley Park neighborhood. Its presence encouraged other industries to locate there. In 1919 Wrigley purchased Catalina Island in California for $2 million, sight unseen, and spent millions more developing the fabled isle. Several years later, he hired Chicago's best architects to construct the Wrigley Building on North Michigan Avenue, completed in 1924, to house the burgeoning chewing-gum empire. In 1921 Wrigley became principal stockholder of the Chicago Cubs baseball team, and in 1926 the team's stadium, formerly called Weeghman Park, was renamed Wrigley Field.

Wrigley was quite an innovator when it came to business. He was the one of the first manufacturers to give employees Saturday off, he provided free medical care to workers for injuries sustained on the job, and he offered life insurance for every employee. He died in 1932 at his winter home in Phoenix at the age of seventy without attaining his life's ambition: seeing his beloved Cubs win a world championship. He was buried on Catalina Island.

Upon his father's death, Philip K. Wrigley assumed control of both the chewing-gum business and the Chicago Cubs baseball club. In 1981 the Tribune Company bought the team for $20.5 million. In April 2008, the William Wrigley Jr. Company announced its sale to Virginia-based Mars, Inc. for $23 billion, operating as a subsidiary of the privately owned Mars. The merger created the world's largest confectionary company, with such popular brands as Extra and Orbit gums, Snickers, and M&M's.

In July 2011, the William Wrigley Jr. Company announced that the company would be moving its global headquarters from its iconic North Michigan Avenue address to a new $45 million research and development center on Goose Island on Chicago's North Side.

See also: Charles A. Comiskey, Bill Veeck

Further reading: William Zimmerman Jr., *William Wrigley, Jr.: The Man and His Business, 1861–1932* (1935).

Charles Tyson Yerkes

Financier

BORN: June 25, 1837
Philadelphia, Pennsylvania

DIED: December 29, 1905
London, England

Charles Tyson Yerkes, an unscrupulous railroad baron, was at the center of a controversy that plagued Chicago for many years: the traction problem—private versus public ownership of the streetcar and elevated lines. Yerkes bribed virtually everyone to obtain franchise rights. The very core of Yerkes's corrupt empire was based on bribery and shady deals. "Buy old junk, fix it up a little, unload it on the other fellow," he once said. That was the Yerkes way of doing business.

The son of a Philadelphia bank president, Charles Tyson Yerkes entered the brokerage business in Philadelphia as a clerk. In 1859 he opened a brokerage house and in 1862 a banking house. He built a sizable fortune until a recession struck in 1871. Yerkes was convicted and sent to prison for embezzlement over the alleged mishandling of Philadelphia municipal funds. He served seven months and then resumed his career by investing in Philadelphia railroads and transit companies.

In 1882 Yerkes, ready for a new life in another city, moved to Chicago. By 1886 he had gained control of the city's streetcar lines and organized his own line, the North Chicago Street Railway, replacing horse cars with trolley cars and building new lines. Yerkes made the easy money while his stockholders were left holding the bag—usually an empty one. Through sly maneuverings and shady deals with corrupt politicians—including the nefarious aldermen from the First Ward, "Bathhouse John" Coughlin and

Michael "Hinky Dink" Kenna—Yerkes obtained franchises. In addition to Coughlin and Kenna, his allies in city hall included Republican chieftain William Lorimer and Johnny Powers, the powerful alderman from the Nineteenth Ward.

In 1895 Yerkes tried to pass a plan through the city council to extend his franchise of the transit lines, which included the newly constructed elevated lines, for another fifty years with no compensation to the city. Yerkes's forces then introduced a bill—the Allen bill—in the state legislature to permit franchise extensions. The *Chicago Tribune* estimated that the passage of such an ordinance would cost the city a massive $150 million. The Allen bill became law in 1897, but the public outcry was so severe that Yerkes decided to wait before renewing his franchises. Two years later he tried again, and nearly succeeded, until Mayor Carter Harrison II and the city council finally turned against him, fueled by spirited attacks from the Municipal Voters League. Pressure mounted for municipal control of the city's transit lines. Protests occurred. Newspaper accounts report of marching in the streets and angry mobs converging on city hall, threatening death to any alderman who sided with the unscrupulous traction king. Succumbing to the will of the people, the Illinois legislature finally repealed the law. A sulking Yerkes blamed his defeat on "socialists, anarchists, and newspapers."

In 1892 Yerkes donated $1 million to the University of Chicago for the construction of the Yerkes Observatory—which still houses the world's largest refracting telescope—in Lake Geneva, Wisconsin. In 1897 he bought the *Chicago Inter-Ocean* newspaper. Yerkes, who lived in a mansion at Michigan Avenue and 32nd Street, was also a serious art collector. His attempts at respectability did not alter his corrupt image, however. Newspapers continued to condemn him as a ruthless and deceitful opportunist.

In 1899 Yerkes sold his interest in the traction franchises, and the following year he moved to London, where he played a significant role in the creation of that city's subway system. He died there in 1905, having squandered most of his wealth.

In 1907 the traction problem was finally resolved when the streetcar operators agreed to give the city the option to buy the transit lines at any time. Eventually a single public agency—the Chicago Transit Authority—was created in 1947.

Yerkes's turbulent career generated interest beyond his lifetime. Writers were fascinated by Charles Yerkes's power and personality. Novelist Theodore Dreiser's "Trilogy of Desire" was inspired by Yerkes's life. The series consists of *The Financier* (1912), *The Titan* (1914), and *The Stoic* (1947). And in 1988 two Chicago playwrights, Michael C. Dorf and Claudia Howard Queen, collaborated on a musical play entitled *Titan*. Based on Dreiser's book of the same name, *Titan* chronicled the life and times of the traction king.

See also: John Peter Altgeld, "Bathhouse John" Coughlin, Theodore Dreiser, Carter Harrison II, Michael "Hinky Dink" Kenna

Further reading: John Franch, *Robber Baron: The Life of Charles Tyson Yerkes* (2008); Ray Ginger, *Altgeld's America: The Lincoln Ideal Versus Changing Realities* (1958); Herman Kogan and Lloyd Wendt, *Lords of the Levee: The Story of Bathhouse John and Hinky Dink* (1943).

Arthur Young
Accountant

BORN: Circa December 1863
Glasgow, Scotland

DIED: April 3, 1948
Macon, South Carolina

Arthur Young was arguably the most important and influential accountant in the city's history. He entered the profession when accounting was still in its infancy, yet within a short time the public accounting firm he founded, Arthur Young and Company—a member of the "Big Eight," became one of the largest accounting firms in the country.

Arthur Young was born in Scotland, the son of a Glasgow shipbuilder. Educated at the prestigious Glasgow Academy, he received a master's degree from the University of Glasgow in 1883. After serving a three-year apprenticeship as a clerk in a Glasgow law firm, he returned to the university and received his law degree in 1887. Young had plans to move to Edinburgh to practice law when he began exhibiting the first signs of deafness, a condition that would grow progressively worse. Heeding the advice of his doctor, who suggested he find a less stressful profession, Young left Scotland. He spent some time in Switzerland and then traveled to the warmer climate of Algiers. There he met an American businessman, Gordon Bennett, who encouraged him to immigrate to the United States.

Young arrived in America in 1890 and settled in New York. He found work at J. Kennedy Tod and Company, an international banking firm on Wall Street, which was run by a fellow Scotsman. Young spent four years at the firm until he decided to pursue a new profession—accounting—in a new city, Chicago. In Chicago, Young met Charles W. Stuart, a comptroller of a Boston-owned copper company, who had also just moved to the city. Together, in 1894, they established their own public accounting firm in a one-room office in the Monadnock Building at 53 West Jackson Boulevard, with a starting capital of $500 and a staff of one stenographer.

When Young started, the accounting profession in the United States was virtually nonexistent. "There was no legal recognition of accountancy; in fact, it was not until 1896 that New York State formally recognized accountancy as a profession," he recalled in his autobiography. Accountancy originated in Young's native Scotland when the Society of Accountants was created by a royal charter in Edinburgh in 1854. The state of Illinois did not recognize accounting as a legitimate profession until 1903—almost ten years after Young entered the field. Young was one of the first people in the state to become a certified public accountant.

In 1906 the firm dissolved when Young parted with Stuart, "who," he explained tersely, "had proved an unsatisfactory partner." With his brother Stanley—also a graduate of the University of Glasgow—Young founded Arthur Young and Company. In 1915 the firm moved into larger quarters in the Borland Building at 105 South LaSalle Street. The firm grew slowly but steadily. Young's main obstacle was locating trained accountants. Since accounting was such a new profession in the United States, very few universities and colleges taught accounting classes. In addition most businesses were reluctant to hire outside employees to handle their bookkeeping tasks—managers preferred to handle accounting matters in-house. Thus, Young was compelled to return to Scotland to recruit good accountants. Young secured important clients during those early years, including Swift & Company, Crane and Company, and the William Wrigley Jr. Company. Others would follow: Montgomery Ward and Company, Encyclopaedia Britannica, and Rand McNally.

In 1911 Young opened a New York branch, which became the home office of the company when Young moved there in 1917. Prior to 1921, the various branches were run as local partnerships, operated independently from one another. In 1921 Young decided to merge all the branches into a single partnership under one firm with Young assuming the position of senior partner. In 1923 the first overseas branches opened in London and Paris. The firm weathered the Great Depression, although not without some difficulty. The advent of World War II brought several significant changes. The firm hired its first women accountants, for example, in 1943. In 1957, its first woman partner, Mary Lanigar, came aboard.

Young died in April 1948 of viral pneumonia in South Carolina at the age of eighty-four. A history of the company, *Arthur Young and the Business He Founded,* was published the same year.

In 1956 the firm moved to the Harris Bank Building at 111 West Monroe Street and, later, as business continued to expand, into the IBM Plaza at 420 North Wabash Avenue. During the 1980s, additional emphasis was placed on the firm's thriving consulting practices. The firm specialized in the entrepreneurial services concept, providing business advice to companies in virtually every industry.

On June 22, 1989, Arthur Young and Company and Ernst and Whinney—two of the country's largest accounting firms—merged to form Ernst and Young, with branches around the world.

See also: Arthur Andersen

Further reading: J. C. Burton, ed., *Arthur Young and the Business He Founded* (1948); Mark Stevens, *The Big Eight: Inside America's Largest Accounting Firms* (1984).

Ella Flagg Young

Educator

BORN: January 15, 1845
Buffalo, New York

DIED: October 28, 1918
Washington, D.C.

Ella Flagg Young was not only the first woman superintendent of the Chicago public school system, a position she held from 1909 to 1915, she was also one of the best educators in the Midwest. Fair and conscientious, Young served as a role model for a generation of young women. In her speeches and in the classroom, she told her students—both girls and boys—that they could be whatever they wanted to be.

In 1858 Ella Flagg Young came to Chicago with her parents. Two years later she enrolled at the Chicago Normal School. Young secured her first teaching position in 1862 when she was assigned to Foster School. On Saturday mornings she attended teacher training sessions to learn the latest instruction methods and theories. In 1863 she transferred to Brown School as assistant principal, and in 1865 she began training neophyte teachers at Scammon School. An

efficient and conscientious administrator, Young quickly advanced in her profession. In 1876 she was elected principal of Scammon School, and in 1879 she became head of the much larger Skinner School on the West Side.

Although women dominated the teaching professions during the 1870s at both the elementary and high school levels, men still pulled the strings and determined hiring practices. In 1879 half of the city's high school teachers and half of the elementary school teachers were women, notes Young's biographer Joan A. Smith. In 1887 Young became assistant superintendent of Chicago Public Schools. Two years later she was appointed to the state board of education. At the same time she was furthering her own education: in the fall of 1895, she enrolled in a seminar at the University of Chicago, where her professor was the noted scholar John Dewey. She was deeply influenced by Dewey.

Young's work as a member of the board of education had taken its toll, however, and her relationship with the current superintendent of schools had become rather strained. In June 1899 she resigned her position as assistant superintendent to protest interference from the board of education. After leaving the University of Chicago, she spent some time abroad, traveling and visiting the various school systems in Europe. Returning to the United States, she received her Ph.D. from the University of Chicago in 1900—by that time, she was in her fifties—and was promoted soon thereafter from associate professional lecturer at the university to professor of education.

In 1900 the new superintendent, Edwin G. Cooley, chose Young as principal of the Chicago Normal School, a training school for teachers located at 68th Street and Stewart Avenue on the South Side. Young was influenced by the "new humanism" promulgated by professors at her alma mater, the University of Chicago. Everything was connected, she believed. Nothing existed in isolation. She became determined to turn theory into practice.

As principal, Young was actively involved in the day-to-day activities of the school. Her influence grew. A progressive thinker, she opposed corporal punishment and allowed teachers flexibility when planning their day's work. She would make the rounds of the school, walking down the hallways, stepping into classrooms, and asking the students questions. The teacher's aim, she insisted, "is the evolution of a character which, through thinking of the right and acting for the right, shall make for right conduct, rectitude, righteousness." She called for less punishment and more individual rewards in the classroom. In such a nurturing atmosphere, she believed, "the strong will be generous, the weak will dare to be true; the gifted and the lowly will strive for the good of all." Among the teaching staff, she attempted to instill a spirit of mutual cooperation.

When Superintendent Cooley resigned in 1909, Young was considered a possible candidate. She had two strikes against her, however: her age—she was sixty-four years old—and her sex. "I only wish Mrs. Young were a man," mused one board member. Ultimately, however, she was elected. Young took to the job with great energy and enthusiasm. Immediately she announced that her door would always be open to teachers.

Her first two and a half years in office were calm and fruitful. She introduced vocational courses in high schools and recommended courses in ethics and morality. Not one to dictate directives to either pupils or staff, she believed that children had the right to make their own choices when it came to their education and insisted that teachers have a say in determining school policy.

Rivalry on the school board disrupted her term in office and forced her, on two occasions, to resign her position as superintendent. In August 1913 she stepped down, convinced that she was "the victim of political intrigue among board members." As evidence, she cited several examples: salaries were approved by the board without her consultation, several of her recommendations for principal were rejected, and a committee was formed to suggest possible revisions in the curriculum from so-called fads and frills courses (sewing and crafts) to the "three Rs." Bowing to public pressure—citizens, many of them women, held protest meetings throughout the city demanding that the popular superintendent be reinstated—the board voted to retain her, and she resumed her duties.

Young achieved many firsts. She was the first woman superintendent of a major American city, the first woman to earn a Ph.D. from the Department of Education at the University of Chicago, the first woman president of the Illinois Teachers Association, and the first woman awarded an honorary LL.D. by the University of Illinois.

Young retired from the superintendency in December 1915. On October 26, 1918, she died of pneumonia in Washington, D.C., while on a speaking tour. She was buried at Rosehill Cemetery.

See also: John Dewey, Margaret Haley, Francis W. Parker

Further reading: George S. Counts, *School and Society in Chicago* (1928); Mary J. Herrick, *The Chicago Schools: A Social and Political History* (1971); Joan A. Smith, *Ella Flagg Young: Portrait of a Leader* (1979).

Florenz Ziegfeld

Theatrical Producer

BORN: March 21, 1869
Chicago, Illinois

DIED: July 22, 1932
Hollywood, California

Florenz Ziegfeld was a native Chicagoan who made a name for himself on Broadway. His *Ziegfeld Follies*, a lavish musical revue, represented good, old-fashioned, wholesome fare, while the *Follies* dancers came to epitomize the ideal American girl—virginal, sweet, and beautiful. "We do not select according to our own conception of beauty," Florenz once said. "No, we keep our finger on the public pulse and give it what it wants."

Florenz Ziegfeld was a product of Chicago's public schools. His father, a musician also named Florenz Ziegfeld, immigrated to the United States from Germany in 1858 and settled in Chicago in 1863. Four years later he founded the Chicago Academy of Music. In the family home at 1448 West Adams Street, the younger Ziegfeld grew up listening to Beethoven and Bach and was active in amateur theater. He entered show business in 1893, producing orchestras and musical shows at the World's Columbian Exposition. He brought a German band, Russian singers and dancers, a Hungarian string orchestra, and an English singer to the world's fair. He also introduced Eugene Sandow, called the "perfect man" due to his finely chiseled athletic build, to the fair and acted as Sandow's manager for several years.

Like many Chicagoans who wanted to make a living in show business, Ziegfeld moved east to New York. In 1896 he introduced a French starlet, Anna Held, in *A Parlor Match*. Held appeared in many of Ziegfeld's musical comedies. One of Ziegfeld's early musical comedies, *Mlle. Napoleon* (1903), was an utter failure and left the showman on the brink of bankruptcy, but he didn't let hard times get in the way of success. Instead, with *The Follies of 1907,* he ushered in a new kind of musical variety program. The *Follies* made their debut at the New York Theatre on July 8, 1907. The show was seen annually on Broadway, with three exceptions, until 1931.

The first *Follies* featured a bevy of beauties in a chorus line, personally chosen by Ziegfeld himself. Ziegfeld wished to "glorify the American girl." He selected not only the girls but also the music; in addition, he approved the costumes and directed the production numbers. Ziegfeld hired many eminent composers to write for his shows, including Irving Berlin and Jerome Kern. Entertainers Sophie Tucker, Eddie Cantor, Fannie Brice, W. C. Fields, Will Rogers, Bert Williams, and Ed Wynn got their start with Ziegfeld. Moreover, in his programs he introduced songs that became American standards, including "Shine On, Harvest Moon" (1908); "By the Light of the Silvery Moon" (1909); "My Man" (1921), sung by Fannie Brice; and "My Blue Heaven" (1927), performed by Eddie Cantor. Other Ziegfeld shows included *Sally* (1920 and 1923), *Show Boat* (1927 and 1932), *Show Girl* (1929), *Simple Simon* (1930), and *Smiles* (1930).

Critics accused Ziegfeld of provincialism and of lacking sophistication, to which he sniffed, "What is sophistication?" Americans, he claimed, preferred good, old-fashioned entertainment, and he, for one, would gladly supply it.

Ziegfeld always considered Chicago his home. Whenever he was in town, he would visit his parents and the old Victorian brick mansion on Adams Street. In 1925 Ziegfeld announced plans to build a huge $1 million playhouse on Michigan Avenue and 8th Street to be known simply as The Ziegfeld. "I intend to inaugurate here an annual musical production, comparable to the *Follies,*" he told reporters. "Chicago is entitled to have just as good entertainment as New York. Any producer who tries to bring second-string casts here will be fooled. Chicago audiences are too wise." But it never came to pass. Neither did Ziegfeld's wish to produce another *Follies* show starring Maurice Chevalier.

Weakened by a bout of pneumonia, Ziegfeld suffered a fatal heart attack in a Hollywood hospital in July 1932. He was sixty-three. In 1936 a movie based on his career, *The Great Ziegfeld*, was released and in 1945, the *Ziegfeld Follies*, starring Fred Astaire, Judy Garland, and Lena Horne, was made.

Several months before he died Ziegfeld produced a national weekly radio program, "Ziegfeld Follies of the Air," that aired in Chicago on WGN on Sunday evenings. Ziegfeld hosted, arranged, and directed the program, which featured talent from past and contemporary Ziegfeld productions.

Further reading: Rudolph A. Hofmeister, *The Germans of Chicago* (1976); Ethan Mordden, *Ziegfeld: The Man Who Invented Show Business* (2008).

Bibliography

Abbott, Karen. *Sin in the Second City: Madams, Ministers, Playboys, and the Battle for America's Soul.* New York: Random House, 2008.

Abt, Jeffrey. *American Egyptologist: The Life of James Henry Breasted and the Creation of His Oriental Institute.* Chicago: University of Chicago Press, 2011.

Ade, George. *Chicago Stories.* Chicago: Henry Regnery, 1963.

Adelman, William J. *Haymarket Revisited: A Tour Guide of Labor History Sites and Ethnic Neighborhoods Connected with the Haymarket Affair.* Chicago: Illinois Labor History Society, 1976.

Alexander, Elizabeth, ed. *The Essential Gwendolyn Brooks.* American Poets Project. New York: Library of America, 2005.

Algren, Nelson. *Entrapment and Other Writings.* Edited by Brooke Horvath and Dan Simon. New York: Seven Stories Press, 2009.

Allsop, Kenneth. *The Bootleggers and Their Era.* Garden City, N.Y.: Doubleday, 1961.

Allswang, John M. *A House for All Peoples: Ethnic Politics in Chicago.* Lexington: University of Kentucky Press, 1971.

Anderson, Brooke Davis. *Darger: The Henry Darger Collection at the American Folk Art Museum.* New York: American Folk Art Museum / Harry N. Abrams, 2001.

Anderson, Margaret. *My Thirty Years' War: The Autobiography; Beginnings and Battles to 1930.* New York: Horizon Press, 1969.

Andreas, A. T. *History of Chicago.* 3 vols. Chicago: A. T. Andreas, 1884–1886.

Angle, Paul M. *Philip K. Wrigley: A Memoir of a Modest Man.* Chicago: Rand McNally, 1975.

Anson, Adrian Constantine. *A Ball Player's Career.* New York: Macmillan, 1900.

Asbury, Herbert. *Gem of the Prairie: An Informal History of the Chicago Underworld.* Garden City, N.Y.: Doubleday, 1942.

Ascoli, Peter. *Julius Rosenwald: The Man Who Built Sears, Roebuck and Advanced the Cause of Black Education in the American South.* Bloomington: Indiana University Press, 2006.

Ashbaugh, Carolyn. *Lucy Parsons: American Revolutionary.* Chicago: Charles H. Kerr, 1976.

Ashmore, Harry S. *Unseasonable Truths: The Life of Robert Maynard Hutchins.* Boston: Little, Brown, 1989.

Asinof, Eliot. *Eight Men Out: The Black Sox and the 1919 World Series.* Chicago: Holt, Rinehart and Winston, 1963.

Atlas, James. *Bellow: A Biography.* New York: Modern Library, 2002.

Austin, Andy. *Rule 53: Capturing Hippies, Spies, Politicians, and Murderers in an American Courtroom.* Chicago: Lake Claremont Press, 2008.

Avrich, Paul. *The Haymarket Tragedy.* Princeton, N.J.: Princeton University Press, 1984.

Axelson, Gustaf W. *"Commy": The Life Story of Charles Comiskey.* Chicago: Reilly & Lee, 1919.

Baatz, Simon. *The Thrill of It All: Leopold, Loeb, and the Murder That Shocked Jazz Age Chicago.* New York: Harper Perennial, 2009.

Bachrach, Julia S. "Jens Jensen." *Chicago Wilderness,* Spring 2001.

Bachrach, Julia Sniderman. *The City in a Garden: A Photographic History of Chicago's Parks.* Foreword by Bill Kurtis. Placitas, N.M.: Center for American Places / Chicago Park District, 2001.

Baim, Tracy, ed. *Out and Proud in Chicago: An Overview of the City's Gay Community.* Evanston, Ill.: Agate Publishing / Surrey Books, 2008.

Baker, Carlos. *Ernest Hemingway: A Life Story.* Princeton, N.J.: Princeton University Press, 1972.

Ballowe, James. *A Man of Salt and Trees: The Life of Joy Morton.* DeKalb: Northern Illinois University Press, 2009.

Barnard, Harry. *Eagle Forgotten: The Life of John Peter Altgeld.* Indianapolis: Bobbs-Merrill, 1938.

Barter, Judith A., ed. *Apostles of Beauty: Arts and Crafts from Britain to Chicago.* With essays by Judith A. Barter, Sarah E. Kelly, Ellen E. Roberts, Brandon K. Ruud, and Monica Obniski. Chicago: Art Institute of Chicago, 2009.

Baugher, Shirley. *Our Old Town: The History of a Neighborhood.* Chicago: Old Town Triangle Association, 2001.

Baum, L. Frank. *The Annotated Wizard of Oz.* Edited with an introduction by Michael Patrick Hearn. Centennial Edition. New York: W. W. Norton, 2000.

Baxter, Charles, Michael Collier, and Edward Hirsch, eds. *A William Maxwell Portrait: Memories and Appreciations.* New York: W. W. Norton, 2004.

Bay, Mia. *To Tell the Truth Freely: The Life of Ida B. Wells.* New York: Hill and Wang, 2008.

Beadle, Muriel. *The Fortnightly of Chicago: The City and Its Women, 1873–1973.* Chicago: Henry Regnery, 1973.

Beck, Frank O. *Hobohemia: Emma Goldman, Lucy Parsons, Ben Reitman, & Other Agitators & Outsiders in 1920s/30s Chicago.* Bughouse Square Series. Edited by Franklin Rosemont. Chicago: Charles H. Kerr, 2000.

Becker, Lynn. "An Odd Way to Honor Burnham." *Chicago Reader,* July 16, 2009.

Benezra, Neal. *Ed Paschke.* Manchester, Vt.: Hudson Hills Press, 1996.

Berger, Daniel, and Steve Jajkowski, ed. *Chicago Television.* Charleston, S.C.: Arcadia Publishing / Museum of Broadcast Communications, 2010.

Berger, Miles L. *They Built Chicago: Entrepreneurs Who Shaped a Great City's Architecture.* Chicago: Bonus Books, 1992.

Berkow, Ira. *Maxwell Street: Survival in an Ethnic Bazaar.* Garden City, N.Y.: Doubleday, 1977.

Bernardin, Joseph Cardinal. *The Gift of Peace: Personal Reflections.* Chicago: Loyola Press, 1997.

Bernstein, Arnie. *Hollywood on Lake Michigan: 100 Years of Chicago and the Movies.* Chicago: Lake Claremont Press, 1998.

Bernstein, Arnie, ed. *"The Movies Are": Carl Sandburg's Film Reviews and Essays, 1920–1928.* Introduction by Roger Ebert. Chicago: Lake Claremont Press, 2000.

Bernstein, Fred. "Rediscovering a Heroine of Chicago Architecture." *New York Times,* January 1, 2008.

Biesenbach, Klaus. *Henry Darger.* Munich: Prestel, 2009.

Bilek, Arthur J. *The First Vice Lord: Big Jim Colosimo and the Ladies of the Levee.* Nashville, Tenn.: Cumberland House, 2008.

Biles, Roger. *Big City Boss in Depression and War: Mayor Edward J. Kelly of Chicago.* DeKalb: Northern Illinois University Press, 1984.

———. *Crusading Liberal: Paul H. Douglas of Illinois.* DeKalb: Northern Illinois University Press, 2002.

———. *Richard J. Daley: Politics, Race, and the Governing of Chicago.* DeKalb: Northern Illinois University Press, 1995.

Black, Timuel D., Jr. *Bridges of Memory: Chicago's Second Generation of Black Migration.* Vol. 2. Evanston, Ill.: Northwestern University Press, 2008.

Blakely, Robert J., and Marcus Shepard. *Earl B. Dickerson: A Voice for Freedom and Equality.* Forewords by John Hope Franklin and Alta M. Blakely. Evanston, Ill: Northwestern University Press, 2006.

Block, Jean F. *Hyde Park Houses.* Chicago: University of Chicago Press, 1978.

Blumberg, Dorothy Rose. *Florence Kelley: The Making of a Social Pioneer.* New York: Augustus M. Kelley, 1966.

Boas, Maxwell, and Steve Chain. *Big Mac: The Unauthorized Story of McDonald's.* New York: E. P. Dutton, 1976.

Bolotin, Norm. *The World's Columbian Exposition: The Chicago World's Fair of 1893.* Urbana: University of Illinois Press, 2002.

Bonesteel, Michael, ed. *Henry Darger: Art and Selected Writings.* New York: Rizzoli, 2000.

Bordin, Ruth. *Frances Willard: A Biography.* Chapel Hill: University of North Carolina Press, 2001.

Bowen, Louis DeKoven. *Growing Up with a City.* Introduction by Maureen A. Flanagan. Urbana: University of Illinois Press, 2001.

Bowron, Bernard R., Jr. *Henry B. Fuller of Chicago: The Ordeal of a Genteel Realist in Ungenteel America.* Westport, Conn.: Greenwood Press, 1974.

Branch, Edgar M. *James T. Farrell.* Minneapolis: University of Minnesota Press, 1963.

———. *Studs Lonigan's Neighborhood and the Making of James T. Farrell.* Newton, Mass.: Arts End Books, 1996.

Bray, Robert, ed. et al. *A Reader's Guide to Illinois Literature.* Springfield: Office of the Illinois Secretary of State, 1985.

Breasted, Charles B. *Pioneer to the Past: The Story of James Henry Breasted, Archaeologist.* New York: Charles Scribner's Sons, 1943.

Brent, Stuart. *The Seven Stairs: An Adventure of the Heart.* New York: Simon & Schuster, 1989 [1962].

Brommel, Bernard J. *Eugene V. Debs: Spokesman for Labor and Socialism.* Chicago: Charles H. Kerr, 1978.

Broonzy, William, and Yannick Bruynoghe. *Big Bill Blues: William Broonzy's Story.* London: Cassell, 1955.

Brooks, Gwendolyn. *Selected Poems.* New York: Harper & Row, 1963.

———. "They Call It Bronzeville." *Holiday,* October 1951.

Brown, Victoria Bissell. *The Education of Jane Addams.* Philadelphia: University of Pennsylvania Press, 2004.

Browne, Maurice. *Too Late to Lament.* Bloomington: Indiana University Press, 1956.

Bruce Graham of SOM. New York: Rizzoli, 1989.

Bruegmann, Robert. *The Architecture of Harry Weese.* New York: W. W. Norton, 2010.

Bruns, Roger A. *The Damndest Radical: The Life and World of Ben Reitman, Chicago's Celebrated Social Reformer, Hobo King, and Whorehouse Physician.* Urbana: University of Illinois Press, 1987.

———. *Preacher Billy Sunday and Big-Time American Evangelism.* New York: W. W. Norton, 1992.

Bukowski, Douglas. *Big Bill Thompson, Chicago, and the Politics of Image.* Urbana: University of Illinois Press, 1997.

Burkhardt, Barbara. *William Maxwell: A Literary Life.* Urbana: University of Illinois Press, 2005.

Burnham, Daniel, and Edward H. Bennett. *Plan of Chicago: Centennial Edition.* Chicago: Great Books Foundation, 2009.

Burns, Peter. *Curtis Mayfield.* London: Sanctuary Publishing, 2003.

Butcher, Fanny. *Many Lives, One Love.* New York: Harper & Row, 1972.

Cahan, Richard. *They All Fall Down: Richard Nickel's Struggle to Save America's Architecture.* New York: Wiley, 1995.

Cahan, Richard, and Michael Williams. *Richard Nickel's Chicago: Photographs of a Lost City.* Chicago: CityFiles Press Publishers, 2006.

———. *Edgar Miller and the Handmade Home: Chicago's Forgotten Renaissance Man.* Chicago: CityFiles Press Publishers, 2009.

Caray, Harry, with Bob Verdi. *"Holy Cow!"* New York: Villard Books, 1989.

Carduff, Christopher, ed. *William Maxwell: Early Novels and Stories.* New York: Library of America, 2008.

Carlozo, Louis R. "The Forgotten Confines." *Chicago Tribune,* May 15, 2008.

Carolan, Nicholas. *A Harvest Saved: Francis O'Neill and Irish Music in Chicago.* Cork, Ireland: Ossian Publications, 1997.

Carson, Mina. *Settlement Folk: Social Thought and the American Settlement Movement, 1885–1930.* Chicago: University of Chicago Press, 1990.

Carter, Steven R. *Hansberry's Drama: Commitment Amidst Complexity.* New York: Penguin, 1993.

Carwardine, William H. *The Pullman Strike.* Chicago: Charles H. Kerr, 1973.

Catrambone, Kathy. *Taylor Street: Chicago's Little Italy.* Chicago: Arcadia Publishing, 2007.

Cawelti, John C., ed. *Leon Forrest: Introductions and Interpretations.* Bowling Green, Ohio: Bowling Green State University Press, 1997.

Century, Douglas. *Barney Ross: The Life of a Jewish Fighter* (Jewish Encounters). New York: Schocken, 2006.

Cheney, Anne. *Lorraine Hansberry*. Boston: Twayne Publishers, 1984.

Chicago Maritime Society, eds. *From Lumber Hooks to the Hooligan Fleet: A Treasury of Chicago Maritime History*. Chicago: Lake Claremont Press, 2008.

Chinen, Nate. "Four Decades of Music That Redefined Free." *New York Times*, May 2, 2008.

Christiansen, Richard. *A Theater of Our Own: A History and a Memoir of 1,001 Nights in Chicago*. Foreword by Brian Dennehy. Evanston, Ill.: Northwestern University Press, 2004.

Ciccone, F. Richard. *Royko: A Life in Print*. New York: PublicAffairs, 2003.

Clayton, Douglas. *Floyd Dell: The Life and Times of an American Rebel*. Chicago: Ivan R. Dee, 1994.

Cohen, Aaron. "History in a Boxed Set." *Chicago Tribune*, December 23, 2007.

Cohen, Adam, and Elizabeth Taylor. *American Pharaoh: Mayor Richard J. Daley—His Battle for Chicago and the Nation*. New York: Back Bay Books, 2001.

Cohen, Rich. *Machers and Rockers: Chess Records and the Business of Rock & Roll*. New York: W. W. Norton, 2004.

Cohen, Richard E. *Rostenkowski: The Pursuit of Power and the End of the Old Politics*. Chicago: Ivan R. Dee, 1999.

Cohodas, Nadine. *Spinning Blues into Gold: The Chess Brothers and the Legendary Chess Records*. New York: St. Martin's Press, 2000.

Coleman, Janet. *The Compass: The Improvisational Theatre That Revolutionized American Comedy*. Chicago: University of Chicago Press, 1991.

Collier, James Lincoln. *Benny Goodman and the Swing Era*. New York: Oxford University Press, 1989.

———. *Louis Armstrong: An American Genius*. New York: Oxford University Press, 1985.

Collis, John. *The Story of Chess Records*. New York: Bloomsbury, 1998.

Condit, Carl W. *The Chicago School of Architecture: A History of Commercial and Public Building in the Chicago Area, 1875–1925*. Chicago: University of Chicago Press, 1998.

———. *The Rise of the Skyscraper*. Chicago: University of Chicago Press, 1952.

Conrow, Robert. *Field Days: The Life, Times, and Reputation of Eugene Field*. New York: Charles Scribner's Sons, 1974.

The Conspiracy Trial: The Extended Edited Transcript of the Trial of the Chicago Eight. Introduction by William Kunstler. Foreword by Leonard Weinglass. Indianapolis, Ind.: Bobbs-Merrill, 1970.

Cowan, David, and John Kuenster. *To Sleep with the Angels: The Story of a Fire*. Chicago: Ivan R. Dee, 1996.

Cox, Martha Heasley, and Wayne Chatterton. *Nelson Algren*. Boston: Twayne, 1975.

Crimmins, Jerry. *Fort Dearborn: A Novel*. Evanston, Ill.: Northwestern University Press, 2006.

Cronon, William. *Nature's Metropolis: Chicago and the Great West*. New York: W. W. Norton, 1992.

Croydon, Michael. *Ivan Albright*. New York: Abbeville Press, 1978.

Curtis, Richard K. *They Called Him Mister Moody*. Garden City, N.Y.: Doubleday, 1962.

Cutler, Irving. *The Jews of Chicago: From Shtetl to Suburb*. Urbana: University of Illinois Press, 1996.

Danckers, Ulrich, and Jane Meredith. *Early Chicago: A Compendium of the Early History of Chicago to the Year 1835 When the Indians Left.* With John F. Swenson, contributing editor, and a contribution by Helen H. Tanner. River Forest, Ill.: Early Chicago, Inc., 2000.

Darnell, Don. "Martie." *Chicago Tribune Sunday Magazine*, January 20, 1991.

Davis, Allen F. *American Heroine: The Life and Legend of Jane Addams*. Chicago: Ivan R. Dee, 2000.

Davis, Allen F., and Mary Lynn McCree. *100 Years at Hull-House*. Bloomington: Indiana University Press, 1991.

Dedmon, Emmett. *Fabulous Chicago*. New York: Random House, 1953.

Dell, Floyd. *Intellectual Vagabondage*. Introduction by Douglas Clayton. Chicago: Ivan R. Dee, 1990.

———. *Homecoming: An Autobiography*. New York: Farrar, 1933.

DeMuth, Jerry. *Small Town Chicago: The Comic Perspective of Finley Peter Dunne, George Ade, Ring Lardner*. Port Washington, N.Y.: Kennikat Press, 1980.

Despres, Leon, and Kenan Heise. *Challenging the Daley Machine: A Chicago Alderman's Memoir*. Evanston, Ill.: Northwestern University Press, 2005.

Destler, Chester McArthur. *Henry Demarest Lloyd and the Empire of Reform*. Philadelphia: University of Pennsylvania Press, 1963.

Dixon, Willie. *I Am the Blues: The Willie Dixon Story*. New York: Da Capo Press, 1990.

Donnell, Courtney, Susan Weininger, and Robert Cozzolino. *Ivan Albright*. Chicago: Art Institute of Chicago, 1997.

Donnelly, Joseph P. *Jacques Marquette*. Chicago: Loyola University Press, 1985.

Dorsett, Lyle W. *Billy Sunday and the Redemption of Urban America*. Macon, Ga.: Mercer University Press, 2004.

Douglas, Paul. *In the Fullness of Time*. New York: Harcourt Brace Jovanovich, 1972.

Drake, St. Clair, and Horace R. Cayton. *Black Metropolis: A Study of Negro Life in a Northern City*. 2 vols. New York: Harper & Row, 1962.

Drew, Bettina. *Nelson Algren: A Life on the Wild Side*. New York: Putnam, 1989.

Duffey, Bernard. *The Chicago Renaissance in American Letters: A Critical History*. East Lansing: Michigan State College Press, 1954.

Duis, Perry. *Chicago: Creating New Traditions*. Chicago: Chicago Historical Society, 1976.

———. *The Saloon: Public Drinking in Chicago and Boston, 1880–1920*. Urbana: University of Illinois Press, 1983.

Dunbar, Olivia Howard. *A House in Chicago*. Chicago: University of Chicago Press, 1947.

Duncan, Hugh Dalziel. *The Rise of Chicago as a Literary Center*. Totowa, N.J.: Bedminster Press, 1964.

Duneire, Mitchell. *Slim's Table: Race, Respectability, and Masculinity*. Chicago: University of Chicago Press, 1992.

Eals, Clay. *Steve Goodman: Facing the Music*. Foreword by Arlo Guthrie. Toronto: ECW Press, 2007.

Eastwood, Carolyn. *Near West Side Stories: Struggles for Community in Chicago's Maxwell Street Neighborhood*. Chicago: Lake Claremont Press, 2002.

Eaton, Leonard K. *Landscape Artists in America: The Life and Work of Jens Jensen*. Chicago: University of Chicago Press, 1964.

Ebner, Michael H. *Creating Chicago's North Shore: A Suburban History*. Chicago: University of Chicago Press, 1988.

Eig, Jonathan. *Get Capone: The Secret Plot That Captured America's Most Wanted Gangster*. New York: Simon & Schuster, 2010.

Elder, Donald. *Ring Lardner*. Garden City, N.Y.: Doubleday, 1956.

Elias, Robert H. *Theodore Dreiser: Apostle of Nature*. New York: Alfred A. Knopf, 1949.

339

Ellis, Elmer. *Mr. Dooley's America: A Life of Finley Peter Dunne*. New York: Alfred A. Knopf, 1941.

Epstein, Dena J. *Music Publishing in Chicago Before 1871: The Firm of Root & Cady*. Detroit: Harmonic Park Press, 1969.

Eskenazi, Gerald. *Bill Veeck: A Baseball Legend*. New York: McGraw-Hill, 1987.

Fabre, Michel, ed. *Richard Wright Reader*. New York: Da Capo Press, 1997.

———. *The Unfinished Quest of Richard Wright*. Urbana: University of Illinois Press, 1993.

Fanning, Charles. *Finley Peter Dunne and Mr. Dooley: The Chicago Years*. Lexington: University of Kentucky Press, 1978.

Farr, Finis. *Black Champion: The Life and Times of Jack Johnson*. New York: Charles Scribner's Sons, 1964.

———. *Frank Lloyd Wright: A Biography*. New York: Charles Scribner's Sons, 1961.

Farrell, James T. *Chicago Stories*. Selected and edited by Charles Fanning. Urbana: University of Illinois Press, 1998.

Farrell, John A. *Clarence Darrow: Attorney for the Damned*. New York: Doubleday, 2011.

Felsenthal, Carol. "Dear Ann." *Chicago Magazine*, February 2003.

Finks, P. David. *The Radical Vision of Saul Alinsky*. Mahwah, N.J.: Paulist Press, 1984.

Fitzpatrick, Tony. *Bum Town*. Chicago: Tia Chucha, 2001.

———. *The Wonder: Portraits of a Remembered City; The Dream City*. San Francisco: Last Gasp, 2006.

Fossett, Steve, with Will Hasley. *Chasing the Wind*. London: Virgin Books, 2010.

Franch, John. *Robber Baron: The Life of Charles Tyson Yerkes*. Urbana: University of Illinois Press, 2008.

Fraser, Steven. *Labor Will Rule: Sidney Hillman and the Rise of American Labor*. Ithaca, N.Y.: Cornell University Press, 1993.

Fraterrigo, Elizabeth. *"Playboy" and the Making of the Good Life in Modern America*. New York: Oxford University Press, 2010.

Freeman, Bud, as told to Robert Wolf. *Crazeology: The Autobiography of a Chicago Jazzman*. Urbana: University of Illinois Press, 1989.

Friedenberg, Richard. *A River Runs Through It: Bringing a Classic to the Screen*. Introduction by Robert Redford. Livingston, Mont.: Clark City Press, 1992.

Frueh, Erne R., and Florence Frueh. *Chicago Stained Glass*. 2nd ed. Chicago: Loyola Press / Wild Onion Books, 1998.

Funchion, Michael F. *Chicago's Irish Nationalists, 1881–1890*. Salem, N.H.: Ayer Co. Pub., 1976.

Gabler, Neal. *Walt Disney: The Triumph of American Imagination*. New York: Random House, 2002.

Ganz, Cheryl R. *The 1933 Chicago World's Fair: A Century of Progress*. Urbana: University of Illinois Press, 2008.

Garden, Mary, and Louis Biancolli. *Mary Garden's Story*. New York: Simon & Schuster, 1951.

Gayle, Addison. *Richard Wright: Ordeal of a Native Son*. Garden City, N.Y.: Doubleday, 1980.

Giddings, Paula J. *Ida: A Sword Among Lions: Ida B. Wells and the Campaign Against Lynching*. New York: HarperCollins / Amistad, 2008.

Giddins, Gary. *Satchmo: The Genius of Louis Armstrong*. New York: Da Capo Press, 2001.

Gies, Joseph. *The Colonel of Chicago: A Biography of the Chicago Tribune's Legendary Publisher, Colonel Robert McCormick*. New York: E. P. Dutton, 1979.

Gilbert, James Burkhart. *Perfect Cities: Chicago's Utopias of 1893*. Chicago: University of Chicago Press, 1993.

Gill, Brendan. *Many Masks: A Life of Frank Lloyd Wright*. New York: Ballantine Books, 1987.

Ginger, Ray. *Altgeld's America: The Lincoln Ideal Versus Changing Realities*. New York: Funk & Wagnalls, 1958.

———. *The Bending Cross: A Biography of Eugene Victor Debs*. New Brunswick, N.J.: Rutgers University Press, 1949.

Giordano, Gus. *Anthology of American Jazz Dance*. 2nd ed. New York: Orion Publishing House, 1978.

———. *Jazz Dance Class: Beginning thru Advanced*. Hightstown, N.J.: Dance Horizons, 1992.

Gleason, Bill. *Daley of Chicago: The Man, the Mayor, and the Limits of Conventional Politics*. New York: Simon & Schuster, 1970.

Glover, Tony, Scott Dirks, and Ward Gaines. *Blues with a Feeling: The Little Walter Story*. New York: Routledge, 2002.

Golden, Harry. *Carl Sandburg*. Cleveland: World Publishing, 1961.

Golus, Carrie, Patrick Welch, and Annie Morse. *Capturing Sunlight: The Art of Tree Studios*. Chicago: Chicago Department of Cultural Affairs, 1999.

Gora, Susannah. *You Couldn't Ignore Me If You Tried: The Brat Pack, John Hughes, and Their Impact on a Generation*. New York: Random House, 2010.

Gosnell, Harold F. *Negro Politicians: The Rise of Negro Politics in Chicago*. Chicago: University of Chicago Press, 1935.

Gottfried, Alex. *Boss Cermak of Chicago: A Study of Political Leadership*. Seattle: University of Washington Press, 1962.

Gottfried, Martin. *All His Jazz: The Life and Death of Bob Fosse*. New York: Da Capo Press, 2003.

Gray, Mary Lackritz. *A Guide to Chicago's Murals*. Chicago: University of Chicago Press, 2001.

Green, Hardy. *The Company Town: The Industrial Edens and Satanic Mills That Shaped the American Economy*. New York: Basic Books, 2010.

Green, James. *Death in the Haymarket: A Story of Chicago, the First Labor Movement, and the Bombing That Divided Gilded Age America*. New York: Random House, 2007.

Green, Paul M., and Melvin G. Holli, eds. *The Mayors of Chicago: The Chicago Political Tradition*. Carbondale: Southern Illinois University Press, 1987.

Grese, Robert E. *Jens Jensen: Maker of Natural Parks and Gardens*. Baltimore: Johns Hopkins University Press, 1998.

Griffin, Constance. *Henry Blake Fuller: A Critical Biography*. New York: Oxford University Press, 1939.

Griffin, Peter. *Along with Youth: Hemingway: The Early Years*. New York: Oxford University Press, 1985.

Griggs, Jeff. *Guru: My Days with Del Close*. Chicago: Ivan R. Dee, 2005.

Grimshaw, William J. *Bitter Fruit: Black Politics and the Chicago Machine, 1931–1991*. Chicago: University of Chicago Press, 1995.

Grossman, James R. *Land of Hope: Chicago, Black Southerners, and the Great Migration*. Chicago: University of Chicago Press, 1991.

Grossman, James R., Ann Durkin Keating, and Janice L. Reiff, eds. *The Encyclopedia of Chicago*. Chicago: University of Chicago Press, 2004. See also the electronic edition.

Grossman, Ron. "Matters of Opinion: Friends to Toast the Late Slim Brundage, Whose College of Complexes Gave Chicago's Thinkers a Forum." *Chicago Tribune*, September 19, 1997.

Grubb, Kevin Boyd. *Razzle Dazzle: The Life and Work of Bob Fosse*. New York: St. Martin's Press, 1991.

Gude, Olivia, and Jeff Huebner. *Urban Art Chicago: A Guide to Community Murals, Mosaics, and Sculptures.* Chicago: Ivan R. Dee, 2000.

Guzman, Richard R., ed. *Black Writing from Chicago: In the World, Not of It?* Foreword by Carolyn M. Rodgers. Carbondale: Southern Illinois University Press, 2006.

Halas, George S., with Gwen Morgan and Arthur Veysey. *Halas: An Autobiography.* Chicago: Bonus Books, 1986.

Halker, Clark D. *For Democracy, Workers, and God: Labor Song-Poems and Labor Protest, 1865–95.* Urbana: University of Illinois Press, 1991.

Halper, Albert. *This Is Chicago: An Anthology.* New York: Henry Holt, 1952.

Hansberry, Lorraine. *A Raisin in the Sun.* New York: Signet, 1958.

Hansen, Harry. *Midwest Portraits: A Book of Memories and Friendships.* New York: Harcourt, Brace and Company, 1923.

Harmon, Larry Bozo, with Thomas Scott McKenzie. *The Man Behind the Nose: Assassins, Astronauts, Cannibals, and Other Stupendous Tales.* New York: HarperCollins, 2010.

Harpster, Jack. *The Railroad Tycoon Who Built Chicago: A Biography of William B. Ogden.* Carbondale: Southern Illinois University Press, 2009.

Harris, Leon. *Merchant Princes: An Intimate History of Jewish Families Who Built Great Department Stores.* New York: Berkley, 1979.

Harris, Michael W. *The Rise of Gospel Blues: The Music of Thomas Andrew Dorsey in the Urban Church.* New York: Oxford University Press, 1994.

Harris, Neil, with the assistance of Teri J. Edelstein. *The Chicagoan: A Lost Magazine of the Jazz Age.* Chicago: University of Chicago Press, 2008.

Harrison, Carter H., II. *Growing Up with Chicago.* Chicago: Ralph Fletcher Seymour, 1944.

———. *Stormy Years: The Autobiography of Carter H. Harrison, Five Times Mayor of Chicago.* Indianapolis, Ind.: Bobbs-Merrill, 1935.

Hart, John Edward. *Albert Halper.* New York: Twayne, 1980.

———. *Floyd Dell.* New York: Twayne, 1971.

Hass, Jeffrey. *The Assassination of Fred Hampton: How the FBI and the Chicago Police Murdered a Black Panther.* Chicago: Chicago Review Press / Lawrence Hill, 2009.

Hayden, Tom, Frank Condon, and Ron Sossi. *Voices of the Chicago 8: A Generation on Trial.* San Francisco: City Lights Publishers, 2008.

Hayner, Don, and Tom McNamee. *Streetwise Chicago: A History of Chicago Street Names.* Foreword by John Callaway. Chicago: Loyola University Press, 1988.

Heap, Jane. *Dear Tiny Heart: The Letters of Jane Heap and Florence Reynolds.* New York: New York University Press, 1999.

Hecht, Ben. *A Child of the Century: An Autobiography.* New York: Simon & Schuster, 1954.

———. *Gaily, Gaily: The Memoirs of a Cub Reporter in Chicago.* New York: Doubleday, 1963.

———. *1001 Afternoons in Chicago.* With a new introduction by Bill Savage. Chicago: University of Chicago Press, 2009.

Heise, Kenan, and Michael Edgerton. *Chicago: Center for Enterprise.* 2 vols. Woodland Hills, Calif.: Windsor Publications, 1982.

Herrick, Mary J. *The Chicago Schools: A Social and Political History.* Beverly Hills, Calif.: Sage Publications, 1971.

Hines, Thomas S. *Burnham of Chicago: Architect & Planner.* 2nd ed. With a new introduction by Neil Harris. Chicago: University of Chicago Press, 2009.

Hirsch, Arnold. *Making the Second Ghetto: Race and Housing in Chicago, 1940–1960.* Rev. ed. Chicago: University of Chicago Press, 1998.

Hirsch, Susan E., and Robert I. Goler. *A City Comes of Age: Chicago in the 1890s.* Chicago: Chicago Historical Society, 1990.

Hise, Beth. *Swinging Away: How Cricket and Baseball Connect.* London: Scala Publishers, 2010.

Hofmeister, Rudolph A. *The Germans in Chicago.* Urbana: University of Illinois Press, 1976.

Holden, Greg. *The Booklover's Guide to the Midwest: A Literary Tour.* Cincinnati: Clerisy Press, 2010.

———. *Literary Chicago: A Book Lover's Tour of the Windy City.* Chicago: Lake Claremont Press, 2001.

Holli, Melvin G., and Paul M. Green. *Bashing Chicago Traditions: Harold Washington's Last Campaign, Chicago 1987.* Grand Rapids, Mich.: William B. Eerdmans, 1989.

———. *The Making of the Mayor, Chicago 1983: Harold Washington.* Grand Rapids, Mich.: William B. Eerdmans, 1983.

Holli, Melvin G., and Peter d'A. Jones, eds. *Ethnic Chicago.* Revised and expanded. Grand Rapids, Mich.: William B. Eerdmans, 1984.

Holt, Glen E., and Dominic Pacyga. *Chicago: A Historical Guide to the Neighborhoods; The Loop and South Side.* Chicago: Chicago Historical Society, 1979.

Horan, James D. *The Pinkertons: The Detective Dynasty That Made History.* New York: Crown Publishers, 1967.

Horwitt, Sanford D. *Let Them Call Me Rebel: Saul Alinsky, His Life and Legacy.* New York: Vintage, 1992.

Hoy, Suellen. *Ellen Gates Starr: Her Later Years.* Chicago: Chicago History Museum, 2010.

Huebner, Jeff. "City Without Art." *Chicago Reader,* November 2, 2001.

———. "The Return of the Magnificent Seven." *Chicago Reader,* September 5, 2002.

Hughett, Barbara. *The Civil War Round Table: Fifty Years of Scholarship and Fellowship.* Dayton, Ohio: Morningside, 1995.

Jablanovec, Ida Therese, Susan James, and Jose Chavez. *Stray Bullets: A Celebration of Chicago Saloon Poetry.* Chicago: Tia Chucha Press, 1991.

Janega, James. "Driven by Soaring Dreams." *Chicago Tribune,* October 3, 2008.

Janowitz, Rebecca. *Culture of Opportunity: Obama's Chicago—The People, Politics, and Ideas of Hyde Park.* Chicago: Ivan R. Dee, 2010.

Jensen, Jens. *Siftings.* Baltimore: Johns Hopkins University Press, 1990.

Jepsen, Cara. "Champion of the Gabfest: Remembering Slim Brundage and the College of Complexes." *Chicago Reader,* September 19, 1997.

Jeuck, John E., and Boris Emmet. *Catalogues and Counters: A History of Sears, Roebuck & Co.* Chicago: University of Chicago Press, 1950.

Johannsen, Robert W. *Stephen A. Douglas.* New York: Oxford University Press, 1973.

Johnson, Geoffrey. "Edgar, the Ape-Man." *Chicago,* December 1989.

———. "Little Captain of the Ragged, the Mad Army of Poets." *Chicago Reader,* September 6, 1985.

Johnson, John H., and Lerone Bennett Jr. *Succeeding Against the Odds: The Autobiography of a Great American Businessman.* Chicago: Johnson Publishing Company, 1992.

Johnson, Ken. "An Insider Perspective on an Outsider Artist." *New York Times,* April 18, 2008.

Johnson, Kim. *The Funniest One in the Room: The Lives and Legends of Del Close.* Chicago: Chicago Review Press, 1999.

Johnson, Mary Ann, ed. *The Many Faces of Hull-House.* Urbana: University of Illinois Press, 1989.

Jones, Chris. "50 Years of Constant Funny." *Chicago Tribune*, December 6, 2009.

Josephson, Matthew. *Sidney Hillman: Statesman of American Labor*. New York: Doubleday, 1952.

Kalmbach, Sally Sexton. *The Jewel of the Gold Coast: Mrs. Potter Palmer's Chicago*. Chicago: Ampersand, 2009.

Kamin, Blair. "Disaster Averted, but . . . Ouch." *Chicago Tribune*, September 12, 2000.

———. "Touched by Genius." *Chicago Tribune*, July 11, 2010.

Kantowicz, Edward R. *Corporation Sole: Cardinal Mundelein and Chicago Catholicism*. Notre Dame, Ind.: University of Notre Dame Press, 1983.

———. *Polish-American Politics in Chicago, 1888–1940*. Chicago: University of Chicago Press, 1975.

Karamanski, Theodore J., and Deane Tank. *Maritime Chicago*. Charleston, S.C.: Arcadia Publishing, 2000.

Karl, Barry D. *Charles E. Merriam and the Study of Politics*. Chicago: University of Chicago Press, 1974.

Katz, Donald R. *The Big Store: Inside the Crisis & Revolution at Sears*. New York: Viking Press, 1987.

Keating, Ann Durkin, ed. *Chicago Neighborhoods and Suburbs: A Historical Guide*. Chicago: University of Chicago Press, 2008.

Keegan, Anne. "Artists in Residence." *Chicago Tribune Sunday Magazine*, March 7, 1993.

Keil, Charles. *Urban Blues*. Chicago: University of Chicago Press, 1992.

Kennedy, Elizabeth, ed. *Chicago Modern 1893–1945: Pursuit of the New*. Essays by Wendy Greenhouse, Daniel Schulman, and Susan S. Weininger. Chicago: Terra Museum of American Art and Terra Foundation for the Arts, 2004.

Kennedy, Eugene. *Himself! The Life and Times of Richard J. Daley*. New York: Viking Press, 1978.

Kenney, William Howland. *Chicago Jazz: A Cultural History, 1904–1930*. New York: Oxford University Press, 1993.

Kent, George E. *A Life of Gwendolyn Brooks*. Lexington: University Press of Kentucky, 1993.

Kersten, Andrew E. *Clarence Darrow: American Iconoclast*. New York: Hill & Wang, 2011.

Kiehn, David. *Broncho Billy and the Essanay Film Company*. Berkeley, Calif.: Farwell Books, 2003.

Kinsley, Philip. *The "Chicago Tribune": Its First 100 Years*. 3 vols. New York: Alfred A. Knopf, 1943–46.

Kittredge, William, and Annick Smith. "The Two Worlds of Norman Maclean: Interviews in Montana and Chicago." *TriQuarterly*, Spring/Summer 1984.

Kleppner, Paul. *Chicago Divided: The Making of a Black Mayor*. DeKalb: Northern Illinois University Press, 1988.

Klinenberg, Eric. *Heat Wave: A Social Autopsy of Disaster*. Chicago: University of Chicago Press, 2002.

Knight, Louise W. *Jane Addams: Spirit in Action*. New York: W. W. Norton, 2010.

Kobler, John. *Capone: The Life and World of Al Capone*. New York: Da Capo Press, 2003.

Kogan, Herman. *A Continuing Marvel: The Story of the Museum of Science and Industry*. New York: Doubleday, 1973.

———. *The First Century: The Chicago Bar Association, 1874–1974*. Chicago: Rand McNally, 1974.

Kogan, Herman, and Robert Cromie. *The Great Fire: Chicago, 1871*. New York: G. P. Putnam's Sons, 1971.

Kogan, Herman, and Rick Kogan. *Pharmacist to the Nation: A History of Walgreen Co*. Deerfield, Ill.: Walgreen Co., 1989.

Kogan, Herman, and Lloyd Wendt. *Lords of the Levee: The Story of Bathhouse John and Hinky Dink*. Introduction by Rick Kogan. Evanston, Ill.: Northwestern University Press, 2005.

Kogan, Rick. *America's Mom: The Life, Lessons, and Legacy of Ann Landers*. New York: Harper, 2005.

———. *A Chicago Tavern: A Goat, a Curse, and the American Dream*. Chicago: Lake Claremont Press, 2006.

———. "Last Call at Ric's: A Final Toast to the Watering Hole Ric Riccardo Left Chicago." *Chicago Tribune*, September 15, 1995.

Kohut, Heinz. *Analysis of the Self*. New York: International Universities Press, 1971.

———. *How Does Analysis Cure?* Edited by Arnold Goldberg with the collaboration of Paul E. Stepansky. Chicago: University of Chicago Press, 1984.

———. *The Restoration of the Self*. New York: International Universities Press, 1977.

Kotlowitz, Alex. *Never a City So Real: A Walk in Chicago*. New York: Crown, 2004.

Kramer, Dale. *Chicago Renaissance: The Literary Life of the Midwest 1900–1930*. New York: Appleton-Century, 1966.

Kroc, Ray, with Robert Anderson. *Grinding It Out: The Making of McDonald's*. Chicago: Henry Regnery, 1977.

Kroty, Paul. *Frank Lloyd Wright and Midway Gardens*. Urbana: University of Illinois Press, 1998.

Kuenster, John. *Remembrances of the Angels: 50th Anniversary Reminiscences of the Fire No One Can Forget*. Chicago: Ivan R. Dee, 2008.

Lanctot, Barbara. *A Walk Through Graceland Cemetery*. Chicago: Chicago Architecture Foundation, 2004.

Lane, George A. *Chicago Churches and Synagogues: An Architectural Pilgrimage*. Chicago: Loyola University Press, 1981.

Larson, Erik. *The Devil in the White City: Murder, Magic, and Madness at the Fair That Changed America*. New York: Vintage, 2004.

Lawrence, Jerome. *Actor: The Life and Times of Paul Muni*. New York: G. P. Putnam's Sons, 1974.

Leech, Harper, and John Charles Carroll. *Armour and His Times*. New York: D. Appleton-Century, 1938.

Leonard, William. "Chicago's New 'Left Bank.'" *Chicago Tribune Magazine*, November 23, 1958.

———. "The College of Cut-Ups." *Chicago Tribune Magazine*, May 13, 1956.

Lester, Robin. *Stagg's University: The Rise, Decline, and Fall of Big-Time Football at Chicago*. Urbana: University of Illinois Press, 1999.

Levinsohn, Florence Hamlish. *Harold Washington: A Political Biography*. Chicago: Chicago Review Press, 1983.

Lewis, George. *A Power Stronger than Itself: The Association for the Advancement of Creative Musicians*. Chicago: University of Chicago Press, 2008.

Lewis, Lloyd. *John S. Wright: Prophet of the Prairies*. Chicago: Prairie Farmer Publishing, 1941.

Lewis, Lloyd, and Henry Justin Smith. *Chicago: The History of Its Reputation*. New York: Harcourt, Brace, 1929.

Lindberg, Richard C. *The Gambler King of Clark Street: Michael C. McDonald and the Rise of Chicago's Democratic Machine*. Carbondale: Southern Illinois University Press, 2009.

———. *To Serve and Collect: Chicago Politics and Police Corruption from the Lager Beer Riots to the Summerdale Scandal, 1855–1960*. Carbondale: Southern Illinois University Press, 1998.

———. *Total White Sox: The Definitive Encyclopedia of the World Champion Franchise*. Chicago: Triumph Books, 2006.

Lingeman, Richard. *Theodore Dreiser: An American Journey 1908–1945*. New York: G. P. Putnam's Sons, 1986.

Linn, James Weber. *Jane Addams: A Biography*. New York: Appleton-Century, 1935.

Littlewood, Thomas B. *Horner of Illinois*. Evanston, Ill.: Northwestern University Press, 1969.

Livingston, Dorothy Michelson. *The Master of Light: A Biography of Albert A. Michelson*. New York: Charles Scribner's Sons, 1973.

Lloyd, Richard D. *Neo-Bohemia: Art and Commerce in the Industrial City*. New York: Routledge, 2005.

Loerzel, Robert. "Reel Chicago." *Chicago*, May 2007.

Logan, John. *Never the Sinner: The Leopold and Loeb Story*. Woodstock, N.Y.: Overlook Press, 1999.

Loncraine, Rebecca. *The Real Wizard of Oz: The Life and Times of L. Frank Baum*. New York: Gotham Books, 2009.

Love, John F. *McDonald's: Behind the Arches*. Toronto: Bantam Books, 1986.

Loving, Jerome. *The Last Titan: A Life of Theodore Dreiser*. Berkeley: University of California Press, 2005.

Lowe, David. *Lost Chicago*. New York: American Legacy Press, 1985.

Lucia, Ellis. *Mr. Football: Amos Alonzo Stagg*. New York: A. S. Barnes, 1970.

Lupoff, Richard A. *Edgar Rice Burroughs: Master of Adventure*. New York: Ace Books, 1965.

Maass, Alan. "The Little Red Book House." *Chicago Reader*, October 17, 1986.

MacAdams, William. *Ben Hecht: The Man Behind the Legend*. New York: Scribner's, 1990.

MacGregor, John M. *Henry Darger: In the Realms of the Unreal*. New York: Delano Greenridge Editions, 2002.

Maclean, Norman. *A River Runs Through It and Other Stories, Twenty-Fifth Anniversary Edition*. With a new foreword by Annie Proulx. Chicago: University of Chicago Press, 2001.

Majer, Gerald. *The Velvet Lounge: On Late Chicago Jazz*. New York: Columbia University Press, 2005.

Maldre, Mati, and Paul Kruty. *Walter Burley Griffin in America*. Urbana: University of Illinois Press, 1996.

Maloney, Cathy Jean. *The Gardener's Cottage in Riverside, Illinois*. Chicago: University of Chicago Press, 2010.

Marjanovic, Igor, and Katerina Rüedi Ray. *Marina City: Bertrand Goldberg's Urban Vision*. New York: Princeton Architectural Press, 2010.

Martin, Robert F. *Hero of the Heartland: Billy Sunday and the Transformation of American Society, 1862–1935*. Bloomington: Indiana University Press, 2002.

Masters, Charles J. *Governor Henry Horner, Chicago Politics, and the Great Depression*. Carbondale: Southern Illinois University Press, 2007.

Matsoukas, Nick J. "The Kogen-Miller Studios." *Western Architect*, December 1930.

Mayer, Harold M., and Richard C. Wade. *Chicago: Growth of a Metropolis*. Chicago: University of Chicago Press, 1969.

McCaffrey, Lawrence, Ellen Skerrett, Michael F. Funchion, and Charles Fanning. *The Irish in Chicago*. Urbana: University of Illinois Press, 1987.

McDonald, Forrest. *Insull*. Chicago: University of Chicago Press, 1962.

McFarland, Ron, and Hugh Nichols, eds. *Norman Maclean*. Lewiston, Idaho: Confluence Press, 1988.

McKinney, Megan. *The Magnificent Medills: America's Royal Family of Journalism During a Century of Turbulent Splendor*. New York: HarperCollins, 2011.

McPhaul, John. *Deadlines and Monkeyshines: The Fabled World of Chicago Journalism*. Englewood Cliffs, N.J.: Prentice-Hall, 1962.

Merriam, Charles E. *Chicago: A More Intimate View of Chicago Politics*. New York: Macmillan, 1929.

Merriner, James L. *Grafters and Goo Goos: Corruption and Reform in Chicago*. Carbondale: Southern Illinois University, 2004.

———. *Mr. Chairman: Power in Dan Rostenkowski's America*. Carbondale: Southern Illinois University Press, 1999.

Metress, Christopher, ed. *The Lynching of Emmett Till: A Documentary Narrative*. Charlottesville: University of Virginia Press, 2002.

Meyer, Ray, with Ray Sons. *Coach*. Chicago: Contemporary Books, 1987.

Miller, Alton. *Harold Washington: The Mayor, the Man*. Chicago: Bonus Books, 1989.

Miller, Donald L. *City of the Century: The Epic of Chicago and the Making of America*. New York: Simon & Schuster, 1996.

Monroe, Harriet. *John Wellborn Root: A Study of His Life and Work*. Park Forest, Ill.: Prairie School Press, 1966.

———. *A Poet's Life: Seventy Years in a Changing World*. New York: Macmillan, 1938.

Moody, Paul D. *My Father: An Intimate Portrait of Dwight Moody*. Boston: Little, Brown, 1938.

Mordden, Ethan. *Ziegfeld: The Man Who Invented Show Business*. New York: St. Martin's Press, 2008.

Morgan, Anna. *My Chicago*. Chicago: Ralph Fletcher Seymour, Publisher, 1918.

Morn, Frank T. *The Eye That Never Sleeps: A History of the Pinkerton National Detective Agency*. Bloomington: Indiana University Press, 1982.

Morrison, Hugh. *Louis Sullivan: Prophet of Modern Architecture*. Westport, Conn.: Greenwood Press, 1971.

Moscato, Mark. *Brains, Brilliancy, Bohemia: Art & Politics in Jazz-Age Chicago*. Portland, Ore.: Eberhardt Press, 2009.

Murray, George. *The Madhouse on Madison Street*. Chicago: Follett, 1965.

Nelli, Humbert S. *Italians in Chicago 1880–1930: A Study in Ethnic Mobility*. New York: Oxford University Press, 1973.

Nelson, Bruce C. *Beyond the Martyrs: A Social History of Chicago's Anarchists 1870–1900*. New Brunswick, N.J.: Rutgers University Press, 1988.

Nemanic, Gerald, ed. *A Bibliographical Guide to Midwestern Literature*. Iowa City: University of Iowa Press, 1981.

Ness, Eliot, with Oscar Fraley. *The Untouchables*. New York: Award Books, 1969.

Nevius, Blake. *Robert Herrick: The Development of a Novelist*. Berkeley: University of California Press, 1962.

Newman, Christine. "An Old Town Odyssey." *Chicago*, October 2000.

Nickel, Richard, and Aaron Siskind, with John Vinci and Ward Miller. *The Complete Architecture of Adler & Sullivan*. Chicago: Meridian Press / Richard Nickel Committee, 2010.

Noyes, Jim. "Fore! Father." *Chicago*, August 2005.

O'Gorman, James F. *Three American Architects: Richardson, Sullivan, and Wright, 1865–1915*. Chicago: University of Chicago Press, 1991.

Old Town School of Folk Music Songbook. New York: Hal Leonard, 2008.

Olson, James C. *J. Sterling Morton*. Lincoln: Nebraska State Historical Society, 1972.

Ottley, Roi. *The Lonely Warrior: The Life and Times of Robert S. Abbott*. Chicago: Henry Regnery, 1955.

Pacyga, Dominic A. *Chicago: A Biography*. Chicago: University of Chicago Press, 2009.

Pacyga, Dominic A., and Ellen Skerrett. *Chicago: City of Neighborhoods; Histories & Tours*. Foreword by M. W. Newman. Chicago: Loyola University Press, 1986.

Palazzolo, Tom, comp. *At Maxwell Street: Chicago's Historic Marketplace Recalled in Words and Photographs*. River Forest, Ill.: Wicker Park Press, 2008.

Palmer, Robert. *Deep Blues*. New York: Penguin, 1982.

Parisi, Joseph, and Stephen Young, eds. *Between the Lines: A History of "Poetry" in Letters, 1962–2002*. Chicago: Ivan R. Dee, 2006.

———. *Dear Editor: A History of "Poetry" in Letters Part I: 1912–1962*. Foreword by Billy Collins. New York: W. W. Norton, 2002.

———. *The "Poetry" Anthology, 1912–2002: Ninety Years of America's Most Distinguished Verse Magazine*. Chicago: Ivan R. Dee, 2002.

Parnell, Sean. *Historic Bars of Chicago*. Chicago: Lake Claremont Press, 2010.

Parson, Julie, Jorjet Harper, Paula Berg, Lillian Anguiano, and Beatriz Badikian, eds. *Naming the Daytime Moon: Stories & Poems by Chicago Women*. Chicago: Feminist Writers Guild, 1987

Pasly, Fred D. *Al Capone: The Biography of a Self-Made Man*, 1930.

Patillo, Mary. *Black on the Block: The Politics of Race and Class in the City*. Chicago: University of Chicago Press, 2007.

Patinkin, Sheldon. *The Second City: Backstage at the World's Greatest Comedy Theater*. Naperville, Ill.: Sourcebooks, 2000.

Payton, Walter, with Don Yaeger. *Never Die Easy: The Autobiography of Walter Payton*. New York: Random House, 2001.

Pearlman, Jeff. *Sweetness: The Enigmatic Life of Walter Payton*. New York, Gotham Books, 2011.

Peditto, Paul. *Sounds of Silents (The Essanay Years)*. Chicago: Dramatic Publishing, 2002.

Peterson, Virgil W. *Barbarians in Our Midst: A History of Chicago Crime and Politics*. Boston: Little, Brown, 1952.

Petrakis, Harry Mark. *Tales of the Heart: Dreams and Memories of a Lifetime*. Chicago: Ivan R. Dee, 1999.

Petterchak, Janice A. *Jack Brickhouse: A Voice for All Seasons*. Chicago: Contemporary Books, 1997.

Phillips, Michael. "When Chicago Created Hollywood." *Chicago Tribune*, July 22, 2007.

Philpott, Thomas Lee. *The Slum and the Ghetto: Neighborhood Deterioration and Middle-Class Reform, Chicago, 1880–1930*. New York: Oxford University Press, 1978.

Pierce, Bessie Louise, ed. *As Others See Chicago: Impressions of Visitors, 1673–1933*. Foreword by Perry D. Duis. Chicago: University of Chicago Press, 2004.

Pierce, Bessie Louise. *A History of Chicago, Volume Two: From Town to City 1848–1871*. Chicago: University of Chicago Press, 2007.

———. *A History of Chicago, Volume Three: The Rise of a Modern City 1871–1893*. Chicago: University of Chicago Press, 2007.

The Plan of Chicago @ 100: 15 Views of Burnham's Legacy for a New Century. Wheaton, Ill.: Ely Chapter, Lambda Alpha International, 2009.

Platt, Harold K. *The Electric City: Energy and Growth of the Chicago Area, 1880–1930*. Chicago: University of Chicago Press, 1991.

Plumpp, Sterling D. *Blues: The Story Always Untold*. Chicago: Another Chicago Press, 1989.

Pollack, Harriet, and Christopher Metress, eds. *Emmett Till in Literary Memory and Imagination*. Baton Rouge: Louisiana State University Press, 2008.

Poole, Ernest. *Giants Gone: Men Who Made Chicago*. New York: McGraw-Hill, 1943.

Pridmore, Jay, and George A. Larson. *Chicago Architecture and Design*. New York: Harry N. Abrams, 2005.

Prince, Sue Ann, ed. *The Old Guard and the Avant-garde: Modernism in Chicago, 1910–1940*. Chicago: University of Chicago Press, 1990.

Pruter, Robert. *Chicago Soul*. Urbana: University of Illinois Press, 1992.

———. *Doowop: The Chicago Scene*. Urbana: University of Illinois Press, 1997.

Quaife, Milo. *Checagou: From Indian Wigwam to Modern City, 1673–1835*. Chicago: University of Chicago Press, 1933.

———. *Chicago and the Old Northwest, 1673–1835: A Study of the Evolution of the Northwestern Frontier, Together with a History of Fort Dearborn*. Urbana: University of Illinois Press, 2001.

Rakove, Milton. *Don't Make No Waves, Don't Back No Losers: An Insider's Analysis of the Daley Machine*. Bloomington: Indiana University Press, 1975.

———. *We Don't Want Nobody Nobody Sent: An Oral History of the Daley Years*. Bloomington: Indiana University Press, 1979.

Rascoe, Burton. *Before I Forget*. New York: Doubleday, Doran, 1937.

Ratliff, Ben. "Honoring Heroes of Jazz, with Words, Silence, and Improvisation." *New York Times*, June 26, 2010.

Reaves, Jessica. "Capone's Legacy Endures, to Chicago's Dismay." *New York Times*, April 23, 2010.

Reed, Christopher Robert. *Black Chicago's First Century: Volume 1, 1833-1900*. Columbia: University of Missouri Press, 2005.

Regnery, Henry. *The Cliff Dwellers: The History of a Chicago Cultural Institution*. Evanston, Ill.: Chicago Historical Bookworks, 1990.

———. *Creative Chicago: From the Chap-Book to the University*. Evanston, Ill.: Chicago Historical Bookworks, 1993.

Reich, Howard. *Let Freedom Swing: Collected Writings on Jazz, Blues, and Gospel*. Foreword by Ellis L. Marsalis Jr. Evanston, Ill.: Northwestern University Press, 2010.

———. "Saxophonist Nurtured Jazz in Chicago." *Chicago Tribune*, June 25, 2010.

Reid, Robert L., ed. *Battleground: The Autobiography of Margaret A. Haley*. Urbana: University of Illinois Press, 1982.

Riesman, Bob. *I Feel So Good: The Life and Times of Big Bill Broonzy*. Chicago: University of Chicago Press, 2011.

Reiss, Stephen A. *City Games: The Evolution of American Urban Society and the Rise of Sports*. Urbana: University of Illinois Press, 1989.

———. *Touching Base*. Westport, Conn.: Greenwood Press, 1980.

Rethford, Wayne, and June Skinner Sawyers. *The Scots of Chicago: Quiet Immigrants and Their New Society*. Dubuque, Iowa: Kendall-Hunt Publishing, 1997.

Rivlin, Gary. *Fire on the Prairie: Chicago's Harold Washington and the Politics of Race*. New York: Henry Holt, 1992.

Roberts, Randy, and Carson Cunningham, eds. *Before the Curse: The Chicago Cubs' Glory Years, 1870–1945*. Urbana: University of Illinois Press, 2012.

Rogak, Lisa. *A Boy Named Shel: The Life and Times of Shel Silverstein*. New York: St. Martin's Press / Thomas Dunne Books, 2007.

Rosemont, Franklin, ed. *From Bughouse Square to the Beat Generation: Selected Ravings of Slim Brundage*. Bughouse Square Series. Chicago: Charles H. Kerr, 1997.

———. *The Rise & Fall of the Dil Pickle: Jazz-Age Chicago's Wildest & Most Outrageously Creative Hobohemian Nightspot*. Bughouse Square Series. Chicago: Charles H. Kerr, 2004.

Rossen, Susan F., ed. *Ivan Albright*. Chicago: Art Institute of Chicago, 1997.

Rowe, Mike. *Chicago Breakdown*. New York: Da Capo Press, 1980.

Rowley, Hazel. *Richard Wright: The Life and Times*. Chicago: University of Chicago Press, 2008.

Royko, Mike. *Boss: Richard J. Daley of Chicago*. New York: Plume, 1988.

———. *Early Royko: Up Against It in Chicago*. With a new foreword by Rick Kogan. Chicago: University of Chicago Press, 2010.

———. *For the Love of Mike: More of the Best of Mike Royko*. Chicago: University of Chicago Press, 2002.

———. *One More Time: The Best of Mike Royko*. Chicago: University of Chicago Press, 2000.

Rubin, Steven J. *Meyer Levin*. Boston: Twayne Publishers, 1982.

Ruff, Allen M. "Socialist Publishing in Illinois: Charles H. Kerr & Company of Chicago, 1886–1928." *Illinois Historical Journal*, Spring 1986.

Russell, Herbert K. *Edgar Lee Masters: A Biography*. Urbana: University of Illinois Press, 2001.

Ryan, Zoë. *Bertrand Goldberg: Architecture of Invention*. Chicago: Art Institute of Chicago, 2011.

Sahlins, Bernard. *Days and Nights at the Second City: A Memoir, with Notes on Staging Review Theatre*. Chicago: Ivan R. Dee, 2002.

Saliga, Pauline A., ed. *The Sky's the Limit: A Century of Chicago Skyscrapers*. New York: Rizzoli Books, 1990.

Sandburg, Carl. *Chicago Poems*. New York: Dover Publications, 1994.

———. *The Chicago Race Riots, July 1919*. New York: Harcourt, Brace, 1919.

———. *Poems for the People: 73 Newfound Poems from His Early Years in Chicago*. Edited with an introduction by George and Willene Hendrick. Chicago: Ivan R. Dee, 2001.

Sautter, R. Craig, and Edward M. Burke. *Inside the Wigwam: Chicago Presidential Conventions, 1860–1996*. Chicago: Loyola Press / Wild Onion Books, 1996.

Sautter, R. Craig, ed. *Floyd Dell: Essays from the Friday "Literary Review," 1909–1913*. Highland Park, Ill.: December Press, 1996.

Sawyers, June Skinner. *Chicago Sketches: Urban Tales, Stories, and Legends from Chicago History*. Chicago: Loyola Press / Wild Onion Books, 1995.

Schabas, Ezra. *Theodore Thomas: America's Conductor and Builder of Orchestras, 1835–1905*. Urbana: University of Illinois Press, 1989.

Schaff, Barbara C. *Mr. Dooley's Chicago*. Garden City, N.Y.: Doubleday, 1977.

Schlesinger, Toni. "Old Town's Mad Masterpiece." *Chicago*, May 1988.

Schmidt, John R. *"The Mayor Who Cleaned Up Chicago": A Political Biography of William E. Dever*. DeKalb: Northern Illinois University Press, 1989.

Schoenberg, Robert J. *Mr. Capone*. New York: Harper, 1993.

Schultz, John. *The Chicago Conspiracy Trial*. Rev. ed. With a new introduction by Carl Oglesby and a new afterword by the author. Chicago: University of Chicago Press, 2009.

Schultz, Rima Lunin, and Adele Hast, eds. *Women Building Chicago 1790–1990: A Biographical Dictionary*. Bloomington: Indiana University Press, 2001.

Schulze, Franz. *Mies Van Der Rohe: A Critical Biography*. Chicago: University of Chicago Press, 1985.

Schulze, Franz, and Kevin Harrington. *Chicago's Famous Buildings*. 5th ed. Chicago: University of Chicago Press, 2003.

Schwieterman, Joseph P., and Alan P. Mammoser, eds. *Beyond Burnham: An Illustrated History of Planning for the Chicago Region*. With a postscript by John A. Shuler. Lake Forest, Ill.: Lake Forest College Press, 2009.

Scott, A. O. "An Appraisal: The John Hughes Touch." *New York Times*, August 8, 2009.

Scroggs, Marilee Munger. *A Light in the City: The Fourth Presbyterian Church of Chicago*. Chicago: Fourth Presbyterian Church of Chicago, 1990.

Scully, Vincent, Jr. *Frank Lloyd Wright*. New York: George Braziller, 1960.

Segrest, James. *Moanin' at Midnight: The Life and Times of Howlin' Wolf*. New York: Da Capo Press, 2005.

Seymour, Ralph Fletcher. *Some Went This Way: A Forty-Year Pilgrimage Among Artists, Bookmen, and Printers*. Chicago: R. F. Seymour, 1945.

Shanabruch, Charles. *Chicago's Catholics: The Evolution of an American Identity*. Notre Dame, Ind.: University of Notre Dame Press, 1981.

Sharoff, Robert. "Reconstructing Harry Weese." *Chicago*, July 2010.

Shay, Art. *Album for an Age: Unconventional Words and Pictures from the Twentieth Century*. Chicago: Ivan R. Dee, 2000.

———. *Chicago's Nelson Algren*. New York: Seven Stories Press, 2007.

Siegel, Allen. *Heinz Kohut and the Psychology of the Self*. Makers of Modern Psychotherapy. New York: Routledge, 1996.

Sinkevitch, Alice, ed. *AIA Guide to Chicago*. 2nd ed. Orlando, Fla.: Harvest / Harcourt, 2004.

Siry, Joseph. *Carson Pirie Scott, Louis Sullivan, and the Chicago Department Store*. Chicago: University of Chicago Press, 1988.

Skerrett, Ellen, ed. *At the Crossroads: Old Saint Patrick's and the Chicago Irish*. Foreword by Richard M. Daley. Chicago: Loyola Press / Wild Onion Books, 1997.

———. *Born in Chicago: A History of Chicago's Jesuit University*. Chicago: Loyola Press, 2008.

Skerrett, Ellen, and Mary Lesch, eds. *Francis O'Neill: Chief O'Neill's Sketchy Recollections of an Eventful Life in Chicago*. Foreword by Nicholas Carolan. Evanston, Ill.: Northwestern University Press, 2008.

Sklar, Kathryn Kish, ed. *The Autobiography of Florence Kelley: Notes of Sixty Years*. Chicago: Charles H. Kerr, 1986.

Slayton, Robert A. *Back of the Yards: The Making of a Local Democracy*. Chicago: University of Chicago Press, 1988.

Smith, Alson J. *Chicago's Left Bank*. Chicago: Henry Regnery, 1953.

Smith, Bryan. "Without a Trace." *Chicago*, March 2008.

Smith, Carl. *Chicago and the American Literary Imagination, 1880–1920*. Chicago: University of Chicago Press, 1984.

———. *The Plan of Chicago: Daniel Burnham and the Remaking of the American City*. Chicago: University of Chicago Press, 2006.

———. *Urban Disorder and the Shape of Belief: The Great Chicago Fire, the Haymarket Bomb, and the Model Town of Pullman*. Chicago: University of Chicago Press, 1995.

Smith, Joan A. *Ella Flagg Young: Portrait of a Leader*. Ames, Iowa: Educational Studies Press / Iowa State University Research Foundation, 1979.

Smith, Sally Bedell. *In All His Glory: The Life of William S. Paley, the Legendary Tycoon and His Brilliant Circle*. New York: Simon & Schuster, 1990.

Solti, Sir Georg. *Memoirs*. Chicago: Chicago Review Press, 1998.

Sorensen, Lorin. *Sears, Roebuck and Co. 100th Anniversary 1886–1986*. St. Helena, Calif.: Silverado Publishing, 1985.

Spear, Allan H. *Black Chicago: The Making of a Negro Ghetto, 1890–1920*. Chicago: University of Chicago Press, 1967.

Spears, Timothy B. *Chicago Dreaming: Midwesterners and the City, 1871–1919*. Chicago: University of Chicago Press, 2005.

Special Collections Department of the Chicago Public Library. *Resetting the Stage: Theater Beyond the Loop 1960–1990*. Chicago: Chicago Public Library, 1990.

Spink, J. G. Taylor. *Judge Landis and Twenty-Five Years of Baseball*. New York: Thomas Y. Crowell, 1947.

Spolin, Viola. *Theater Games for Rehearsal: A Director's Handbook*. Evanston, Ill.: Northwestern University Press, 2010.

Sprague, Paul E. *Guide to Frank Lloyd Wright & Prairie School Architecture in Oak Park*. Oak Park, Ill.: Village of Oak Park, 1986.

Stagg, Amos Alonzo, as told to Wesley Winans Stout. *Touchdown*. New York: Longmans, Green, 1927.

Stamper, John W. *Chicago's North Michigan Avenue: Planning and Development, 1900–1930*. Chicago: University of Chicago Press, 1991.

Starkey, David, and Richard Guzman, eds. *Smokestacks & Skyscrapers: An Anthology of Chicago Writers*. Chicago: Loyola Press / Wild Onion Books, 1999.

Starrett, Vincent. *Born in a Bookshop: Chapters from the Chicago Renascence*. Norman: University of Oklahoma Press, 1965.

Stegner, Wallace, "Haunted by Waters," in *Where the Bluebird Sings to the Lemonade Springs: Living and Writing in the West*. New York: Random House, 1992.

Stern, Richard. *Still on Call*. Ann Arbor: University of Michigan Press, 2010.

Stevens, Mark. *The Big Eight: Inside America's Largest Accounting Firms*. New York: Macmillan, 1984.

Stone, Irving. *Clarence Darrow for the Defense*. Garden City, N.Y.: Doubleday, 1941.

Stone, Melville E. *Fifty Years a Journalist*. Garden City, N.Y.: Doubleday, Page, 1921.

Stone, Steve, and Barry Rozner. *Where's Harry?* Dallas, Tex.: Taylor, 1999.

Storr, Richard J. *Harper's University: The Beginnings*. Chicago: University of Chicago Press, 1966.

Stricklin, David. *Louis Armstrong: The Soundtrack of the American Experience*. The Library of African-American Biography. Chicago: Ivan R. Dee, 2010.

Strozier, Charles B. *Heinz Kohut: The Making of a Psychoanalyst*. New York: Farrar, Straus & Giroux, 2001.

Sullivan, Frank. *Legend: The Only Inside Story About Mayor Richard J. Daley*. Chicago: Bonus Books, 1989.

Sullivan, Louis H. *The Autobiography of an Idea*. New York: Dover Publications, 1924.

Sustar, Lee. "When Speech Was Free (And Usually Worth It). Con Men and Communists, Lowlife and Literati, Blowhards and Bohemians: Reminiscences of Chicago's Soapbox Society." *Chicago Reader*, October 21, 1983.

Sutton, William A. *The Road to Winesburg: A Mosaic of the Imaginative Life of Sherwood Anderson*. Metuchen, N.J.: Scarecrow Press, 1972.

Swanberg, W. A. *Dreiser*. New York: Charles Scribner's Sons, 1965.

Sweet, Jeffrey. *Something Wonderful Right Away*. New York: Avon Books, 1986.

Swift, Louis F., with Arthur Van Vlissingen Jr. *The Yankee of the Yards: The Biography of Gustavus Franklin Swift*. Chicago: A. W. Shaw, 1927.

Taylor, Benjamin, ed. *Saul Bellow: Letters*. New York: Viking, 2010.

Taylor, Graham. *Chicago Commons Through Forty Years*. Chicago: Chicago Commons Association, 1936.

———. *Pioneering on Social Frontiers*. Chicago: University of Chicago Press, 1930.

Taylor, Troy. *Murder & Mayhem on Chicago's North Side*. Charleston, S.C.: The History Press, 2009.

———. *Murder & Mayhem in Chicago's Vice Districts*. Charleston, S.C.: The History Press, 2009.

Teachout, Terry. *Pops: A Life of Louis Armstrong*. New York: Houghton Mifflin Harcourt, 2009.

Tebbel, John W. *An American Dynasty: The Story of the McCormicks, Medills, and Pattersons*. Garden City, N.Y.: Doubleday, 1947.

———. *The Marshall Fields: A Study in Wealth*. New York: E. P. Dutton, 1947.

Tesser, Neil. "A Jazz Great Who Left More than His Music." *New York Times*, June 27, 2010.

Thomas, John L. *Alternative America: Henry George, Edward Bellamy, Henry Demarest Lloyd, and the Adversary Tradition*. Cambridge, Mass.: Harvard University Press, 1983.

Thomas, Mike. *The Second City Unscripted: Revolution and Revelation at the World-Famous Comedy Theater*. New York: Villard Books, 2009.

Tierney, Kevin. *Darrow: A Biography*. New York: Thomas Y. Crowell, 1979.

Till-Mobley, Mamie, with Christopher Benson. *Death of Innocence: The Story of the Hate Crime That Changed America*. New York: One World Books, 2004.

Thorn, John. *Baseball in the Garden of Eden: The Secret History of the Early Game*. New York: Simon & Schuster, 2011.

Townsend, Kim. *Sherwood Anderson*. Boston: Houghton, Mifflin, 1987.

Tracy, Steven C., ed. *Writers of the Black Chicago Renaissance*. Urbana: University of Illinois Press, 2011.

Travis, Dempsey J. *An Autobiography of Black Chicago*. Chicago: Urban Research Institute, 1981.

———. *An Autobiography of Black Jazz*. Chicago: Urban Research Institute, 1983.

———. *An Autobiography of Black Politics*. Chicago: Urban Research Institute, 1987.

———. *Harold—the People's Mayor: An Authorized Biography of Mayor Harold Washington*. Chicago: Urban Research Institute, 1989.

Tucker, John I. "Tarzan Was Born in Chicago." *Chicago History*, Spring 1970.

Tuttle, William. *Race Riot: Chicago in the Red Summer of 1919*. New York: Atheneum, 1970.

Twombly, Robert C. *Louis Sullivan, His Life and Work*. New York: Viking Press, 1986.

Upton, George P., ed. *Theodore Thomas: A Musical Autobiography*. New York: Da Capo Press, 1964.

Vander Weele, Maribeth. *Reclaiming Our Schools: The Struggle for Chicago School Reform*. Foreword by John Callaway. Chicago: Loyola University Press, 1994.

Van Zanten, ed. *Marion Mahony Reconsidered*. Chicago: University of Chicago Press, 2011.

Vass, George. *George Halas and the Chicago Bears*. Chicago: Henry Regnery, 1971.

Veeck, Bill, with Ed Lynn. *Veeck—As in Wreck: The Autobiography of Bill Veeck*. New York: G. P. Putnam's Sons, 1962.

Vlahos, James. "Steve Fossett: The Aviator." *New York Times Magazine*, December 28, 2008.

von Hoffman, Nicholas. *Radical: A Portrait of Saul Alinsky*. New York: Nation, 2010.

von Rhein, John. "Legendary Promoter of Lyric, the Arts." *Chicago Tribune*, December 3, 2007.

Wade, Louise Carroll. *Chicago's Pride: The Stockyards, Packingtown, and Environs in the Nineteenth Century*. Urbana: University of Illinois Press, 1987.

———. *Graham Taylor, Pioneer for Social Justice 1851–1938*. Chicago: University of Chicago Press, 1964.

Waldrop, Frank C. *McCormick of Chicago: An Unconventional Figure*. Englewood Cliffs, N.J.: Prentice-Hall, 1966.

Wallach, Jennifer Jensen. *Richard Wright: From Black Boy to World Citizen*. The Library of African-American Biography. Chicago: Ivan R. Dee, 2010.

Walljasper, Jay. "Those Vagabond Days." *Chicago Tribune Sunday Magazine*, August 15, 1982.

Walsh, Justin E. *To Print the News and Raise Hell: A Biography of Wilbur F. Storey*. Chapel Hill: University of North Carolina Press, 1968.

Ward, Geoffrey C. *Unforgivable Blackness: The Rise and Fall of Jack Johnson*. New York: Alfred A. Knopf, 2004.

Washburn, Charles. *Come into My Parlor: A Biography of the Aristocratic Everleigh Sisters of Chicago*. New York: National Library, 1936.

Webb, Constance. *Richard Wright: A Biography*. New York: Putnam, 1968.

Weese, Kitty Baldwin. *Harry Weese Houses*. Chicago: Chicago Review Press, 1987.

Weinberg, Arthur, ed. *Attorney for the Damned: Clarence Darrow in the Courtroom*. New York: Simon & Schuster, 1957.

Weinberg, Arthur, and Lila Weinberg. *Clarence Darrow: A Sentimental Rebel*. New York: G. P. Putnam's Sons, 1980.

Weininger, Susan, and Kent Smith. *Gertrude Abercrombie*. Springfield: Illinois State Museum, 1991.

Weissmuller, Johnny. *Water, World, and Weissmuller*. Los Angeles: Vion Publishing, 1964.

Weltzien, O. Alan, ed. *The Norman Maclean Reader*. Chicago: University of Chicago Press, 2008.

Wendt, Lloyd. *"Chicago Tribune": The Rise of a Great American Newspaper*. Chicago: Rand McNally, 1979.

———. *"Swift Walker": An Informal Biography of Gurdon Saltonstall Hubbard*. Chicago: Henry Regnery, 1986.

Wendt, Lloyd, and Herman Kogan. *Big Bill of Chicago*. Foreword by Rick Kogan. Evanston, Ill.: Northwestern University Press, 2005.

———. *Bosses in Lusty Chicago*. Bloomington: Indiana University Press, 1976.

———. *Give the Lady What She Wants! The Story of Marshall Field and Co.* Chicago: Rand McNally, 1952.

Werner, Craig. *Higher Ground: Stevie Wonder, Aretha Franklin, Curtis Mayfield, and the Rise and Fall of American Soul*. New York: Crown, 1995.

Werner, Morris R. *Julius Rosenwald: The Life of a Practical Humanitarian*. New York: Harper & Bros., 1939.

Whitfield, Stephen J. *A Death in the Delta: The Story of Emmett Till*. New York: Free Press, 1988.

Wideman, John Edgar. "In Memoriam: Leon Forrest, 1937–1997." *Callaloo* 21 (Winter 1998).

Wiener, Jon, ed. *Conspiracy in the Streets: The Extraordinary Trial of the Chicago Eight*. Foreword by Tom Hayden. Drawings by Jules Feiffer. New York: New Press, 2006.

Wilkinson, Alec. *My Mentor: A Young Writer's Friendship with William Maxwell*. New York: Mariner Books, 2003.

Willard, Frances. *Glimpses of Fifty Years: Autobiography of an American Woman*. Chicago: Woman's Temperance Publication Association, 1889.

Wille, Lois. *At Home in the Loop: How Clout and Community Built Chicago's Dearborn Park*. Carbondale: Southern Illinois University Press, 1998.

———. *Forever Open, Clear, and Free: The Struggle for Chicago's Lakefront*. Chicago: University of Chicago Press, 1991.

Williams, Dana A. *"In the Light of Likeness-Transformed': The Literary Art of Leon Forrest*. Columbus: Ohio State University Press, 2005.

Williams, Ellen. *Harriet Monroe and the Poetry Renaissance: The First Ten Years of "Poetry," 1912–22*. Urbana: University of Illinois Press, 1977.

Williams, Juan. *Eyes on the Prize: America's Civil Rights Years, 1954–1955*. New York: Viking Press, 1987.

Williams, Kenny J. *In the City of Men: Another Story of Chicago*. Nashville: Townsend Press, 1974.

———. *Prairie Voices: A Literary History of Chicago from the Frontier to 1893*. DeKalb: Northern Illinois University Press, 1980.

———. *A Storyteller and a City: Sherwood Anderson's Chicago*. DeKalb: Northern Illinois University Press, 1988.

Wilson, William Julius. *There Goes the Neighborhood: Race, Ethnic, and Class Tensions in Four Chicago Neighborhoods and Their Meaning for America*. New York: Vintage, 2007.

Wolff, Daniel, with S. R. Crain, Clifton White, and G. David Tenenbaum. *You Send Me: The Life & Times of Sam Cooke*. New York: William Morrow, 1995.

Wood, Debora, ed. *Marion Mahony Griffin: Drawing in the Form of Nature*. Evanston, Ill.: Mary and Leigh Block Museum of Art / Northwestern University Press, 2005.

Wood, James, ed. *Saul Bellow: Novels 1970–1982*. New York: Library of America, 2010.

Woodward, Bob. *Wired: The Fast Times and Short Life of John Belushi*. New York: Simon & Schuster, 1984.

Woolley, Lisa. *American Voices of the Chicago Renaissance*. DeKalb: Northern Illinois University Press, 2000.

Wright, Frank Lloyd. *An Autobiography*. New York: Horizon Press, 1977.

Yardley, Jonathan. *Ring: A Biography of Ring Lardner*. New York: Random House, 1977.

Young, David M. *Chicago Maritime: An Illustrated History*. DeKalb: Northern Illinois University Press, 2001.

———. *Chicago Transit: An Illustrated History*. DeKalb: Northern Illinois University Press, 1998.

Zorbaugh, Harvey Warren. *The Gold Coast and the Slum: A Sociological Study of Chicago's Near North Side*. With a new introduction by Howard P. Chudacoff. Chicago: University of Chicago Press, 1976.

Zukowsky, John, ed. *Chicago Architecture 1872–1922, Birth of a Metropolis*. Munich: Prestel-Verlag / Art Institute of Chicago, 1987.

———. *Mies Reconsidered: His Career, Legacy, and Disciples*. New York: Rizzoli Books, 1986.

Periodicals

Chicago Daily News
Chicago Defender
Chicago Sun-Times
Chicago Tribune
New York Times

Private Papers

Robert Abbott–John Sengstacke Family Papers. Woodson Regional Library of the Chicago Public Library. Part of the permanent collection of the library's Vivian G. Harsh Research Collection of Afro-American History and Literature.

Ivan Albright Archives. Ryerson & Burnham Archives, Art Institute of Chicago.

Elizabeth Jenks Clark Collection of Margaret Anderson. Yale Collection of American Literature, Beinecke Rare Book and Manuscript Library, Yale University.

Mary Bartelme Papers. Part of the Jane Addams Memorial Collection, University of Illinois at Chicago.

Ann Barzel Papers. Newberry Library, Chicago.

Daniel Burnham Collection. Ryerson & Burnham Archives, Art Institute of Chicago.

Fanny Butcher Papers. Newberry Library, Chicago.

Cyrus Colter Papers. Northwestern University Archives, Evanston, Illinois.

Clarence Darrow Digital Collection. University of Minnesota Law School.

Floyd Dell Papers, Newberry Library, Chicago.

Dil Pickle Club Records. Newberry Library, Chicago.

Leon Forrest Papers. Northwestern University Archives, Evanston, Illinois.

Bertrand Goldberg Archive. Ryerson & Burnham Libraries and Bertrand Goldberg Collection, Department of Architecture and Design, Art Institute of Chicago; http://www.artic.edu/aic/libraries/research/specialcollections/goldberg/index.html.

Ernest Hemingway Archives and Research Room, Oak Park Library, Oak Park, Illinois.

Margaret Hillis Collection, Rosenthal Archives, Chicago Symphony Orchestra, Chicago.

Robert Kennicott Papers. Northwestern University Archives, Evanston, Illinois.

Victor Lawson Papers, Newberry Library, Chicago.

Agnes Lee-Edgar Lee Masters Papers, Newberry Library, Chicago.

William Maxwell Papers, University of Illinois Rare Books and Manuscript Library, University of Illinois at Urbana-Champaign.

Ludwig Mies van der Rohe Collection. Ryerson & Burnham Archives, Art Institute of Chicago.

Morton Family Papers, Chicago History Museum.

Sterling Morton Library Archives. Morton Arboretum, Lisle, Illinois.

Newberry Midwest Manuscript Collection (includes the papers of Ben Hecht and Kenneth Sawyer Goodman). Newberry Library, Chicago.

Francis O'Neill Collection. Hesburgh Library, University of Notre Dame, Notre Dame, Indiana.

Ruth Page Nutcracker Papers, Newberry Library, Chicago.

Mike Royko Papers, Newberry Library, Chicago.

Florence Scala Collection. Part of the Jane Addams Memorial Collection / Midwest Women's Historical Collection, University of Illinois at Chicago.

Louis Sullivan Collection. Ryerson & Burnham Archives, Art Institute of Chicago.

Graham Taylor Papers. Newberry Library, Chicago.

Lambert Tree Papers. Newberry Library, Chicago.

Harry Weese Collection. Ryerson & Burnham Libraries, Art Institute of Chicago.

Frank Lloyd Wright Collection. Ryerson & Burnham Archives, Art Institute of Chicago.

Richard Wright Papers. Beinecke Library, Yale University.

Libraries and Museums

Chicago History Museum

DuSable Museum of African American History

Harold Washington Library

Newberry Library

Woodson Regional Library of the Chicago Public Library (Vivian G. Harsh Research Collection of Afro-American History and Literature)

Index

Photography Credits

Photographs of Daniel H. Burnham and Louis Sullivan are reproduced by permission of the Art Institute of Chicago:

Daniel H. Burnham, c. 1891. *The final official report of the Director of Works of the World's Columbian Exposition, June, 1894*, vol. 1, pp. 47–49. Ryerson and Burham Archives, The Art Institute of Chicago. Digital File #DFRWCE.Port_Burnham.jpg © The Art Institute of Chicago.

Louis H. Sullivan, 1900. Sullivaniana Collection, Ryerson and Burnham Archives, The Art Institute of Chicago. Digital File #193101.LHS_Portrait_1900.jpg © The Art Institute of Chicago.

The photograph of Carl Sandburg was provided courtesy of Arnie Bernstein.

The following images are courtesy of the Library of Congress: Grace Abbott (National Photo Company Collection), Gertrude Abercrombie (Carl Van Vechten Collection), Nelson Algren (*New York–World Telegram* staff photo), Margaret C. Anderson (*New York–World Telegram* staff photo), Cap Anson (early baseball card), Louis Armstrong, Mary Bartelme (Bain Collection), L. Frank Baum, Edgar Rice Burroughs (*New York–World Telegram* staff photo), Clarence Darrow, Charles Gates Dawes, Eugene Debs, Oscar De Priest (National Photo Company Collection), Earl Dickerson (U.S. Farm Security Administration), Paul Douglas (Harris and Ewing Collection), Stephen A. Douglas, Theodore Dreiser (Carl Van Vechten Collection), Elmer E. Ellsworth, Eugene Field, Marshall Field, Morris Fishbein (Harris and Ewing Collection), Mary Garden (*New York–World Telegram* staff photo), Hamlin Garland, Red Grange (National Photo Company Collection), Walter Burley Griffin (Bain Collection), William Rainey Harper, Carter Henry Harrison I, Carter Henry Harrison II (Bain Collection), Mahalia Jackson (Carl Van Vechten Collection), Florence Kelley, Edward J. Kelly (Harris and Ewing Collection), Kenesaw Mountain Landis, Victor Lawson, Vachel Lindsay, Mary Livermore, Edgar Lee Masters (Arnold Genthe Collection), Cyrus H. McCormick, Mary McDowell, Charles E. Merriam (Harris and Ewing Collection), Dwight Moody, Willard Motley (Carl Van Vechten Collection), James Mulligan, George Mundelein (Bain Collection), Paul Muni, Agnes Nestor, Bertha Honore Palmer, Potter Palmer, Allan Pinkerton, Ben Reitman, Julius Rosenwald (National Photo Company Collection), Richard W. Sears, Philip Sheridan, Albert G. Spalding, Amos Alonzo Stagg, Ellen Gates Starr, Gustavus F. Swift, David Swing, Lorado Taft, Lambert Tree, Muddy Waters (*New York–World Telegram* staff photo), Frances E. Willard.

Photograph of Ben Hecht is reproduced courtesy of the Newberry Library, Chicago. Call # Midwest, MS Hecht, Box 107, Folder 2798.

The following images are reproduced with the permission of the *Chicago Tribune*: Jane Addams, John Belushi, Joseph Bernardin, Al Capone, Harry Caray, Richard J. Daley, Leon Despres, Willie Dixon, Ann Landers, Harriet Monroe, George Pullman, John Wellborn Root, Mike Royko, Gene Siskel, Georg Solti, Studs Terkel, Bill Veeck, Harold Washington, Richard Wright, William Wrigley Jr.

The photograph of Edgar Miller is courtesy of the photographer, Michael Williams.

The photograph of Frank Lloyd Wright is reproduced by permission of the Frank Lloyd Wright Preservation Trust:

Frank Lloyd Wright, c. 1904–1906. Collection of Frank Lloyd Wright Preservation Trust (H&S H 273).